Linux Routers

Second Edition

ISBN 0-13-009026-3

90000

9 780130 090263

Prentice Hall Series in
Computer Networking and Distributed Systems
Radia Perlman, Series Editor

Linux Routers
A Primer for Network Administrators
Second Edition

Tony Mancill

PH PTR

Prentice Hall PTR
Upper Saddle River, NJ 07458
www.phptr.com

A Cataloging-in-Publication Data record for this book can be obtained from the Library of Congress.

Editorial/Production Supervision: Faye Gemmellaro
Acquisitions Editor: Mary Franz
Editorial Assistant: Noreen Regina
Marketing Manager: Dan DePasquale
Manufacturing Manager: Maura Zaldivar
Cover Design Director: Jerry Votta
Cover Designer: Anthony Gemmellaro
Cover Illustration: Tom Post
Compositor: Lori Hughes

©2002 Prentice Hall PTR
A division of Pearson Education, Inc.
Upper Saddle River, NJ 07458

Prentice Hall books are widely used by corporations and government agencies for training, marketing, and resale.

For information regarding corporate and government bulk discounts, contact:

Corporate and Government Sales: (800) 382-3419 or corpsales@pearsontechgroup.com

All products mentioned herein are trademarks or registered trademarks of their respective owners.

Printed in the United States of America
10 9 8 7 6 5 4 3 2 1

ISBN 0-13-009026-3

Pearson Education Ltd.
Pearson Education Australia Pty., Limited
Pearson Education Singapore, Pte. Ltd.
Pearson Education North Asia Ltd.
Pearson Education Canada, Ltd.
Pearson Educación de Mexico, S.A. de C.V.
Pearson Education—Japan
Pearson Education Malaysia, Pte. Ltd.

CONTENTS

PREFACE

The first edition of this book was the culmination of over two years of dodging the obvious: I needed to write a HOWTO to document the things that I was using Linux for in my work, particularly concerning the use of Linux as a router in a variety of scenarios. The second edition of the book presents the rare chance one gets to temper and revise one's words based upon reflection and experience.

The book is not only about routers, it's about running Linux in production and all of the nontechnical details which go along with it. This book is not intended to be the authoritative "be-all end-all" of what can be accomplished with Linux routers, but a HOWTO describing what has worked for me and my employers over the past few years. I have tried to record all of the stupid mistakes I have made along the way, and I've taken pains to include the arbitrary parts of configuring and running a Linux router so that you won't have to learn them on your own. I fully expect you to move far beyond the contents of this book as you further the state of the art.

Acknowledgments

I had the opportunity to hear Richard Stallman speak in 1998 about the Free Software Foundation and his work to develop, support, and promote the GPL. I found his talk very inspiring, and although this book is not released under the GPL, it is nevertheless inspired and made possible by the work of Richard Stallman, Linus Torvalds, and the GNU/Linux community at large.

Specifically, I would like to thank the technical reviewers Todd O'Boyle, Tom Daniels, Mark Thomas, Radia Perlman, and David Mandelstam for working through the manuscript repeatedly and for setting me straight on technical inaccuracies. Radia Perlman gets double thanks, along with Jim Markham, for the thankless job of helping me improve my writing. Mary Franz and David Mandelstam (again) are to thank for being constant sources of encouragement and putting the idea of a book in my head in the first place. Last, and certainly not least, thanks to Melissa, Java, and Grommit for support and for dealing with my weird writing schedule and moodiness due to sleep deprivation.

Feedback

As an active professional in the IT industry and an advocate of Linux, I am interested in your commentary about the contents of this book. Please feel free to contact me by email to provide feedback, contribute ideas, or discuss your criticisms of either the material or my method of presenting it. The following address should find me: <tony@mancill.com>.

Happy Hacking!

INTRODUCTION

Router configuration has long been an arcane art possessed by the few (and the lucky—at least in the eyes of the interested yet unchosen). One reason for this is that routers were expensive, and required specialized training. They were also found only in small numbers in larger companies. Unix, while not quite as inaccessible in terms of cost, has also frequently been considered a black art for the few. Linux, of course, has turned all of this on its ear and delivered a GNU[1] operating system to the masses. There used to be only a few big-city bookstores that had a decent selection of Unix books. Now every mall bookstore has a Unix/Linux section.

Routers, although not quite ubiquitous, are also much more prevalent in recent times too. The explosive growth of the Internet has every business, large and small, scrambling to get connected. Even completely nontechnical organizations POP their email from their ISP over a dial-up link several times a day. And people use more networked computers in general nowadays. People even have routers in their homes, perhaps to provide Internet connectivity via a cable modem to multiple computers in the home.

Interestingly (but not surprisingly), Linux delivers a router platform accessible by the many, almost as easily as it has resurrected the word "Unix." Although what folks think of as "traditional" routers are special-purpose hardware running embedded real-time operating systems, there has always been a group using Unix-based operating systems running on general-purpose hardware. Linux has helped expand this group immensely by providing a full-featured and robust TCP/IP stack and hundreds of device drivers—all of which run on commonly available computing hardware. Another important factor is the GNU/Linux community's basic tenet of sharing ideas and knowledge instead of hoarding them. The truly amazing part is that all of this is available without expensive licensing costs or nondisclosure agreements. With these good tools and some know-how, anyone can build an inexpensive, stable router platform capable of performing a variety of functions within any organization.

If you're asking yourself, *What's a router?*, do not despair! This book will cover most topics in enough depth and with enough references that you will not be left stumped. If it fails to do this, please let me know. Traditionally, a router is defined as a layer 3 switch. That is, it looks at the layer 3 packet headers and decides where to forward them. (Layer 3 refers to the OSI "network" layer.) For TCP/IP networks, the router examines the IP headers to determine the destination IP address of the packet and the TTL (Time To Live), among other things. In this strict definition, the type of packet—TCP, UDP, ICMP, etc.—is immaterial. However, as routers accumulate functionality, they can now take into account the layer 4 (transport layer)

---

[1] "GNU's Not Unix," although it's more Unix than anything else that claims to be. The complete text of the GNU General Public License appears in Appendix E.

headers (as well as those above layer 4 and below layer 2) when deciding what to do with a packet. Some other things that routers do:

- Transfer traffic between two different types of physical networks. An example of this is forwarding packets from Ethernet to Frame Relay and vice versa, as is done by a WAN router.

- Restrict the flow of traffic to/from certain addresses or networks. This is commonly known as **packet filtering**. Often the router will examine more than just the IP headers to make filtering decisions. TCP and UDP headers and other layer 4+ packet fields are fair game.

- Rewrite source addresses so that traffic appears to originate from an address other than that of the original sender. Under Linux, this is accomplished through **masquerading** and **network address translation** (or **NAT**). The task includes unmasquerading replies flowing in the other direction.

- Act as a BOOTP or DHCP server issuing IP addresses and other configuration parameters for workstations on your network. Throughout this book we will use Linux routers to perform these tasks and much more.

The focus of this book is admittedly not on academic definitions, but on how to accomplish (or at least get started on) a certain task. You may find that knowing the correct technical definition for something is not the same as successfully configuring and administering it in a production environment. If you're just getting started as a network administrator, be confident that a lot of technical know-how can be learned only through experience (a.k.a. "the hard way"). Do not be intimidated by the lack of a formal body of knowledge; just admit it to yourself when you don't know the answer and strive to figure it out.

From Whence Linux?

The progress on operating-systems implementation, in my opinion, has been quite dramatic during the 1990s thanks to Linux. If you are interested in the "early" history of Linux, the Ur-history, and can stomach discussions of OS design, you should check out the following:

- *http://www.educ.umu.se/~bjorn/mhonarc-files/obsolete/* This is a thread that features a heated exchange between Linus Torvalds and Andy Tanenbaum, a well-established researcher, professor, father of *MINIX*, and author of several (good) OS-design books. (I read somewhere that Linus Torvalds isn't particularly proud of the bravado he displayed in these messages. I find the characteristic of being passionate about something and then later being able to admit having been caught up in the heat of the moment, and to rise above it, to be magnanimous indeed.)

- *http://www.educ.umu.se/~bjorn/linux/misc/linux-history.html* This is a collection of Linux-relevant postings made to comp.os.minix about building an OS.

The way I understand the early history of Linux, it boils down to this: Linus Torvalds had an Intel 80386-based PC and some free time. He set out to write an operating system that would capitalize on the new features of this processor, ignoring backward compatibility with the 8088 and the 80286. (Other PC operating systems of that era were struggling with some design trade-offs that were imposed by the limitations of the 386's predecessors. In all fairness, they did this to maintain backward compatibility with software written to run on those systems.)

Another incentive for writing his own OS from scratch was to take advantage of the large body of excellent "free" software being developed by the Free Software Foundation. This is the (first) connection between Linux and Richard Stallman, who founded the GNU project in 1984 and has lent both philosophy and code to the effort. The system software which Linus used for his new kernel is commonly known as the GNU toolset. These tools implement most of what is commonly thought of as standard "Unix" system tools.[2] This collection of software had the tremendous advantage of being available in source-code form and being delivered with a license that allowed early Linux developers to modify that source and redistribute it.

In the early 1990s, the Internet made the transition from an academic/scientific tool to the most powerful communications medium ever available to the general public. The ability to communicate, collaborate, share, discuss, and debate has never before been available to such a large percentage of the world's population. Why the sentimentality about the Internet? If Linus Torvalds conceived Linux, and it spent a while in the "womb" of academia, then the Internet is its home—where it will play, grow, and mature. But Linux has become more than a user of the Internet; it has become part of it, and thus is now being used to propagate itself.

Why a Linux Router?

At this point, you may be thinking that this is all well and good and apropos in some sort of cosmic sense—the child has grown up to take care of the parent, etc., and so on—but what makes a Linux router any better or different than other routers? As with most interesting questions, the answer is: "It depends." Primarily, it depends upon what your definition of "better" is.

- *Linux routers are inexpensive.* For about $500 plus a meagerly equipped PC, you have a WAN router capable of running several different protocols at T1 (1.5Mbps) speeds and higher. For a bit more, you can route multiple T3s. License costs are typically nil. Ongoing hardware maintenance costs are nil to minimal. Linux runs on an amazing variety of hardware platforms, from the latest low-cost commodity gear to systems that haven't been manufactured in a decade.

- *Linux routers are flexible.* Try running a copy of *Apache* (the world's most popular HTTP daemon) on a "traditional" router, or integrating a "traditional" router into your in-house-developed security infrastructure. At best, you will pay your router vendors handsomely for the privilege of letting them port your code to their systems. Otherwise, you're probably out of luck.

- *Linux routers are stable.* Whereas the TCP/IP implementation of many others has been reviewed by, at most, a few hundred capable programmers, Linux's TCP/IP stack has been reviewed by literally thousands. (It even has its own book; see *TCP/IP and Linux Protocol Implementation* in the Bibliography.) And because Linux is a "labor of love" for most of its contributors, its quality is based on pride and technical excellence, not hampered by deadlines and office politics.

---

[2]Remember, "*GNU's Not Unix.*"

- *Linux routers are easy to administer.* If you can navigate a shell (you can pick the shell of your choice), you have already completed level one of your router training. With other solutions, you need to learn a new command environment and set of tools. Linux is the same whether it's acting as a web server, workstation, or router.

- *Linux routers are based on proven, widely available technology.* Because the system hardware and adapters are being produced for such an enormous market, costs are low and time-to-market cycles are as short as possible.

- *Linux routers provide investment protection beyond that of their "traditional" counterparts.* If you've worked in computer support for any length of time, you've probably experienced a vendor's discontinuing a product line, phasing out support for a particular version, failing to add features that you desperately need, or simply not responding to bug reports. With Linux, there is no vendor who can strong-arm you into accepting any of these frustrations. You always have the option of modifying the source yourself or choosing not to upgrade and remaining at the version which suits you best.

- *Linux routers are expandable.* Because you can use almost anything that you can attach to a general-purpose computer, you never have to worry about whether or not your router chassis can support a third BRI ISDN adapter. Just add a serial expansion card and attach the third adapter.

- *Linux routers are adaptable.* One thing the computer industry has shown us by now (or taught us the hard way) is to expect change. Where is IBM's MCA? Whatever happened to 100VG-LAN? Did VoIP (Voice over IP) really ever catch on? The next big thing to hit the market will be ??. Since a Linux router is not a proprietary "point-in-time" solution, you can retrofit to meet your technology needs without replacing your entire router hardware.

Goals of This Book

This book aims to promote Linux as a router by telling you how to set up and manage your own Linux router based on my experiences using them in production environments. Different "types" of routers are illustrated through a series of examples, each of which introduces the functionality and configuration of that router. For instance, Chapter 3 describes a router used to route traffic between two LAN subnets, while Chapter 5 details the configuration of a Frame Relay (WAN) router. Because the fine details of "how" change continually, every attempt is made to maintain a level of detail that will be useful for more than just the next point-release of the kernel. (However, the specific examples in this, the second edition of the book, are for the 2.4.x kernel series. See Chapter 10 for information on prior kernels.)

Alongside the configurations are general discussions about running Linux in production, as well as coverage of some applications that help support the network infrastructure (like traffic analysis and system monitoring). For me, Linux is about enabling people to do things that they would not have been able to do or afford to do otherwise. Really. I mean that quite sincerely. Sometimes "afford" means more than having sufficient money—it means having sufficient time. Linux can help you craft tailor-made solutions by building on the work of others. The book also contains some background information suited for "newbie" administrators who have never done network administration. While this information will be familiar to experienced network administrators, I feel that it's important, because technical elegance is pointless without sound administration practices, or if you don't even know where to start.

To exhibit what I believe is the "true spirit" of Linux—sharing information, ideas, and accomplishments instead of hiding them—references to publicly available resources will be made whenever I am aware of such sources. Several of these are collected as a list of links in Appendix A. Much of what you read in this book is made possible by the existence of openly available documentation. Another element of this spirit is the attitude that "whatever it is I need to accomplish, Linux is a sufficient toolset to succeed." Having faith in your toolset and in your ability to use it effectively to solve business problems is crucial to your performing your work well and enjoying it, too. This book aims to help you establish some faith in the toolset by offering knowledge about how to use it. It will help you find ways in which you can:

- Reduce the total cost of ownership (TCO) of your current environment. Very few businesses are so wealthy that they disregard the bottom line.

- Deploy Linux routers in organizations which might not be able to afford the "traditional" hardware or the associated license and maintenance costs.

- Solve problems not addressed by "traditional" routers.

- Keep your Linux production environment healthy, saving yourself time and unexpected trips into the office.

The Linux Documentation Project

The *Linux Documentation Project*, or *LDP* as it's commonly known, is an invaluable resource for Linux documentation. The project aims to make high-quality documentation freely available to all. This means not only covering a wide range of topics at various depths and skill levels, but also making sure that the documentation is current and correct.

This documentation covers a wide variety of topics, from general hardware compatibility to specialized software configurations. The documentation takes several forms, from the informal FAQs and mini-HOWTOs to the regular HOWTOs and the longer guides. If you're not already familiar with this site, bookmark it—I will refer throughout this book to documentation found there.

http://www.linuxdoc.org/

Nongoals of This Book

This book does not aspire to incite the masses to riot and replace all "traditional" routers with Linux systems. (Throughout this book the term "traditional" should be taken to mean router product offerings based on a closed, proprietary system interfaces or "operating systems." This would include the fine family of Cisco products, Nortel, Ascend Communications, et al.) These products have their place, and they have paved the way for the existence of Linux and the Linux router. In many instances, depending upon either the specific application or your corporate culture, traditional routers are the right choice for your production environment. On the other hand, a sound business principle is to pick the least expensive tool capable of satisfying all of the operational requirements—the tool that will result in the lowest total cost of ownership. Realistically, cost is the overriding factor for most business ventures, and Linux-based solutions will often have the advantage.

This book does not attempt to thoroughly teach TCP/IP or fully explain routing protocols used in TCP/IP networks. Nor does the book thoroughly address firewall configuration or security. These topics are simply beyond the scope of this book, and other people have done fantastic jobs of covering them (much better than I could). I do heartily recommend a thorough understanding of TCP/IP and networking in general for anyone considering administering a TCP/IP network, regardless of the equipment used. For an authoritative treatment of networking and routing, see *Interconnections* by Radia Perlman. Finally, the book you now hold covers only routing with TCP/IP (although Linux is capable of handling other protocols). If you need to support something other than IP, know that you are not alone, and that much of the software and hardware specifically supports protocols besides IP.

Layout of This Book

Chapters 1 and 2 discuss topics which are generic and applicable to all Linux routers, while Chapters 3–9 each cover a type of Linux router as I have used it in production and highlight what I learned in the process.[3] Of the latter seven chapters, the first three are basic LAN, extranet, and WAN routers, while the remaining four address more advanced topics such as connecting to the Internet and making routers do more than just route.

Within each router chapter, first the router is introduced by its function, and then technical details of configuration are discussed. Throughout the book, several threads of related topics are presented and developed alongside the routers themselves. These topics include choice of hardware, choice of software, strategies for high availability, TCP/IP niceties of Linux available in the kernel, and monitoring configurations and software. Different chapters have different components and requirements, but generally have the following layout:

- hardware
- software required and configuration
- kernel configuration
- support/high availability
- monitoring

The appendices address topics either too general or too specific for the main text, from how to compile the Linux kernel (Appendix B) to using *VMware* to augment your testing strategies (Appendix C) to ethical considerations of a network admin. Finally, there may not be a single "flavor" of router presented in this book that fits your application. If that is the case, do not shy away from combining configurations presented here into something new.

Typographical Conventions

Every technical book has this section and I almost never read it, as it seems that all of the publishers must have sat down together a few years back and worked this out once and for all. On the other hand, I find that I am free to use conventions of my choice. Hopefully, you will find these to be straightforward. If you're still reading, here goes:

---

[3]There should probably be a chapter called "Franken-router" for the router configurations that did not work—a HOWNOTTO of sorts. Adventurous readers will be able to write this chapter themselves.... :)

bold text	is used to introduce new terms and keystrokes which are not command names (e.g., **CTRL-D** or **ESC**).
italics	indicate file, directory, and command names when they appear in the body of a paragraph. They also are used to highlight options to commands appearing in the body of the text. Beside that, they carry the normal meanings of *emphasizing* a word or phrase and marking URLs and email addresses, etc.
`fixed font`	is used for the contents of files, the output from commands, and general things that appear on the shell prompt.
fixed bold	is used for things that should be literally typed by you if you are following along with an example.
fixed italics	signify keywords, options, or other text which are variable and should be replaced by the user to fit the situation at hand.

A Note to 2.0.x and 2.2.x Kernel Users

Initially, the first edition of this text encompassed the 2.0.x and the 2.2.x versions of the kernel. As that book went through various stages of editing (and time passed), it became clear that the main text should appeal to the broadest userbase without forcing the reader to switch back and forth between the details of two different kernel versions. This is particularly true for the sections on masquerading and firewalling (Chapters 4, 7, and 9).

In the second edition the focus is on the 2.4 kernel, since all of the major Linux distributions at the time of writing run on 2.4 kernels. However, notes for 2.0 and 2.2 kernel users remain and are scattered throughout the text, including many of the first edition materials for the 2.2.x kernels collected in Chapter 10. If you support an environment running on an older kernel and need assistance, check *http://mancill.com/linuxrouters/*.

Naming of Chapters

You might have already noticed a common thread in the names of the chapters in this book. Maybe they make you want to check the cover to make sure that this isn't a science textbook. Selecting a naming motif for Unix systems is a tradition that seems to have been around for quite a while. Perhaps one of the hacker subculture deities knows its origin. (See *The New Hackers Dictionary* by Eric Raymond if this sort of trivia interests you.) If you haven't already guessed, I've named my routers after elements in the periodic table.

The periodic table has characteristics that render it useful as a system naming scheme. First of all, there is a large pool of names, many of which sound cool. Next, every name has a short yet unique "symbol name" associated with it, e.g., *gold* is **Au**, *carbon* is **C**. These can be used as a sort of shorthand, along with aliases (CNAMEs) in DNS to save keystrokes.

Chapter 1

ROUTING BUILDING BLOCKS

What *is* a Linux router? What does it look like on the inside? How would you recognize one if you saw it? And where did it originate? (Or, for those of us with philosophical aspirations, which came first, the router or the packets?) Well, a Linux router is nothing more than a computer, sometimes with additional special-purpose hardware, configured to perform a special purpose. We'll spend most of our time talking about configurations, but right now we're going to focus our attention a layer below that. For the purposes of this chapter we will want to conceptualize a router as consisting of three different components:

- The **hardware**, the tangible bits of metal and plastic upon which the software runs and which connects to the network via various electrical and optical interfaces.

- The **environment**, which does not include the hardware or software conducting the routing of packets but is important all the same. Without it, the router hardware and software may not be able to perform their specific tasks.

- The **software**, which receives packets and directs them along their way and may perform other useful functions, such as logging, filtering, and much more.

This chapter will cover aspects of Linux routers common to most variations on the theme. Having the right mixture of these three basic building blocks is important for building the stable elements described in later chapters. A large part of administering high-availability systems successfully is strategy and organization. Effort put into this up front can save a lot of (down)time and rework down the road. As we talk about the hardware, environment, and software, I will introduce some principles I have picked up while administering production systems. As with most opinions, YMMV (Your Mileage May Vary), so take the applicable parts and expand on them. Leave the rest.

1.1 Router Hardware

What may first come to mind when you think about "hardware selection" are things like processor generation and speed, RAM, and Ethernet adapters. All of these are important to a router, but there are some even more fundamental aspects you should take into consideration. A router has different uptime requirements than a workstation. If a workstation is down for an hour, you've affected only a single user, or at most a single group of users. The same outage with a router will affect all of your users and will not go unnoticed. Maintenance windows are also smaller, since any nightly batch job or system backup that relies on the network may also depend upon the router. Should a component in a router fail, chances are that you will be

1

under considerable stress to return it to service as quickly as possible. Therefore, consider the following when selecting your hardware.

1.1.1 Case

The case should be easy to open and have a consistent type and size of screw-head. The main components—hard drive, add-on cards, power supply, and RAM—should be easy to reach without having to remove other components such as daughterboards, etc. Typically, big-name manufacturers do a better job of this than the low-cost providers, but not always. Also, different product offerings from the same manufacturer can vary greatly. Probably the only way to know if the case is suitable for you is to take a system apart yourself. In environments where you will have multiple production systems, use the same case/vendor for all systems, if possible. The more alike the cases are in size and in configuration, the easier it will be to find a way to neatly stack or shelve them. Rack-mounted systems can make for extremely tidy installations, but they can be expensive and difficult to service while still mounted in the rack unless you have rail kits and sufficient space in front of the rack.

1.1.2 Power Supply and Fans

The power supply should have adequate wattage for all of the components in your system. Redundant power supplies are, without a doubt, well worth the expense if downtime is expensive, embarrassing, or both. If your power supply is difficult to replace, realize that you might be stuck migrating the hard drive and add-on cards to another system if it fails. (There are other, better ways around this in most cases; see Section 9.6.1.) The case fans should provide adequate airflow in case of harsh environmental conditions (typically, extreme heat) outside of the system. Remember that a good fan is worthless if you place the entire unit in such a way that air cannot enter and exit the case. Finally, keep in mind that the moving parts, unlike the vast majority of the highly complex technology found in a computer nowadays, are subject to the laws of Newtonian physics and you should keep spares on hand lest Murphy's Law also assert itself.

1.1.3 Architecture and Motherboard

I must admit that in the first edition of the book, I wasn't even thinking about architectures other than Intel-based x86. I have since experienced the variety firsthand—Linux runs very well indeed on a *lot* of different architectures. Therefore, instead of allowing this section to balloon into a novella of uninteresting details and quickly outdated compatibility quirks, let's talk about what is important regardless of the flavor of CPU under the hood.

The choice of main system board for your router is usually not something to agonize over. If you have experience with a certain architecture or vendor, stick with it. If you're starting from scratch or would like to redeploy older equipment, take the time to load your version of Linux (perhaps several times) before you implement a solution. Keep in mind that a router is less likely to use some of the fancier motherboard features, such as AGP bandwidth, USB support, or on-board soundcards. So whether or not these work with your version of the kernel is immaterial (as long as they do not interfere with the operation of other components in the system). I recommend disabling all system components you will not be using (with the except of serial ports, which can come in quite handy in a pinch), either through BIOS, if your motherboard has such a concept, or by not loading the corresponding device driver module into your running kernel. Along these same lines, the more exotic the hardware (which often correlates with propriety), the more painstaking it may be to configure under Linux (or any operating system).

If you are worried about a motherboard's compatibility with Linux, a good starting point is *http://www.linux.org/help/beginner/platforms.html.* If you are starting completely from scratch, some motherboard features listed below are worth consideration during your selection process.

Bus Architecture

A lot of theory goes into a discussion about the relative strengths of different bus architectures. I believe that much of the dispute can only be resolved empirically—testing a given application on a given piece of hardware. If your application is going to be sensitive to submillisecond packet latency, get busy researching IHA (Intel Hub Architecture) vs. Northbridge/Southbridge chipsets and go for the fastest FSB (Front Side Bus) available. But don't be discouraged, especially in the x86 world, if you find that many bus optimizations focus on multimedia performance. And don't worry if your router platform can't play Quake3 at 50 frames per second.

- For equipment with ISA expansion slots, PCI >> ISA 16-bit > ISA 8-bit (where "greater than" means "faster than"), so use PCI adapters when possible. Hopefully, there are not many 8-bit ISA Ethernet cards out there, but if there are, find some other use for them besides in your router.

- EISA support wasn't really big for Linux during the period that EISA-based systems were still being marketed, and I've never had the opportunity to use it. If you need to deploy EISA, be sure you do your homework on device support. I'd recommend physically testing before you commit to that bus architecture.

- Interrupts *are* important—you should particularly avoid having an Ethernet adapter at a lower interrupt priority than a slow device, such as a parallel port or a serial port. Typically, interrupts 3, 4, 5, 7, 9, 10, 11, and 12 are available to you. The relative priorities, from highest to lowest, are 9, 10, 11, 12, 3, 4, 5, and 7.[1]

- Sbus and beyond—See the comment on EISA support.

Remote Management—Service Processors

One fairly recent development may benefit those of us running Linux in mission-critical applications. Hardware manufacturers are finally starting to realize that not all x86-based servers are administered by walking up to a GUI console attached via a KVM switch. For admins of more traditional Unix platforms, the need to have a keyboard and mouse to manage a system in the data center made x86-based hardware a little laughable. Many of these systems have on-board service processors that allow a range of actions to be performed remotely, from reading LEDs to cycling power on the system. The service processor is a wholly contained embedded system that continues to perform its function regardless of the state of the operating system running on the host system. Service processors also provide functions such as monitoring CPU and ambient temperature and operating-system health (really, whether or not the system has crashed) and can be programmed to send out alerts, shut a system down if the temperature exceeds a given threshold, or automatically reboot a system. For platforms without a service

---

[1]For more information about interrupts, see *http://www.linuxdoc.org/LDP/LG/issue38/blanchard.html.*

processor, the motherboard firmware is such that the system can be managed entirely through
the serial console, including all boot options and CMOS settings.

Admittedly, this isn't necessary for every environment, but its utility strikes home the first
time you absolutely have to power-cycle a system that is not physically accessible by you or
a co-worker, and it's something to take into consideration when purchasing a system. IBM's
x-series line (also known as Netfinity) comes with service processors and remote management
tools (potentially either network or serial-based). You can also purchase third-party add-on
cards, such as DarkSite by Crystal Group, Inc. (*http://www.crystalpc.com/darksite*). These
cards can be added to any system with a free PCI or ISA slot but are most useful for motherboards that allow their BIOS setup screens to be accessed via a serial port. (This is a handy
feature in a motherboard whether you're going to use a remote management card or not.)
We'll talk more about serial consoles in Section 1.1.6.

x86 BIOS Settings

Linux does very little, if anything, with BIOS after the machine bootstraps itself and starts
loading the operating system. Up until that point, the BIOS is involved in assigning base
addresses and IRQs to your PCI devices and assigning a precedence to the various potential
boot devices it recognizes. Note the implication: although you might be able have your root
partition on a USB-attached microdrive in your digital camera, the initial loading of the
kernel must be off a device the BIOS recognizes as a boot device. So your major concern
with your motherboard's BIOS is that it can start loading the kernel. Beyond that, a BIOS
that supports a password to get into its configuration menu might be useful, as are power-on
passwords if physical security is a concern. (And physical security is a concern for your network
infrastructure—see *Hacking Linux Exposed, Chapter 5* for a good treatment of this topic.)

There are a few BIOSes that are just a pain and possibly not worth the effort it takes to
work around their shortcomings. You're not likely to find such a thing marketed today, but
the BIOS on some older Compaq systems (Deskpro XLs) relocates the PCI address space to
a location in memory that Linux will never find. There is a documented work-around for this
which you can find via the *LDP*. Another source of annoyance is a BIOS that won't allow the
system to boot without a keyboard (or sometimes, <shudder>, a mouse) attached. These are
more common and very annoying.

For the BIOS that's made it this far, you will still need to configure it. Every BIOS is
different, but here are some basic configuration guidelines for standard desktop PC fare:

- Turn off any "Windows *XX*" features.

- Turn off any "15–16MB memory hole" features.

- Turn off all of the APM (Advanced Power Management) features; routers never sleep.
  The BIOS should not be continually stopping and restarting your hard drive, as this will
  definitely shorten the drive's lifespan. Also, a router should be able to process an interrupt from a communications adapter quickly, and waiting for APM to wake up system
  components may take too long to avoid packet loss. If you are environmentally conscious,
  try to purchase components with low power requirements, or use fewer components.

- Disable unused on-board adapters such as integrated USB ports or parallel ports. These
  use interrupts, which you may need for communications adapters. (On the other hand,
  do not disable things that you may need, since reenabling them will require you to reboot
  the system while at the console.)

- Use the PCI bus controller configuration (if available) to explicitly set the interrupt to be given to a PCI slot. This will prevent quirky things from happening, like adding an Ethernet adapter and then discovering on your next reboot that the IRQs assigned to your adapters have changed (and no longer match the values you are using when loading device-driver modules).

- As alluded to earlier, *consider* using power-on passwords and BIOS configuration passwords. I would tend to shy away from power-on passwords unless you have a facility that is staffed 24×7. These are a good idea for physical security but can be troublesome when you desperately need to reboot a router from a remote site or suffer a power failure.

  A BIOS configuration password is a good idea as long as you can find the password when you need it. One way to keep these passwords safe without having to keep track of many (potentially dozens of) different passwords is to send a GPG-encrypted email containing the password to yourself (and your backup administrator or manager).

- Disable any "virus-detection" feature in the BIOS. All this does is detect changes to the MBR (Master Boot Record) on your hard drives. LILO, *grub*, et al. are going to modify this from time to time, and it's a hassle to have a machine hang on a reboot because the BIOS doesn't like the fact that the MBR has changed.

1.1.4   Hard-Drive Subsystem

In most applications, a router should not be disk I/O bound,[2] and this makes your choice of hard drive fairly arbitrary. The only reason I qualify this statement is that there are conceivable situations where the system could be performing a lot of disk I/O—say if one of your routers is the target of a DoS (Denial of Service) attack and that system is configured to perform detailed logging of the network traffic it encounters. (In fact, it doesn't take long to realize that bringing a system to its knees with logging could itself comprise the DoS attack. We'll talk about some of features in Linux's netfilter code that limit or negate the effect of this sort of attack in Section 7.3.6.) But in general, your router shouldn't be be performing such excessive logging that your choice of hard drive will make a difference.

Many people swear by SCSI drives for both reliability and performance. I typically have used IDE drives for routers due to their low cost and easy configuration, but have had good luck with both. (It seems that drives have improved greatly in the past decade anyway.) SCSI drives can certainly be faster, but unless you anticipate needing that performance (are you sure this is a router?), it's doubtful that you'll take advantage of it.

One recent advent is the availability of IDE controllers with support for mirroring and/or RAID. Some motherboards feature these controllers integrated right onto the motherboard. Although you can perform mirroring and RAID in software, via the Linux kernel, why go to the trouble (or pay the overhead) when the hardware will do it for you? SCSI-based hardware RAID adapters, which have been around a little longer, are also becoming popular with Linux. In both cases you need to double-check to make sure that your hardware mirroring chipset/adapter is supported by the version of the kernel you'll be running. (The same goes for SCSI adapters in general, although there aren't too many SCSI adapters out there that still aren't supported under Linux.)

---

[2] A state when other system activities must frequently wait for the completion of reads and/or writes to the disk subsystem. This waiting is also known as **blocking**.

Drive Reliability in the Real World

Donald Becker, the author of a large number of the Ethernet drivers in the Linux kernel and leader of the *Beowulf* project, had some interesting things to say about IDE hard drives during a talk about Beowulf clusters at the 1998 Atlanta Linux Showcase. In his experience, which includes large numbers of IDE drives running continuously for long periods of time, drive failures are unrelated to the MTBF statistics listed by the manufacturer.

According to him, drives come in either good batches or bad batches—i.e., different production runs, regardless of manufacturer, are a more important factor in drive reliability than the manufacturer. He went on to say that power consumption also seems to play a very important role in drive reliability, and that the lower the average power consumption, the more reliable the drive. (Power consumption is a product of the spindle speed [RPM] and the mass of the platters themselves.)

In case you are wondering, a Beowulf cluster is a group of Linux machines networked together to build a system capable of performing like a supercomputer. What started as an experiment in the cost-efficiency of such a solution has been very successful, and many dozens of such clusters are now in use. See *http://www.beowulf.org/* for more information.

Partitioning Hard Drive Space

Overall drive capacity is not a primary concern for most router applications. It depends primarily on the amount of logging required. Many of my production routers use a single 1GB or 2GB drive (absolutely miniscule by today's standards), some as small as 300MB. If there is a second drive, it is a backup for the primary drive. The question of how to partition drive space is a common one among those new to Linux and Unix. There are lots of opinions, each founded upon its owner's experience, and you're about to hear another one. If you have a single 2GB disk, assign 600–800MB for the root partition, between 64–128MB of swap space, and everything else to */var*. The resulting partition table looks like the following:

Device Bootflag	Mount point	Size (MB)	File System
/dev/hda1 *	/	800	ext2 (Linux native)
/dev/hda2	n/a	128	Linux swap
/dev/hda3	/var	all remaining	ext2 (Linux native)

If you have a very small drive, dispense with the separate filesystem for */var*; you don't want to create arbitrary boundaries that will cause headaches later. Make your first partition a swap partition and allocate the rest to root. Just be aware that a full root filesystem makes for an unhappy Unix box and invites code that doesn't behave nicely when a write fails to fail in whatever manner it sees fit. You may want to have a cronjob frequently cleaning up logfiles in */var*.

On the other hand, the typical COTS (Commercial Off-The-Shelf) drive capacity has increased literally tenfold in the last few years, making partitioning decisions correspondingly less difficult. However, even with very large drives, you should still give the matter some thought. Most boot loaders aren't partial to booting from disk offsets deeper than 2GB into the drive (refer to the *Large Disk HOWTO* at the LDP). Therefore, I'd recommend a partition table closer to the following:

```
Device Bootflag    Mount point  Size (MB)      File System

/dev/hda1    *         /boot        10          ext2 (Linux native)
/dev/hda2              n/a          384         Linux swap
/dev/hda3              /            3000        ext2 (Linux native)
/dev/hda4              /var         6500
```

The table above represents a 10GB disk. If your drive is larger than that, you may want to hold off and simply leave some space unallocated until you're sure what scheme works best in your environment. Also, sometimes there really can be too much of a good thing; waiting 5 minutes for *fsck* to finish checking a 20GB partition can seem like a half-hour during a production outage. Here are some general principles to use when considering how to slice a disk:

- Size your root partition large enough so that you won't be low on space any time soon. Migrating root to another partition, while not overly difficult, can be time consuming.

- All logging is done to */var*. Even if you use *syslog* to log remotely, you should have enough space to log locally for cases when you need to do some serious debugging or packet capture.

- Several distribution package managers do all of their work in */var*, including using it for a cache of recently loaded packages. You'll need some space here if you want to upgrade between releases.

- Packages you may add to your routers, such as *sendmail*, *Apache*, and *Squid*, all use space under */var* to hold their spool files.

- Without users, */tmp* space is not a concern. Well-behaved Linux packages do not use */tmp* for anything of consequential size.

- Compared to */var*, */usr* remains fairly static, although it does grow when you add more packages (and therefore system executables). You will want enough space in */usr* to hold a copy (perhaps two copies) of your kernel source tree if you plan to build your kernels directly on your machine. Note that you can always symlink */usr/src* to somewhere with lots of space, e.g., */var/tmp*. [3]

- Many folks swear by a separate filesystem for */usr*, but if forced to choose between that and a separate filesystem for */var*, I strongly recommend */var*.

- There is little point in carving your disk up into eight or ten different partitions for the various filesystems. This creates boundaries that serve no purpose other than to trip you up at some later date. Having many filesystems *does* make sense on systems that must organize a large amount of data, but an excessively large disk subsystem should tip you off to the fact that it is no longer a router.

- Some controllers/drives require reboots before the new partition can be recognized.

---

[3] The kernel keeps growing—sizes at the time of writing can be found in Appendix B.

The panacea for all of this partitioning hassle is the appearance of LVM (logical volume manager) tools for Linux in combination with filesystems which can be dynamically grown and shrunk. At the time of writing, these tools are not quite ready for prime-time, but are imminent. Along with filesystems that support resizing, Linux has several journaling filesystems to chose from. These can combat that potentially long *fsck* by implementing a transactional model with respect to how filesystem metadata are maintained.

1.1.5   SCSI Adapter

Since I normally do not use SCSI devices in my routers, I should probably just hush. But if you do require a SCSI adapter in your system, check the *LDP*'s *Linux Hardware Compatibility HOWTO* and consider an adapter that supports bus-mastering DMA transfers. Bus-mastering greatly reduces the load on the processor and the bus while accessing the device(s) by allowing the adapter to read and write data from memory directly. Without bus-mastering support, the CPU has to manage these transfers, which necessitates transferring the data from the device to the CPU and then from the CPU to memory to complete a read.

1.1.6   Video Adapter

This is an area where almost nothing is more than enough. You merely need an adapter capable of supporting an 80×25 text-mode console. Starting with version 2.2 of the kernel, the use of a serial port as a console is supported—thus eliminating the need for any video adapter whatsoever (almost). The caveat is that you won't be able to modify the system BIOS without a video adapter on x86 architectures that don't support text-based BIOS configuration over the serial port—refer back to Section 1.1.3—and a few systems may refuse to boot without a keyboard attached.[4] Configuring your system to use a serial port as the console requires three steps:

1. You need to enable serial console support in the kernel. (Although you can compile the serial support as a module, I recommend against it, since you will want to see the boot messages before any modules are loaded.)

```
Character devices --->
    <*> Standard/generic (dumb) serial support
    [*]     Support for console on serial port
```

2. Configure your boot loader to tell the kernel which serial port to use as the console by supplying console=device,baudrate as an argument to the kernel during the boot sequence. You should use the device name shown by *dmesg* (not the path to the device in */dev/*). Use 9600 for the baudrate. If you are using LILO, add the following line to your configuration and then rerun *lilo* to update the boot sector:

```
append = "console=ttyS0,9600"
```

3. Configure a getty process to run on this port by adding the appropriate line to */etc/inittab*.

```
T0:2345:respawn:/sbin/getty -L ttyS0 9600 vt100
```

---

[4]If you are stuck dealing with such a system, you may be able to get by with a keyboard dongle that fakes the system into believing that a keyboard is attached.

After you reboot so that these settings are active, you can access your serial console by attaching the specified port to any dumb terminal or to the serial port on another system or a terminal server. If you're using another Linux system, you'll need a terminal emulator, such as *minicom* or *cu* (which is part of the **uucp** package).

1.1.7   CPU

Processor speed can be quite important for certain types of routers, while others seem to barely touch the CPU at all. Routers that need more processing power are ones with lots of firewalling or NAT/masquerading rules and those that must also perform heavy statistics collection or monitoring. CPU requirements depend not only upon load, but also upon the number and type of adapters in the system. Adapters capable of DMA (and having Linux drivers which support bus-mastering) can significantly reduce the CPU requirements by being able to move data to and from main memory without involving the CPU. In the case of WAN adapters, some of these are capable of running the link protocol on the card itself, which means less code in the device driver and correspondingly lower CPU requirements.

In this matter, my recommendations are based purely on experience. At the time of writing, I have never needed to use anything faster than a Pentium II/233 (which was for a packet-filtering firewall). For WAN routers, a 486/66 has proved itself adequate, exposing its relative sloth only during kernel compiles. Because it really does depend upon your application, you should keep a close watch on marginally sized systems using tools like *top* and *vmstat*. Remember that routing and network transfers that occur in the kernel are recorded as system CPU time.

Linux Router Shootout!

Several people have suggested conducting a benchmark to determine the relative speed of Linux routers compared to traditional offerings. This is a good idea, because I believe it would allay the fears of those reluctant to consider Linux as a router. On the other hand, speed is only part of the equation, since Linux offers low cost and unprecedented flexibility. Furthermore, speed is relative; a couple of milliseconds may be intolerable latency for a gigabit switch, but it's peanuts for a 128kb ISDN link.

1.1.8   RAM

You should have enough RAM to ensure that your router will not be swapping at any point during normal day-to-day operations. With the 2.4 kernel, this means at least 16MB for an access router on a low-speed link and definitely more if you intend to run other services, perform firewalling, or do any monitoring. Of course, faster memory is better, more memory is better, and better memory is better. Since you're not going to be able to solve an equation that minimizes the cost of all three of those at the same time, I'd opt for quantity and quality (ECC) before I'd get the fastest memory available.

1.1.9   Network Interface Card (NIC)

Your choice of network adapter is a topic that warrants some discussion, although much less nowadays than it used to.[5] The Linux kernel natively supports a wide variety of adapter types,

---

[5]Many thanks to all of the people who have contributed to the impressive amount of support and stability of the network device drivers for Linux.

including ATM, FDDI, ISDN, token ring, Wireless LAN, ARCnet, Appletalk, infrared, amateur radio, WAN, and a slew of Ethernet cards from 10Base-T to all different flavors of gigabit and beyond. The amount to which different devices are supported seems to be proportional to the probability of encountering those devices; i.e., the more popular the device, the more fully developed and tested the driver. Ethernet, of course, reigns supreme, but there is an impressive amount of support for the other types of devices too.

If you're interested in trying something new or perhaps a bit out of the ordinary, check for driver availability in the most recent stable kernel release. (When possible, I'd shy away from using development kernels for routers.) If the driver is not in the kernel source, you should check with the hardware manufacturer to determine if they have Linux support. Sometimes they have drivers that either have not yet made it into the source, or have license restrictions which prevent them from being incorporated into the main source.[6] You can also refer to the *Linux Hardware Compatibility* or to the *NET-HOWTO* on the *LDP*.

1.1.10   Ethernet Adapters

Because Ethernet is so ubiquitous, let us spend a moment talking about it specifically, although some of the comments apply to all adapters. For most applications, a well-known PCI 10/100 card is the right choice. Here are things to keep in mind:

- Look for PCI cards that support bus-mastering DMA. You can also look for cards with more on-board RAM. This is used for buffers and can normally be found on the "server" cards. The extra buffer space is a Good Thing when your router gets busy.

- On average, you're not going to be able to send or receive data at rates any higher than the rate of the slowest interface in your packet flow. When one side of the router hosts a relatively slow communications link (like ISDN, a cable modem, or a T1), a well-performing 10Base-T card is more than adequate. At the same time, if you anticipate heavy use of the Ethernet interface for DNS lookups or the router performs some sort of store-and-forward function (such as a caching proxy or a mail-gateway), use the fastest card that your network supports (and that you can afford).

- Always compile your device drivers as modules. In many cases, this will allow you to upgrade the device driver without having to generate a new kernel or reboot your machine. It also makes it possible to unload and reload the device driver should you need to reinitialize the driver for some reason. For a more in-depth discussion of kernel modules, see Section B.6 in Appendix B.

- To get the most out of your device driver (modular or not), you should read the comments at the beginning of the driver source code in the kernel. This is traditionally where the most current (and complete) driver documentation is kept. The drivers are stored in `./drivers/net/driver_name.c` relative to the root of the Linux source tree. Of particular interest for router admins will be documentation on initializing more than one card of the same type per system and options that allow tuning memory buffer sizes and link speed/duplex autonegotiation. (Another benefit of using modular drivers: If you specify the parameters incorrectly for a built-in driver, you'll have to reboot to test another syntax or combination—with modules, you keep trying until you get it right.)

---

[6] If they provide no Linux support whatsoever, take the time to send them a polite note. It may be that someone in-house has developed the driver, but it has not yet been made public. Also, companies don't know about demand unless you make that demand known.

- Plug-and-Play (PnP) ISA cards are not going to save you any time whatsoever. They only confuse the issue of base address and IRQ selection, and there are some behaviors that are very difficult to troubleshoot if the card is left in PnP mode. If you have a PnP card, immediately disable the PnP functionality and set the base address and IRQ manually. Typically, this can be done with the DOS-based setup utility which comes with the card. A few cards have their configuration utilities ported to Linux, and most of these seem to be available at *http://www.scyld.com/diag/index.html*. If you're wondering how to find out what IRQs and base addresses are already in use on your system, check `cat /proc/interrupts` and `cat /proc/ioports`, respectively.

- WOL (Wake-On-LAN) cards—cards that can be remotely controlled to "wake up" your system—are not worth the extra expense unless you have a specific application in mind where you'd like to have the router remain powered down until a certain situation occurs.

- Spend some time reading through the materials at *http://www.scyld.com/network/*. Besides being the foremost Linux Ethernet driver guru, period (IMO), Donald Becker does a good job of explaining complex topics and has collected a wealth of valuable information at this site. Unless you're a member of the IEEE 802.3 working group, consider it mandatory reading.

- If you're annoyed at the huge selection available and tired of this already and just want me to pick a card for you, try one of these:

  - 3Com 3c905B-TXNM. This card uses the `3c59x` kernel driver module. Note that 3com supplies a vendor driver for some of the newer cards in this line. This driver is `3c90x` and is *not* the driver to which I refer in the sidebar about vendor-supplied drivers.

  - Intel EtherExpress Pro 10/100. This card uses the `eepro100` kernel driver module.

1.1.11   Other Networking Adapters

As convenient as Ethernet is, it's not the only thing out there. Many companies have made large investments in LAN topologies like token ring and FDDI, and LANs are just the beginning of networking with Linux. If you intend to use something other than Ethernet, don't feel left out. Flexibility is Linux's middle name, and several chapters in this book specifically address other technologies. Since our primary focus right now is on hardware selection, here are some pointers that may help in research for other types of hardware:

- *http://www.linuxtr.net/* is the URL for the Linux Token Ring Project's website. This site has detailed information about card compatibility and documentation about how to get those cards running.

- *http://linux-atm.sourceforge.net/* has information for running ATM on Linux.

- Visit *http://www.worldvisions.ca/~apenwarr/arcnet/index.html* for information on running ARCnet.

- **Synchronous serial adapters** is an ominous sounding term for high-speed serial adapters that normally interface dedicated telco circuits, like T1s. They're typically designed to be general-purpose enough to run several protocols, including Frame Relay,

---

A Bad Experience with a Vendor-Supplied Driver

Sometimes a box that carries the phrase "Supported on Linux" is less helpful than the box that doesn't say anything about Linux support at all. I was in a hurry to get a 100Mbit PCI card for a home system, and in typical consumer fashion—I wanted it to be cheap but hadn't done sufficient research beforehand. I was at my local electronics warehouse and had sorted out the really expensive cards (ironically the ones I *knew* would work, since I had used them at the office) and had a couple of relatively inexpensive cards in hand. One of them indicated that it worked with Linux and even listed RedHat 5.2. Assuming that the box had been printed a year or two earlier during the period when that version of RedHat would have been current, I took the "Supported on Linux" card, trying to reward the vendor that recognizes Linux. Bad idea....

That card was supported on RedHat 5.2, meaning that a binary module and a copy of the driver source for the 2.0 kernel were located on the driver disk. The vendor's website did have a version for the 2.2 kernel that, to put it mildly, performed pitifully. (Going from a 10Mbit card on a hub to a 100Mbit card on a switch shouldn't result in a performance decrease!) All's well that end's well, I suppose; Donald Becker, the great guru of Ethernet device drivers, had been working independently on a driver for the chipset in question and had incorporated this into the upstream 2.4 kernel sources. Why can't the manufacturers just list the chipset on the side of the box?!?

PPP, X.25, BiSync, and perhaps protocols like SNA. We will talk more about these adapters when we cover Frame Relay implementations in Chapter 5.

Analog Modems

Although some might find analog modems a low-tech topic, several aspects of this ubiquitous peripheral warrant discussion when you're going to deploy one in a production Linux environment. At all costs avoid *Winmodems*, modems that require a device driver because they utilize the host system's processor to provide their functionality. Very few of these DSP-based modems have device drivers available for Linux, and the idea of having the router's CPU involved in the modem's compression negotiation is distasteful anyway. To save yourself from continually having to write business justifications that explain the difference between K65Flex, V.90, and V.92, spend a little extra for a modem with upgradable firmware (ideally the upgrades should be software-based, i.e., via flashing an EEPROM). Unless you're buying modems in large quantities, spend a little extra money to get a good-quality modem. A less expensive modem might seem like a good deal, but when you are trying to establish a connection over a very noisy, high-latency satellite link, you will find out what was sacrificed to lower the price.

Finally, use external modems, unless this causes a great deal of hassle with your physical installation. External modems can be replaced and moved between systems without having to shut anything down. Nicer ones may have DIP switch settings that can be adjusted without having to crack the case. External modems are easily power-cycled if need be, remove a potential source of RF noise from within your computer case, and have cool blinking lights. If your modem firmware does need updating but your vendor does not provide a mechanism for doing this within Linux, you'll be less peeved about the situation if you don't have to reboot your box (probably twice—again to reinstall the modem) to perform the upgrade.

xDSL Adapters and Cable Modems

Consumer broadband is truly a wonderful thing. For $50 USD per month you can have unlimited downloads at T1+ speeds, and some providers will allocate you a static IP address so that you can offer network services from a server or servers running in your home. Although providers are gradually becoming more Linux savvy, you're still very likely to hear the automaton's drone *Linux is not a supported platform*, even if your question is completely unrelated to Linux. Your main objective when evaluating devices to interface one of these services is to avoid any sort of device driver at all, if that's possible. In other words, insist upon an external device that connects to your system via Ethernet. By doing this, you limit your device driver responsibility to the Ethernet card in your router or workstation.

If you're adventurous (<cough> foolhardy), you may have luck employing a USB-based device, but I would advise against it. Supposing that you are able to get it to work, you're trading good networking performance with low system overhead (Ethernet) for a lower-performance solution. Also, some services, such as SDSL, can achieve downstream speeds of 6Mbits/second, far more than I want to pump through a USB port.

Another thing to consider when shopping for DSL services is whether or not you have to run PPPoE (PPP over Ethernet) to use the service. Although there is established support for this under Linux, it burns cycles that could just as well have been doing something else. Take your time and research your prospective provider to make sure Linux is supported (or at least known to work) with their service and that the product offering suits your needs. You may find *http://www.dslreports.com/* a good source of information beyond the provider's sales pitch, including feedback from current customers.

That completes the general hardware selection notes for your Linux router. Unless you like to roll up your sleeves and hack driver and kernel code, it is advisable to stick with devices that are supported in the stable kernel releases for your production systems. Although the preceding section may seem to be full of caveats and gotchas, you shouldn't belabor your decision about hardware for too long. The items noted are meant to save you time if you have something specific in mind. Most of the work and decision making takes place during the software configuration, so save your time and energy for that.

1.2   The Environment around Your Router

Now we will step back and look not at the router itself, but at some of the elements that surround it. Our view encompasses not only the physical space the router occupies, but also procedures and policies surrounding access to it and management of it.

1.2.1   Power Source

You should have a good, stable source of adequate grounded power. If you are not familiar with the ratings of the outlets where your systems are located, try to spread the load out across as many different outlets (and hopefully different circuits) as is feasible without creating a mess of extension cables. Beware power strips/surge protectors with nice big flat paddle switches on them. I cannot tell you how many times I've inadvertently powered off everything plugged into one of those things by grabbing the thing and accidently throwing the switch. (No, really, I can't tell—people would be angry if they found out!) Purchase a bag of nice long zip-ties and affix the power strip to the inside of your rack, a table leg, wherever. Then take some black electrical tape and tape that paddle switch into the *on* position.

In the United States, be mindful of the difference between 110 volts and 220 volts, lest your power supply spit the answer at you in a pall of blue smoke. Many data centers have 220-volt circuits for the larger systems, which draw less current at the higher voltage. Most x86-based systems have power supplies that can run at either voltage, but not many I've used have auto-sensing supplies.

A UPS is an important investment toward keeping your system up and protected from power outages, brownouts, lightning strikes, and other enemies of electronics. Several major UPS vendors provide Linux versions of their software, and there are many open-source monitors available. If you're buying a UPS, be sure that it can be managed over a serial port, or in the case of larger models, via a network-attached management module that speaks TCP/IP— typically then telnet and/or SNMP. Some UPS hardware can generate statistics regarding the quality of the utility power in case you need some facts to take to your provider about the quality of their service. You may also be able to monitor the temperature in your computer via your UPS.

1.2.2   Physical Installation

Like any other production system, your router(s) should be in an area which is able to be physically secured (i.e., locked), is temperature-regulated, and is low-traffic. (By a "low-traffic" area I mean one where people are seldom to be found.) You should use a rack or a cabinet to house the system, if possible, and make sure that there is adequate airflow around the case. It may sound pedantic, but a neat installation is less likely to be accidentally taken offline by a clumsy mistake. Also, people who should not be messing with your systems are less likely to be inclined to touch or disturb a neat installation. You should use every trick in the book to keep **lusers** from defiling (pun intended) your systems.

1.2.3   Testing and Planning

No matter how good you are, or how careful you try to be, everybody makes mistakes. I have heard it said that *human error* is the cause of over 80% of production computer outages. It is important to recognize this fact from the very beginning if your production environment is to have a minimum of downtime. You should always be mindful of it in your work. Any change should be thoroughly tested before you roll it out to your production environment, and there should be a fallback plan in case things get sticky in the middle of a change.

The problem is that networks are not always easy to test adequately. It is often difficult and/or expensive to duplicate certain aspects of your environment, such as network load and circuit types. This is particularly true when you are making changes to systems that are part of a larger whole, involving networks controlled by others—for example, testing bandwidth filters for Frame Relay links and automatic failover for your Internet firewall. Special circumstances aside, you can limit your vulnerability by being confident about any changes you make. One confidence builder is testing, while another is following sound **change-management** procedures. The first part of change management is planning.

Examples include the planning of upgrades, scheduled outages, migrations, and the like. Take the time to list out the steps required to complete some task—say, for example, adding an NIC to a router, migrating a remote office to a larger Frame Relay link, or upgrading the hubs in your equipment room without affecting the users. You may never use the list, but the act of writing out the steps required is worth the time it takes. It will often lead you to consider how those actions will interact with your environment, and remind you of things you might have overlooked had you started the task without explicitly listing the steps required. Roadblocks take many forms—a piece of hardware that wasn't ordered, a hostname that should have been registered with the InterNIC, or simply a lack of ports on a hub. Speaking from personal experience, you can save yourself a lot of frustration by just jotting down the sequential actions you need to take to complete a job and then reviewing these before you start the task.

Although I'm not big fan of bureaucratic processes or procedural formalisms, you may want to generate a checklist for yourself, or in some cases a set of change documentation for peer review. At a minimum, make sure you consider these aspects before embarking on major changes:

- *Plan out your change beforehand.* Document what you hope to accomplish, obtain approval, and notify any affected parties. You'll find that users are much more sympathetic when they've been given advance notice that there could be an issue. (Another bit of psychology: the *permission/forgiveness equation* is reversed when it comes to outages during change windows.)

- *Have a clearly documented fallback plan.* If your change goes south, you should be able to return the environment to its prior state without having to rebuild from scratch and restore your backups.

- *Set milestones and reasonable time limits to achieve those milestones.* If a change does go south, you need plenty of time to execute your fallback. Working under pressure only makes mistakes more likely.

- *Have a postchange test script* that exercises not only the functionality the change was to provide, but also the other capabilities provided by that equipment. More than once I've done user group A a favor only to realize after it was implemented that group B was going to be ticked.

- *Use a revision-control tool,* such as *RCS*, to track all changes to important configuration files—say, everything in */etc*. If there are multiple administrators, make sure that everyone is clear on the policy surrounding use of the tool.

One could write an entire text on best practices with respect to change control. (Well, I couldn't, but I'm sure several folks already have.) As opposed to providing a lengthy discussion on change management, I have relegated some material on testing strategies and change control to Appendix C. Let's get on with it so that we can talk about routers.

1.2.4   Backups

It's a boring job, but *you* have to do it. There are methodologies surrounding what to back up and how often to do it. Some are simply more useful than others, and some are going to be more appropriate for your environment than others. I recommend reading the section on Unix backups in *Practical UNIX and Internet Security* by Garfinkel and Spafford[7] before deciding on a strategy.

As for backup hardware and software, things have come a long way since the first edition of the book. At that time, the major backup software vendors were still scoffing at Linux, and I performed my backups to 4mm DAT tapes using *BRU 2000* from EST, Inc. (and had good experiences with that solution). Now you can't turn around without tripping over a major software vendor peddling their revolutionary Linux port of their enterprise-class product. And

---

[7]See the Bibliography for the complete reference.

I've used them, too, to back up my Linux systems to a beast of a tape library, an IBM 3494 with about 10TB of capacity. So you should have plenty of options, including integrating with the backup solution already in place at your facility.

But backups to removable media are not your only option. Maintaining orthogonality between the files that comprise the operating system and those that make your system unique can help to make the concept of a *full backup* obsolete. Why bother restoring a box when you have a redundant spare already loaded and can lay your configuration files down on it in a matter of minutes? (Your tape robot could still be mounting the tape by the time you were back online.) Because routers are dataless or very nearly so, you can adopt other strategies that result in reproducibility in your environment. We will discuss this further in Section 8.5.2.

1.2.5   Runbooks

You should maintain a log, or **runbook**, of all significant changes you make to your production systems, including software loads and configuration changes, password changes, hardware changes, in addition to any outages, odd behavior, security breaches, etc. Even if the event is not directly related to your system(s), you might want to note it. (<cough>.... This is really another aspect of change management.) Keep a runbook per system and, depending upon the size of your environment, one or more overall logs related to each service you provide your users. These logs will help you see how changes in one part of the network affect the other parts.

You may store these as files, but you should keep them in a safe place, possibly encrypted, and definitely back them up at regular intervals. Some stress hardcopy as a necessary component, but you cannot *grep* hardcopy, nor can you quickly transfer it to other members of your team, nor does it stay current for very long. One thing that has worked for me is to post the runbook entries as newsgroup articles on an internal NNTP server. This generates a nice threaded discussion forum and time-stamps everything submitted to it. Then I use *namazu*, a feature-rich full-text search engine tool (see *http://www.namazu.org/*), to generate a searchable index of this and other documentation and HOWTOs I have available on an internal website. Whatever the final format is, for your routers, don't forget to include things like essential system files, a copy of a working routing table, and any known bugs or odd behaviors.

1.2.6   Scripting and Version Control

No matter what your choice of scripting language, thoroughly document your scripts; well-documented code saves time down the road. Your code should contain comments within the code and a modification history at the top which tracks changes made to the script over time. You can save yourself some typing by developing or borrowing a script template to use as a starting point for all of your scripts. I use a header like this:

```
#!/usr/bin/perl
#
# <name of program>
#     <description of program>
#
# <license/copyright information (if needed)>
#
# modification history:
#
```

```
# 19990914/tm  initial release
# 20000608/tm  reworked error message code
# 20011103/tm  ported script from ksh to perl
################################################################
```

The main point is that changes in the script are noted so that others (or even you) will not have to guess at what changes have occurred when the script suddenly stops doing what you expect it to do. Use a common date format so that changes can be quickly spotted by a human and match regular expression searches. If you didn't notice, I'm partial to date patterns that sort correctly regardless of what century this is.

Other very important friends of the system administrator are version-control tools, namely *RCS* and *CVS*. I have to admit that I went far too long without these tools, simply because I hadn't set aside the paltry fifteen minutes or so needed to figure out how to use them. To what extent you use them—for every configuration file on your system, for a few frequently changing configuration files, or only for your scripts—depends on your work habits and the environment in your shop, but don't avoid them because they seem complicated.

1.2.7   Security

While password and network security receive a lot of attention, physical security is often neglected. Different types of organizations have differing needs, but at a minimum you should have a room with a lock on the door and a list of those who have the key. Where you go from there, be it to cameras or biometrics, know that a box that is openly accessible to nontrusted members of your IT staff is as good as lost, hacked, owned . . . . There is an excellent treatment of this topic in *Hacking Linux Exposed* (see the Bibliography entry on page 427). I highly recommend reading the entire book.

And thus concludes our brief discussion of system environmentals. Much of being a good system administrator is being conscientious about things like documentation and backups, being aware of how changes to one system might affect the systems around it, and having a contingency plan should things go wrong. (And things *will* go wrong.) Therefore, it is prudent to control the things you can, since there will be many that you cannot. This leads us to our next topic: software.

1.3   Distributions—Router Software

The term *router software* might be a bit misleading, since it is the Linux kernel itself that performs the actual routing of network packets. In other words, there is no program, per se, that has to be running for routing to occur. The routing takes place in **kernel-space** (as opposed to daemons and most services which run in **user-space**). Still, there are a host of programs which help make this happen and make it easier for humans to manage. This section contains a discussion of the different Linux distributions and what you might want to consider when you go about selecting one.

The selection of a Linux distribution can be the source of great anguish and gnashing of teeth, and you will find that it is as much a religious debate as a technical one. If you're asking yourself, *What's a distribution?*, it is a set of precompiled binaries and **package tools** (tools that are used to load and upgrade software on the system) which work together and have been tested as a whole to give us a complete operating system. In Linux lingo, they are called **distros**. Realize that the Linux kernel itself is only a small part of the distribution (or what we commonly think of a "Linux"). The remainder is comprised of compilers, shells, applications, servers, and systems software so that we can actually do something useful with the kernel. I've divided the discussion of distribution into two parts: *full-sized distributions*—distributions that are intended to be run from a hard drive and are general-purpose in nature—and *mini distributions*, which normally fit on a single floppy (or at most a few) and are often special-purpose.

1.3.1 Full-Sized Linux Distributions

At least a half-dozen very stable, successful full-sized distributions are available. You are not likely to go wrong with any of these, and your choice is largely a matter of personal preference. Since routing is performed in the kernel, I am not aware of a distribution that couldn't act as a router. However, keep in mind that the requirements of production systems differ from those of a personal workstation or home system, so some distros are better suited than others. The following is a list of properties which I believe are important for a production Linux distribution:

- **dependencies**—Be sure to choose a distribution that supports package dependencies (i.e., uses a scheme to notify you when you are loading software that depends upon some other software or library, or perhaps a certain version of a library). Most of the "modern" distributions do this automatically via their **package manager**. It is vital for this piece of software to prevent you from upgrading pieces of software which may have adverse effects on other software on the system.

- **upgradability**—Closely related to dependencies, make sure you choose a distribution which is committed to providing upgrade paths between versions. There is a certain sinking feeling you might be familiar with—that feeling you get when you realize that there is no (or at least no sane) upgrade path between the OS version that you currently have and the next supported version. Don't be bitten.

- **support**—Unless you have a lot of free time on your hands or very special requirements, choose a distribution which is being actively maintained and developed. There should also be a forum for submitting bugs, asking questions, and making suggestions for improvements. For an active distribution, users beget questions, which beget FAQs, which beget gurus. If you (or your management) require it, do some research to determine if commercial support is available.

- **stability**—The better tested the distribution, the less "testing" you'll do on your own. This also points toward the more popular distributions, although another aspect to consider is the value of simplicity over complexity. The more complicated a piece of software, the less likely that any organization or number of people will be able to test it thoroughly. Of course, you can quickly make a stable distribution unstable by taking matters into your own hands and deciding to upgrade software outside the confines of the package management scheme.

- **security**—Security goes hand-in-hand with testing and support. A distribution should have provisions for you to file security bugs against it, and provide documentation for running a (more) secure version of the base distribution.

- **licensing**—Because Linux is inexpensive in the grand scheme of things, an extra copy here or there should not break the bank. However, you should be cognizant of the licensing policy of the distribution you use.[8] Software piracy continues to exist, even in the world of OpenSource.

- **extensibility**—Although you might not initially be thinking of writing your own software packages, when you do, it would be nice to be able to distribute your custom software via the same mechanism as the rest of the OS. Therefore, your distribution should make available to you the same tools used to build packages for the released version, so that you can also build packages. This saves you the time and effort of producing documentation about how to compile, install, and configure software which is not available in the distribution.

- **target audience**—Linux is growing in popularity, and distributions are emerging with specific target audiences in mind. Not all of these will be the right choice for your production router.

Loading Linux

As I stated earlier, any of the modern distributions should suffice for a router. Choose what suits you and learn how to use that distribution's tools and features. Being able to find what you're looking for when you're trying to fix things is more important than whether or not the file is in the "right place." When you load your system, remember to select tools and avoid unnecessary toys. With the variety of distributions and their various schemes for loading software, it is difficult to list exactly what you should select from your system. The following guidelines should help:

1. You will very likely need C development environment (at least *gcc*, *make*, and the *bin86* tools [assembler, etc.]—in other words, enough to compile a kernel). Some distributions will automatically load the required tools if you select a kernel source package. If you find that loading an entire development environment just to compile a kernel is overkill, you can forego this and compile your kernels on another system. In my experience, having the ability to compile a kernel on the router is useful.

2. You should not need an X-server or a window manager, although X libraries are not a bad idea if you will be throwing xterms and running other X clients from your system.

3. Load all of the networking tools you can find, at least until you learn which ones you like and don't like. Examples of what to load are mentioned throughout the book.

4. Do not load "network server" parts of the distribution unless you know that you need these things—typically, packages like *Samba*, *Apache*, and other things for network *servers*. Once you're up and routing, you can go back and add individual packages as needed. Until then, they are a security risk and an extra load on your router.

Once you have loaded your system, take some time to familiarize yourself with what you have loaded. Sometimes, the distribution will come with tools that you were not even aware existed. All of the distributions that support dependencies will place information specific to the packages loaded somewhere on your system. For example, if you're running Debian, you can use `dpkg -l` to see what packages are loaded. For every package loaded, there is a directory */usr/share/doc/package* which contains documentation for that package (or a pointer to it), in addition to the license and a changelog.

---

[8]Furthermore, I think that you should fundamentally agree with it.

1.3.2 Mini Linux Distributions

The minidistributions offer several advantages over their full-sized counterparts. Many are small enough to fit on a single floppy disk and can be tried without disrupting the system configuration on the hard drive. They can be easier to master because there is less to learn, and they are small enough that you can take them completely apart and look at how they work. Their size also makes them more likely to be both secure and fully tested (less to crack and less to break). Because they can be placed on removable media, they are not subject to hard drive failures. For this reason, they are an excellent choice for physically demanding environments which might be too rough for a hard drive.

Of course, these advantages come at a certain cost. Namely, these distributions lack some of the flexibility and conveniences of their larger cousins. (Do not expect to find half a dozen different shells plus a Perl interpreter.) Also, many of the commands have to be scaled down and recompiled against leaner versions of *libc* to save space. This means that some commands might behave a little differently than they do on the full distributions. Still, for a router, they can be a good fit. You can prepare upgrades and fixes at your desk and send them to remote sites, either on floppies or as an email attachment. (If you do the latter, make sure you trust the person on the other end, and include a copy of *rawrite2.exe* along with instructions if they're running a Microsoft-based operating system.) They can serve as rescue disks—either enough to get you back up and running while you piece your normal router back together, or as the toolset used to boot the failed (perhaps hacked) router to poke around the filesystems and assess the situation. They are also excellent instructional aids; several of them cater to this purpose. And you can try them out in a matter of minutes; if you don't like what you see, just format the floppy and try another. Here is a partial list of the mini distro offering:

- **LRP**—The Linux Router Project. This distribution is directly targeted at the network administrator of production routers. It is well done and capable of supporting more than just basic routing. Examples include packages for *Bind*, *GateD*, and an *SNMP* daemon, among others. You can find out more about it at *http://www.linuxrouter.org/* as well as in Section 3.5.

- **tomsrtbt**—*http://www.toms.net/rb/*—This single floppy distribution provides a nice set of commands which can be used to perform rescue activities as well as configure a router. I have used this distribution in the past to put together single-purpose diskettes—for tasks at remote sites without sysadmin staff for which some special action is needed, which cannot be performed over the network.

- **Trinux**—*http://www.trinux.org/*—This is based on multiple floppies (two or three) and focuses on providing network security and monitoring tools. It supports an impressive amount of network tools and is ideal for quickly producing a working sniffer on almost any machine without damaging the host OS.

- **muLinux**—*http://sunsite.auc.dk/mulinux/*—This fits on a single floppy with optional "add-on" floppies. Like Trinux, it is also targeted for workstation and educational use but contains enough tools to be useful as a basis for a router.

- **floppyfw**—*http://www.zelow.no/floppyfw/*—Here is another networking-centric single floppy distribution which is designed to act as a packet-filtering router. It caught my eye since it stays very current with respect to kernel releases (and because it also happens to be based on Debian).

- **Coyote**—*http://www.coyotelinux.com/*—This distribution is another single-floppy mini distro focused on network connectivity. The distribution is aimed at configuring your system as an access router/firewall for cable modem and DSL installations.

This list is by no means complete. A more comprehensive list can be found on the **tomsrtbt** homepage. To my knowledge none of the minidistributions is a commercial effort or has any sort of financial backing. Keep this in mind if you find that they are lacking some of the gloss and polish that the full commercial distributions have. Since the authors volunteer their time, they might not be able to incorporate features or answer questions as quickly as you would like. Do not let this dissuade you from their use. Like so many other things involved with Linux, they have merit *because* they are noncommercial. They are usually a labor of love, and their high quality reflects this. If you really want to see something in the distribution, submit a patch, get involved.

1.3.3   Debian, My Distribution of Choice

If your mind wasn't already made up on the question of distribution before you started reading this section, things are probably about as clear as mud. The choice of distribution can seem unwieldy when you first get started, but to a large extent it's arbitrary (and yes, even my choice is arbitrary). Different distributions appeal to folks for a variety of reasons, and my advice is to try several of them until you find the one that feels right. Unlike other operating systems, where when you run Solaris, there is no question that you're running Sun Microsystems' copy of Solaris, Linux is available in more flavors than the number of other currently available operating systems combined. Each of these can be thought of as an interpretation of how an operating system should work for its system administrators and users. Some workplaces may be keen on commercial support directly from the distribution. (But know that you can purchase commercial support for all of the major distributions if you need it.) Some system administrators may insist on GUI installers, while others loathe the idea. Some are available only for specific hardware platforms, allowing the distribution to focus on the strengths of a given platform.

I use Debian GNU/Linux; I have used it since 1996 and will undoubtedly still be using it when the information in this book has been depreciated by the march of new features and kernel routing mechanisms. Why I started using it is an uninteresting historical factoid, a decision that now I can hardly consider informed but was nonetheless suitable. Debian is completely open, from its toolset to its bug list to the (often hotly debated) discussion of what features should be in the next release. Debian is entirely noncommercial and free—not only in terms of cost, but in terms of the licensing and source-code availability. Having the source code for both the binaries and the packaging greatly aids its extensibility. Should you require a slight modification or a backport, all you need do is retrieve a copy of the source package, make the desired changes, and use the Debian developer's tools to repackage the software. Debian's target audience seems to be those who agree with the philosophy of a 100%-free Linux distribution and who value the technical precision that is fostered by openness and constructive criticism. (They claim no particular target.) And Debian runs on just about anything, hardwarewise. See *http://www.debian.org* for more information.

All that being said (and my plug for Debian finished), the examples in this book should run on any of the distributions. Every now and then I'll throw in some value-added information about Debian, since I know it better than the other distros. Since Debian consists solely of freely available software, there won't be mention of anything that you cannot easily find and get running on your distribution of choice.

1.4   Summary

This concludes the section on router software, and with it the chapter. We have covered a large range of topics, trying to provide an overview of things to keep in mind for newcomers before we dive into the tech-talk of the later chapters. If you're new to this, I hope that you feel you have enough knowledge to get started. Let's quickly review where to find information on the tasks of:

- gathering hardware (page 1) and selecting a network adapter card (page 9).

- justifying to your management why you need budget dollars for environmentals—the UPS, the rack, the support system and internal documentation web server. . . . (page 13).

- selecting a Linux distribution (page 17), whether full-sized or miniature.

This knowledge classifies you as a *Linux Router Acolyte*. The next chapter continues talking about routers in general but is generally more interesting than change control (regardless of how vital it is). It covers IP subnetting and basic routing principles and then terminology surrounding digital telephony. After that, we'll start routing.

Chapter 2

IP, ETHERNET, AND
TELEPHONY BASICS

This chapter covers some necessary background concepts before we dive into configuring a router. First, we'll review some IP subnet terminology and the related base-2 math. The math is a prerequisite for the discussion on principles of IP subnetting used by workstations and routers and for successful day-to-day work with TCP/IP networks. After that, we'll switch gears for a short discussion of Ethernet, including how machines find each other and the difference between Ethernet hubs and switches. The chapter concludes with an introduction to WAN links based on digital telephone circuits.

2.1   Routing 101

For the purposes of this book, a router is anything that transfers TCP/IP packets between different IP subnets, regardless of their physical media type or the media protocol. In short, a router is something used to connect two distinct IP subnets.

What's an IP subnet? What's a physical media type? What's a link-layer protocol? These are all questions first of terminology, but also of *layers*. Networking can be discussed in terms of layers and how each layer acts as an interface, performing communication between the layer above and below it. This is done for numerous reasons, but I believe the most important are reuse and flexibility. It is useful to be able to differentiate between the layers and to agree on a common terminology in order to talk clearly about building networks and routers. The most common taxonomy for networks is defined by the OSI networking model. If you are not familiar with the OSI networking model, see the first chapter of *Interconnections* by Radia Perlman or *Computer Networks* by Andrew S. Tanenbaum. (Complete references can be found in the Bibliography.) To get started with routing, you don't need to memorize all seven layers of the model. Just understand the concepts in the following definitions:

physical medium—in most cases a wire, or perhaps an RF link. It is generally associated with a specific physical interface. As an example, think of a normal serial cable used to connect a DB9 serial port to a DB25 external modem.

physical protocol—the protocol (normally electrical or optical) which runs on the **physical medium**. RS-232 is an example for a serial cable, or IEEE 802.3 for Ethernet.

link-layer protocol—the protocol used to negotiate a connection (or a **link**) between two machines sharing the same physical medium. Examples are PPP, HDLC, Frame Relay, and Ethernet. The link-layer does not dictate which networking protocol you run on top of it, but it does need to know about it. This is why you might find different PPP implementations for IP and IPX.

networking protocol—the protocol that dictates addressing of nodes and packets, and the way that packets are routed across the network between any two endpoints. Examples are IP and IPX.

transport protocol—the protocol which interfaces the networking protocol to the operating system and processes within it. In the case of TCP/IP, there are multiple protocols which comprise the **protocol suite**—namely, TCP and UDP.

application protocol—the level of protocol created by applications programmers, often where users get involved. They invoke commands such as *telnet*, which define a sequence of TCP transactions, which in turn are realized through a series of IP events (which define transmissions between Ethernet hosts, which in turn result in electromagnetic waveforms propagating through a piece of twisted-pair). Other application protocols are NFS, HTTP, SSH, NNTP, SNMP, SMTP, FTP, and many others.

Figure 2.1 illustrates each layer encapsulating the layer above it. When everything is configured properly, the different layers work together as a cohesive whole, and the user doesn't even think about these things. In contrast, you need to understand what's happening at the different layers to be able to effectively design and troubleshoot your network. As an example, not being able to make a connection to a remote machine does not necessarily mean the network's *down*, at least not if the problem is with the user's DNS configuration. By correctly assessing the level at which the problem exists, you eliminate the need to test other layers, whose problems are merely symptomatic of the root problem. The end result of a good understanding is less time spent on wild goose chases.

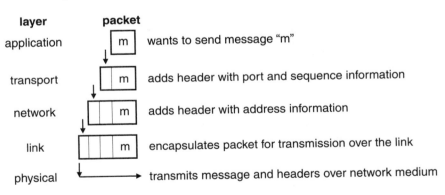

Figure 2.1 Layered Network Model

2.1.1 IP Subnetting

An IP subnet is a collection of network addresses which can communicate directly with each other without having to refer to a router to accomplish the communication. In other words, the media-protocol drivers support direct communication between all systems in the same subnet. Transmitting data between two separate subnets requires a router, often called a **gateway** in this context. To determine whether or not two systems are in the same subnet, do the following:

> Perform a binary AND of the IP address of machine A and the subnet mask of machine A. Now do the same for machine B. If the resulting network addresses are identical for both machines, then these machines can speak over TCP/IP to each other without using a gateway.

If this is Greek to you, you should review the remainder of this section. It introduces enough base-2 math to get you started with IP addresses, the subnet mask, what is meant by a network and broadcast address, and how to calculate them.

The IP Address and Base-2 Mathematics

An IPv4 address[1] is a collection of 32 bits, divided into four groups of 8 bits for convenient presentation in the form of 4 unsigned integers. (Really, those unsigned integers are more appropriately called *decimals*, since the presentation is in base-10.) Each grouping of 8 bits can be expressed as a value between 0 and 255. Almost everyone is familiar with the dotted-decimal notation used for 32-bit IP addresses: $w.x.y.z$, where $0 \leq$ w,x,y,z $\leq$ 255. This is done primarily for humans; the computers couldn't care less about the decimal values. Here is an example IP address:

As you see it (base-10): 215.38.181.126

As the computer sees it (base-2 or binary): 11010111001001101011010101111110

Split into 4 groups of 8 bits: 11010111 00100110 10110101 01111110

Each bit represents a successively greater power of two as you move from right to left. Note that the powers of two, which are listed below, start at 2^0.

$$2^7 \quad 2^6 \quad 2^5 \quad 2^4 \quad 2^3 \quad 2^2 \quad 2^1 \quad 2^0$$
$$128 \quad 64 \quad 32 \quad 16 \quad 8 \quad 4 \quad 2 \quad 1$$

A 1 in a given bit position indicates that the corresponding power of two counts toward the final value. A 0 in a given bit position means to ignore that position. If we label the bit positions b_7–b_0 (moving from left to right), we can write out a formula for our binary-to-decimal conversion.

$$128*b_7 + 64*b_6 + 32*b_5 + 16*b_4 + 8*b_3 + 4*b_2 + 2*b_1 + 1*b_0$$

Thus, the binary-to-decimal conversion of 11010111 works as follows:

128*1	+	64*1	+	32*0	+	16*1	+	8*0	+	4*1	+	2*1	+	1*1
128	+	64	+	0	+	16	+	0	+	4	+	2	+	1

which equals 215.

As you can see, the bit positions where there was a 1 contributed to the final value; the positions containing 0 did not. Converting the other three values in our initial example (often referred to as **octets**, as they are groupings of 8, but most commonly known simply as **bytes**) yields:

---

[1] Note: We will discuss IPv6 later on in the book in Section 6.5. For the time being, all of the material that refers to simply IP implies IPv4.

$$00100110 = 38$$
$$10110101 = 181$$
$$01111110 = 126 \tag{2.1}$$

The reason the computer does not use the decimal representation is that it is easier only for humans. The hardware in the computer (and on the NIC) is designed to operate on bits. In fact, it can work *only* with bits. One good thing about bits is that digital hardware can do things with them incredibly quickly. Routers like speed and efficiency, so router admins get to work with bits.

To review, an IP address is 32 bits that are often represented as four groupings of 8 bits each. At least, that's the simple answer. The next section covers how these 32 bits can be split into network and address fields.

> ## Tip: Help with Base-2 Conversions
>
> If you are not accustomed to making these conversions (or counting in 2's), I encourage you to perform these conversions on your own so that you can be certain about how they work. Most scientific calculators can help, as will some calculator programs—notably *calctool* (written by Rich Burridge).

The Subnet Mask

The topic of the subnet mask seems to cause considerable confusion when it comes to configuring a TCP/IP stack. The **subnet mask** is used to divide the 32 bits into two parts. The left portion is the **network address**. The remaining part is the **host address**. The subnet mask simply tells the computer how many bits (from left to right) are in the network address. The remaining bits comprise the host address. This can be seen in Figure 2.2.

In the olden days there were three types of networks: class A, class B, and class C, each with its own fixed subnet mask. Period. This meant that there were three ways to divide the 32 bits in an IP address into a network and a host address. Because this resulted in extremely restrictive groupings of IP addresses, **CIDR** (Classless Inter-Domain Routing) was born. With CIDR, you can divide the IP address almost anywhere within its 32 bits. You can think of it

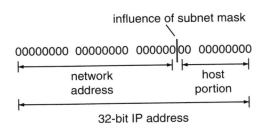

Figure 2.2 Network and Host Portions of the IP Address

as drawing a line in the sand and proclaiming: *"All bits to the left of this line comprise the network address, and all bits to the right of this line comprise the host address."*

The delineation between the two fields of the IP address is presented with the subnet mask. The idea is similar to cutting a hole in a piece of paper and then placing it over a page of this book. The larger the hole, the more of the book you can see through it. In the case of a subnet mask, the part you see through the hole is controlled by the number of 1s, and corresponds to the network address of the subnet. The remainder is the host address. To "look through the mask," the computer performs a binary-AND operation of the IP address and the subnet mask. Here is a quick example:

	11010111 . 00100110 . 10110101 . 01111110			*IP address*
bitwise-AND	11111111 . 11111111 . 11111100 . 00000000			*subnet mask*
	11010111 . 00100110 . 10110100 . 00000000			*network address*

As you can see, where there is a 1 in the subnet mask, the bit in the IP address is copied into the network address. 0s in the subnet mask remain 0s. That's **masking**, and it is something that can be performed very quickly by computer hardware. Although the subnet mask is always a string of bits inside the computer, people get tired of writing out all of those ones and zeros, so there are three different representations for human use.

- The first is just like a dotted IP address—For example, **/255.255.252.0**. This is easy for humans, and it is the most common format used when specifying the subnet mask in commands and configuration files.

- The second is the format used in the example—i.e., all bits written out as four groups of eight bits (**/11111111.11111111.11111100.00000000**). It is rarely written out except when you need to calculate network addresses by hand.

- The third representation counts the number of 1s before the 0s start, which we can call **maskbits** notation. The subnet mask in our example has 22 1s and would be written simply as **/22**.

Note that there cannot be a 0 followed by a 1 in a subnet mask. Recall that the subnet mask is telling us how many bits (from left to right) are in the network address. Because the **network** and **host** fields are contiguous, and all bits must be used, there are no gaps. For all three representations it makes no sense to specify a network address without a subnet mask, or vice versa, so a slash (/) is used to separate the two.

Converting Between Subnet Mask Representations

Table 2.1 contains a list of subnet mask numbers that can help you perform conversions between the different subnet mask formats. Use this for each octet in your mask separately. If you encounter 255.255.224.0 as a subnet mask, you can use the table to quickly calculate that it is equivalent to $8+8+3 = 19$, or /19, or if you need the binary, 11111111.11111111.11100000. 00000000.

Parameters Related to the Subnet Mask

Given an IP address and its associated subnet mask, we can determine anything we need to know about the properties of the IP subnet. In addition to the network address, which we calculated in the prior example, the following parameters can be calculated:

Table 2.1 Subnet Mask Lookup Table

dec	binary	# of bits
255	11111111	8
254	11111110	7
252	11111100	6
248	11111000	5
240	11110000	4
224	11100000	3
192	11000000	2
128	10000000	1
0	00000000	0

host address—This is the portion of the IP address that does not correspond to the network address. If you were to invert the subnet mask (exchange 0s with 1s and 1s with 0s— this is known as the **1's complement**), and calculate the bitwise-AND of this with the IP address, the result would be the host portion. There is no point in calculating this parameter, because people never use it.

broadcast address—The broadcast address is a reserved address in each IP subnet which can be used to speak to all of the IP hosts via a single packet (called a **broadcast**). For a given subnet, it is the network address together with the bits in the host portion of the address all set to 1. Put another way, it is the highest (or last) host address in the subnet. It is easiest calculated by performing a bitwise-OR of the IP address and the 1's complement of the subnet mask.

number of host addresses in this IP subnet—This quantity is used for planning deployment of address space. (We will use it later, on page 31, for this purpose.) The value is calculated by raising two to the power of the number of 0s in the subnet mask. But because the first address in the subnet is always reserved for the network address, and the last address for the broadcast address, you should subtract two from this value to find the maximum number of hosts. You can use these formulae:

$$\# \ of \ host \ addrs \ = \ 2^{(32-maskbits)} \tag{2.2}$$

$$max \ \# \ of \ hosts \ = \ 2^{(32-maskbits)} - 2 \tag{2.3}$$

Calculating Network Parameters with CIDR

The rub when working with network addresses is that humans do not like counting in twos as much as computers do. The way the subnet mask splits the string of 32 bits is pesky for the human operator's decimal-to-binary and binary-to-decimal conversion circuits. It may clear things up to work through a few examples:

> ## Tip: A Shortcut for Calculating Host Addresses
>
> A colleague of mine pointed out a nice trick for calculating the number of host addresses in a subnet, given the decimal representation of the subnet mask. If your subnet mask is 255.255.255.x, there are $256 - x$ host addresses. For example:
>
> 255.255.255.240 yields $256 - 240$, or 16 host addresses per subnet
> 255.255.255.192 yields $256 - 192$, or 64 host addresses per subnet
>
> You still need to remember to subtract 2 for the network and broadcast addresses, and if the first non-255 value in the subnet mask falls in the third octet, multiply by 256; in the second octet, multiply by 256^2, and so on. But for subnetting class C addresses (that is, 24 or more maskbits), this is quite handy.

Example 1

IP address: 192.168.40.31
subnet mask: 255.255.255.0 (or /24)

Calculation of the network address

	11000000	.	10101000	.	00101000	.	00011111	*IP address*
bitwise-AND	11111111	.	11111111	.	11111111	.	00000000	*subnet mask*
	11000000	.	10101000	.	00101000	.	00000000	*network address*

or **192.168.40.0/24** (converted to dotted-decimal notation)

Calculation of the broadcast address

	11000000	.	10101000	.	00101000	.	00011111	*IP address*
bitwise-OR	00000000	.	00000000	.	00000000	.	11111111	*! subnet mask*
	11000000	.	10101000	.	00101000	.	11111111	*broadcast address*

or **192.168.40.255** (converted to dotted-decimal notation)

This example is easy because the subnet mask ends on a dot-boundary, so you can just read off the answers by knowing how the subnet mask works. Note that "!" is a way of indicating the inverse or 1's complement of a value. For single bits, it means to flip the bit. For multiple bits, flip each of them individually, as was done with the subnet mask. For the next example, let's use the same IP address but with a different subnet mask. ∎

Example 2

IP address: 192.168.40.31
subnet mask: 255.255.240.0 (or /20)

Calculation of the network address

	11000000	.	10101000	.	00101000	.	00011111	*IP address*
bitwise-AND	11111111	.	11111111	.	11110000	.	00000000	*subnet mask*
	11000000	.	10101000	.	00100000	.	00000000	*network address*

or **192.168.32.0/20**

Calculation of the broadcast address

	11000000	.	10101000	.	00101000	.	00011111	*IP address*
bitwise-OR	00000000	.	00000000	.	00001111	.	11111111	*! subnet mask*
	11000000	.	10101000	.	00101111	.	11111111	*broadcast address*

or **192.168.47.255**

Now, just for the sake of completeness, how about the host portion of the address? You can calculate it by ANDing the complement of the subnet mask with the IP address.

Calculation of the host address

	11000000	.	10101000	.	00101000	.	00011111	*IP address*
bitwise-AND	00000000	.	00000000	.	00001111	.	11111111	*! subnet mask*
	00000000	.	00000000	.	00001000	.	00011111	*host address*

or **0.0.8.31**

So the host address is 0.0.8.31?!? I can assure you that no one writes out host addresses this way. In fact, no one really bothers with host addresses at all when working with CIDR. ■

Class A, B, and C Networks

Now that you've learned the right way to think about subnets, it is safe to introduce the traditional "classed" subnet definitions. In the early days, these conventions dictated the values of the first four bits in the address (known as the **prefix**), which, in turn, implied how the 32-bit address space was separated into network and host portions. This way, routers could share network route information with each other without including the subnet mask (an initial savings that would end up costing a lot later in terms of confusion and rework to implement CIDR).

The different designations split the address on octet boundaries, which lessened the need for base-2 math skills on the part of the network administrator. The designations are listed in Table 2.2.

Table 2.2 Subnet Class Designations

class	prefix	bits in subnet mask
A	0	8
B	10	16
C	110	24
D	1110	n/a
E	1111	n/a

Thus, a class A address must have the first bit set to zero, and it uses the first 8 bits for the network address and the remaining 24 bits for the host address. Classes B and C each set another bit in the prefix and shift the subnet mask over by 8 bits. Class D is used for multicast addresses (11100000 in binary equals 224 in decimal, if that rings a bell). Class E is reserved for future use.

Because the prefix places certain limitations on the network address, you can easily identify which class an address is in by looking at the first octet. So if you see 151.30.22.12 and you know that your network is following the class conventions, you instantly know that this is a class B network and that the subnet mask is /16. The ranges are listed in Table 2.3.

Although I'm not much of a fan of the class designations, it is important to be familiar with them in order to communicate with others who use the terminology.[2] Probably the most frequently used term is "class C." People often use this to refer to any network with a 24-bit subnet mask and 8-bit host address, although properly it includes only those network addresses that begin with 110.

Table 2.3 Class Address Ranges

class	network address range	host address range
A	0–126	0.0.1–255.255.254
B	128.0–191.255	0.1–255.254
C	192.0.0–223.255.255	1–254

Carving Up IP Address Space with CIDR

Sometimes you will need to take address space allocated to you and divvy it up into several IP subnets. You have to choose either the number of separate subnets you want to create, or how many hosts should be in each subnet. To divide the original subnet, you add bits to the network address (thereby removing bits from the host portion of the address) until you have the desired number of subdivisions in the original address space. It should come as no surprise that everything happens in powers of 2, and that more base-2 math is lurking around the corner.

If you choose to create N subnets, you need an additional $m = \log_2 N$ 1s in the subnet mask. An easier way to think about the math is to realize that adding m bits to the subnet mask will result in 2^m additional subnets.

Example 3

Let's take the address space 192.168.18.0/24 and carve it up into 8 subnets. $N = 8$, so $m = \log_2 8 = 3$, which is the number of bits to add to the subnet mask. The result is 8 subnets with network addresses of 192.168.18.x/27.

Now we need the 8 values for x: x_1, x_2, x_3, x_4, x_5, x_6, x_7, x_8, so that we can write out the network address for each subnet. The first one always starts where the original address space started, in this case 0. The subsequent values for x_n are found by adding the number of hosts in each subnet to the preceding value of x. To calculate the number of hosts, refer back to the equation on page 28. In this case, the number of host addresses is $2^{(32-27)} = 2^5 = 32$, and we can write out our network addresses accordingly:

---

[2]I have to admit that I also use them sometimes due to laziness on my part.

$$
\begin{array}{ll}
x_1 & 192.168.18.0/27 \\
x_2 & 192.168.18.32/27 \\
x_3 & 192.168.18.64/27 \\
x_4 & 192.168.18.96/27 \\
x_5 & 192.168.18.128/27 \\
x_6 & 192.168.18.160/27 \\
x_7 & 192.168.18.192/27 \\
x_8 & 192.168.18.224/27
\end{array}
$$

The number of usable host addresses in each subnet is 30. You could calculate the broadcast address for each of these, although they can be written down by inspection. Since the broadcast address is the last address in the subnet, it must be one lower than the next network address. For x_1, it would be 192.168.18.31; for x_6, 192.168.18.191, and for the special case, x_8, 192.168.18.255 (because the next network address would be 192.168.19.0/255).

You won't be able to use the maskbits representation of the subnet mask for most networking commands, so you should go ahead and convert it back to decimal (using the chart on page 28, if needed). Remember that the 27 bits must be contiguous, from left to right, so they must be 11111111.11111111.11111111.11100000, which is 255.255.255.224. You don't really have to write out the full 32 bits each time, just start subtracting 8 from the maskbits. Each time you can subtract 8, copy down 255. When you are left with a number less than 8, look it up in the table and copy down the decimal representation. If you have not yet written down 4 decimal values, then write down 0s for the rest.   ∎

Before we move on to the next example, let's look at one more property of the subnet mask and the network address that you can use to double-check your work.

$$
\begin{array}{llll}
11000000 & . \quad 10101000 & . \quad 00010010 & . \quad 01100000 \quad \textit{network address } (192.168.18.96) \\
11111111 & . \quad 11111111 & . \quad 11111111 & . \quad 11100000 \quad \textit{subnet mask } (255.255.255.224)
\end{array}
$$

Notice, when you line up the network address and the subnet mask, that the network address is all 0s to the right of the subnet mask's last 1. This will **always** be the case. If it's not, then you have made a mistake. Simply put, you are in a completely different subnet. Recall that the purpose of the subnet mask is to divide the IP address into network and host fields. The bits in the host field are reserved for hosts, so let not network bits appear there, lest the stack complain bitterly and functioneth not.

Example 4

When we started this section, I said that you could also pick the number of hosts you would like in the subnet and use this to calculate the subnet mask and network address. Let's assume that you need a subnet with at least 1400 addresses. Since we have to pick a power of two, and 1024 is not large enough, we have to take 2048. A subnet that has 2048 host addresses in it needs to have $\log_2 2048 = 11$ bits to hold the host address. There are 32 bits total, so this leaves 21 bits for the network address.

Now that you know the subnet mask, chances are good that you'll need to carve it out of some private address space. If you want to take this space from the RFC 1918[3] allocation for private class A (10.x.x.x) or class B (172.16-31.x.x) networks, you have no worries. The class A network space has 24 bits of host address—more than plenty. The same is true for any of

---

[3]More information about RFC 1918 can be found in Section 2.1.5 on page 39.

the 16 different private class B networks. They each have 16 bits of host address. (Remember that we need only 11.) Just choose an unused one, slap on the /21, and start CIDRing.

However, if you want to use an aggregate of private class Cs (the 192.168.x.x address space), things can get a little sticky. The last example included a prologue which showed that the network bits cannot run over into the host portion of the IP address. That wasn't so tough when we had a network and wanted to carve out addresses. But now we have addresses and want to fit them into a network. The first thing to do is to write out the subnet mask in binary.

$$11111111.11111111.11111000.00000000$$

Now, we want to find a network address that does not have a 1 in any of the last 3 bits of the third octet. (If a 1 appears here, the network address is spilling into the host position.) This is not as difficult as it sounds, once you write out the subnet mask in binary. Using 0 (binary 00000000) for the third octet will meet the criterion. If this address space is not available, then the next choice is to copy down the octet with the rightmost 1 in the subnet mask intact, and everything else 0—so in this case 00001000 (8). Any multiple of this value will also meet the requirements, up to copying down the octet from the subnet mask itself (11111000). So we are free to choose from:

192.168.0.0/21	11000000 .	10101000 .	00000000 .	00000000
192.168.8.0/21	11000000 .	10101000 .	00001000 .	00000000
192.168.16.0/21	11000000 .	10101000 .	00010000 .	00000000
192.168.24.0/21	11000000 .	10101000 .	00011000 .	00000000

$$\vdots$$

192.168.248.0/21	11000000 .	10101000 .	11111000 .	00000000

Each of these has room for 2046 hosts and will have its own broadcast address. If you are still unclear on calculating the broadcast address, try calculating it for 192.168.64.0/21. You should come up with 192.168.71.255.

If you try to start anywhere in the address space, e.g., at 192.168.2.0/21, you'll have problems. Let's write this network address out in binary and align it with the subnet mask:

network address	11000000 .	10101000 .	00000010 .	00000000
subnet mask	11111111 .	11111111 .	11111000 .	00000000

As you can see, the network address spills over into the host portion of the address (to the right of the last 1 in the netmask). By doing this, you specified a host within the subnet, and not a network address. If you ever try something like this with Linux, it will let you know:

```
$ route add -net 192.168.2.0 netmask 255.255.248.0 eth0
route: netmask doesn't match route address
```
■

More Subnet-Related Definitions

The material covered in Section 2.1.1 may have seemed a bit obtuse, but it truly is useful when designing networks. Here are a few more notes on terminology before we get to routing.

- The term **supernet** can be used to refer to subnets containing more addresses than a normal class C. Sometimes this helps to remind people that 255.255.255.0 is not always the subnet mask.

- I have attempted to be consistent in my use of terms. The term **subnet mask**, however, is equivalent to **netmask** (as it appears in most command names), **network mask**, and sometimes even just **mask**. In the routing table, it appears as **Genmask**.

- An **IP subnet** and a **network** are the same thing, unless some special distinction is made about the type of network.

- A **workstation** is a generic term for any node on a network that is not part of the routing infrastructure. It sounds better than saying **PC**, and **node** is being saved for Frame Relay routers. Sometimes I call workstations **machines**.

- The next session talks about **gateways** and **routers**, which are equivalent. Typically, users configure their workstations with a **gateway**, whereas a router talks to another router.

- **Forwarding** and **routing** are, in most cases, the same thing.

2.1.2   Workstations—To Gateway or Not to Gateway

Every machine on your network with a TCP/IP stack has a configuration setting for *gateway*. This is so that it can reach IP networks other than its own. When it detects that the destination is part of a remote network, it sends the packet to the gateway for forwarding. For destinations in the same subnet, it will send the packet directly to the other machine. How does a workstation determine if a destination is part of the same or a different IP network?

First it ANDs the destination address of the packet with its own subnet mask. If the resulting address matches its own network address, then the destination is in the same subnet, and the TCP/IP stack tells the card to send the packet directly to the destination machine. (Actually, more than this occurs in order to send the packet directly, but it's no longer part of TCP/IP, but Ethernet. This is covered in Section 2.2.2.) If, however, the calculation shows that the destination is part of another network, then the sender makes use of its gateway to transmit the packet. In effect, the sender is saying, *"I do not know how to deliver this packet; can you please deliver it for me?"* The gateway accepts the packet and then goes through a similar procedure. (That procedure is known as **routing**, and there will be plenty more about it later.) Here are a few examples of the workstation's decision-making process (the workstation IP and network information is in Table 2.4):

workstation A sends to workstation B   Workstation A knows its own network address/subnet mask is 192.168.16.0/22. Workstation A calculates the *local-subnettedness* of the destination packet as follows:

Table 2.4 Address Information for Workstation Routing Examples

workstation	IP address	network/netmask	gateway
A	192.168.16.4	192.168.16.0/22	192.168.16.1
B	192.168.17.20	192.168.16.0/22	192.168.16.1
C	192.168.30.4	192.168.30.0/24	192.168.30.1

Are A and B in the same subnet?

	11111111	.	11111111	.	11111100	.	00000000	*subnet mask of A*
bitwise-AND	11000000	.	10101000	.	00010001	.	00010100	*IP addr of dest (B)*
	11000000	.	10101000	.	00010000	.	00000000	*network of dest*
compare	11000000	.	10101000	.	00010000	.	00000000	*network of A*

they are equal—both **192.168.16.0**

Because the network address of the sender matches the result of this calculation, the packet is sent directly to machine B.

workstation C sends to workstation B   Workstation C knows its network address/subnet mask is 192.168.30.0/24. Machine C checks to see if the destination packet falls within its subnet:

Are C and B in the same subnet?

	11111111	.	11111111	.	11111111	.	00000000	*subnet mask of C*
bitwise-AND	11000000	.	10101000	.	00010001	.	00010100	*IP addr of dest (B)*
	11000000	.	10101000	.	00010001	.	00000000	*network of dest*
compare	11000000	.	10101000	.	00011110	.	00000000	*network of C*

they are not equal—**192.168.17.0 ≠ 192.168.30.0**

In this case, the comparison fails. The sender, C, has no choice but to send the packet to its gateway. (If you take the time to do the calculation, you discover the gateway is in machine C's subnet. In fact the gateway must always be in the sender's subnet; otherwise, the sender could not send to it either!)

2.1.3   A Workstation's Routing Table

Even workstations with a single interface have a routing table and must scan it before deciding what to do with a packet. The tests above are performed multiple times—once for each entry in the workstation's routing table. Note that having a routing table does not necessarily mean that the workstation can route; it is simply the means for determining how to send packets. Here is an example routing table from a workstation. The `Destination` field contains the network address, and the `Genmask` field contains the subnet mask. By reading this table from top to bottom, you make decisions about what to do with a packet just as the kernel does.

```
$ route -n
Kernel IP routing table
Destination      Gateway         Genmask         Flags Metric Ref    Use Iface
192.168.18.0     0.0.0.0         255.255.254.0   U     0      0      869 eth0
127.0.0.0        0.0.0.0         255.0.0.0       U     0      0        2 lo
0.0.0.0          192.168.18.1    0.0.0.0         UG    1      0      182 eth0
```

1. All packets for the network 192.168.18.0/23 (remember that /23 is just another representation of /255.255.254.0) are sent out via interface *eth0* without using a gateway. This is denoted by `0.0.0.0` in the `Gateway` field and the lack of a `G` flag in the `Flags` field.

2. All packets for the network 127.0.0.0/8 are sent out via interface *lo*. This is known as the **loopback interface**, and it is reserved for sending packets to the local machine.

3. Any other packet will be forwarded to the gateway address (192.168.18.1), which is accessible via interface *eth0*. If you look at the `Destination` field, you will notice that the network is 0.0.0.0 with a `Genmask` of 0.0.0.0. This matches every packet and is known as a **default route**.

   When the kernel encounters this entry, it notices that the `G` flag is set, which means that the packet is to be sent to the IP address listed in the `Gateway` field for forwarding.

Note that the table is sorted in reverse order by the number of bits in the `Genmask` (subnet mask) field. This is so that the kernel walks the table in most-to-least restrictive order (the last entry will always be the default route). As soon as a suitable `Destination` and `Genmask` (really, subnet and subnet mask) pair is found, the packet is sent via that interface. The routing table on a router functions exactly the same way, which is the topic of the next section.

2.1.4 A Gateway's Routing Table

To forward packets, a router consults its routing table much as a workstation does and sends the packet on its way over the appropriate interface. Where a router differs from workstation is in what sort of traffic it will accept. When routing is enabled in the Linux kernel, the router will accept packets destined for its Ethernet address, but with IP destination headers pointing somewhere else. A machine without routing might accept these packets from the wire (because of the correct Ethernet address) but would then discard them when it discovered that they were not destined for its IP address. The router knows that its job is to forward, so it accepts the packet and examines its headers to find out where it's headed. A routing table on a router looks like this and is taken from the router depicted in Figure 2.3.

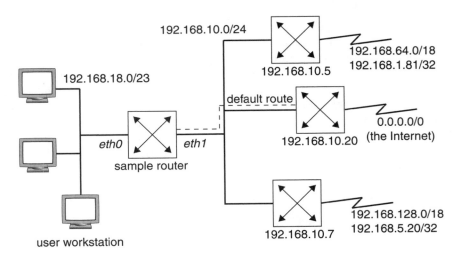

Figure 2.3 Sample Router

```
$ route -n
Kernel IP routing table
Destination      Gateway          Genmask         Flags Metric Ref    Use Iface
192.168.5.20     192.168.10.7     255.255.255.255 UGH   1      0      180 eth1
192.168.1.81     192.168.10.5     255.255.255.255 UGH   1      0      187 eth1
192.168.10.0     0.0.0.0          255.255.255.0   U     0      0    63311 eth1
192.168.18.0     0.0.0.0          255.255.254.0   U     0      0   753430 eth0
192.168.64.0     192.168.10.5     255.255.192.0   UG    1      0    47543 eth1
192.168.128.0    192.168.10.7     255.255.192.0   UG    1      0    89011 eth1
127.0.0.0        0.0.0.0          255.0.0.0       U     0      0      564 lo
0.0.0.0          192.168.10.20    0.0.0.0         UG    1      0   183436 eth1
```

We can tell a lot about this router by looking at the routing table (even without the aid of the illustration).

- The first two entries are known as *host routes*; they can be used to access only a single destination IP. This is denoted by the H in the `Flags` field and the fact that the `Genmask` is 255.255.255.255 (or /32). Both of these routes have a metric of 1 and a gateway on the 192.168.10.0/24 network, which is why the `Iface` is set to `eth1`. When the kernel encounters a packet destined for one of these exact IP addresses, it forwards it to the specified gateway over the *eth1* interface.

- The next entry is just like the one that a workstation has for its network interface. It is a network route for the locally connected network, 192.168.10.0/24. You can tell this because the gateway is set to 0.0.0.0 (which implies a local interface), and there is no G in the `Flags` field. We can safely assume that the *eth1* interface has an IP address in the 192.168.10.0/24 subnet. The figure confirms this; the interface is 192.168.10.1.

  For those of you familiar with other Unices, this is one point where Linux differs. It does not need to use the IP address of the interface as the gateway for locally connected networks (although this type of configuration will also work). It automatically uses the interface listed in the `Iface` field. By looking at the figure, we might surmise that the 192.168.10.0/24 network is a network for routers.

- The fourth entry is just like the third, except that it is for interface *eth0*, which we can see is connected to the 192.168.18.0/23 network. This is the network where the workstations are—the LAN.

- The next two (fifth and sixth) entries are network routes which point out over gateways on the router network. All traffic which falls into IP address ranges denoted by the network address (**Destination**) and subnet mask (**Genmask**) will be forwarded to the appropriate WAN router. A safe bet would be that these correspond to IP address space in use in other locations. If you notice their **Genmask**, you will understand why they first appear now in the routing table. The table is sorted from most restrictive to least restrictive, and 255.255.192.0 is the *widest* subnet mask yet.

- The next-to-last entry in the table is for the loopback device, *lo*, just as on a workstation.

- The last entry is the **default route**. Just like workstations, routers have these in case they do not know where else to forward a packet. In our example, the default route points to the 192.168.10.20 machine and is heavily used (note the `Use` field). 192.168.10.20 could be the Internet router or a firewall.

Preference for Two Equivalent Routes

Note that the table is sorted in reverse order by the number of bits in the `Genmask` field (just as it is on a workstation). The kernel checks each entry in the table against the destination IP address of the packet it received, and it forwards the packet on the first match it finds. This means that multiple (static) routes to the same destination are not used if you have simple static routing. In the case of a tie—two entries with identical `Destination` and `Genmask`—the one with the lower metric value is chosen. Should the metrics be equal, the more recent entry is chosen. The kernel doesn't remember when the entries were made for static routes, but it knows that when someone enters a route equivalent to an existing route, the intention is most likely to use the new route. This is convenient if you need to temporarily route around a particular gateway or have some other testing in mind. You can enter the temporary route, and it will be used. When you delete it, the previous route is used.

Unroutable Packets

Each of the other routers must also have routing table entries for the network(s) and host(s) it is expected to forward. If they don't, then they will either use their default route, or, if no default route exists, they will reply with an `ICMP: host unreachable` message. In the pathological case the route points back to the sending router, which forms a loop. (Router$_A$ sends to router$_B$, which sends to router$_A$, and so on ....) Fortunately, IP packets all contain a TTL (Time To Live) field which is decremented every time the packet is forwarded. Eventually (actually, very quickly), the packet will be discarded. Nonetheless, such misconfigurations mean that the packet will not find its destination, which results in performance degradation for correctly routed packets on the network. Just say *No* to routing loops!

Misconfigured Routes—ICMP Redirects

Another situation arises when router$_A$ forwards a packet to router$_B$ when it could (and should) have forwarded it directly to router$_C$. That is, all three routers are on the same subnet, but router$_A$ is ignorant of (one or more of) router$_C$'s routes. When router$_A$ forwards a packet to router$_B$, and router$_B$ notices that the packet should have been sent directly to router$_C$, it forwards the packet, but alerts router$_A$ to the fact with an `ICMP: redirect` message telling router$_A$ how to forward packets of that type in the future. Router$_A$ notes this by adding a new (host route) entry in its routing table. You can quickly spot these entries because they have the `UDGH` flags all set. Of note is the D, which indicates that the route was added either dynamically or due to a redirect.

Static vs. Dynamic Routing

There are two methods of configuring a routing table. If the table is populated by you (or by a script on your behalf) using the *route* command, then it is known as **static routing**. If it is populated automatically by a daemon such as *routed*, you are using **dynamic routing**.

I am a fan of static routing, because the reassurance of knowing exactly what the router will do with a packet at all times is worth the extra effort on my part. However, static routing cannot be used in every situation and is by no means the only way to do things with Linux. (More information about dynamic routing daemons for Linux can be found in Section 9.4.)

If this material is new to you, hopefully you're feeling more acquainted with TCP/IP routing than you were before. If you're not, there are many good tutorials on TCP/IP subnetting available on the Internet, as well as numerous books on the subject. One such tutorial is at *http://www.sangoma.com/fguide.htm*; another is the *IP-Subnetworking mini-HOWTO*, part of the *LDP*.

Being able to calculate network addresses and subnet masks and to convert subnet masks from binary to the # of maskbits representation are important day-to-day skills for network admins. The next section is about private address space—address space which you can use to build your own IP network, as long as you keep it isolated from the Internet.[4]

2.1.5   RFC 1918 Private Address Space

Under the current IP addressing scheme (often known as IPv4, eventually to be replaced by IPv6), the address space is divided into two types: public address space and private address space. Understanding the difference is important and useful for a network administrator, especially if your organization is connected to the Internet.

All of the **public address space** (IP addresses) routable via the Internet are managed by one of the three *Regional Internet Registries* (RIRs). Each of these is responsible for a geographic region. (Don't confuse these with the InterNIC [*http://www.internic.net*] and its designated registrars, such as *Network Solutions, Inc.* They handle **domain name** registration, not address registration.)

- North and South America, the Caribbean, and sub-Saharan Africa are managed by the *American Registry for Internet Numbers*, or simply: *ARIN. http://www.arin.net*

- Europe, the Middle East, and other parts of Africa are managed by *RIPE* (*Réseaux IP Européens*). *http://www.ripe.net*

- *APNIC*, the *Asia Pacific Network Information Centre*, handles the Asia Pacific region. *http://www.apnic.net*

You must request address space, and they will either grant or deny your request. Alternately, you can request the address space from your ISP (who then, in turn, allocates you from its ARIN-allotted address space or makes the request on your behalf).

This is done to preserve address space and provide a central authority to prevent address-space collisions. When you are using a public address, you can send to and receive from all (nonbroken) parts of the Internet. This means that all routers in the Internet have an idea about how to route your IP address toward you. Because of this, not all address space is **portable**. If you own your address space, you can authorize an ISP to route it for you, but when you change providers or locations there is a chance that it will no longer be possible to route your IPs to that new location. (So you might want to check before you travel with your address space.)

In any event, the public address space has been divvied up and allocated to countries, companies, universities, ISPs, other organizations, and individuals. A small part of the overall address space has been classified as **private address space**. It is also known as **RFC 1597** or **RFC 1918** address space, after the RFCs that describe its proper use. Private address space is intended for use by anyone, but on private networks. The subnets themselves will be familiar to many of you, even if you were previously unaware that they corresponded to private address space. According to RFC 1918 (which obsoletes the well-known RFC 1597), the private subnets are:

---

[4]Several sections of this book deal with *how* to keep your private networks isolated from the Internet. They are the sections on IP masquerading (Sections 4.2–10.6) and proxy servers (Section 9.1).

IP address range	network/mask	number of address
10.0.0.0–10.255.255.255	10.0.0.0/8	16,777,216 (2^{24})
172.16.0.0–172.31.255.255	172.16.0.0/12	1,048,576 (2^{20})
192.168.0.0–192.168.255.255	192.168.0.0/16	65,536 (2^{16})

The 10.0.0.0/8 network is a single class A network. 172.168.0.0/12 is a set of sixteen class B networks. 192.168.0.0/16 represents 255 contiguous class C networks. For organizations with private networks which are connected to the Internet, this means:

1. They can run TCP/IP without any danger of address conflicts with the outside.

2. They can allocate address space from the private address space in a manner which makes sense for them (perhaps geographically, maybe organizationally).

3. Their internal networks are (somewhat) shielded from Internet-based attacks. An attacker has more difficulties launching an attack against IP addresses which cannot be routed.

4. Their machines with private addresses cannot directly communicate with the Internet. This necessitates the use of a proxy or masquerading mechanism, which can help perform logging and prevent unauthorized access.

5. They do not have to go through the hassle of changing IP addresses should they change ISPs, nor do they have to apply for address space when they need more.

Every network admin should have a copy of the latest RFC describing the private address space (for IPv4). An official source for this document is *http://www.ietf.org/rfc*. Debian has provided a copy if you've loaded either the **bind-doc** or the **doc-rfc** package.

Allocating Private Address Space Internally

Keep private address space in mind when planning your network. If you work with other network admins at your organization, draw up an allocation scheme for your environment and have all involved agree to abide by it. The time savings down the road could be substantial. Another benefit is that you can prevent clutter in your routing tables. If you use CIDR to divide the address space into large aggregates of subnets which are based on geographic boundaries, you can reduce the number of routing entries at each router.

For example, imagine a Frame Relay router located in Europe with PVCs to North America and the Pacific Rim. The site in Europe acts as the hub—i.e., the two leaf sites send data to each other via the site in Europe. Each site has four class C subnets, and all sites communicate with all other sites. If all three sites grew up at about the same time, and you allocated the subnets sequentially, you would have:

Europe	North America	Pacific Rim
192.168.10.0/24	192.168.14.0/24	192.168.18.0/24
192.168.20.0/24	192.168.24.0/24	192.168.28.0/24
192.168.30.0/24	192.168.34.0/24	192.168.38.0/24
192.168.40.0/24	192.168.44.0/24	192.168.48.0/24

The router in Europe would then have four class C subnets to route per PVC. But the router in North America would have eight, as would the router on the Pacific Rim. At this scale, the issue is still a manageable one, but consider what happens when each site has 10–15 class C networks. If you plan ahead and assign each location a larger block of class C networks, you could have the following:

region	range of addresses	subnet	# of subnets
Europe	192.168.0.0–192.168.63.255	192.168.0.0/18	64
Pacific Rim	192.168.64.0–192.168.71.255	192.168.64.0/21	8
North America	192.168.128.0–192.168.159.255	192.168.128.0/19	32

Now Europe has only two routing-table entries: 192.168.64.0/18 (all 64 class Cs toward the Pacific Rim) and 192.168.128.0/17 (the remaining 128 class Cs toward North America). North America has only a single routing entry, 192.168.0.0/17, which points toward Europe. And the Pacific Rim also has two routing-table entries: 192.168.0.0/18 and 192.168.128.0/19. A little time spent up front can alleviate the need for large static routing tables or dynamic routing daemons for your internal network.

When you're allocating network space, leave yourself room for growth. It is difficult to know in advance how much address space a site will need, so spread things out at first. (If you need to reclaim the unused address space later, it will still be there.) As a rule of thumb, allocate a class C for every existing 100 devices, and if the site expects growth, double the existing address space by taking another bit from the subnet mask.

2.2   Ethernet 101—Switches and Hubs

This section drills down and looks at how packets flow across an Ethernet LAN, and specifically how machines on the same Ethernet segment communicate with each other. This case is analogous to the concept of IP subnets, except that Ethernet segments are groupings based on physical topology, while IP subnets are groupings based on configuration. This communication is the same mechanism used by the workstation to contact the router (or gateway) for that segment—which is why the gateway must be on the same physical Ethernet segment.

A common mechanism for connecting machines together nowadays is over twisted-pair (either 10-BaseT or 100-BaseT), where each machine is connected via its own dedicated wire to a port on some sort of "network port concentrating device." This "device" comes in two basic flavors. A **hub** emulates a broadcast bus—what is sent to one port is available for all ports to see. (Technically, this is a **repeater**.) Most of the time, a **switch** emulates a crossbar switch—the sending port and receiving port are directly connected to each other for the length of the packet transmission. (In this operation, the switch acts like a very short-lived **bridge**.) However, for certain types of packets—for example, broadcasts—a switch will turn itself back into a hub for the duration of that packet. Section 2.2.3 gives more detail on the differences between a hub and a switch.

2.2.1   The MAC Address

Of primary interest is how communication takes place between two systems on the same Ethernet segment, since it's a quantum of much of the network communications we're concerned about in this book. The answer is that machines send Ethernet packets directly to one another by specifying the 6-byte Ethernet address of the destination system. This address is often called the **hardware address** or the **MAC address** of the Ethernet card. *MAC* is an abbreviation for *Media Access Control*. On any given LAN, every MAC address must be unique. This should not be a problem, because the MAC address is programmed in by the NIC vendor, and there is a system by which NIC vendors ensure that the addresses they program into their cards are unique.

All vendors have their own address block(s), designated by the first 3 bytes of the address field. IEEE acts as a registrar for these addresses and calls this field of the MAC address the **Organizationally Unique Identifier** or **OUI**. If you'd like to see who owns a particular block—in other words, determine who really manufactured the NIC you're using—visit IEEE's website at *http://standards.ieee.org/regauth/oui/* to view the registry of assigned addresses. Each vendor code or OUI encompasses $2^{24} - 2$ (16,777,214) addresses after you take out the reserved *ff:ff:ff* broadcast address, and many vendors have multiple codes. (To be completely accurate, not all cards have their own MAC address—on some systems, such as Sun Microsystems, the MAC address is stored in NVRAM and assigned to whatever network interface is plugged into the system. This way, the MAC address for a system doesn't change, even if the physical card does.)

To determine the **hardware address** of the NIC corresponding to *eth0* on your system, use the command **ifconfig eth0** and look at the HWaddr field. It should look something like:

```
$ ifconfig eth0
eth0      Link encap:Ethernet  HWaddr 00:80:5F:7D:56:20
          inet addr:192.168.1.1  Bcast:192.168.1.255  Mask:255.255.255.0
          UP BROADCAST RUNNING MULTICAST  MTU:1500  Metric:1
          RX packets:1702854 errors:0 dropped:0 overruns:0 frame:0
          TX packets:1987005 errors:0 dropped:0 overruns:0 carrier:0
          collisions:0 txqueuelen:100
          RX bytes:287146186 (273.8 Mb)  TX bytes:1372224993 (1308.6 Mb)
          Interrupt:11 Base address:0x1420
```

The hardware address is normally expressed with each byte represented in hexadecimal format and separated by colons, like *ff:ff:ff:ff:ff:ff*. The chances of having two Ethernet cards with the same MAC address are quite slim, but it seems to happen occasionally. The result is chaos on the affected segment and some nasty commentary on a given hardware company's quality assurance department.

2.2.2 Address Resolution Protocol (ARP)

ARP, the Address Resolution Protocol, is the means by which a sender finds the desired recipient on an Ethernet segment. The ARP protocol uses a simple broadcast mechanism to learn the address of the recipient. This Ethernet broadcast packet is called an **ARP request**, and it is seen by all systems connected to that Ethernet segment. To generate an Ethernet broadcast, the system sets all of the bits in the destination address to one (which yields *ff:ff:ff:ff:ff:ff*, similar to an IP broadcast) and the IP address of the recipient it desires. The host that has that IP address replies—all others remain silent (even if they know the answer)—with an **ARP reply**. Unlike the request, the reply is sent directly to the machine that issued the ARP request.

Now the sender knows the MAC address of the recipient, so it stores it in a cache called an **ARP table.** (You can save your system the step of using broadcasts to find MAC addresses by storing the mappings in */etc/ethers*, but this is rarely done nowadays.) Periodically, a host will expire entries in its ARP table to prevent it from having old information should the MAC/IP relationships of machines on the network change, or to prevent that host from trying to directly contact MAC addresses that have dropped off the network.

For the 2.2 version of the kernel, the default timeout is 5 minutes; for the 2.4 version it seems to vary and from about 6 to 10 minutes. You can view the contents of your system's ARP table using the command *arp*, as in the following example (the -n switch suppresses name resolution of the IP addresses), or by listing the information directly from the */proc* filesystem:

```
tmancill@java:~$ /usr/sbin/arp -n
Address         HWtype   HWaddress            Flags  Mask   Iface
65.0.44.1       ether    00:02:FC:81:38:54    C             eth0
192.168.1.2     ether    00:02:E3:02:A2:DD    C             eth1
192.168.1.8     ether    08:00:20:B5:D7:F3    C             eth1

tmancill@java:~$ cat /proc/net/arp
IP address      HW type  Flags  HW address        Mask   Device
65.0.44.1       0x1      0x2    00:02:FC:81:38:54   *     eth0
192.168.1.2     0x1      0x2    00:02:E3:02:A2:DD   *     eth1
192.168.1.8     0x1      0x2    08:00:20:B5:D7:F3   *     eth1
```

If you'd like to know what those hexadecimal values in the HW type and Flags fields mean, you can take a gander at *./include/linux/if_arp.h* in the kernel sources.

Packet-Sniffing ARP Requests

Packet sniffers are programs that "watch" everything that flows across the network segment; they are covered later (Section 3.3). If you're monitoring your network and watching for ARP traffic, your sniffer will report them with messages like:

```
arp who-has 192.168.16.1 tell 192.168.16.2
arp reply 192.168.16.1 is-at 0:50:56:8a:0:0
```

The first packet is the ARP request, issued by 192.168.16.2 in an attempt to contact 192.168.16.1. 192.168.16.1 replies that it has hardware address 00:50:56:8A:00:00. Because ARP is a link-layer protocol, there are different specifications for each type of link. For example, FDDI uses a different ARP specification than the one for Ethernet. If you would like to read the ARP specification for Ethernet, it is *RFC 826*.

RARP

RARP, or Reverse ARP, can be used by a machine that does not know its own IP address to learn it from a machine that does. It generates a broadcast which appeals to a machine running *rarpd* (the Reverse ARP Daemon) to answer back with its IP address. The answering machine has a list of MAC addresses along with the corresponding IP addresses to assign to them. It is typically used in environments with diskless workstations and Xterminals. If you need this functionality, you should look into the **BOOTP** and **DHCP** protocols, too. If nothing else, you should be aware of its existence and function.

Proxy ARP

Proxy ARP is a term that describes a configuration where a given machine will reply to ARP requests for IPs other than its own. It is then up to that machine, the *proxy* as it were, to make sure that the packets are delivered to the real owner of that IP address. This is often used if you would like to insert a firewall between an access router and a group of machines on a segment that was previously connected directly to the access router. You can find a good practical discussion on how to use it at *http://www.sjdjweis.com/linux/proxyarp/*, but we are getting ahead of ourselves.

2.2.3 Ethernet Switches and Hubs

Although, from the users' perspective, there is little difference between switches and hubs (perhaps additional performance when using a switch), there are significant differences for network administrators.

A switch differs from a hub in that the former maintains a mapping of ports to the MAC address(es) attached to them. It uses this table to "switch" packets between ports by connecting the sending and receiving port using its crossbar circuitry. In contrast, a hub is simply an electronic conduit, which forwards anything received on one port to all other ports. In general, switches can do everything that a hub can do, plus the following:

- Switches should always offer the same performance as hubs, and they typically offer much better performance. Why not always better? Imagine a configuration where all systems on the switch want access to the same port. An example is when all of the ports on the switch are allocated to clients, except for one, which is the server. If all clients speak only to the server, and not to each other, then the performance gain by using a switch will be marginal. Some clients may even be worse off than with the hub, depending upon the algorithm that the switch uses to choose the next user.

- Switches often allow you to mix 10Mbps and 100Mbps ports (as well as media types, like gigabit fiber) on the same unit. This is relatively easy for them to do, since they have to be able to perform buffering. (There are some hubs which provide this capability, too—you could call them hybrids.)

- Because more circuitry and higher costs are involved, many switches come with features such as network-based management modules for configuration and statistics gathering. (Many hubs offer this, too.)

- Some offer the ability to partition sets of ports into multiple isolated segments. This can be useful in the server room, when you might need several different segments with only a few machines on each but realize that an isolated segment will now need to traverse your router to access other segments. Some switches offer **layer 3 switching**, which simply means routing between separate IP subnets.

- They provide *some* protection against people running packet sniffers on other ports connected to the same device. See Figures 2.4 and 2.5 for the idea. To compensate for this loss of monitoring capability, some switches have an optional monitoring port that can be used to see all traffic traversing the switch (if you have a sniffer that can keep up with it all!).

In that last bullet point, unfortunately, the reality of the situation is that a switch may prevent your legitimate monitoring of the wire, but not deter a hacker who has a port on that same switch. There are some quite advanced hacking tools out there that can trick systems connected to the switch into communicating with the hacker's system instead of the intended system. They are even sophisticated enough to turn around and communicate with the intended

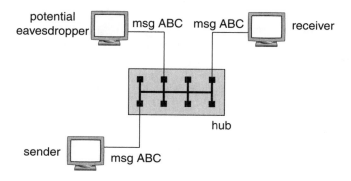

Figure 2.4 Eavesdropping with a Hub

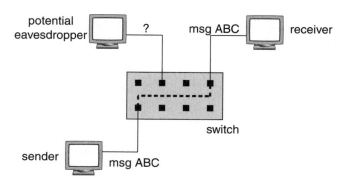

Figure 2.5 Preventing Eavesdropping with a Switch

system so that no one is the wiser (known as **connection hijacking**). The two more popular of these tools are *hunt* and *dsniff*; if you're looking for them, it won't take long to find copies on the Internet. In Section 3.3, we'll talk more about using sniffers for troubleshooting purposes and discuss a few tools that can detect unauthorized usage of packet sniffers on your network.

The moral is that to prevent this sort of eavesdropping, you must physically secure access to your switches and must not allow unmanaged user machines on the same segment. Still, you should certainly be using switches for your servers and your router(s) if they are available to you. Just don't consider them as contributors to network security. There are cases where I think that plain old vanilla hubs are still useful. As an example, a **perimeter net** or **DMZ** (the network outside the firewall where external web servers and mail gateway, etc., are located) might only have three or four machines on it. If the hub can be physically secured (i.e., no one can walk up and plug into one of its ports), then a simple hub may have advantages over a switch, such as the following:

1. Beyond the initial cost savings, hubs are inexpensive enough to allow keeping spares in stock.

2. Any of the machines on the perimeter net can act as a sniffer. This relieves the router from having to do all of the monitoring work. Note that the router may not be able to see all of the traffic anyway. For example, there may be DNS traffic between two machines on that network which would not be visible to the router.

3. At its simplest, a hub is truly *dumb* in that it doesn't look at the packets, it just passes them. Many switches being sold today offer features such as network-based configuration and statistics. While this might be neat and handy, it also poses a security risk. If hackers attack the switch itself, they can reconfigure it, monitor data undetected, cause outages, etc.

4. Along those same lines, switches have firmware, i.e., software packaged in silicon. This software occasionally has bugs—bugs that potentially cause network outages and security holes.

In summary, you should understand the difference between hubs and switches and keep them in mind when deploying them in your network. My advice is to get the right equipment for the task at hand and avoid the trap of believing that more features are better, or that expensive hardware is somehow always worth it. If you're not going to use any of its extra capabilities, then you're only wasting money and increasing the probability of failure of your network.

2.3   WAN Basics 101

Many organizations need to span greater physical distances than those possible using normal LAN technologies, so they deploy a **WAN** (Wide Area Network). Linux routers feel right at home acting as LAN or WAN routers or as an interface between the two. Because Linux routers can provide functions in addition to routing, WAN links are an application where they shine in comparison to the alternatives. More about this in Chapter 8. But before you start deploying them as WAN routers, you will need to be familiar with some of the terminology and technologies used in a WAN environment.

An impressive number of communications technologies are available today, and I cannot profess to having mastered even a reasonable subset of these. Therefore, I present only the

Step One

Call this toll-free number
1-800-569-5572
on any touch-tone phone
within 5 days of your visit.

Step Two

You will be asked to respond to questions
regarding your experience at *Jo-Ann etc.*
Following is the rating scale used
on most of the questions.

Excellent   Satisfactory   Poor
5   4   3   2   1

Step Three

At the completion of the telephone survey, a validation code will be given to
you. Please write this code in the space provided below. You may then redeem
this coupon at any participating *Jo-Ann Fabrics and Crafts* or *Jo-Ann etc* store.

Expiration Date: 8/24/02   Serial Number: **81906**

24 0308240202 030 6

Validation Code

TELL US HOW WE'RE DOING
& RECEIVE

30% OFF

J@ANN
experience the creativity®

THE REGULAR PRICE OF ONE ITEM ON YOUR NEXT PURCHASE*

TO VALIDATE THIS COUPON, FOLLOW THE THREE EASY STEPS ON THE BACK.

Limit one per customer. Cannot be combined with any other discount. Must be surrendered at time of checkout.
*Offer excludes special orders, previous purchases, purchase of gift cards, classes, custom services (custom bedding, window treatments, framing & floral services), Viking White Machines, irons & leased department merchandise. A single cut of by-the-yard fabric or trim equals one item (present coupon at cutting counter)..

2S2-91 etc

mainstay for use in corporate WANs today—namely, the digital T-carrier and its common variants. After introducing it, we will talk about how you tie yourself into public and semi-public networks, including interface equipment and billing. This section concludes with a few potential issues to keep in mind when planning your WAN links.

2.3.1   Telephony 101

When you use an ordinary telephone in the United States, you are using what is generally referred to as an **analog line** or **POTS** (Plain Old Telephone Service). The analog telephone network was designed for carrying voice conversations of frequencies up to 4000Hz.[5] In fact, it attenuates frequencies outside of the 300 to 3400Hz range so effectively as to filter them out almost completely. Digital data will not pass unless it is encoded to "fit" in this frequency range, known as the **passband**.

Because of its bias toward human voice frequencies, a POTS line is often referred to as a **voicegrade** circuit. This is where a modem comes into play; it converts digital pulses into a format compatible with voicegrade circuits. But forget for the moment about modems, bandwidth, and signal waveforms. There is something else special about the ordinary telephone network.

Switched Access

A POTS circuit is an example of **switched access**, which means it is a connection to a public network that can make a connection to any of multiple other sites. In the case of the public telephone network, you can connect to literally hundreds of millions of destinations (one at a time) using your single connection. This is the **switched** part, meaning that the network can switch your destination for you based on your input. **Access** in this context is a noun and refers to the facility you are using to connect your telecommunicating device (in this case, the device is a telephone) to the public network. One property of switched access is that you need to tell the network where you would like to go, i.e., you must *dial* it before you make a connection to it. The most commonly used switched networks are the analog telephone network, ISDN (which is integrated into the analog network), and the X.25 packet-switching network. Costs for switched services normally include a base rate plus usage charges—you pay for it when you use it. Also, switched networks are not necessarily designed so that every node can be used simultaneously (as in the infamous *I can't get a line out on Mother's Day* problem). To save costs, there is limited capacity in the backbone (or the "switch") of the network.

Dedicated Access

Compare switched access to its counterpart, **dedicated access**. Here, you have a circuit which runs from point A to point B. (Note that point B is not necessarily the remote location you are trying to connect to—more on this later.) This circuit does not need to be dialed, because its endpoints are fixed. Dedicated access is often known as a **leased line**, because you are paying for all of the bandwidth of the circuit, all of the time. Leased lines are typically digital **telco** circuits, but you can also lease a copper pair or a fiber-optic cable running between two points from any suitable provider.[6]

---

[5] Have you ever wondered why music sounds so different (and bad!) over a telephone? It's because the higher (and lower) frequencies have been filtered out. Try turning the treble and bass controls of your stereo all the way down. This setup acts like a bandpass filter similar to that used on an analog voice circuit.

[6] But often the only providers are PTTs, an acronym for Post, Telegraph, and Telephone, frequently used generically to refer to the service provider in an area.

There are two overall categories of telco leased lines in the United States: analog and digital. While analog circuits were widely used in the past and may still be very cost-effective for certain applications, advances in analog modem technology (for use on voicegrade circuits) and the proliferation of digital circuits (due to the decreasing cost of broadband telco infrastructure) have made them less common. You may still want to use them for point-to-point links which span large physical distances, but the number of data network service providers in the United States which will allow you to connect to their networks using such a circuit is decreasing.

Still, a dedicated analog circuit has several advantages over a switched one (i.e., a POTS circuit). First, it is not subject to the same bandpass filters that voicegrade circuits are. Because more frequencies are allowed to pass, the result is higher bandwidth and through-put. Another advantage is that these are four-wire circuits, which means that they can operate at full-duplex (they can send and receive simultaneously at the full bandwidth of the circuit—voicegrade analog modems present the illusion of doing this as best they can over two wires). If you know you're going to need to use analog leased lines, you should do some research about the capabilities and equipment.

Dedicated Digital Access

The second category of dedicated access is digital access, and it represents a much broader class of circuits. Examples of service offerings are DDS (DS0), T1s, T3s, and so on, up to things like an OC-48 (a 2.5Gb SONET standard). The proliferation of digital circuits is largely due to advances in fiber-optic technologies used in the backbone of the world's telecommunications networks (and to some changes in industry regulation). The benefits to you are lower bandwidth costs and improved reliability. The results are that more and more digital telco circuits are being used to build wide area networks. Although costs have decreased, they may still constitute a sizable fraction of your connectivity bill, and because most services are priced based on the length of the access circuit, what might be reasonable for one location may be cost-prohibitive for another.

Despite the advances in fiber optics, the legacy of the voice network is still present—in fact, the two are still largely integrated. The T-carrier was originally designed to allow a single digital circuit to simultaneously carry 24 voice conversations. This reduces the number of circuits required between a residential area and a **CO** (central office), and also between COs. It is achieved by digitizing the voice waveform via **PCM** (Pulse-Code Modulation) and using **TDM** (Time-Division Multiplexing). The T1 communicates by sending frames—a frame can be sent in a fixed amount of time and contains a fixed number of bits. Each of the 24 conversations is periodically sampled and the results are loaded into the frame, which is sent to the receiver. The receiver demultiplexes the signal by separating the frame into 24 pieces, each of which is decoded to reconstruct the voice signal corresponding to each of the 24 conversations being sent. Each of these "conversation channels" is commonly referred to as a **channel** (and sometimes as a **trunk**). Under normal conditions, a channel carries a single voice conversation.

If you bypass the PCM conversion, you can send digital data directly over the circuit, as long as the other end knows when to expect the digital portion and when to expect the voice portion. Each of the 24 timeslots in a frame can be virtualized as a channel, labelled 1–24, each of which can be used independently. This is what makes the T-carrier so versatile. You can mix voice and data on a single circuit simply by allocating a subset of channels (really just timeslots) to different applications. For example, you may want to use 8 channels for local telephone service, 4 channels for a Frame Relay circuit, leave 4 channels free for growth of that data circuit, and then assign the last 8 channels to route calls to your long-distance provider.

As long as both ends agree about how to multiplex and demultiplex the applications, no one will ever know the difference.

T-Carrier Bandwidth

The bandwidth of each channel is 64kbps. Although it may seem to be a nice round number, designed with data applications in mind, the origin is the PCM conversion, which samples each voice conversation 8000 times per second (at 8000Hz) and encodes the result in an 8-bit value.[7] Furthermore, data applications are not limited to using one channel at a time. The circuitry which interfaces with the digital circuit can aggregate channels to achieve higher data throughput. It is safe to say that the T-carrier scheme has been wildly successful and ubiquitous. Here are some common flavors of digital circuits:

- A **DDS** (or **DS0**), which is a digital circuit running at 56/64kbps (or one channel). (Note that this is not the same as a POTS circuit.)

- The **T1** (or **DS1**), which is $N \times 56/64$kbps, where $1 \leq N \leq 24$, up to 1536Mbps in increments of either 56kbps or 64kbps. The quantum is 56 or 64, depending upon the signalling protocol used on the T1.

  A T1 can be viewed as (24) DS0s, each of which is called a **channel**. A **full T1** is all 24 channels. A **fractional T1** is a subset of these channels.

- A **T3** (or **DS3**) is a digital circuit designed to carry 672 simultaneous voice conversations (channels). When used for digital transmission, it has a bandwidth of almost 45Mbps.

- An **E1** is a European standard similar to the T1, but instead of 24 trunks it has 32, corresponding to a data rate of 2.048Mbps.

- **FT1 access**, or **fractional T1 access**, is a service offering that does not correspond to a physical circuit. Still, the jump from 64kbps to 1.536Mbps is too wide a gap for some applications, so it is in the PPT's interest to provide such a product. If you order fractional T1 service, then the telco will run a full T1 and give you part of it. If possible, it will use the remaining bandwidth for another customer at the same facility. This sort of offering is common in Europe.

  Note: Do not confuse fractional T1 *access* with fractional T1 *ports*, which are data services that use less than all 24 channels.

Digital circuits are your friends, your lifeline connecting you to the world. It helps to know the terminology, because you will find that the people maintaining the access circuit are not the same ones selling you the circuits or the same ones responsible for the data services which ride them. (Services often "ride" T1s, in the jargon.) The next section takes this piece of the puzzle and places it in the context of a data link like one you would use to connect to a network service provider (such as an ISP).

---

[7] The Nyquist sampling theorem states that you need to sample a waveform at a frequency at least 2 times the highest frequency in the waveform to be able to faithfully reconstruct it without data loss. If you recall, the original voicegrade circuit may have frequencies up to 4000Hz, so 8000Hz is the "magic number."

2.3.2   Data Links and Digital Access

Consider the situation where we have a group of machines in locations A and B—separated by 800 km—that would like to speak TCP/IP to each other. We're going to need some way to tie our routers together so that they can speak to each other and trade packets. Unless you have the capability to build the network infrastructure yourself, meaning everything from erecting microwave towers to burying cable, configuring repeaters, bribing the local officials, and who knows what else, you're going to have to get your bandwidth from some sort of provider. What you purchase, and why, depends on myriad factors, so let's try to take this apart, step by step.

There are many different physical methods of moving bits from point A to point B. The partial list includes fiber-optic cable, copper cable, satellite up-links, microwave, coaxial cable, and other forms of RF, either through the air, a wire, or some other waveguide. What you use is often dictated by economics and physics, so unless you really can build your own network, you do not always have control over what will be used. For most circuits, your data will end up traveling over a combination of these anyway. This should not be an issue unless you have an application which is sensitive to latency, as discussed in Section 2.3.5.

To establish a link between our sites, we could order a dedicated digital circuit which connects them directly to each other. This is known as a point-to-point configuration. It is depicted in Figure 2.6.

In this scenario, we would be leasing 100% of the circuit between the sites and could run whatever protocol we like over the link (as long as it is compatible with being used over a digital telco circuit—e.g., CHDLC, Frame Relay, or PPP). This is also known as a **back-to-back** configuration, because you control both ends and all of the active network elements between them. You also have the full bandwidth of the circuit at your disposal, and you can perform whatever type of compression suits you. This arrangement is great, because we are confident that the only other people who have access to the circuit are telco technicians, whom we trust not to monitor our packets. If we think even they might be snooping, we can always use some sort of encoding or encryption. However, with most access circuits, you pay the telco based on the distance between the sites and the bandwidth of the circuit. If locations A and B are distant from each other, this can become prohibitively expensive.

An alternative is to turn to a service provider which has **POPs** (Points of Presence) near both locations and purchase two access circuits—one between location A and its nearest POP, and the other between location B and its corresponding nearest POP. We then pay the provider to route traffic on its internal network between the POPs (and thus between our sites).

Now our dedicated access circuit costs are lower, because we only have to pay for the distance between each location at its nearest POP. The difference now is that we don't own

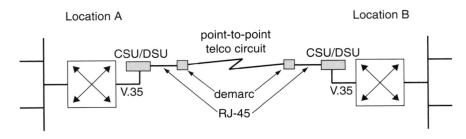

Figure 2.6 Point-to-Point Connection of Remote Sites

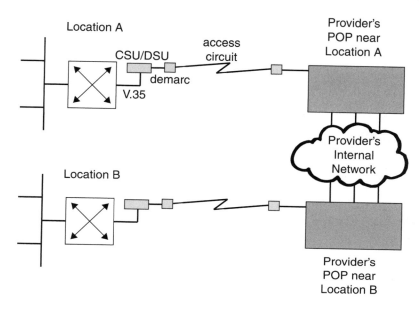

Figure 2.7 Connection of Remote Sites via Provider POPs

the entire path between our sites. This has its own benefits and drawbacks. Apart from cost savings, the benefits are that the provider will have many POPs, and it becomes quite easy to add locations C, D, and E to our network. We also do not have to worry about maintaining anything more than the node (endpoint) routers.

However, because there are other routers (which belong to our provider) between our sites, we have to comply with their protocols and configuration guidelines. This means that we cannot use all types of data compression (we can still encrypt and/or compress IP payloads, but not link-layer protocol packets). More noteworthy, however, is that because we are using the provider's network, we have to pay for that bandwidth. And the more we want to use, the more it will cost. But, because our provider has orders of magnitude more bandwidth than we want, she can offer us equivalent bandwidth for far less than what it would cost us to lease the same dedicated bandwidth using a point-to-point. In this scenario, our WAN link looks like Figure 2.7. In the case of Internet access, the cloud is the Internet, and many providers are connected.

The Path Between You and the POP

The path your packets take between your router and the provider's POP for a typical T1 access circuit includes the following pieces of hardware and steps:

1. A synchronous WAN interface card in your router. This is typically an add-on adapter which has a high-speed serial port and a processor on-board to handle the protocol for synchronous communications.

2. A CSU/DSU which interfaces the synchronous WAN interface to the digital telco circuit. Details about CSU/DSUs are given in Section 2.3.3.

3. An RJ-45 connection between the CSU/DSU and the telco access point, often known as either **demarc** or a **smart-jack**. The term *demarc* has its basis in the fact that everything on your side of that interface belongs to you and is referred to by the telco as **CPE** (Customer Premise Equipment). The demarc is either a self-contained unit (normally a metal box mounted on the wall) or a card in a chassis which holds several demarcs. A smart-jack is the same as a demarc, except that the interface card (the circuitry which terminates the access circuit) is in a closet somewhere, and only the RJ-45 jack has been extended out to your site. When the circuit is installed, it should be labelled with the circuit ID of the access circuit.

4. The CSU/DSU handles the **channelization** of your data—i.e., it takes the stream of bits from the WAN interface and builds frames (with data only in the timeslots which correspond to the channels in use on the circuit). The CSU/DSU also converts the electrical signals for transmission over the T1.

5. This bit stream is transmitted through the telephone network through some combination of central offices and switches until it reaches its destination, which is the demarc at the POP. Because the data are digital, they can be reconstructed any time it is required to rebuild the signal strength or to switch media within the telco network (for example, if a portion of the circuit is on fiber instead of copper).

6. The process is reversed on the other side. The bit stream flows through the demarc into their CSU/DSU, where it is converted into signal levels that their router's WAN interface understands and expects.

7. From there, the packets flow on the provider's internal network until they find the appropriate exit point (also known as **egress**). The egress point from the provider's network depends upon the type of service you have. If this is your ISP, then your packet should end up on the Internet. If this is a Frame Relay link, then it will appear on your provider's router at the POP on the remote end of the link, so that it can be transmitted to your location B.

Looking back at the block diagram (Figure 2.7), it is functionally very similar to that of analog modems. The cables are new, the protocols are different, and what is really happening on the line is *entirely* different, but it feels the same (if you squint at the picture).

2.3.3   CSU/DSUs

As you noticed in the previous section, a T1 circuit requires an interface before it can be attached to your router. This device is known as a **CSU/DSU**, or a Channel Service Unit/Data Service Unit. CSU/DSUs range from a simple black box that interfaces the two media types to complicated devices containing multiplexers, inverse multiplexers, SNMP daemons, "phone home" functionality, and circuitry to failover to back up access circuits. CSU/DSUs range in cost from a few hundred dollars to several thousand.

Some routers come equipped with an integrated CSU/DSU, and many service providers will provide a CSU/DSU as part of your service or will lease one to you. You should be aware that some T1 CSU/DSUs can interface only a full T1—i.e., they are permanently configured for all 24 channels. There are also T1 CSU/DSUs called "drop-and-add" units, which can be used to multiplex a single T1 for multiple applications. For example, you can order a T1 that has 8 channels of long-distance voice circuits and 16 trunks (1024kbps) of Frame Relay. The "drop-and-add" CSU/DSU makes sure that the signalling is not confusing to either your router or your PBX. Like a T1, a DDS circuit also requires an interface, but it contains only a DSU (since there is only one channel and is therefore not compatible with the T1 variety).

The CSU/DSU almost always interfaces to the telco circuit via a straight-through twisted-pair cable with RJ-45 connectors on each end. In other words, any CAT5 Ethernet cable that isn't a crossover cable will do. On the "router side" of the CSU/DSU there is typically a V.35, RS-232, or X.21 connector. Make sure that you get the right cable to interface your router.

Configuring the CSU/DSU

If your service provider does not do it for you, you'll have to configure the CSU/DSU yourself. This is done through either a (second) RS-232 interface or the front panel. Things you will need to know from your provider about your T1 access circuit are:

- framing (ESF or D4) [**ESF**]

- encoding (B8ZS or AMI) [**B8ZS**]

- line build-out (expressed in either distance in feet or dB signal loss) [**0–133 ft** or **0 dB**]

- which channels carry the data circuit, in the case of fractional T1

- clocking (internal or external) [**external**] (For anything not in a test lab, the clocking must be driven externally, i.e., from the telco circuit.)

Once you have these values, you'll configure the CSU/DSU to multiplex/demultiplex frames on the T1 as required for the circuit. If you haven't a clue what the values should be, try the bolded values in the list. For the channels, if there is no other application on the circuit, they are typically configured consecutively from channel 1 to N, where $N = $ bandwidth/64kb. If this material is new to you, don't worry too much about it. The configuration will be intuitive, once you understand the background.

2.3.4   Billing of Digital Services

As the network administrator, you will probably have to validate the charges on the invoices, since you are best prepared to interpret them. Although it sounds like a mundane task, it is important to understand where your money is going. You will need this to be able to compare offers from other service providers.

Access can be expensive, and it is often a source of confusion. Some providers will try to hide access charges by charging a single price for the service, regardless of its distance from the POP (within reason, say 10 miles). This could be a good deal for those relatively distant, and a bad deal for others. Other vendors will separate the access out—perhaps even invoicing it separately. If your organization has contracts for voice service, the access circuits may fall under that contract. Because the FCC tariffs access and data services differently, access may be discounted separately, too.

Other potential complications arise when access is provided by a third party. Often the data service provider will not own the "last mile" and will lease the access circuit on your behalf. In this case, you may see things like "COC" or "Central Office Coordination" charges on your bill. These charges represent the fees your provider has to pay the access provider for co-locating in their facility. They are often not subject to discount terms in your contract.

Finally, there is often an opportunity to save costs by multiplexing a single access circuit for both voice and data.

Once you get beyond access costs, there are fees for the data services themselves. In general, the cost of using a vendor-provided service with a leased line includes:

- monthly access costs (possibly including COC fees)

- one-time access install charge (sometimes waived)

- monthly port costs (for the service itself)

- one-time port install/setup charge (sometimes waived)

- per-byte charges if your port/service is usage-based

It adds up quickly. A vendor should be able to explain all of the costs related to the service. It is in your best interest to collect and organize as much documentation as possible about the link and the various vendors' services which comprise it. When there are troubles and questions, you may be ultimately responsible within your organization.

2.3.5   Potential Datacomm Issues

Between having to decide what to order, solve CSU/DSU configuration problems, cope with physically down circuits, and audit incorrect billing, you'd think that a WAN administrator had enough to worry about. (After all, you're just supposed to configure the router.) The following sections address other topics which you may need to consider.

Latency

When you are working with extreme physical distances, the different media paths your packets take through a provider's network become important. Latency is a measure of the time it takes for a packet to travel from location A to location B, and is independent of bandwidth. For example, you can place a small packet into a very large pipe (say, a 45Mbps link) between two points, but it could still take a "long" time (maybe 600-800ms) for a packet sent to emerge from the other end. Latency is partially due to the delays introduced by switching elements, which require some time to look at the packet and pass it on. But a significant cause of latency is a physical limitation—namely, the speed of light.

A satellite geosynchronous orbit has an altitude of almost 38,000 km. If you could beam light directly at it in a vacuum, it would take about an eighth of a second to get there. Multiply this by two to go up and come back down. And because you won't be directly under the satellite for both trips (otherwise, you'd be sending it to yourself), you should factor in another $\sqrt{2}$, plus the switching delays. Now you're well past 350ms, and all of this just to get to the destination. If you're working interactively, you'll need to wait for a reply, too.

Compare this to the latency for fiber-optic halfway across the face of the earth, and you'll see why it makes good sense to stay on the ground. Of course, with fiber-optic, you'll be taking more hops (more switching time) and not travelling directly from location to location. Fiber-optic links can also be more expensive to deploy (and therefore more expensive to use) than RF or satellite links. In most circumstances you have little control over the path your packets take once they leave your facility, but be aware that more bandwidth does not always equate to "fast" for your users.

Link Security

Where there is networking, it seems that a security discussion is not far behind. The basic goal is always to exchange data between two or more machines, but the security measures required vary, based on the nature of the connection (and the data).

When you dial up an ISP and use the Internet to connect to your office, you are establishing a connection via a public network that is, for the most part, unregulated. You must guard not only the data you transfer, but also the machines themselves.

Compare this to some of the private IP networks, which are known as dial-IP solutions. Access to a private network is controlled, either physically or by some authentication mechanism. The users of these networks all know each other; at least that is the illusion. At least they may all be customers of the same service provider. Furthermore, the service provider should go to some effort to ensure that customer X cannot take a peek at the traffic customer Y is sending. Therefore, a better classification would be a **semiprivate** network. If you are dealing with very sensitive information, you cannot completely guarantee that an acutely interested competitor might not find a way to infiltrate your provider's network (admittedly paranoid, but conceivable).

Frame Relay is also a semiprivate network, although most treat it as a private network. Once your packets are on your provider's network, they travel alongside packets from anyone else. It is conceivable that through some social engineering someone on the inside could be listening. My guess is that most providers would wag their heads very convincingly that these sorts of things never happen, but then again, you never know. This very topic came up during the deployment of a worldwide personnel system which was to be used only on the internal network. The objection was that the use of the WAN violated the German data security law (*Datenschutzrecht*), because it allowed information about employees to pass between sites over unencrypted links—an interesting proposition, even though the links between our sites belonged to an uninterested third party.

Are these sorts of links truly insecure? That will be for you to decide, depending upon your application. My personal belief is that there are far easier (and less expensive) methods of spying, but that may be my naiveté. If these sorts of things make you perk up, consider using a strong method of encryption of your IP packet payloads. There are several **VPN** (Virtual Private Network) solutions for Linux; here are a few links to get you started in the meantime:

- **CIPE** (Crypto IP Encapsulation) is a lightweight protocol that allows you to connect two subnets via an insecure middle network. It encapsulates all of the applicable traffic within UDP packets using a Linux kernel module. See its homepage at *http://sites.inka.de/sites/bigred/devel/cipe.html* for more information.

- *vpnd* (the Virtual Private Network Daemon—*http://sunsite.dk/vpnd/*) uses a TCP session to tie together two machines running *vpnd* and encrypts the packets between them using the Blowfish algorithm. When the daemon is running, it creates a local SLIP device which can then be used for secure routes to the remote network.

- **Linux *FreeS/WAN*** is an implementation of the IETF's IPsec (Internet Protocol SEcurity) for Linux. It is also implemented in the kernel (like CIPE) and comes with a set of tools and utilities for its use. Its homepage has some very good documentation about configuring and using the software (*http://www.freeswan.org/*).

- The **VPN HOWTO**, part of the *LDP*, covers using Secure Shell (*ssh*) and a pty redirector to easily build a private network using the standard PPP daemon. Sort of a *poor* *man's VPN*, it is a good example of an *IP-encapsulated-within-IP protocol* similar to **PPTP** (Point-to-Point Tunneling Protocol).

2.4 Summary

This chapter covered some of the background material which, hopefully, will help you increase your comprehension of what you are doing as a network administrator. It began by defining the difference between a physical (media) protocol, a link protocol, and a networking protocol. While the definition presented is somewhat informal, the concept should stick in your mind. *Frame Relay* is a link protocol which ties routers together. *IP* is a networking protocol which supports the TCP and UDP transport protocols. *V.90* is a physical protocol (used by two modems talking to each over an analog telephone line).

The next topic was IP subnetting. You should revisit that section or appeal to other sources if the concepts and math of CIDR are not clear. You cannot balance a checkbook without being able to add and subtract; you cannot design a network without being able to calculate subnet masks.

The next topic was, *How does a workstation decide if it needs to use a router, and how does a router make its decisions?* We then talked about the hardware—hubs and switches—used to glue routers and workstations together when using Ethernet and discussed some security considerations when using them.

Zooming out from the LAN, we looked at the WAN, including general types of access, information about digital telco circuits, the interfaces required to use them, and the general layout of a WAN link. The section also noted a few gotchas about billing, round-trip packet delay, and link security. From here on out, we'll build routers!

Chapter 3

SILICON—A LAN ROUTER

"Silicon" is the name of one of the most heavily used Linux routers I have ever administered. As the main LAN router and the primary internal DNS server in an office with several hundred users, this system is involved with almost every action that a user in that office may perform with a networked computer. Silicon was initially deployed somewhat tentatively, "just to see" how it would perform. It was worth a shot, because it cost about one-tenth of what it would cost to add a single 100BaseT interface to the existing router. That it could act as the DNS server was a bonus, since we were going to need one anyway. The fact that silicon was so successful helped widen my perspective on where all Linux routers might find a home in the network.

The first part of this chapter covers configuring a Linux router to route between two separate physical subnets. Since some of you may be first-timers, we will work through this configuration in detail to make sure that all goes well. (Later examples build on this groundwork and will go much more quickly.) After we configure our LAN router and play with it a little bit, we extend the idea of routing between physically separate subnets and introduce **IP aliasing** and the idea of **multinetting**. This can be used to route between multiple logical IP subnets that exist on a single physical segment, a technique that can ease migrations from one set of IP addresses to another. After this, we'll delve into the topic of **packet sniffers** available for Linux. These programs are used to "see what's on the wire" and are invaluable tools for learning and troubleshooting. With these topics under your belt, you're ready to go out and accomplish some real work. The chapter concludes with an introduction to the **LRP** Linux distribution. LRP is networking-centric and fits on a single floppy diskette, making it an alternative to using a full Linux distribution for your router.

3.1 Configuring a LAN Router

Silicon is a good place to start talking about production Linux routers, because its hardware configuration is very simple and it requires no software other than the Linux kernel and the network utilities that are included in the base installation of all common distributions.

In Section 2.1.2 we studied the degenerate case of how a single workstation sends a packet directly to another workstation on the same subnet. We noted that if the destination's IP subnet does not match that of the sender, then the sender needs to use a gateway. Here we configure that gateway, routing between two physically separate Ethernet segments, each with its own IP subnet. (Connecting two physically separate physical segments which are part of the *same* logical IP subnet is known as **bridging**. The Linux kernel provides bridging support, but it is not covered in this book.)

3.1.1 Defining Our LAN Router

The first thing you should do when starting a project is figure out what you need to accomplish, noting any specific conditions which must be met or limitations you must take into account. This will help you map out your solution and keep you from losing sight of your goal as you become engrossed with the myriad details and smaller obstacles which may present themselves. (I cannot tell you how many times I have realized upon completion of a project that I spent 80% of the time working on 20% of the functionality and forgot to implement another 20% of the functionality altogether.)

Our goal in configuring silicon is to

> enable communication between two separate IP subnets via a router. Each IP subnet is on its own physical Ethernet segment. Subnet$_A$ is 192.168.16.0/24; subnet$_B$ is 192.168.18.0/24. Both subnets are to have full access to each other. The IP addresses 192.168.16.1 and 192.168.18.1 have been reserved as the gateway addresses for subnet$_A$ and subnet$_B$, respectively.

Often it can be quite helpful to draw a picture. Even if you understand how a given topology solves the problem at hand, a diagram will aid others who want to grok it (and may help you identify mistakes before you make them). Try to be consistent when depicting your network graphically—a simple set of conventions makes for clearer communication of ideas, especially with more elaborate topologies. A picture *can be* "worth a thousand words" (of documentation), but spending eight hours to produce a fancy drawing with a bunch of part numbers is usually a waste of time. The conventions I use are in Figure 3.1. Using these conventions, silicon's topology is depicted in Figure 3.2.

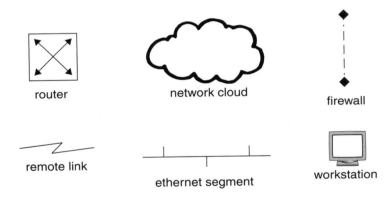

Figure 3.1 Conventions Used When Drawing Networks

3.1.2 Configuring the Base Platform

Now that we have a plan and a picture, we can roll up our sleeves and get busy with some hardware. We need a system with (at least) two Ethernet adapters, one connected to each physical segment, and enough disk space to hold whatever distribution of Linux you're running (and possibly a copy of the kernel source for the examples down the road). As we discussed back in Section 1.1, the CPU itself doesn't need to be particularly powerful to provide acceptable

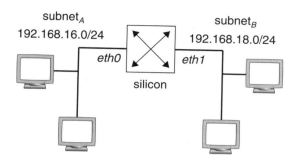

Figure 3.2 LAN Router with Two Subnets

performance. (The silicon of this chapter was a 166MHz Pentium with 32MB of RAM.) There is no need to load a slew of packages on your router; even the most minimal set of system binaries will be enough to make things happen. Once we're connected and the software is loaded, we need to make sure the kernel can detect the individual interfaces, configure them, and then instruct it on how to direct the flow of packets between them. Detection and configuration of the interfaces are done in precisely the same manner as you would do for a **single-homed** workstation (a system with only one network interface), only you're going to do it twice for this **multihomed** system. To keep things moving along I'm going to assume that you're running a reasonably generic Linux kernel of version 2.0.x, 2.2.x, or 2.4.x. (*Reasonably generic* means that you haven't pared down the kernel to the point where it's lacking TCP/IP, sysctl, and */proc* support. We'll address the specific kernel requirements in Section 3.1.6.)

Note: Privileges for Networking Commands

For much of the procedure in this chapter (and throughout this book) you will have to become the superuser on your system to be able to execute most of the commands. Save yourself some hassle and make sure that your **PATH** contains both */sbin* and */usr/sbin*, since most of the network configuration commands are in these directories. If you'd like to keep a record of the commands executed, try the *script* command.

Alternately, load and use the *sudo* command to become the superuser when need be instead of running a shell as root. It may seem like a hassle at first, but having to prefix superuser commands triggers you to *think* about whether or not you really need to run as root and reminds you to take care. (The horror stories I could tell about fat fingers and root ....) The *sudo* command provides a useful audit trail, especially in environments where there are multiple system administrators.

3.1.3   Detecting Ethernet Interfaces

An Ethernet adapter or **NIC**, be it an add-on card or integrated into the motherboard, is based on some particular **chipset** that interfaces an IEEE 802.3 LAN to the bus in your computer. Because there are several types of buses and many manufacturers, each chipset has its own distinct device driver. Notice that I didn't say adapter manufacturer; cards from several different vendors may share a common chipset and thus driver. While this can occasionally lead to confusion, a much more frustrating practice of some vendors is to change the chipset without changing the model of the card. Sometimes the only thing to do is to physically examine the card and jot down the designation of the chip itself. (After a while, you'll learn which specific chip is the most likely candidate.) All of this talk about chipsets is simply to say that you need to know which one you have in order to be able to select the correct device driver.

Why should you have to explicitly select the device driver? Many Ethernet device drivers can autodetect the presence of a given card they support by **probing** for it. (For ISA cards, this involves writing to a particular address (control port) and then trying to read the response back from another address in the appropriate address range; for PCI/on-board cards, the driver scans the list of PCI devices which have registered themselves, searching for the unique signature(s) of devices it supports. Try `lspci` or `cat /proc/pci` if you're interested.) However, due to the sheer number of them available for Linux, these device drivers are typically not compiled directly into the kernel. Instead they are made available as dynamically loadable modules, and as such, they cannot perform any sort of probing until somebody (or something) invokes them by loading that module.

Once you know the name of your chipset, you need to cross-reference this to the name of the Linux device-driver module that supports it. This is not always straightforward, but you should be able to find the module/driver name by visiting the Linux Documentation Project's Ethernet-HOWTO (*http://www.linuxdoc.org/HOWTO/Ethernet-HOWTO.html*), reading the `<Help>` while compiling the kernel, browsing through */usr/src/linux/Documentation/networking/*, or in the worst case by searching the source itself: **grep -i** *chipsetname* **/usr/src/linux/drivers/net/*.c**.

When you discover the right module name, use **modprobe** *modulename* to load it into your running kernel. Do this only once if you have two cards with the same chipset; for two separate drivers, load both of them now. Next you need to make sure that the kernel recognized and initialized the adapters correctly. The kernel always names the first NIC it finds *eth0*. Subsequent adapters are numbered consecutively as *eth1*, *eth2*, etc. There are several different ways to determine whether the kernel has already detected your NICs.

1. The contents of */proc/net/dev* will show all network devices which are currently configured on the system.

   ```
   silicon:/root> cat /proc/net/dev
   Inter-|   Receive                    |  Transmit
    face |packets errs drop fifo frame|packets errs drop fifo colls carrier
      lo:    4378   0    0    0    0      4378   0    0    0    0     0
    eth0:   27520   0    0    0    0     26367   0    0    0    1     0
    eth1:      31   0    0    0    0        17   0    0    0    0     0
   ```

   This shows that the devices *eth0* and *eth1* do exist (along with the *lo*, the **loopback** device which by convention always has the IP address 127.0.0.1). If a device appears in this table, then we can configure it with an IP address and use it. Unfortunately, */proc/net/dev* does not tell us much about settings of the device driver or the NIC.

2. The *dmesg* command, which displays messages generated by the kernel during the boot sequence and thereafter, often gives more information. Sample *dmesg* output corresponding to three separate Ethernet card initializations follows:

```
silicon:/root> /bin/dmesg

eepro100.c:v1.09j-t 9/29/99 Donald Becker
    http://cesdis.gsfc.nasa.gov/linux/drivers/eepro100.html
eepro100.c: $Revision: 1.36 $ 2000/11/17
    Modified by Andrey V. Savochkin <saw@saw.sw.com.sg> and others
eth0: OEM i82557/i82558 10/100 Ethernet, 00:08:C7:0A:AD:96, IRQ 9.
    Board assembly 692290-002, Physical connectors present: RJ45
    Primary interface chip i82555 PHY #1.
    General self-test: passed.
    Serial sub-system self-test: passed.
    Internal registers self-test: passed.
    ROM checksum self-test: passed (0x24c9f043).
    Receiver lock-up workaround activated.

natsemi.c:v1.05 8/7/2000  Written by Donald Becker <becker@scyld.com>
    http://www.scyld.com/network/natsemi.html
    (unofficial 2.4.x kernel port, version 1.0.2,
     October 6, 2000 Jeff Garzik, Tjeerd Mulder)
eth1: NatSemi DP83815 at 0xc482e000, 00:02:e3:02:a2:a7, IRQ 11.
eth1: Transceiver status 0x7869 advertising 05e1.

pcnet32_probe_pci: found device 0x001022.0x002000
PCI: Enabling device 00:12.0 (0001 -> 0003)
       ioaddr=0x001040  resource_flags=0x000101
divert: allocating divert_blk for eth2
eth2: PCnet/PCI II 79C970A at 0x1040, 00 50 56 e2 00 21
pcnet32: pcnet32_private lp=c0d09000 lp_dma_addr=0xd09000 assigned IRQ 10.
pcnet32.c:v1.25kf 26.9.1999 tsbogend@alpha.franken.de
```

dmesg does display more information about the driver and initialization, but there is no fixed format for what you'll get. Different device-driver authors display various aspects of the initialization at their discretion, and in the order of their choosing. For the example output above, I added spaces between each initialization of each driver. You might have to take a careful look to separate the output of one driver from that of another.

Note that you can control which physical card is known to the operating system by the name *eth0*, *eth1*, etc. simply by rearranging the order in which device-driver modules are loaded. In the situation where you have multiple cards of the same type, this is not as straightforward. As you can see in the sample output below, loading the 3c59x module detects and initializes both of cards. Now, which card is *eth0*? Truth be told, I don't know, and I believe the quickest way to resolve the question is to plug one of the cards into a known subnet, *ifconfig* it up with an IP on that subnet, and try to ping another address. (Alternately, you could sniff the traffic flowing across a given interface to determine which card was which. If this doesn't make sense to you, it will be made clear in Section 3.3.)

```
3c59x.c:v0.99E 5/12/98 Donald Becker
  (http://cesdis.gsfc.nasa.gov/linux/drivers/vortex.html)
```

```
eth0: 3Com 3c905 Boomerang 100baseTx at 0xfcc0, 00:60:97:da:8d:91, IRQ 11
  8K word-wide RAM 3:5 Rx:Tx split, autoselect/NWay Autonegotiation interface.
  MII transceiver found at address 24, status 786b.
  Enabling bus-master transmits and whole-frame receives.
eth1: 3Com 3c905 Boomerang 100baseTx at 0xfc80, 00:60:97:26:6b:c7, IRQ 10
  8K word-wide RAM 3:5 Rx:Tx split, autoselect/NWay Autonegotiation interface.
  MII transceiver found at address 24, status 782b.
  Enabling bus-master transmits and whole-frame receives.
```

Be aware when using *dmesg* that it reads from a circular buffer. If there have been a lot of kernel messages generated since bootup, the messages may have "wrapped around" and started overwriting the earlier messages. Many Linux distributions save the output of *dmesg* just after system startup so that it can be referenced later; try */var/log/dmesg*. Finally, do not be misled into thinking that *dmesg* contains the startup messages for other subsystems (e.g., daemons and services) on your router. It shows only kernel messages.

3. The results of *ifconfig* are useful if the devices are, in fact, not being initialized by the kernel. If the command returns an error like:

```
silicon:/root> ifconfig eth3
eth3: error fetching interface information: Device not found
```

then you know that either the driver module is not loaded, or it is being loaded but is not detecting the NIC. On the other hand, if the kernel does detect the devices and they are not yet configured, then *ifconfig* will return something like:

```
silicon:/root> /sbin/ifconfig eth2
eth2      Link encap:Ethernet  HWaddr 00:50:56:E2:00:21
          BROADCAST MULTICAST  MTU:1500  Metric:1
          RX packets:0 errors:0 dropped:0 overruns:0 frame:0
          TX packets:0 errors:0 dropped:0 overruns:0 carrier:0
          collisions:0 txqueuelen:100
          RX bytes:0 (0.0 b)  TX bytes:0 (0.0 b)
          Interrupt:10 Base address:0x1040
```

ifconfig tells us a lot about the interface—ironically, everything except for the driver type. Normally it also shows the IP configuration, but at this point the IP address has not been configured.

4. *netstat -ia* will show you an abridged version of *ifconfig*'s output. Note that with just -i, you will see all of the interfaces which are **up**, along with some statistics. Using the -a switch shows all of the network interfaces registered with the kernel, regardless of whether they are **up** or **down**.

```
silicon:/root> netstat -in
Kernel Interface table
Iface   MTU Met RX-OK RX-ERR RX-DRP RX-OVR TX-OK TX-ERR TX-DRP TX-OVR Flg
eth0   1500   0   133     0    0  0    105     0      0      0 BMRU
lo    16436   0    48     0    0  0     48     0      0      0 LRU

silicon:/root> netstat -ina
Kernel Interface table
Iface   MTU Met RX-OK RX-ERR RX-DRP RX-OVR TX-OK TX-ERR TX-DRP TX-OVR Flg
eth0   1500   0   140     0    0  0    109     0      0      0 BMRU
eth1   1500   0     0     0    0  0      0     0      0      0 BM
eth2   1500   0     0     0    0  0      0     0      0      0 BM
lo    16436   0    48     0    0  0     48     0      0      0 LRU
```

5. In a roundabout way, *lsmod* will show us what is going on, too. Since we are using modules for our NIC device drivers, our NICs will not be detected until the module is loaded. For each *ethX* device detected by that module and configured **up** by *ifconfig*, the **Used by** field is incremented by one. Thus, in the following output, we would surmise that two 3c59x devices are **up**.

```
silicon:/root> lsmod
Module          Pages    Used by
serial            7          0
3c59x             4          2
```

The converse, however, does not hold true. The fact that the module name does not appear in the output of *lsmod*, or the value of **Used by** is 0, does not mean that the NICs have not been detected. Devices that have not yet been configured "up" or have been deconfigured with `ifconfig` *ethX* **down** will not be counted in the **Used by** field. Last but not least, the driver support could simply already be compiled into the kernel.

3.1.4   Loading Modular Device Drivers

OK, what if you've read the previous section and run all of the various commands to locate your Ethernet interface, but your system still cannot detect them? We're going to talk here in a bit more detail about working with modular device drivers with Linux. Until you have security concerns that encourage you to do otherwise, I recommend the use of modules over device drivers built directly into the kernel. For a list of reasons why, see the discussion in Section B.6.

In the 2.4 kernel, modular device drivers are placed by default in the directory */lib/modules/ version/kernel/drivers/*category, where `version` is the currently running kernel (given by `uname -a`) and `category` is *net* for our purposes here, but in general may represent any broad class of device. These directories are created and populated during the `make modules_install` phase of the kernel build. The module itself is the file `modulename.o`—say *3c59x.o* for example—and to load it, you can typically use **insmod** *modulename*. *Typically* means that there is a fair amount of work going on behind the scenes to allow this; see the manpage for *insmod* for the details of how it knows where to find the module you're asking it to load.

Dependent Modules

Be aware that some modules use services (really, code) from other modules and must be loaded in what is called a **stack of dependent modules**. A very common case involves cards based on the NE2000 chipset. The module *ne.o* cannot be loaded until a module it depends upon, *8390.o*, is present in the kernel. Fortunately, you do not have to memorize this. Every time the system boots, *depmod* is called and writes the current list of module dependencies to */lib/modules/$*(uname -r)*/modules.dep*. You can look in this file to see what dependencies exist between modules. Each line in the file lists a module in the first field followed by a ":" and then a list of space-delimited module names. If nothing follows the ":", then the module has no dependencies. Otherwise, the dependent modules are required.

modprobe uses the contents of the *modules.dep* file to load any dependent modules that might be required before loading the module name you specify. You simply give it the name of the module to load as its argument, followed by any options you would normally specify to that module when using *insmod*. For example, `modprobe ne` will load *ne.o* and *8390.o*. Using the `-r` switch reverses the sense and removes a module along with any of its dependent modules (as long as they not in use by other modules or processes).

Module Parameters

Many modules accept configuration parameters which can be specified on the command line when they are loaded. The parameters often tell the driver where to search for the card (at what IRQ and base address), as well as set options such as whether or not the card should use full-duplex mode, which transceiver to activate, and so on. Not all modules use the same keywords, although most support `io=`*baseaddr* and `irq=`*irq* for setting these values. Unfortunately, the manner in which options must be specified when you have multiple interfaces is completely up to the driver author. In these cases, it is best to refer to the documentation accompanying the driver or in the driver source code itself. These may be found in the kernel source tree (usually */usr/src/linux*) in *./Documentation/networking/* and *./drivers/net/**driver**.c*, respectively. Since not all driver names are the same as the card they support, it is helpful to *grep -i* through this directory for the name of your card to locate the right file(s). It also may not hurt to read through */usr/src/linux/Documentation/modules.txt*.

Problems Loading Modules?

What to do if you have the correct driver support and the cards still are not recognized? Chances are it has to do with incorrect parameters or a resource conflict (IRQ or base address). First, recognize that PCI and ISA cards are different. PCI cards receive their IRQ assignments from the BIOS on the motherboard at boot time, and most (worthwhile) BIOSes produce a list of IRQ assignments to PCI devices just before booting the operating system. If you still suspect an IRQ conflict with a PCI device (probably with an ISA device), check the contents of */proc/interrupts* to see if the interrupt you are using to initialize the card is already in use. (This is not foolproof, because the ISA card causing the conflict may not be initialized by the OS either.) The base address should rarely pose a problem. The range of addresses assigned to PCI devices is different from that used for ISA cards.

ISA cards are another matter altogether. For one thing, be certain than **PnP** (Plug and Play)[1] is turned **off** for any card in the system. Many network cards come with a configuration utility (which typically runs under MS-DOS) that will do this for you and let you set the

---

[1] "Plug and Pray" for those who have suffered its arbitrary nature.

IRQ and base address. Some of these tools are available for Linux; I would start my search at *http://www.scyld.com/network/index.html*. Older cards have jumpers, which you can use to set to the base address, IRQ, or sometimes both. In the worst case, just use two interfaces with different driver types. Keep in mind that most cards of the same brand and model default to the same **base address** and IRQ settings, so you will have to take some action to avoid the conflict.

If none of these things helps, break down and RTFM to find out if the card is supported by Linux at all. Odds are that others have had the same problem, and perhaps they documented their experience at the *LDP* site (either in the *Ethernet HOWTO* or the *Hardware Compatibility HOWTO*). You can also pose the question to the support structure(s) of your Linux distribution. (See Appendix A.)

3.1.5 Configuring Ethernet Interfaces

Before you can go any further, make sure you have a system where *dmesg* shows that both *eth0* and *eth1* are recognized; i.e., you should be able to execute **ifconfig eth0** and **ifconfig eth1** and not receive `Device not found`. If you do receive this error message, make sure that you have support in your kernel for the NICs you are using, and that you've loaded the appropriate modules.

Now that we have gone through all of this material on Ethernet cards and modular device drivers, you might be wondering, "What was the question again?" Refer back to Figure 3.2 on page 59 to see the picture of our problem statement. We need to configure our router to route between the 192.168.16.0/24 and the 192.168.18.0/24 subnets, and we have reserved the .1 address in both subnets for the router.

So the next step is to assign IP addresses to *eth0* and *eth1*. Different Linux distributions provide different ways to do this, although the underlying mechanism for configuring a card with a fixed IP address is the same and is based on *ifconfig*. Despite its potentially confusing manpage, *ifconfig* is easy to use once you get the hang of it. (The myriad options derive from a long history and the fact that *ifconfig* isn't used only for Ethernet interfaces running TCP/IP.) For configuring our adapters, the usage is:

ifconfig *device ipaddr* `broadcast` *bcastaddr* `netmask` *netmask* `up`

Let's configure *eth0* first:

```
silicon:/root> ifconfig eth0 192.168.16.1 broadcast 192.168.16.255 \
                        netmask 255.255.255.0 up
```

Verify that the device is correctly configured by entering **ifconfig eth0**. The results should look something like this:

```
silicon:/root> ifconfig eth0
eth0      Link encap:Ethernet  HWaddr 00:50:56:E2:00:69
          inet addr:192.168.16.1  Bcast:192.168.16.255  Mask:255.255.255.0
          UP BROADCAST RUNNING MULTICAST  MTU:1500  Metric:1
          RX packets:3015 errors:0 dropped:0 overruns:0 frame:0
          TX packets:2262 errors:0 dropped:0 overruns:0 carrier:0
          collisions:0 txqueuelen:100
          RX bytes:743497 (726.0 Kb)  TX bytes:226314 (221.0 Kb)
          Interrupt:9 Base address:0x1000
```

The important bits at this point are that the IP address (`inet addr:`) and the subnet mask (`Mask:`) are set correctly, and that the `UP` flag is present (on the third line of output). If the interface settings do not look correct, you can run *ifconfig* repeatedly until things are right. Let's look at the output listed above line-by-line to learn about the command and what parameters it controls.

Line 1 shows the interface name, the type of interface, and the **MAC address** of the interface. Nothing on this line is controlled by *ifconfig* (for an Ethernet card).

Line 2 shows the IP address, broadcast address, and subnet mask of the interface—all of which are controlled by *ifconfig*. You may notice that the broadcast address is calculated from the IP of the interface and the subnet mask directly. Note, however, that if you specify a broadcast address using the keyword **broadcast**, and miscalculate, you will receive no warning of your error. Furthermore, once the broadcast address is set (either by you or by *ifconfig*), it will not change until you explicitly change it with the keyword **broadcast**.

Hint: Automatic Assignment of the Subnet Mask

If you are not using CIDR networks, there is no need to specify the broadcast address or the subnet mask. As with most Unices, *ifconfig* will assume you want a class A, B, or C network, depending upon the IP address assigned, and assigns the subnet mask and broadcast values accordingly. See Section 2.1.1 (page 30) to refresh your memory on what default class submasks are. (Unlike some Unices, there is no support for */etc/netmasks*—a Good Thing IMO, since I've seen that file cause more problems than it solves.)

Line 3 shows which flags are set for the interface name, along with the **MTU** and **metric**. MTU stands for Maximum Transfer Unit, or max size in bytes for a packet which will be generated by this interface. The metric is a way of specifying which of two (or more) similarly configured interfaces is preferable and should be used by the kernel first. The flags for an Ethernet device are:

UP indicates that the interface is available to be used for sending and receiving packets.

BROADCAST indicates that this interface can receive all broadcasts. You can disable this by issuing **ifconfig eth0 -broadcast**.

RUNNING indicates that the driver for the interface is running.

MULTICAST indicates that the interface is capable of multicast. You can set[clear] this (for some devices) with **ifconfig eth0 [-]multicast**.

PROMISC indicates that the interface is listening to *all* traffic on the network visible to it. This effectively turns the interface into a network sniffer. *tcpdump*, *ethereal*, and other programs use this mode to have a look at all of the packets flowing past the interface. (See Section 3.3.) You can set[clear] this by issuing the **ifconfig eth0 [-]promisc** command.

ALLMULTI indicates that the **all-multicast** mode has been set, and that all multicast packets on the network will be received by the interface. This is similar to **promiscuous** mode, but for multicast.

Lines 4, 5, 6, and 7 are mostly statistics for the interface. Zero values in these fields (except **RX packets** and **TX packets**) are Good Things. The **txqueuelen** field is the number of packets allowed to buffer in the send queue before the sending process blocks. This value can be tuned down for low-speed/high-latency links to prevent file transfers from continuously filling the queue and disrupting the performance of other (interactive) protocols, say like an *ssh* session.

Line 8 contains information from the driver about the IRQ and base address of the hardware. (Some drivers support changing these values with *ifconfig*, but I would recommend using driver module parameters.)

Now we have one interface up and configured. Before moving on, we need to do a little housekeeping. We have *eth0* configured, but which card in the PC is *eth0*? Take a moment now to label the physical interface card corresponding to *eth0* so that there is no confusion later on about which card corresponds to which interface. This is a good time to do this, because the second card is not initialized with an IP address, so even if you have both cards attached to the same hub, only the first card could be the one being used. You should attach the card you believe (or guess) to be *eth0*, and `ping` an IP address on that network. (Note that the Linux version of *ping* must be terminated with **CTRL-C** [unless you use the **-c** *count* option].) If you did not specify IRQs or base addresses when loading the device-driver modules, use *dmesg* (or *ifconfig*) to note the IRQ of *eth0* so that you can specify it explicitly in the future. This way, you can be certain that the kernel's *eth0* is the same card you expect it to be. Once you know which interface is which, label them both, and connect them to their respective hubs. (Also note that users of the 2.0 or earlier versions of the kernel will need to add a **network route** for 192.168.16.0/24 before you'll be able to ping an address on that subnet. See Section 3.1.6 for more information.)

Moving onto the second interface .... We simply repeat the process for the *eth0*, but for *eth1* and changing IP addresses and network addresses as appropriate. First, *ifconfig* the interface with **ifconfig eth1 192.168.18.1 netmask 255.255.255.0 up**, and check to see that all is well by examining the output of *ifconfig* and pinging a workstation on the 192.168.18.0/24 subnet.

3.1.6   Adding Routes—The *route* Command

If you have worked with some other flavors of Unix, you may be wondering how we've made it this far without adding routes for the locally attached subnets. The reason is that, starting with version 2.2 of the Linux kernel, the kernel adds a network route automatically when the interface is *ifconfig*ed up. (The route added is based on the IP address and subnet mask of the interface.) OK, what's a network route? In general, a **network route** tells the kernel how to find a given IP network. Even when an IP subnet is directly attached, the kernel needs to know which interface or gateway to use to speak to that subnet. You can verify this automatic addition of the appropriate network route by checking the contents of the **routing table** before and after configuring your interfaces. Do this with either **route -n** or **netstat -rn**—the command results are almost identical.

```
### before any interfaces are configured
silicon:/root> route -n
Kernel IP routing table
Destination   Gateway Genmask         Flags Metric Ref   Use Iface
```

(Note that users of version 2.2 and prior kernels typically have a route present for their loopback interface—i.e., a route to destination 127.0.0.0 with a netmask of 255.0.0.0 that uses interface *lo*. This seems to have quietly disappeared starting with 2.4, yet the system is still able to reach that interface and 127.0.0.0/8 network.)

```
### after eth0 has been configured, and before eth1
silicon:/root> route -n
Kernel IP routing table
Destination   Gateway Genmask         Flags Metric Ref   Use Iface
192.168.16.0  0.0.0.0 255.255.255.0   U     0      0       0 eth0
```

Note that you do not need a **host route** for the interface as you do for some other Unix variants. (A host route indicates how the kernel is to find a specific IP; some operating systems require that there be a routing table entry for each specific interface, including interfaces local to the system in question.) If you inadvertently remove the network route for a given interface or are running a kernel prior to version 2.2, you can (re)add the network route (in this case for *eth0*) with:

route add -net 192.168.16.0 netmask 255.255.255.0 eth0

Note that the *route* command for Linux has some slight differences when compared to other versions of Unix. Mainly, you can add network routes directly to interfaces, bypassing the step of establishing a host route for the interface before adding the network route via the gateway of the IP address of the adapter. This "trick" also works for point-to-point links. (More about this in Section 5.3.4.) Also, the syntax is a little different. Let's cover some of the options.

route [add|del] [-net|-host] *target* **netmask** *nm* **[gw** *gw]* *intf*

Basically, you can either **add** or **del**ete routes, of type either **-net** or **-host**.[2] For network routes, you will want to use the **netmask** keyword unless you are using only class A, B, or C networks, in which case the command will look at the **target** and determine a default value for the netmask (like *ifconfig* will do when configuring the interface). Because many applications are a mix of CIDR and standard class C networks, I recommend that you always specify the netmask explicitly, or at least until you're comfortable with the mix of subnets in play at your site. The **netmask** must be specified in dot notation.[3]

If you need to specify a gateway, use **gw** followed by either the IP address or the hostname of the gateway. Once again, you should be explicit and type out the IP address. If you get into the habit of using hostnames, make sure that they are in the local */etc/hosts*, not DNS or NIS names. Although these names will work fine as long as the name resolution succeeds, you may have to wait through some long timeouts if you specify a DNS name for the gateway for a route, and your DNS server is somewhere beyond that gateway. In a more hostile environment (really, any environment where you have users), you may find yourself the victim of DNS

---

[2] Host routes are typically used for a single IP address, in which case you do not have to specify a netmask.

[3] Anyone want to write a patch to let you use */maskbits*?

poisoning—when an attacking system poses as the DNS server and returns bad information in response to your DNS queries—and inadvertently using an attacker's system as your gateway.

The last argument is the *interface* to use for this routing-table entry. You may use the **dev** keyword before it and list it anywhere in the command line,[4] but placing it at the end of the line and omitting the **dev** seems to be a popular convention. If you do not specify a gateway, you will have to specify an interface, but in most other cases the kernel can figure out which interface it should use from the IP address of the gateway.

Moving back to our example, with both of the interfaces configured up, the routing table should look something like:

```
silicon:/root> route -n
Kernel IP routing table
Destination   Gateway   Genmask          Flags Metric Ref   Use Iface
192.168.16.0  0.0.0.0   255.255.255.0    U     0      0       0 eth0
192.168.18.0  0.0.0.0   255.255.255.0    U     0      0       0 eth1
```

Or, if you want to get to the real source of things, you can view the routing table in much the same light as the kernel does by executing `cat /proc/net/route`. Notice in the sample output below (which I've compressed a bit to have it fit the page) that the values are displayed in hexadecimal, and that they are ordered a bit differently than you might expect. In the case of the **Destination**, **Gateway**, and **Mask** fields, it will be easier (for us humans) to look at the value as 4 pairs of 2-byte words, with the least significant word starting on the left, and running left to right.

```
silicon:/root> cat /proc/net/route
Iface Destination Gateway  Flags RefCnt Use Metric Mask     MTU Window IRTT
eth0  0010A8C0    00000000 0001  0      0   0      00FFFFFF 40  0      0
eth1  0012A8C0    00000000 0001  0      0   0      00FFFFFF 40  0      0
```

If we break down the **Destination** for *eth1*, we find:

$$00 \,_{base16} == 0 \,_{base10}$$
$$12 \,_{base16} == 18 \,_{base10}$$
$$A8 \,_{base16} == 168 \,_{base10}$$
$$C0 \,_{base16} == 192 \,_{base10}$$

And if we put that back together along with the **Mask** for that entry, we find that we have 192.168.18.0/255.255.255.0.

Now that both interfaces are up, and workstations on either segment can ping the router addresses of 192.168.16.1 and 192.168.18.1, the 64-thousand-dollar question is, *Are we routing?* If you have the time and patience, I would encourage you to see for yourself by using one of the workstations on one of the segments to ping a workstation on the other segment (and vice versa). To do this, you should configure workstations in each subnet to use the gateway address presented by the router—either 192.168.16.1 or 192.168.18.1. If you have Linux workstations, you can add a route to a workstation in subnet$_A$ to find subnet$_B$ with **route add -net 192.168.18.0 netmask 255.255.255.0 gw 192.168.16.1 metric 1**. Alternatively, you could add a default route to that workstation in subnet$_A$ with **route add -net default gw 192.168.16.1 metric 1**. Use a similar command for a workstation in subnet$_B$ so that it can

---

[4]In fact, most of the options may be shifted around to suit your taste.

find subnet$_A$ before you test. Note that it is not enough to test pinging the gateway interface for the other subnet (i.e., the "far side" of the router); by default, a multihomed Linux box will respond to those connection attempts even if no routing is configured. Specifically, being able to ping 192.168.18.1 from a workstation on the 192.168.18.0/24 segment means nothing other than if you hit any of the interfaces on a Linux box asking for any of the other interfaces, you'll get a response. (Try it and see.)

When you try to ping that workstation on the other segment, you should notice that there is a whole lot of nothing going on. If the ping across the router does succeed—i.e., a nongateway system on 192.168.16.0/24 can reach a nongateway system on 192.168.18.0/24—then the startup scripts that came with your Linux distribution have taken the next step for you.

Enabling IP Forwarding (Kernels ≥ 2.2)

By default, the Linux kernel does not automatically configure itself to forward packets between interfaces, hence it will not act as a gateway until you tell it to do so. (The exception is the one we noted in the prior section; all local interfaces, by default, can respond regardless of their subnet affiliations.) You must indicate to the kernel whether it is allowed to route packets—i.e., accept packets sent to the system but not destined for its IP address(es), and forward these packets according to the system's routing table—by setting the value of */proc/sys/net/ipv4/ip_forward* appropriately. By writing a value of 1 to this file, you are setting the bit in the kernel that indicates that forwarding is allowed. Whether or not that forwarding actually occurs depends on a long list of other factors, such as any packet filtering that may have been configured, IP spoofing detection that is in effect (should the source be spoofing its address), and so on. These topics will be discussed later in the book. In the general case, a 1 here allows IP forwarding, while a 0 clears the bit and prevents any forwarding from occurring.

Once you've enabled IP forwarding, **that's it!** You now have a router. If for some reason you are not forwarding, make sure that the interfaces on the router and the workstations are configured correctly, and double-check that IP forwarding is enabled and that no firewalling is currently active. If things still don't work, you're allowed to let out a long `<sigh>`, but keep reading. You will route yet. A little further along, Section 3.3 discusses how to take a peek under the covers, as it were, to see what's actually happening on the network.

3.1.7   Making Configuration Changes Permanent

But before you announce your victory, you need to make sure that what you have done will be there the next time the machine is restarted. One common question I hear is: *Where is the routing table stored?* To a certain extent, the answer is *nowhere*, or at least *nowhere safe*. In the case of static routes, the routing table is stored in memory, and unless you record the same commands you issued during the example in a startup script somewhere, you will be starting over again from the beginning whenever you reboot your router. Let's review what we have done, thereby noting the configuration changes which need to be made permanent:

- We loaded modular device drivers for our network interfaces. Recall that the order in which you load your drivers is significant in two senses. If your modular device driver is dependent upon other modules, all modules must be present for the driver to load—use `modprobe`. If you have cards that require different drivers, the order in which they are loaded dictates which physical card is known to the kernel as *eth0* and *eth1*. Making this change permanent is easy, and you have several options:

The /proc Filesystem and Sysctl

The /proc filesystem offers a quick way to control many of the kernel features on a Linux system, provided that you have superuser access and the kernel is compiled with Sysctl and /proc support. Although it is mounted like other filesystems—you can see it when you execute a df—it does not truly represent a filesystem. Instead it is an access mechanism into the kernel's datastructures via the filesystem interface. This is unbelievably handy compared to having to modify the kernel parameters in a configuration file and then reboot (or worse yet, not being able to modify some parameters at all). The filesystem is a good choice of an API, if you will, to access the running kernel, because it is the lowest common denominator of interfaces on a Unix system. Having a GUI to modify these parameters is well and good, but having *only* a GUI is not. Being able to read from and write to a file, however, is well understood, by command-line jockeys and GUI programmers alike. For those of us on the command line, manipulating /proc is as follows.

- `cat /proc/sys/net/ipv4/ip_forward` will display the current value of the parameter.

- `echo "1" > /proc/sys/net/ipv4/ip_forward` enables the facility.

- `echo "0" > /proc/sys/net/ipv4/ip_forward` disables it again.

Because of its great utility, we will talk about the information to be found in /proc as well as actions to be taken by modifying it throughout this book.

1. You can add the module names needed to /etc/modules. Since the modules listed there will be loaded sequentially, be aware of which module represents *eth0* and *eth1* when populating this file.

2. You can add an `alias` line to your *modules.conf* file. This line associates a device name like *eth0* with a module name. When the kernel needs the given device, it will try to load the indicated module. You can also specify options required for that module at load time. For the three cards initialized earlier in the chapter, the entries in this file would be:

```
alias eth0 eepro100
alias eth1 natsemi
options natsemi debug=2 full_duplex=1
alias eth2 pcnet32
```

3. You can load the modules explicitly during your own custom network startup script. An example script is provided on page 72.

- We configured each of the network interfaces with the appropriate static IP address. The act of configuring the cards automatically added the appropriate network routes to the kernel's routing table. How this is done on your system is distribution dependent, which is why we're going to stick to our homegrown network startup script.

- We instructed the kernel to forward packets between interfaces by setting the value of */proc/sys/net/ipv4/ip_forward* to 1. Again, how you make this change permanent depends upon your distribution. It's better to know how to do things by hand anyway.

Basic Network Configuration in Debian

The previous configuration can be achieved on a Debian 2.2 (or newer) system as follows:

- Add the modules required to */etc/modules* or */etc/modules.conf*.

- Edit */etc/network/interfaces* to configure the IP settings for the interfaces:

```
auto eth0 eth1
iface eth0 inet static
        address 192.168.16.1
        netmask 255.255.255.0
        network 192.168.16.0
        broadcast 192.168.16.255
iface eth1 inet static
        address 192.168.18.1
        netmask 255.255.255.0
        network 192.168.18.0
        broadcast 192.168.18.255
```

You can then use the *ifup ethX* and *ifdown ethX* to configure individual interfaces up and down, or use */etc/init.d/networking* {*start|stop*} to start/stop the entire subsystem. Other options can be specified in this file—see the manpage for *interfaces*.

- The value of */proc/sys/net/ipv4/ip_forward* is controlled by the setting of ip_forward parameter in */etc/network/options*.

Since we're router admins and not workstation jockeys, I believe that we're sophisticated enough to keep all of the network configuration in our own script. This means disabling our distribution's specific network startup, but gives us complete control over the process. A version for the configuration of silicon so far would look like this:

```
#!/bin/sh
#
# /etc/init.d/local_network
#
# modification history:
#
# 19990213/tm    complete rework for new silicon box
# 20000417/tm    mod for 2.2 kernel: no longer need to add network routes
#                - they are added automatically by ifconfig up
################################################################################
```

```
Intf_up()
{
   [ -z ${INF} ] && echo "failure - INF not set" && return 1
   [ -z ${IPADDR} ] && echo "failure - $INF IPADDR not set" && return 1
   [ -z ${NETMASK} ] && echo "warning - $INF NETMASK not set"
   [ -z ${BROADCAST} ] && echo "warning - $INF BROADCAST not set"

   print "   configuring ${INF}=${IPADDR}"
   ifconfig ${INF} ${IPADDR} netmask ${NETMASK} broadcast ${BROADCAST}
   if (($? != 0))
   then
      print "*** error configuring ${INF} - please investigate ***"
   fi
   return
} # end Intf_up()

case "$1" in
   start)
      print "Starting Ethernet networking support:"
      print "   configuring lo"
      ifconfig lo 127.0.0.1

      print "   loading device drivers"
      modprobe eepro100        # eth0
      modprobe pcnet32         # eth1

      INF=eth0
      IPADDR=192.168.16.1
      NETMASK=255.255.255.0
      NETWORK=192.168.16.1
      BROADCAST=192.168.16.255
      Intf_up                  # eth0

      INF=eth1
      IPADDR=192.168.18.1
      NETMASK=255.255.255.0
      NETWORK=192.168.18.0
      BROADCAST=192.168.18.255
      Intf_up                  # eth1

      print "   enabling IP forwarding"
      echo "1" >/proc/sys/net/ipv4/ip_forward

      echo "end of network start"
      ;;
   stop)
      print -n "Stopping Ethernet networking support:"
      ifconfig eth1 down
```

```
      ifconfig eth0 down
      modprobe -r pcnet32
      modprobe -r eepro100
      ;;
  restart)
      echo -n "Restarting networking driver support:"
      $0 stop ; $0 start
      echo "."
      ;;
  *)
      echo "Usage: $0 {start|stop|restart}"
      exit 1
      ;;
esac
exit 0
```

Realize that the script is not meant to illustrate best scripting practices, but instead to be very clear (in other words, linear) and thus easy to follow. The script could also be made more robust by adding code to check the return code of *modprobe*, etc.

3.1.8   Kernel Talk: IP Forwarding and General Routing

In this chapter, we jumped right in and started using the kernel's networking and routing functionality, taking for granted that this functionality was available in the running kernel. Actually, assuming these facilities are available in the running kernel is not that much of a stretch, but we should take a moment to cover our bases.

I refer to the kernels that come with the various Linux distributions as **stock**, since they're configured by the folks building the distribution. Stock kernels have come a long way, largely thanks to modular device drivers. These allow a kernel to be compiled with all kinds of device support enabled yet without bloating the kernel to the point where it would be a memory hog (and far too large to fit onto a single floppy disk). Furthermore, the kernel developers started making some sound assumptions and changes with the 2.2 series[5] that made the kernel more versatile without sacrificing flexibility. Much of this is done via the */proc* filesystem, which we will talk about throughout this book.

Note, however, that stock kernels are often compiled for the lowest common denominator of machine hardware (e.g., for a 386 on Intel i32 architectures) and probably contain device support and options you do not need. To decrease the size of the kernel's memory footprint and to fine-tune other options to suit your environment, you should get into the habit of compiling your own. Refer to Section B.5 in Appendix B for detailed instructions on building kernels. If you're new to building kernels, note that the examples thus far depend upon the following options being compiled into the kernel.

```
Loadable module support --->
    [*] Enable loadable module support

General setup --->
    [*] Networking support
    [*] Sysctl support
```

---

[5]Which is not to imply that they were making unsound assumptions before! Things just started getting easier with 2.2.

```
Networking options --->
    [*] TCP/IP networking

Filesystems --->
    [*] /proc file system support
```

Of course, these options won't be nearly enough—there is no device support for your networking adapters, nor filesystem support, and so on—but you'll need at least these to have a kernel capable of networking. (If you're going to use the alias trick for module loading in */etc/modules.conf*, you'll also need `Kernel module loader` underneath `Loadable module support`.)

3.2   IP Aliasing for Multinetting

The Linux kernel supports a functionality called **IP aliasing** that allows you to assign multiple IP addresses to a single interface. Behind the scenes, what's happening is that when the kernel sees an ARP request on the wire, it will respond not only to the card's primary address but also to any of its aliases. Understandably, all of the aliases share the same MAC address. IP aliasing is useful for situations when you want to create the illusion of having more interfaces than physically exist. One such use is **multinetting**. The term refers to running multiple logical IP subnets on a single segment. Useful examples of this capability include preparing for and executing piecewise migrations to other IP address space (as opposed to having to work all weekend for a flash-cut), and planning for future growth by using more IP address space than you currently need to support your clients.

First take the IP address-space migration . . . . If you need to migrate to a different address-space, you can create additional "virtual" interfaces (really aliases) on top of your existing interface(s) and convert your users to their new IP addresses and gateways over time. Another scenario: If you are planning network growth at some point in the future, you might want to assign separate IP ranges to different departments or physical areas in your building. If there are currently only 10–15 people in each department, it would be overkill to have a separate router interface for each department. However, if you expect growth to 80–100+ devices in this area, you would be wise to go ahead and assign a class C subnet address space to this department (254 IP addresses) so that you will not have to go back and reassign addresses later when you do decide to give that department its own segment and interface. Finally, if you have no free slots for additional interfaces in your router, but need to add an IP subnet, you can use IP aliasing as a stopgap measure.

In this section we will use the second case as our example and add an IP subnet to the 192.168.18.0 segment of silicon. Once again, let us begin with a short description of the work to be completed and a sketch of how the network will look after the configuration change (Figure 3.3).

Create a new IP subnet, 192.168.20.0/24 which will share physical Ethernet segment B with 192.168.18.0/24. The 192.168.20.0/24 subnet, subnet$_C$, should have full access to the other subnets.

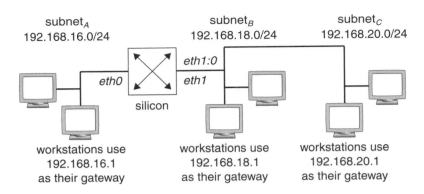

Figure 3.3 Multinetting LAN Router

IP Aliasing for Kernel Versions Prior to 2.4.x

If you're running a 2.4 version of the kernel and have networking support, you're set. For those of us running an older kernel, we must first enable IP aliasing in the kernel before we can use it. It should go without saying that we'll need the options listed previously, plus for a 2.2 kernel:

```
Networking options --->
+ [*] IP: IP aliasing support
```

And if you're running a 2.0.x kernel, you'll also have to select `Network aliasing` in order to be able to select `IP aliasing support`. Another difference—the 2.0 series kernels were the last to offer this as a loadable module. For the 2.2 kernel, if you select it, it is compiled directly into the kernel. In both cases you will have to rebuild your kernel and reboot your system before you can use the new functionality.

You'll know that you do not have IP aliasing support in your 2.2 kernel if, when you try any sort of access to the aliased device, you receive error messages like those listed below. The corresponding 2.0 kernel error message is very similar.

```
coyote# ifconfig eth0:0 192.168.20.1 up
SIOCSIFADDR: No such device
SIOCSIFFLAGS: No such device
```

3.2.1 Using IP Aliasing

IP aliasing works by assigning additional virtual interface names to existing interfaces. IP aliases for a given interface are indicated by appending *:alias* to the interface name. Thus, the syntax *ethX:alias* is used to specify the aliased interface name, indicating that the virtual interface is associated with physical interface *ethX*. The *alias* portion of the interface name must be an integer N, where $(0 \leq N \leq 9)$, for the 2.0 kernel series. For the 2.2 and 2.4 kernel, the *alias* can be almost any string, including numbers, letters, and punctuation characters.

Almost anything after the first ':' is tolerated, including more ':' characters. In a way this is pretty nifty, but you have to work with these things. A word to the wise: use integers and lowercase strings and no more than 4 characters. The output from *ifconfig* is going to truncate anything past the fourth character and lead to confusion.

After you've spent the afternoon coming up with the perfect alias, you use *ifconfig* to actually create the virtual interface(s). For example, to add a virtual interface to the real interface *eth1*, use:

```
silicon:/root> ifconfig eth1:0 192.168.20.1 netmask 255.255.255.0 \
               broadcast 192.168.20.255 up
```

Check the interface with *ifconfig* just as you would any real physical interface. Note that all of the address settings and flags are present but the interface statistics are not. (If you need to keep track of these, you can do so with **IP Accounting**, introduced in Section 10.1.)

```
silicon:/root> ifconfig eth1:0
eth1:0  Link encap:Ethernet  HWaddr 00:60:97:26:6B:C7
        inet addr:192.168.20.1  Bcast:192.168.20.255  Mask:255.255.255.0
        UP BROADCAST RUNNING MULTICAST MTU:1500  Metric:1
        Interrupt:10 Base address:0xfc80
```

Just as with a real interface, the kernel will automatically register a network route for the aliased interface when you configure it up.[6] However, if you look in the routing table, you'll notice that it uses the real name of the interface, not the IP aliased name.[7] If we take another look at the routing table, we'll see that our new subnet is routed out over *eth1*:

```
silicon:/root> route -n
Kernel IP routing table
Destination     Gateway     Genmask         Flags Metric Ref   Use Iface
192.168.16.0    0.0.0.0     255.255.255.0   U     0      0       0 eth0
192.168.18.0    0.0.0.0     255.255.255.0   U     0      0       0 eth1
192.168.20.0    0.0.0.0     255.255.255.0   U     0      0       0 eth1
127.0.0.0       0.0.0.0     255.0.0.0       U     0      0      24 lo
```

You can delete an IP aliased interface the same way you would a real interface—in this case, *ifconfig eth1:0 down*. Appropriately, this also removes only the network route corresponding to the virtual interface. As with any actions you take which modify the running kernel, you need to incorporate them into your startup script(s) in order for them to be consistently executed upon startup. They can also be added to your distribution's configuration files—for example, */etc/network/interfaces* in Debian—and used like any other interface, just as long as the alias interface is configured after the physical interface of which it is a part.

IP aliasing is quite a useful tool to have at your disposal. Should a group of contractors show up onsite and require immediate access to the network, you can add a virtual interface, with its own firewalling and accounting rules, in a matter of minutes. It can also be useful for high-availability situations, where once you detect that system$_X$ is down, you would like system$_Y$ to quickly assume IP$_X$ and to provide a meaningful error message to your userbase (or perhaps a redundant version of the services on system$_X$) while you investigate the outage.

---

[6]For the 2.0 kernel, you need to do this by hand.

[7]This changed between kernel versions 2.0 and 2.2; I thought it was clearer to be able to see the virtual interfaces in the routing table.

Speaking of investigation, let's say that problem with system$_X$ wasn't some obvious hardware problem, but instead, the system seemed to be up and healthy. Everything looks OK, so why can't your users access it? In many cases, the best way to get to the bottom of things is to determine what's happening on the network.

3.3   IP Monitoring Tools

Having access to the data on the line is invaluable when you are troubleshooting a variety of network problems. Sniffers can operate on all different network layers or be configured to operate at only a certain layer. Imagine all that is happening on an Ethernet segment when machine$_A$ tries to telnet to machine$_B$ and everything works as it should:

1. First, machine$_A$ might need to resolve the hostname of machine$_B$, requiring it to perform a DNS hostname lookup. When it calls `gethostbyname()`, a UDP packet is formatted to be sent to the DNS server.

2. For our example, let's assume that the DNS server is on the same IP subnet and is known as machine$_C$. This means that the IP stack is not going to use a gateway to transmit the packet. It will send the packet directly to the DNS server. To contact the DNS server, machine$_A$ will have to issue an **ARP request** to locate the address of machine$_C$. The ARP request is sent to media address *ff:ff:ff:ff:ff:ff*, which is the broadcast address for the Ethernet segment. The ARP request is `Who has the IP address of machine C?`

3. Machine$_C$ will answer with an **ARP reply** which contains its Ethernet hardware address.

4. Machine$_A$ can now send its UDP packet to port 53 on machine$_C$ as an IP packet. Machine$_C$'s reply goes out immediately, because machine$_C$ already knows machine$_A$'s Ethernet hardware address. The **ARP table** on machine$_C$ should have been updated with this information when it received the packet from machine$_A$.

5. Now machine$_A$ has the IP address of machine$_B$ (it took long enough, eh?), which is located in another IP subnet. The telnet client on machine$_A$ formats its TCP packet to send to port 23 of machine$_B$.

6. The IP stack on machine$_A$ looks in its *routing table*. (Machine$_A$ has a routing table of sorts. Although it is not necessarily a gateway, it uses the same mechanism to determine where to send a packet as a router would.) Machine$_A$ notes that the destination address is not part of the IP subnet attached to its *eth0* and it has only one NIC, so it will have to use the default gateway.

7. Now the process to contact the default gateway (which is known by its IP address) begins with another **ARP request**, assuming that either machine$_A$ has not used the gateway before, or it has, but the entry in the ARP table has already expired.

8. Once machine$_A$ has the MAC address of the default gateway, it can format its packet and send it to the gateway, in hopes that the gateway will forward it on to machine$_B$.

9. Once the gateway receives the packet, it checks the packet's destination and sees that the packet must be sent to machine$_B$, which (thankfully!) is on an Ethernet segment directly connected to another interface on the gateway.

10. The gateway must perform an **ARP request** on the segment where machine$_B$ is located to learn machine$_B$'s Ethernet. When machine$_B$ answers with the MAC address needed, the gateway finally delivers the packet from machine$_A$.

11. The entire process starts anew when machine$_B$ goes to reply to machine$_A$, except that machine$_B$ has a bit of a headstart. It already knows the MAC address of the gateway because it stored that information in its ARP table when it received the packet from the gateway. Also, it already knows the IP address of machine$_A$, so it will not have to perform a DNS lookup to reply (although the telnet daemon on machine$_B$ may need to perform a DNS lookup anyway for logging purposes or to determine if the IP-to-name mapping [a.k.a. **reverse mapping**] matches the name-to-IP mapping for machine$_A$).

Simple, eh? With a packet sniffer, you can watch all of this unfold before your eyes in frighteningly verbose detail. Use packet sniffers to explore what is happening at the **link-layer** (Ethernet), the **network-layer** (IP, ARP, RIP, etc.), and the **transport-layer** (TCP, UDP, etc.). If that doesn't pique your interest, other examples of uses follow:

- You can detect Ethernet segment problems such as hosts configured with incorrect gateways, hosts which are continually generating broadcast messages, and even hosts which are generating malformed packets.

- You can quickly detect routing and firewalling problems by seeing if the packets you expect are on the line. If there is a lot of activity on the segment, use a filter to restrict what is monitored to only the IP address of host(s) in question. You can further restrict what is monitored by specifying a certain protocol and/or port. (If you are connected via the network to the machine where you are performing the sniffing, be sure to exclude traffic to and from your machine unless you want to see all of the results of the trace *in* the trace.)

- You can measure the volume and latency of the packet exchange required to complete a transaction. Because a sniffer prints very precise timestamps along with the packet headers, it is not difficult to write another script to calculate where in the sequence there are delays, and from that to present a detailed analysis of where the latency was occurring.

- As the network administrator, sometimes you will be asked to perform odd functions. A user once came to me because he had forgotten the password for a POP3 account a mail client had been automatically checking from his workstation at the office. The user asked me if I could sniff the password when the mail client checked his mail the next time. `ipgrab -i eth0 port 110 and host` *userip* to the rescue . . . .

I will introduce a few of the popular packet sniffers, of both command-line and GUI flavors. All of these are based on *libpcap*, a packet-capture interface library originally from the Network Research Group at the Lawrence Berkeley National Laboratory (or LBL). If you can handle wading through the source, visit *http://www.tcpdump.org/*. Note that some kernel support is required to use sniffers. Namely, in the 2.4 tree, you'll need the `Packet socket` option enabled (the second option is not required, but can benefit performance):

```
Networking options   --->
   <*> Packet socket
   [*]    Packet socket: mmapped IO
```

There are a few things to remember when using packet-capture programs. First, they can show you only what they see on the wire. If you are plugged into a switch, you may see only IP broadcasts, some Ethernet broadcasts, and traffic to and from your workstation. (Refer to Section 2.2.3 for a more detailed description of why this is.) Second, sniffers work only when they are run as the superuser. Unless they are being run as root, they cannot put the interface into **promiscuous mode**. (And no, that's not a stage you go through in your bar-hopping days.) Third, it isn't ethical to go about sniffing other people's packets just because you can. See Section D.1 in Appendix D for more on this.

A good way to start is with one of the command-line sniffers. They can unlock the details of the network without generating a lot of overhead on the system they are running on, and they spit out packets as they receive them.

3.3.1 *tcpdump*

tcpdump could be called the *original* packet sniffer, first being introduced in January of 1991. It was written by the same folks responsible for *libpcap*—Van Jacobson, Craig Leres, and Steven McCanne—and it runs a slew of different versions of Unix. In its most basic form, you can start it without any arguments and it will dump the packet headers being sent and received on the first Ethernet interface it finds (normally *eth0* for Linux) onto *stdout*. Of course, you can adjust where the sniffer gets its input, how the output looks, where the output goes, and what sort of filter the sniffer should use. Here are some of the common options used with *tcpdump*:

```
tcpdump [-adeflnNOpqRStvxX] [-c count] [-F file]
        [-i interface] [-m module] [-r file]
        [-s snaplen] [-T type] [-w file]
        [-E alogorithm:secret] [expression]
```

Controlling Where *tcpdump* Gets Its Input

-i *interface*—a network interface with an encapsulation format supported by *libpcap*. For Linux, this is almost anything you'll come across, including link protocols like PPP and Frame Relay.

OR

-r *file*—read the *file* for input. *file* should have been created by `tcpdump -w` or a program that writes the same format. Specify "-" to read from *stdin*.

-c *count*—read only *count* packets from the input source before exiting.

-s *snaplen*—specify a different number of bytes to be read from each packet. Typically, *tcpdump* reads only enough bytes to make sure that the headers are saved, but you may want to increase this value, especially if you intend to use `-x` down the road.

[**expression**]—is an expression used to limit the scope of the patterns matched by *tcpdump*. By default, all packets are displayed. The format is known as the *Berkeley packet-filter expression* format. Although it is different from the filtering expressions you use with the Linux packet-filtering tools and a few other tools you're likely to use, this one is very intuitive and is used by several popular sniffers. The expressions often look like English phrases. We'll dive into the expression syntax in a moment. First let's look at an example using the syntax so far:

```
root@vivaldi:~# tcpdump -c 4
tcpdump: listening on eth0
13:40:07.506722 hund.ntp > bach.ntp:  v4 client strat 0 poll 10 prec -16 (DF) [tos 0x10]
13:40:07.510846 bach.van > hund: icmp: bach udp port ntp unreachable [tos 0xd0]
13:40:07.540552 hund.1026 > bach.domain:  15769+ PTR? 1.1.168.192.in-addr.arpa. (42) (DF)
13:40:07.544570 bach.domain > hund.1026:  15769* 1/1/1 PTR[|domain] (DF)
```

With no interface specified, *tcpdump* opens up the first interface it finds, *eth0*, and starts listening. In this case we've limited it to capturing 4 packets, but even in the span of 0.04 seconds we can see some interesting things going on. The NTP daemon on hund attempts to contact the NTP server on bach. NTP must not be running, because bach replies that the port is unreachable. Then hund decides it needs to do a reverse DNS lookup for 192.168.1.1. Here, again, bach is its DNS server and responds to hund with the requested data. That's a lot of information, and that's just from reading only the headers and for a very short time period indeed. So that we don't have to wade through hundreds and hundreds of megabytes of this to find a given interchange between two systems, we'll need a way to tell *tcpdump* to limit what it displays. This is done via expressions.

The expression syntax is one or more **primitives**, combined by **and**, **or**, or **not**, which are also known by **&&**, **||**, and **!**, respectively. Primitives may be grouped using parentheses, but when you do this, you will need to either quote or otherwise escape the *(* and *)* characters to prevent the shell from misinterpreting them. So you can do things like p_1&&!$(p_2||p_3)$. But what exactly is a **primitive**? It consists of an **identifier**, potentially preceded by a **qualifier**. And this is where it gets complicated .... The authoritative source on this subject is the manpage and whatever works for you on the command line. A synopsis is provided below:

Berkeley Packet-Filter *qualifiers*

type—specifies the type of the *identifier*. It can have the values of **host**, **net**, or **port**, with **host** being assumed.

direction—is one of **src** or **dst**, with the default (when no direction is specified) being **src or dst**. Therefore

```
tcpdump -n -i eth0 src or dst port 110
tcpdump -n -i eth0 port 110
```

are equivalent. Keep in mind that **src** and **dst** do not apply to just IP headers. They can also apply to other protocols, such as **ether** (and thereby indicate a source or destination Ethernet address).

protocol—when used alone (without a qualifier), is one of **ether**, **fddi**, **tr**, **ip**, **ip6**, **arp**, **rarp**, **decnet**, **tcp**, and **udp**. There are more protocol specifications if you qualify them with protocol family. For example, you can specify **ip proto igrp** to match Interior Gateway Routing Protocol packets, or **ip proto esp** to capture IPsec Encapsulated Security Payload packets. There are a lot of permutations, and your needs will guide you to the protocols you need to sniff, so curl up with the manpage and a cup of coffee when you need something exotic. If you do not specify a **protocol**, then any protocol type which makes sense for the identifier will match. Therefore, if you specify only a **port**, then both *tcp* and **udp** protocols are implied.

Types of Berkeley Packet-Filter *identifiers*

host *host*—indicates the IP address of *host*. Qualifiers that make sense with this are **src** and **dst**—remember that the default means that *host* can be either the source or the destination. *host* can also be a DNS name which resolves to multiple IP addresses, in which case all of them will match. Note that **host** is the keyword and *host* is the value of the identifier.

ether host *ehost*—indicates an Ethernet address. Once again, **ether host** is the keyword and *ehost* is either a 6-byte Ethernet (MAC) address in the format *xx:xx:xx:xx:xx:xx* or a name from */etc/ethers*. The **dst** and **src** qualifiers apply as they do for a **host**.

gateway *host*—generates a match if the packet being examined was forwarded by *host* acting as a gateway or is about to be (next hop *only*) forwarded by *host*. The *host* specified must appear in both */etc/hosts* and */etc/ethers*. BTW, */etc/ethers* is not so wonderfully documented. The only whitespace that seems to be allowed between the Ethernet address and the ehostname is a single space.

The reason *tcpdump* needs those two files for this feature to work is that what it's really using for an expression is **ether host** *ehost* **and not host** *host*, so it needs the MAC address of the gateway to pick up off the wire (the *ehost*) as well as the host IP of that gateway (the *host*) to ignore traffic with that source IP address in the headers. Because of the touchiness of */etc/ethers* and because, at the time of writing, versions of *tcpdump* with IPv6 support enabled won't let you use **gateway** anyway, use the alternate expression supplied above.

Note that you must specify the MAC address of the interface on the segment you're on for the *ehost*, and that if you have services bound to specific IPs on your gateway, you may want to supply both of the *host* addresses of the gateway (by tacking on an additional **not host** *othergatewayIP*.

net *net[/masklen* | **mask** *mask]*—is merely one of several different ways to specify an IP subnet. The keyword **net** is required, while the */masklen* (the same "number of ones" format covered back in Chapter 2 and used by *ipfwadm* and *ipchains*) and the **mask** *mask* (the dot-format used by *ifconfig*) are optional. The **dst** and **src** qualifiers apply.

port *port*—indicates *port* is on one end (or both) of an IP packet. *port* can be an integer port number or a service name from */etc/services* or equivalent. The **dst** and **src** qualifiers apply as usual, optionally *preceded* by **tcp** and **udp**. Note that the order of the qualifiers before the keyword **port** is important, as in the following examples:

```
tcpdump -n -i eth0 tcp src port 110    # correct
tcpdump -n -i eth0 src tcp port 110    # WRONG
```

less *length*—matches packets with a length (in bytes) less than or equal to *length*. Note that the length is the payload + the transport headers, so you cannot use *less 1* to catch empty packets (ACKs and whatnot). Because different protocols have different header lengths, you might have to experiment a bit to find the magic number. My rule of thumb is to add 64 to whatever length you are looking for when you're sniffing an Ethernet device, and 40 for PPP devices.

greater *length*—matches packets with a length (in bytes) greater than or equal to *length*. The same comment about headers made for **less** applies.

ip broadcast—matches three different types of IP broadcasts.

> packets sent to 255.255.255.255 (all ones)
>
> packets sent to 0.0.0.0 (all zeros)
>
> packets sent to the local subnet broadcast address (as is applicable for the **-i** interface being listened upon).

ip multicast—matches ip multicast packets.

ether broadcast—matches the packet if it is an Ethernet broadcast—any packet with an Ethernet destination address of *ff:ff:ff:ff:ff:ff* (e.g., an **ARP request**). The keyword **ether** is optional, but to avoid confusion with **ip broadcast**, I recommend using it.

ether multicast—matches Ethernet multicast packets (I've personally never come across one of these ....).

expr relbinop expr—Last but not least, this syntax is a way to get inside the packets to compare either 1, 2, or 4 bytes of the packet header with some known quantity. The first *expr* should be a *protocol*[*offset*:*size*] where:

- *protocol* is one of the protocols listed among the protocols in *types of qualifiers*
- *offset* is the number of bytes from the beginning of the header implied by the *protocol*
- *:size* is optional, as *size* will default to 1

relbinop is a relative binary operator from the list of **>, <, >=, <=, =, !=**, and the second *expr* is an integer mathematical expression (no variables!) in C syntax.

If that sparks your interest, then go for it. It might be useful as a training aid, or to watch for some rare condition (perhaps a suspected protocol violation). I consider it to be for full-blown gurus, so I'll leave it up to you to figure out how to make use of it.

Before we move on to output options, let's look at a couple more examples that contain expressions. In this first example, we want all packets either to or from vivaldi, but no packets with a source port of 22 in the TCP header. Because we happened to be *ssh*'d into vivaldi from bach, we see half of that *ssh* connection, namely, the traffic sent to port 22 (which is ssh in */etc/services*). We also see a DNS request being made by vivaldi. If you're wondering, you normally won't use **-c** very often in the real world; you would forego the count and simply hit **CTRL-C** when you'd seen enough. It's used here only to keep the results brief, as is **-t**, which suppresses printing timestamps.

```
root@vivaldi:~# tcpdump -t -c 3 host vivaldi and not tcp src port 22
tcpdump: listening on eth0
bach.41509 > vivaldi.ssh:     \
    . ack 1961648478 win 63712 <nop,nop,timestamp 58424771 8438456> (DF) [tos 0x10]
bach.41509 > vivaldi.ssh:     \
    . ack 65 win 63712 <nop,nop,timestamp 58424778 8438463> (DF) [tos 0x10]
vivaldi.1026 > java.domain:  11746+ PTR? 1.18.168.192.in-addr.arpa. (43) (DF)
```

In this example, we want to observe the traffic on the subnet we created using IP aliasing. Easy, right? The catch is that `tcpdump -i eth1:0` shows us everything on that physical segment, not just the traffic for the IP subnet that we intended by specifying `eth1:0`. The reason is that, without any more clarification, *tcpdump* takes the card indicated by the interface given with **-i** and puts that physical card in promiscuous mode. (What other card could it use?) To get the results we want, we'll use **-net** to indicate only the traffic on our "virtual" subnet. Furthermore, we don't want to be bothered with ARP traffic.

```
drone3:~# tcpdump -i eth1 net 192.168.20.0/24 and not arp
tcpdump: listening on eth1
20:10:21.099529 192.168.20.15.1024 > 192.168.20.13.telnet:      \
     S 209094949:209094949(0) win 512 <mss 1460> [tos 0x10]
20:10:21.100696 192.168.20.13.telnet > 192.168.20.15.1024:      \
     S 1065737340:1065737340(0) ack 209094950 win 5840 <mss 1460> (DF)
20:10:21.106609 192.168.20.15.1024 > 192.168.20.13.telnet:      \
     . ack 1 win 32120 (DF) [tos 0x10]
20:10:21.132447 192.168.20.15.1024 > 192.168.20.13.telnet:      \
     P 1:25(24) ack 1 win 32120 (DF) [tos 0x10]
```

As you can see, we picked up a telnet session between 192.168.20.15 and 192.168.20.13. Why didn't we get pretty hostnames as in the other examples? Because we haven't set up a reverse PTR map for the zone 20.168.192.in-addr.arpa on our DNS server yet. If you notice some lag waiting for traffic to show up while running *tcpdump*, it could be that the monitoring machine is trying several DNS servers to obtain an IP-to-host mapping. By default, *tcpdump* resolves IPs to hostname and port numbers to the symbolic equivalent in */etc/services*. You can use **-n** and other options in the next section to control this behavior.

Controlling How *tcpdump* Formats Its Output

-e—extend the output to include the link-layer headers for each line of output. (You can also remember this by thinking of **e**thernet headers.)

-E *algorithm:secret*—decrypt IPsec ESP (data payload) packets. Read the manpage for the algorithms supported in your version of *tcpdump*. The *secret* is the string, or password if you will, required to decrypt the payload. As noted in the manpage, use this for debugging purposes and only with secrets you don't mind sharing with others. The secret will be available to all in the output of a *ps* command.

-n—**n**o name resolution of IP addresses or service names (ports). This can save a lot of time, especially when running *tcpdump* with output going to *stdout*.

-N—do not print FQDNs (Fully Qualified Domain Names), but instead only print the hostname portion. Obviously, this makes no sense if you have specified **-n**. (I cheated in some earlier examples and trimmed the FQDNs myself to make them fit the page.)

-q—**q**uiet, a less verbose mode of output. This skips the sequence numbers and a lot of the protocol flags. The output (when used with **-n**) will fit nicely in an 80-column terminal window.

-S—print absolute TCP sequence numbers, which might be useful for calculating packet counts during a given session.

-t—do not generate a timestamp on each line.

-tt—display the 32-bit timestamp value instead of the wall-clock time. (Warning—only useful until the year 2038!).

-v—display more verbose output, including IP TTL and TOS header information.

-vv—display even more verbose output, including protocol information when *tcpdump* knows about the protocol.

-x—print the packet payload in hexadecimal, up to the number of bytes set by **-s** *snaplen*. This is one reason why *tcpdump* might be considered more polite than other sniffers that display the data in ASCII. You will not just happen across the contents of someone's email or his/her password with the data in hex without making an effort to decode it. If you can *read* hex-formatted ASCII, you need to get out of the office more.

-X—a nicer version of **-x** when used in combination with **-x**, this prints the output in both hex and ASCII, for when you have the RFC on one knee and don't want to have a hex-to-ASCII table on the other.

-w *file*—write the output to *file. file* will be in binary and can be parsed by specifying it as the input for **tcpdump -r**. This eliminates the overhead of writing to a terminal, so you might prefer using **tcpdump -w** and then **tcpdump -r** on busy machines. *tcpdump* is clever enough not to even try to perform host or service name lookups while in this mode to further increase performance. It will do them for you while reading the file back in if you do not turn them off. Specify "-" to write to *stdout*.

If you didn't absorb all of those options all at once, here are a couple more examples that illustrate their usage. The first captures all traffic other than *arp* and *ssh* (port 22). If I tell you that *eth1* is connected to the 192.168.18.0/24 subnet, you can surmise from the third packet that drone3 is acting as a gateway. In the second example, we capture everything on the segment to a file and then use *tcpdump* to parse the contents as we see fit:

```
#
# Example 1
#
drone3:~# tcpdump -nXq -i eth1 not arp and not port ssh
tcpdump: listening on eth1
21:17:59.369273 192.168.18.15.1030 > 192.168.18.13.21: tcp 0
0x0000   4500 002c 004d 0000 4006 d512 c0a8 120f   E..,.M..@.......
0x0010   c0a8 120d 0406 0015 67d6 97ff 0000 0000   .......g.......
0x0020   6002 0200 ecc8 0000 0204 05b4 0000        '..............
21:17:59.369438 192.168.18.13.21 > 192.168.18.15.1030: tcp 0
0x0000   4500 0028 0000 4000 ff06 d662 c0a8 120d   E..(..@....b....
0x0010   c0a8 120f 0015 0406 0000 0000 67d6 9800   ............g...
0x0020   5014 0000 0672 0000                        P....r..
21:20:15.478752 192.168.1.1 > 192.168.16.55: icmp: 192.168.1.1
                                 udp port 123 unreachable
0x0000   45d0 0068 6ec7 0000 fe01 ba74 c0a8 0101   E..hn......t....
0x0010   c0a8 1037 0303 8fcf 0000 0000 4510 004c   ...7........E..L
```

```
0x0020    0000 4000 3e11 aa08 c0a8 1037 c0a8 0101    ..@.>......7....
0x0030    007b 007b 0038 ba2f e300 0af0 0000 0000    .{.{.8./........
0x0040    0001 59d9 0000 0000 0000 0000 0000 0000    ..Y.............
0x0050    0000                                        ..
```

```
#
# Example 2
#
drone3:~# tcpdump -w /tmp/tcpdump.out -i eth1
tcpdump: listening on eth1
^C
1610 packets received by filter
0 packets dropped by kernel

# now let's look at UDP traffic on that segment
drone3:~# tcpdump -r ./dump.out -Nq udp
14:48:14.274728 192.168.18.15.1046 > java.domain:   udp 37
14:48:14.276317 java.domain > 192.168.18.15.1046:   udp 84 (DF)
14:50:02.340543 vivaldi.1026 > java.domain:   udp 32 (DF)
14:50:02.417371 java.domain > vivaldi.1026:   udp 86 (DF)
14:50:02.422828 vivaldi.1026 > java.domain:   udp 32 (DF)
14:50:02.505450 java.domain > vivaldi.1026:   udp 394 (DF)

# how about http traffic?
drone3:~# tcpdump -r ./dump.out -qt port http
192.168.18.15.1054 > bigfoot.eecs.umich.edu.www: tcp 0 (DF)
bigfoot.eecs.umich.edu.www > 192.168.18.15.1054: tcp 1460 (DF)
bigfoot.eecs.umich.edu.www > 192.168.18.15.1054: tcp 1460 (DF)
192.168.18.15.1054 > bigfoot.eecs.umich.edu.www: tcp 0 (DF)
bigfoot.eecs.umich.edu.www > 192.168.18.15.1054: tcp 1460 (DF)
bigfoot.eecs.umich.edu.www > 192.168.18.15.1054: tcp 569 (DF)
bigfoot.eecs.umich.edu.www > 192.168.18.15.1054: tcp 1460 (DF)
vivaldi.mancill.van.1034 > klecker.debian.org.www: tcp 0 (DF)
klecker.debian.org.www > vivaldi.mancill.van.1034: tcp 0 (DF)
...
(argh - there's too much)

# how about http traffic
drone3:~# tcpdump -r ./dump.out -qt port http and  \
              host pandora.debian.org
192.168.18.15.1052 > pandora.debian.org.www: tcp 0
pandora.debian.org.www > 192.168.18.15.1052: tcp 0 (DF)
192.168.18.15.1052 > pandora.debian.org.www: tcp 0 (DF)
192.168.18.15.1052 > pandora.debian.org.www: tcp 157 (DF)
pandora.debian.org.www > 192.168.18.15.1052: tcp 0 (DF)
pandora.debian.org.www > 192.168.18.15.1052: tcp 509 (DF)
```

As you can see, use -w *filename* to perform noninteractive monitoring. This generates less system overhead than redirecting the formatted normal output on stdout to a file, and it also gives you more than one chance to get your filter express right when you review the file. You may also want multiple runs to produce different views of the data.

Learning how to use *tcpdump* is probably half the battle. The other part is learning efficient ways to parse and condense its output into reports and other things consumable by humans. Computers can generate meaningless data extremely quickly. *Perl* is a natural choice, but don't overlook its capable forerunners, *awk* and *sed*. It all depends upon how you look at the problem. A few nice example scripts are included with the *tcpdump* package (in */usr/share/doc/tcpdump/examples* on Debian boxen) that I wish I had known about before trying to imitate their functionality.

3.3.2 *ipgrab*

ipgrab is another command-line packet sniffer available for Linux based on *libpcap*. IMHO, it is a good example of a program which has not succumbed to creeping featurism. It is very much like *tcpdump* and uses the same Berkeley Packet-Filter expression syntax. If you look at its manpage, you'll see that most of the options center around whether or not to print out certain headers and fields.

So why use *ipgrab* instead of *tcpdump*? It is smaller than *tcpdump* and has an uncomplicated command-line interface. Its output is also nicely formatted and easy to follow, making it a bit less imposing than *tcpdump*. It does this without sacrificing detail, since it goes to great lengths to *dump every relevant header field possible*, as the author states in the README file that accompanies the package. Mr. Borella goes on to say:

> I expect that this code can be used for detailed packet level debugging of existing or new protocols. Also, I imagine that it could be a useful teaching and instruction tool for TCP/IP or security courses. I've made an effort to make the code readable, sometimes even at the expense of efficiency, so that one can use it to learn about the *pcap* library calls and the header field data structures.

I looked over the source code for *ipgrab*, and it is indeed well documented and easy to follow. This makes it good reading for those who want to know what is really happening, bit for bit, at every step along the way (i.e., at the link, session, and protocol/transport layers). Instead of being condensed, the output format is designed for human consumption. If you want to grab the latest copy of the sources for *ipgrab*, SourceForge has it at *http://ipgrab.sourceforge.net/*.

```
**************************************************
      Ethernet (1002752661.291498)
--------------------------------------------------
Hardware source:         00:50:56:ad:01:02
Hardware destination:    00:50:56:c0:00:02
Type / Length:           0x800 (IP)
Media length:            66
--------------------------------------------------
                         IP Header
--------------------------------------------------
Version:                 4
Header length:           5 (20 bytes)
TOS:                     0x00
Total length:            52
Identification:          15113
```

```
Fragmentation offset:    0
Unused bit:              0
Don't fragment bit:      1
More fragments bit:      0
Time to live:            63
Protocol:                6 (TCP)
Header checksum:         40460
Source address:          192.168.16.55
Destination address:     198.186.203.20
-----------------------------------------------
                         TCP Header
-----------------------------------------------
Source port:             1045 (unknown)
Destination port:        80 (http)
Sequence number:         2688083666
Acknowledgement number:  866989241
Header length:           8 (32 bytes)
Unused:                  0
Flags:                   FA
Window size:             26064
Checksum:                48774
Urgent:                  0
Option:                  1 (no op)
Option:                  1 (no op)
Option:                  8 (timestamp)
   Length:               10
   Timestamp value:      9363147
   Timestamp reply:      80222142
*************************************************
```

3.3.3   sniffit

sniffit is actually a hybrid—it supports a great many options on the command line, making it similar to *tcpdump*, but it also has an *ncurses* interface which runs in a terminal window. According to the documentation, *sniffit* was written *to demonstrate the unsafeness of TCP.* *sniffit* does make it simple to look at the packet payloads because by default it stores 300 bytes from the start of each session it sees. It even has a logging mode specifically configured to catch FTP and telnet session passwords. Also of note is that *sniffit* will summarize duplicate information about connections. It supports packet filtering via its configuration file format (**man 5 sniffit**) and it has support for (application layer) protocol plugins. The package ships with a DNS plugin.

When I was working on the first edition of this book, I recall there being some hubbub about *sniffit*'s built-in support for collecting passwords. As a system administrator, I have to admit that it does not comfort me to think about users sniffing passwords off the network. However, the author's point is well taken—many TCP/IP application protocols, as implemented, offer an entirely false sense of security. In the Linux tradition, the belief is that exposing security holes is healthier in the long run than ignoring them or trying to hide them. Some people have called *sniffit* dangerous and a hacker's tool. They do this because it takes even *less* skill to sniff passwords with *sniffit* than with other packet capture tools. (See Figure 3.4.) There is

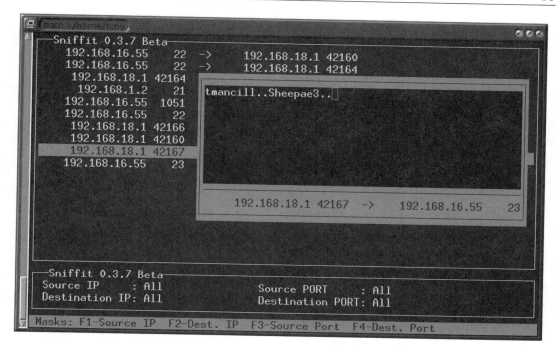

Figure 3.4 Capturing a *telnet* Password with *sniffit*

little point in this. Any of the comparable tools are capable of the same thing, and the skill required is very slight indeed.

One thing for certain about *sniffit* is that, although it performs a very similar function, it is completely different code from *tcpdump* and *ipgrab*, and it takes some getting used to if you normally use *tcpdump*. *Sniffit* does have a filtering mechanism, but it is not the Berkeley packet-filter syntax. It supports writing to *stdout* and logging to a file. The naming convention for the output files is *x.x.x.x.p-y.y.y.y.o*, where *x.x.x.x* is the sender's IP address and *p* is the sending port. *y.y.y.y.o* indicates the same for the receiver. So, instead of having one file with all of the traffic in it, the traffic is already separated into each connection.

You may not use *sniffit* as your primary network debugging tool (those #$% options!), but some of its features would be time-consuming to implement on top of other sniffers, so keep it in mind. Of particular interest is the interactive *ncurses* mode, which is updated in real time and doesn't have nearly the memory and CPU overhead of a full-blown GUI sniffer.

3.3.4   *hunt*

If you thought *sniffit* was bad, you ain't seen nuthin' yet! A true hacker's toolkit, *hunt* is in an entirely different class from *sniffit*. I mention it here because, as a network administrator, you may end up explaining to your management how some incident of network hijinks and treachery actually occurred. With some 80% of all security break-ins coming from within the organization, you need to be aware of what you're up against. The thing that makes *hunt* special is that it's really a collection of disparate tools stitched together with an interface for ease of use. It's

- A sniffer, much like *sniffit* in terms of collecting passwords, and also like *karpski* in that it can build a library of MAC addresses active on a given segment. (*karpski* was covered in the first edition of the book, as it was the forerunner in the Linux-compatible GUI-sniffer arena at that time. Since then, *ethereal* has come along and asserted itself, and *karpski* is no longer being developed. It was and still is a useful tool—many thanks to Brian Costello for sharing his work with the community—*http://mojo.calyx.net/~btx/karpski.html*.)

- A DNS server daemon, used in this case for the illegitimate purpose of spoofing DNS information.

- A tool to watch client-server TCP/IP connections and reset them if desired (in hopes that the user will simply log in again).

- An **ARP-relay daemon**—a coined term for a redirector that puts data back onto the network after it has been consumed by the sniffer/connection-hijacker.

- The connection hijacker itself, with the ability to insert itself into an active TCP stream such that neither of the legitimate ends of the connection is aware of the intrusion. The tool is sophisticated enough to that it can even resynchronize the legitimate client and server and bow out of the exchange *without* resetting either end.

OK, so it's pure evil. I present *hunt* only as a learning tool. If you don't have the willpower to abstain from using it for unethical purposes, that's just lame. If you have unethical intentions to start with, no printed work will stop you anyway.

3.3.5   *ethereal*

ethereal, by that name, is a full-blown GUI sniffer. As such, it requires quite an entourage of libraries for its operation—it took about 10MB of disk space on my box—and won't be something you'll want to run from your 486/66 access router with 8MB of memory. By the way, there is also a text-based version called *tethereal*. Both programs support reading a great many different file formats, from the *libpcap* format used by *tcpdump* to a number of commercial sniffer formats, including those from Microsoft and other Unixes. *ethereal* has a large number of other features (enough that the manpage calls it a *protocol analyzer*), but I think the best way to get started with it is to dive in.

To start monitoring with *ethereal*, you toggle the capture function via the menu section **Capture → Start**. This will present you with a dialog box where you can select the interface and, if you like, a filter, as well as some options about name resolution. The filters use the same syntax as a *tcpdump* **expression**, and you can name a filter and save it, so that you can recall it during other sessions. You may also specify the number of packets you would like to collect. Once the sniffer is in capture mode, a window pops up and displays protocol statistics for the data being captured. This window has a **Stop** button that you can use to toggle off the capture.

Once the capture has stopped, the packets will be displayed in the upper section of the main window, which is divided into three sections: synopsis, protocol, and raw data. The upper section contains a synopsis line for each of the packets captured, and when a given line is highlighted, the corresponding protocol and raw data (in both hex and ASCII) are displayed in the other two sections of the window. Here is where things get very neat. The middle, or protocol, section of the window presents detailed information about the packets and protocols via expanding hierarchical lists. (The *ethereal* calls them *protocol trees*.) As you traverse the protocol tree, you can expand and collapse the detailed view of the headers for each layer in the packet—for example, the link-layer, IP layer, and then the TCP or UDP layer for a standard TCP/IP application packet. When a given header is expanded, your view is a complete list of header flags for that layer. For things like flags which are part of a bitmap, you will see the value of the flagword, and then when you click on that, you'll see the status of each of the bits in the flag. The top-level choices for a TCP packet are:

+ Frame (# of bytes on wire, # of bytes captured)

+ Ethernet II

+ Internet Protocol

+ Transmission Control Protocol

If you watch carefully, you will notice that when you highlight a given header or field, the exact amount of data corresponding to that portion of the packet is highlighted in the raw data portion of the window. This is a fantastic way to learn what the given RFCs mean when they describe a given field; it's about as tangible as you're going get with networking. Very cool!

But wait, there's more! Another handy feature is the ability to select a packet in the upper portion of the window and then pull down the Tools menu and select Follow TCP stream. This will walk the TCP stream from start to finish, stripping away headers and protocol information, and present just the data payloads in a dialog box. Say goodbye to any unencrypted passwords you may use (but that shouldn't surprise you after the other material in this section). Besides all of this functionality, *ethereal* sports some aesthetic features that give it a mature, almost commercial feel. You can select which fields should appear in the synopsis window, and in what order. You can change the color of the text displayed when a stream is followed. You can move the scrollbars around. Et cetera, und so weiter . . . .

And if you download in the next 10 minutes, we'll even throw in complete IPv6 protocol support, just in time for learning hands-on about IPv6. Seriously, this a professional tool. Visit *http://www.ethereal.com/* or load the package **ethereal** via your distribution. Also take a few moments to glance through the *Ethereal User's Guide*.

Before we conclude the section on packet sniffers, there is one point I would like to make about the nice GUI sniffers and your routers. Sniffers are a natural fit for laptops, because often you would like to go to the area where someone is reporting the trouble. This way, you can plug the sniffer into the same hub where the problem exists to get an idea of what is happening. However, for environments with switches instead of hubs, many times you will want (or need) to run the sniffer directly on the router itself to obtain the information you require. This can place extra load on the router, especially if you use something beefy like *ethereal*. Consider running a thinner client, like *tethereal* or *tcpdump*, writing the raw data to a file. You can then parse and reparse this file at your leisure on a workstation. Alternately, if you do take that laptop with you to the problem spot, have a cheap 4-port hub with an uplink port/switch and a couple of cables in the laptop bag. Plug the laptop into the hub along with the workstation where you'd like a protocol trace, and uplink the hub to the port that connects the workstation to the LAN. Add Tux the Penguin stickers on the hub and laptop, and you're set.

3.4   The *mii-diag* Utility

As far as technologies go, Ethernet gives a lot of bang for the buck, in that it doesn't take a lot of configuration or tuning to keep Ethernet purring along at a good clip. There are a few areas where you might run into problems, though, and one of the most common I've encountered is the failure of a 10/100-BaseT link to autonegotiate link speed and duplex settings. The symptom is that the interface will configure properly and work fine when you test it to make sure it's up—in fact, everything works fine—but performance is miserable, and it gets worse the more load you try to put on the link. When I first encountered the problem, I performed some benchmarks and obtained a measly 20kB/s over what should have been a 100BaseT-FD (100Mbps, full-duplex) link. The next indication that things are wrong is the existence of collisions (which shouldn't occur at all with a switch) and transmit overruns as in the *ifconfig* output below.

```
eth1    Link encap:Ethernet  HWaddr 00:06:29:1F:5D:79
        inet addr:192.186.96.171  Bcast:192.168.96.255  Mask:255.255.255.128
        UP BROADCAST RUNNING MULTICAST  MTU:1500  Metric:1
        RX packets:19175450 errors:0 dropped:0 overruns:0 frame:0
        TX packets:16248694 errors:0 dropped:0 overruns:12 carrier:0
        collisions:13 txqueuelen:100
        RX bytes:369591157 (352.4 Mb)  TX bytes:456681132 (435.5 Mb)
        Interrupt:25 Base address:0x2000
```

Now take a look at the difference in performance between this same interface when allowed to autonegotiate and when forced to run at 100Mbps, full-duplex. By the way, FTP, despite its inherent evilness, i.e., throwing passwords and usernames around in cleartext, is a better way to test link bandwidth than *scp* unless you're absolutely sure that both ends of the link can keep up with encryption and decryption at link speeds.

```
ftp> get wtmp
local: wtmp remote: wtmp
200 PORT command successful.
150 Opening data connection for wtmp (37876608 bytes).

receive aborted - waiting for remote to finish abort
426 Transfer aborted. Data connection closed.
226 Abort successful
26116128 bytes received in 1363.52 secs (18.7 kB/s)

## I gave up - it was too painful to wait for my 38MB file.
## But after using "mii-diag eth1 -F 100BaseTx-FD"...

ftp> get wtmp
local: wtmp remote: wtmp
200 PORT command successful.
150 Opening data connection for wtmp (37877376 bytes).
226 Transfer complete.
37877376 bytes received in 3.25 secs (11371.5 kB/s)
```

When you encounter this, you can handle the situation in one of two ways. The first is to read up on the device driver and set the options accordingly when loading the module. The second, which I find more convenient, is to use *mii-diag* to set the appropriate flags in the card to the type of link you're supposed to have. Once you get the card the way you want it, don't forget to add those same statements to the appropriate (perhaps local) network configuration script. The basic synopsis on how to use the tools is mii-diag *dev* -[A|F] *setting*, where *dev* is the Ethernet device and *setting* is one of 100baseTx-FD, 100baseTx, 10baseT-FD, or 10baseT. The presence of FD indicates full-duplex; otherwise transmit and receive share the same physical bandwidth. The difference between -A and -F is whether you're going to advertise or force the link to the setting specified. Note that you can advertise more than one setting.

You can invoke *mii-diag* to view the status of a card, too. Note, however, that not all cards and drivers are equipped with support for the MII (Media Independent Interface). (Also note that **MII** is used to refer to a physical 40-pin connector available on some Ethernet transceivers.) In the output below, we see that *eth0*, an on-board controller based on the ThunderLAN chipset, cannot be tuned with *mii-diag* because the ioctl() call to open that interface failed. The second card on that system is supported, though, and is ticking along at 100Mbps, full-duplex.

```
root@java:/proc/net# mii-diag eth0
SIOCGMIIPHY on eth0 failed: No such device
root@java:/proc/net# mii-diag eth1
Basic registers of MII PHY #1:   1000 782d 7810 0000 01e1 41e1 0003 0000.
 The autonegotiated capability is 01e0.
The autonegotiated media type is 100baseTx-FD.
 Basic mode control register 0x1000: Autonegotiation enabled.
You have link beat, and everything is working OK.
Your link partner advertised 41e1: 100baseTx-FD 100baseTx 10baseT-FD 10baseT.
 End of basic transceiver information.
```

After never having had a problem like this for probably 4 or 5 years, I ran into several instances both at work and at home where I would have been dead in the water without *mii-diag*—which goes to deepen my debt of gratitude to Donald Becker for the great things he does for Linux networking. If *mii-diag* is not part of your distribution, you can obtain it along with many other good networking hardware diagnostic tools and information at *http://www.scyld.com/diag/*. The site has detailed documentation on *mii-diag*, including information about what the various flags signify. By the way, this is not a Linux-specific problem. I've seen Sun and IBM RS/6000 equipment have difficulties autonegotiating, which leads me to believe that there's something amiss with the Cisco Catalyst 5000 switch on the other end of the wire.

Tunnelling alone can be used to solve a class of routing problems, to *extend the network*, as it were, and to handle things like IPv6 over IPv4, as we'll see in Section 6.5.4. But perhaps the most compelling motivator to development of tunnelling protocols came from the need for establishing secure communications over insecure links. The most common of these *insecure links* is the Internet, and secure tunnels erected across the Internet are commonly known as VPNs (Virtual Private Networks). The entire VPN standards soup was pretty much out of hand at first, with vendors pushing *their* solution in the normal fashion. Meanwhile, the Linux camp started work on standards-based tools. It's difficult to emphasize how difficult system integration tasks can be when portions of your environment are based on tools using closed standards. I believe that the TCO of any sizable deployment should include the cost of the inevitable retrofit. But I digress . . . .

Several standards-based tunneling protocols offer security, the foremost of which is Internet Protocol Security, commonly known as **IPsec**. When you start talking about useful security, things get complicated pretty quickly, thus there is an overwhelming abundance of documentation for this protocol. A good starting place for the standards themselves is *http://www.ietf.org/html.charters/ipsec-charter.html*. The next section introduces *FreeS/WAN*, a popular IPsec implementation for Linux, and includes further links to information about IPsec and IPsec on Linux.

3.5   LRP—The Linux Router Project

Silicon has an emergency floppy diskette which waits patiently for the day when it will be used to resurrect the system after a catastrophic hard-drive failure. The rescue floppy was created using the Linux Router Project (LRP) distribution, which is homed at *http://www.linuxrouter.org/*. LRP is certainly more than just for rescue floppies; it's a router-centric minidistribution versatile and capable enough to be used as the basis for all of your routers. I'd also have to say that it's one of the more widely used minidistributions, meaning a wide range of support and add-ons. In this section, we are going to configure silicon again, but this time using LRP.

LRP is a distribution that fits on a single 1.44MB floppy disk. (Actually, it uses 1.44MB media formatted to hold anywhere from 1.44MB to 1.73MB. We'll cover how to do that momentarily.) Unlike a router based on a full-sized Linux distribution, you will need to build your LRP boot disks on another machine. This machine does not necessarily have to be a Linux machine, since any machine that can unzip the gzipped files and write a disk image to a floppy will work to create the LRP disk from the *idiot images* provided on the LRP site. And, since the LRP boot disks are FAT (MS-DOS) formatted, they can usually be worked with on the same machine used to create them.

I recommend getting a copy of the latest distribution *sans* the source tree and the kernel sources. If you have some free disk space and are serious about working with LRP, *lftp* can mirror the entire directory tree with a single command, and it supports some nice extensions, such as extended regular expressions in the filespecs and restarting an interrupted mirror job. (If you aren't familiar with it, *lftp* is a nice command-line FTP client.)

The commands to retrieve LRP version 2.9.8 are:

```
$ lftp ftp.linuxrouter.org
lftp ftp.linuxrouter.org:~> cd linux-router/dists/2.9.8
lftp ftp.linuxrouter.org:/linux-router/dists/2.9.8> mirror -x source/* -x kernel/*
```

Once you have the files that make up the package, you will need the floppy tools mentioned below to make your LRP boot floppy. The general idea is:

> Build the floppy, boot from it, configure the system the way you see fit, and then use the LRP provided utilities to back up your configuration changes to the boot floppy. The next time you boot from this floppy, your saved configuration is used to configure the system.

This section presents two different ways to configure your LRP boot disk. The first is the easy way, using the *idiot image* available the *linuxrouter.org* site. The standard trade-off applies—the second way is more complex than the idiot image, but also more flexible. The second method will also give you more insight into how LRP works. Before diving into the two examples, there are a few tools you will need to have on your system to be able to work the LRP disks, listed in Table 3.1.

As previously mentioned, the LRP disks are standard MS-DOS formatted disks, and they use *syslinux* as the boot loader. For this reason, it is helpful (but not necessary) for your

Table 3.1 Packages Useful for Working with LRP Images

syslinux	supplies *syslinux*, used to make the LRP boot disk bootable.
mtools	contains the *mformat* command, which provides the same functionality as the *mkdosfs* command listed in the LRP documentation.
fdutils	contains the *superformat* command for low-level formatting of floppy disks.
lftp	FTP client able to retrieve entire directory trees in a single command (optional).

workstation to have FAT filesystem support in the kernel. If you do have MS-DOS compiled into your kernel, you will be able to mount your LRP disk and copy files to it as needed. Both examples presented here assume that you have FAT filesystem support.

3.5.1   Quick-n-Dirty LRP Configuration

The quick-n-dirty configuration is a shortcut to getting an LRP system running (at the expense of understanding why or how it works like it does). To build this configuration, you need to retrieve the disk image from the LRP FTP site, and also the corresponding kernel tarball, found in the *kernel/* directory. The tarball I retrieved was named *kernel/2.2.19-1-LRP.tar.gz*, only to find out that the idiot images run the 2.2.16 kernel. So go back and get the *kernel/2.2.16-1.tar.gz* if you haven't already.

Start with two 1.44MB floppy disks; label one *LRP root* and the other *LRP modules*. Perform a low-level format of both with **superformat /dev/fd0**. Note that you will have to be the superuser (or have access permissions to write to */dev/fd0*) for this procedure. Also, the device file given is for the first floppy drive on your system. Adjust */dev/fdX* accordingly.

Creating an Idiot Image Diskette

You need to transfer the idiot image to a floppy disk. Notice the word *transfer* and not *copy*. The image is a complete image of the floppy disk used to boot LRP. You do this with *dd*. Insert the *LRP root* disk, and from the directory where you have the LRP files,

```
$ dd if=./idiot-image_1440KB_2.9.8 of=/dev/fd0 bs=8192 conv=sync ; sync
```

You can use this command to duplicate any 1.44MB disk, regardless of the filesystem on it, simply by reversing `if` (input file) and `of` (output file) as required. The last *sync* ensures that all of the data blocks to be written to the floppy drive are flushed before the command prompt returns. This will prevent you from ejecting the floppy disk from the drive prematurely.

The LRP root image already has the kernel and all commands needed for a fully bootable Linux system. What it lacks are the device-driver modules needed for your specific Ethernet cards, and possibly other devices. If these were all included in the idiot image, it would be too large to fit on a single floppy.

---

dd—The Multipurpose Diskette Duplicator

You can use *dd* to create an exact duplicate (or **image**) of any floppy disk (or other type of disk or file), regardless of the operating system on it.

To read in the image, specify the device file of the device with the data to be read as the argument for `if=`. The block size (`bs=`*blocksize*) is the quantum of data to be read—use either 512 or 8192 for floppy disks. The output file (`of=`*/path/to/image*) will contain the image being read.

To write the image to another diskette, make sure that the disk has been low-level formatted and then call *dd* again, swapping the arguments for `if` and `of`.

Creating a Modules Diskette

The reason you need an *LRP modules* disk is to transfer any needed device drivers over to your LRP system. Create it as follows:

Go to the start of the directory tree where you downloaded the different LRP files, and **export LRP=$(pwd)**. This way, you can refer to this directory as `$LRP` throughout the session. The command paths assume that you downloaded LRP with the directory tree intact. Take the *LRP modules* disk (which is already low-level formatted), insert it in your floppy drive, and create an MS-DOS FAT filesystem on it with `mformat a:`.[8] With our modules floppy formatted and ready to go, we need to copy over the precompiled kernel modules from the LRP distribution.

```
$ cd $LRP/kernel
$ tar xzvf 2.2.16-1.tar.gz
$ cd 2.2.16-1/modules

### Customize the following module name for the interface cards
### on your router.

$ mcopy net/pcnet32.o a:
$ mdir a: # just to make sure things are there

### OR

$ mount -t msdos /dev/fd0 /floppy
$ cp net/pcnet32.o /floppy
$ umount /floppy
```

A note on using *mcopy*: It works great and saves time by not making you mount and unmount the disk, but it mangles filenames longer than the DOS 8.3 naming convention, so beware.

---

[8] Note that this depends upon */etc/mtools.conf* being properly configured for your floppy drives. The default configuration on my system required me to add the string *1.44m* along with the *exclusive* flag so that the line looked like `drive a:file=''/dev/fd0''` `exclusive 1.44m` before it worked without supplying all of the various command-line switches to describe the geometry of a 1.44MB FAT format.

Configuring LRP to Be Silicon

To configure the LRP-silicon, just follow these steps:

1. Boot your router system with the *LRP boot* floppy. You will notice the banner message which can be customized by replacing *syslinux.dpy* (on this diskette) with your own ASCII art.

2. Login to the router as *root*. Initially, there is no root password, but we will set it soon.

3. You will be presented with the LRP configuration menu. This menu allows you to edit your configuration without having to navigate the filesystem manually. You can (**q**)uit the configuration menu and work directly on the command line and return to the configuration menu at any time with **lrcfg**.

4. Hit **q** to exit to the command line.

5. Use the *passwd* command to change the root password.

6. Eject the *LRP root* floppy and insert the *modules* floppy. Mount it with **mkdir /tmp/ mnt ; mount -t msdos /dev/fd0 /tmp/mnt**.

7. Copy the required modules from */tmp/mnt* into place in */lib/modules*. Do **not** create *net/*, *ipv4/*, etc., subdirectories underneath */lib/modules*. All modules must be in */lib/modules*, as this is where the LRP version of */etc/init.d/modutils* expects them to be. For silicon:

```
myrouter# cd /tmp/mnt
myrouter# cp * /lib/modules
myrouter# cd
myrouter# umount /tmp/mnt
```

8. Go ahead and eject the *LRP modules* so that you do not inadvertently try to write to it later on when you back up your configuration for your *LRP root* disk.

9. Edit */etc/modules* to load both of these modules by adding/uncommenting the lines **3c59x** and **ip_alias**. The editor that comes with LRP is *ae*.[9] It is has *vi*-esque and *emacs*-esque modes; the one you get depends upon how you invoke it. **vi** will act like *vi*, while *ae* is the *modeless* mode. If you need help, hit **F1**.

10. Next you need to configure networking on your system. You can either edit */etc/network. conf* from the command line or restart *lrcfg* and select **1)** Network settings, **1)** Network Configuration (auto). In either case, you need to make the following changes:

   (a) set IPFWDING_KERNEL to YES

   (b) CONFIG_HOSTNAME=YES

   (c) uncomment IF0_IFNAME=eth0

   (d) set IF0_IPADDR to 192.168.16.1

   (e) set IF0_NETMASK to 255.255.255.0

---

[9]The same editor found on Debian and other rescue floppies.

(f) set IF0_BROADCAST to 192.168.16.255

(g) modify IF1 as you did IF0, except use the correct values for 192.168.18.0/24

(h) set HOSTNAME to a name of your liking

11. If you'd like to add a default route, set GW0_IPADDR. For more complicated routing setups, use the *lrcfg* menu and select **2) Network Configuration (direct)**; then add the commands needed to achieve the desired configuration.

12. Your work is almost done. All you need to do is to save your configuration to your *LRP root* disk and test. To write your configuration, go back to the main menu (or restart *lrcfg*) and hit **(B)ack-up ramdisk**. Then select **2) etc** and **5) modules**. When queried as to whether or not there will be enough space on the *LRP root* disk, answer **y**.

13. Reboot the system, either with **CTRL-ALT-DEL** or by logging into a shell prompt and executing **shutdown -r now**. Test your system after the reboot to make sure that it functions as you would like it to.

14. If you find that you need other commands to be executed during the router configuration, it's easiest to add these to */etc/network_direct.conf*. Do not forget to back up your **etc** configuration after you make the changes.

3.5.2 Manual LRP Configuration

Manual configuration of LRP is really not so bad, and you gain the personal satisfaction of having not used the idiot image. (At the time of writing, you can use the 2.2.19 version of the kernel, too.) Instead of starting with the idiot image, you are going to build your own disk and then copy over the LRP packages you would like. The procedure after that is similar. But to help illustrate how the LRP packages (the .lrp files) work, we will assemble our *modules.lrp* on our workstation and then transfer it to the *LRP root* disk. By knowing how to take apart the LRP packages, you can do much of your configuration on your own workstation. The basic steps are:

1. Use *superformat* and *mformat* to prepare your *LRP root* floppy. Mount it on your workstation with **mount -t msdos /dev/fd0 /floppy**. (Alternately, you can use *mcopy* if you don't mount the floppy.)

2. Using the LRP tree you retrieved earlier, **cd $LRP ; cp base/* /floppy ; cp boot/* /floppy**. The *base/* directory includes the files you need for a minimal LRP system. The *boot/* directory contains the files needed for *syslinux*.

3. Copy the LRP kernel to your *LRP root* disk. Depending upon the version of LRP you are using, there may be several different kernels.[10] The kernel images are in the *$LRP/kernel/2.2.19-1-LRP.tar.gz* tarball. Extract this archive and copy the image to the floppy disk, making sure to name it *linux* on that filesystem. For example:

```
$ cd $LRP/kernel
$ tar xzvf 2.2.19-1-LRP.tar.gz
$ cd 2.2.19-1-LRP
```

---

[10]If you have an older 486-class machine without a built-in FPU (Floating Point Unit), you need use the kernel with FPU emulation support.

```
# there are several different kernel images for various
# architectures in the LRP kernel package
# adjust the exact kernel image you are using
$ cp 2.2.19-1-LRP.486 /floppy/linux
```

Note that the LRP kernel image file is just like any other normal kernel image, except that it was built from LRP-patched sources. For those of you who want to build your own kernel images, make sure that you used the LRP patch, or else your system will not know where to find *init*. There is a -config file in kernel tarball which will help you get started.

4. Extract a copy of the *modules.lrp* in a safe place where you can work on them. I chose *$LRP/work*. Note that the .lrp files are gzipped tarballs in disguise.

```
$ mkdir $LRP/work
$ cd $LRP/work
$ tar xzvf $LRP/etc/modules.lrp
```

5. Now add the files that you would like to include in the modules LRP package. You can do this by copying the file to its destination. Do not add completely new directory trees unless you know what you are doing and want to hack the files in *var/lib/lrpkg/*. For the silicon configuration, all we need is the module with our NIC driver, and we'll throw in the IPv4 modules for posterity. Continuing from the example above:

```
$ cd $LRP/work/lib/modules
$ cp $LRP/kernel/2.2.19-1-LRP/modules/net/pcnet32.o .
$ cp $LRP/kernel/2.2.19-1-LRP/modules/ipv4/* .
$ cd ../..
```

6. After you make sure that you have changed the current directory back to *$LRP/work/*, you can build your new *modules.lrp* tarball and write it directly to the floppy: **tar czvf /floppy/modules.lrp ***.

   You can perform this same step for any of the LRP packages; just make sure that you do not move or delete important parts of the system. One application of this would be to localize the *etc.lrp* module (or edit the *local.lrp* module).

7. To make your *LRP root* floppy bootable, run *syslinux*. The only argument it requires is the device name of your floppy drive (probably */dev/fd0*). It automatically knows to look for the *syslinux.cfg* in the root of the filesystem on that device.

8. Unmount the floppy disk from your workstation, configure, and then test your LRP system.

The ultramanual LRP configuration would mean starting from scratch. Thanks to Dave Cinerge and other volunteers at the LRP for creating such an attractive alternative to this option. There is a selection of *packages* available for LRP from their website. If you would like a quick introduction on how to use packages which are not part of the base LRP distribution, see Section 5.6.1 in Chapter 5. For more information about LRP, visit the LRP webpage and subscribe to the LRP mailing list.

3.5.3 LRP and High Availability

High availability is not always an easy goal to obtain. Many (<cough> "sales") people think that it can be accomplished with a showcase of hardware redundancy and their latest *Gee Whiz HA 9000 Software*. In reality, the hardware, software, and administrative practices all need to be mature and working in concert to realize the goal. In my experience, it's rarely slick software that makes for high availability, but instead preparedness and simple ideas. For instance, let's say that silicon's power supply fails. More important than anything else, you need your network to be back up immediately. If you have an LRP disk for silicon, that's all well and good, but it's not the hard drive that failed. But if you have an LRP disk with silicon's configuration *and* modules for all of the common Ethernet cards at your site, you can easily shave 15 minutes off your outage. You may want to keep a spare box lying around with a pair of NICs already installed—just make sure you have the drivers for those NICs on your rescue disk. (Knowing where your rescue disk can be found is another important, if not obvious, suggestion.)

You can base your entire Linux router infrastructure on LRP. Because of its widespread use, it is well tested, and because it is smaller than a full-sized Linux distribution, it is easier to test more completely. A side-effect of its size is that it is easier to document, customize, and harden (with respect to security). Because it is open, you can review *all* of the code used to build the distribution to check it for security holes, etc. There are LRP mailing lists, and the author is actively involved in support. If you decide to do this, do not forget to contribute when and where you can. Answering common questions on the mailing list might not seem like a lot, but it reduces the workload on others who might be contributing to development.

3.6 Summary

As the first router chapter concludes, we have covered how to do some fairly general things with our Linux router. Silicon can route physical and virtual IP subnets. We can use a sniffer to monitor traffic, troubleshoot certain types of workstation and application problems, collect transaction performance statistics, and learn about the protocols running on our network. Silicon can be implemented on a low-end system without a hard drive.

If you have set your sights on loftier achievements, don't let the simplicity of this example implementation discourage you. A Linux LAN router can be used to connect two or more Ethernet subnets together, connect 10Base-T to coax Ethernet, connect Ethernet to token ring, Ethernet to FDDI, FDDI to ATM, or almost any conceivable combination. (In the next chapter we're going to tie Ethernet to an analog modem.) Use your imagination, and let the solution fit the problem at hand. And don't forget to keep track of how much money and time you've saved . . . .

Chapter 4

ERBIUM—AN EXTRANET ROUTER

Erbium is an example of an **extranet** router, which is used to connect your network to other networks of other organizations (in this case, not including the Internet). It was configured in response to the need for a dial-out point for a product support group at my employer's so that they could access client networks to validate and research problems. Although the support staff had access to a modem server from their desktops, which provided them PPP and terminal dial-out capabilities, this arrangement had certain limitations:

1. Access into a client site was limited to a single person/machine, making collaborative efforts difficult.

2. Direct access from the Unix development servers was not possible without undertaking extensive configuration efforts and opening questionable security holes.

3. All users who required access to the remote system had to set up the access themselves, an inefficient use of time which further resulted in more time spent assisting with configuration (and repairing broken configurations).

4. Controlling use of the dial-out connections via a modem-server solution in use was difficult. Users could dial anywhere, potentially creating security holes or accumulating excessive toll charges.

In summary, the environment was not conducive to productive troubleshooting for the support staff. They spent more time making their tools work than using them to help clients. We needed a method of dialing into the client sites and reconfiguring the network so that access from all of the support group's workstations and the Unix servers over that single dial-up link was possible.

This chapter presents a solution that addresses these capabilities both as they apply to erbium and in general. Key to that solution is the ability to *masquerade* the IP addresses of the workstations connecting via the extranet router, since the target network is not expecting them. This feature is often known as **NAT**, or Network Address Translation, and is frequently used to allow Internet access from private address space. In the 2.4 Linux kernel, this capability is provided through a kernel mechanism called *netfilter*, which bears a decent introduction before we actually start masquerading. After we do configure masquerading, we'll conclude the chapter with a brief introduction to IPv6 and its support under Linux. Specifically, the chapter is divided into the following major sections:

- Erbium's hardware, software, and scripting configuration

- IP masquerading in general

- Linux's *netfilter* concepts

- Configuring IP masquerading on Linux

- Using IP masquerading every day

Note: Linux as a Modem or Dial-In Server

Note that this chapter is not a discussion of using Linux as a true modem server—
although support for this is available. Likewise, using Linux as a dial-in server, either
for an ISP or as a remote access server, is not covered. Many people are using Linux
very successfully in this role, and you should be able to find ample documentation
concerning this configuration. You can start with the *LDP* if you are looking for
resources.

Why Linux for an Extranet Router?

An extranet router is faced with a daunting list of tasks. Its job after establishing a connection
is to make *n* different workstations appear as a single dial-up client. It needs to be flexible in
terms of both security and networking standards. After all, you cannot tell your clients that
they must implement protocol XYZ with product ABC so that you can access their network
for support. They have several other vendors who need access, their own security policies to
enforce, and their own dial-in solution investment. An extranet router should be customizable,
so that you can cater to the needs of your users and their needs, and it should be able to grow
along with the rest of the technology world. Finally, it should offer some security, even though
its primary role is to connect your network to external ones.

Linux has a lot to offer in this role, since many have long prized how effectively you could
connect it to other machines. Open standards for dial-up connectivity are already implemented,
and in dire cases, you have the source to roll your own. Using a popular hardware architecture
means that your selection of interface devices is plentiful and economical. You can customize
your dial-out server with your own shell scripts, Tcl/Tk, or a full-blown GTK-based GUI front
end. And if you need to, you can lock it all down with packet filtering and integration to the
security mechanism of your choice.

4.1   Erbium's Design

The basic idea is to have a router configured to dial up analog and ISDN links so that we can
connect to customer networks as if from a single workstation. This allows support links to be
set up very quickly, since most of the target networks already have provisions for point-to-point
remote access. In this case, erbium dials the connection and appears to the target network as
a single workstation. In reality, it populates the routing table on our local LAN router with
information about systems in the customer's network available for support access.

When a user accesses destinations in the remote network, the LAN router forwards this traffic to erbium and then out over the dial-up link toward the destination in the customer's network. However, this accomplishes only half of the goal; **IP masquerading** does the second half. The issue is that the customer's machine doesn't know how to respond to an IP address in our internal network. After all, remote access typically wasn't designed for this type of use. IP masquerading takes care of this by modifying all packets destined toward the remote network so that they appear to have originated from erbium's dial-out interface. Because the customer network knows this IP (it issued it), it can respond. When erbium receives the response, it knows what traffic is for it and what is for our internal workstations and forwards the workstation traffic appropriately.

4.1.1   Choose Your Weapons—Dial-Out Hardware

Erbium's hardware won't come as any surprise. It's off-the-shelf equipment, similar to what you might use for a home PC.

- A Pentium 90 with 32MB of RAM—which is more than adequate. The system has very little overhead or CPU demands.

- A 2GB IDE hard drive—we need a little bit of space for logfiles and as a staging area for file transfer between the networks.

- Two external analog modems, both of them *U.S. Robotics V.Everything* modems for analog dial-out. Whatever you do, do not go out and buy the cheapest modems you can find. (And remember that Winmodems will not work because their manufacturers provide no drivers for Linux.) Refer back to the discussion about modems on page 12.

- A SpellCaster Datacommute/BRI ISDN board in the machine for ISDN dial-out. This is an adapter card, so it doesn't require a third serial port (the two we have are taken by the modems). The vendor is committed to providing Linux driver support, which is a pleasant surprise when shopping for ISDN adapters in North America.

4.1.2   Dial-Out Software

Once the hardware is set up, you need something to glue it all together. Before anything else, you need a way to dial out. (The boldfaced items are Debian package names.)

- **ppp**, which contains the PPP daemon, *pppd*.

- **minicom** for dialing into terminal servers, gettys, and BBS-style systems.

- **uucp**, which contains the venerable *cu* utility for connecting to serial ports without the fuss of a full-screen dialer like *minicom*.

- *Babylon*, which is a product from SpellCaster. It contains drivers for the *Datacommute/BRI* and programs to configure and dial ISDN PPP and MPPP links.

- A utility for configuring PPP links. (Actually, not a necessity, but potentially a big time-saver. Some of these are introduced in Section 4.1.3.)

In order to enable your users to perform certain superuser actions associated with bringing the link up and configuring the routing and masquerading, you need a controlled mechanism for allowing normal users to execute commands with root privileges. (On erbium, the only commands users may execute as root are the custom shell scripts which dial the link and set up the routes.) The following packages are related to this purpose:

- Access is regulated with **sudo**. (There are several other choices, such as **super** and **secure-su**.)

- **ssh** is needed as a secure alternative to *rexec* for running commands on nearby routers.

Last but not least, we turn to another cool feature of the Linux kernel, IP masquerading NAT (covered in Sections 4.2–4.4), and employ some custom scripts to make it easier for the user to set up and tear down connections.

4.1.3 *pppd*—The PPP Daemon

At the heart of our analog dial-out capability is the ability to connect to other dial-in solutions. Many such solutions assume that remote users will connect to their networks using a machine running a Microsoft operating system,[1] so we have to accommodate this. Enter *pppd*, the Point-to-Point Protocol Daemon, which does a pretty good job of pretending to be almost any type of PPP dial-up client. It supports the **PAP**, **CHAP** (or **CHAP-5**), and **MS-CHAP** (also known as **CHAP-80**) forms of PPP-based authentication, in addition to being flexible about chat-based (`ogin: assword:`) mechanisms. It is, of course, compatible with other (non-Microsoft) dial-in solutions as well.

Instead of going into a droll description of *pppd* and how to configure it for dial-out, I offer you references to some nice configuration utilities. (Just let me tell you that it used to be much more difficult—barefoot in the snow, 20 miles, uphill in both directions, all that good stuff.) To get *pppd* running on your system, you will need the *pppd* software and probably one of its configuration utilities. *pppd* itself is in the **ppp** package, which is part of the Debian base installation. The configuration packages available will vary, based on the distribution you are using; the list below uses the names of the Debian packages.

PPP Configuration Packages

pppconfig is the tool I use most frequently. It has an *ncurses* interface and supports any number of different connection configurations. Once the package is loaded, you invoke it by running *pppconfig* as the superuser. The rest is self-explanatory.

xisp is a nice GUI-based dial-out tool, suitable for standard PPP links and links which require a combination of terminal interaction (e.g., use of a hard token) and PPP. It's not designed to be used to build configurations for use by other dialers, but it is very useful for one-off situations.

ppxp was not available when I was configuring erbium, but had it been, I think I would have taken a very close look at it. According to the package description:

> PPxP is a user-space PPP program. It provides easy setup, on-demand dial-up, IP masquerading, IP filtering, DNS relaying, and more. It can work as a PPP server, using either the *userlink* or *ethertap* kernel modules.

---

[1] A silly assumption, if you ask me.

There are X11 and Tck/Tk console (management) packages available (**ppxp-x11** and **ppxp-tcltk**), as well as a development package, **ppxp-dev**, for building your own management console interface. If it delivers all that it claims to, then it could save an impressive amount of work.

wvdial was the first of these configuration tools I encountered to support automatic modem detection. It is (currently) geared toward a single dial-up connection, so it's not that well suited for an extranet server.

Hint: Finding Software for Non-Debian Users

If you're having trouble locating the source of a package, meaning that the usual *http://freshmeat.net/* and *http://sourceforge.net/* don't come up with anything, you might try the following. Visit Debian's website and search for the package. The original upstream source is always stored in Debian's archive along with the copyright and diffs required to build the Debian package.

To do this, point your browser to *http://www.debian.org/* and select the *Debian Packages* link. Scroll to the bottom of this page, and use either *Search Package Directories* or *Search the Contents of the Latest Release*. The former will search through the list of package names and present you with a clickable link to any packages which match. The latter searches through all files in the current distribution and will show you the filename, section, and package name which contains the package. Once you have located the package, you can download the source or view the copyright file to try to locate the original upstream source.

4.1.4   Kernel Support for PPP

To be able to use any of these, you will need PPP support in your kernel. The default kernel supplied with most Linux installations should already have this compiled into it. Since you may well be rolling your own by Chapter 4, don't forget to include the PPP support you'll need. The options changed a bit between the 2.2 and 2.4 kernels. For analog modems, you're going want something like this:

```
Network Device Support --->
  <M> PPP (point-to-point protocol) support
  [ ] PPP multilink support (EXPERIMENTAL)
  <M>PPP support for async serial ports
  < >PPP support for sync tty ports
  <M>PPP Deflate compression
  <M>PPP BSD-Compress compression
  < >PPP over Ethernet (EXPERIMENTAL)
```

If you're running a 2.2 kernel, support is provided via the single PPP (point-to-point) support option under the Network Device Support heading. If you compile PPP support into the kernel as a module, realize that it is part of a dependent module stack, so load it with *modprobe*. On a 2.2.x system, because I used to always forget to load the *bsd_comp* module (which provides software compression if it is supported on the other side), I learned to use modprobe bsd_comp, which loads everything:

```
ppp_deflate            38516   0
bsd_comp                3468   0
ppp                    19324   2  [ppp_deflate bsd_comp]
slhc                    4128   1  [ppp]
```

Things are not quite that easy in 2.4, since *bsd_comp.o* no longer depends upon *ppp_async.o*. To obtain the module stack I wanted, I had to issue modprobe for each of the top three modules listed below. (Maybe I should just break down and use */etc/modules* ....)

```
root@vivaldi:~# lsmod
Module                  Size  Used by
ppp_deflate            39040   0  (unused)
ppp_async               6496   0  (unused)
bsd_comp                3968   0  (unused)
ppp_generic            20584   0  [ppp_deflate ppp_async bsd_comp]
slhc                    4352   0  [ppp_generic]
```

4.1.5 Using Debian's PPP

OK, now that you have compiled support in the kernel and have loaded the PPP modules, you need to configure a dial-up link for each client. We're going to use these configurations in the dial-out script we write for our users. Debian's **ppp** package comes with two handy commands: *pon* and *poff*. Despite their funny names, they are useful abbreviations for the most common tasks involved with PPP links—bringing them up (*pon*) and shutting them back down (*poff*). A third command, *plog*, will *tail* the last bits of */var/log/ppp.log* so that you can see what is going on. Their usage is simple.

- *pon* takes one argument, the name of the link to dial. This is the same name of the file which appears in */etc/ppp/peers/* and is the name you gave the connection while configuring it with *pppconfig*. If you do not specify an argument, the PPP peer of "provider" is assumed.

- *poff* can take several options followed by the name of the link to disconnect. See the *poff* manpage for details. Be aware that without any options, it kills all active *pppd* connections.

- *plog* displays the last 10 lines of */var/log/ppp.log* so that you can see what is happening. *pppconfig* by default configures all of your PPP option files (the files in */etc/ppp/peers/*) with the keyword **debug**, so there should be something in the file. *plog* optionally takes any argument that *tail* takes. Of these, -f to follow the file is probably the most useful.

Configuration of PPP links can be frustrating. When things don't work, sometimes it is not abundantly clear how to fix them. Be sure to use the documentation resources at your disposal before you get too irritated. As unlikely as it may seem, someone else really has already run into the problem you are experiencing; hopefully they were thoughtful enough to share their experience in a HOWTO somewhere. The documentation in */usr/share/doc/ppp* can be very helpful. There are several HOWTOs as part of the *LDP* which cover PPP, modems, serial ports, etc., in detail. Also, do not forget to enable debugging if you turned it off in the configuration file. You can do this quickly, without having to stop the link and edit the file with **poff -d** *linkname*. This way, you'll know what to look for in the documentation.

Before we start configuring the actual links for erbium, we should take a moment and consider the network surrounding erbium and how the different components should interact with each other.

4.1.6   A Sample Network Topology for an Extranet Router

One key to erbium's functionality is the fact that it requires no changes to the user workstations whatsoever. Once the link is up, a user can *telnet* to the client's machine as if it were part of the local network. But for this to function, you need to make sure that the client can find the remote machines, and this takes a little bit of design work. Because a typical workstation network configuration consists of a routing entry for the local subnet and another for the default gateway, your choices are to update either the workstation or the gateway (or other gateways upstream of that gateway). Because modifying the client's configuration is tricky at best, and potentially downright foolhardy, I opted for the latter. The topology is displayed in Figure 4.1.

In this topology the extranet router is located at least one **layer** removed from your local LAN. When extranet links are active, erbium updates silicon's routing table to include routes to the customer's network. When the link goes back down, erbium removes the routes. In both cases, the changes are performed using shell scripts which invoke *ssh* to make the changes on silicon.

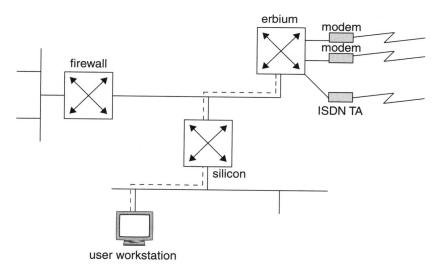

Figure 4.1 Erbium Network Topology

4.1.7   A Dial-Out Script for Extranet Connections

Now that we know where erbium fits into our network, we can start the configuration. So that we can focus on the integration piece, let's assume that we already have PPP configurations so that you can connect to our client(s). Furthermore, we'll take for granted that we have worked out any required routing and masquerading statements. Now we need a way to let our users start and stop these links.

Scripting dial-out access presented a few challenges. First, a lot of the documentation about *pppd* was geared toward dial-in solutions, and I couldn't find any documentation about dynamically choosing from a pool of available modems for dial-out. After choosing a modem and dialing the link, masquerading had to be configured on erbium and routes had to be added to both erbium and silicon. Finally, I wanted the script to be easy to use. For analog PPP dial-out, the result was a single script with the following properties:

1. A single script without requiring the user to remember options necessitated a "script of many names." The script infers the action to be taken based on the name by which it was invoked.

   The usage is simple—either **dial_***client* or **hangup_***client*. The code to accomplish this is:

```ksh
#!/usr/bin/ksh
prog=$(basename $0)       # program name without a path component
ACTION=${prog%*_*}        # get the string up to the '_'
TARGET=${prog#*_*}        # get the string past the '_'

case $ACTION in
    dial)
        pon $TARGET
        ;;
  hangup)
        poff $TARGET
        ;;
    *)
        # a user should not be able to call this script such that
        # their intention is not known - we control the arguments!
        echo "something is wrong!"
        ;;
esac
```

   To add links, simply create symbolic links or hard links back to the main script. Having one script is useful because when you want to make changes or add functions—for example, to perform extra logging—everything is updated for all connections simultaneously.

2. Using more than one modem for dial-out is one of the few options you cannot set in a *pppd options* file. The device name listed in the file is the one which will be used. To remedy this, the script went under the knife again to take advantage of UUCP device-locking semantics. *pppd* and other well-mannered applications which use the modem will write lockfiles to */var/lock/* as long as you don't configure them not to.

   All we need to do is to find out which devices are not locked, and then fix up the options file to use one of these. The result is a function which uses *sed* to fix the options file before the link is dialed. The function is added to the beginning of the prior code snippet; the code below it is called as part of the *dial* case.

```
    MODEMS="ttyS0 ttyS1"        # list of available devices

    # function to walk the list of MODEMS to see which
    # have lock files
    Find_Free_TTY()
    {
        FREE_TTY="none"
        for TTY in $1
        do
            if [[ ! -f /var/lock/LCK..${TTY} ]] ; then
                FREE_TTY=${TTY}
            fi
        done

        echo ${FREE_TTY}
        return
    }


    # a cheap hack to find a free modem
    MODEM=$(Find_Free_TTY ${MODEMS})
    if [[ $MODEM == "none" ]] ; then
        Error "Sorry... all modems are currently in use"
    else
        # fixup the options file with the right tty
        cp -p ${OPTFILE} ${OPTFILE}.presed
        echo "s/^\/dev\/ttyS./\/dev\/$MODEM/" >${SEDFILE}
        cat ${OPTFILE}.presed | sed -f ${SEDFILE} >${OPTFILE}
    fi
```

3. Now add routes and configure masquerading. This is done by calling an additional function. First, routes are added to the local system, then masquerading is configured and routes are added to silicon. Tearing down a connection is the same set of steps in reverse.

```
    Setup_Connection()
    {
        # assert:  TARGET is a global, and is set
        case $TARGET in
            client1)
            route add -net 10.34.2.0 netmask 255.255.255.0 $DEV
            route add -host 209.54.2.2 $DEV
            ipchains -A forward -j MASQ -i $DEV
            ssh silicon route add -net 10.34.2.0   \
                    netmask 255.255.255.0 gw erbium
        ;;
    client2)
        :
        ;;
        esac
    }
```

4. Hold on a minute! How did the value of $DEV get set to the right value? You know that it's the name of the PPP device created by *pppd*, but the catch is that the name is not always *ppp0*, since you may have multiple concurrent sessions. The work-around is to take advantage of the */etc/ppp/ip-up.d/* directory, which executes all scripts located in it after the link is dialed and configured up. We will add a script, */etc/ppp/ip-up.d/list_device*, which looks something like:

```
# the PID was just patched by sed - watch out for race conditions
CALLER_PID=123
# write the device into this file
echo $PPP_IFACE >/tmp/pppdevice.${CALLER_PID}
```

Our main script can modify the script above with *sed* to set the PID to its executing PID and then read the device as */tmp/pppdevice.$$*. Once it's read, delete the temporary file.

Mocked up into its final form, the script looks like:

```
# header with modification history
# function definitions
# code to get $ACTION and $TARGET

case $ACTION in
    dial)
        # code to find a free modem
        # code to sed the "list_device" script with our PID

        pon $TARGET          # dial the link
        sleep 30              # wait for it to connect
        Setup_Connection     # set up masquerading
        ;;

    hangup)
        poff $TARGET         # hang up the modem
        Teardown_Connection  # unconfigure masquerading
        ;;
esac
```

Once everything is coded and tested, we cannot forget that giving users dial-out privileges is not sufficient if they also have to add routes, run masquerading commands, etc. To do this, we need to configure *sudo* to allow our users to **sudo dial_***client*. A little bit of user education and we're ready to turn them loose ....

4.1.8   ISDN Dial-Out with SpellCaster's Babylon

Erbium also needed to be able to dial ISDN links. Because both of the serial ports on erbium are used for analog modems, I had to find an ISDN solution other than the standard terminal adapter (TA) with a serial interface. One such device is the *Datacommute/BRI* from SpellCaster, Inc., an ISA add-on card with Linux driver support.

Although it is a complete departure from the status quo Linux support for ISDN, the board works well. The folks at SpellCaster have put a lot of effort into designing an entire system around their cards. You use their utility to configure the card once with the SPID information for the ISDN circuit, and then edit a configuration file which sets the parameters for your various dial-out (or dial-in) sessions. After that, you dial the link with one of their software commands—similar to using *pon* and *poff* with *pppd*. The software, which is called *Babylon*, has support for multiple devices, which can be grouped into pools, and MPPP (bridging the two BRI B-channels to form a 128kb link).

The Babylon software is very easy to use. Note that SpellCaster produces a range of ISDN equipment, including PRI boards which could be used for larger-scale dial-in or dial-out solutions. For more information, visit its website at *http://www.spellcast.com*.

Erbium in Retrospect

How well did all of it work? The IP masquerading works like a charm, at least for all of the applications we were using (normally FTP, telnet, IRC, and SQLnet connections). The biggest single problem I had was the users forgetting to hang up the connection after using it. This ran up toll charges and left the routing tables and masquerading entries cluttered. It is easy enough to script around this—probably the easiest thing to do is to issue an *at* job to bring the link down automatically after a period of time.

If I'm allowed a complaint, it would be that *pppd* didn't have exit codes (at the time) to tell you the results of the command. What I was looking for was the ability to check the return code to see whether the link dialed, or whether no modem was available, etc. This would have made things easier on the user, who sometimes had to use the *plog* command to see what was going on. But I shouldn't complain, since I have the source and can compile my own version to suit my needs. The privilege of having the source code comes with the responsibility of making things better instead of just griping about them .... And with that, we conclude the discussion of erbium and shift the focus to more general topics useful for extranet routers. The first of these is IP masquerading, a topic crucial not only for this type of router, but also for many Internet routers.

4.2   IP Masquerading Concepts

IP masquerading is a facility in the Linux kernel which can manipulate packets so that they appear to originate from addresses other than the original source. Before you think that this is some hacker tool, the masquerading is performed only during the *forwarding* of a packet. (It would make no sense if the router itself originated the packet or if the router were the destination of the packet.) The kernel performs some acrobatics to make the process transparent to both the sender and the receiver. It does a good job in all but a few rare cases. Masquerading is actually a special case of **NAT**, Network Address Translation, where a many-to-one mapping occurs at the router on the behalf of a set of clients. There are several other types of NAT supported by Linux that we will cover later in the book.

Before we talk about configuring IP masquerading, let's start with an example of why one might need it, and what happens to a packet when it is masqueraded. The primary function of masquerading is to obscure the IP address of a client from a server located on a separate network. The reasons for doing this vary. The most common one is that the client has an address such that the server either would not or could not respond to a connection request originating from that client. This situation is depicted in Figure 4.2, where the client can contact the server, but the server response will never reach the client.

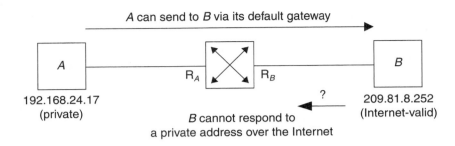

Figure 4.2 A Scenario for IP Masquerading

Remember that the private address space may be used by any private net, and as such, may be routed internally at B's network to some other machine with the address 192.168.24.17. To remedy the situation, the router alters the packet so that it appears to have originated from its external interface R_B, which is an Internet-valid address. When the server sends a response, it is routed to R, which then forwards the packet on to client A. The topology, of course, is usually much more complex than that depicted; there may be many hops between the router and the server. The result, however, is the same. The packet appears to have an Internet-valid source address and will find its way back to the router to be unmasqueraded.

4.2.1 IP Masquerading Under the Hood

Now that we are motivated to use masquerading, we can talk about what is really happening to the packet when it is masqueraded. As an example, let's say that client A would like to connect to server B using either TCP or UDP.[2] The client is going to send from port x to port y on the server. In order to reach B, A first sends the packet to its gateway, which has address R_A. The gateway interface on the B side is R_B.

If you take a close look at such a transaction, three different types of addresses are involved. First, each machine has an Ethernet address (or really, any link-layer address), useful only for transmission of frames to other machines on its local subnet. The next layer includes the IP address of the source and the destination. Finally, for the TCP and UDP protocols, there is a specific port on both the client and the server. Normally, the client port is not significant and is a value between 1024 and 65534, arbitrarily chosen by the operating system.[3] However, the server response must arrive on the port where the client expects it—otherwise, the client doesn't know that the packet is a response to its send.

Forwarding without Masquerading

Let's list the sequence of a send/respond transaction when no masquerading occurs, and then follow the values of the three addresses in Table 4.1:

1. Client A wants to send to the service running on port y on server B, so it builds a packet with B's IP address as the destination. Because B is part of a different subnet, client A

---

[2]The client/server designations refer to the system's role in the transaction. The client originates the connection request with the server, and the server responds to it.

[3]If the send port is not specified in the code, Linux starts at 1024 and simply increments the value each time a client binds to a new port for sending.

Table 4.1 Packet Headers during Normal Forwarding

Ethernet addr		IP addr		TCP port	
src	dst	src	dst	src	dst
A	R_A	A	B	x	y
router forwards					
R_B	B	A	B	x	y
B	R_B	B	A	y	x
router forwards					
R_A	A	B	A	y	x

knows to forward the packet to its gateway, R. It does this by setting the destination in the Ethernet frame to R.

2. R receives the packet and notes that its destination is a remote IP address. Because R is configured to forward, it accepts the packet and determines which interface to use to forward the packet. It then places B's Ethernet address as the destination address in the Ethernet frame and sends the packet. (In the general case where B is still several hops away, it determines which gateway is the next hop and sends to it, where the same procedure takes place.)

3. Server B receives the Ethernet frame and notes that the destination address for the packet is its own. Therefore, it accepts the packet and sends it to the process which has a socket bound and listening to the destination port y in the TCP packet header.

4. The same procedure is executed in reverse for the response. This time, the TCP header destination port is x, and the source port is y. The IP packet header has B as the source and A as the destination. The Ethernet frame headers take on the appropriate values as the packet makes its way back to client A.

Forwarding with Masquerading

Now take the same situation and configure the router to masquerade traffic from subnet$_A$ or traffic to subnet$_B$. The following steps will occur during a transaction between client A and server B:

1. **client send/router receive**—A sends a packet to B via its gateway R.

2. **router masquerade**—The packet pattern-matching on the router R notices that this connection should be masqueraded. It builds a new set of IP headers for the packet payload in which the source IP address of the packet is replaced by the IP address of the forwarding interface on R. R opens a free port, z, and fixes up the packet so that it now originates from R:z.

3. **router forward/server receive**—The newly massaged packet is forwarded to B.

4. **server reply/router receive**—B's server process receives the packet and builds a packet to reply to it. The reply is to R at port z, because these are the source values B sees in the packet headers. B puts this packet on the wire to R.

5. **router unmasquerade**—The kernel on R recognizes the packet as a response to a previously masqueraded send by the destination IP and port tuple (R, z). When it opened the socket corresponding to port z, it left special instructions there to forward responses to that port to A at port x. Therefore, it **unmasquerades** the packet by fixing up the headers and then forwarding it to client A. The fix-up includes replacing the source IP address to be that of B, and the sending port to be y.

6. **router forward/client receive**—R puts the packet on the wire. A receives the server response, which automagically appears to have come directly from the server at B. Neither A nor B is the wiser.

In summary, forwarding involves fixing up the link-layer headers, while masquerading is the act of fixing up network-layer headers (IP address) and transport protocol-layer headers (port). Table 4.2 and Figure 4.3 illustrate the step-by-step exchange explained above. The items in the table which are changed by the masquerading router are marked with an asterisk.

The values reported in the tables are the same values you would see in the output of a packet sniffer (covered in Section 3.3) if you traced such a transaction. In this case, there are four different points where you could monitor the packet flow (at A, R$_A$, R$_B$, and B). If you were to watch all four, you would see that both interfaces on subnet$_A$ see the same traffic, as do both interfaces on subnet$_B$. I point this out to show that the kernel modifies the packets *in-between* the interfaces—i.e., while it internally forwards the packet from one interface to another. The upswing is that you can perform your monitoring directly on any interface on the masquerading router.

Table 4.2 Packet Headers while Masquerading

	Ethernet		IP		TCP	
	src	dst	src	dst	src	dst
(1)	A	R$_A$	A	B	x	y
(2)	router masqs					
(3)	R$_B$	B	R$_B$*	B	z*	y
(4)	B	R$_B$	B	R$_B$	y	z
(5)	router unmasqs					
(6)	R$_A$	A	B	A	y	x*

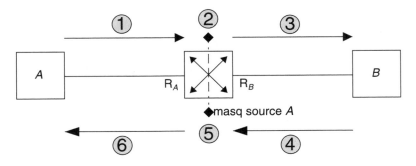

Figure 4.3 IP Forwarding and Masquerading over Ethernet

4.2.2   Protocol-Specific Masquerading

You can fool some of the packets some of the time,
but you can't fool all of the packets all of the time.

The prior example represents one class of TCP/IP connection: a TCP stream. What about masquerading UDP and ICMP? As long as they are *well-mannered*, the IP masquerading code in *./net/ipv4/ip_masq.c* (in the 2.2 kernels) or *./net/ipv4/netfilter/ipt_MASQUERADE.c* (in the 2.4 kernels) handles all three without any additional configuration. What do we mean by *well-mannered*? IP masquerading works out of the box for all TCP and UDP-based applications based on a single fixed server port and an arbitrarily chosen client port, where the machine being masqueraded (the client) is the initiator of the connection.

How far does this get you? It handles telnet, *ssh*, rlogin, HTTP, pings (ICMP) and traceroutes (a combination of ICMP and UDP), DNS (often UDP, but can be TCP), NNTP, and many others. But, as you already know, it's what *doesn't* work that people notice. The first notable exception is FTP. FTP likes to open connections from the server back to the client, contrary to the direction you are trying masquerade (and/or firewall).

To handle a case like this, the masquerading/NAT code needs to understand something about the application protocol so that it can watch for the beginning of a transfer and know to connect the inbound socket connection to the client, not to the router. Remember, the process running on the client is expecting that inbound connection, not the router. To make things even more complicated, the FTP protocol also has a **passive mode** in which this inbound connection does not occur. The client and server negotiate a new pair of ports and use these to build a stream connection for the data transmission. For more information on protocol-specific masquerading, see Section 10.4.1 in the chapter on 2.2 networking goodies. The 2.4 kernel solves this as a special case of connection tracking and utilizes the *ip_conntrack_ftp* module in conjunction with the *ip_nat_ftp* module.

Huh? What modules? What is **connection tracking**? Before we start configuring our box for masquerading, we need to dig into some background information about the kernel code that implements this function and the tool used to control it.

4.3   Linux's *netfilter*—Concepts

The Linux kernel's firewalling, masquerading/NAT, and general network packet management code is known as *netfilter*. It is a complete rewrite and departure from the interface used in the 2.2 series kernels, *ipchains*. This constitutes the third major rewrite of this code for Linux since packet filtering was introduced in the 1.1 version of kernel. Although it's too early to say (so far, there's no news about what might show up in the 2.5 kernel), I tend to believe that the *netfilter* code is going to stay with us for a while. It's very modular and flexible, in terms both of its functionality and the programming interface, and it's fast.

Frequently folks will dive into using the kernel's filtering and NAT facilities before they fully understand its underlying structure. This is completely understandable—when you want (or desperately need) to accomplish a task, knowing all the details about how something works is secondary. In the first edition of this book I took the view that it would be better to *back into* the theoretical part by covering the practical application first. Based on reader feedback and reflection, I think that *netfilter* is best introduced by talking about its design and structure, and then filling in the details about usage.

We understand how a packet traverses a network, with each network element along the way making decisions about whether and/or how to pass it along the path toward its destination.

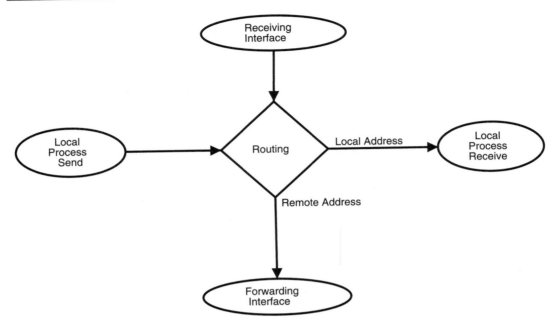

Figure 4.4 Packet Path without *netfilter*

That decision-making process performed by each network element can also be considered a path—a path through the kernel of the machine handling the packet. Let's take a moment to consider and document that path for Linux. First off, for a Linux system without any packet-manipulation code, the situation is depicted in Figure 4.4.

The routing decision is the same process we described in Section 2.1.4 and includes whatever the *iproute2* code in the kernel is configured to do. Keep this in mind for later. So far, so good. Now, let's think about what we might want to do to a packet while it's in our router, before it's forwarded on to wherever it says it needs to go.

- We may want to throw the packet away because we don't allow that kind of traffic around here.

- We may want to change where it's headed, its destination address, to enforce policies about using HTTP proxy servers.

- We may want to change the address whence the packet appears to originate, i.e., masquerade its source, because we know it originated from private or otherwise unroutable address space.

- We may want to note that the packet traversed our router, either via a counter for that type of packet, or by logging that (and every) specific instance of that type of packet.

You'll notice from the list above that our potential actions often imply some knowledge about the packet. We don't want to throw away all packets (or we wouldn't have much of a router), just packets that match a given set of criteria. So what are those criteria?

4.3.1 Packet-Matching Criteria

With *netfilter*, you can specify the criteria to match just about any part of the headers on
an IPv4, IPv6, or DECnet packet (the list of protocols that have *netfilter* hooks at the time
of writing). We'll focus on IPv4 for the time being. Furthermore, you can add criteria based
on the link-layer as well (such as the MAC address of the sending interface). Within an IPv4
packet, you have IP headers and then either TCP or UDP headers. Examples of things to
match against:

- source or destination IP address (or a range of IP addresses, specified in network/subnet
  mask notation)

- source or destination port (or a list, or range, of ports), which in turn implies the application protocol being used, e.g., TCP port 80 is HTTP traffic, UDP port 53 is DNS
  traffic

- protocol of TCP, UDP, ICMP, or *all (all is the default when no protocol is listed)

- physical interface used to send or receive the packet

- the status of certain flags, such as the **SYN** and **ACK** bits, or the TOS (Type Of
  Service) flag. The significance of **SYN=1 & ACK=0** is that this type of packet is the
  first packet used to establish a TCP/IP connection. If ACK is set (equal to 1), then this
  packet is part of an established connection.

- whether or not the packet is a fragment of larger packet. This isn't a problem if you're
  also doing masquerading or NAT, as that code requires that all fragments be reassem-
  bled before they are forwarded, but in some performance-conscious packet-filtering-only
  situations, there may be use for matching fragments.

4.3.2 *netfilter*'s Terminology

As we mentioned, *netfilter* is *modular*, and central to this idea is the use of **tables**. Tables are
implemented via hooks into the kernel's networking code and cannot be created by userspace
tools. For now, the tables available are `filter`, `nat`, and `mangle`. Each implements a certain
class of actions you may perform on a packet: acting as a filter, performing network address
translation, or modifying the packet in other ways, such as marking the packet to enforce
a particular queuing algorithm later on. There are five different points (the aforementioned
hooks) in the packet's path where the *netfilter* tables get a chance to examine and affect the
fate of a packet. A table may inhabit one or more of these hooks with its built-in chain(s),
which take the name of hook. I mention this to avoid any confusion with how some of the very
good Internet resources explain *netfilter*, and so that you don't confuse the `PREROUTING` chain
in the `mangle` table with `PREROUTING` for `nat`. These hooks, without any table associations,
are depicted in Figure 4.5. Don't puzzle too long over them now; their purpose will be clearer
once we talk about the various tables.

Within a table is a collection of *chains*, which in turn contain *rules*. Some of these chains
are built into the kernel and cannot be removed or renamed (but you can add rules to them).
These are the *built-in* chains. Chains also have **policies**, which indicate what default action to
take with a packet that doesn't match any of the rules on the chains. Every rule within a chain
has a single **target**, which indicates what to do with packets that match that rule. A target
can be be another user-defined chain, one of the predefined targets valid for that table, or a

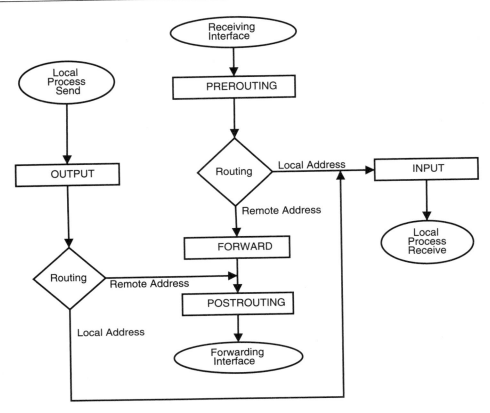

Figure 4.5 *netfilter* Hooks

return to the calling chain. If it sounds complicated, don't be intimidated. It's just because it is such a flexible scheme for dealing with packets, and when you want to do something interesting with your router, you'll be thankful for that flexibility.

A point of clarification: A packet does not traverse a table, so don't think that a packet enters a table, which consists of chains, which are composed of rules and targets. A table implements a set of functionality by enabling one or more built-in chains at opportune points in a packet's path through the kernel. Those built-in chains have default policies and may contain rules. These rules, in turn, may have user-defined chains as targets (and there can be as many layers of user-defined chains as needed). So think of a table as a functionality space, while chains are collections of rules which a packet must traverse.

4.3.3   2.4 Kernel Support for *netfilter*

To be able to use it, you need to know how to get *netfilter* support into your running kernel. The options listed below are the bare minimum required to have *netfilter* support—I don't even think you can do anything with *netfilter* with only these options. But unless you select these, you won't have access to the other options required to use various components of *netfilter*. My recommendation if you don't want to be continually compiling kernels is to select everything underneath the IP: Netfilter Configuration as a module. This won't bloat your kernel much and will help you learn which modules are needed for a given function (especially if you disable the `Kernel module loader` so that you have to load the modules by hand before they can be used). IPv6 is, of course, optional, and I'll introduce the specific modules needed for examples.

```
Networking options --->
   [*] Network packet filtering (replaces ipchains)
   [*] TCP/IP networking
      IP: Netfilter Configuration  --->
         <M> Connection tracking (required for masq/NAT)
         <M> IP tables support (required for filtering/masq/NAT)

   <M>   The IPv6 protocol (EXPERIMENTAL)
      IPv6: Netfilter Configuration  --->
         <M> IP6 tables support (required for filtering/masq/NAT)
```

4.3.4   *iptables*—**The Interface to** *netfilter*

The user-space tool used to control *netfilter* is *iptables*. Like its predecessor *ipchains*, it gives us plenty of syntax to learn, so we'll break it down into sections. Also like *ipchains*, but to a far greater extent, some of the arguments to *iptables* are applicable only when certain modules are loaded (or certain functionalities are compiled into the kernel). Finally, you must specify the table upon which you'd like the command to apply, or the default table of `filter` is assumed. I suggest always supplying the table name using `--table [filter|nat|mangle]` (or `-t` for short). The first set of commands (really, arguments) we'll cover are shown in Table 4.3. These are used to manipulate chains as a whole.

Notice that for some commands, if you don't specify a chain, the command affects all of the chains in that table. The next set of commands (Table 4.4) manipulate rules within a given chain, and therefore all require that a chain be specified, typically along with a rule. As you've noticed from the first column of the reference tables, (almost) all of *iptables'* command-line options are available in both short and long form. These can help make network configuration scripts more self-documenting, especially when we get into the long list of rule specifiers in Table 4.5. For the rule specifiers, you can mentally insert a *packet is [not] of* or *packet matches* before all of the descriptions.

Part of the rule specification is that rule's **target**, specified with `-j` or `--jump`. The valid list of targets depends upon three factors: what table you're using, what extensions you might have loaded (for example, there is a *LOG* target that provides a packet-logging facility), and

Table 4.3 Commands that Manipulate Chains

switch	argument(s)	description
-N or --new	*chain*	Create a new user-defined chain
-E or --rename-chain	*old-chain new-chain*	Rename a new user-defined chain
-X or --delete-chain	*[chain]*	Delete *chain*/all chains
-Z or --zero	*[chain]*	Zero *chain* counters/all chains
-P or --policy	*chain target*	Set *chain* policy to *target*
-F or --flush	*[chain]*	Flush rules in *chain*/all chains

Table 4.4 Commands that Manipulate Rules

switch	argument(s)	description
-A or --append	*chain rule*	Append *rule* to *chain*
-D or --delete	*chain rule*	Delete *rule* from *chain*
-D or --delete	*chain [n]*	Delete *nth*/first rule from *chain*
-I or --insert	*chain [rulenum] rule*	Insert *rule* into *chain* (or at location *n* if given)
-R or --replace	*chain n rule*	Replace *chain* rule *n* with *rule*

Table 4.5 Specifying Rules

switch	argument(s)	description
-j or --jump	*target*	action to take if packet matches
-s or --source	*[!] address[/mask]*	[not] source address
-d or --destination	*[!] address[/mask]*	[not] destination address
-i or --in-interface	*[!] dev[+]*	[not] input interface + is a wildcard, e.g., *eth+*
-o or --out-interface	*[!] dev[+]*	[not] output interface
[!] -f or --fragment		(un)true if fragment number ≥ 2
-p or --proto	*[!] protocol*	[not] protocol *protocol* (see notes in text)

what other user-defined chains you have created in that table. Note that you can create a set of rules that forms a loop (or forms a loop only under certain conditions). The following is a silly example where I configure a chain to watch telnet traffic, configure another chain to log telnet traffic, and then have them call each other. They utilize the `filter` table, which we don't cover until Section 7.3 and requires kernel support for packet filtering, but the point of the example is to show how to link chains together. (And a rule like this would make no sense whatsoever in the *nat* table!)

```
drone3:~# modprobe iptable_filter
drone3:~# modprobe ipt_LOG
drone3:~# iptables -t filter -N tonytest
drone3:~# iptables -t filter -A OUTPUT -j tonytest
drone3:~# iptables -t filter -A tonytest --proto tcp --dport 23
drone3:~# iptables -t filter -N testchain2
drone3:~# iptables -t filter -R tonytest 1 --proto tcp --dport 23 --jump testchain2
drone3:~# iptables -t filter -A testchain2 --proto tcp --dport 23 -j LOG
drone3:~# iptables -t filter -I testchain2 --proto tcp --dport 23 -j tonytest
iptables: Loop found in table
```

In this next case I replace rule number 1 in the tonytest chain with a rule to jump to testchain2, but testchain2 hasn't been created yet. Since the kernel cannot find that name, it assumes that this is a target module to be loaded (just as with the *LOG* target). Hence the perhaps misleading error message. But we learn something from the error message too—*iptables* dynamically links in code at invocation time to perform parsing of arguments and the configuration of some rules. This helps *iptables* to be extensible without our having to rebuild or bloat the main binary. It's pretty clever stuff IMO.

```
drone3:~# iptables -t filter -R tonytest 1 --proto tcp \
        --dport 23 --jump testchain2

iptables v1.2.2: Couldn't load target 'testchain2':
/lib/iptables/libipt_testchain2.so:
cannot open shared object file: No such file or directory
```

When matching source or destination addresses, you can use hostnames as well as IP addresses. If the hostname resolves to multiple addresses, all of them will match. You can also specify a subnet mask in the maskbits notation. If source or destination addresses are not specified, then any address (equivalent to 0.0.0.0/0) will match. Being able to match an input or output interface, or any interface except this one (with '!'), can be quite handy. Use '+' as a wildcard just as you would an asterisk in a filespec. (The shell doesn't expand '+', so you don't have to worry about quoting it or otherwise escaping it.) The fragment flag matches packets that are fragments of an originally larger packet. Note that it doesn't match the first fragment, so ! --fragment indicates the first fragment or an unfragmented packet.

If the variety of rule specifiers so far seems a little weak—for example, we cannot even match a TCP source port or destination port yet—don't worry, there are many still to come. The options in Table 4.5 are merely the specifiers applicable to all packets, regardless of table or optional extension modules that may be loaded. We can specify a packet's protocol with --proto *protocol*, where protocol may be the string tcp, udp, icmp, or all, or a protocol found in */etc/protocols*. Note that this file provides a mapping similar to */etc/services* but between protocol names and the protocol number (found in an 8-bit field in the IPv4 header). The complete list of valid protocol numbers can be found at *http://www.iana.org/assignments/protocol-numbers*. If no protocol is specified, then all is assumed. When you *do* specify a particular protocol, you enable additional command-line arguments specific to that protocol. Instead of presenting yet another table of syntax, we'll introduce those protocol-specific specifiers when we need them, during the discussion of firewalling later in Section 7.3.

Hint: Command-line Help for *iptables*

If you're beginning to think about tattooing all of the *iptables* arguments and switches down the length of both of your forearms, don't go for it quite yet. Because of its modular nature, *iptables* can offer context-sensitive command-line help. When --help is given, it looks at the other command-line options specified to determine what to display. For example, if you execute iptables --proto icmp --jump LOG --help, you will receive three usage statements on stdout. (Thank you *iptables* developers for spitting this out on stdout and not stderr. With so many options, we need to be able to use *more*, *less*, or our $PAGER of choice.)

The first is the usage information common to all *iptables* commands, the Usage:, Commands:, and Options:, preceded by the version. The next two statements are specific to the jump target (LOG) and protocol specified, also prefaced by the extension version. This is very handy if you don't keep a list of all of the ICMP types or TCP flags handy. One thing I did notice is that you need to specify --help as the last argument in order for it to list the extension help as well, otherwise you'll only get the common usage information.

The last bits of *iptables* syntax we want to cover at this time are the options used to display chains and rules. Actually, the only argument needed is -L (or --list), optionally followed by a chain name. If you don't specify a chain, you'll get all chains for the table table specified, and if you don't specify a table, as you already know, filter is assumed. Therefore, the basic command form is iptables --table nat|filter|mangle --list [chain] [modifiers], with the modifiers listed in Table 4.6.

Table 4.6 Displaying *iptables* Rules

switch	description
-v or --verbose	include packet and byte counters
-x or --exact	counters are in bytes (no K, M, etc.)
	(only when used with -v)
-n or --numeric	numeric addresses and ports
--line-numbers	list rule numbers (for R, I, and D)
-Z or --zero	zero counters in [chain]
	(all chains if none given—be careful!)
--set-counters PKTS BYTES	preload counters for chain or rule

It is, I know, a fair amount of syntax to try to absorb in one chunk. I cover it here so that you'll have it for reference, and so that options will be familiar to you when we cover them in examples. Now let's pull together the ideas about *netfilter* and masquerading to see how *netfilter* provides this functionality. Once we have that, we begin to put this tangle of *iptables* command options to work for us.

4.4   Masquerading and NAT with *netfilter*

Hey, didn't we need to connect erbium to some other networks without exchanging any routing information? In other words, we needed erbium to connect to the foreign network as a client, and to alter any packet from behind erbium (i.e., on our side) to appear to have originated from that one valid client IP address on the foreign network. This is no different from the situation where you have one valid IP address (say on your cable modem router) and a network using RFC 1918 address at your home or office. Or you may have a handful of Internet-valid addresses, but not enough for all of your clients (or servers) to each have one. Because this is such a common need, Linux makes it easy, and because every situation may possess unique nuances, Linux gives the administrator a great deal of leeway in just how this done. As always, we'll need some kernel support, in this case in the form of modules. A typical set of kernel options follows. You certainly want the NAT and MASQUERADE targets; the FTP and IRC modules are optional.

```
Networking options --->
    [*] Network packet filtering (replaces ipchains)
    [*] TCP/IP networking
      IP: Netfilter Configuration  --->
        <M> Connection tracking (required for masq/NAT)
        <M>   FTP protocol support
        <M>   IRC protocol support
```

```
<M> IP tables support (required for filtering/masq/NAT)
<M>   Full NAT
<M>      MASQUERADE target support
```

Figure 4.6 illustrates the paths a packet may take through the kernel when the `nat` table has been loaded. (You can accomplish this with `modprobe iptable_nat`, and if you have the kernel configured to autoload modules, it will automatically load this module when you execute `iptables -t nat`.) As you can see, the hooks for this table are located both before and after routing decisions are made. Why both locations? Wouldn't one be enough? In the 2.2 series kernel, there was a single hook into the forwarding code. In other words, if you weren't forwarding a packet, you couldn't modify its source address. This is sufficient when you want to modify the source address, but if you need to change the destination address (where the packet is headed), you need to know about it *before* you hit the routing code so that you can route it appropriately. This is known as **DNAT**, Destination NAT, for when you have servers on IPs you need to hide. This will be the topic of Section 9.2.3. To change the source address, the `POSTROUTING` chain is the place to be, so let's start with a simple (and not very useful) example.

```
iptables -t nat -A POSTROUTING -j MASQUERADE
```

If we look at the command, we're selecting the table `nat` and the `POSTROUTING` chain, and the target to jump to is `MASQUERADE`. What type of packets? All kinds of packets. From

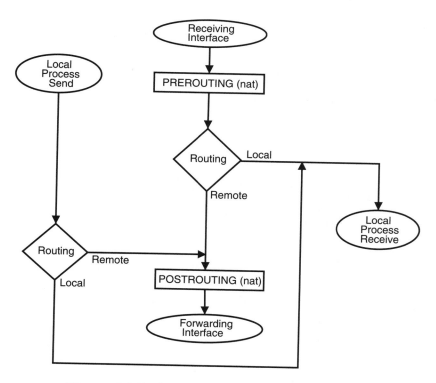

Figure 4.6 Packet Path with *netfilter*'s `nat` Table

what source address? From any source address. To what destination? To any destination. Remember that parameters left unspecified default to *any*. So will this do what we want for erbium? Surprisingly, yes. Because it masquerades only when it forwards, and it remembers what connections it has masqueraded (via the connection tracking code), this will get the job done. It may, however, have some unexpected side-effects if erbium is used to route packet flows other than those from our internal clients out into the foreign extranet. First of all, without any firewalling in place, any connection attempted from extranet side that was routing back over the extranet link would make it to erbium, and based on erbium's routing table, be routed into our network, but sporting erbium's IP address. OK, firewalling is an entirely different issue (taken up in Section 7.3), but can't we at least make sure that we're masquerading only the packets we send? This is easily done by specifying the sending interface with -o *intf* or --out-interface *intf*. But erbium is a little special in that we're not always sure what the output device name will be (in the case of a PPP connection, it will *pppN*, but our ISDN links have another device name altogether). Here are a couple more examples of the command form:

```
# masquerade all packets output on ppp*
erbium:~# iptables -t nat -A POSTROUTING -j MASQUERADE -o ppp+

# masquerade all packets to a given destination address/subnet
erbium:~# iptables -t nat -A POSTROUTING -j MASQUERADE -d 10.10.34.216
erbium:~# iptables -t nat -A POSTROUTING -j MASQUERADE -d 10.10.34.216/25

# masquerade only from a certain local subnet to a given dst subnet
erbium:~# iptables -t nat -A POSTROUTING -j MASQUERADE        \
                -d 10.10.34.216/25 -s 192.168.16.0/24

# masquerade only to a given port
erbium~# iptables -t nat -A POSTROUTING -j MASQUERADE        \
                -d 10.10.34.216/25 --proto tcp --dport 22
```

In that last example, we specify that we're only going to allow packets destined to port 22 (normally used for *ssh*). You may also specify a range of ports using --dport *start:finish*, where either *start* or *finish* may be omitted to imply *all ports up to* or *all ports greater than*. (Note to *ipchains* users: the ability to list out multiple distinct ports, e.g., 22,25,110, is available when using the multiport match extension, provided by the *ipt_multiport.o* module. We'll talk more about match extensions in Chapter 7.) Sometimes it is easier to specify what it is that you do not want to masquerade. For example, you may have a topology where the firewall is performing masquerading, but there are several machines located outside the firewall that have routes for your internal networks. You do not want connections to these machines from internal machines to be masqueraded because any meaningful information about the source IP address is lost. If the internal network you need to masquerade is 192.168.0.0/16, and the external network is 172.16.12.64/255.255.255.192, you can set the rules as follows:

```
# masquerade all connections not bound to special net Z
erbium~# iptables -t nat -A POSTROUTING -j MASQUERADE        \
                --source 192.168.0.0/16                      \
                --destination ! 172.16.12.64/255.255.255.192
```

```
# alternately, use ACCEPT to forward traffic without masquerading
erbium~# iptables -t nat -A POSTROUTING -j MASQUERADE          \
                --source 192.168.0.0/16
erbium~# iptables -t nat -I POSTROUTING -j ACCEPT              \
                --source 192.168.0.0/16                        \
                --destination 172.16.12.64/255.255.255.192
```

In the first command above, we're creating a rule that masquerades everything not destined for our special net Z (and note that we can specify the subnet mask in dotted-quad notation if we prefer). In the second set of commands, we use two rules to accomplish the same effect. The first masquerades everything, and the second, which is inserted into the POSTROUTING chain so as to come before the MASQUERADE rule (which matches everything from this source), uses the standard target ACCEPT to allow these packets to pass normally. This sort of rule specification can be used to create very fine-grained rulesets, especially useful for firewalling.

4.4.1   Kernel Modules Required for Masquerading

netfilter's modularity can really be felt when you compile a kernel without automatic module loading support and you go to use masquerading. There are quite a string of module dependencies, not all of which you'd guess at first glance. Here are the modules required for a basic masquerading setup on my 2.4.12 box that includes support for FTP:

- ip_tables

- iptable_nat

- ip_conntrack

- ipt_MASQUERADE

- ip_conntrack_ftp

- ip_nat_ftp

Now, if your kernel does have support for automatic module loading, then the modules will be brought into the kernel as soon as they are required (normally by *iptables*). One exception are the _ftp modules, which need to be loaded explicitly for passive-mode FTP to work. By all means you should be using *modprobe*, and I suggest `modprobe ip_nat_ftp`, which, by nature of its dependencies will get all of the above.

4.4.2   Viewing Rules with *iptables*

As with any virtual space you work in, be it filesystems or routing tables, or favorite Infocom text adventure, you need a way to explore the lay of the land, to *see*, as it were. *netfilter* is certainly no exception. In fact, I think having a clear mental picture of what's going on with the rulesets is the single largest hurdle to overcome when you start working with packet-mangling and filtering (the second being a lack of understanding about how TCP/IP ports and IP protocols work). So we'll want to look around us frequently and from as many different perspectives as possible. The first is to take a look at what `iptables -L` can show us.

```
root@java:/tmp# iptables -L -t nat -v
Chain PREROUTING (policy ACCEPT 52940 packets, 9875K bytes)
 pkts bytes target       prot opt in   out  source          destination

Chain POSTROUTING (policy ACCEPT 5709 packets, 381K bytes)
 pkts bytes target       prot opt in   out  source          destination
19424 1193K MASQUERADE   all  --  any  any  192.168.0.0/16  anywhere

Chain OUTPUT (policy ACCEPT 5780 packets, 385K bytes)
 pkts bytes target    prot opt in    out   source          destination
```

By default, you get all of the chains in the **nat** table if you specify -L without specifying a chain. (If you forget the **-t nat** you'll be looking at the chains in the **filter** table, or at nothing if that table isn't loaded.) From the output above, the system only has a single rule in the POSTROUTING chain, and no user-defined chains at all. If you omit the verbose flag, you'll lose the input and output interfaces and all of the counters. Another way to view the active rules on the system is with the *iptables-save* command. This has the advantage of listing out the rules in a format (mostly) suitable as an argument to *iptables* (and completely suitable as input to *iptables-restore*). Chains are listed on lines starting with ':'—tables are listed on lines starting with '*'. Note that chain lines indicate the policy for that chain, and that counters for chains are always displayed. If a default policy has not been specified for a user-defined chain, you'll see a '-' where the policy is normally displayed. Rules used to create user-defined chains are not explicitly found in the output. However, the existence of a chain other than a built-in implies its creation.

```
root@java:/proc/net# iptables-save --table nat
# Generated by iptables-save v1.2.3 on Fri Nov  9 00:24:29 2001
*nat
:PREROUTING ACCEPT [53069:9889882]
:POSTROUTING ACCEPT [5719:381229]
:OUTPUT ACCEPT [5790:385825]
-A POSTROUTING -s 192.168.0.0/255.255.0.0 -j MASQUERADE
-A POSTROUTING -s 193.101.146.0/255.255.255.0 -j MASQUERADE
COMMIT
# Completed on Fri Nov  9 00:24:29 2001
```

This command is useful if you've been trying different things to get a configuration working and would like to be able to track what you did without taking notes along the way. If you omit the **--table** option, all tables, chains, and rules are displayed. And if you redirect the output of *iptables-save*, you have instant rules in a can—just add *iptables-restore*.

4.4.3 Viewing Active Connections with */proc/net/ip_conntrack*

Now, iptables -L can show you rules and counters, but it doesn't show you actually what's being masqueraded at that moment. Put more precisely, it doesn't show you what connections are actively being tracked (similar to what ipchains -M -L did for those of you familiar with the 2.2 kernel). This information is available in */proc/net/ip_conntrack*.

```
root@java:~# cat /proc/net/ip_conntrack
tcp 6 209921 ESTABLISHED src=192.168.1.12 dst=206.220.21.7 sport=1182 dport=1352
   [UNREPLIED] src=206.220.21.7 dst=65.0.44.4 sport=1352 dport=1182 use=1

udp 17 36 src=192.168.1.2 dst=10.10.1.1 sport=32990 dport=53
   src=10.10.1.1 dst=192.168.1.2 sport=53 dport=32990 [ASSURED] use=1

tcp 6 431999 ESTABLISHED src=192.168.1.2 dst=161.58.178.38 sport=42262 dport=2000
   src=161.58.178.38 dst=65.0.44.4 sport=2000 dport=42262 [ASSURED] use=1
```

I am not aware of a tool that parses and prints this file for you (a bit of Perl and you'd have it, though). In the sample output above, I've broken the lines pretty much in half and added some spaces. The first two fields are the protocol and the protocol number (from */etc/protocols*). The next pair contain the number of seconds remaining before the connection tracking for this connection times out and the current state of the connection. The timeout is reset to the maximum value for the current state any time there is traffic over that connection, or the state changes. Here's the list of timeouts for TCP connections, taken straight from the kernel source tree (*./net/ipv4/netfilter/ip_conntrack_proto_tcp.c*):

```
static unsigned long tcp_timeouts[]
= { 30 MINS,    /*      TCP_CONNTRACK_NONE,      */
     5 DAYS,    /*      TCP_CONNTRACK_ESTABLISHED,*/
     2 MINS,    /*      TCP_CONNTRACK_SYN_SENT,  */
    60 SECS,    /*      TCP_CONNTRACK_SYN_RECV,  */
     2 MINS,    /*      TCP_CONNTRACK_FIN_WAIT,  */
     2 MINS,    /*      TCP_CONNTRACK_TIME_WAIT,        */
    10 SECS,    /*      TCP_CONNTRACK_CLOSE,     */
    60 SECS,    /*      TCP_CONNTRACK_CLOSE_WAIT,       */
    30 SECS,    /*      TCP_CONNTRACK_LAST_ACK,  */
     2 MINS,    /*      TCP_CONNTRACK_LISTEN,    */
};
```

By the way, there are also timeouts for UDP *connections* (since UDP is stateless, the word *conversations* may be more appropriate). The kernel also makes an attempt to detect streaming UDP, in which case it triples the connection tracking timeout. (See *./net/ipv4/netfilter/ip_conntrack_proto_udp.c*.) After that, you have the client-side source and destination IP address and ports, or the values of these fields from the perspective of the client (the system behind the masquerading router), potentially any additional state information from the connection-tracking code's point of view—for example, [UNREPLIED]—and then source and destination information as seen on the remote side of the connection. The flag [ASSURED] indicates that the TCP handshake was successful and that packets have been received and acknowledged by the client. The last field, use, does not provide a counter, but instead another flag to indicate that the connection has been used (as opposed to being set up, but not utilized).

Port Ranges for Masquerading

When you're using the MASQUERADE target, the masquerading code uses the client's source port for the masqueraded side of the connection, if that port is available. If that port isn't available, it will select an unused port, pretty much at random. This may not go over too well with the firewall folks at your organization, since it would be nice to lock down traffic (both source and destination) as much as possible. The MASQUERADE target allows for this with the `--to-ports` *port[-port]* option. Because you can specify a range for each rule containing the MASQUERADE target, client traffic can be classified and restricted to specific ranges. You can also use this to ensure that the same port will be used on the outside as on the inside for cases where the server is finicky about the source port on the client (a generally evil practice on the part of the server, IMHO).

4.4.4   Comparing the MASQUERADE and SNAT Targets

An important feature of the Linux 2.4 kernel is the ability to perform true **NAT**, Network Address Translation. You can probably imagine the potential for stickiness with the way that client ports are managed with masquerading. For instance, if the server on the outside really is sensitive to the client port used—let's say it absolutely requires that the client send from a single well-known port—and we have many clients, we cannot provide very good service to our user community with just masquerading. Fortunately, most client-server protocols don't exhibit this behavior, but there other limitations to masquerading. Another is that the packet's apparent source address is always the single IP address of the output interface used to forward the packet. This is where **SNAT**, Source Network Address Translation, enters the picture. With SNAT, you indicate explicitly what source address should be placed into the packets that match the rules with an SNAT target. As far as what you need to configure SNAT, you already have it if you can use the MASQUERADE target. Masquerading is actually a special case of NAT, both in its functionality and in the modules that provide it, designed for cases when the IP address of the output interface on the masquerading router is not known beforehand (or perhaps is changing), and you want to be sure that the packet is masqueraded. Because the masquerading feature in the 2.4 kernel is designed for use with things like dialup links, the code drops all of the connection tracking for existing connections, the assumption being that next time the link is up, you'll have a different IP anyway. So, a basic SNAT configuration that maps all output packets to the IP address of the output interface is the same as masquerading, except that you won't lose all of your connection tracking if the link bounces.

Up to this point, erbium has been a good example of a topology where masquerading is appropriate. SNAT makes more sense if you think about applications where you have a fixed IP address for your access link, like many **SOHO** (Small Office/Home Office) networks using a cable modem for access. In this topology, there is one Internet valid IP address but several clients accessing the Internet, which is depicted in Figure 4.7. Many larger shops are set up essentially the same way, but often have multiple IP addresses available (some portion of their allocated Internet-valid IP address space).

SNAT adds the `--to-source` *addr[-addr][:port-port]* switch, which can be specified one or more times for a given rule and tells the kernel what IP(s) to map output packets as. (You will often see `--to-source` abbreviated as `--to` in the examples in the documentation available online.) Here are some examples of SNAT configurations:

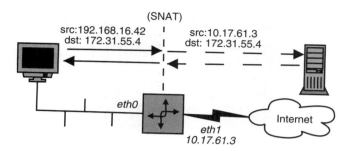

Figure 4.7 Simple SOHO Topology

```
# SNAT all connections forwarded through our router
# to the single IP address on our router
soho~# iptables    -t nat -A POSTROUTING -j SNAT       \
                   --out-interface eth1                \
                   --source 192.168.0.0/16             \
                   --to-source 10.17.61.3

# SNAT internal addresses to our Internet valid range
# not already taken by other boxes
office~# iptables -t nat -A POSTROUTING -j SNAT        \
                   --out-interface eth1                \
                   --source 192.168.0.0/16             \
                   --to-source 10.17.61.5-10.17.61.9   \
                   --to-source 10.17.61.11-10.17.61.126

# SNAT, knowing that the firewall restricts the port range
office~# iptables -t nat -A POSTROUTING -j SNAT        \
                   --out-interface eth1                \
                   --source 192.168.0.0/16             \
                   --to-source 10.17.61.5:35000-45000
```

The first and third examples potentially map a large number of addresses onto a single IP address. SNAT attempts to use the same source port that the client used, if it can. In the first example, this will occur until two clients attempt to use the same source port, at which time the connection-tracking code will detect the potential clash on the *outside* of the route and assign another source port from the unused source ports on that system. In the third example, it's unlikely that this can be achieved (most TCP stacks start with 1024 as the first client port and increment from there), so the mapping is arbitrary. In the middle example, multiple addresses are available for remapping the client addresses. If you want a one-to-one mapping of a client address to a source address, add as many rules to the POSTROUTING chain as needed with the appropriate values in the `--source` and `--to-source` fields. (There are other, easier ways of doing this, though, depending on exactly what you're trying to accomplish. One such method is **DNAT**, Destination NAT, which we'll talk about in Section 9.2.3.)

In the second example, we give the SNAT 120-odd addresses to use for mapping client addresses. Be aware that if *eth1* is configured with a single IP address, you'll need to take other actions for this configuration to work. You need to for *eth1* to respond to ARP requests for all of these addresses when the next router up the chain looks for them. This is trivial to do, using the *ip* command with `ip addr add dev eth1 10.17.61.11`, which is covered in Section 6.3. (But you'd need to do it 120 times ....) When you have several addresses available for NAT, the kernel will try to honor the client's choice of source port by using the next available SNAT address where that source port hasn't been assigned. What happens when the 121st client connect wanting to use source port 1352 comes along? Well, the kernel can't honor that source port, but it can still make the connection, so it just remaps the source port as it does when only a single SNAT address is available. When this remapping occurs, another port from the same **port class**, to borrow a term from Rusty Russell's excellent *Linux 2.4 NAT HOWTO*, is used. The three port classes are the traditional ranges you'll find in the Stevens books: less than 512, between 512 and 1023, and 1024 and greater. Recall that you must be the superuser to bind to any port less than 1024, known as **privileged** ports, and those first 1024 ports are split into half, with the upper range being designated as **authenticated**. (Authenticated ports really don't mean as much as they did way back when. When Unix boxes were much less plentiful, it was a pretty big deal to have root on one, and since you might very well know the administrator on the other side, you would grant an elevated level of trust to programs with users who could originate from ports in the range of 512–1023. This is, nowadays, foolhardy, unless it is used in conjunction with a *lot* of other security measures.)

4.4.5   SNAT and Masquerading Resources

Each time the Linux kernel interface to packet-mangling has changed, it has taken a while for some folks to divest themselves of their investment of time and intellectual capital in the previous mechanism and migrate over to the new. As I've said previously in this book, a good system administrator is cautious and skilled at managing change as well as technology. I have to admit that I wasn't terribly thrilled about things changing *again* with introduction of the *netfilter* code to the 2.4 kernel, but after overcoming my initial reluctance, I can appreciate why the change was necessary. The connection-tracking code, with all that it provides, takes Linux's networking functionality to a new level. Fortunately, a good number of people took the plunge early and have built a good body of practical knowledge concerning this toolset. You can dig around on *http://google.com/* and find relevant material quite quickly. In any case, I recommend visiting *http://netfilter.samba.org/unreliable-guides/*, the site that houses Rusty Russell's *Unreliable Guides*. (I them find very accurate, despite the moniker.) Especially pertinent to this chapter is the *Linux 2.4 NAT HOWTO* mentioned previously, but all of his documents make for good reading. Also, there are a few general tips I'd like to list:

- Remember always to tell *iptables* what table you'd like to operate on. Even if the chain name is unambiguous, you'll get an error message like that below when the table is not specified:

```
root@drone3:~# iptables -I POSTROUTING -s 192.168.16.55 -j MASQUERADE
iptables: No chain/target/match by that name
```

- */proc/net/ip_conntrack* is your friend. Between its contents and the output of *tcpdump*, you should be able to track down problems without too much head scratching and hair pulling.

- Don't forget that you can use *iptables-save* to take several snapshots of your configuration while you are testing. With a little scripting work, you should be able to use this output directly to configure *netfilter*.

- Make a mental note of Figure 4.5 back on page 118. Things can get tougher to conceptualize when the same system is performing routing, NAT, and filtering. Having a clear picture of the path which a packet follows can help.

- If you're using the 2.2 kernel, refer to Section 10.4 for instructions on how to configure *ipchains*. That section also contains some information that might be helpful for users of the MASQUERADE target, if you have reason not to use SNAT.

4.4.6   Why Masquerade?

This chapter introduces IP masquerading in conjunction with the configuration of erbium. It was used to overcome a technical snag in connecting two corporate networks. Whether the IP addresses were private or not was not always the issue; it was often a question of coordination with the other network administrator. Neither of us wanted to exchange network information, worry about address-space collisions, or expend efforts reconfiguring our networks for an infrequent (although important) application. In short, erbium uses IP masquerading because of its convenience.

The most common motivation for its use, however, is for Internet access from clients on private subnets. If your organization is using any of the private subnets listed in RFC 1918 (see Section 2.1.5), you will be required to either provide proxy servers or perform masquerading for these clients to access the Internet. Even if you can get Internet routable address space, you may choose to use private address space. After all, it is nice to have all of that address space at your disposal when planning your network. For both of these reasons, you will often see IP masquerading discussed side-by-side with packet-filtering firewalls and proxies in discussions for using it on an Internet gateway. But aside from allowing access from machines where access would not normally be possible, you may find yourself using IP masquerading for applications where the traffic could have been routed normally. In essence, you are obscuring the identity of the sender from the receiver, which has a couple of tangential benefits. First, it is a security measure. Second, it can be used to *condense* traffic.

IP Masquerading as a Security Measure

Say that a user on your network is using a web browser to access a less-than-reputable website. Web browsers have loose tongues and almost always reveal the operating system of the sender. Should someone on the receiving side have unscrupulous ideas with regard to users of this particular operating system, he/she may launch an attack against the sender. In the case of masquerading, he/she will not have access to the IP of the true sender. Instead, he/she will launch an attack against the wrong system. Although perhaps not the most quieting of examples, it is the Right Thing to limit attacks against users.

IP Masquerading to Condense Traffic

Although its applications are less frequent, there may be times when you do not want to know the IP address(es) of those who are contacting you, even if routing is not a problem. In this case, you are purposefully masquerading incoming traffic before it enters your network. One

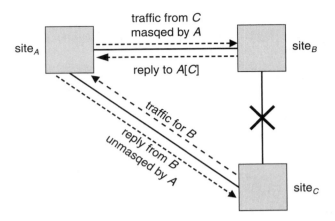

Figure 4.8 Rerouting Traffic with IP Masquerading

reason may be because your servers are having a hard time performing (reverse) name lookups on the IP address coming over the link, resulting in long DNS timeouts for client connects. Another reason may be for logging purposes, when you would like all connections from a certain site or IP range to appear to originate from a single point. If you wanted to get an idea of the amount of web traffic the group on the second floor generated on the proxy server, you could configure IP masquerading from that router interface to the HTTP proxy server at port 80. This might not be your *modus operandi*, but you could configure it for a day just to generate statistics. A third reason would be to bypass a problem in your network. Refer to Figure 4.8 as part of the following scenario.

When everything works, each site routes over its link directly to the other site. Now imagine that the link$_{BC}$ goes down in the middle of B's night. C is in the office and unhappy about not being able to access B, and A is on the phone and unhappy about being the only WAN admin available for comment. Here's one solution:

- Log into C's router and reroute traffic toward A over link$_{AC}$.

- Configure the router$_A$ to masquerade all traffic originating from C and bound for B.

- B's servers will see traffic from router$_A$ and respond to it, avoiding link$_{BC}$. Make sure that you have the protocol modules loaded on router$_A$ so that things like FTP will work.

- Send an email to the users at C that not everything is going to work wonderfully in this scenario, but most services (anything that can be masqueraded) will.

- Go back to bed, but make sure that you get the password for router$_B$ for future reference.

By nature of its incredible usefulness, and therefore popularity, many resources are available to assist you in configuring IP masquerading. A quick search on almost any web search engine should produce hundreds of hits (in at least a dozen languages), so you should not have any problem locating resources. If you do, try the Linux Documentation Project.

4.5   Summary

So now we have a Linux router taking care of the LAN and dial-up connections to external networks. We can hide the identity of our clients (or at least their IP addresses) by using masquerading and SNAT, placing the entire RFC 1918 address space at our disposal for our internal networks. We can troubleshoot configurations by looking at the kernel's data structures via the */proc* filesystem, or by viewing the contents the traffic "on the wire" with packet-capture tools like the sniffers mentioned in the previous chapter. The next step is a general-purpose WAN router, which is the topic of Chapter 5. This router can be used to connect our network to others (public or private) over high-bandwidth connections and long distances.

Chapter 5

ZINC—A FRAME RELAY ROUTER

Zinc has been up and routing IP over Frame Relay since late 1996 and has proven itself a *bread-and-butter* production Linux application. The heart of the router is an S508 router card manufactured and sold by Sangoma Technologies, Inc. This card, a 90MHz Pentium-based PC with 16MB of RAM,[1] and a little Linux kernel glue make an excellent low-cost Frame Relay router—one which is easy to administer, even for the first-time WAN administrator, yet offers the flexibility of a general-purpose platform. Zinc's configuration should give you a good basis for building your own Frame Relay router.

Before we begin building, we first cover some concepts of Frame Relay for those of you who have not worked with it before, then briefly introduce the Sangoma card and other WAN adapters available for Linux. The bulk of the chapter discusses configuring a Frame Relay router using *WANPIPE*, the software drivers and toolkit that accompany the Sangoma cards, and troubleshooting using this software. Related topics covered at the end of the chapter include using *MRTG* to monitor link performance and running *WANPIPE* in conjunction with *LRP*.

5.1 Frame Relay Basics—DLCIs, PVCs, and CIRs

Frame Relay for the WAN admin is pretty simple stuff, once you get the hang of it. The only confusing part is getting a handle on the terminology and understanding the different layers which make up a link. Essentially, you are dealing with an easy-to-configure version of PPP (although it's more complicated for network providers and other more complex topologies). First, let us define some terms (some of which are a review of Section 2.3.1); these terms are put to use in Figure 5.1.

access—This refers to the digital telco circuit that runs between your location and your Frame Relay provider's nearest **POP**. Access is also known as the **local loop**.

POP—Point Of Presence means any sort of network service provider (not just Frame Relay) facility which is available for you to connect to its network. This connection is your **access**.

port—This is the card or port on your provider's switch that is connected to your router via your **access**. Ports have speeds associated with them, indicating the maximum speed

---

[1] Actually, zinc ran fine on a 486/66 with 8MB for almost two years.

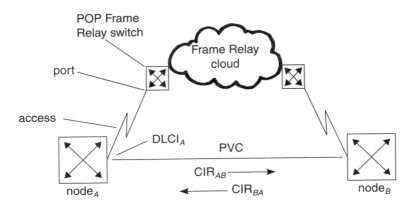

Figure 5.1 Frame Relay Terms

at which your provider's switch will accept packets from you. Note that the port speed does not always coincide with access speed.

DLCI—Data Link Connection Identifier is the address used to specify the endpoint of a PVC (which corresponds to one of your **nodes**). This address is single integer and is used by your router to indicate which of potentially several different PVCs configured at your provider's switch is the correct recipient of the frame. (Note that you still need DLCIs, even if you have a single PVC in your network.) The DLCI should be a value between 16 and 1023. Many providers will allow you to request the DLCIs you would like to use for your network.

CPE—Customer Premises Equipment is a term for your router.

node—This is another term that refers to your router. A Frame Relay node typically has a single DLCI associated with it. Of these, **CPE** is probably better terminology, since your provider may use **node** to refer to network entities other than your router.[2]

PVC—Permanent Virtual Circuit is a path between two nodes on the network, set up by the provider so that they can talk to each other. (Actually, how the packets are routed through the provider's network is not known to you, but the PVC gives the illusion that the two nodes are directly connected to each other.) From your vantagepoint, a PVC can be thought of as a network pipe running between two **DLCI**s. PVCs are not directional, nor are they strictly associated with bandwidth. Although many like to talk about the "speed of the PVC," they should be talking about the CIR associated with that PVC.

CIR—Committed Information Rate (expressed in bits per second) is the maximum rate at which your provider guarantees that you can transmit packets over your PVC without any packet loss. (Actually, this guarantee is often a "best efforts" type of service.) **CIR**s, unlike **PVC**s, *are* directional, which means that the guaranteed bandwidth from router$_A$ to router$_B$ does not have to equal the guaranteed flow in the reverse direction. Not all providers allow you to specify this sort of **asymmetrical CIR** for a PVC. If they are

---

[2]I frequently use the term **node** for my routers, however, and do so throughout this chapter.

available, CIRs are a good way to save costs while still providing adequate bandwidth for your application.

LMI—Local Management Interface is the method by which Frame Relay routers keep each other notified regarding the status of the network. This involves the exchange of status messages between your node and the router at the POP. These messages may conform to one of three different standards: **LMI**, **ANSI** (also known as **Annex D**), and **Q.933** (also known as **Annex A**).

NNI—Network-to-Network Interface is a term used by providers when they connect two disparate networks. An NNI enables them to provide a PVC between routers located on different Frame Relay networks. (If you need a PVC between one of your nodes and a business partner who uses a different provider, ask your provider if he/she has an **NNI** with the other provider.)

5.1.1   Frame Relay Bandwidth

One thing that confuses first-time Frame Relay administrators is the question, *How much bandwidth do I have?* The question is important because ordering Frame Relay services can get complicated (and expensive), and you want to know what to expect. There are different parameters in a Frame Relay network which dictate the end-to-end bandwidth. Some scenarios which affect this bandwidth are:

1. You may be saving telco costs by multiplexing applications on a single piece of digital access. In this case, your access is necessarily larger than your port.

2. If access is inexpensive, you may choose a port smaller than your access to avoid paying for a port which fills up the access.

3. Once your data enter your provider's network, they become subject to the CIRs you have selected for your PVCs. Different providers may enforce the CIR upon ingress (entering the network) or egress (exiting the network). Still others never enforce the CIR at all, in which case link speed equates to the lower of the two associated port speeds.

4. You may have different port sizes at each end of a PVC, which limits throughput to the lesser of the two. (However, depending upon how your provider's network performs buffering, you might not notice this limitation until the differences in port speed are pronounced.)

5. Some nodes in your network might be **oversubscribed**, a situation where the sum of the ports attached to a node via PVCs exceeds the port speed at this node. If you are oversubscribed, and all of the nodes on the other ends of your PVCs burst (send data at their full port speed) to you simultaneously, things may slow down and/or get lost.

In the case of a simple two-node network, your average throughput in a given direction will be the smallest value found between points A and B. Figure 5.2 illustrates this. Note, however, that this is the **guaranteed rate**. The **burst rate**, the maximum speed at which an interface can transmit data, is equal to the port speed for that interface. The **burst throughput** for a PVC, assuming that your provider does not enforce the CIRs, is the lesser of the two port speeds for that PVC.

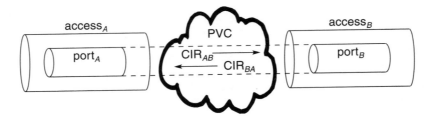

Figure 5.2 Frame Relay Bandwidth

Exceeding Your CIR

When you exceed your CIR, the ugly truth is that your provider may discard some of your packets. Whether or not it does so is determined as follows. The upstream switch (at your provider's POP) continuously monitors how much bandwidth you are using. If you exceed your CIR, the packets are marked by setting a bit in the packet header. If any other node in the cloud is heavily congested, it can discard packets with this bit set. So, while exceeding your CIR can squeeze more bandwidth out of your link for a lower cost, doing so also puts you at risk for packet loss. Of course, TCP-based applications will notice the missing packet and correct the situation, but at the expense of retransmitting the packet, which wastes time and bandwidth. The situation can be particularly bad for geographically remote locations which already experience high packet latency. If you habitually exceed your CIR, your provider may request or force you to increase the CIR for which you are subscribed.

5.1.2   Reviewing Frame Relay Concepts

Let's review what we've covered so far and add a few finishing details.

- Each **node** is connected via a piece of **access** to a **port** at your provider's **POP**. Your *node* is a **CPE** router.

- A **node** (or **CPE**) is designated by its **DLCI**, which is an integer used as an address.

- A **PVC** builds a path through your provider's network (the **cloud**) between two **nodes**.

- A **PVC** has a **CIR** associated with it. **CIR**s may be used to discard data being sent over the **PVC** when it exceeds predefined bandwidth limitations.

- **CIR**s are directional. If your provider indicates that they are not, ask whether a 64kbps **CIR** is 64kbps in *each* direction, or 32kbps in each direction. Different providers sell bandwidth differently.

- A **PVC** with the same **CIR** in each direction is said to have a **symmetrical CIR**. An **asymmetrical CIR** has a different data rate in each direction. This can be useful for sites which pull more traffic than they push, as is the case for sites which do a lot of Internet browsing.

- A node can **burst** at the **port speed**.

- A node is **oversubscribed** if it cannot satisfy the potential bandwidth requirements of the nodes attached to it.

For those of you who would like to know more about Frame Relay, there are numerous tutorials available on the web. As a starting point, visit *http://www.frforum.com/*. This is the home of *Frame Relay Forum*, an association of assorted commercial members who have an interest in promoting Frame Relay. They have a document for download called *The Basic Guide to Frame Relay Networking*. The 86-page document of general information is a bit cutesy, but useful nonetheless.

5.2   Linux WAN Adapters

For our purposes, a **WAN adapter** is an add-on card that is essentially the equivalent of an "async" port on a traditional router. These cards support WAN protocols such as Frame Relay, synchronous PPP, X.25, Bisync, HSSI, and others. They typically have their own processor to run the link-layer protocol on the card. This offloads this task from your system's CPU and simplifies the device drivers needed. When the card has a decoded frame available for the operating system, it triggers it via an interrupt and passes it to the device driver in the same way that an Ethernet card would. These WAN adapters connect to the outside world through a high-speed serial port (usually V.35 or RS-232), suitable for connecting to a CSU/DSU and then to a digital telco access circuit. Some cards are available with an integrated CSU/DSU so that they can be connected directly to a digital access circuit. The cards available now have between one and four ports and support speeds from 56kbps to 52Mbps.

Interfaces of this type offer several advantages over a simple data pump or modem. The first I've already mentioned: Since the link-layer protocol is being executed on the card itself, the host processor is free to do other things. (Because of this, zinc was able to handle a T1 running Frame Relay on a 66MHz 486-based system.) Second, the code run by the card's processor (the adapter's firmware) is stored on a EEPROM or similar device which is downloaded to the card when it is initialized. The upswing of this is that the link-layer protocol can be changed or upgraded simply by reinitializing the adapter with new firmware (and can take effect without your ever rebooting the router). Finally, in an emergency, almost anything can host these adapters, even your workstation.

This section lists manufacturers of cards who have Linux driver support (at the time of writing). Of these, I have experience only with the Sangoma products. When you start to research the card for your application, use these manufacturers as a starting point; they have solid reputations for providing Linux solutions.

5.2.1   Sangoma—The S508 and S514

Sangoma offers two WAN interface cards: the PCI-based S514 and its ISA-based predecessor, the S508. Currently, there is protocol support for running IP over Frame Relay, PPP, X.25, and Cisco HDLC. In the event that you do not want to be hindered by the limitations of TCP/IP, you can use the Bisync and HDLC LAPB API interfaces to develop your own protocol specific to your application. All of these protocols and cards are supported by their freely available *WANPIPE* software. As I mentioned, I have been a longtime user of Sangoma cards, and I've enjoyed working with them so much that I took over the Debian package of their driver utility software (called **wanpipe**). A brief rundown of the cards follows. For more information, visit *http://www.sangoma.com*.

- The S508 comes with two ports: a high-speed (up to E1 speeds, 2Mbps) port, and a second port which can run CHDLC (only) at up to 256kbps. The high-speed port uses a DB25 connector and a special cable to connect it to RS-232, V.35, EIA530, or X.21 external devices. The low-speed port uses a DB9 to connect to a RS-232 device. Internally, the card connects to a 16-bit ISA bus.

- The S5141 is the single-CPU version of the S514. Like the S508, it is a dual-port card. In this case, the high-speed port can handle link speeds up to 4Mbps, while the second port is limited to 512kbps.

- The S5142 is a quad-port, dual-CPU version of the S514. It is equivalent to two S5141 cards (i.e., two high-speed ports and two low-speed ports) but occupies a single slot.

- The S514/FT1 and S508/FT1 are variants of their respective cards with an integrated fractional T1 CSU/DSU. These cards come with a single port which connects to the digital access directly.

Hint: Integrated CSU/DSUs Save Money, Space, and Time

You should consider cards with integrated CSU/DSUs when ordering your router cards. The additional cost is less than that of the least expensive external CSU/DSU on the market. Because the integrated card connects directly to the demarc provided with your leased line, your installation is neater—fewer boxes, fewer cables, fewer power outlets. This allows for a tidy rack-mounted installation.

5.2.2 ImageStream

ImageStream Internet Solutions offers SDL Communications' adapters in combination with their Linux drivers. They also offer Linux-based routers, firewalls, and servers outfitted with these adapters. These systems run ImageStream's own Linux distribution (*Enterprise Linux*) which includes a full set of standard server daemons, including dynamic routing support for RIP2, OSPF, and BGP4. Linux standards such as IP masquerading and firewalling are, of course, accessible. All of their *All-in-One* offerings include redundant RAID disk configurations, and some are equipped with hot-pluggable components.

If you would rather build your own router, you can choose from a variety of adapters they offer, ranging from an ISA model with a single 2Mbps port up to PCI adapters with (eight) 8Mbps ports and dual-port HSSI-capable cards (52Mbps per port). If space is an issue, they have another line of 3U format CompactPCI adapters. Most cards are available with integrated CSU/DSUs.

All cards support the following protocols: PPP, HDLC, Frame Relay, X.25, and raw IP. Electrical interfaces are V.35, RS-232, RS-422 (EIA530 or X.21), and HSSI or T1 or DDS CSU/DSU (as appropriate). X.21 will be a welcome sight if your plans include deployment in areas other than the United States. You can visit ImageStream at *http://www.imagestream-is.com/*.

5.2.3 Cyclades

Cyclades has been a long-time player in the Linux market, offering high-density serial-port products with Linux driver support since the Linux 1.x days. They also produce Linux-based terminal servers and have sponsored several Open Source development efforts. In the Linux-WAN world their offering is the PC300 card, a standard PCI adapter card that comes in a variety of flavors and is capable of driving up to a pair of T1/E1s, depending on the exact model of the card you purchase. Similar to other cards, the PC300 supports PPP, Frame Relay, Cisco HDLC, and X.25 via RS-232, V.35, X.21, or integrated CSU/DSUs. The card is also available in a PMC (PCI Mezzanine Card) format for use in ruggedized applications. More details on the PC300 can be found at *http://www.cyclades.com/*. (Don't confuse Cyclades' PR router products, which run their CyROS embedded OS product on PowerPC chips with the PC300, which is the add-on adapter with Linux support.)

5.2.4   Gcom

Gcom, Inc. offers an add-on card for ISA and PCI architectures supporting up to four ports. In addition to Linux, they support several other commercial x86 Unix flavors. They also have some heavy-duty protocol support for those who need to interface systems using link protocols other than Frame Relay or PPP. Taken from their website, they support:

- Frame Relay, X.25, and SDLC/HDLC

- SNA LU0, LU2, LU4, LU6.2 over SDLC or QLLC/X.25

- LAPB, LAPD, and LLC

- Available upon request are Bisync and X.3, X.28, X.29 PAD protocols

In addition to producing these boards and driver software, they champion and host the Linux implementation of STREAMS, known as *LiS*. This source is released primarily under the LGPL (the less restrictive library version of the GNU Public License). (Cool!) It is implemented as a Linux kernel module, with drivers for use above or below the IP stack—i.e., it can use an existing device driver and present a DLPI interface to another STREAMS driver (above the IP stack), or it can interface a STREAMS device driver to the IP stack (below). (Very cool!) For more information on their boards, protocol support, or *LiS*, visit Gcom's website at *http://www.gcom.com/*.

5.2.5   Emerging Technologies

Emerging Technologies produces PCI adapters and drivers and bandwidth management software for Linux and FreeBSD. Like so many others, they have the good taste to release their driver source to the public. Their products include:

- The ET/PCISYNC, a PCI interface card which supports up to four T1 ports running PPP, Frame Relay, or Cisco HDLC.

- The ET/HSSI, also a PCI card which can support two 52Mbps HSSI links on a single card.

- If you would like a complete routers solution, you can purchase one of their ET/R1000 or ET/R1500 systems. These use the cards mentioned above and come preconfigured to dual-boot Linux and FreeBSD.

- They also offer *ET/BWMGR*, their *Bandwidth Manager* software, used to throttle bandwidth used by addresses or interfaces. The software is provided free of charge to those who purchase one of the synchronous adapters or prepackaged solutions, but potentially has applications beyond those in conjunction with their cards.

Router Physical Installation

Once you have your router loaded with a basic Linux install and have installed your interface card(s), you need to find a good place to put it. Physical installation is often a secondary thought, but is important with WAN routers for several reasons.

- If you have an integrated CSU/DSU, you should be within 40 meters (133 feet) of the demarc installed by your access provider—less if they installed a smart-jack which is run over a twisted-pair to somewhere else in the building. If you cannot be within this distance, you will need to program your CSU/DSU to compensate for the drop in signal strength (attenuation) due to the distance. This setting is known as **LBO**, Line Build Out.

- If you have an external CSU/DSU, take into consideration the length of the V.35 cables that run between the CSU/DSU and the router. If possible, make sure that you can move the PC without having to reposition the CSU/DSU. (Otherwise, you might find yourself there late at night trying to hold three things at once.)

- Most technicians value *function over form*, as do I, but a neat installation is worthwhile. If you ever have problems with your access circuit, you might receive a visit from your local access provider. An accessible, clean installation will make it easier for these people to test the circuit and minimize the chance that they trip over that dangling wire you have been meaning to do something about for so long.

You can contact them at *http://www.etinc.com/*. As a side note, their Linux routers run *zebra*, a dynamic routing daemon, which is introduced in Section 9.4.2 in Chapter 9.

5.3   Linux and *WANPIPE* for Frame Relay

In this section we build a Frame Relay router using Linux, a Sangoma S508, and Sangoma's *WANPIPE* software. We will assume that the link has been ordered and correctly provisioned by our Frame Relay provider and that the link on the other side is up and running, waiting for our router to come online and complete the project. (If this is not the case, configuring two Linux routers for Frame Relay is not any more difficult than configuring the first one.) The first time through the configuration is presented as a quickstart. For those who are experienced with Linux and Frame Relay, this should be enough to attach to the cloud and start routing. The sections following the quickstart cover the configuration in more detail, and Section 5.3.2 explains *WANPIPE's* main configuration file line by line.

5.3.1   Frame Relay Router Quickstart

Here is a recipe for zinc using Sangoma's *WANPIPE* software as it is distributed from their site, and as such, suitable for all Linux distributions. It's worth noting that the great tossed salad of Linux distributions out there does make things more difficult for commercial vendors who write software for the Linux community. It's evident that the developers at Sangoma have taken pains to make this process as easy and foolproof as possible.

WANPIPE **Quickstart**

1. Retrieve the latest *WANPIPE* tarball from *ftp://ftp.sangoma.com/linux/current_wanpipe/* and extract it using `tar xzvf tarball` in the root directory of your filesystem.

2. Execute the script `/usr/local/wanrouter/Setup install`. This script checks to make sure that your system has the requisite tools, applies the kernel patches as necessary, and then builds the module and binary tools, if it can. If it cannot, it will indicate what tools should be installed on the system so that it can.

3. If your kernel needs to be recompiled, you'll be instructed on how to do so. After you've built the new kernel, reboot.

4. Invoke */usr/local/wanrouter/wancfg* to have the curses-based tool walk you through the creation of the configuration files required for your router. You should end up with:

   - */usr/local/wanrouter/wanrouter.rc*

   - */usr/local/wanrouter/wanpipe1.conf*

   - and one interface file for each PVC on your Frame Relay link in the */usr/local/ wanrouter/interfaces/* directory

5. Start your link with `/usr/sbin/wanrouter start`. Add routes as appropriate.

You can check the progress of the startup by looking at the output in */var/log/wanrouter* and */var/log/messages*. You should also be able to `ifconfig` *wan_interface* to see that your interface is up. If your link did not come up immediately and the logfiles do not indicate the problem, you can use *fpipemon* to glean loads of information about the link and what might be wrong (see Section 5.4.3 for more details about using this command). If you're still not up and running, read over the next few sections, especially the detailed configuration information starting with Section 5.3.2, to see if you can spot the problem.

Hey, What-All Did *Setup* **Do to My System?!?**

If you experienced some nervousness while letting the *Setup* do its thing, this is the healthy byproduct of not wanting one piece of software on your router to adversely affect another. One thing experience has taught me is that subsystem components should be as orthogonal as is possible. In other words, installing package *x* shouldn't break seemingly unrelated package *y*. In the case of *WANPIPE*, you're going to end up with some patches against your kernel source tree, so make a backup beforehand if you're worried. Next you'll get a handful of binaries dropped into */usr/sbin/*. Finally, you'll get an initialization script dropped into */etc/init.d/* (or similar) along with the corresponding links in */etc/rc2.d/* (or its analog on your distribution). Everything else stays neatly under */usr/local/wanrouter/*, as it should. (By the way, when I gave `./Setup remove` a test run, it left the binaries in */usr/sbin/*. This isn't a serious problem by any means, but the moral is to take the the time to know what third-party software does before you install it.)

During the heyday of the 1.2 and 2.0 kernels there was a lot of fluctuation in the kernel, and seemingly less coordination between the driver authors and the kernel authors/maintainers.

The 2.2 series did a good job of putting the brakes on the chaos of constant change. The vote's still out on 2.4, but so far, it feels like we're back to days of greater volatility. When a new patch level of the kernel is released, Sangoma has to test their drivers, make any necessary changes, and potentially release a new set of patches. Because of this, *WANPIPE* is distributed along with a set of kernel patches and the source code for the utilities (which would need to be compiled by the end user against their specific version of the kernel).

Issues such as this make it relatively difficult for vendors to distribute precompiled binaries for Linux. (Let's not even get into glibc versions and sensitivity to the version of the ld.so, the linker loader.) The beauty of Linux, of course, is that the price you pay for all its flexibility is merely a bit of disk space for the compilers and tools required to build your own binaries. Even though there is added complexity, and therefore more to break, it's hard to beat openness when things don't go as planned.

5.3.2   Editing *wanpipe1.conf* **for Frame Relay**

Once you install the Sangoma card, build your system, and load the software, you need to configure it to correspond to the settings for your Frame Relay link. The configuration file that controls this is *wanpipeN.conf*, where *N* is the *n*th Sangoma card in your system. For our purposes (a single card), this is *wanpipe1.conf*. (If you are familiar with *WANPIPE*, this file was named *router.conf* until the 2.1 release.) This file can be created using the *wancfg* utility, which provides detailed help on the meaning of each parameter. We're going to cover the format of the file so you'll understand what's going on beneath the covers in case you'd like to edit by hand. The default install location for this file is in */usr/local/wanrouter/*, although you might find it under */etc/wanpipe/* with older versions of the software. The file controls:

- Physical parameters about the Sangoma card, such as the type of interface to the CSU/DSU, the baudrate of the port, and the interrupt of the card.

- The firmware loaded during card initialization (and therefore the WAN link-layer protocol) to run on the card.

- The name(s) of the interface(s) to be created by the kernel to correspond to the link(s) configured for this card: *wan0*, *wan1*, and so on ....

- Special parameters about those interfaces. For example, do they allow multicast? Should they try to adhere to a provider's CIR?

wanpipe1.conf's **Structure**

The file might seem a little imposing at first, but it is easy to follow once you understand the different sections and how they chain together. The format is very similar to that of an *.ini* file used on other operating systems. The sections are denoted by keywords enclosed in [ ]s. Comments start with the # character and continue to the end of the line.

The file has a hierarchy with two main sections, [devices] and [interfaces]. Both of these sections must appear, and each contains one line for each device or interface you would like to configure, respectively. For each line (i.e., device or interface) in these two sections, there will be a subsection later in the file denoted by the *name* of the device or interface. A brief example of the format should make this clear. In the mock *wanpipe1.conf* file below, there is one **device** and two **interfaces**.

```
[devices]
# this machine contains one device/physical card, wanpipe1
wanpipe1
.
.
.

[interfaces]
# there are two interfaces
wan0
wan1

[wanpipe1]
# configuration settings for the physical device wanpipe1
.
.
.

[wan0]
# settings for the interface wan0
.
.
.

[wan1]
# settings for the interface wan1
.
.
.
```

wanpipe1.conf—[devices]

A **device** in this case refers to a physical Sangoma card. In previous versions of *WANPIPE*, the number entries in the [device] section would correspond to the number of S508 or S514 cards in your system. Starting with *WANPIPE* version 2.1, you no longer configure more than one device in this file, but instead create another *wanpipeN.conf* file.

If you do have multiple cards, you must name the cards (and configuration files) *wanpipeN*, where ($1 \leq N \leq 8$), and you must number these **consecutively!** On the device line, you also specify the protocol that the card will be running. You may optionally include a comment which will appear in your system logfiles during startup and shutdown. For a system running Frame Relay the [devices] section looks like:

```
# start the [devices] section
[devices]
wanpipe1 = WAN_FR, myframecircuit - cktid MCI ZAW828360001, DLCI 100
# end [devices]
```

wanpipe1.conf—[interfaces]

An **interface** refers to the entity used by the kernel to communicate over the link. This can be a source of confusion, as many people commonly refer to these as **devices**. Just remember that an interface is an entity similar to *eth0*—it can support routes, have different subnet masks, etc.

A single Frame Relay device (or **port**) may have multiple PVCs configured in the provider's network. On your router, each of these PVCs is an **interface** in *wanpipe1.conf*. These interfaces behave like point-to-point interfaces with an IP at each end, except that you address the remote endpoint here by specifying the corresponding DLCI in the configuration file. Think of this as indicating the link-layer address at the remote end, although we'll find out that this is not how your Frame Relay provider refers to them. Once you take care of this here, the interfaces are addressed by IP with respect to the rest of the operating system. For a location with two PVCs, the [interfaces] section looks like this:

```
# wanpipe1.conf for location A
#
# start the [interfaces] section
[interfaces]
#intf = device,   DLCI, WANPIPE, comment
#----   ------    ----  -------  ------------------------------
wan0  = wanpipe1, 200,  WANPIPE, location A <-> location B PVC
wan1  = wanpipe1, 300,  WANPIPE, location A <-> location C PVC
# end [interfaces]
```

In the above file, frames addressed to DLCI 200 will be routed by the Frame Relay switch to location *B*, while frames addressed to DLCI 300 will go to location *C*. When the link is up and *WANPIPE* is running, you add routes to location *B* via interface *wan0*, and routes to location *C* via interface *wan1*.

Whose DLCI Is It, Anyway?

The preceding example configuration indicates that location *A* needs to address frames to DLCI 200 to get them to location *B*. From the information given, we cannot tell what the locations *B* and *C* will have in their configuration files to send frames to location *A*. Perhaps they both *call* location *A* DLCI 100, maybe not. This is because DLCIs have only *local* significance—i.e., your router sees only the DLCIs presented to it by the provider's switch at your POP.

This means the DLCI only has meaning for your router and the switch at your provider's POP, and *not* that DLCI 200 is the "address of the node at location *B*" in any absolute sense. The concept is simple, but the implications can be confusing. For example, your provider could quite easily set up the switch at location *B* to use DLCI 200 to refer to the PVC that transmits frames to location *A*. In this case, both configuration files would list DLCI 200 as the media address to access the remote site. This situation is depicted in Figure 5.3, where site *B* accesses site *C* via 600, and site *C* accesses site *B* via 600. But site *A* accesses site *B* via 200, and vice versa. To make things even more confusing, site *A* accesses site *C* via 300.

For this reason, I ask my provider to supply a unique DLCI for each router, but to reuse the same DLCI for routers that have more than one PVC. In other words, the switches at locations *B* and *C* both refer to location *A* by the same DLCI. This, in essence, gives each router its own DLCI (or address) and is an intuitive way to approach the matter. (See Figure 5.4.) Now, no matter what node you configure to talk to location *A*, it uses the same DLCI to get there.

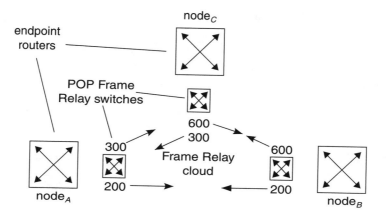

Figure 5.3 A Potentially Confusing Way to Allocate DLCIs

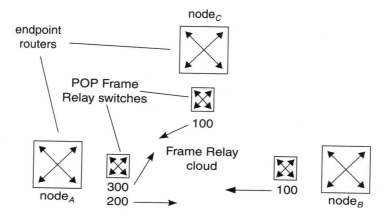

Figure 5.4 A More Intuitive Way to Allocate DLCIs

The [wanpipe1] Device Configuration

OK, both the top-level sections in *wanpipe1.conf* are complete. But remember that there is a subsection for every named **device** which details the physical attributes of the Sangoma card and other characteristics of the link that are applicable to the link/port as a whole. An example for a 512kb Frame Relay link on a Sangoma S508 connected to a CSU/DSU with a V.35 follows:

```
[wanpipe1]   ###### Sample Frame Relay Configuration ########
             ### ----- Hardware configuration ------------###
IOPort       = 0x360    # I/O port base              (S508 only)
IRQ          = 12       # interrupt request level    (S508 only)
#S514CPU     = A        # S514 PCI Card CPU: A or B   (S514 only)
#PCISlot     = 0        # PCI Slot num: 0 for autodetect (S514 only)
#Memaddr     = 0xD0000  # commented out enables auto memory selection

             ### ----- Adapter firmware for Frame Relay --###
Firmware     = /usr/local/wanrouter/firmware/fr514.sfm

             ### ----- Physical interface configuration --###
Interface    = V35      # physical interface type, RS232/V35
Clocking     = External # Tx/Rx clock source, {External|Internal}
BaudRate     = 512000   # data transfer rate in bps, 1200..20480000

             ### ----- Media-specific configuration ------###
MTU          = 1600     # maximum data transfer unit, bytes
UDPPORT      = 9000     # for UDP management

             ### ----- Protocol specific configuration ---###

Station      = CPE      # station type, {CPE|Node}
Signalling   = ANSI     # In-channel signalling {ANSI|LMI|Q933}
#NUMBER_OF_DLCI = 2     # (for "Node" operation only)
T391         = 10       # Link Integrity Verification Timer
T392         = 15       # Polling Verification Timer
N391         = 6        # Full Status Polling Cycle Counter
N392         = 3        # Error Threshold Counter
N393         = 4        # Monitored Events Counter
TTL          = 0x7F     # Time To Live parameter for UDP packets
```

What does it all mean? Let's define each of the keywords, with the keywords grouped as they are in the configuration file.

Hardware Configuration Portion of *wanpipe1.conf*

These values apply to the adapter itself and how it will interact with the host computer.

IOPort—This is the base address of the S508 adapter. It must be set using the jumpers on the card, and each card must have a unique address. (The default is 0x360.) Be sure to change the jumper setting on the second and subsequent cards if you have multiple cards. If you suspect an ioport conflict, check */proc/ioports* for ports already in use. This parameter is required, but only for S508 cards.

IRQ—This is the interrupt the card will use to notify the device driver that it needs to be serviced. Whatever you specify here is the interrupt that the card will try to use. A listing of interrupts already taken can be found in */proc/interrupts*. (If you ever receive an `interrupt counter test failed` message in *syslog* related to *WANPIPE*, you have selected an interrupt already in use.) This parameter is also required and is applicable only to S508 cards.

S514CPU—This is the CPU to be used—either `A` or `B`—applicable only to S514 cards. Unless you purchased an additional CPU, use `A`.

PCISlot—This is the PCI slot number of the S514 card. For a router with a single Sangoma card, always use `0`. For multiple Sangoma cards, the driver needs to know which of these cards corresponds to this configuration file (this wasn't a problem with the S508, because the jumpers set the base address). Refer to Sangoma's documentation for setting this value. (The process is a little complicated and may soon be changed.)

Firmware—This is the absolute path to the software which will be loaded onto the onboard processor at initialization time. For the default Sangoma distribution, it can be found in */usr/local/wanrouter/firmware/*.

Memaddr—This is the value of the (dual) memory port that the device driver uses to access adapter memory. The autoselection performed during driver initialization works well under Linux, and I have never had to use this parameter.

Physical Interface Configuration Portion of *wanpipe1.conf*

This [`wanpipe1`] section controls how the adapter talks to the outside world (i.e., the CSU/DSU).

Interface—This must either be `RS232` or `V35` and is dictated by the type of external CSU/DSU you have. Notice that there is no '.' in `V35`.

Clocking—This determines whether or not the Sangoma card should generate the clocking signal for the CSU/DSU (`Internal` clocking). It must be either `External` or `Internal`. Typically, the CSU/DSU slaves its clock off the signal on the access line, so this parameter should always be set to `External`. (The only time that you might want to change this is if you were in a lab environment testing a back-to-back configuration.)

BaudRate—This value is set to your **port speed** (in bps) provided by your Frame Relay provider and corresponds to the CSU/DSU configuration for the number of channels times 56 or 64kbps. (Remember that this might not be equal to the access speed.) The parameter is required.

Media-Specific Configuration Portion of *wanpipe1.conf*

This section specifies link-layer protocol attributes required for negotiation with the port at your Frame Relay provider. Some of these parameters control how often your router will send/expects status information to/from your provider's equipment. Finally, there are a few additional parameters related to the *fpipemon* monitoring utility. Here is a rundown of what they mean.

MTU—This is the maximum data transfer unit in bytes. It is equivalent to the MTU setting for an Ethernet or other network device.

Station—This is your router's station type. This must be set to CPE (Customer Premise Equipment) unless you are running a back-to-back configuration (without a provider), in which case you set it to Node. It is required.

Signalling—In the Frame Relay world, there are several different types of signalling used to communicate between your router and your provider's equipment at the POP. This value can be ANSI, LMI, or Q933. Your provider should specify the type of signalling you should use when you order your link. When in doubt, try ANSI.

T391 [range 5–30, default is 10]—This is the Link Integrity Verification Timer (in seconds). It asks the question, "How often do we check to see if the link is still good?" It applies only to routers with the Station parameter configured to be CPE.

T392 [range 5–30, default is 15]—This is the Polling Verification Timer (in seconds). It is applicable only to routers with the Station parameter set to Node.

N391 [range 1–255, default is 6]—This is the Full Status Polling Cycle Counter, and it is applicable only to **CPE** routers.

N392 [range 1–10, default is 3]—The Error Threshold Counter is the limit of the number of consecutive Status Enquiry Message exchange failures before the link is marked *inactive*. In other words, it controls how many times we'll let something bad happen before we'll start complaining about it. It is applicable to both **CPE** and **Node** Station types.

N393 [range 1–10, default is 4]—This refers to The Monitored Events Counter. When a network becomes active, you need *N393* successful exchanges of Status Enquiry Messages (keepalives) before the link is considered *active*. Like N392, it is applicable to both **CPE** and **Node** Station types.

NUMBER_OF_DLCI [range 0–100, default is 0]—This is the number of DLCIs on the network. This is not necessary for normal CPE links and should not be used for **CPE** Station types. It is useful only for back-to-back configurations.

UDPPORT [range 1–65534, default is 9000]—This is the UDP port used by the various pipemon programs to talk to the drivers. You should change it only if you have already committed to using port 9000 for some other service. Note that if you do not specify this value, the driver will default to using 0, which is probably not what you want. (It would be more correct to say that the "normal" value is 9000.)

TTL [range 0x01–0xFF, default is 0x7F]—This is the Time To Live parameter for the UDP packets being sent to and from the **UDPPORT** in the previous setting. This is a security feature of *WANPIPE*, as it limits the distance (in network hops) from which you can run the monitoring programs. The lower the TTL, the *closer* (in terms of hops) you need to be in order to be able to access the monitoring port. If you are too far away, you can send to the monitoring port, but replies will be discarded by the network before they reach you.

Logical Interface Configuration Portion of *wanpipe1.conf*

Before you heave a sigh of relief, there is still one more section of the file. Remember that each named [interface] requires its own section, delimited by the name of the interface. For our example file, we have interfaces *wan0* and *wan1*.

```
[wan0]
# wan0 interface specific information (Frame Relay)
MULTICAST           = NO        # Multicast Enabled?   (YES/NO)
CIR                 = 16        # Committed Information Rate   1 - 512 kbps
BC                  = 16        # Committed Burst Size         1 - 512 kbits
BE                  = 0         # Excess Burst Size            0 - 512 kbits
INARP               = NO        # Inverse ARP Requests?        (YES/NO)
INARPINTERVAL       = 0         # sec. between INARP requests - default 10
DYN_INTR_CFG        = NO        # auto determine interface state?
TRUE_ENCODING_TYPE = NO         # lie to libpcap about link encoding?


[wan1]
# wan1 interface specific information (Frame Relay)
# (nothing to say, since the parameters settings are optional)
# but do not omit the [wan1] part so the file parses correctly
```

The interface-specific section sets up parameters unique to an individual Frame Relay PVC. These parameters apply to either IP configuration.

CIR [range 1–512, default 16]—This is the Committed Information Rate in kbps. It limits how quickly the interface will transmit data when it has a large amount of data to send. If this parameter is used, **BC** and **BE** must be set also. Otherwise, you should comment out all three lines (**CIR**, **BC**, and **BE**). Because your provider may deal with network congestion by discarding packets which exceed your CIR (see the discussion of CIR on page 138), you may want to use this parameter to throttle transmission at your router to prevent packet loss and retransmission.

BC [range 1–512, default 16]—This is the Committed Burst Size in kbits (do not forget to multiply the kB/sec by 8 to get kbits/sec). This is the number of bits that the interface knows it will try to send to the CIR before it starts counting using the next parameter, **BE**. When used, this value is nearly always set to the CIR.

BE [range 0–512, default 0]—This is the Excess Burst Size in kbits (once again, watch your bits and bytes). Once **BC** kbits have been sent to the **CIR**, your interface will try to sneak in many more kbits before throttling itself to honor the **CIR**.

MULTICAST [YES or NO, default is NO]—This indicates whether or not to accept packets with a multicast source address. Setting this to **YES** indicates that you allow multicast on your WAN.

INARP [YES or NO, default is NO]—Should this interface periodically send INverse ARP requests? The purpose of inverse ARP is for an interface at one end of PVC to learn the IP of the interface at the other end of the PVC. (In general, the idea is to learn the **protocol address** of the interface on the other end—it doesn't have to be an IP address.) Inverse ARP is a type of ARP because both sides know the DLCI to reach the other end (analogous to the MAC address for Ethernet). Using Inverse ARP, they can learn of the IP(s) of interfaces at the other end of the PVC.[3]

INARPINTERVAL [0–65535, default 10]—If **INARP** is set to **YES**, this parameter indicates the number of seconds between the transmission of these requests. 0 indicates that they should never be sent.

DYN_INTR_CFG [YES or NO, default is NO]—Should the interface be marked administratively down if the physical link (between the Sangoma card and the CSU/DSU, or the T1 itself in the case of an integrated CSU/DSU) is detected down? This is here to help SNMP-based monitoring to detect a link-down condition, since it merely goes by the interface state in the kernel. (This is equivalent to setting up a monitor that will `ifconfig` *intf* `up|down` to reflect the physical state of the local link. If this is enabled and the link is administratively up, that doesn't necessarily mean that communications are OK. There could be a problem at the other end. But it will help indicate that there is a local problem.

TRUE_ENCODING_TYPE [YES or NO, default is NO]—Should the interface report its true link-layer protocol to the kernel? The default is NO, which sets the protocol type to raw/pure IP. The upshot is that tools based on *libpcap* will be able to sniff the interface because it's simply a raw IP device. The downside is that autoconfiguration of link type may not be possible (and might be required if you don't own the other end). Leave this as NO until you are forced to do otherwise.

Minimal Frame Relay *wanpipe1.conf*

Let's trim some of the comments and optional parameters and see how our *wanpipe1.conf* looks.

```
# /etc/wanpipe/wanpipe1.conf (for Frame Relay)
############################################

[devices]
wanpipe1 = WAN_FR, myframecircuit - cktid (my DLCI)

[interfaces]
wan0  = wanpipe1, 200, WANPIPE, loc A <-> loc B PVC
wan1  = wanpipe1, 300, WANPIPE, loc A <-> loc C PVC

[wanpipe1]
IOPort        = 0x360      # I/O port base (jumper setting)
IRQ           = 12         # IRQ (software selectable)
Firmware      = /usr/lib/wanpipe/fr514.sfm
Interface     = V35        # physical interface: RS232/V35
Clocking      = External   # clock source: External/Internal
BaudRate      = 512000     # port speed in bps
Station       = CPE        # station type: CPE/Node
Signalling    = ANSI       # signalling: ANSI/LMI/Q933
UDPPORT       = 9000       # required because the default is 0
```

---

[3]See RFC 2390 for more information about INARP.

```
# interface specific configuration
[wan0]
[wan1]


# end of /etc/wanpipe/wanpipe1.conf
#####################################
```

5.3.3   *interface* Files for Frame Relay

Our link is almost completely configured, but there is still the matter of configuring the interfaces with the IP addresses for their point-to-point connection to the other end of the PVC. If you are accustomed to other Frame Relay router configurations, you may think that this step is optional. Theoretically, you needn't have IP addresses assigned to each of the Frame Relay interfaces—the Frame Relay cloud knows where to route your packets (based on the DLCIs and PVC). However, when you are using *WANPIPE*, you need to assign each end of each PVC an IP address. This is so the kernel can treat these interfaces just like any other point-to-point interface with respect to routing, displaying its properties with *ifconfig*, etc.

Each end of the PVC is issued an IP address, and the PVC itself can be treated like a network with only two nodes. (In fact, you can configure the point-to-point link to be a network with zero nodes by specifying a subnet mask of 255.255.255.255. See Section 5.3.4 for more information on this method.) For each interface in [interfaces] there is a file bearing its name in */etc/wanpipe/interfaces/* or */usr/lib/router/interfaces/* for non-Debian. For our example file, that means */etc/wanpipe/interfaces/wan0* and */etc/wanpipe/interfaces/wan1*. Looking into this file, you will find:

```
DEVICE=wan0
ONBOOT=yes
IPADDR=192.168.20.2
NETMASK=255.255.255.255
POINTOPOINT=192.168.20.3
GATEWAY=
```

The file is **sourced** by the startup script, which means that the file must follow basic Bourne shell syntax. (Actually you do not need to worry much about the syntax, since *wancfg* will create the file for you.) The parameters are:

DEVICE—The device name.

ONBOOT [yes or no]—This can be used to temporarily disable an interface upon startup without having to remove it from *wanpipe1.conf*. Otherwise, it should be **yes**.

IPADDR—The IP address of your side of the point-to-point link representing the PVC.

NETMASK—The netmask of the *network* between the two routers. (More on this in Section 5.3.4.)

POINTOPOINT—The IP address of the router on the other side of your PVC. Your counterpart should have the same values reversed.

GATEWAY—A gateway address which will be used to configure a default route, if it's specified.

5.3.4   Saving Time with Zero-Node Networks

When I first started deploying Frame Relay links, I used subnets carved out of the 172.16.*.* private address space with 255.255.255.252 subnet masks. After setting up and maintaining these links for a while, I found this small IP *network* between the Frame Relay routers to be an annoyance. Let's call these *frnets* for this discussion. Specifically, I encountered these problems.

- First, you have to go to the trouble of assigning some IP address space and noting its usage so that it does not pop up somewhere else in your network. Extra documenta- tion ....

- Second, if you want to *traceroute* over a link end-to-end, the traceroute command will want to be able to find the *frnet* (so that it does not print out '*'s). This means that there must be routing-table entries for the *frnet* on (almost) every router in your network. If you use static routes, extra routing-table entries mean real work.

- You'll need to update your DNS maps—possibly create entirely new zones, both forward and reverse (or at a minimum reverse). If you don't, and you forget to specify the −n switch to *traceroute*, then you will have to wait for DNS lookups for the IPs in the *frnet* to time out.

My solution was to take a pair of IP addresses from the Ethernet subnet on one side of the link. (The choice of side is arbitrary—I took the addresses from the remote side, since it was typically a smaller office.) The convention is to reserve addresses .2 and .3 for the point-to-point link. For example, if the remote office is subnet 192.168.18.0/24, the hub side of the point-to- point receives 192.168.18.2, and the remote gets 192.168.18.3. To complete the configuration, assign a subnet mask of 255.255.255.255 (/32) to both interfaces when you configure them.

From this we can coin the term **zero-node network**, since this includes nothing but the IP address of the interface—not even the interface on the other end of the link. However, the configuration works well. If you are running *WANPIPE* on both ends of your link, try it and see. The situation looks something like that depicted in Figure 5.5. This configuration has these advantages:[4]

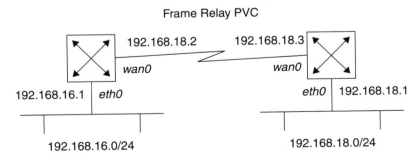

Figure 5.5 Frame Relay PVC Using a Zero-Node Network

---

[4]Actually, you may be able to get away with even fewer IPs—you'll see this later on page 318.

1. Configuring DNS maps for location *B* either has already been done or is on your to-do list. You can quickly modify the reverse DNS zone for location *B* (18.168.192.in-addr.arpa) to have meaningful names for the ends of the PVC, such as

```
1.18.168.192          IN      PTR          frlocB.yourdomain.com.
2.18.168.192          IN      PTR          pvc100-200.yourdomain.com.
3.18.168.192          IN      PTR          pvc200-100.yourdomain.com.
```

Having these items in DNS also helps any IP-based authentication mechanism which utilized reverse lookups.

2. Packets to and from the point-to-point IPs will be recognizable to all by their IP addresses.

3. Say that you are logged onto router *B* and want to talk to a workstation in network *A*. You know the route to subnet *A*—it is out over the Frame Relay link. This means that your packets will have a source address of 192.168.18.3 (not 192.168.18.1, as some may assume). When the workstation in network goes to reply, it can easily find 192.168.18.3, since this is just one of the machines in location *B*. (If you had used a separate network for the link, then the workstation in *A* might not have been able to find you as quickly, or not at all.)

4. You have potentially saved a routing-table entry for every PVC in your network, on every router in your network.

5. You have saved at least 4 IP addresses (one for each node plus the network address and the broadcast address). If IP addresses are in short supply for some reason, this becomes meaningful.

5.3.5   Starting *WANPIPE*

If you are like I am, then you are probably too impatient to read the documentation before trying something. You can test your configuration with /etc/init.d/wanrouter start or /usr/sbin/wanrouter start. If your link comes up, great! If it does not, we'll need to do some troubleshooting. First of all, let's review what the *WANPIPE* startup script does.

1. Reads the contents of *[wan]router.rc* into the environment. This file tells *WANPIPE* where to find certain files and whether or not it should start the router at all.

2. Checks to see if **$ROUTER_LOCK** exists. If it does, then *WANPIPE* is currently running and should be stopped before restarting.

3. Calls the function router_up(), which logs all of its output to **$ROUTER_LOG**. router_up() does the following:

   (a) Checks to see if the configuration files for each of the $WAN_DEVICES exist in $WANPIPE_CONF_DIR. Obviously, whatever is not present is not started.

   (b) Checks to see if $ROUTER_BOOT is set to **NO**. If it is, then *WANPIPE* does not start.

(c) Loads each module in $WAN_DRIVERS, checking first to make sure that the module is not already loaded. The results of the *modprobe* are noted with either *ok* (success) or *fail* (failure) in the logfile. The script will fail automatically if $WAN_DRIVERS is an empty string.

(d) Calls *wanconfig* with *wanpipe1.conf* (and others) as an argument. This is the point where the interfaces listed in [interfaces] are created.

(e) Looks in $IFCONF_DIR to find the IP configuration for each of the interfaces. When *wanconfig* creates an interface and successfully registers it with the kernel, an entry is created in */proc/net/dev*. The script checks each interface file $IFCONF_DIR; when it finds a match in */proc/net/dev*, it calls the function interface_up for that interface.

(f) interface_up reads the interface file (previously discussed in Section 5.3.3) and uses the values therein to *ifconfig* the interface with the values in $IPADDR, $NETMASK, and $POINTOPOINT address.

(g) A host route for the $POINTOPOINT interface is added to the kernel routing table with *route*.[5]

(h) A default network route is added over the $GATEWAY (if it is set).

Starting *WANPIPE*—Loading Modules

Now that you know what is supposed to happen, we can talk about what can go wrong. The loading of the driver modules must occur. If the modules are not found in */lib/modules/ version/net* (2.2 kernels) or */lib/modules/version/kernel/drivers/net* (2.4 kernels), or are compiled for the wrong version of the kernel, you will have to take some corrective action.

In the first case, perhaps you neglected to perform the last step in kernel compilation, make modules_install. It could be that you have built the kernel but *depmod* has not been run since the kernel build. *depmod* normally runs during system startup, so one way to ensure that it occurs is to reboot your system. This should also correct the second problem, as long as you boot from the same place where lilo is writing your kernel (are you using make zlilo during your kernel build?). When the modules are loaded, the output of *lsmod* should look like the output below:

WANPIPE modules for the 2.2.x kernel

Module	Size	Used by	
wanpipe	124148	1	
wanrouter	7940	2	[wanpipe]
sdladrv	12768	0	[wanpipe]
syncppp	9004	0	[wanpipe]

After the modules load, *syslog* should contain messages like:

```
zinc kernel: Cronyx Ltd, Synchronous PPP and CISCO HDLC (c) 1994
zinc kernel: Linux port (c) 1998 Building Number Three Ltd & Jan "Yenya" Kasprzak.
zinc kernel: SDLA Support Module v3.0 (c) 1995-1999 Sangoma Technologies Inc.
zinc kernel: Sangoma WANPIPE Router v1.1 (c) 1995-2000 Sangoma Technologies Inc.
zinc kernel: WANPIPE(tm) Multiprotocol Driver v5.0 (c) 1995-2000 Sangoma Technologies Inc.
zinc kernel: wanpipe: Probing for WANPIPE hardware.
zinc kernel: wanpipe: S508-ISA card found, port 0x360
zinc kernel: wanpipe: Allocating maximum 2 devices: wanpipe1 - wanpipe2.
zinc kernel: wanpipe1: Starting WAN Setup
```

---

[5]Kernel 2.0 systems only.

Starting *WANPIPE—wanconfig*

wanconfig must read and parse *wanpipe1.conf* and configure the card and drivers with this information. It logs its output in the $ROUTER_LOG, so any errors in the format of the file will show up there. If all goes well, you should have the following in */var/log/wanrouter*:

```
Mon Nov 12 16:56:23 MST 2001: starting WAN router
Loading driver wanpipe ... ok
Starting up device: wanpipe1
WAN Router Configurator. v2.1.0 (c) 1995-1999 Sangoma Technologies Inc.
 * Parsing configuration file /usr/local/wanrouter/wanpipe1.conf ...
 * Reading section [devices]...
 * Reading section [wanpipe1]...
 * Reading section [interfaces]...
 * wan0 to be used by WANPIPE
 * Reading section [wan0]...
 * Configuring device wanpipe1 (Comment)
 * Setting IOPORT to 0x360
 * Setting IRQ to 7
 * Reading 25084 bytes from /usr/local/wanrouter/firmware/fr514.sfm ...
 * Setting INTERFACE to V35
 * Setting CLOCKING to External
 * Setting BAUDRATE to 1540000
 * Setting MTU to 1500
 * Setting UDPPORT to 9000
 * Setting NUMBER_OF_DLCI to 1
 * Setting STATION to CPE
 * Setting SIGNALLING to ANSI
 * Setting T391 to 10
 * Setting T392 to 16
 * Setting N391 to 2
 * Setting N392 to 3
 * Setting N393 to 4
 * Setting TTL to 255
 * Reading DLCI(s) Included : 16
 * Configuring channel wan0 (WANPIPE). Media address: 16
 * Setting MULTICAST to NO
 * Setting INARP to NO
 * Setting INARPINTERVAL to 0
 * Setting TRUE_ENCODING_TYPE to NO
 * Setting DYN_INTR_CFG to NO
```

The activities of *wanconfig* also generate messages in *syslog*. A loaded session (*sans* the output created by the modules noted above) has information that looks like the following:

```
zinc kernel: Processing WAN device wanpipe1...
zinc kernel: sdladrv: found S5080 card at port 0x360.
zinc kernel: sdladrv: assuming CPU clock rate of 16000 kHz
```

```
zinc kernel: sdladrv: dual-port memory window is set at 0xD0000.
zinc kernel: sdladrv: found 128K bytes of on-board memory
zinc kernel: sdladrv: loading Frame Relay for S508 (T1/E1) (ID=6800)...
zinc kernel: wanpipe1: Initializing for SMP
zinc kernel: wanpipe1: Starting Frame Relay Protocol Init.
zinc kernel:
zinc kernel: wanpipe1: running Frame Relay firmware vT.00
zinc kernel: wanpipe1: Global CIR enabled by Default
zinc kernel: wanpipe1: End of Interrupt Test rc=0x0  count=101
zinc kernel: wanpipe1: Interrupt Test Passed, Counter: 101
zinc kernel: wanpipe1: link connected!
zinc kernel:
zinc kernel: wanpipe1: Running in WANPIPE mode.
zinc kernel: wanpipe1: CIR disabled for DLCI 16
zinc kernel: wanpipe1: Inverse ARP Support Disabled
zinc kernel:
zinc kernel: wanpipe1: Interface wan0: DLCI 16 disconnected!
zinc kernel: wanpipe1: link disconnected!
zinc kernel:
zinc kernel: wanpipe1: link connected!
zinc kernel: wanpipe1: Interface wan0: DLCI 16 connected!
```

5.3.6   Starting *WANPIPE*—Other Potential Problems

If everything in *syslog* and in the */var/log/wanrouter* seems OK, but the connection still doesn't work, then you'll have to dig a little deeper. Although none of these will immediately fix the problem, they are ways to check your work and understand how *WANPIPE* works with your system.

Once *WANPIPE* has started, you can use *ifconfig* to view the interfaces it created for each PVC. If they do not exist (an error message like wan0: unknown interface), then review the logfiles carefully. Make sure that you see a message like wanpipe1: Interrupt Test Passed, Counter: 101, which indicates that the interrupt you select is available for the S508. If you see wanpipe1: Interrupt Test Failed, then you have specified an interrupt which is already in use. **cat /proc/interrupts** works to find an unused interrupt and edit the IRQ setting in *wanpipe1.conf* with your new selection.

```
zinc:/root> ifconfig wan0
wan0  Link encap:Point-to-Point Protocol
      inet addr:192.168.20.2  P-t-P:192.168.20.3  Mask:255.255.255.255
      UP POINTOPOINT RUNNING NOARP  MTU:1500  Metric:1
      RX packets:473135 errors:0 dropped:0 overruns:0 frame:0
      TX packets:488143 errors:0 dropped:10 overruns:0 carrier:0
      collisions:0 txqueuelen:100
      RX bytes:0 (4.6 Mb)  TX bytes:0 (3.9 Mb)
      Interrupt:7 Base address:0x360 Memory:c00d0000-c00d1fff


zinc:/root> route -n | grep wan0
Destination     Gateway   Genmask          Flags Metric Ref    Use Iface
192.168.20.3    0.0.0.0   255.255.255.255  UH    0      0     4552 wan0
192.168.20.0    0.0.0.0   255.255.255.0    U     0      0    77727 wan0
```

If you take a close look at the output from *ifconfig*, you'll notice that our link is encapsulated as PPP, and this is Frame Relay. Why's that? Recall the parameter TRUE_ENCODING_TYPE back on page 152, which controls what link encapsulation is reported to the kernel. It defaults to NO (and we took the default), which means that the kernel sees this link as a point-to-point. The upshot is that we don't have to worry about any of our network monitoring tools being tripped up by the Frame Relay packet headers.

Is everything working? Routers do not live by *ifconfig*s alone; you must also have routes over your link to be able to use it. And it bears repeating, if only for the number of times that I've scratched my head and wondered what's wrong: Make sure that IP forwarding is enabled in the kernel by checking the value of */proc/sys/net/ipv4/ip_forward*, just as we did in Chapter 3.

When *WANPIPE* starts, it creates its own directory in the */proc* filesystem. The directory is */proc/net/wanrouter/* on 2.2 and 2.4 systems. The files are *config*, *status*, and *wanpipeN* (one for each physical device in the system). Each of these should contain meaningful information—the values of the first two files should jibe with what you entered into the configuration files, while the third contains statistics about usage of the card.

```
zinc:/proc/net/wanrouter> cat config
Device name| port |IRQ|DMA| mem.addr |mem.size|option1|option2|option3|option4
wanpipe1   |0x360 |  7|  0|0xC00D0000|0x2000  |   5080|  16000| 131072|   6800

zinc:/proc/net/wanrouter> cat status
Device name|protocol|station|interface|clocking|baud rate| MTU |ndev|link state
wanpipe1   | FR     | CPE   | V.35    |external|   512000| 1600|   1 |connected

zinc:/proc/net/wanrouter> cat wanpipe1
          total packets received:     81010211
       total packets transmitted:     86599548
           total bytes received:   56464117067
        total bytes transmitted:   21996285192
            bad packets received:            0
        packet transmit problems:          902
        received frames dropped:             0
        transmit frames dropped:           412
      multicast packets received:            0
             transmit collisions:            0
           receive length errors:          138
        receiver overrun errors:             0
                     CRC errors:             0
     frame format errors (aborts):           45
            receiver fifo overrun:            0
          receiver missed packet:             0
       aborted frames transmitted:            0
```

If you are still stuck, do not despair! This section is about configuration and system problems. Many factors contribute to the functioning of your Frame Relay circuit. Please review the information in Section 5.4, which covers other scenarios which can result in your link being down.

If your link is up, congratulations! I always find bringing up new links exciting. You add routes simply by listing the interface at the end of the route statement—no **gw** *gateway* required—as we did with Ethernet devices in Chapter 3.

5.4   Troubleshooting Frame Relay with *WANPIPE*

Problems with Frame Relay links can occur at many points along the path between your routers at locations A and B. Effective troubleshooting involves using (often limited) information to deduce the root cause of a problem. Once the problem has been located, you devise a strategy to repair it, and then test the repair. Because WANs span large distances by their very definition, your strategy is to first determine *where* the problem is occurring. I use the following list:

- your router at location A

- the access between location A and your provider's POP near A

- your provider's router at POP A

- the network between your provider's POPs

- your provider's router at POP B

- the access between your provider's POP near B and location B

- your router at location B

Because there are a lot of steps, the first thing to do is to reduce the possibilities. The following sections list items you can check at each of these locations. They also mention some uses of the *fpipemon* utility, which is more fully introduced in Section 5.4.3.

5.4.1   Frame Relay Troubleshooting—Your Router

- Did your router recently reboot? Use *uptime* to see. Because of the number of nodes along the way between locations A and B, it can take 30–40 seconds before an interrupted link starts passing traffic again. If your router has just rebooted, it could be negotiating link parameters and waiting for its peer to notice that it is back on the network.

- Have you recently genned a new kernel which perhaps does not have *WANPIPE* support? Have you done this accidentally and then rebooted?

- Is *WANPIPE* started? After stopping and restarting it, are there error messages in */var/log/wanpipe.log* or *syslog*? Most *syslog* messages are lines containing the string "wanpipe," so you can look at them all with `grep -i wanpipe /var/log/messages | more`.

  Use *last* and *lastb* to determine who has logged into the router and *whom* to see if someone else may be logged in, performing maintenance.

- Does an *ifconfig* show the interface(s) as up?

- Does `route -n` show a routing-table entry for the point-to-point link?

- Does `route -n` show the route(s) for the remote subnet?

- Is there a network admin in another location performing maintenance? Sometimes you cannot determine whether the problem is in the provider's network or on the other side— you will just be able to say for certain that it is not between you and the provider's POP for your location. In this case, check with your counterpart in the remote location, or use analog dial-in to check the status of the router there. (If you always immediately open a trouble ticket with your provider and release the circuit for testing, your provider may bring the circuit down as part of his problem-determination procedure. If it turns out that the problem is on the other end of the link and could be quickly resolved, you have, in effect, created two outages from one.)

- Have you recently made changes to *wanpipeN.conf* or upgraded the *WANPIPE* software? Is this the first time that you have restarted *WANPIPE* since either of those activities?

- Have you (very) recently added another device to the system? A second S508 card (without remembering to change the base address)? An ISA card that wants the IRQ of your *WANPIPE* card? An ISA PnP device? There should be a message about `Interrupt Test Passed` in */var/log/messages*—otherwise, you probably have an interrupt conflict.

- Is your system otherwise sick? Out of disk space? Did the kernel panic? (Word to the wise: If you have panics that make no sense whatsoever, fall back to a kernel that you know has worked in the past. If that doesn't help, change out all of the memory in the system.)

- Last but not least, the dreaded: Did you check the cables? Unfortunately, this is often a source of trouble in server rooms and telecom closets which experience a lot of foot traffic.

OK, I admit that none of those was rocket science, but you have to start somewhere. Spending a few seconds reflecting upon what changes you might have recently made to the system and performing a quick sanity check can save much time barking up the wrong tree. The fact is, once your Linux/*WANPIPE* router is up and running, there are very few things to troubleshoot with the router configuration itself. Still, it makes sense to check out the router first. Now we move on to the next potential point of failure: the digital circuit between you and the POP.

5.4.2   Frame Relay Troubleshooting—Access Problems

Without the local loop (so aptly known as **access**) functioning properly, you are not going to be able to get your traffic to your provider and into the cloud. Access is simple and tricky at the same time. While it may be easy enough to locate access problems, it can take quite a while to get them solved. For one, they are telco circuits, so you are at the mercy of your local access provider. The issue is more complicated when your Frame Relay provider does not provide the access circuit. In that situation, your Frame Relay provider leases the **last mile** from the local access provider, which makes your Frame Relay provider the *customer* as far as the local access provider is concerned. To troubleshoot the access circuit, even if you *know* that the access is down, you normally have to contact your Frame Relay provider, wait for him to go through his preliminary testing, and have him call the access provider. The problem can exist the other way around, too. In either case, all of this takes time, during which you have a link down. Ways to detect access problems are:

- Does `fpipemon -i` *interface* `-u 9000 -c xm` show the circuit up? (Note: *interface* is either the name of the interface of the IP address or the IP address of the *other* end of the point-to-point link.) Good output looks like that below.

```
zinc:/root> fpipemon -i wan0 -u 9000 -c xm

        ----------------------------
                 MODEM STATUS
        ----------------------------

DCD is HIGH
CTS is HIGH
```

  Bad output lists either of the signals as `LOW`. If you get an error from *fpipemon* about checking the IP address and the port, then either you are not specifying the correct IP address or interface, or *WANPIPE* is not running.

- If *fpipemon* thinks that the circuit is down, is there any problem indicated on the CSU/DSU or on the circuit's demarc? If there is, contact your Frame Relay provider. You will need to have your circuit ID when you call, which is why I put this information directly into *wanpipe1.conf*.

- If the circuit looks fine at your end, maybe the problem is not the access. You should be able to use *fpipemon* in trace mode to see some traffic between your node and the switch at the POP. At a minimum, you should see the status messages (keepalives), full status enquiries, and possibly data packets being traded.

fpipemon **Tracing Status Messages, FSEs and Data Payloads**

```
zinc:/root> fpipemon -i wan0 -u 9000 -c ti

Starting trace...(Press ENTER to exit)
OUTGOING  16   19821  Link Verification      Request Sx 7C  Rx 06
INCOMING  16   19823  Link Verification      Reply   Sx 07  Rx 7C
OUTGOING  16   7727   Full Status            Request Sx 1D  Rx 1B
INCOMING  21   7730   Full Status            Reply   Sx 1C  Rx 1D  \
                                             DLCI 600 PRS 600ACT

INCOMING  293  49726  Data Frame on DLCI 600
INCOMING  52   30939  Data Frame on DLCI 600
```

If you see outgoing traffic, but no incoming traffic, then the card thinks that the access is OK. Perhaps the problem is with your provider's equipment or with the access on their side. When it cannot talk to the provider's router, *WANPIPE* marks the circuit as down in */var/log/messages*, because it does not receive any replies to its keepalives and status enquiries. It will continue to generate `OUTGOING` LMI messages in hopes that the circuit will come back up, but it will not try to transmit TCP/IP data.

- If you call in a problem and there is not something else obviously wrong, your provider will probably want to perform a **loopback test**, or "loop up the CSU/DSU." If the provider cannot loop up your CSU/DSU, he or she will surely ask you if your equipment is powered-up and connected. As demeaning as it is, you should check all of your cables, and, if you have an external CSU/DSU, check to make sure that it is on and properly connected. If your side looks good, then there is a problem with the access circuit.

What's a Loopback?

A **loopback** refers to a provision for automated testing built into all T1 interface equipment. What happens is that the provider sends a special sequence of bipolar violations down to your equipment that instructs it to complete the circuit between the transmit and receive pairs. Now that he has a "loop," the provider can send test patterns down the circuit and see them. This is done to determine how much noise there may be on a circuit, and that the circuit is complete.

   Don't confuse this with the local loopback network interface found on every Unix system—interface *lo* with IP address 127.0.0.1.

Problems in the Cloud

The **cloud** refers to the portion of your provider's network that lies beyond your routers and access. Once packets make the trip from your router along your access to your port on the provider's equipment, you basically have no control over them until they egress on the other side. This means that it is difficult to actually detect a problem in the cloud. The more likely scenario is that you will exhaust all of the other possibilities and deduce that the problem is there.

   The "symptom" is that routers on both ends are up and sending and receiving keep-alive messages (so that you know that LMI is up and your ports are active) but you cannot pass packets end-to-end. If both sides believe that the remote DLCI is active, then the problem could be with buffering in the provider's network. If one side cannot see its partner DLCI, then the provider has probably built the PVC incorrectly (or not built it at all).

   In either case, there is nothing you can do except to open a trouble ticket with your provider. Because most Frame Relay networks have multiple redundant paths, problems in the cloud often mean something bad is afoot. Alternately, the problem could be with the switch or PVC configuration within the provider's network.

Problems with Access at Location B and Router B

Any problems on the other side can be evaluated in the same manner that you did on the A-side of the link. The only sticky point might be that you cannot get to router *B* (because the link is down!), or that router *B* is not a Linux router. If you are responsible for problem resolution on the *B*-side of the link, you should make provisions for emergency access.

5.4.3   Using *fpipemon*

The *fpipemon* utility is the "window into your router"—it displays card status and acts as a general-purpose sniffer for link-layer packets (known to *fpipemon* as **protocol** packets). Several common uses of *fpipemon* were introduced in Section 5.4.2. In this section we'll cover all the options of the utility. First, let's look at the general command form:

fpipemon -i *interface* **-u** *port* **-c** *command* [**-d** *dlci*]

When invoking *fpipemon*, you must list an interface, the UDP monitoring port,[6] and a command. Optionally, you can specify a DLCI modifier for the command. The *interface* can be the (local) interface name (as it shows up in *ifconfig* on this router) or the IP address of the far end of your point-to-point interface in decimal format. Because the monitor uses UDP to communicate with the driver, the device you are monitoring does not have to be local to your system. As long as the IP address is routable, you can run *fpipemon* against a remote machine.

fpipemon **Commands**

After you specify the interface and the monitoring port, you have to tell *fpipemon* what you'd like it to do. The command follows the -c switch and is either two or three characters. The first character specifies the type of command and can be one of the following:

fpipemon **Command Types**

command type	meaning
x	card status
c	card configuration
s	card statistics
d	driver statistics
T	FT1 configuration and statistics
f	flush (statistics)
t	interactive trace

Now we will introduce all the commands for each of these command types, grouped into tables. The flush command forms are presented alongside the parameters they affect. Note that there is no space between the command-type character and the command specifier(s). A valid command looks like `fpipemon -i wan0 -u 9000 -c trp`, which is command form "t" (for trace) with specifier "rp" (for raw protocol).

You can use the "f" command form to flush (reset) each of these statistics individually. Use the same specifier (g, c, or e) to zero the corresponding statistic. To zero a DLCI's stats, use i for the specifier, as in `-c fi -d` *dlci*.

---

[6]The Debian version of the command doesn't require the UDP port. It assumes the default of 9000.

fpipemon **Commands–Card Status Forms (x)**

specifier	meaning
xm	modem status—This shows the status of the DCD (Data Carrier Detect) and CTS (Clear To Send) pins of the S508's interface to the CSU/DSU. These should both be HIGH. If one of these is LOW, then there is a problem with either the access circuit or the CSU/DSU.
xl	link status—This shows the driver's opinion of the status of the link. It should say OPERATIVE.
xru	router uptime—This returns the time elapsed since you last started *WANPIPE*. (Note that this does not always equal the uptime of the machine.)

fpipemon **Commands–Card Configuration (c)**

specifier	meaning
cl	active DLCIs for this adapter—This lists all active DLCIs as reported in your provider's reply to the last FSE (Full Status Enquiry). If there are DLCIs missing, then either you have a problem on the other side of your link or there is a configuration problem with your provider.

fpipemon **Commands—Card Statistics (s)**

specifier	meaning
sg	global statistics—This displays the data regarding the link management (LMI) taking place on your link. You might use this to troubleshoot an incompatibility or settings mismatch between your router and the switch at your provider's POP. CRC errors indicate errors during packet transmission, while ABORT refers to errors detected while the line was idle.
sc	communications error statistics—This will list the number of times that CSU/DSU dropped out or otherwise told the Sangoma card to hush. It is useful for noting packet loss/bandwidth loss due to communications errors (potentially noisy access or otherwise).
se	error statistics—This displays counts of the instances when sends or receives failed due to problems with the Frame Relay headers (e.g., invalid sequence numbers, frames with invalid lengths, or other formatting errors).
sd	DLCI-specific statistics—For the DLCI specified on the command line, statistics about frames sent to or received from that DLCI are displayed. You must use the -d *dlci* switch to indicate which DLCI you would like see.

Example *fpipemon* **Statistics Output**

```
zinc:/root> fpipemon -i wan0 -u 9000 -csd -d 200
                            Information frames transmitted: 837911
                             Information bytes transmitted: 354079392
                              Information frames received: 810404
                               Information bytes received: 118737889
               Received I-frames discarded due to inactive DLCI: 4
 I-frames received with Discard Eligibility (DE) indicator set: 5480
                       I-frames received with the FECN bit set: 0
                       I-frames received with the BECN bit set: 12223
```

The frames and bytes counters are self-explanatory. `Received I-frames discarded due to inactive DLCI` are packets which come from a DLCI that this router did not know (in our case, not from DLCI 200). `I-frames received with Discard Eligibility (DE) indicator set` is a count of the number of frames that we *received*, although they were eligible to be thrown away in the cloud if they had encountered sufficient congestion—in other words, how many of the received frames sent by the indicated DLCI were done so while that router was exceeding the CIR for the link—in the case above, 5480 out of 810404, or about 0.7%. (Not bad.) FECN stands for Forward Explicit Congestion Notification. The FECN bit is sent to the next hop in the Frame Relay network (the cloud) when a router there is experiencing congestion. It makes sense that this counter would be zero, since our router is leaf node and is not situated so that it could be the forward router in the cloud. The BECN count is more interesting, as it indicates the number of times that the provider's switch told our router that it was congested and asked it if it could possibly throttle what it was sending onto the network. If you know that you are never exceeding your CIR, yet you received packets with the BECN bit set, then there is a possibility that your provider has oversold its network.

fpipemon **Commands–Driver Statistics (d)**

specifier	meaning
ds	If_Send driver statistics—This option gives you access to the statistical variables in the driver related to sends. It can tell you some interesting things about what is happening to your packets, especially if you suspect packet loss or other foul play.
di	interrupt driver statistics—This displays more statistics like those shown with ds, but these are related to interrupts (which are packet receives).
dg	general driver statistics—This shows even more driver statistics.

Don't be alarmed if these don't make a lot of sense to you. They are normally used by Sangoma's technical staff for support and driver debuggings. Still, it's nice to have access to the interesting bits. Use the `fd` command form to flush (reset) all of the driver statistics.

fpipemon **Commands–FT1** (T)

specifier	meaning
Tv	view status
Ts	self-test
Tl	line loop test
Td	digital loop test
Tr	remote test
To	operational mode

Note that these commands are valid only if you have an FT1 version of a Sangoma card with an integrated CSU/DSU. Better descriptions of the output are available in the documentation that comes with *WANPIPE* and are therefore not presented here. A warning: If you loop up your CSU/DSU while your router is running, you will undoubtedly bring down your link, at least for a short while. Except for Tv (view status), you should use these commands only when *WANPIPE* is stopped.

fpipemon **Commands–Traces** (t)

specifier	meaning
i	interpret/all—This shows both data (IP) and protocol (link-layer) frames in an easy-to-read "cooked" format.
ip	interpret/protocol—This shows protocol frames only in an easy-to-read "cooked" format.
id	interpret/data—This shows data payloads only in the easy-to-read "cooked" format.
r	raw/all—This shows the contents of all data (IP) and protocol (link-layer) frames in hexadecimal.
rp	raw/protocol—This displays the raw link-layer frames. This might be useful as a learning aid. (Sit down with the applicable RFC—probably RFC 1490—and decode the values in the frame headers.) You should do the same if you suspect some sort of incompatibility with your provider's equipment.
rd	raw/data—This displays the frame payloads in hexadecimal format.

For all of the trace modes, you toggle tracing on when you issue the command with *fpipemon*, at which point it starts tracing to *stdout*. To turn off the trace, hit **ENTER**. Depending upon the options used to invoke *fpipemon*, the output is Link Verifications or Status Requests (protocol), various replies to these (also protocol), or INBOUND or OUTGOING data.

The interpreted protocol trace is an excellent source of troubleshooting information. The output is the **LMI** (Local Management Interface) information being exchanged between your router and the equipment at the POP. Once you learn how to decipher the output, you can tell from the **FSE** (Full Status Enquiry) messages which DLCIs are active, available, and missing. The exact format of the messages depends upon which of the status-polling (LMI) protocols you are running. The original LMI is known simply as **LMI**. This protocol has the limitation of being unidirectional (your node router had to ask the questions, and the POP router would answer them). After some updating, the newer choices are Q.933 (Annex A) and ANSI (Annex D).

Your router will periodically send out an **enquiry** to the effect of *Are you alive?* The upstream router should reply within a certain timeout period (T391). Your node may send a Full Status Enquiry to the POP router, requesting more information about the status of the network. The POP should reply within the timeout period specified by T392. The POP router may also originate messages. These messages may be things like *DLCI 600 is no longer active* or *DLCI 400 has become active.*

Hint: Sangoma's SNOOPER Utility

Sometimes so many things have gone wrong, or documentation is so scarce, that you just want to establish some confidence that your access circuit is functioning. For these situations you can use Sangoma's *SNOOPER* utility. (If you do not have the floppy disks that came with your card, you can get a copy of it at *ftp://www.sangoma.com/snooper/*. Note that it operates only with Sangoma ISA cards, such as the S508.)

SNOOPER is a DOS executable. To use it, place it on a bootable DOS floppy diskette and boot your router from this floppy. It will diagnose many problems with a T1 link, including a noisy T1. It can also tell you if the router on the other side is talking PPP or Frame Relay. When you're stumped as to why things aren't working, it's a convenient way to establish the validity of your CSU/DSU configuration and eliminate the access circuit from suspicion.

That concludes the discussion of *fpipemon* and Frame Relay troubleshooting. Documenting troubleshooting procedures and strategies is difficult when you consider the range of different situations one may encounter. I have tried to emphasize the knowledge gained during my experiences with *WANPIPE* Frame Relay links. You may come across completely new and mind-boggling issues to solve. If this happens, you should not be discouraged or assume that the problem is automatically on your side. I've seen providers make mistakes configuring a circuit where I had to all but solve the problem for them before they finally corrected it. This is one of the advantages of Linux and *WANPIPE*—you are armed with information and tools. A lot of this information may be available on Sangoma's troubleshooting webpage. The URL is *http://www.sangoma.com/linedebug.htm*.

Once you are up and running, you'll want some way to determine how much and how effectively you are using your link. The next section covers a web-based tool to monitor bandwidth.

5.5   *MRTG*—Monitoring Link Utilization

MRTG is short for *Multi Router Traffic Grapher*. It is a network monitoring tool which specializes in presentation of traffic data graphically, both in real time and over intervals, such as hourly, daily, weekly, monthly, and yearly. It uses the **SNMP** protocol[7] as its data-collection mechanism, so it can be used with more than just Linux routers. **SNMP** is an acronym for Simple Network Management Protocol, which can be used to gather statistics and perform configuration changes. It is the basis upon which many embedded systems routers' management tools are built, plus some enterprise management tools, such as HP's *OpenView*—Linux is willing to play along with any open standard.

---

[7]Note that the SNMP code is built into *MRTG*, so there is no need for an external SNMP collection mechanism on the server.

In this instance, you will need to load the **snmpd** Debian package (or the equivalent for your distribution) to any system which you would like *MRTG* to monitor. You can think of the *snmpd* as a server (listening on port 161), willing to serve up information about the system to any SNMP client who connects and has the required credentials to get the information it requests. *MRTG* can be configured to produce graphs for anything that will respond to an *snmpget*. It presents its traffic summaries via GIF images in HTML pages, so they may be viewed by any standard web browser that supports images. An example of the output is shown in Figure 5.6.

To view the graphs via a browser, you also need to load some sort of HTTP daemon. I suggest *Apache*, since it is readily available and has excellent documentation and support. It will also allow you to configure some security around your *MRTG* statistics pages by using *.htaccess* files. Figure 5.7 gives an overview of the architecture. Note that *MRTG* and the web server need not be loaded on your router but can be put on an intranet server or on your workstation. In this way, you spare your router the overhead of calculating statistics, drawing graphs, and serving up webpages.

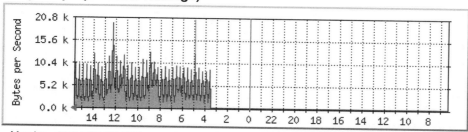

Traffic Analysis for wan0

System:	zinc
Maintainer:	tony@mancill.com
Interface:	wan0 (3)
IP:	atl-sfo-pvc.mydomain.com (172.16.1.9)
Max Speed:	192.0 kBytes/s (frame-relay)

The statistics were last updated **Sunday, 18 July 1999 at 15:40** at which time **zinc** had been up for **12:17:23**.

Daily Graph (5 Minute Average)

Max In:	20.5 kB/s (10.7%)	Average In:	5377.0 B/s (2.8%)	Current In:	2982.0 B/s (1.6%)
Max Out:	19.5 kB/s (10.2%)	Average Out:	5350.0 B/s (2.8%)	Current Out:	2992.0 B/s (1.6%)

GREEN ### Incoming Traffic in Bytes per Second
BLUE ### Outgoing Traffic in Bytes per Second

MRTG MULTI ROUTER TRAFFIC GRAPHER

2.5.4-1998/10/13 Tobias Oetiker <oetiker@ee.ethz.ch> and Dave Rand <dlr@bungi.com>

Figure 5.6 MRTG Sample Output

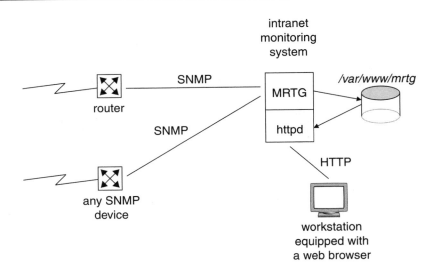

Figure 5.7 MRTG Architecture

5.5.1 Configuring *MRTG*

It takes only about an hour to set everything up, including loading the software, and the system needs practically no ongoing maintenance. The logfile format used by *MRTG* is efficient and self-pruning. Let's walk through a sample configuration to monitor one or more of our routers. Remember that *MRTG* is useful for more than just Frame Relay routers.

1. On the system that will be performing statistics collection, the **support system**, you will need to load *MRTG* and *Apache* (Debian packages **mrtg** and **apache**). If this system will also be monitored, add the SNMP daemon (**snmpd** for Debian).

2. On each of the routers to be monitored, load and configure the SNMP daemon. Most Linux distributions now come with the *UCD SNMP* daemon, but a few may still run *CMU SNMP*. By the time you're reading this, *UCD SNMP* will have migrated over to SourceForge and will be released under the name *net-snmp*.

   - For *CMU SNMP*, the configuration file is */etc/snmpd.conf*. You'll need to add an `interface:` line for your Frame Relay interfaces along with their type (from Section 3.5 of RFC 1213—also known as MIB-II) and speed. For a 512kbps interface named *wan0*, I use:

     ```
     interface:     wan0    32           512000
     ```

     Once you restart the daemon, the SNMP agent programs should recognize your interface, and *MRTG* will be able to judge its speed correctly.

   - For *UCD SNMP*, you'll need to open up the default security a little bit to be able to use it. By default, only *localhost* is allowed access, but you'll need read-only access for the system running *MRTG* so that *MRTG* has access to read the statistics. Resist the temptation to open *snmpd* up to other systems, as this can produce gaping security holes. You may also want to establish your own community names and passwords. This is all controlled in the */etc/snmp/snmpd.conf* (or better yet, in the */etc/snmp/snmpd.local.conf*) file. Refer to your system's documentation for more information about the options in this file.

After changing either of these, you'll need to restart the daemon to read the new configuration file: **/etc/init.d/snmpd reload**.

3. Go back to the support system and configure *Apache* to suit your tastes. The out-of-the-box configuration will work fine, and the remaining steps assume that your `DocumentRoot` is */var/www* and that you have created */var/www/mrtg* for your *MRTG* data. When you create this directory, make it group-readable by at least `www-data` so that *Apache* can get to it. It should be writable by the user you will run the *mrtg* executable as.

4. Now you need to create the *MRTG* configuration file, which is located in */etc/mrtg.cfg*. The configuration file syntax is not difficult, but the *MRTG* authors decided to make the process even easier by providing *cfgmaker* and *indexmaker* utilities. You invoke *cfgmaker* once for each router you would like to monitor. It goes out and queries the router about how many interfaces it has and of what type and speed. (This is why we needed to configure *snmpd* to know the speed of our *wan0* interface.) Do this with `cfgmaker public@`*router* `>>/etc/mrtg.cfg` for each *router* you would like to monitor.

The configuration file format is easy enough to decipher, and you can read the *MRTG* documentation if you need to fine-tune the configuration for a particular router or interface. You will also need to review the documentation if you want to monitor MIB values not included by *cfgmaker*. The only other value required in *mrtg.cfg* is the `WorkDir:`, which you should set to */var/www/mrtg*.

5. Once you have the configuration file, you have to configure a way to invoke *mrtg* periodically with the path to the configuration file as the argument. Note that *MRTG* is not a daemon.[8] Every time that it runs, it reads its configuration file to know which systems to query and where to write the results. The Debian package comes with a cronjob already set up for this in */etc/cron.d/mrtg*. You can see that it executes once every five minutes.

6. At this point, you could point your browser at your support system and access the HTML pages created for each router. You would do this with a URL like *http://support/mrtg/ipofrouter.intf.html*. Look at the contents of */var/www/mrtg* to see what I mean.

Just so that you cannot complain about having to type all of this into your browser, the authors of *MRTG* included an easy way to generate an index to the routers you have configured—*indexmaker*. Review its manpage, and run it every time you make changes to *mrtg.cfg*. Now you can point your browser at *http://support/mrtg* to see an overview, and click on the links provided to view details of each router and interface.

If you followed along with the example, I hope that your configuration went smoothly. It is not a difficult package to configure and is well worth the effort, once you see the nice graphs of router traffic. By default, *MRTG* produces daily, weekly, monthly, and yearly graphs, so it is immediately useful for watching trends in network traffic develop. Because it is based on SNMP (and you have the source code!), it can become the backbone of your monitoring infrastructure. There are many potential "next steps" with *MRTG*. One possibility I find

---

[8]This is a good example of keeping the code focused on the task at hand. Leave the coding of *cron* to *cron*.

interesting is making IP accounting counters available via SNMP. With this and a little time spent configuring *MRTG*, you could produce traffic graphs for certain protocols, or certain subnets—anything you can configure with IP accounting. Cool, eh?

5.6   LRP with *WANPIPE*

If you are a fan of LRP and need the functionality of *WANPIPE*, you are in luck. The LRP maintainers have already packaged a version of Sangoma's driver software like the Debian **wanpipe** package. The package is available at the LRP site, *ftp://ftp.linuxrouter.org*, and can be added to your LRP root disk as explained in the following section. Note that there are a few differences between the LRP and Debian **wanpipe** packages, in the interest of saving space. The trimmings include documentation, the verbose startup and shutdown script, the kernel patches, etc. If you plan to use the LRP *wanpipe*, you should obtain the documentation from elsewhere (e.g., Sangoma's FTP site). From a configuration perspective, here are the major differences:

- The main configuration file is */etc/wanpipe/wanpipe.conf*.

- There are no interface files. You will need to configure your *WANPIPE* interfaces with *ifconfig* as part of your startup, after *wanconfig* parses the configuration file.

- There is an additional command called *wanstat*, which displays some status information from the */proc* filesystem.

- The *cfgft1* is not included. If you want to have it on your LRP root disk, do not copy the binary compiled on your system or from Sangoma's tarball. Because these are dynamically linked, they are not likely to run on the LRP system with its pared-down libraries. Instead, either compile a statically linked version (edit the makefile to use the `-static` switch) or configure your S508-FT1 on another system before installing it in your LRP system. Because the configuration is stored in nonvolatile memory, it will remain intact while you transfer the board.

5.6.1   Adding LRP Packages to Your LRP Root Disk

Adding a package to LRP is straightforward; the steps are listed below. If you have problems with the command syntax for any of these, refer back to Section 3.5 in Chapter 3.

1. Make any changes you require to the *.lrp* tarball, e.g., for *WANPIPE*, you can provide your specific *WANPIPE* configuration file, and then reassemble the tarball.

2. Mount the LRP root floppy on your workstation (remember that it is a DOS formatted floppy) and copy the *.lrp* file into the root directory of the floppy. Use a command such as `mount -t msdos /dev/fd0 /floppy` to mount the disk as */floppy*.

3. Edit */floppy/syslinux.cfg* and modify the `LRP=` portion of the *append=* line to reflect the package(s) you added. For the base packages plus *WANPIPE*, the list looks like `LRP=etc,log,local,modules,wanpipe`.

4. Unmount the floppy with `umount /floppy` and rerun *syslinux* against it to update the configuration.

Using mtools to Work with MS-DOS Filesystems

Alternatively, you can use *mcopy* (part of the **mtools** package) to copy files to and from the LRP floppy. These tools allow you to work with MS-DOS formatted filesystems without explicitly mounting and unmounting them as part of your filesystem. The tools include most of the basic DOS file-manipulation commands and use */etc/mtools.conf* to assign "drive letters" to devices and partitions on your system.

For example, in */etc/mtools.conf*, I have:

```
drive a: file="/dev/fd0" exclusive
```

This allows me to use commands like:

```
# copy the file over so that I can edit it
zinc:/root> mcopy a:syslinux.cfg /tmp/syslinux.cfg
zinc:/root> vi /tmp/syslinux.cfg
zinc:/root> mcopy /tmp/syslinux.cfg a:syslinux.cfg
# check the new configuration file
zinc:/root> mtype a:syslinux.cfg
```

5.7   Summary

When I configured my first Linux Frame Relay router with *WANPIPE*, I immediately felt as if I were better off with Linux than with the traditional Frame Relay routers we had in production at the time. My comfort level with using a Unix shell as the command interface, the accessibility of information, and the ease of configuration were all factors. This experience really brought me onto the Linux router bandwagon. This chapter has covered a lot of ground regarding Linux Frame Relay routers:

- Basics of Frame Relay for a CPE (endpoint) router. There is a lot more to Frame Relay if you are a provider or want to run voice-over-IP applications alongside your data. The material presented is geared toward basic WAN applications—you don't have to be a Frame Relay expert to deploy it effectively for your organization.

- Various WAN adapters available for Linux. These range from single-port ISA cards running 56kbps to quad-port HSSI boards at 52Mbps. Protocol support also covers the spectrum, from LU6.2 to Cisco HDLC.

- Configuration of *WANPIPE* Frame Relay, using both the Debian **wanpipe** package and Sangoma's general version of the software. Depending upon the current version of the kernel and *WANPIPE*, you may get into patching your kernel with new driver code. Once you have the necessary support, you configure *wanpipe1.conf* and the appropriate *interface* files to match your link parameters.

- Troubleshooting a Frame Relay link running *WANPIPE* using *fpipemon* can be a pleasurable experience, especially when you use the information from the utility to quickly isolate the location and cause of the outage.

- Configuring *MRTG* to monitor link performance and establish a web-based reporting engine—free software keeps looking better and better.

Chapter 6

CESIUM AND XENON—TUNNELING ROUTERS

Cesium and xenon are the routers that didn't know they were going to be routers. They were yanked out of their retirement jobs as door stops and dust collectors and impressed into service to save us large sums of money. The basic story is that my group is located in a work center amidst service reps and other folks who need, at best, a single network connection. So every cube is wired with a single network drop, and (gasp) it's all token ring. The group was fortunate enough to be allocated some Sun Ultra5 workstations by the budget gods, but the systems didn't include token ring cards (over a thousand-dollar add-on if purchased directly from Sun). There are a few third-party token ring cards that will operate under Solaris, but we still only had one network drop per cube. Wiring costs, if you've never had to pay them or budget for them, are astronomical. You would think that wireless LAN technologies like 802.11b would price themselves out of the market when compared to the cost and performance of CAT5, but wireless technologies suddenly become attractive when you're faced with funding a crew of electricians pulling cable for a week. Furthermore, we didn't want to pour company money into more token ring drops on the principle of the thing. Well, a Sun workstation without a network connection is only fun for about a day, after which it becomes a very expensive screensaver platform. All Sun systems come with Ethernet ports, so we chipped in on a 10Base-T hub and built our own network segment between the machines, but we were geographically limited to a single row of cubes—you cannot have CAT5 cables running across walkways in work centers.

Although we were short on network connections, we had literally stacks of old 486 and older Pentium boxes, and cartons full of token ring cards. (At the risk of dating myself, a 90MHz Pentium was once a wickedly fast computer—probably at about the same time that token ring was a *strategic* technology.) Enter cesium to tie the row$_A$ segment to the token ring, and not long afterward, xenon for row$_B$, and so on. Each **token ring gateway**, for lack of a better term, needed a token ring card to tie to the main network and an Ethernet card for the local workstation segment. Once we were physically tied to both networks, they had to talk to each other. And sometimes, just sometimes, you're *not* the network administrator. In this instance, it meant that we were not free to request from the local network administrator that a subnet from the local address space be routing to our token ring gateway so that we could route it to our Ethernet-based workstations. In the general case, you may find yourself needing to construct (sometimes elaborate) network topologies solely because you are not in a situation to request a simple change from the network powers that be.

Fortunately, the networking stack in Linux provides several facilities that make these sorts of configurations possible. (I guess I wasn't alone in needing this sort of configuration.) In this chapter we'll briefly revisit **masquerading** and talk about how we might let a few things from the outside in. We'll also talk about **tunnelling**, which can be used to connect two or more networks separated by an intervening network with no knowledge of/support for those networks. As part of the discussion on tunnelling we'll introduce *iproute2*, a powerful replacement for the traditional network-configuration commands like *ifconfig* and *route*. Then, we're going to put it all together to build secure tunnels, also known as VPNs, using *FreeS/WAN*, an IPsec implementation for Linux. Finally, we'll sink our teeth into some IPv6.

6.1   Linux and Token Ring

In terms of networking hardware, cesium and xenon don't look much different from our basic Ethernet router, silicon, save that they have a token ring card in place of the second Ethernet adapter. There's a long story about not being able to boot Compaq Deskpro XL90s directly into Linux because of some craziness about a DOS-based device driver that has to be loaded to map the BIOS into memory. Instead of going into that, I'll summarize by saying that the best way to boot one of these beasts is to boot off of a DOS diskette, load the silly device driver, and then use *syslinux* to load the Linux kernel from that same floppy and boot the box into Linux. And find a HOWTO . . . . There is another equally long story about getting a PCI-based Madge token ring card running under Linux. At the time, the drivers were not part of the upstream kernel, and I had another relatively discouraging experience with vendor-supplied drivers. Not that I'm ungrateful that Madge offers Linux support—that's the card I had on hand—and I was able to get things running. (And token ring cards remain expensive. I suppose they never reached critical mass in the marketplace.) But things just seem to take longer with vendor-supplied drivers. The precompiled binary versions are invariably for a kernel other than the one you need to run (and there always seems to be a good reason for that), and the source kits can suffer from odd build dependencies (in this case *newt*) or general libc or kernel version touchiness. I'll take a driver from the upstream kernel over a vendor driver any day.

Since this is a networking book, token ring itself deserves a little attention. Although much maligned—sysadmins who join my group always react with *You're running what?*—token ring is a little like the Rodney Dangerfield of LAN link-layer protocols. The protocol is actually much like FDDI, both in its token passing (only the person holding the token is permitted to speak, or transmit) and in its stability during peak-load situations. Token ring has the ability to weather very high load without any nasty drops in throughput as on a bridged Ethernet segment, and without expensive concentrators like Ethernet switches. If you're interested in learning more about the protocol, try *http://www.networkuptime.com/faqs/token-ring/*, which is a collection of questions and answers from the `comp.dcom.lans.token-ring` Usenet newsgroup. You can also go straight to the source and try *http://www.8025.org/*, but it's a tad dry for my tastes.

If you do happen to be running token ring on Linux, you can expect the same stability from it that you do with Ethernet. You may notice that a few tools lag behind their Ethernet counterparts. For example, older versions of *tcpdump* won't decode the packets on the wire for you, so you're stuck with a timestamp plus station addresses, flags, and then raw packet data as shown here. Newer versions work as you'd expect. Here is what the old output looks like:

```
cesium:~$ tcpdump -n -i tr0
22:21:30.643295 0:0:90:0:5a:7d 10:40:c0:0:0:1 609e 352:
                            c220 aaaa 0300 0000 0800 4510 0148 792d
                            4000 4006 e5db ab88 23f0 ab88 5f96 0016
                            03ec 77f0 03e8 7847 968f 8018 7d78 94ec
                            0000 0101 080a
22:21:30.643295 60:9e:0:6:7c:97 10:40:10:0:5a:7d 7ac1 74:
                            aaaa 0300 0000 0800 4510 0034 e54e 4000
                            3e06 7cce ab88 5f96 ab88 23f0 03ec 0016
                            7847 968f 77f0 03e8 8010 7c70 9bb2 0000
                            0101 080a 99a9
```

6.2   Cesium's Environment

Let's get back to our Ethernet/token ring gateways and take a look at what we need to build to get our workstations talking to the rest of the network. The basic topology is depicted in Figure 6.1. So at first glance it seems all we need to do is assign addresses to our token ring cards, pick a private subnet for our Ethernet segments, and configure IP forwarding. But recall that the token ring network was built for individual clients, and we're not going to be able

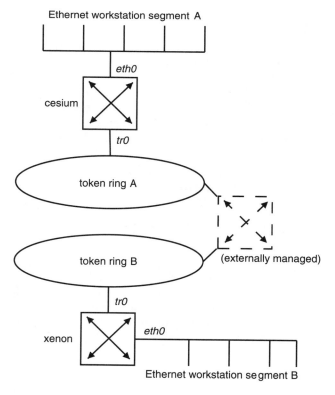

Figure 6.1 Cesium/Xenon Network Topology

to get traffic from the token ring side forwarded via cesium. In fact, because the token ring segments are set up for DHCP, we cannot even get a fixed IP address for cesium! So any traffic exiting the Ethernet segments will have to be marked with the IP address of *tr0* so that the reply will find its way back. In other words, we're masquerading again.

To complicate matters, the RFC 1918 address space has been assigned for use to other systems within the corporation and is routable across the WAN (don't laugh—this is a true story). So we shouldn't pick this address space for our private segments because we can't be sure that we won't need to route to 192.168.0.0/16 some day to access resources on the network. Now what? Well, in a way, I cheated. I took a handful of class C subnets from Internet valid address space and used them. This was safe for the following reasons: access to the *real* outside, the Internet, was via proxies, so the workstations would not need to access that address space in any context other than the local usage; the workstation IPs would be masqueraded by the token ring gateways, so there wasn't any danger of their freaking out any internal (but external to us) routers or traffic monitors; and finally, I happened to know that the Internet valid IPs were sitting behind a firewall on the other side of the planet (which is largely irrelevant). Anyway, that's where the address space comes from, although I'll be using RFC 1918 address space for all the example addresses in this chapter.

Now, what if a workstation on Ethernet segment$_A$ would like to connect to a workstation on Ethernet segment$_B$? Can't we just add a route to cesium that forwards all packets for segment$_B$ to xenon? As tempting as this is, the answer is no. Cesium and xenon are separated by a router (and therefore aren't on the same subnet), and you cannot specify a route that uses a gateway remote to the segment you're on. Think about it for a moment, and you'll realize that there aren't enough address fields in a normal IP packet to do this. Well, strictly speaking, the prior statement is not true. This is possible with **source routing**, a feature of IP that allows the sender to specify the network path to take to the destination. Source routing, though, is Evil because it can be used in all kinds of spoofing attacks and therefore is typically disabled. We're certainly not going to count on its being available to us for passing traffic between cesium and xenon. By the way, don't confuse **source routing** with **source-based routing**. The latter refers to the practice of taking the source address into consideration before forwarding a packet and can be used to provide differentiated levels of service to clients based on the IP address of the sender.

Hint: Disabling Source Routing on Linux

If you'd like to make sure that your Linux router will not be party to an attack that utilizes source routing, make sure that the feature is disabled (it is by default) by checking the value of:

$$/proc/sys/net/ipv4/conf/\textit{interface}/accept\_source\_route$$

where *interface* represents the network interface which should not accept source routes. Better yet, use the interface *all* to disable this feature for all interfaces on the system. As with other files in */proc*, 0 means off/disabled, and 1 means on/enabled.

I hope you'll discover that the primary reason to have Linux in your network is for its flexibility, not its low cost. The cost is just icing on the cake. Good technicians demand good tools, which is how I explain the growth and long-standing popularity of the GNU toolset. Integral to flexibility are choices, and Linux often offers you choices about how to complete a task so that you can select what suits you best. In that vein we head into the next section, which introduces us to the **iproute2** toolset.

6.3   The *iproute2* **Toolset**

The *iproute2* package of utilities, written by Alexey Kuznetsov, is a very powerful set of tools for managing network interfaces and connections on Linux boxes. It completely replaces the functionality of *ifconfig, route,* and *arp* tools in the more traditional net-tools toolkit. The term *traditional* really refers to the toolset that mimics interface and routing-table management found on other Unices, the toolset we've been using so far. Because it is tightly integrated with the kernel, *iproute2* is available only for Linux. I'm afraid this is one of the reasons that *iproute2* hasn't received a lot of mainstream attention—old fogey network administrators like myself have been comfortable with the 15–20-year-old toolset we grew up with and look outside that framework only when we need something special. Well, no more. *iproute2* is worth the trouble of learning, even if it is only for Linux.

To help introduce the syntax, we'll revisit some of the tasks we've already completed and then strike out from there. First off, you'll need the toolset loaded on your system. The package name is **iproute** for both Debian and RedHat. If you'd like to pull it from the upstream source and build it yourself, the main site is *ftp://ftp.inr.ac.ru/ip-routing/*. You'll be presented with a list of mirrors when you connect; you should be polite and use a nearby mirror if one is available. You'll also need to ensure that your running kernel was compiled with the following options:

```
Networking options --->
  [*] Kernel/User netlink socket
  [*]    Routing messages
```

If you don't have these, you'll receive one of the following error messages when trying to use the tools, depending upon what exactly your kernel is missing:

```
tony@vivaldi:~$ /sbin/ip addr show
Cannot open netlink socket: Address family not supported by protocol

tony@bach:~$ /sbin/ip addr show
Cannot send dump request: Connection refused

tony@vivaldi:~$ /sbin/ip rule list
RTNETLINK answers: Invalid argument
Dump terminated
```

Once you have the tools built and/or installed, and you're running a 2.2 or 2.4 kernel with the appropriate support, you fire up *ip* and get the potentially bewildering:

```
tony@bach:~$ /sbin/ip
Usage: ip [ OPTIONS ] OBJECT { COMMAND | help }
where OBJECT := { link | addr | route | rule | neigh | tunnel |
          maddr | mroute | monitor }
      OPTIONS := { -V[ersion] | -s[tatistics] | -r[esolve] |
            -f[amily] { inet | inet6 | ipx | dnet | link } | -o[neline]  }
```

At first, this doesn't seem much better than what `ifconfig -?` spits out. It might be helpful to list out some of the common COMMAND keywords and to indicate that if no command is given, the default keyword is **show** or **list** (which are identical). The complete list of valid COMMAND keywords contains **add**, **delete**, **set**, **flush**, **change**, **replace**, **get**, and **show** or **list**, plus abbreviations for these. However, not all of those keywords are applicable for all OBJECTs. Fortunately, the command syntax is well designed and very regular (consistent). It will take you little time to pick it up, and you can always issue `ip OBJECT help` to view help for that option. But if you're like me, you're not going to remember the syntax diagrams presented by **help**; you remember things by using them.

6.3.1   *iproute2*: **Common** *ifconfig, route,* **and** *arp* **Forms**

```
tmancill@drone4:~$ /sbin/ip addr show dev eth0
2: eth0: <BROADCAST,MULTICAST,UP> mtu 1500 qdisc pfifo_fast qlen 100
    link/ether 00:50:56:40:40:92 brd ff:ff:ff:ff:ff:ff
    inet 192.168.16.1/24 brd 192.168.16.255 scope global eth0
```

The usage in this first form should be pretty clear. We want to view the *address* object corresponding to device *eth0*. There are several things to note here:

- The very first 2: is a unique **interface index**. Later on, we'll change the name of our interface, but the interface index always sticks with the same physical device.

- The `mtu` and device flags are directly from the *ifconfig* output.

- `qdisc` is short for **queuing discipline**, which is Greek for *What algorithm do we use for this interface to determine what is the next packet to be sent?*

- The `qlen` is the maximum depth of the queue in packets. This can be tuned to allow for greater bursts at routers acting as the boundary between high-speed and low-speed interfaces. Note that larger buffers are not always a good thing.

- The *link* line shows detail about the link-level hardware, including the type (`ether`), the link-layer address (in this case, a MAC address), and the link-layer broadcast address.

- The `inet` line is actually an address line for an `inet` family adapter, which is synonymous with IPv4. There may be multiple lines here—a given link (adapter) may have several addresses of one or multiple types. (If you surmise that this foreshadows IP aliases, you are correct, and there is more than that.)

- The interface's IP address is indicated together with the netmask, which is displayed in the **maskbits** notation we talked about on page 27. The *network* is not explicitly indicated, although we know how to calculate this quickly by taking a look at the combination of the IP address and the number of bits in the subnet mask. The `brd` address on this line is the IP broadcast address.

- Protocol addresses have a `scope`, set in this case to the default `global`. Don't worry about this for now, but it's part of policy-based routing, which we will touch on briefly in Section 8.4.1.

There's a lot of information in there, but unlike *ifconfig*, you get interface statistics only if you ask for them explicitly with `-statistics`, which can be abbreviated with `-s`. The next command displays the routing table.

```
tmancill@vivaldi:~$ /sbin/ip -statistics link show dev eth0
2: eth0: <BROADCAST,MULTICAST,PROMISC,UP> mtu 1500 qdisc pfifo_fast qlen 100
    link/ether 00:50:56:40:40:86 brd ff:ff:ff:ff:ff:ff
    RX: bytes  packets  errors  dropped overrun mcast
    18196332   50205    0       0       0       0
    TX: bytes  packets  errors  dropped carrier collsns
    33017745   55970    0       0       0       0


tmancill@vivaldi:~$ /sbin/ip route show
192.168.18.0/24 dev eth1  proto kernel  scope link  src 192.168.18.13
192.168.16.0/24 dev eth0  proto kernel  scope link  src 192.168.16.13
default via 192.168.18.1 dev eth1
```

If you're asking yourself *What's the point? I knew how to do these things before*, please bear with me. We're not even scratching the surface with *iproute2* yet. As you've probably noticed, all of the addresses are displayed as dotted IP addresses. If you want hostname/network name resolution, you'll have to use the -r switch to enable it. (This is a nice change; if I had a nickel for every time I've meant to add the -n switch when invoking *route* ....) What about configuring an interface?

```
# assign the IP address and subnet mask
root@vivaldi:~# ip addr add dev eth1 192.168.64.55/24

# double check to make sure it looks OK
root@vivaldi:~# ip addr list dev eth1
3: eth1: <BROADCAST,MULTICAST> mtu 1500 qdisc pfifo_fast qlen 10
    link/ether 00:50:56:40:40:87 brd ff:ff:ff:ff:ff:ff
    inet 192.168.64.55/24 scope global eth1

# check the routing table - hey, where's the route for 192.168.64.0/24!
root@vivaldi:~# ip route show
192.168.16.0/24 dev eth0  proto kernel  scope link  src 192.168.16.55
default via 192.168.16.13 dev eth0

# doh - the link layer has to be brought up
root@vivaldi:~# ip link set dev eth1 up

root@vivaldi:~# ip route show
192.168.64.0/24 dev eth1  proto kernel  scope link  src 192.168.64.55
192.168.16.0/24 dev eth0  proto kernel  scope link  src 192.168.16.55
default via 192.168.16.13 dev eth0

# add route with nice compact /maskbits notation
root@vivaldi:~# ip route add 10.0.0.0/8 via 192.168.64.12
```

The gotchas I noticed when I first started using *iproute2* were either not initializing a link as up, or not indicating the subnet mask along with the IP address. When this occurs, *ip* assumes you meant /32 (the only safe assumption to be made—far better than using the class A, B, and C subnet semantics). The end effect is that you don't automatically get an entry in the routing table for that subnet, and you can't ping anything even though the device is up.

***iproute2* Documentation**

The primary documentation available with the package is *doc/ip-cref.tex*, a TEX source formatted file.[1] You can compile the source into a DVI (DeVice Independent) file using LATEX. However, loading a complete TEX distribution to format a single piece of documentation may be out of the question for some folks. The Debian package includes a PostScript formatted version of this file in */usr/share/doc/iproute/*, and I have made the latest version of the file available via my site at *http://mancill.com/linuxrouters/ip-cref.ps*.

   See *http://www.linuxdoc.org/HOWTO/Adv-Routing-HOWTO.html* for a fantastic HOWTO using *iproute2*.

iproute2 is very much in tune with the link-layer, and as you might expect, offers *arp* functionality and more. You can determine what machines are visible via the various links on your system with `ip neigh list`, the `neigh` being short for neighbor or neighbour. In the output below, the first entry indicates that drone3 tried to contact 192.168.16.51 but didn't receive a reply to its ARP requests. The `reachable` state means that all is well—this system is an active member of our ARP cache. An entry in the `stale` state was recently *reachable* but will need to be checked before use again. The `delay` state indicates that the kernel is in the process of checking a `stale` neighbor at the moment. In case you're wondering, `nud` is Neighbor Unreachability Detection, as in `NUD_STATE` in the kernel.

```
drone3:~# ip neigh list
192.168.16.51 dev eth0   nud failed
192.168.16.55 dev eth0 lladdr 00:50:56:40:40:86 nud reachable
192.168.16.12 dev eth0 lladdr 00:50:56:40:40:bf nud stale
192.168.18.1 dev eth1 lladdr 00:50:56:c0:00:02 nud delay
```

6.3.2   *iproute2* **Parlor Tricks**

By now you should be getting used to `ip [OPTIONS] OBJECT COMMAND [ARGS]`, so let's use it to do some things we haven't done yet. From the discussion of the hacker tool *hunt* in Section 3.3.4, you may recall that *hunt* sports an ARP spoofing module that can wreak havoc, even on switched networks. And DNS spoofing just makes it worse. Now, the hacker can spoof an ARP address but cannot very easily spoof a MAC address, so let's add a permanent entry into our ARP cache for the IP address of our DNS server. Assuming that you know the current mapping is OK, do the following.

```
drone3:~# ip neighbor change dev eth1 to 192.168.18.1 nud permanent
drone3:~# ip neighbor list
192.168.16.55 dev eth0 lladdr 00:50:56:40:40:86 nud stale
192.168.18.1 dev eth1 lladdr 00:50:56:c0:00:02 nud permanent
192.168.16.12 dev eth0 lladdr 00:50:56:40:40:bf nud stale
```

   If you're paranoid (and it's healthy to be a little bit paranoid), use the additional `lladdr` *macaddress* argument to explicitly indicate the MAC address. (Just don't mistype the MAC address or you'll create an instant outage.)

---
[1]The same format I'm using to write this book.

You can use `ip addr add` to add IP aliases like those in Section 3.2 by supplying the address with subnet mask and indicating the correct physical link with `dev dev`. However, you need to consider whether or not you (or others) may use *ifconfig* to look at the status of the aliased interfaces. Unless you also use the `name dev:alias` argument when you add the address, the alias will exist but won't be visible via *ifconfig*.

What if we'd like to completely rename an interface? It may sound arbitrary to run around renaming interfaces—maybe I'm vain or have nothing else to do. But suppose I work in a pretty big IT shop with a large number of systems, all of which are connected to a network we refer to as the *shadow lan*. That network is used for backups and NFS traffic, and we like to keep tabs on network utilization of those interfaces via SNMP. The machine names of the interfaces might be anything, requiring us later to correlate the correct interface name with the function. Not so if we rename the interface. Here's how you would rename *eth2* to *shadow*:

```
root@drone2:~# ip link set dev eth2 down
root@drone2:~# ip link set dev eth2 name shadow
root@drone2:~# ip link set dev shadow up
root@drone2:~# ifconfig shadow
shadow    Link encap:Ethernet  HWaddr 00:50:56:40:40:81
          UP BROADCAST RUNNING MULTICAST  MTU:1500  Metric:1
          RX packets:32 errors:0 dropped:0 overruns:0 frame:0
          TX packets:95 errors:0 dropped:0 overruns:0 carrier:0
          collisions:0 txqueuelen:100
          RX bytes:2984 (2.9 Kb)  TX bytes:5558 (5.4 Kb)
          Interrupt:10 Base address:0x10a0
```

You can determine what route or interface a packet is going to take by using forms of *ip route get ADDR*. For the address you must specify a single IP address or a network range in *network/maskbits* notation. Because the TOS field is a crucial part of policy-based routing (deciding how to route a packet based on either its source address or the value of its TOS field), you can set it for your test, too. You may also specify a source address using `from ADDR` and ask the tool to assume that the packet is going to be received via a particular interface with `iif`, or sent via the interface specified with `oif`.

```
ip route get ADDR [from ADDR iif STRING] [oif STRING] [tos TOS]
```

The ability to specify the sending interface is interesting, because it gives you the ability to ask yourself *what if the packet were actually sent via this other interface?* This includes the source address that will be placed on the packet and the gateway to be used. (By the way, there is a good section on the source-address selection algorithm in Appendix A of Kuznetsov's *IP Command Reference*, the documentation that accompanies *iproute2*.) In the example below, you'll note that the first time I specify the network to reach, the command indicates that the packet will be sent on interface *vmnet4* with a source address on that network. However, if the packet were to be sent via *eth0*, it would have a different source address and would utilize the gateway 192.168.1.1 (indicated by `via`). If we're experiencing problems, perhaps it's because that gateway is masquerading everything passing through it, or the hosts on 193.101.146.0/24 don't have a route to respond to 192.168.1.2. YMMV, but I think it's a nice tool.

```
tony@bach:~$ ip route get 193.101.146.0/24
broadcast 193.101.146.0 dev vmnet4  src 193.101.146.1
    cache <local,brd>  mtu 1500
```

```
tony@bach:~$ ip route get 193.101.146.0/24 oif eth0
193.101.146.0 via 192.168.1.1 dev eth0   src 192.168.1.2
    cache  mtu 1500
```

For our final trick, `ip route list cache [ADDR]` is going to list out routing decisions made in recent history by our system. Basically, this file is a notepad for the routing decisions performed by the kernel. Because the kernel considers many criteria when selecting a route, there may be more entries in the output than you expect. For instance, whenever packets flow between a given source and destination, that constitutes an entry. For packets following this same path, but with a different TOS value, you'll see another (very similar) entry. There's a lot of information here, and I encourage you to play with the command on a system where you're familiar with the sort of traffic (that should be) flowing through it. Piecing together why entries are there (and how they got there) is a good exercise. I'd recommend that you grep out the local entries initially, since they can trip you up trying to grok them at first, or specify an *ADDR* explicitly:

```
tony@java:~$ ip -s route list cache 172.16.5.79
172.16.5.79 from 192.168.1.2 via 10.0.0.1 dev eth0   src 192.168.1.1
    cache <src-direct> users 1 used 11 age 202sec mtu 1500 iif eth1
172.16.5.79 via 10.0.0.1 dev eth0   src 10.0.0.25
    cache users 1 age 206sec mtu 1500
```

In the output above, the entries matching 172.16.5.79 are displayed. It may help to know that java is a masquerading router, with two interfaces 10.0.0.25 (on the outside) and 192.168.1.1 (the inside). 192.168.1.2 is a client contacting 172.16.5.79. The first line tells us that we reached the 172.16.5.79 address via the gateway 10.0.0.1, with a packet that originated from 192.168.1.2. The input interface for that packet was *eth1*, which is further confirmed by `src`, the IP address of the gateway used by the next hop (or the `from` address if it's on the same network). So we can conclude that 192.168.1.2 and 192.168.1.1 are on the same network (which we already knew) and that 192.168.1.2 is using 192.168.1.1 as its gateway to reach 172.16.5.79. The use of `-s` displays additional statistics about the entry in the cache, including how many different IPs used the route and how recently the route was used.

The second line of output tells us something about the return path. Packets from 172.16.5.79 came via java's default gateway, 10.0.0.1 over device *eth0*, which received the packet on address 10.0.0.25. Although we already knew that 10.0.0.25 is the address of *eth0*, the `src` field is more interesting when you're working with a device that has multiple IP addresses. So *ip* knows a lot about routing on our systems, eh? Actually, it's parsing */proc/net/rt_cache* and */proc/net/rt_cache_stat* for us, but we won't quibble because it's very convenient, and this is how most of the networking commands get their information anyway. I know that there are a mind-numbing lot of numbers flying around in this example, but that's really all routers do, sling numbers around. If you really want to melt your brain, take a look at the output of `ip -6 -s route cache` on a moderately busy IPv6 router.

If browsing routing table minutiae doesn't strike your fancy, *ip* can also be used to configure tunnels. We will use this functionality throughout the rest of the chapter to build various types of tunnels.

6.3.3   *iproute2*: **Tunneling IP over IP**

The *ip tunnel* command is (alarmingly!) one of the simplest of the *ip* command forms. It covers three types of IPv4 tunnels (the modes): ipip, which is IPv4 inside of IPv4, gre (Generic Routing

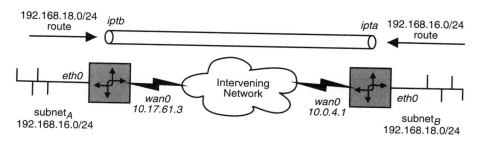

Figure 6.2 General Tunneling Setup

Encapsulation), another IPv4 within IPv4 protocol, and sit (Simple Internet Transition), which is IPv6 inside IPv4 and intended for phased migration to the IPv6 protocol. Tunnels are typically deployed when the pathway between two networks cannot route the traffic for those networks directly because the IP address space of one or both of the networks is not routable along the pathway. Conceptually, it's a little bit like the packet is masqueraded on one end so that it can traverse the tunnel and then unmasqueraded on the other end so that it can continue on toward its destination. But in reality, the IP payload on the tunnel is packaged up inside another perfectly normal packet that is sent from one end of the tunnel to the other. Take a gander at Figure 6.2 for an artist's rendition of what's happening here.

Simple enough, right? We have two boxes separated by an arbitrarily complex network, the key attribute of which is that we can count on most of our packets sent from the external interface (*wan0*) of router$_A$ to reach the external interface of router$_B$. We would like systems on subnet$_A$ to be able to reach subnet$_B$ and vice versa. So we configure a tunnel to carry this traffic between the two routers and add a route to router$_A$ to send all traffic destined for 192.168.18.0/24 via the tunnel device on that box, and a corresponding route to router$_B$ for the 192.168.16.0/24 traffic.

Now, what do I mean by the term *tunnel device*? This is a virtual device—it shows up in an *ifconfig*, it has an IP address, and you can assign a route to it—but it doesn't correspond to a real physical device. By being a device (and not merely a set of rules in the kernel) it provides a handy abstraction in a paradigm that network administrators are used to manipulating. When you send something via a tunnel device, say from 192.168.16.45 (client$_A$) to 192.168.18.27 (client$_B$), the packet is wholly encapsulated (source and destination address included) into another packet that has source address 10.17.61.3 and destination 10.0.4.1. Now, the intervening network knows how to find 10.0.4.1, and when the packet arrives, it is examined by router$_B$, the headers are peeled off, and it is forwarded on to client$_B$, just as if it had traversed the path without the tunnel. Of course, for client$_B$ to respond to client$_A$, the same procedure must be followed in reverse. The nice bit is that the clients need not be aware that this is occurring.

Configuring an IPIP Tunnel

As you've come to expect, you'll need kernel support for this example. The feature is compiled into the kernel if you have a message like `IPv4 over IPv4 tunneling driver` in the output of *dmesg* after boot or after you load the *ipip* module. The module is enabled by compiling support for:

```
Networking options --->
  <M>   IP: tunneling
```

Constructing a tunnel consists of the following steps:

1. Create a tunnel device, specifying the type of tunnel as well as the local and remote ends of the table. You must specify a name for your tunnel device. I use *iptb* to indicate a tunnel to subnet$_B$ and *ipta* for the tunnel to subnet$_A$. The mode tells *ip* what type of encapsulation to use. The local address is what you want as the source address for any tunneled packets from this router—in other words, the address of *wan0* on router$_A$. The remote address is the address to which the tunneled packets are to be sent.

2. Assign an IP address to our tunnel device. Although you are free to choose almost anything within reason here, the convention is to use the same IP address as the internal address on the router (i.e., *eth0* on router$_A$). The best reason for this is that when you initiate a packet directly from router$_A$, it won't have yet another IP that needs to be resolved and routed. Also, these addresses are incorporated already into the routes we're going to add.

3. Configure the interface to be administratively up. (This can be easy to forget until you become accustomed to it.)

4. Add a route for the distant subnet that points to the tunnel. The commands for both ends of the tunnel are spelled out below.

```
routera:~$ ip tunnel add iptb mode ipip local 10.17.61.3 remote 10.0.4.1
routera:~$ ip addr add 192.168.16.1 dev iptb
routera:~$ ip link set iptb up
routera:~$ ip route add 192.168.18.0/24 dev iptb

routerb:~$ ip tunnel add ipta mode ipip local 10.0.4.1 remote 10.17.61.3
routerb:~$ ip addr add 192.168.18.1 dev ipta
routerb:~$ ip link set ipta up
routerb:~$ ip route add 192.168.16.0/24 dev ipta
```

Now, there had better be something on the other end expecting the IP-within-IP encapsulated packets, or they're not going to get very far. Therefore, we need to perform an almost identical configuration on router$_B$. This type of tunnel is not like a PPP device where the devices speak a link-layer protocol with each other. Router$_A$ has no idea whether router$_B$ (or the IP address specified by `remote`) is going to do anything with the encapsulated IP packets. It just knows to perform the encapsulation, slap the remote IP address on the header, and send the packet on its way.

I encourage you to set up a tunnel and then use a packet sniffer to take a look at the packets generated in comparison to normal IPv4 traffic (*ethereal* is great for this). *Note:* Be careful about adding default routes over your tunnels. While this may be what you want to do, keep in mind that unless you're using some source-based routing (separate routing tables, a topic in Section 8.4.1), you cannot have multiple default routes, and your router still has to be able to find the remote end of the tunnel without using the tunnel itself! Invariably, when I make these kinds of mistakes, I'm on the far end of the tunnel, which is where it really hurts, because then I need another way in. Fortunately, the first time I configured this, both ends were located in the same building, so it didn't take too much walking back and forth before I got the procedure straight.

IPIP Tunnel Deployment Considerations

Hopefully it's evident how to approach the tunneling between the Ethernet segments behind cesium and xenon. The combination of media types is immaterial. You can use *tcpdump* and friends to monitor the tunnel device itself—a great way to troubleshoot a configuration that isn't working the way you expect it to. Also, there's no reason to stop at a single tunnel between two routers. You can build arbitrarily complex topologies where a packet may traverse several tunnels before reaching its destination, the only requirements being that routes exist along the way (you'd have to have that anyway) and that there aren't any firewalls that take offense to IP protocol 4 (the packet type used for IPIP) or prevent two-way communication between the tunnel endpoints. If you might be tunneling across a firewall, realize that the IPIP protocol consists of raw IP packets of protocol 4, no UDP or TCP, and thus no ports. If you own the piece in the middle and would like, for some reason, to block tunnels (maybe because folks are using them to run telnet after the big boss made it clear that telnet was dangerous and not to be tolerated?), you can use the following *iptables* command on the intervening router to prevent IPIP tunneling from occurring:

```
iptables -t filter -A FORWARD --proto 4 -j DROP
```

GRE Tunnels

If you're interested in running GRE instead of IPIP, you have merely to indicate `mode gre` when you configure the tunnel. (Well, you'll need to `modprobe ip_gre` after enabling this option as a module in the kernel.) If you don't change anything else, you'll end up with essentially the same tunnel, but this time using raw IP protocol 47. This brings up a good point about IPIP tunnels and security. They're not the least bit secure in the sense of a VPN (we'll get to that later in the book); everything you send through the tunnel is available to folks in the intervening network. GRE addresses this to some extent. Take a look at the syntax for *ip tunnel* and you'll notice the three options on the third line that are applicable only to GRE tunnels.

```
tony@bach:~$ ip tunnel help
Usage: ip tunnel { add | change | del | show } [ NAME ]
          [ mode { ipip | gre | sit } ] [ remote ADDR ] [ local ADDR ]
          [ [i|o]seq ] [ [i|o]key KEY ] [ [i|o]csum ]
          [ ttl TTL ] [ tos TOS ] [ [no]pmtudisc ] [ dev PHYS_DEV ]
```

By specifying `key KEY`, where `KEY` is a 32-bit integer, you can prevent folks from arbitrarily inserting traffic into the tunnel. The tunnel device will only accept GRE packets containing the correct key. This buys you something if the hacker doesn't have access to capture packets in the stream between the tunnel endpoints, because the key will have to be guessed by brute force. But the key is stored in cleartext in the packet header. The `csum` option tells the tunnel device to generate checksums for outgoing packets and require that incoming packets contain valid checksums. Finally, the `seq` flag indicates that sequence numbers should be included in the GRE headers (used for sequential packet numbering). This is a counter that starts at one and increments for each packet. This actually provides somewhat better security against someone trying to slip random packets into the stream, because they have to get the sequence number correct. (*Note:* I noticed that you cannot use `ip tunnel change` to enable sequence numbers after the tunnel has been configured up, so use this option when you first add the tunnel.) The [i|o] indicates whether the parameter is to be applied to inbound or outbound traffic on the tunnel. Not specifying a direction means that the parameter should be used for both directions.

GRE is a more complicated protocol than IPIP and therefore supports more options, such as multicast routing, recursion prevention, the options discussed in the previous paragraph, and others. The cost compared to that of IPIP is a larger header, and you're still missing the security of full-blown encryption that we'll talk about in Section 6.4. Still, it's an invaluable tool to have on your Linux router when you need to communicate with a traditional router that speaks GRE.

Various Other *ip tunnel* Commands

You can add, change, del,[2] and show (or list) tunnels on your system. You can specify specific ttl and tos values for the packets while they traverse the tunnel. If you do not, the encapsulating header inherits whatever value the packet has just before it enters the tunnel. You can indicate PMTU (Path MTU discovery) is not to occur on this tunnel, which means that the system will not negotiate an MTU. By default this is off, and it cannot be used in conjunction with setting a fixed ttl (since PMTU needs the TTL field to do its job). If you'd like to set the MTU of the tunnel interface, you can always use ip link set dev *TDEV* mtu *MTU*, just as you would for a real interface. If you receive an error message like ioctl: No buffer space available while working with your tunnel devices, make sure that you're not re-adding a tunnel device that hasn't been deleted. You can use ip -s tunnel list *[dev]* to list some statistics specific to the tunnel protocol you're running. Finally, by using dev *DEV*, you tie a tunnel device to transmit only via particular interface on the system, meaning that if your route to the endpoint changes to point out a different physical device, the tunnel won't follow. (If you do not specify a device, the tunnel will use any device it can reach at the far endpoint.)

Tunneling Gedanken Experiments

Can you create a tunnel across a masquerading router/NAT? Does it matter if there is more than one NAT in the path between the tunnel endpoints? Can you make it work for a single tunnel, but not if there are multiple tunnels? What about if there are multiple tunnels with a common endpoint? (You may want to use more than just your *Gehirn*—I found it necessary to fire up at least four different copies of *tcpdump* before I was satisfied with what I saw.) Think about it, try it.

6.4 *FreeS/WAN*—An IPsec Implementation for Linux

FreeS/WAN is the project name of Linux's IPsec implementation. The *Free* part is obvious; *S/WAN* is the Secure Wide Area Network project, which is working to ensure that the various IPsec implementations really do interoperate when the time comes. (The VPN Consortium, *http://www.vpnc.org/*, is also involved in this effort.) One important aspect of the *FreeS/WAN* project is the emphasis on using code and algorithms free from patent problems, and, insofar

---

[2]Annoyingly, you cannot use the full word delete. If I weren't so lazy, I'd scare up a C compiler and fix that . . . .

as possible, free from export (or at least use) restrictions in countries that view cryptography as a weapon. In the United States, where I am writing this book, things seems to have taken a tiny step forward and two giant leaps backward with the new regulations from the Commerce Department's Bureau of Export Administration (or BXA) and the DMCA (Digital Millennium Copyright Act). As inconceivable as it is, it is illegal for any American to contribute code (or even a patch) to the *FreeS/WAN* project. The *FreeS/WAN* documentation makes a point of noting that *the U.S. government has very little sense of humor about this issue and does not consider good intentions to be sufficient excuse. Beware.* Instead of going off on a rant about how very misguided I believe some of these laws to be, you should research the matter and form your own opinion. Therefore, those of you who live in free countries are spared, and all of us can focus on using *FreeS/WAN*, which has been graciously provided by contributors in countries without these sorts of restrictions. *FreeS/WAN* consists of several components that must mesh to make everything tick. These are listed here so that you can start building a mental map of how the pieces fit together.

- The IPsec protocol itself, the part that encrypts packets before sending them and decrypts them on the other side, is implemented by **KLIPS**, or Kernel Level IP Security. This is a set of kernel patches distributed with *FreeS/WAN*.

- A public-key exchange service, somewhat similar to public GPG and PGP key servers. As with any public-key algorithm, public keys can be made openly available and freely distributed, but the burden is still on you to verify the authenticity of the key before using it. This portion of IPsec is handled by the **IKE** (Internet Key Exchange), which has been implemented within *FreeS/WAN* by a daemon named *pluto*. (I'm not sure, but would guess that this is a humorous reference to Kerberos, a.k.a. Cerebus.) If you're going to support large numbers of users, say in the case where you're using IPsec as your VPN protocol for all of your field users, the IKE component is often referred to as **PKI** (Public Key Infrastructure), or X.509.

- A set of user-space tools to configure and manage the kernel module. This is */usr/sbin/ipsec* itself, which thankfully can be used as the the single interface to the tools used to generate keys, configure the links, start IPsec, start *pluto*, gather statistics, etc.

There is a lot to *FreeS/WAN* and IPsec, enough to write a book on it easily, especially when you get into the details of deployment using different types of keys and different implementations. I'm certainly not the person to write that book, and I don't want to confuse the issue by presenting information that cannot be adequately covered. We're going to set up *FreeS/WAN* as a tunnel between two Linux systems so that we can enjoy the routing benefits of the tunnel and the safety of encryption for the traffic flowing over it. Therefore, we are necessarily only scratching the surface.

6.4.1   *FreeS/WAN* **Distribution—Obtaining and Building**

The primary source for the upstream package is *ftp://ftp.xs4all.nl/pub/crypto/freeswan/*. Since the cryptography export laws of various countries are continually in flux, there aren't many mirrors. Note this also means that the distribution CD that comes with your favorite Linux CD may not have the distribution's version of the package either, so you may have to search a little, since the package will need to be pulled from a network site (possibly not the primary site for the distribution). You may also have problems with support (at least from distributions based in the United States), since such activity is all regulated. This is a shame, because building and installing *FreeS/WAN* from the upstream source takes time and resources that would be better spent not duplicating effort. I was able to get the Debian package installed and running in a matter of minutes (most of those minutes being the part where I had to patch my kernel, since the upstream kernel does not contain the KLIPS code, once again due to legal restrictions). If you're using your distribution's packages, follow the included instructions. We'll walk through the steps to build *FreeS/WAN* using the upstream tarball.

1. Have a copy of the recent kernel source tree in */usr/src/linux/*. If you're pulling a copy of the kernel source just for this, you should go ahead and configure your kernel once, using the configuration method of your choice.

2. Locate and install copies of **libgmp3-dev** and **libgmp3** (these are the Debian package names), as these are required for the build and run time, respectively. GMP is the GNU Multi-Precision math library and is required by *FreeS/WAN* for key calculations. If you're really working from scratch, you can pull the source for the libraries from *http://www.swox.com/gmp/*.

3. Extract the tarball and `cd freeswan-1.91`. Invoke `make menugo`, which will patch the kernel source and give you another chance to review the configuration, or `menu ogo` if you're quite sure that the kernel configuration is how you want it. By default (and if you use the latter), IPsec will be compiled directly into the kernel, so use menugo if you'd prefer it to be a module. The options you're concerned with are:

```
Networking options --->
  <*> IP Security Protocol (FreeS/WAN IPSEC)
  --- IPSec options (FreeS/WAN)
  [*]     IPSEC: IP-in-IP encapsulation (tunnel mode)
  [*]     IPSEC: Authentication Header
  [*]        HMAC-MD5 authentication algorithm
  [*]        HMAC-SHA1 authentication algorithm
  [*]     IPSEC: Encapsulating Security Payload
  [*]        3DES encryption algorithm
  [*]     IPSEC: IP Compression
  [*]     IPSEC Debugging Option
```

4. Get a cup of coffee, catch up on email, or take a nap (which depends upon how long it takes your box to build a 2.4 kernel). The kernel build should complete without error, and it will also install the user-space tools into the default location of */usr/local/lib/ipsec/*. You'll still need to `cd /usr/src/linux ; make bzlilo` or similar to get the new kernel into a place where you can boot from it. Alternatively, try `make kinstall` from the freeswan-1.91 directory.

After these steps, you should have the files */etc/ipsec.conf* and */etc/ipsec.secrets* (which will already contain a generated key pair for this system), the tools as noted above, and a system startup script called *ipsec* in */etc/init.d/* or wherever your system startup directory is. But don't reboot yet. If you do, *ipsec* will start at boot time. You have a halfway working configuration at this point, a configuration that will add routes to the *ipsec0* virtual device and could possibly make for a long boot process waiting for DNS lookups (or worse, mounts) to time out. Plus, you'll probably need console access to get back on the machine.

6.4.2   Configuring *FreeS/WAN* and *ipsec*

Although there is potentially quite a lot to configuring *FreeS/WAN*, to achieve a basic two-system topology you need only generate key pairs on the routers at each end of the tunnel, place these into */etc/ipsec.secrets*, exchange the public keys from these key pairs, edit */etc/ipsec.conf* on one system and copy it to the other (nice touch, IMO), and then fire it up. The first step is done for you automatically when using the upstream package. If you're using a distribution package, check to see if keys were generated (they aren't in the current Debian package). If they weren't, or you'd like to generate a new keypair at any time, you can use `ipsec rsasigkey 2048 >./myipseckey` to generate your key. You'll need to add the contents of *myipseckey* to the appropriate place in */etc/ipsec.secrets* for that system only. You can use a number other than 2048, the number of bits in the key, but I couldn't get *FreeS/WAN* to use a key shorter than 512 bits. In general, you need to protect the contents of */etc/ipsec.secrets* just as you would your own GPG private key. The file contains the private key that identifies your system as you, so if someone has it, they can spoof that system's identity. (Therefore, destroy the *myipseckey* file, watch file permissions on the file in */etc/*, think about who has access to backup media, and so on.)

To view the usage statement for `ipsec rsasigkey`, invoke it with the `--help` argument, which is valid for any `ipsec command` form, much like `ip`; `ipsec` alone will show you the allowed commands. If you're looking for the command itself, the upstream package drops this executable into */usr/local/sbin/*, so you may want to add this to your `PATH`. Before we dig into the configuration file, let's take a look at our simple topology in Figure 6.3. The default configuration file uses the labels of **left** and **right** to differentiate between the two systems in a peer-to-peer topology like the one we're going to build here.

The figure labels interfaces the way that */etc/ipsec.conf* does, so if your topology is similar, you can simply plug in the values and go. Note that you need not have two separate gateways between your two systems—there may be one router, or the left and right systems may be part of the same subnet. The same is true for the **leftsubnet** and the **rightsubnet**; if they don't exist, just comment them out in the configuration file. Both the subnet and nexthop values are there so that *FreeS/WAN* can configure routes over the *ipsecN* devices accordingly. In the following example configuration, we're configuring a single workstation, vivaldi, to set up a secure connection to drone1, and to route 192.168.0.0/16 over that secure tunnel.

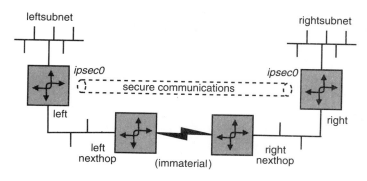

Figure 6.3 *FreeS/WAN* Basic Configuration Topology

```
# basic configuration on drone1
config setup
        interfaces=%defaultroute
        klipsdebug=none
        plutodebug=none
        plutoload=%search
        plutostart=%search
        uniqueids=yes


conn %default
        keyingtries=0        # be persistent
        authby=rsasig        # use rsakeys

conn vivaldi-drone1
        leftid=@vivaldi.mancill.com
        leftrsasigkey=0sAQO8...
        left=192.168.16.55
        leftnexthop=192.168.16.13
        rightid=@drone1.mancill.com
        rightrsasigkey=0x0103....
        right=192.168.18.11
        rightnexthop=192.168.18.13
        rightsubnet=192.168.0.0/16
        auto=start
```

The first section contains general parameters global to the entire setup and probably will not need to modified. *FreeS/WAN* logs a good bit of information via syslog, even when the debug modes are set to *none*, so you probably won't need to set these to their full value, which is *all*. The `uniqueids` parameter is used to indicate that if a second connection comes in from the same ID, the first connection should be torn down. Leave it like that to avoid confusion (otherwise you may need to restart *ipsec* on both ends of a connection after a parameter change). The second section contains parameters to be applied to all connection (`conn`) sections in the file. In this file we have only one connection defined, but you can list as many as you'd like. Note that you'll need to assign a unique id to every node that will be running IPsec, so the use of a DNS name is a natural choice. There is another reason for this as well. DNS can be configured to serve those rsasigkeys, so that you aren't constantly trying to cut and paste them between systems. (Just take the necessary precautions to ensure that someone doesn't spoof your DNS.) After placing the same file on vivaldi, we're ready to test our configuration.

6.4.3   *FreeS/WAN* **in Use**

To start *FreeS/WAN*, use either */etc/init.d/ipsec start* or `ipsec --setup start`, both of which actually run the same script. You'll need to do this on both ends and be patient while *pluto* figures things out. Most likely you will receive some warning messages during the startup about needing to disable reverse path (or route) filtering on all of the interfaces involved with your configuration. This is necessary basically because, in a way, you're communicating over two interfaces simultaneously, the *ipsecN* interface along with your physical Ethernet device. You may send something from vivaldi to drone1 while restarting *FreeS/WAN* on vivaldi, and therefore before the IPsec link is up, but once vivaldi has that, it can respond via the tunnel. By disabling the reverse path filtering, you're saying that this is OK and allowing **asymmetrical routing**. (In general, this is to be avoided, but there are situations where it is required, this being one of them.) Execute `echo "0" >/proc/sys/net/ipv4/conf/`*intf*`/rp_filter` for each of your physical and virtual *ipsec* devices used in the *ipsec* configuration, as the warning messages will instruct you (although it's not abundantly clear to me why the startup script can take care of the *ipsec* devices for you). A successful startup will look something like:

```
tmancill@drone1:~# sudo /etc/init.d/ipsec start
ipsec_setup: Starting FreeS/WAN IPsec U1.9/K1.91...
ipsec_setup: 102 "vivaldi-drone1" #1: STATE_MAIN_I1: initiate
ipsec_setup: 104 "vivaldi-drone1" #1: STATE_MAIN_I2: from STATE_MAIN_I1; sent MI2, expecting MR2
ipsec_setup: 106 "vivaldi-drone1" #1: STATE_MAIN_I3: from STATE_MAIN_I2; sent MI3, expecting MR3
ipsec_setup: 004 "vivaldi-drone1" #1: STATE_MAIN_I4: ISAKMP SA established
ipsec_setup: 110 "vivaldi-drone1" #6: STATE_QUICK_I1: initiate
ipsec_setup: 004 "vivaldi-drone1" #6: STATE_QUICK_I2: sent QI2, IPsec SA established
```

If you've set up a sniffer somewhere along the path between the two systems, you can watch the key negotiations occur on port 500 (which will obviously need to be allowed to pass through intermediary firewalls and NATs). If you are behind something that may hinder this communication, specify this in the configuration file under the connection-specific information with `rightfirewall=yes` for the right side, left for the left. I include some sniffer output that details the key exchange as well as some encapsulating security paylog (ESP) packets, which is now as much as any eavesdropper will determine about the communication between these two systems.

```
tmancill@drone3:/tmp$ sudo tcpdump -n host vivaldi and host drone1
tcpdump: listening on eth0
vivaldi.500 > drone1.500: isakmp: phase 1 I ident: [|sa] (DF)
drone1.500 > vivaldi.500: isakmp: phase 1 R ident: [|sa] (DF)
vivaldi.500 > drone1.500: isakmp: phase 1 I ident: [|ke] (DF)
drone1.500 > vivaldi.500: isakmp: phase 1 R ident: [|ke] (DF)
vivaldi.500 > drone1.500: isakmp: phase 1 I ident[E]: [|id] (DF)
drone1.500 > vivaldi.500: isakmp: phase 1 R ident[E]: [|id] (DF)
vivaldi.500 > drone1.500: isakmp: phase 2/others I oakley-quick[E]: [|hash] (DF)
drone1.500 > vivaldi.500: isakmp: phase 2/others R oakley-quick[E]: [|hash] (DF)
vivaldi.500 > drone1.500: isakmp: phase 2/others I oakley-quick[E]: [|hash] (DF)
.
.
.
drone1 > vivaldi: ESP(spi=0x2c525b1b,seq=0x1)
vivaldi > drone1: ESP(spi=0xf1a4e13d,seq=0x8)
```

If you are so inclined, now would be the perfect time to try out that −E option for *tcpdump*, where you supply the secret key to decrypt the contents of the ESP packets. Note that your distribution's copy of *tcpdump* might not be able to handle the crypto code (due to the same export regulations mentioned earlier), so you may have to dig around to find a binary, or compile your own.

Once you have your link up and running, you can use the *ipsec0* device like most any network device, adding routes to it and starting packet sniffers to monitor it (which will give you access to the unencrypted packets on the wire). You can use several of the *FreeS/WAN* tools to get your bearing. `ipsec eroute` will display routes on your system that will result in use of the encrypted communications channels. By the way, if you set up multiple connections and mistakenly configure the leftsubnet or rightsubnet so that there are multiple routes to the same subnet, you may see an error message about an eroute being unavailable (as it's masked by another). `ipsec look` will show you a goodly amount of information about your IPsec connection(s), and `ipsec barf` gives you a ton of information, including configuration details, that can be used as part of a bug report or request for assistance. (Look carefully at the output and you'll see that it does not share your keys.) Even if you don't plan on filing a bug, you can use this command as a starting point for exploring what's pertinent to your *FreeS/WAN* configuration.

6.4.4   More Elaborate *FreeS/WAN* Configurations

It is trivial to add additional connections to */etc/ipsec.conf*. Each connection will begin with the `conn` *lname-rname* statement (actually, the connection name is arbitrary, but using the lname-rname convention makes good sense). Since your first connection always starts up on *ipsec0*, don't expect to have the second connection in the file attach to the virtual device *ipsec1*. That's not how it works. Connections will share a given *ipsecN* interface as long as that is the interface being used to transmit and receive for that connection. This is because each *ipsecN* is bound to a physical device (see `ipsec tncfg` for the bindings). You'll note that the current KLIPS implementation allows for four *ipsecN* interfaces, meaning four different physical interfaces—likely more than enough for most systems. When adding connections, there is no need to maintain consistency in the left/right semantics other than for your own sanity. If you build a topology with a closed path, e.g., a triangle, someone who is a lefty will have to be a righty in at least one of the connections.

FreeS/WAN can also be configured to support what is known as **opportunistic** connections. In this configuration, the system will attempt to establish IPsec communications for outgoing connections (or incoming connections, if it is configured for such), once again using DNS as a mechanism for retrieving the public key for the system on the other end. This demonstrates the real potential of IPsec—no more TCP wrappers, the reverse DNS lookup will be replaced by a key lookup (which can be compared to a cache of keys on our local system for an added layer of protection, similar to how *ssh* clients work), and once that checks out, you will have secure communication between the two endpoints without any further configuration required.

If we want to (i.e., we're truly paranoid enough), we can go back to cesium and xenon and, with just a little more work, replace our IPIP tunnels with IPsec using *FreeS/WAN*. When you really start working with *FreeS/WAN*, take the time to read the excellent documentation included in the *doc/* directory of the source tree. And to reiterate, we're merely scratching the surface with *FreeS/WAN* and with secure tunneling software in this section. If you control both ends (and have a compiler on both ends), I'd recommend taking a look at *VTun*, which not only provides security, but incorporates compression and traffic shaping into the same tool. It is available at *http://vtun.sourceforge.net/*. If you're not sure what you want, but you haven't come across it yet, there is an excellent site specializing in cryptography software (all types, not just tunnels) for Linux at *http://munitions.vipul.net/*.

Now we're going to switch gears a little bit and talk about IP version 6. It may seem like a change in direction, but the IPsec protocol used in *FreeS/WAN* is actually a backport of the security features designed into IPv6. You'll also see that eventually we're going to end up tunneling again—this time to run IPv6 within IPv4 over links that don't yet speak IPv6.

6.5   A Brief Introduction to IPv6 on Linux

IPv6 has been around for several years now. The original proposal was made in 1994 and was approved that same year by the Internet Engineering Steering Group (IESG). In 1998 the basic protocols were approved as drafts by the IETF (Internet Engineering Task Force), which means that the protocols were officially RFCs. The protocol seeks to address some of the shortcomings with IPv4 while retaining features that allow the migration from IPv4 to occur piecewise (meaning that you can run both protocols simultaneously on the same interface and there is a proposed mapping of IPv4 address space to IPv6). IPv6 has the following features:

- The new addressing scheme has 128 bits, as opposed to IPv4's measly 32 bits. Instead of a horrendous *dotted-sixteen*, in accordance with IPv4's dotted quad, addresses are represented in hexadecimal using a colon to separate each 16 bits. This still results in 8 fields of 4 hex digits—for example:

  3ffe:0b00:0c18:1fff:0000:0000:0000:0286

  However, you're allowed to drop leading zeroes and to coalesce as many adjacent fields of all zeroes into a single *::* as you can. So the address above becomes:

  3ffe:b00:c18:1fff::286

  That might not make you feel a lot better, but then again, users typically won't be typing them out (leave that to the poor lummox running the routers, eh?)

- IPv6's header structure is extensible, unlike IPv4's fixed-length (and for many people's tastes, somewhat cramped) header. The minimum header length in IPv6 is 40 bytes, but 32 of those are used for the source and destination addresses alone. The remaining 8 bytes contain the **version**, **priority**, **flow label**, **payload length**, **next header**, and **hop limit** fields. The priority and flow label fields are worth mentioning. The former is a 4-bit field meant to be populated by the sender to categorize the traffic for use by queuing and congestion management facilities within the network. The latter is 3 bytes long and is meant to identify a specific traffic stream. This is intended to work hand-in-hand with QoS mechanisms, where a level of service is negotiated for that particular stream when the connection is initiated. The next header field is used to indicate whether or not the data payload begins a TCP or UDP packet, or perhaps more headers.

- There is a concept of an **anycast address**, which is a way of the sender's saying *please deliver this packet to **any** of the machines configured with this anycast address*. When this packet is routed, it's delivered to the closest routable interface configured with that anycast address. Providing redundancy and ease of configuration has just become much easier. You may want to provide three or four proxy servers on different segments in your network and configure them with the same anycast address. Users will always get the nearest one, even if that means that 3 of the 4 are down for maintenance. And there is no more haggling with what's the right name for multihomed boxes. Assign the same anycast address to all of the interfaces and advertise the anycast address via DNS.

- The semantics of the **multicast address** have been refined to include a **scope** and to do away with broadcast addresses. This makes sense, since a broadcast is just a special case of a multicast anyway. BTW, a regular unique address assigned to a single interface is called a **unicast address** in IPv6.

- IPv6 offers better support for security and authentication (IPsec) and takes advantage of that extensible header format in that only routers that care to look at the extended headers in a stream must do so. Other routers along the packet's path can process the 40-byte header and ignore the rest.

- The ICMP portion of the protocol, ICMPv6, has options for automatic assignment of unique **link-local**, **site-local**, and **global** addresses. As its name implies, the first of these is valid only on the physical link to which that interface is attached, implying uniqueness only within the realm of that specific link-layer space. Such addresses cannot be routed across subnet boundaries. The site-local address is routable only within a site. And a global address is just that—a unique routable address, anywhere IPv6 is spoken. Obviously the assignment of the global address requires some information from routers at your site with your routable IPv6 address allocation, which is done via an ICMPv6 Router Solicitation. See Table 6.1 for some special IPv6 addresses/networks, or **prefixes** as they are commonly called.

Table 6.1 Common IPv6 Addresses and Prefixes

prefix/address	significance
2000::/3	provider-based prefix
3ffe::/48	part of the Test pTLA
fe80::/10	link-local prefix
fec0::/10	site-local prefix
ff00::/8	multicast prefix
::192.168.15.14	IPv6 mapping of IPv4 address
::1	loopback address
::/0	default route

Note that you may also see fe80::/10 expressed as fe80::/64, as the convention is to fill the intervening 54 bits with zeroes and use the last 64 bits for the unique link-local address.[3] fec0::/10 similarly is often seen as fec0::xxxx/64—the convention being to fill the address with zeroes until you get to the 16-bit subnet field, which you'll populate for this local address space. The next 64 bits are for a unique host id within one of those 65 thousand subnets.

6.5.1   IPv6 Test Drive

If you aren't already experimenting with IPv6, stop what you're doing (er, finish reading this section first) and set up an IPv6 test lab so that you can start building skills with IPv6. Linux provides a quite capable testbed, and by the time you're reading this, the Linux implementation is far from bleeding edge. We'll work through a couple of examples in this chapter to whet your appetite for further exploration.

You'll need to compile IPv6 support into your kernel (if it's not already there). While it's not an absolute necessity, you'll probably want to have the *iproute2* toolset loaded on

---

[3]I'm still trying to fathom a link with 2^{64} hosts on it.

your box. Its syntax is easier to follow, and more and more of the examples and HOWTOs you find will be using it. Finally, you'll need some applications that support IPv6. This last bit might prove the most difficult, but applications with IPv6 support compiled into them are becoming more prevalent for Linux. Although you might not have all of your favorite tools, there should be enough on a modern Linux system to at least test things. At the bare minimum, you'll want to have *ping6* and *tracepath6* (or *traceroute6*). The first two are part of the *iputils* package by Alexey Kuznetsov, the networking genius of *iproute2* fame, and both can be found at *ftp://ftp.inr.ac.ru/ip-routing/*. (Most distributions have an **iputils** package; Debian has **iputils-ping** and **iputils-tracepath**.) To configure your kernel for IPv6 support:

```
Code maturity level options  --->
   [*] Prompt for development and/or incomplete code/drivers
Networking options  --->
   <M>   The IPv6 protocol (EXPERIMENTAL)
```

Then rebuild and boot from the new kernel. To check to see if your kernel already has IPv6 support, look for the existence of the */proc/sys/net/ipv6/* directory in the */proc* filesystem, or try `modprobe ipv6` (and then check in */proc*). You should also be able to ping your loopback address with `ping6 ::1` (and notice how, on reasonably fast machines, *ping6* returns the time in μsec for submillisecond ping responses).

Configuring Interfaces and Routes for IPv6

In order to become familiar with the syntax and accustomed to working with the new addresses, let's configure something basic and very much like the router *silicon* in Chapter 3. First let's get two systems on the same subnet speaking to each other by assigning them IPv6 unicast addresses. The systems are drone3, which is our router box with two interfaces, and vivaldi, which is a Linux workstation. We'll use address space from the site-local prefix and invent a subnet following the fec0::xxxx/64 convention mentioned previously. If we assign our network address to be fec0:0:0:1/64, we can take the first two IPs from this, which are fec0:0:0:1:0:0:0:1 and fec0:0:0:1:0:0:0:2. To illustrate how to use both *ip* and *ifconfig*, drone3 will be configured with the former and vivaldi with the latter. (Refer to Section 6.3 for more details on *ip*.)

```
root@drone3:~# ip -6 addr show
1: lo: <LOOPBACK,UP> mtu 16436 qdisc noqueue
    inet6 ::1/128 scope host
2: eth0: <BROADCAST,MULTICAST,UP> mtu 1500 qdisc pfifo_fast qlen 100
    inet6 fe80::250:56ff:fee2:69/10 scope link
3: eth1: <BROADCAST,MULTICAST,UP> mtu 1500 qdisc pfifo_fast qlen 100
    inet6 fe80::250:56ff:fead:102/10 scope link

root@drone3:~# ip addr add fec0::1:0:0:0:1/64 dev eth0

root@drone3:~# ip addr list eth0
2: eth0: <BROADCAST,MULTICAST,UP> mtu 1500 qdisc pfifo_fast qlen 100
    link/ether 00:50:56:e2:00:69 brd ff:ff:ff:ff:ff:ff
    inet 192.168.16.13/24 brd 192.168.16.255 scope global eth0
    inet6 fec0:0:0:1::1/64 scope site
    inet6 fe80::250:56ff:fee2:69/10 scope link
```

```
root@drone3:~# ip -6 route show
fe80::/10 dev eth0   proto kernel   metric 256   mtu 1500
fe80::/10 dev eth1   proto kernel   metric 256   mtu 1500
fec0:0:0:1::/64 dev eth0   proto kernel   metric 256   mtu 1500
ff00::/8 dev eth0   proto kernel   metric 256   mtu 1500
ff00::/8 dev eth1   proto kernel   metric 256   mtu 1500
default dev eth1   proto kernel   metric 256   mtu 1500
default dev eth0   proto kernel   metric 256   mtu 1500
unreachable default dev lo   metric -1   error -101
```

There are a few details to notice in the four prior commands. First, we display only the IPv6 addresses for the interfaces on our system using the -6 option for *ip*. Note that when the ipv6 module is loaded an IPv6 address is automatically added to all the interfaces, the ::1 by convention to the loopback, and automatically generated local-link addresses for the Ethernet adapters. The second command performs the address assignment. Note that I used :: to save typing a few zeroes. The next command is just another form of ip addr list that shows all of the interfaces on *eth0* that I'm using to check my work. The fourth command displays the IPv6 routing table on drone3. It looks like a mess, with duplicate entries for fe80::/10, ff00::/8, and the default route. I include it to make a point about Linux IPv6 (at least at the time of writing). Although the functionality is there, some of the polish and fine-tuning is yet to be done. In this case, it seems that the interface initialization code assigns these routes to every interface it finds. (Besides the default route, there aren't any really negative side-effects, and you can use ip -6 route flush root *prefix* to clean these up.) The route that we did want, the one for fec0:0:0:1/64, was added correctly when the IPv6 address was added to *eth0*. Now let's configure vivaldi with another address on this subnet using *ifconfig* and *route*.

```
root@vivaldi:~# ifconfig eth0 add fec0:0:0:1::2/64

root@vivaldi:~# ifconfig eth0
eth0      Link encap:Ethernet  HWaddr 00:50:56:40:40:86
          inet addr:192.168.16.55  Bcast:192.168.16.255  Mask:255.255.255.0
          inet6 addr: fec0:0:0:1::2/64 Scope:Site
          inet6 addr: fe80::250:56ff:fe40:4086/10 Scope:Link
          UP BROADCAST RUNNING MULTICAST  MTU:1500  Metric:1
          RX packets:1447 errors:0 dropped:0 overruns:0 frame:0
          TX packets:1103 errors:0 dropped:0 overruns:0 carrier:0
          collisions:0 txqueuelen:100
          RX bytes:178627 (174.4 Kb)  TX bytes:200231 (195.5 Kb)
          Interrupt:9 Base address:0x1080

root@vivaldi:~# route -A inet6
Kernel IPv6 routing table
```

Destination	Next Hop	Flags	Metric	Ref	Use	Iface
::1/128	::	U	0	0	0	lo
fe80::250:56ff:fe40:4086/128	::	U	0	0	0	lo
fe80::/10	::	UA	256	0	0	eth0
fec0:0:0:1::2/128	::	U	0	0	0	lo
fec0:0:0:1::/64	::	UA	256	0	0	eth0
ff00::/8	::	UA	256	0	0	eth0
::/0	::	UDA	256	0	0	eth0

Using *ifconfig* isn't terribly different from using *ip*—I tend to believe that the version of *ifconfig* in the more recent netkits was influenced by **iproute2**. To view the IPv6 routing table, you have to tell *route* to use address family *inet6*. Try displaying the routing table using both *route*[4] and *ip* and you'll notice some subtle differences. For example, *route* displays host routes for the loopback, link-local, and our newly added unicast address, and indicates that all of these are tied to the loopback device, while *ip* shows none of these. The last entry in the table is the prefix that designates the default route, ::/0 in IPv6 notation. At this point, we should be able to test communications over our link.

```
root@drone3:~# ping6 fec0:0:0:1::2
PING fec0:0:0:1::2(fec0:0:0:1::2) from fec0:0:0:1::1 : 56 data bytes
64 bytes from fec0:0:0:1::2: icmp_seq=0 hops=64 time=837 usec
64 bytes from fec0:0:0:1::2: icmp_seq=1 hops=64 time=492 usec
64 bytes from fec0:0:0:1::2: icmp_seq=2 hops=64 time=521 usec

--- fec0:0:0:1::2 ping statistics ---
3 packets transmitted, 3 packets received, 0% packet loss
round-trip min/avg/max/mdev = 0.492/0.616/0.837/0.158 ms
```

Now we need to configure the system on the other side of our router. I chose fec0:0:0:8/64 for that network, just so the 1::2 and 2::1s wouldn't be confusing. Of course, anything between 0–ffff would be valid in the 16-bit subnet field. We'll assign fec0:0:0:8::1 to *eth1* on drone3, and fec0:0:0:8::2 to our interface on the workstation bach. After testing to make sure that bach can ping the address on drone3 and vice versa, we need to enable forwarding for IPv6 packets on drone3. This is done with the command echo "1" >/proc/sys/net/ipv6/conf/all/ **forwarding** (because we're lazy and don't want to have to echo the value more than once into the */proc/sys/net/ipv6/conf/ethX/forwarding* files). So now vivaldi should be able to communicate with bach, right?

```
root@vivaldi:~# ping6 fec0:0:0:8::2
ping: bind icmp socket: Invalid argument
```

Chances are that you caught my mistake right away. We need network routes. But the error message you receive if you don't have an appropriate route is worth noting, as I don't find it particularly intuitive. If we had tried a telnet, we would have seen a more helpful No route to host. The next two statements illustrate how to add a network route using a gateway.

```
root@vivaldi:~# ip route add fec0:0:0:8::/64 via fec0:0:0:1::1
root@bach:~# route -A inet6 add fec0:0:0:1::/64 gw fec0:0:0:8::1
```

6.5.2   *radvd*—IPv6 Autoconfiguration

If you found typing out those long IPv6 IP addresses and routes in the previous section tedious, good for you; good computer administrators have to possess a certain type of laziness in order

---

[4]Note that I've pared down the output from route considerably, and that the formatting can be confusing on an 80-column terminal. The output from *route -A inet6* is very wide and requires almost 120 columns to display correctly. It is done this way so that the output can have constant field widths without ever truncating long IPv6 addresses.

to achieve greatness.[5] Plus, IPv6 hasn't yet begun to live up to its promise of ease of administration with autoconfiguration. The *Router ADVertisement Daemon*, or *radvd*, is alleged to deliver on that promise. Freely available from *ftp://ftp.cityline.net/pub/systems/linux/network/*
ipv6/radvd/, I recommend that you obtain the patched version from *http://v6web.litech.org/*
radvd/. I loaded the Debian package **radvd**.

After an initial glance at the configuration file for *radvd*, */etc/radvd.conf*, it reminds one
of DHCP. On drone3 I set up the basic default configuration to see if I could autoassign an
address to vivaldi. Start *radvd* with -d3, place it into the background, and then `tail -f`
`/var/log/syslog` so that you can watch the action.

```
drone3:~# cat /etc/radvd.conf
interface eth0
{
    AdvSendAdvert on;
    prefix fec0:0:0:1::/64
    {
        AdvOnLink on;
        AdvAutonomous on;
    };
};
```

Then, I rebooted vivaldi to make sure I was starting with a clean configuration, since once
the IPv6 module is loaded, it cannot be unloaded, and it's more work to configure all of the
interfaces down and back up than it is to reboot. Upon loading the IPv6 module on the new
system, I noticed some *radvd* activity on drone3. Checking on vivaldi, a pseudorandom IPv6
address from the correct prefix was applied, and a default route was configured. (I say *pseu-*
dorandom because you can tell that it's a mangled version of the MAC address of the card
configured.) I was able to ping drone3's address on the same link, so that was good. But the default route was not via the site-local gateway address I had configured for drone3, fec0:0:0:1::1,
but instead over drone3's link-local address. Although unexpected, it works, making another
point for starting to play with IPv6 now, before you actually have to start deploying it, so
that you're familiar with how it really works.

If you recall from the configuration of drone3, there were all kinds of unexpected IPv6
routes automatically configured for each interface. Now it was time to see if those collided
with each other when I configured *radvd* to advertise one of the router interfaces. I was afraid
that this

```
drone3:~# ip -6 route list
fe80::/10 dev eth0   proto kernel   metric 256   mtu 1500
fe80::/10 dev eth1   proto kernel   metric 256   mtu 1500
```

was going to spell trouble for drone3 when it tried to respond to clients for replies forwarded
back over the gateway. My concern was completely unfounded. Although the gateway address
autoassigned via the IPv6 router advertisements contains the local-link address of the router
on a given interface, it turns out that clients sending packets always use their local-site unicast
address. In fact, you cannot even ping a local-link address (not even your own), most likely
because you cannot assign your local-link address as the packet source address.

---

[5]Often, the sort of laziness that leads to four hours of scripting to solve a problem that would have been
two hours of mundane effort with a text editor . . . .

At this point, you should have a basic IPv6 routing configuration up and running along with some minimal autoconfiguration capabilities. I highly encourage you to load a copy of *ethereal* onto your equivalent of drone3 and watch some IPv6 traffic traverse your router. Also, drill down on some of the *Router solicitation* and `Router advertisement` packets (preferably with copies of the IPv6 RFCs available) to get a feeling for what's happening.

6.5.3   IPv6 Application Support

So far we've gone to a lot of trouble to set up IPv6, and all we can do with it is transmit pings back and forth. What about actually accomplishing some work with IPv6? For that, you'll need applications compiled with IPv6 support as well as some sort of DNS support. In both cases, I believe that including any significant amount of HOWTO detail here in this book is pointless, as the state of the applications will have changed drastically by the time you are reading this. I can, though, at least give you some pointers on where to start.

- Recent versions of the *Bind* DNS server software support forward IPv6 address resolution via its AAAA record format (as compared to the A records used for IPv4 addresses). Reverse mappings are still via PTR records but use the designation `.ip6.int.` instead of `.in-addr.arpa` when specifying the origin. For more detailed instructions, refer to *http://www.isi.edu/simbmanning/v6DNS.html.*

- You should refer to Peter Bieringer's site (*http://www.bieringer.de/linux/IPv6/*) for a fairly up-to-date matrix of application support available for Linux, including which distributions include IPv6-enabled versions of given applications. Much of the application support is available via patches to apply against the source. One of the primary repositories for these patches is *ftp://ftp.kame.net/pub/kame/misc/.* (Although the site focuses on BSD support, many of the applications use the same code base.)

- Keep in mind that network services typically bind to all available network interfaces on startup by listening to *0.0.0.0:port.* (This is the convention for binding to all interfaces using the `AF_INET` address family, which is IPv4.) However, some daemons may be explicitly configured to bind only to a certain interface/address, and these you will need to configure for your IPv6 interfaces. (This isn't specific to IPv6, so don't let this bite you with regular IPv4 either.) The best way to tell if your application is listening for an IPv6 connection is to use either `netstat -pln` or `lsof -Pni` to list all of the ports open for listening on your system.

  Some applications currently support either IPv6 or IPv4, but not both simultaneously. At the time of writing, the *openssh* daemon is like that, so I have a separate instance for IPv6 running on port 44. Notice how *netstat* also detects *radvd* listening on an IPv6 socket for raw IPv6 protocol 7.

```
drone3:~# lsof -i | grep IPv6
sshd      391 root   3u  IPv6  6657       TCP *:44 (LISTEN)

drone3:~# netstat -pnl | grep ::
tcp   0     0 :::44 :::* LISTEN       391/sshd
raw   0     0 :::58 :::* 7        175/radvd
```

6.5.4 IPv6 over IPv4 Tunnel Broker Setup

You may be thinking to yourself, *This is a lot of work for nothing. My boxes could communicate just fine over IPv4.* In this example, we're going set up a system to communicate with the rest of the IPv6 world using a tunnel broker to ferry our IPv6 traffic over our existing IPv4 ISP connection. While this won't open up an entire new world of Internet sites, several sites have been kind enough to set up a few Internet servers to be accessible only via IPv6, which helps us to validate our setup. It's also a taste of how things will be in the (perhaps distant) future. A good number of IPv6 tunnel brokers out there offer free tunnelling accounts to allow you to get your feet wet with IPv6 without having to purchase anything. Most of the tunnel providers will even provide a ::/64 or ::/48 prefix delegation. The only requirements are that you have a valid Internet IPv4 address (a masqueraded private address won't do), that you are not behind a firewall that filters IP protocol 41 traffic (the protocol used by the tunnel), and that you don't mind registering with the tunnel broker provider. (If you're very concerned about privacy, try *http://www.freenet6.net/*, where you can obtain an anonymous tunnel for a single address.) You'll also need IPv6 support and will want the *iproute2* toolset.

Of the tunnel broker setups I have tried, I have to recommend *Hurricane Electric*'s as being by far the simplest to get running quickly. After you register with them, they give you explicit instructions for several different operating systems. The commands are surprisingly simple.

1. `modprobe ipv6`

2. `ip tunnel add sb0 mode sit remote tbaddr local laddr ttl 255`
Here we use *ip* to create a tunneling interface named *sb0* (for sixbone0) using the mode *sit* (which is specifically for IPv6 over IPv4) between the tunnel broker's IPv4 address and our local IPv4 address. We also specify that the TTL field for packets traversing this link should be set to 255.

3. `ip link set sb0 up`
Administratively mark the tunnel as up.

4. `ip addr add ipv6-addr/127 dev sb0`
Add the IPv6 address assigned to you by the tunnel broker to the *sb0* interface. The /127 subnet mask should make sense, as there are only two addresses on the tunnel, yours and the tunnel broker's on the other end.

5. `ip route add ::/0 dev sb0`
Add a default route via the tunneling interface. Note that at the time of writing, Linux doesn't seem to like the default route over the tunnel interface—it works fine using IPv6 over nontunnelled devices. So you may have to replace this with *ip route add 2000::0/3 dev sb0*, which, if you work out the math, is all of the provider-based IPv6 address space.

6. `ip -f inet6 addr`
Display all of the IPv6 addresses on your system; just a sanity check. The `-f inet6` is equivalent to using `-A inet6` with *route* and can be abbreviated as simply `-6`.

Once you've configured the tunnel, make sure that you can *ping6* the tunnel broker's end of the tunnel, and then start accessing IPv6-only sites. Perhaps try `lynx ipv6.research.microsoft.com` for your first visit. Then *http://www.normos.org/*, which has quite a number of IETF standards online.

And that concludes our introduction to IPv6 on Linux. If you think the addresses are a pain to type, let's step back and try to get some perspective on the size of the address space now, as compared to before. It wasn't *that* long ago that I had to write up a formal justification to my ISP to request a block of eight class C addresses. After all, they couldn't be handing out address space willy-nilly. Fortunately for everyone involved, it was a lot easier to dole out private address space for most user needs and reserve my precious routable IPs for machines that actually needed server interaction with the Internet. Now via an IPv6 broker I can quite easily obtain a /48 prefix from the RFC 2471 *IPv6 Testing Address Allocation*. This means that the broker allocates a unique address out of their portion of the first 48 bits of the address,[6] leaving me with 16 bits for subnets and another 64 bits for hosts. Let's see, with 2^{80} bits of address space, I could host the entire IPv4 Internet address space 281 *trillion* times. And that's just my /48 prefix .... Seriously, it's a lot of addresses. I've heard several folks make comments about IPv6 being ready for nanotechnology. With the NLA ID (Next Level Aggregate Identifier) field of 32 bits, we could steal a couple of bits from the TLA ID field and allocate every person on the planet their own /48 prefix. If you read RFC 2471 carefully, you note that the TLA ID may change in the future and that users may have to *renumber*. (Sounds ominous.) Realize that readdressing in the IPv6 world means changing a couple of values on your router, not having to touch every client in your network (unless you've done something very strange indeed internal to your network with your allocation). Here are a few links for further research on IPv6:

- *http://www.hs247.com/*—a metaresource page, this site has lots of links to other sites with information about IPv6.

- *http://www.6bone.net/*—the main page for the administrative body for the test IPv6 allocation (RFC 2471).

- *http://playground.sun.com/ipv6/*—specifications and general protocol information.

- *http://www.bieringer.de/linux/IPv6/*—Peter Bieringer's site, an IPv6 site specifically for Linux.

6.6   Summary

Tunneling, *iproute2*, IPv6 ... and token ring?!? This chapter started with a simple problem of deploying a Linux box as an interface between two LAN technologies to save some money. It then paid brief homage to a network configuration tool poised to supplant the venerable *ifconfig* and *route* and used that tool to make our token ring gateways a little spiffier. Next we let our paranoia get the best of us. And finally, the chapter ended with the future protocol of the Internet, the widespread deployment of which is who knows how far in the future. It serves to make a point about the flexibility of Linux as your networking tool—I don't want to be burdened by having to switch between network operating systems to work with different technology families. To be honest, sometimes I like to turn off my monitor and go outside (for a little while, anyway). If I had to learn the nuances and bugs of four or five different vendors' toolsets **and** integrate them to work in concert with each other, I'd never get to go home. Does that mean I propose that the IT world should be Linux, Linux, everywhere? No, it's merely that I feel confident developing my skillsets for an environment that allows me to leverage them in the router, network server, and workstation worlds. Next up, we're going to start talking about an Internet access router in more depth (beyond the mention of SNAT in Chapter 4), including packet filtering.

---

[6]Actually, the first 16 bits are fixed by the RFC to be *3ffe*, so the broker probably has 32 bits to dole out.

Chapter 7

OXYGEN—INTERNET ROUTER

Once upon a time, our Internet link was connected with a BigName router. One day this router decided to die in a very poetic "it just will not boot" sort of way. In total, it took about an hour to get a technician from BigName on the phone; we whiled away the time scrambling around looking for our support ID, wading through the "press six if you'd like to use our fax-back server" menus, waiting on hold, and fending off frantic users. After a short discussion about my abilities to configure a terminal program (peppered with a few curt remarks of my own about what sort of idiot cable was needed to access the BigName router console), the technician decided that we needed a new motherboard.

Since we had paid dearly for our support contract, a new board was to arrive the next day. We informed our users of the situation and eagerly awaited our package. A package did arrive promptly the next day. However, much to our dismay, we had received a new power supply and case—no motherboard. Now we were in trouble. BigName was going to send us our part, but that meant at least another 24 hours of downtime. Based on our experience with our Linux Frame Relay router, we decided to bring up the T1 link with our spare Sangoma S508 card. We were loaded and configured in about an hour. Everyone took a deep breath and let out a sigh of relief—for now we had oxygen.

Because there is a lot of territory to cover when connecting a system to the Internet, the topic is spread across two chapters.[1] This chapter begins by getting our access router up and running using Sangoma's *WANPIPE*, this time for synchronous PPP. Then we review general network security for Linux (and Unix in general). Once the system no longer has any gaping security holes due to services running on it, we'll turn to IP firewalling to protect our networks and our router even further. There are two basic ways to use IP firewalling: by preventing forwarding of traffic across the router or by blocking it altogether from entering (or exiting) the router. We will cover both of them. They are the kernel facilities which form the basis of **packet filtering** and all of the tools which can help you configure it. Finally, we'll talk about notification tools available for Linux so that you can monitor your environment and receive notification when something is wrong.

7.1 Connecting to the Internet

Unlike some networks, which may have only a few different types of access media and corresponding link-layer protocols, you can connect to the Internet in literally dozens of ways. (You might recall the discussion of access and protocols back in Chapter 2.) This section presents a Linux-based router which uses synchronous PPP over a fractional T1 to connect to an ISP and the Internet.

---

[1]The second chapter that relates to Internet routers is Chapter 9.

Synchronous PPP, as a protocol, is not actually any different from vanilla PPP. The name qualifier is an abridged way of saying " I'm running PPP over a dedicated digital access circuit to my ISP." Running over a leased line simplifies some aspects of the protocol. First, you don't have to dial anything. When your router is running and your ISP's router is running, you're on the Internet. Second, the security of the PPP link itself is less of an issue, because the access circuit is terminated at your site and at your ISP. They know who you are, and you know who they are. Thus, most connections dismiss the familiar PAP or CHAP-based authentication and just start routing traffic. The third difference is that you shouldn't need to run *pppd*. I say "shouldn't" because there are scenarios where you might run *pppd*—for example, if your synchronous data pump was merely that—a data pump. In this case, the device driver would present itself to the Linux kernel as a tty instead of a network device. To my knowledge, this is rarely the case, and for the Sangoma S508 card it's definitely not so. It runs the protocol on the board itself and presents itself to the system as a network interface. As you will see, it is very similar to the Frame Relay router from Chapter 5.

7.1.1 An SPPP Router with *WANPIPE*

Ingredients:

- (1) x86-based PC, 486/66 or faster with 16MB RAM

- (1) 1GB IDE hard drive

- (1) Sangoma S508/FT-1 adapter card

- (1) Ethernet adapter

- (2) CAT5 cables

- media for your favorite Linux distribution

Once you have installed the S508/FT-1 adapter card and the Ethernet adapter and performed a base load of the operating system, you're ready to configure the *WANPIPE* software. When loading your Linux distribution, you'll want pretty much just the "Basic" installation plus some networking tools and compilers and kernel source so that you can get *wanpipe* running. Once installation is complete:

1. Use */usr/local/wanrouter/wancfg* to configure your Sangoma card and create an interface named *sppp0*; use the IP configuration given to you by your service provider.

2. Use the */usr/local/wanrouter/cfgft1* utility to configure the integrated CSU/DSU on the Sangoma card.

3. Connect the S508/FT-1 to the T1 smart-jack (or demarc) installed by your provider using a CAT5 cable.

4. Execute the script **/etc/init.d/wanrouter restart**.

5. Use *ifconfig* to verify that the *sppp0* interface is up and operational.

6. Add a default route to the Internet with **route add -net default sppp0**.

7. Take the rest of the day off!

Once you return to the office (or, if you're so equipped, while dialed-in from home), add your default route statement to */etc/wanpipe/wanpipe_routes*. If you are the paranoid type, you should break into a cold sweat at this point. You're on the Internet without any security in place! (We'll address this later.) The configuration process for *WANPIPE* and PPP is very much like it is for Frame Relay. Procedurally, they are identical, so you can review Chapter 5 for more detailed instructions. In a nutshell, PPP has the following differences:

- There are different parameters in *wanpipe1.conf*, which are covered below in Section 7.1.2.

- You will not be inventing IP addresses for your */usr/local/wanrouter/interfaces/sppp0* file. The IP address and network will be given to you by your ISP.

- Later on, there is more emphasis on security for the router in general.

7.1.2   Configuring *wanpipe1.conf* for Synchronous PPP

The *wanpipeN.conf* file for PPP follows the same format as for Frame Relay (covered in Section 5.3.2), except for some new parameters which are applicable to PPP. A sample configuration file is listed below and contains a summary of the new parameters and changes after each section.

```
#
# /usr/local/wanrouter/wanpipe1.conf
#
# ============================================================
# wanpipe S508 sample router configuration for PPP
# ============================================================
#
# ------------------------------------------------------------
# The [devices] section
#  device = config_id,description
# ------------------------------------------------------------
[devices]
wanpipe1 = WAN_PPP, **edit router.conf with your ckt id/vendor info**
```

Devices which will run the PPP firmware modules need **WAN_PPP** as their **config_id**. You should edit the comment field to contain your circuit ID, and perhaps even the telephone number for support at your ISP.

SPPP [interfaces] Configuration in *wanpipe1.conf*

```
# ---------------------------------------------------------
# The [interfaces] section defines logical channels and
# corresponding network interfaces created by the router.
#
# name=device,media_addr,description
#
# ---------------------------------------------------------
[interfaces]
sppp0 = wanpipe1, , WANPIPE, ** edit router.conf - sppp link **
```

sppp0 is the interface name I use for synchronous PPP WAN interfaces, but the choice is arbitrary. If you would like to change it, do not forget to change it in the interface-level configuration section that follows. The *device* is any device you have already defined in the [devices] section that has a config_id of **WAN_PPP**. PPP links do not have media addresses,[2] so media_addr remains blank. This is because there will be only one [interface] per [device] for PPP. The PPP is not designed to share the line with any other protocol or link—it wants to use all of the link for itself. The comment field can be used as you see fit. I recommend placing here the IP addresses of your PPP configuration or more contact info for your ISP.

SPPP Device-Level Configuration in *wanpipe1.conf*

```
# ----------------------------------------------------------
# device-level link configuration section.
# ----------------------------------------------------------
[wanpipe1]                              ### WAN_PPP interface ###
IOPort          = 0x360         # I/O port base
IRQ             = 12            # IRQ
Firmware        = /usr/lib/wanpipe/ppp508.sfm    # adapter firmware
Interface       = V35          # physical interface type, RS232/V35
Clocking        = External     # Tx/Rx clock source: External/Internal
BaudRate        = 512000       # data transfer rate in bps
IP_MODE         = STATIC       # PEER/STATIC: do/not request address
MTU             = 1500         # maximum data transfer unit, bytes
UDPPORT         = 9000         # for UDP management
AUTHENTICATOR   = NO           # initiate PAP or CHAP authentication?
TTL             = 0x7F         # TTL for UDP monitoring packets
```

The device-level configuration prepares the driver for PPP. It is largely the same as the device-level configuration for Frame Relay. The Memaddr has been omitted, since we want the driver to autoselect the memory range to use. Note that the Firmware path has changed from the Frame Relay configuration to reflect the fact that this is a PPP link. (If you remember back to the general discussion of the S508 card in Section 5.2.1, you will recall that this card runs the WAN protocol on the card itself, offloading much of the work from the CPU of your router.) The two new parameters for PPP device-level configuration are:

IP_MODE [STATIC or PEER, default is STATIC]—When set to STATIC, the IP addresses in the */etc/wanpipe/interfaces/sppp0* file are used to configure the link. PEER indicates that the peer on the link, i.e., your ISP's router, should provide the IP addresses for the link.

AUTHENTICATOR [YES or NO, default is NO]—If set to YES, your router will request authentication information from the peer router. This is configured in the interface-level configuration for this interface. For most digital access (leased-line) circuits, this is set to NO (or simply omitted from the configuration), since the physical termination of the link at your facility is enough to convince the ISP that you are the party using the link and will therefore pay the bill. There may, however, be security applications where this option is useful.

---

[2]Apart from the IP addresses of the PPP interfaces themselves.

SPPP Interface-Level Configuration in *wanpipe1.conf*

```
# ----------------------------------------------------------
# interface-level configuration section
# ----------------------------------------------------------
[sppp0]
MULTICAST  = NO      # Multicast Enabled?
PAP        = NO      # Enable PAP?    (YES/NO)
CHAP       = NO      # Enable CHAP?   (YES/NO)
#USERID    =         # If not the authenticator then enter your login name
                     # If you are the authenticator then provide a list of
                     # all login names.  (USER1 / USER2.../ USER10...)
                     # The login name are separated by "/"
#PASSWD    =         # if not the authenticator then enter your passwd for
                     # your login name.  If you are the authenticator then
                     # provide a list of all the passwd for all the login
                     # names in the SAME ORDER. For e.g.  (PASS1 / PASS2.../
                     # PASS10...)
#SYSNAME   =         # If you are the authenticator then enter your local
                     # system name.  Otherwise keep it commented out
```

The only things new in the interface-level configuration for PPP interfaces are related to authentication. A caution about authentication—if you find that you need to be able to authenticate yourself to the peer, then make sure that the peer speaks either PAP or CHAP. Otherwise, you could be out of luck or requesting a special patch from Sangoma. If you are the authenticator (i.e., you set **AUTHENTICATOR=YES**), then you can specify *one* of the protocols. You must also set the name of your system with **SYSNAME**.

USERID=*username* [/ *username* [/ *username*...]]—If you are asked to authenticate yourself, then you should supply a single *username*. If acting as an authenticator, you can list the usernames to be used by your peer(s).

PASSWD=*password* [/ *password* [/ *password*...]]—Use this in the same manner as **USERID**.

SYSNAME=*sysname*—Use this only if you are the authenticator. This is the same as the second field in a *pppd pap-secrets* or *chap-secrets* file.

Configuring the default Route on Your Internet Router

The final step to configuring *WANPIPE* is to tune your interface file created by *wanpipeconfig*. You can edit the file directly: */etc/wanpipe/interfaces/sppp0*. Your ISP should provide you with IP addresses, network address, and subnet mask for the point-to-point link. If the ISP indicates that its router will supply yours with the IP information, then you need to make sure that you set IP_MODE=PEER in */etc/wanpipe/wanpipe1.conf*.

In the case of an Internet router, you want the default route to point to the *sppp0* interface— i.e., out to the Internet. For this application, it does make sense to configure the NETWORK and GATEWAY parameters in the interface file, since once you have a default route pointing to an interface (not the same as a gateway), any other routes over that interface are redundant. NETWORK should be set to 0.0.0.0, and the GATEWAY is the IP address of your ISP's side of the point-to-point interface (the **peer**). If your IP address is being set by the peer, you can just as easily add the statement route add -net default sppp0 to */etc/wanpipe/wanpipe_routes*.

Troubleshooting SPPP—*ppipemon*

If your link doesn't work right off the bat, then you'll need to do some troubleshooting. Fortunately, *WANPIPE* provides a monitor program for each of the WAN protocols it supports. For synchronous PPP, that command is *ppipemon*, and its operation is very similar to that of the *fpipemon* utility in Chapter 5. You can use the monitor to determine a range of information about your link, from the status of the modem to statistics about the interface, to the contents of the IP data packets themselves. Invoke the command without any options to see the usage statement.

7.1.3   Internal Routes on Your Internet Router

The way you configure the remaining routes on your system depends upon your firewall topology, what sort of address space you have and how much of it, and whether or not you will be using a dynamic routing daemon. I've included Figures 7.1–7.4 (all explained below), which cover a few of the possibilities for topologies but really only begin to scratch the surface. This book is not the right forum for a detailed analysis of firewall topologies; I heartily recommend *Building Internet Firewalls* by Chapman and Zwicky (see the Bibliography for the complete reference) if you require this sort of information.

My idea of configuring routes on an Internet router is to make it the ultimate authority on what networks exist inside your network, but not necessarily to advertise that information to the world (aside from what the world already knows because of your presence on the Net). This way, everyone on the inside can use the router (indirectly as a gateway), and troubleshooting is easy. If you intend to proxy all services you provide your users, allowing no masquerading (of users) or direct outbound connections (perhaps with a topology like that in Figure 7.1), then you'll want to do something else. For a few ideas, briefly review each of the topologies in this section, starting with Figure 7.1, which we will call the **perimeter net topology**.

This topology logically separates the functions of the Internet router and the firewall (although you may also perform firewalling on the Internet router, too), which makes the configuration of both easier. The **perimeter net** is the network between the Internet router and your firewall, on the *perimeter* of your network. This is a good place to place your external DNS server, SMTP gateways, and external web servers. The firewall can function as a packet filter, perform masquerading, or both. You may want to place proxy servers on the perimeter net (so that users may access the proxies only through the firewall).

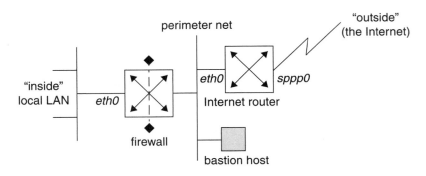

Figure 7.1 Perimeter Net Internet Router Topology

The Chapman and Zwicky book refers to these external hosts as **bastion hosts**. They are located outside the firewall, so that crackers[3] who hacked into them would still be limited in the network attack they might launch against your corporation, although much better off than they were before .... For this reason, you shouldn't be storing the secret formula or any other trade secrets on the perimeter net. You should be prepared for the worst case, that these systems will be completely destroyed by an attack from the outside. (You always have your backups, right?)

Maybe this isn't as bad as it sounds, after all. Linux boxes are great at doing lots of things at once. If a system is compromised, you can configure another system to act like it until you get it back online. In the not-so-bad case, you can spend some time beforehand configuring packet-filtering rules on the Internet router itself. Remember that the distinction between firewall and Internet router is more for the users and network diagrams than a statement about which systems have security measures installed. Your Internet router can have strict policies, just like your firewall; they simply have different policies.

Combination Firewall and Internet Router

Another way of having a perimeter net, without having a separate firewall is to use a topology like that in Figure 7.2. This results in one less system to maintain and protect but is more demanding in terms of configuration. To make this configuration work, you will definitely want to use both **forwarding** and **input/output** firewalling rules to control the flow of traffic through your firewall. This sort of configuration is complicated, so after you're up and running you should test it thoroughly from a shell account on the outside, or by using a security tool such as *Firewalk* or *Satan*.

If you have no need for a perimeter net and want to run your site with a single Internet firewall router, you have something that looks like Figure 7.3, which is a degenerate case of the previous example. Because you do not have to control forwarding between three different networks, this is much simpler to configure.

Isolating the Router from the Perimeter Net

Finally, if you really want to do something different, you can isolate your router from your perimeter net with a private network, as depicted in Figure 7.4. The idea here is configure the subnet between the Internet router and the firewall to be a private network, completely unroutable on the LAN (inside of the firewall).

You should also configure the firewall to reject any traffic with the source IP address of the Internet router. The effect is that, even if someone compromised the Internet router, he would be no better off than he was from the outside. This works because the packet-filtering code on the firewall will be blocking traffic from the Internet router's IP address (i.e., traffic that originated there), and not traffic that was forwarded by the Internet router (and bears only its MAC address). The firewall's default gateway is the Internet router, and the Internet router knows to forward packets for the inside to the IP address on the external interface on the firewall. The cost for this extra protection is that managing the Internet router remotely is not possible without introducing some sort of hole in the firewall between the management workstation and the Internet router. This might be OK, but an attacker will quickly see the portal to the management system and start attacking there. A better idea would be to perform all management of the Internet router on the console of the router itself. To keep management tasks to a minimum, you could use the LRP distribution or some other mini Linux distribution

---

[3]The term *hacker* means *good programmer*, and *cracker* refers to a person of malicious intent.

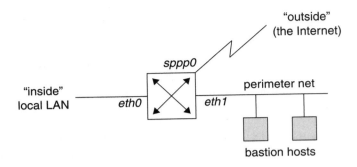

Figure 7.2 Combination Firewall/Router with Perimeter Net

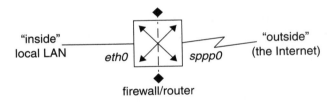

Figure 7.3 Combination Firewall/Internet Router

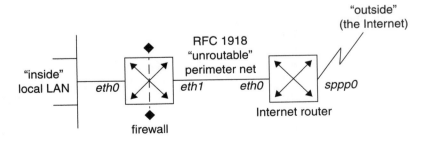

Figure 7.4 Isolation of Internet Router with an Unroutable Network

where you can prepare the configuration in the relative comfort of your workstation and then *hand-lib* it over to the router. Because the security depends upon there being no way to communicate directly between the Internet router and the inside, you will have to think about how you want to perform logging and system problem notification.

That concludes our short tour of Internet router topologies. Remember that they are not meant to be inclusive, or even representative, of the most common configurations. The first three are probably pretty common, and I've used the first two. The fourth is meant to serve as an example of how a little creative thought on your part can add security to this vital portion of your network (however nonintuitive your topology may be). A stable Internet router is not worth much if your network is easily compromised. Nor is a secure network useful if you cannot maintain it. Choosing your configuration is really just a bunch of trade-offs, with security and ease of administration often being diametrically opposed to each other.

Internet Routes—The "Inside" versus the "Outside"

As I stated before, the configuration of your routes will depend on your topology. It will, however, consist of at least three components: the *loopback*, the *inside*, and *everything else*. *Everything else* is the default route that points out toward the Internet over your *sppp0* interface. The *inside* includes everything that is *behind* the Internet router—the portion of the Internet that is yours. At the very minimum, it should include the networks allotted to the private address space,[4] as shown in Table 7.1. You should also configure packet-filtering rules to not allow these IP addresses to originate from outside your network, in case your router advertises them and somebody nearby (in terms of netspace—say, at the same ISP) notices and decides to see just how open your network is. These will be among the examples later in this chapter.

What you will configure in your routing tables also includes the Internet address space which has been allocated to you by your ISP, since it will not automagically be known to your Internet router. This is obvious, but I didn't want you to forget it in your excitement of bringing up the link. Note that the IPs for the point-to-point connection normally do not need to be routed by your internal network. Unless this is the only Internet-valid address space you have (which is problematic, as will be explained in Chapter 9), you can forget that they exist, since you should not have to contact either of the routers on the network directly via those IPs. Finally, your routing table might include any *other* address space, e.g., IPv6 address space or Internet-valid address space, which is not allocated to you, but which you somehow know is not being used or will never be accessed from your site. If you're going to configure a dynamic routing daemon, now's the time to do so.

Otherwise, add the gateway for your default route to */usr/local/wanrouter/interfaces/sppp0* by setting `GATEWAY=IP`, if you don't already have it with your other localized network configuration in */etc/init.d/local_network*. Once everything is up and working, you're probably about

Table 7.1 Private Routes

network	dotted netmask	abbreviated netmask
10.0.0.0	255.0.0.0	/8
172.16.0.0	255.240.0.0	/12
192.168.0.0	255.255.0.0	/16

---

[4]See Section 2.1.5.

20% done (although it might feel like 80%); you still have to configure your security. Much of the remainder of this chapter discusses security. First comes a section on general network host security, which will hopefully help you prevent people on the outside from hijacking your router for their own personal (ab)use. The section following that deals with how to configure two variants of firewalling (really, packet filtering) for Linux, limiting IP forwarding and blocking packets from entering or exiting the system.

7.2   General Network Security Measures

Security is no light matter on a system exposed to the Internet today. If you think that your system will be safe, either because your organization is benevolent or no one knows that your link exists, you may be in for a rude awakening to life on the Internet. Even if no one targets your site, a cracker might like to use it as a convenient launching point for attacks on others. People may want to use your systems to generate spam. Or they may just want to destroy something. As for people not knowing about your presence on the Net, don't count on it. I set up a cable modem at a noncommercial location one afternoon and was quite surprised to see a port scan (originating from a university on another continent!) being run against the system only three hours after it first came online.

You will have to form your own philosophy about how to deal with such incidents. My personal reaction was to make sure that the port scan did not result in anything useful and to review *syslog* logfiles more carefully than normal for the next few weeks. In my opinion, there was no need to actively confront the scanner until a more intrusive attempt to access the system was made. Of course, this was a private system, and the consequences of a security breach would have been inconvenient, but not devastating to my livelihood. In general, I recommend that you consider your reaction carefully, unless you know that you have the resources and know-how to lock horns with a wily cracker. Depending upon your workload or your organization's policies, you may not have a choice.

The remainder of this section is divided into two subsections—one that deals with general network host security, i.e., how to keep people from hacking services which run on your router, and a somewhat longer one on how to configure packet filtering with Linux. Although the sample router configuration in this chapter is for an Internet router, the security measures apply to all routers. Attacks from the inside are just as likely, and typically more devastating, because the attacker already knows something about your network and what he would like to target.

7.2.1   Generic Host Security

Developing a comprehensive security model is not the purpose of this book, nor do I believe that I would be the right person to do so. My recommendations are colored by my experiences. Host security for Unix is an exceedingly complex topic and the subject of several books much thicker than this one. One of the best ways to mitigate the risk of this complexity, and the unnerving fact that crackers trying to break into your systems will invariably be better equipped with tools and have more time than you do, is to eliminate it whenever possible. Simply put, any services which are not required to be running on your router should be disabled. Because Unix has a history of being exposed to the Internet, university campuses, and corporate data centers, some good measures have already been taken, e.g., logging, *tcpd*, etc. I'll introduce those as appropriate. Consider these few points as food for thought. If you do not already have a security strategy, you should do these things at the very minimum. More would be better.

1. Be aware that network security is meaningless if you do not have any physical security for your systems. Why would a **social engineer**, sent to do some corporate raiding, go to great lengths to break into your system over the network when she could casually walk by with a floppy disk, quickly bounce the system, and add herself to */etc/passwd* and */etc/shadow*? You'll notice the reboot, but nothing in *syslog* is going to tell you what happened. *Your* instance of the operating system isn't the one that made the change. It just knows that it went down and came back up. This was mentioned in Section 1.2, but it bears repeating: Physically isolate your routers from the general public whenever possible. If you cannot do that, then use power-on (BIOS) passwords, case locks, and any other method you can think of to prevent unauthorized access to your machine.

2. Do not be naive about the dangers of sending passwords in cleartext over the network. The Linux version of *login* prohibits you from logging in as a superuser via *telnet* or *rlogin*, but by default it does not go so far as to prevent you from logging in as a normal user and then performing a *su* to root. If you do this, you will be sending the root password in cleartext via the telnet session. Your login mechanism should be such that you are able to login to your router(s) from any location securely (unless you are restricting access to the console only, which is not a bad idea). In any event, do not fall into the trap of believing that network access to your systems is safe if there is not some form of session encryption taking place at every step along the way. Otherwise, your password could traverse one link encrypted, only to be unencrypted and sent in cleartext over the next hop. I am referring to the situation when you are using machine A to access machine B via a secure mechanism, and then log into machine C from the shell you have running on machine B. Even though A → B is secure, B → C is not necessarily so.

OpenSSH can help you out of the predicament immensely, because it encrypts the entire session, allows *rexec*-style execution of commands, and also comes with *scp* (a secure form of *rcp*) and *sftp* (which disappointingly doesn't support recursive gets and some of the other features that fancier ftp clients have spoiled us with). *OpenSSH* is a fork of version 1 of the original *ssh*. The *ssh* license is not compatible with all forms of use or philosophies, nor is *ssh* version 2. If for some reason you cannot use *OpenSSH*, you should probably invest in licensed commercial copies of *ssh*. You might also look into *telnet-ssl* in lieu of *ssh*.

If your world includes Win32-based systems, there are some excellent open-source terminal emulators that will speak the SSH protocol. The first of these is *putty*, available at *http://www.chiark.greenend.org.uk/~sgtatham/putty/*, and which comes with clients for *scp*, *sftp*, and *ssh-agent* and *ssh-keygen* as well. These last two, *ssh-agent* and *ssh-keygen*, allow you to generate a public/private key pair and distribute the public key to hosts running the *sshd* server daemon. By possessing the private half of the key pair, you can authenticate yourself to those hosts without a password. In order to protect your private key, however, a passphrase should be required to use it. At this point, you've traded typing passwords on a bunch of hosts for typing it every time you use your private key, so you're still constantly typing passwords. But, if you can trust others not to be sifting through the process memory space on your workstation, you can use *ssh-agent* on that workstation to "remember" the passphrase for you for a limited period of time. The one feature that *putty* lacks is X-forwarding, which you may need, say, if your company's VPN client runs only on Windows-based machines. (Can you hear the collective <sigh>?) Luckily, there is another very good terminal emulation package, *TeraTerm Pro* (*http://hp.vector.co.jp/authors/VA002416/teraterm.html*), with an extension module called *TTSSH* that can handle X11 port-forwarding. You can obtain it from *http://www.zip.com.au/~roca/ttssh.html.*

Note: There are some countries where certain types (often strengths) of encrypted communication are illegal, regardless of the intent or scope of usage. It doesn't quite make sense to me, but you've been warned.

3. Equally as dangerous as sending passwords in cleartext over the network is storing them where they can be retrieved or sending them via email. But it can be tough to remember a long list of passwords, especially those which you use only rarely. For example, you may need to exchange a set of passwords with another administrator in the company in case something happens to you.

GnuPG—GNU Privacy Guard

For securing files, documents, and emails, *GnuPG* is free world's answer to *PGP* (*Pretty Good Privacy*)—a public-key encryption mechanism which has been embroiled in legal issues surrounding export restrictions from the United States and multiple patent holders in different locations. I mention *PGP* by name because it is probably the best known of this type of software. Having dealt with 2^N incompatibilities with this type of software over the years, I suggest you try to stick with *GnuPG* or another OpenPGP/RFC 2440-compliant tool. For more information, visit *http://www.gnupg.org/.*

The procedure I use is a *PGP*-like mechanism. I sign the email containing the password(s) using my private key, so that it can be verified using my public key, which I have already exchanged with the other admin in a secure manner, and then encrypt the email with the other admin's public key, so it is for her eyes only. This way, she can store the email in her email system, but not access it without using her PGP key. If she cannot be trusted with the security of her own PGP key, then you have bigger problems. You can add a layer of security by encrypting the contents of the email with a conventional (single-password) mechanism, sending the email, and then disclosing the password when you talk to the valid recipient of the email. The step confirms that the email was received by the right person. Public-key cryptography is also a handy way to send things to yourself, i.e., to store them securely on your workstation. Even if someone were to physically remove the hard drive, take it somewhere else and mount it, he wouldn't get the passwords, because he wouldn't know how to unlock your private key.

If you need to leave the passwords in a safe place in case something happens to you, you should either use a PGP mechanism or, to get computers out of the loop altogether, put the passwords in a sealed envelope in a fireproof safe with your signature on the outside. If someone opens the envelope, you'll notice, and if someone steals it, you'll notice, and if someone steals it and tries to replace it with a forgery, you'll notice. Of course, you have to check the status of the envelope regularly, say, once a week.

Password choice is also important, but you *already* know this. Still, I'm amazed at the passwords that some people, even system administrators, use. At one environment I worked in, you could get into most of the back office systems by guessing from a list of three or four passwords which we had *retired* from use in the Linux environment over a year prior. Maybe they're still valid. If you're completely at a loss for picking passwords, try either the **pwgen** or **makepasswd** packages, which include binaries of the same name. These will produce passwords which are not based on dictionary words and contain sufficient variation to be considered nontrivial by */bin/passwd*. They are also a good method of automatically generating passwords for users.

4. Be careful about which packages you load on your Internet router. If you load **samba**, you will have the *smbd* daemon listening on port 139, and the *nmbd* daemon broadcasting your existence to the world. This does not say that I am aware of any problems with the Samba daemons. There are many server packages which run as root, open ports, and have potential security exploits. Basically, anything that is not needed should not be loaded. If there are servers which you would like to have loaded on the system, but do not want to be executed upon startup, you should script these not to be started. Every service on your system should be started either from *inetd* or from the system startup directories, e.g., */etc/init.d/* for Debian systems. One way to quickly disable a service is to edit its startup script and add **exit 0** as the first executable statement. This leaves the software and startup script intact and can easily be reversed. Two notes of caution about this, though. First, you should stop the service with **/etc/init.d/**service **stop** before editing the script. This way, you won't have to try to stop the process(es) by hand. Second, for Linux distributions which support the concept of local configuration files, you may have to take manual intervention when upgrading the packages which own these startup files. This is a mixed blessing. On the downside, it requires manual intervention when upgrading the package. On the upside, this reminds you about customizations you have made to your system, allowing you to revisit them as necessary.

5. Subscribe to, read, and participate in a security mailing list or newsgroup, either for your distribution or for Linux/Unix in general. Security is a moving target, and keeping abreast is not easy to do when you have other duties to perform. When working with management, it is often the sort of topic that receives a lot of verbiage, but little support when it comes down to requesting the time, training, or money to perform security enhancements. It is also the sort of thing where the technology is complex enough that it may preclude meaningful decision making on the part of your management, and they will lean upon you to set the direction (and maybe the policy, too). For all of these reasons, it is good to stay in touch with others who have similar interests. For Debian, see *http://www.debian.org/security/*.

6. Get into the habit of using the *last* and *lastb* commands regularly to determine when and from where people have been logging into your system, or failing to log into your system. If it appears that no one ever logs into your systems, then attackers could be removing these logs to cover their tracks. There is plenty of information created by *syslog* (in */var/log/*)—learn what is there and how to read it so that if you suspect something has occurred, you can quickly spot something unusual in the logfiles. I like to configure *syslog* to dump everything into a single file, */var/log/messages*, so that I do not have to keep going from file to file. I can also watch this one file, either interactively with **tail -f**, the "old-fashioned way" with *grep*, using custom Perl scripts, or using one of the Debian packages listed below. The security conscious will consider using the built-in facility in syslog to log both locally and to a remote system.

xlogmaster is a GUI logfile viewer which is customizable to support triggers and even audible alerts.

gnome-admin contains *logview*, which is a nice GUI logfile viewer that contains descriptions of many common *syslog* messages (see the **zoom** feature).

since is a *stateful* version of *tail*. It adds useful functionality for scanning low-volume logfiles by displaying the logfile *since* the last time it was viewed.

syslog-summary incorporates similar functionality to that described above with *since* (with the `--state` switch), has a filtering mechanism (with `--ignore`), and delivers on its name by summarizing the occurrences of a message in the logfile.

xwatch can color-code a logfile being watched to make more important events easier to notice.

7. Read *Practical UNIX and Internet Security* from cover to cover. This book is filled with valuable information based on extensive experience. A reference is available in the Bibliography, which starts on page 427.

8. If you become paranoid that someone within your group (another administrator, perhaps) is doing Not Good Things, you can use the **ttysnoop** (and **ttylog** if your system is accessible via a serial interface) to record every telnet and login session.

7.2.2   Network Service Security

You want your systems to be secure. You have made sure that the passwords are secure. You never send your password over the network unencrypted. Better yet, you login only to the console. The system is physically secure. You have taken every measure possible to make sure that nothing logged by *syslog* eludes you. What about network-based attacks? Unfortunately, you cannot completely hide your router from the network—it *is* the network. To limit your exposure, you should disable any (network) services.[5] To see which network ports are open on your system, use the *netstat* command with various options.

- Review */etc/inetd.conf* and turn off any services which are not needed. These are security holes waiting to happen. Decide between *telnet* and *rlogin*, or better yet, if you are compatible with the license, use *ssh*. You turn off a service by commenting out the appropriate line in *inetd.conf* and then stopping and restarting *inetd*. The same applies for *xinetd*, a more configurable replacement for *inetd*, should you choose to run it. You can ask *inetd* to reread the configuration file with either `/etc/init.d/netbase reload` (Debian), `kill -HUP $(pidof inetd)`, or go for the gusto and `kill $(pidof inetd) ; /usr/sbin/inetd`.

- `netstat -a | more` is the old standby that will be familiar to most Unix hacks. It displays all `family inet` (i.e., TCP/IP) sockets in use, in addition to `family unix` sockets (which are not of concern to us here). It resolves service names using */etc/services* (or whatever mechanism is indicated in */etc/nsswitch.conf*). Use `-n` to prevent the lookups from occurring. (This is more commonly done as part of `netstat -rn`, which displays the kernel's routing table.)

---

[5]Network services are often referred to as just **services**, due to their connection with the */etc/services* file.

- `netstat --inet -a` will display just the TCP and UDP ports and the ICMP services to which our machine will respond. This is better suited to our task of finding potential weaknesses.

- Linux, in keeping with the ideal that providing information about the functioning of the system is a better policy than hiding it, has made some nice improvements to *netstat*. They include:

  — `-p`—lists the PID/process name associated with the socket, à la *lsof* functionality.

  — `-e`—creates extended output. For network sockets, it lists the UID associated with the socket.

  — `-v`—is the obligatory verbose switch. Oddly enough, it does not result in any additional output.

netstat looks like:

```
### active TCP connections between this system and other systems

oxygen:root> netstat --inet -n
Active Internet connections (w/o servers)
Proto Recv-Q Send-Q Local Address       Foreign Address       State
tcp      0       0 192.168.18.1:2089   192.168.18.2:113      TIME_WAIT
tcp      0       0 192.168.16.1:23     192.168.18.2:1107     ESTABLISHED
tcp      0       0 192.168.18.1:2086   192.168.18.2:23       ESTABLISHED
tcp      0       0 192.168.101.2:23    192.168.16.2:1026     ESTABLISHED
tcp      1       1 38.29.61.100:1995   209.81.8.242:80       LAST_ACK
tcp     57       0 38.29.61.100:1809   207.179.18.134:21     CLOSE_WAIT

### active TCP connections AND
### all "server" processes listening for connections on this system
### just look at all those potential security holes...

oxygen:root> netstat --inet -a
Active Internet connections (including servers)
Proto Recv-Q Send-Q Local Address       Foreign Address       State
tcp     57       0 oxy.mancill.com:1809 ftp.kde.org:ftp      CLOSE_WAIT
tcp      0       0 *:auth              *:*                   LISTEN
tcp      0       0 *:exec              *:*                   LISTEN
tcp      0       0 *:login             *:*                   LISTEN
tcp      0       0 *:shell             *:*                   LISTEN
tcp      0       0 *:telnet            *:*                   LISTEN
tcp      0       0 *:ftp               *:*                   LISTEN
tcp      0       0 *:time              *:*                   LISTEN
tcp      0       0 *:daytime           *:*                   LISTEN
tcp      0       0 *:discard           *:*                   LISTEN
tcp      0       0 *:sunrpc            *:*                   LISTEN
tcp      0       0 *:ssh               *:*                   LISTEN
tcp      0       0 *:printer           *:*                   LISTEN
tcp      0       0 *:snpp              *:*                   LISTEN
```

udp	0	0 *:bootps	*:*
udp	0	0 *:791	*:*
udp	0	0 *:2049	*:*
udp	0	0 *:talk	*:*
udp	0	0 *:ntalk	*:*
udp	0	0 *:time	*:*
udp	0	0 *:daytime	*:*
udp	0	0 *:discard	*:*
udp	0	0 *:sunrpc	*:*
raw	0	0 *:1	*:*
raw	0	0 *:1	*:*
raw	0	0 *:6	*:*
raw	0	0 *:1	*:*
raw	0	0 *:6	*:*

- Get acquainted with *lsof*, which, among other things, is a more capable version of *netstat*. It walks the kernel's list of open file descriptors, collecting detailed information about how that file descriptor is being used. If you're wondering what good that does you, you should realize that many things in the Unix kernel are represented internally as file descriptors. Taken from the *lsof* manpage:

  > An open file may be a regular file, a directory, a block special file, a character special file, an executing text reference, a library, a stream or a network file (Internet socket, NFS file, or Unix domain socket.)

  Although many Unices have their own methods for obtaining this information (with Linux, you can get it by walking the individual file descriptor files in */proc/pid/fd/filedes*), *lsof* uses the same switches and formats the information consistently across the different flavors. It also supports dumping its output in a format easily read by scripts. See the **-F** option.

  It is available for virtually every Unix dialect around (currently 18 different dialects, often two or three different kernel versions per dialect). It is extremely useful for debugging client-server problems and network application performance problems, especially when you do not have access to the source code. (I've often used it on HP-UX because their version of *netstat* does not show the port number on the other end of a socket, only the IP address). With nothing sensible coming from *inetd* or the application, how else are you going to find out what's connected to you? You're better off with the basic networking tools that come with Linux, but you still might like some of the features of *lsof*.

  — When using the **-i** to list `inet` sockets, you can filter the output by specifying a particular [*protocol*] [@*host*] [:*port*]. There is also limited AND and OR functionality— see the manpage for details.

  — *lsof* has a **r**epeat mode (**-r**), where it will run itself iteratively. When used in conjunction with **-i**, it is an easy way to watch for a connection to start or die.

  — You can list file descriptors based on PID with **-p**, UID with **-u**, and PGRP (Process GRouP ID) with **-g**. The PGRP is the set of all child processes of parent. Just specify the PID of the parent as the argument to **-g**. Note that you'll probably want to use the **-a** (AND) option to see the intersection of the file descriptors matched by the options (as opposed to the union). For example, to see all of the `inet` file descriptors open for processes spawned by *inetd* on your system, you can use:

```
oxygen:/root> lsof -a -g $(pidof inetd) -i
COMMAND      PID PGRP USER     FD    TYPE DEVICE NODE NAME
inetd        241  241 root     4u   inet    162  TCP *:discard (LISTEN)
inetd        241  241 root     5u   inet    163  UDP *:discard
inetd        241  241 root     6u   inet    164  TCP *:daytime (LISTEN)
inetd        241  241 root     7u   inet    165  UDP *:daytime
inetd        241  241 root     8u   inet    166  TCP *:time (LISTEN)
inetd        241  241 root     9u   inet    167  UDP *:time
inetd        241  241 root    10u   inet    168  TCP *:ftp (LISTEN)
inetd        241  241 root    11u   inet    169  TCP *:telnet (LISTEN)
inetd        241  241 root    12u   inet    170  UDP *:talk
inetd        241  241 root    13u   inet    171  UDP *:ntalk
inetd        241  241 root    14u   inet    172  TCP *:shell (LISTEN)
inetd        241  241 root    15u   inet    173  TCP *:login (LISTEN)
inetd        241  241 root    16u   inet    174  TCP *:exec (LISTEN)
inetd        241  241 root    17u   inet    175  TCP *:smtp (LISTEN)
inetd        241  241 root    18u   inet    176  TCP *:finger (LISTEN)
inetd        241  241 root    19u   inet    177  TCP *:auth (LISTEN)
in.telnet   6528  241 root     0u   inet  27557  TCP 10.1.1.2:telnet->10.1.1.1:2013 (EST)
in.telnet   6528  241 root     1u   inet  27557  TCP 10.1.1.2:telnet->10.1.1.1:2013 (EST)
in.telnet   6528  241 root     2u   inet  27557  TCP 10.1.1.2:telnet->10.1.1.1:2013 (EST)
in.telnet  26341  241 root     0u   inet 132753  TCP 10.1.1.2:telnet->10.1.1.1:3824 (EST)
in.telnet  26341  241 root     1u   inet 132753  TCP 10.1.1.2:telnet->10.1.1.1:3824 (EST)
in.telnet  26341  241 root     2u   inet 132753  TCP 10.1.1.2:telnet->10.1.1.1:3824 (EST)
```

— Use the **-t** option to get (very) terse output, i.e., just the PIDs which match the criteria given. If you want to kill not only *inetd*, but every process it might have spawned (say, to get **everybody** off the box), you can specify the command above along with **-t**. (Take care that you don't kill your own connection to the router.)

You should understand the function of every service running on your router. If you are not familiar with a service, you should do some research about the service and its security configuration, and disable it until you are certain that you can provide it securely or that you need it so badly that you are willing to take the risk of running it as is.

tcpd—Access Control Wrappers

The *tcpd* program monitors incoming network requests via *inetd* and determines whether the requestor may access that service. If it is allowed, it spawns the normal network daemon to deal with the service requested. Otherwise, the connection attempt is rejected, and in either case the attempt is logged via *syslog*. It uses the files */etc/hosts.allow* and */etc/hosts.deny* as configuration files to filter requests on one or more of the following criteria:

1. pattern-based access control (such as IP address ranges, DNS names, and netgroups)

2. client username lookups with the RFC 931 (*authd*) protocol

3. forward and reverse lookups for hostname/IP correlation

4. source-routed clients, systems that are using source routing and therefore possibly address spoofing (i.e., pretending to be a different IP address)

Many *inetd* services make use of the *tcpd* wrappers by default. This allows you to configure your security once and have it apply to multiple services. This satisfies the principle of letting the application programmer focus on the programming of the application (in this case, say, a telnet daemon) and letting the network security guru concentrate on designing network security. *tcpd* should be part of the base network installation of any full-sized Linux distribution.

An Alternative to *inetd*—*xinetd*

Often you are not able to escape using some of these standard services, but you need more protection than they provide or than can be had using *tcpd*. After all, what good is a network computer which cannot interact with the network safely? Rewriting all of them would be a lot of work, and any time a new service becomes available, you have to modify it to comply with your security architecture. Why not cut them off at the source, before the service starts? You can do this to a certain extent with the kernel's packet filtering, but the kernel code should remain lean and fast, and the problem predates GPLed kernels, which come with source anyway. (Imagine being responsible for this big Unix system with no source code available anywhere. Feel the bugs! <shudder>) Panagiotis Tsirigotis had the same ideas you have and came up with *xinetd* back in 1992. Since that time, it's been ported and maintained by Charles Murcko and Jan Wedekind. *xinetd* is a drop-in replacement for *inetd* that offers a very complete network access control mechanism to be executed before a network service even starts. This list of features is taken from the Debian package notes:

1. Access control on all services based on:

   (a) address of remote host

   (b) time of access

   Access control works on all services, whether multithreaded or single-threaded, and for both the TCP and UDP protocols. All UDP packets can be checked, as well as all TCP connections.

2. Hard reconfiguration:

   (a) kills servers for services that are no longer in the configuration file

   (b) kills servers that no longer meet the access control criteria

3. Prevents denial-of-access attacks by:

   (a) placing limits on the number of servers for each service (avoids process table overflows)

   (b) placing an upper bound on the number of processes it will fork

   (c) placing limits on the size of logfiles it creates

4. Extensive logging abilities:

   (a) for every server started it can log:

       i. the time when the server was started (*)

       ii. the remote host address (*)

       iii. who was the remote user (if the other end runs an RFC 931/RFC 1413 server) (*)

       iv. how long the server was running
           (*) each of these can be logged for failed attempts, too.

(b) for some services, if the access control fails, it can log information about
the attempted access (for example, it can log the user name and command
for the *rsh* service)

These features are quite useful for a production environment, and impressive compared
to the normal *inetd*. The distribution also contains *itox*, which can convert your existing
/etc/inetd.conf to a format suitable for */etc/xinetd.conf*.

7.2.3   IP Event Loggers

Sometimes you like to monitor services which are not started via *[x]inetd* at a level similar to
what *xinetd* offers. Once again you face the same issue: needing to perform your own logging
hacks on several system daemons. Even if the servers provide adequate logging, suppose you
would like *all* connections to the system to be logged in the same format, regardless of whether
they were made through *inetd* or directly to the daemon running on the service port. For this
situation, you can employ one of the IP event loggers described below. None of them provides
access control or extensive amounts of logging. For one, they do not pretend to understand the
protocol being used; they simply watch incoming connections. Each is denoted by its Debian
package name, but you can use the URLs listed to visit their home sites.

iplogger provides two separate daemons, one to log TCP and the other to log ICMP events.
It performs its logging through *syslog*. Of note is its ability to detect the FTP server
bounce attack, for which a white paper is included in the documentation. Its source code
is available from several Linux mirrors, including Sunsite as *iplogger-ident-1.1.tar.gz*.

jail (Just Another IP Logger) is also for logging TCP and ICMP events and is originally
based on *iplogger*. It performs its logging via *syslog* and is configurable to log different types of events at different *syslog* levels. You might find it interesting that *jail* is
distributed under the *Artistic License*, which is different from the GPL, but is not ex-
tensively different in its effect. A copy of this license is included with the distribution.
(See *http://www.wiw.org/~ams/jail/*.)

ippl is the IP Protocols Logger and is capable of logging TCP, ICMP, and UDP. It is similar to *iplogger* and is based upon it, but provides some additional features such as
being configurable with *Apache*-like rules and having a built-in DNS cache. Instead
of logging through *syslog*, it writes to its own logfiles (configurable). Its home site is
http://www.via.ecp.fr/~hugo/ippl/.

net-acctd advertises itself as a "usermode IP accounting daemon. . . , similar to what tcpdump does." While I worked with the package, I found it more similar to the IP event
loggers, but offering more information (much more, in some cases). The output fields it
generates are configurable, and output is to filenames listed in the configuration files, as
with *ippl*. It is also the only program listed which will associate traffic to a particular
local user (e.g., for slip or PPP connections). See *http://www.bladesinger.com/net-acct*.

If any of these event loggers detects anything interesting on a regular basis, say an excessive
amount of telnet requests from an external system to a system which does not support external
user accounts, or a great number of connection attempts in a short interval, you will want to
find out more about the packets triggering the event logger. You might need a better tool to
do this—I suggest that you use one of the packet sniffers described in Section 3.3. You might
find that someone is using one of the programs described in the next section, a **port scanner**,
to detect a way to infiltrate your network.

7.2.4 Port Scanners

A **port scanner** is a program which looks for holes in a server or firewall. It is called a port scanner because it walks through the entire list of TCP and UDP ports (ICMP, too) trying to find available services or types of traffic which are allowed to pass. It also tests the system for known vulnerabilities of services and TCP/IP itself. The most famous port scanner is *Satan*, which received a large amount of media attention because it was publicly released and effective. At that time, people were afraid that releasing such a tool to the public instead of only to the network administration community would result in a rash of cracked sites. The problem with this logic is that there isn't a very good way to release software only to system administrators except by making it very expensive, which means that only large/rich corporations will be able to afford it—this is regressive. It also assumes that the hacker community doesn't already have tools this sophisticated or more, which is a poor assumption. Since that time, people (seem to) have come to understand that the only way to make things more secure is to expose their problems, and not cover them up, hoping that you'll get a patch before a *script kiddie* ruins your day.

You can (and should) employ port scanners to periodically check your configuration and services for weaknesses. If possible, you should try to run them from the *complete* outside of your network. If you have a good source for access on the outside, such as a cable modem, then you're in luck. Another alternative is to strike up a rapport with a system administrator at another organization and work out a deal wherein the admin sets up a Linux box outside his firewall with a shell account for you, and vice versa. This sort of configuration could be used for more than just testing your network security. Examples include testing your SMTP gateway configuration (as a place to originate external messages), checking your external DNS configuration, and verifying that Internet services are functioning as they should.[6]

If you cannot find a system completely external to your site, then a system on the perimeter net is acceptable (if you have one). Whatever you do, you should consider using one. If you worry that it will detect holes in your configuration and then mail them off to some hacker organization, pull down a copy of the source and review it for code which might do something like that. This is part of the beauty of free software. *Use the Source, Luke.* I introduce three such port scanners which are freely available. Sorry, I'm not going to tell you any more about how to use them. I live in a very litigious country and would hate to have to recall all of the printed copies of this book to plaster a *warning: contents discuss networking* sticker on them.

- *Satan* is the original. It is written largely in Perl and uses a browser for its user interface (preferably a graphical one). It is likely the best tool to try first, because it comes with HTML-based documentation and a tutorial. It is available as a Debian package **satan** (which is part of the *non-free* of the archive because of *Satan*'s license) or *http://www.fish.com/satan*.

- *SAINT*, the Security Administrator's Integrated Network Tool, is the follow-up to *Satan* and is released under the same license. The program focuses on security but generates a significant amount of general network information in the process. According to its webpage, it aims to be "the best investigative security network tool available, at any price." (*SAINT's* license is similar to the GPL except that neither it nor derivative works can be sold.) See *http://www.wwdsi.com/saint/* for more information. Even if you

---

[6]If I had a dime for every time an employee at a client site would call up and ask me why the FTP server was down, only to find out that they were behind a firewall on their end . . . .

Hint: Package Sources with Debian

Debian's *apt* package manager provides a way to pull the complete sources of a package with a single command (once you set it up properly). All you need to do to set it up is to add a `deb-src` line to */etc/apt/sources.list* for each source repository you would like to access. For the packages included with the base distribution, this line looks like:

```
deb-src http://http.us.debian.org/debian stable main contrib non-free
```

Once you add this line, you need to run `apt-get update` so that *apt* can refresh the list of packages. Then, any time you want to retrieve a set of sources (for any package in the archive category for which you set up a `deb-src` line—there can be multiple `deb-src` lines in your */etc/apt/sources.list*), you can do so with a command such as `apt-get source` *packagename*. This retrieves the original source and the `.diff.gz` file which contains the *debianizations* and extracts them into the current directory. (Debianizations include everything done to make the package compatible with Debian, and everything required to compile your own version of the package by using the Debian developer tools, also available in the standard archive.)

---

are not interested in the software, you should spend some time working through the vulnerability tutorials available at this website.

- *nmap* is a command-line port scanner which supports a wide variety of scanning techniques. It is available from *http://www.insecure.org/nmap*. You should retrieve this package even if you have no intention of using the binary just so that you can read the manpage and the documentation that accompanies it. The current version supports these scanning techniques:

  — Vanilla TCP connect() scanning,

  — TCP SYN (half open) scanning,

  — TCP FIN (stealth) scanning,

  — TCP FTP proxy (bounce attack) scanning,

  — SYN/FIN scanning using IP fragments (bypasses packet filters),

  — UDP recvfrom() scanning,

  — UDP raw ICMP port unreachable scanning,

  — ICMP scanning (ping-sweep), and

  — Reverse-ident scanning.

  — OS detection via TCP stack fingerprinting

The last of these is an interesting hacking technique whereby *nmap* makes an educated guess at the flavor of the operating system running on the target merely by observing how it responds to particular sequences of specially crafted packets. By the way, despite its more devious uses, *nmap* is quite handy for quickly determining what hosts are on a segment (using the relatively benign -sP).

7.3 IP Firewalling

IP firewalling takes many forms and is a topic which covers many facets of TCP/IP networking. For our purposes, I will associate IP firewalling directly with mechanisms which are used to restrict the flow of packets into or out of a host or through a router. The first of these can be termed **packet filtering** and the second **conditional forwarding**. The term **conditional forwarding** has been coined only to separate it from input/output ruled-based packet filtering. In the Real World, people interchange the terms **packet filtering** and **firewalling** freely to mean both of the functions listed above, and several others, such as **proxying** and **masquerading**. And more often than not, **conditional forwarding** is lumped in with **packet filtering**. This is because they do the same thing, but under different circumstances, which is why I present them separately.

Before we get started with our discussions of forwarding and packet filtering, remember that they are not the only game in town for firewalls. Depending upon your application(s) and firewall topology, you can have a firewall or Internet router which does not route or forward at all (*/proc/sys/net/ipv4/ip_forward* = 0). Instead, your users will use proxies to access what they need. This type of topology can be very secure and will work for smaller organizations where a single system can function as the router, firewall, and proxy server. If you implement this type of firewall, you will still use packet filtering to protect the proxy daemons and the host itself, but you will not need to specify any restrictions on forwarding, since none is taking place.

What you do with the rules can be logically separated from *how* you do it. This section concentrates on *how*. *What* varies wildly from application to application and is left as a topic for a book on firewalls, although some examples will be scattered throughout this section and Chapter 9. Both packet filtering and conditional forwarding are supported in the Linux kernel and are applications of our friends *ipchains* (for the 2.2.x kernels) and *iptables* (for 2.4 kernels). Instead of modifying packet source headers with IP masquerading and NAT, you now decide the fate of a packet by allowing it to pass, throwing it away, or replying to the sender that the packet is not allowed to pass. You may decide that you'd like to log the packet to see if you get any more. Or you may want to redirect the packet to a port on the local system or to another port on another system (covered in Section 9.2).

7.3.1 A Look at *netfilter's* `filter` Table

As with the masquerading/NAT rules in Chapter 4, the order in which the firewalling rules are encountered is significant. If the first rule blocks all packets, there is no point in even having the following rules. And if there is a rule which forwards all packets before any of the rules that might block its forwarding, why bother with packet filtering at all? The difference is that you're likely to have dozens of packet-filtering rules, so there's more motivation for being well organized and using multiple user-defined chains to keep things manageable. Once again, it is quite helpful to refer to a graphical depiction of the path a packet takes through the kernel. Recall that the NAT rules were part of the **nat** table and, for our examples, used the POSTROUTING hook and built-in chain; well, our filtering rules fall under the `filter` table (`modprobe iptable_filter`).

For the filter table, the built-in chains are shown in Figure 7.5. As you can see, there are three different places where `filter` registers itself with the kernel: for any packet being sent out of the local box, for any packet being delivered to the local box, and for any packet being forwarded by this system. For that last case, note that */proc/sys/net/ipv4/ip_forward* can be thought of as enabling use of this chain. That is, you cannot forward packets if *ip_forward* is set to 0, regardless of the rules you have in place.

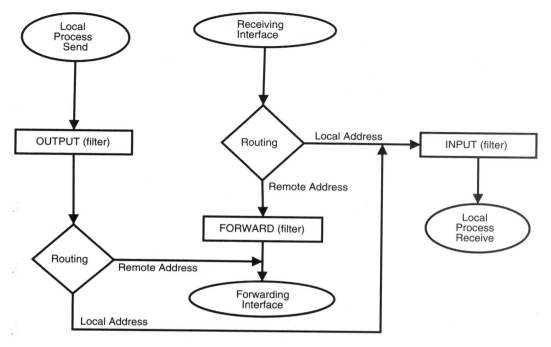

Figure 7.5 Packet Path with the *netfilter* `filter` Table

So, if you wanted to stop inbound telnet traffic to this host only, you would add a rule to `INPUT` that blocked any tcp traffic to port 23. If you want to make sure that no SMTP mail originates from this host, you could add a rule to the built-in `OUTPUT` chain that blocked tcp port 25. (Make sure that your MTA is disabled, or you could end up with a mess of retry and delivery failure notifications in */var.*) To be sure that no one from inside your organization connects directly to the access router (assuming that this system was the gateway between the two), add a rule to the `FORWARD` chain specifying the source addresses of your internal network in a subnet notation, and the destination address of the access router. But, just as with masquerading, you need targets to apply to packets that match a given rule. The list of targets normally used with filtering is:

- `ACCEPT`—allow the packet to pass (be forwarded, allowed to input, or be output) without traversing any other rules (in the current chain).[7]

- `DROP`—throw the packet away, meaning to blackhole the packet (like `DENY` in the 2.2 series kernel).

- `REJECT`—throw the packet away, but reply to the sender with an ICMP port unreachable message. This notifies the sender that there is some sort of firewall in place. (With `DROP`, the sender receives no such notification and will continue to try to establish the connection until the timeouts expire.)

---

[7]If you're familiar with `ipchains`, you'll find that `netfilter` is much more intuitive because of the order in which the hooks are called.

- **LOG**—log the packet via the syslog facility. This does not affect the flow of the packet at all, meaning that the packet will be matched against the next rule in the chain.

- **MIRROR**—quite literally, return (or reflect) the packet back to the sender.

- **RETURN**—return the packet to the calling chain in the case of user-defined chains, or immediately enact the policy for a built-in chain.

- **QUEUE**—queue the packet into user-space, where a program coded with the *libipq* API (part of *iptables*) should be waiting to pass judgment on the packet. This really opens a world of possibilities for self-adjusting filters, automatic response to attacks, and so on. We won't discuss it further in this book, but keep it in mind if you are considering a very specialized application. I think you'll find you can do an incredible amount with what comes standard.

We'll match packets and specify targets. Simple enough, right? As always, the devil's in the details. We're going to start using the `filter` table, first focusing only on the `FORWARD` chain, and then using all three of the chains available to `filter`.

7.3.2   Conditional IP Forwarding—The `FORWARD` Chain

Conditional IP forwarding is a term used for a router configuration that rejects the forwarding of certain packets, or vice versa, one that allows only certain packets to be forwarded. It is typically used when you have more than two network interfaces, as is often the case with firewalls, and need some IP forwarding to occur, but not in all cases (or directions). Refer to Figure 7.6 to view the topology for this example, which represents one basic configuration of the oxygen router where we have a combination firewall and Internet router with a perimeter net to boot. The *sppp0* interface is our point-to-point connection to our ISP and is configured as the default route in the kernel. The perimeter net (connected to *eth1*) hosts our site's proxy servers, web servers, mail server, what-have-you. The inside (physically cabled to *eth0*) should have access only to the perimeter net, and for the time being we will allow the perimeter net to speak freely to the Internet.

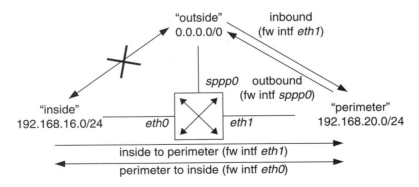

Figure 7.6 Conditional Forwarding Example

An Example of Conditional Forwarding with *netfilter*

First we need to get our kernel compiled with the options required to support packet filtering. The option `Packet filtering` generates the `iptables_filter.o` module. We'd also like to have support for the `REJECT` target, which will be loaded by *iptables* as soon as we add a rule with this target. The `LOG` target isn't strictly part of the `filter` table, but it's very useful, and we want it to be available. If you're compiling a kernel to work up your ruleset, select all of the modules within the `IP: Netfilter Configuration` submenu. The extra time spent compiling the kernel with these extra modules is negligible compared to the time it takes to compile another kernel. For your production firewall, you may decide that you're more comfortable with a monolithic kernel, i.e., a kernel that lacks the ability to load modules dynamically, for security reasons. Chapter 10 in *Hacking Linux Exposed* makes a pretty good case for this precaution by demonstrating the simplicity with which hackers can cover their tracks by using kernel modules. If you're going to do away with the modules, use a modular kernel until you've identified everything you need (because once you're running without modules you'll have to recompile and reboot to get new functionality). If you've got plenty of memory, compile all of the features into your kernel. In any event, we're going to use the following for now:

```
Networking options --->
   [*] Network packet filtering (replaces ipchains)
   [*] TCP/IP networking
      IP: Netfilter Configuration  --->
         <M> IP tables support (required for filtering/masq/NAT)
         <M>    Packet filtering
         <M>      REJECT target support
         <M>    LOG target support
```

We want to prevent traffic from flowing between the *inside* and the *outside* in either direction but to allow traffic to flow between the *perimeter* and the *inside* and between the *perimeter* and the *outside*.

```
### (1)
### flush any existing rules on the FORWARD chain
oxygen:root> iptables --table filter -F FORWARD

### (2)
### our default forwarding policy is DROP
### at this point, no forwarding works
oxygen:root> iptables --table filter -P FORWARD DROP

### (3)
### expressly prohibit those on the inside from reaching
### the outside, but be polite about it ("reject")
oxygen:root> iptables --table filter -A FORWARD -j REJECT  \
                      --in-interface eth0                  \
                      --out-interface eth1                 \
                      --source 192.168.16.0/24
```

```
### (4)
### allow anyone to send to the perimeter net
oxygen:root> iptables --table filter -A FORWARD -j ACCEPT  \
                      --out-interface eth1                 \
                      --destination 192.168.20.0/24


### (5)
### allow the perimeter net to send to the inside
### (*mega-primitive* and dangerous)
oxygen:root> iptables --table filter -A FORWARD -j ACCEPT  \
                      --in-interface eth1                  \
                      --out-interface eth0                 \
                      --source 192.168.20.0/24             \
                      --destination 192.168.16.0/24


### (6)
### allow the perimeter net to forward to the outside
oxygen:root> iptables --table filter -A FORWARD -j ACCEPT  \
                      --in-interface eth1                  \
                      --out-interface sppp0                \
                      --source 192.168.20.0/24


### (7)
### log any direct packet attempts from the outside -> inside
oxygen:root> iptables --table filter -A FORWARD -j LOG     \
                      --log-tcp-options                    \
                      --in-interface sppp0                 \
                      --destination 192.168.16.0/24
```

1. This rule initializes us in a known state. All rules in the built-in FORWARD chain are flushed.

2. Configure the default policy for forwarded packets to be DROP. This black-holes anything that tries to traverse the router.

3. Prohibit any direct communication between the inside and the outside. This isn't strictly necessary, since the default policy already excludes this communication, but dropped packets are a maddening trick to play on your internal clients (and perhaps yourself!). It's better to have the connection attempt fail right away when the firewall returns an ICMP unreachable message.

4. Allow both the outside and the inside to send to the perimeter net. This gives the inside access to the proxies and allows the outside to deliver mail, etc. Notice how by not specifying an input interface, as we did in the previous rule, *iptables* assumes all input interfaces. There is no logical OR for *iptables*, so if we wanted to explicitly list out the interfaces for some reason, we would do this with two separate rules.

5. Allow the perimeter net to communicate with the inside. This is not a terribly good idea, since if one of the perimeter net systems is compromised, then the inside is completely accessible. If we don't anticipate the systems on the perimeter net initiating connections

to the inside, then we can add `--proto tcp ! --syn` to this rule to only allow responses to TCP connection requests from the inside; in other words, the connection must be initiated from the inside. If we did this, and there was some UDP service on the perimeter net (<cough> DNS), we'd want to add a rule to allow access for just that service. But let's stick to forwarding for now.

6. Allow the perimeter net to send freely to the outside.

7. Log any packets received on *sppp0* with a destination address of the inside network. The logging occurs via syslog and can be quite voluminous if there is a lot of traffic that matches the rule. After logging the packet, the `LOG` target does not alter the flow of the packet. It continues on through the chain, and in this example it falls off the chain (meaning that the default policy of `DROP` is enforced—just what we want). We'll cover this target in more depth in Section 7.3.8.

So, that's a bit of conditional forwarding. Please realize that this example is intended only to be illustrative, not to serve as even the basis for your firewall. Also, note that forwarding rules do not, in any way, affect connections to the router/firewall itself. Referring back to Figure 7.5, you'll note that `INPUT` is used to control what reaches the router, even if the packet is destined for an interface other than the one that received it. For example, a host on the outside attempting a connection to the IP to *eth0* (as per our configuration in Figure 7.6) will succeed, despite our rule to prevent forwarding. Regardless of IP subnet or your logical designations, all interfaces on the box are accessible to all others without forwarding. I encourage you to "prove" this to yourself with the following test:

```
iptables --table filter -A FORWARD -p tcp --dport 22 -j DROP
```

Then try to *ssh* across your router (i.e., to something beyond it), which will fail, and attempt to *ssh* to any other interface on your router, which will succeed. It works the other way around, too; `INPUT` has nothing to do with forwarding. If you're familiar with the prior kernel tools for packet filtering, this is a welcome change for situations where you want distinctly different policies for connections *to* your router as opposed to *through* your router. One more note about configuring these rules before we move on. Remember to use the `--verbose` switch (`-v`) when listing rules with `-L`. If you fail to do this, the input/output interface fields won't be listed, which gives rules an entirely different feel at first glance. (OK, honestly, it can be confusing.) Another alternative is to just use *iptables-save* to display the active rules (and counters).

7.3.3   IP Packet Filtering

Packet filtering is a term that often goes hand-in-hand with firewalls, although it can be used almost everywhere. But before it can be used, we should answer the question *What is packet filtering?* Everything that enters and exits our routers via the network is in the form of a packet. Normally, there are no restrictions on which hosts may use the router as a gateway; if the router can forward the packet, it will. In the previous section we placed some basic restrictions on this forwarding by telling the kernel that certain packet flows were not to be allowed. So in that sense we've already done some packet filtering in the previous section.

But now we want to focus on the packets that are destined for the local system. Systems configured with *tcpd* aside, there are few restrictions as to which hosts may attempt to contact a system on any given port via any particular protocol. If the packet can get there and the system can answer, i.e., it has a daemon or service ready to answer on that port, it will. In this section we're going to restrict the packets entering and exiting our system by adding rules to the INPUT and OUTPUT chains of the filter table. This differs from NAT and conditional forwarding in that we'll operate only on input and output from the system, not on packets selected for forwarding by the kernel's routing table. Once again, you might find it helpful to take a glance at Figure 7.5 on page 227.

Adding rules to the INPUT and OUTPUT chains to block undesirable packets can be useful for any system, but it's absolutely crucial on our Internet access router. There are a lot of off-kilter folks out there who would rather knock what you build over than invest their time in building something meaningful. (It doesn't take much of an armchair psychologist to spot the deep-rooted insecurity in their senseless destructive acts.) The harsh reality is that leaving your Linux system open to the Internet is probably worse than leaving it logged in at a root console in a shopping mall. So, let's take a look at paring down what's accessible to whom from the network.

7.3.4   *netfilter's* filter:INPUT **Chain**

The INPUT chain of the filter table is traversed by any packet that is going to be received by the local system, before any of the user-space processes on that system are even aware of it. The rules are matched against all packets that will be received by the local host, even if they are locally generated. In this way, it acts like a protective layer that shields your system from having to process traffic you already know you don't want. (I wish I could get a spam filter that worked as effectively.) Recall the test we proposed back on page 231, where I wanted you to prove to yourself that a packet received on any interface of a multihomed system could reach the IP of any other interface on that same system regardless of any rules in the FORWARD chain. This may have seemed unfortunate at the time, but from the perspective of setting up filters for inbound traffic, rules in the INPUT chain do exactly what you'd hope with a minimum of fuss. Say, for example, that you know you don't want anyone physically on the outside to make any connection to your router whatsoever. You can add a rule like the following:

```
oxygen:root> iptables --table filter -A INPUT -j DROP --in-interface sppp0
```

Seems simple enough, right? What's so magical about this, especially for folks who have used the previous kernel facilities, is that it acts on all packets received on via *sppp0* and bound for the local system. You can be confident that no matter what IP address is in the destination field of the packet, if it matches one on your router, it will be dropped. So even if someone on the outside spoofs their source address and routes a packet toward oxygen using one of the internal IP addresses as the destination, there's no way around the fact that the packet arrived via *sppp0*. Adding rules to the INPUT chain is just like adding rules to the FORWARD chain. If you'd like, you can even set the policy for this chain to be REJECT or DROP. (But you'd better be on the console when you do that, or have already added enough rules to allow your current session to continue. In other words, watch out for the order in which you add your rules.) Let's add a few more rules to our INPUT chain:

```
# set policy to DROP (by default, nothing is allowed in)
oxygen:root> iptables --table filter -P INPUT DROP

# allow ssh connections from any IP on the inside
oxygen:root> iptables --table filter -A INPUT -j ACCEPT    \
                       --in-interface eth0                 \
                       --proto tcp --dport 22
```

```
# allow ssh (only) from the outside from this one host
oxygen:root> iptables --table filter -A INPUT -j ACCEPT    \
                      --in-interface sppp0                 \
                      --source 10.17.63.191/32             \
                      --proto tcp --dport 22

# we want to be able to be able to use our DNS server
oxygen:root> iptables --table filter -A INPUT -j ACCEPT    \
                      --in-interface eth1                  \
                      --source 192.168.20.8                \
                      --proto udp --sport 53

# use REJECT for connection attempts from the inside
oxygen:root> iptables --table filter -A INPUT -j REJECT    \
                      --in-interface eth0
```

The first command sets the default policy. Then we allow *ssh*, since we have confidence that it's sufficiently well protected and will log any mischief. The next rule allows a single host on the Internet side to connect to the firewall using *ssh*. This is a bit of a security trade-off, but we're more willing to do this than to build some other back door into our network. Any compromise like this should be coupled with as stringent an *sshd* configuration as you can tolerate, including limiting hosts that connect to that instance of the SSH server daemon with the `from=` configuration option. The third rule (fourth command) says that we'll allow the IP of our DNS server on the perimeter net to send us traffic from port 53. (Otherwise, we'd be getting timeouts everytime we tried to perform a DNS lookup from this host [or any other host, as we've drastically limited what will be allowed into the box].) Finally, we opt for immediate error messages instead of long timeouts when machines on the inside try to connect to the firewall directly. Notice that the ordering of this last rule is important. If we place this rule before the rule that allows *ssh* from the inside, all packets from the inside, including *ssh* connection attempts, will match this rule and be rejected. Because this rule needs to come at the end of the chain (as sort of an additional default policy), either it must be specified last, or subsequent rules that match the same packets must be inserted using `-I` into the chain.

7.3.5 *netfilter*'s `--match state`

In the previous section we greatly enhanced the security of our firewall by severely limiting the number of packets it would accept. This is a Good Thing, but in some cases we may come to think that we've cut off our nose to spite our face. For example, what happens on that configuration if cron needs to send an email message? The MTA (Mail Transfer Agent) may perform an MX lookup (which will succeed because we are allowing DNS), but when it attempts to forward the email toward its destination, we run into a problem. There's no problem connecting to the next MTA up the line (after all, we haven't even talked about the `OUTPUT` chain yet), but when that remote mail server responds to our connection request, the packet is discarded because it doesn't match any of the rules in the `INPUT` chain. The same is true for any client program on this system, be it *lynx*, *ssh*, or *ftp*. Do we need to start adding rules to allow the responses, opening up pinholes in our firewall for each client protocol we might want to use? We can do this with a set of rules like this one:

```
# we need to be able to send SMTP mail
oxygen:root> iptables --table filter -A INPUT -j ACCEPT    \
                      --in-interface eth1                  \
                      --proto tcp --sport 25 ! --syn
```

By the way, the ! --syn option tells the rule to match packets only where the SYN flag is clear, indicating TCP packets *not used* to initiate a connection. So, even if we have this rule, somebody cannot attempt to open a connection to our system by using port 25 as their sending port, because in that TCP protocol handshake, the first packet always has the SYN flag set. So we can add a bunch of rules like this, but we'll need one for each network protocol (and in the 2.2 kernel facility and before, this is what we'd do). But *netfilter*'s connection tracking code offers a much simpler alternative. By matching the state of a TCP connection, we can construct a rule that will allow responses to any connection we initiate from this system. You can view the state of all connections being tracked by the kernel by looking at */proc/net/ip_conntrack*—refer back to Section 4.4.3 for more information. The rule we desire is simply:

```
# allow responses to locally initiated connections
oxygen:root> iptables --table filter -A INPUT -j ACCEPT    \
                      --match state --state ESTABLISHED
```

The option --match *typeofmatch* is new to us. It is another example of the extendable architecture of *netfilter*. It indicates that a new code should be linked in to help match packets (just as -j can link in new targets). In the case of **state**, or the *ipt_state.o* kernel module, the argument --state *STATE* can now be used to specify a state from the connection tracking code. The states that can be matched are:

- NEW—the packet is initiating a connection.

- ESTABLISHED—the packet is part of a negotiated connection.

- RELATED—the packet is associated with a connection, such as an ICMP error. There's no point in frustratingly long timeouts instead of immediate ICMP port unreachable errors when it can be helped. This state also has specific meaning in conjunction with the very pesky FTP protocol when used together with *ip_conntrack_ftp.o.* (If you're interested in how we had to do it in the olden days, the challenges of the FTP protocol for firewalls is discussed in the 2.2.x kernel material on page 355.)

- INVALID—the packet is not associated with a packet flow, or is otherwise problematic. These packets should be dropped (if the default policy doesn't do so already).

Now, of course, you know that you'll need kernel support for this if you haven't already worked up a superkernel with all of the *netfilter* options. The minimum modules required for stateful rules in the filter table are the following (you'll want to add the FTP and IRC modules if you intend to use them):

```
Networking options --->
    [*] Network packet filtering (replaces ipchains)
    [*] TCP/IP networking
```

```
IP: Netfilter Configuration  --->
   <M> Connection tracking (required for masq/NAT)
   <M> IP tables support (required for filtering/masq/NAT)
   <M>   Connection state match support
   <M>   Packet filtering
```

7.3.6   --match limit

In the previous section we looked at matching connection state to make our router a little more usable (at least for us, not for potential crackers). In this section we'll introduce another match extension, the `limit` extension, which sets a rate at which the rule will match packets that otherwise match the criteria in the rule. To use this feature, you'll need a kernel very much like the one used to match `state` along with `Networking options -> IP: Netfilter Configuration -> limit match support`. If you don't allow autoloading of modules, load the resulting module with `modprobe ipt_limit`. So how does it work? Once the match extension is specified with `--match limit`, two additional command-line arguments are available:

- `--limit` *rate* specifies the average rate at which the match is allowed to occur. By default, the unit for *rate* is hertz, Hz, or 1/second (not to be confused with the kernel's internal concept of HZ, defined in `./include/asm/param.h`). You can also specify rates in terms of `/minute`, `/hour`, `/day`, as well as explicitly specify `/second`. If not specified, the rate defaults to 3 per hour.

- `--limit-burst` *burstquantity* modifies the base rate by allowing *burstquantity* packets to match before the limit is applied. The default burst is 5.

This target is often used to prevent DoS (denial of service) attacks. For example, say that our service provider needs to be able to ping our router from the outside as part of their service-level monitoring, but we don't always know what IP will initiate the ping on their side. So we need to allow ping, but we don't want folks flood-pinging us.

```
# 2 pings per second should be enough for most purposes
oxygen:root> iptables --table filter -A INPUT -j ACCEPT      \
                       --in-interface sppp0                  \
                       --proto icmp --icmp-type echo-request \
                       --limit 2/s --limit-burst 3


# the rest are dropped
oxygen:root> iptables --table filter -A INPUT -j DROP        \
                       --in-interface sppp0                  \
                       --proto icmp --icmp-type echo-request
```

Note that you're specifying a condition upon which the rule matches packets. Therefore, in order to really block unwanted traffic, for example flood pings, you have to specify a limit in conjunction with an `ACCEPT` target, and then make sure that another rule in the chain prevents packets of that type from passing, once the limit has been exceeded. Another common application is to specify a limit in conjunction with a `LOG` target to prevent someone from purposefully filling up your drives with logging information. Also remember that the rule above affects input to the router, not what is allowed to traverse the router (via the `FORWARD` chain). You should also understand that this is not a mechanism to limit bandwidth; we'll look at limiting bandwidth in Section 8.4.

7.3.7   The OUTPUT Chain

We've spent some time talking about the INPUT and FORWARD along with some special mechanisms for matching rules. Now let's look at the other side of INPUT, the OUTPUT chain. With *netfilter*'s separation between forwarding and local system input/output, there may be less motivation for limiting output than with the previous kernel facilities. Still, several uses come to mind, and you'll have this in your toolbox when you need it. As you've surely surmised, the OUTPUT chain is followed by all packets leaving the local system, and as such, it can be used to block (or rate-limit) outbound packet flow. One approach here is to limit output to what you think should be allowed to originate from your router (and then see what breaks). Another is to use output rules to specifically block packets from network services provided on your router as a second line of defense. (You wouldn't want a misconfigured routing daemon broadcasting all kinds of information about your network topology to the outside.) A third approach, sufficient disk space willing, would be to log all of the output from your router (save perhaps DNS lookups). If this really is your firewall, you should have a very good idea of what's being run on it locally. Rules may be added to the OUTPUT chain as long as *iptables_filter* is loaded, and you may additionally use the --out-interface *intf* to indicate the output interface(s) for the rule. Here are some examples:

```
# we don't want to respond to many pings
oxygen:root> iptables --table filter -A OUTPUT -j ACCEPT         \
                      --proto icmp --icmp-type echo-response \
                      --out-interface sppp0                      \
                      --limit 5/s --limit-burst 10
oxygen:root> iptables --table filter -A OUTPUT -j DROP           \
                      --out-interface sppp0                      \
                      --proto icmp --icmp-type echo-response

# no cleartext password protocols!
oxygen:root> iptables --table filter -A OUTPUT -j REJECT         \
                      --proto tcp                                \
                      --match multiport --dport 21,23
```

The first pair of rules implements the other half of the rules we added while discussing --match limit, just in case someone somehow circumvents our input limit and tricks the router into generating a stream of ping replies (or **pongs** in the vernacular). We mentioned --match multiport while introducing *netfilter* back in Chapter 4, but this is the first time we've used it. It allows us to specify a comma-delimited list of ports instead of generating two separate rules. In this case, we don't want an admin to initiate a telnet or ftp from the firewall for fear that an eavesdropper may monitor the connection and obtain one of the administrator's passwords.

Along the lines of controlling what a user can do on the system, there is another match target that can be used to match the user ID, group ID, process ID, or session ID. You'll need to enable Owner match support in the kernel (found within IP: Netfilter Configuration) and have the *ipt_owner* loaded to access to the extension. It should make sense that this match extension is valid only for output from the local system—if the traffic weren't from this system, it wouldn't be traversing OUTPUT. And in any case, we wouldn't want to be asking other systems, using facilities such as *identd*, who originated the packet. This is expensive in terms of time, and you can't really trust any system that you don't administer to tell you what user ID is originating the packet anyway. But to enforce local policies on a system, say that only members of the *netmins* group (gid 17) may originate *ssh* connections from this box, this is a handy match extension. In this example, we utilize both the owner and the state match extensions to allow *ssh* connections to originate only for members of our network administrators group.

```
# allow orginating ssh for members of the netmins group
oxygen:root> iptables --table filter -I OUTPUT -j ACCEPT      \
                      --match owner --gid-owner 17            \
                      --match state --state NEW,ESTABLISHED   \
                      --proto tcp --dport 22
```

After `--match owner`, you may specify one of the following: `--uid-owner` *uid*, `--gid-owner` *gid*, `--pid-owner` *pid*, or `--sid-owner` *sid*, where the ids are specified numerically. (Don't make the kernel go walk through */etc/passwd* to match a username to a uid for every packet you send!) Finally, although we haven't discussed it yet, the `mangle` table also hooks into the `OUTPUT` chain, so I'll reiterate my suggestion of always using `--table` or `-t` to indicate the table desired.

7.3.8   The *netfilter* LOG Target

The last bit of *netfilter* we'll cover in this chapter is the aforementioned `LOG` target. This target, specified with `-j LOG`, simply records the passage of the packet. It can be used in conjunction with any of the tables and chains, both built-in and user-defined. The minimal kernel configuration includes only support for iptables and the `LOG` target itself.

```
Networking options --->
    [*] Network packet filtering (replaces ipchains)
    [*] TCP/IP networking
        IP: Netfilter Configuration  --->
            <M> IP tables support (required for filtering/masq/NAT)
            <M>  LOG target support
```

Once you load the resulting module (`modprobe ipt_LOG`—notice how targets are differentiated from match extensions by always being uppercase, both in the module name and on the command line), you can use the following arguments together with the table, chain, and your packet-matching criteria:

```
LOG v1.2.3 options:
  --log-level level     Level of logging (numeric or see syslog.conf)
  --log-prefix prefix   Prefix log messages with this prefix.
  --log-tcp-sequence    Log TCP sequence numbers.
  --log-tcp-options     Log TCP options.
  --log-ip-options      Log IP options.
```

You control the syslog level with the `--log-level` *level*, where *level* is one of the syslog levels, listed here from lowest to highest priority: DEBUG, INFO, NOTICE, WARN, CRIT, ALERT, and EMERG. The default level is WARN (meaning that any *syslog.conf* entry for kern.warn will catch these messages); facility is fixed at KERNEL. Other options are shown below. When specifying a prefix for your messages, you get up to 30 characters that will be tacked between the facility (always `kernel:`) and the fields logged. You'll probably want to specify a trailing space and think about delimiters so that your parsing script can easily key off your prefix. The last three options give you the ability to log additional protocol header fields sniffer-style. You'll end up with a line like this in your syslog's output file:

```
Nov 23 00:01:12 drone3 kernel: chain=filter:OUTPUT IN= OUT=eth1
                SRC=192.168.16.13 DST=192.168.18.1 LEN=100 TOS=0x10
                PREC=0x00 TTL=64 ID=36736 PROTO=TCP SPT=22 DPT=52724
                WINDOW=8216 RES=0x00 ACK PSH URGP=0
```

The "chain=filter:OUTPUT" is my prefix, and the remainder corresponds to a single SSH packet. The line breaks are arbitrary so that the text will fit the page in this book, so don't worry about what sort of regular expression you'll need to match these lines. The other thing to keep in mind about the logging target is that it can easily consume massive amounts of disk space in short periods of time. Either choose carefully what you log, or better yet, use the `limit` target to enforce a limit on how much logging can take place. Also keep in mind that logging a packet doesn't affect its path, so if you want to log drops, you should log them in the rule right before the drop, or in the case of the default policy, as the last rule in the chain.

7.3.9   Firewalling Rules in the Real World

Now it's time for the big disclaimer. I'm trying to teach you the basics of fishing in this chapter, not giving you a fish. The firewalling rules we've covered up to now aren't even a skeleton of the ruleset you should be running on a production system. The types of rule do, however, represent the components that will comprise a packet-filtering firewall. In fact, you can use these rules on any Linux system to provide a higher level of security, or to help enforce organizational policies, such as weaning folks off telnet and ftp. I don't present a comprehensive firewall ruleset here for two reasons. First, there is no such thing, even if we were to settle on a fixed topology and list out the exact services we want to provide. Network security invariably involves trade-offs, and vendors or administrators who maintain otherwise are either naive or needlessly arrogant. You'll need to gauge your ruleset to strike a balance between the needs of your users and the level of security you hope to attain. Second, there are better materials out there, more thorough configurations, than what I could cook up here, and they are available in electronic form via mechanisms that lend themselves to much more frequent updates than a book. The rulesets are often offered together with startup/shutdown/log-rotation scripts and other useful tools. While you may not find a ruleset that is a perfect match for your environment, odds are that you can come pretty close—the configurations available are getting better—and you're going to learn a lot in the process of searching and comparing. Here are a few links to some good starting places:

- *http://www.linuxguruz.org/iptables/*—This site hosts multiple firewall configuration scripts along with a nice collection of information for network admins and some user-submitted tutorials.

- *http://people.unix-fu.org/andreasson/iptables-tutorial/iptables-tutorial.html* —There are several decent firewall configuration scripts toward the end of this tutorial.

- *http://www.malibyte.net/security/fwscripts.html*—A good starting point for your firewall configuration, "ported" from a popular *ipchains*-based script.

- *http://heimdall.asgardsrealm.net/linux/firewall/*—A single script/package, but written for *iptables* from the start.

- *http://www.fwbuilder.org/*—If you like (or require) GUI configuration tools, you're not alone. There are a slew of GUI front ends available for firewall configuration; *Firewall Builder* happens to be one that I like. It is also already available as packages for several distributions. Search on *http://freshmeat.net/* if you're interested in others.

- *http://www.niemueller.de/webmin/*—If you need an entire suite of graphical configuration interfaces, take a look at the *Webmin* family of tools. At the time of writing, the *iptables* interface isn't complete, but Tim Niemueller does really nice work, so I have high expectations.

7.3.10   Testing Packet-Filtering Rules

Regardless of what you use to configure your rules, you're going to need a way to test your ruleset. And what do you do if you want to test your packet-filter before placing it in production? There are several alternatives. Perhaps the most thorough is to set up an identical environment and test. The problem with this, as when testing any sort of Internet service, is that it is difficult to simulate the Internet without really having the Internet. If you have perimeter net topology, this is still an option. You can configure a test firewall and add a route to your Internet router for your test workstation via the test firewall. The test workstation will use the test firewall for its default gateway. See Figure 7.7 for the topology. This will work, but you should be careful not to weaken your security by allowing another way into your network via the test firewall. It is also a lot of work. The pros are that it is an accurate test of many client-server type connections and that your method of testing/problem detection is identical to your day-to-day firewall activities.

If this is too time consuming, or if you would like to quickly test a rule, there is an easier option. *ipchains*, the utility for the 2.2 kernel, has the ability to generate test packets which will be checked against the rules configured in the kernel. At the time of writing, this hasn't been implemented in *iptables* yet. (I get the error message shown below.)

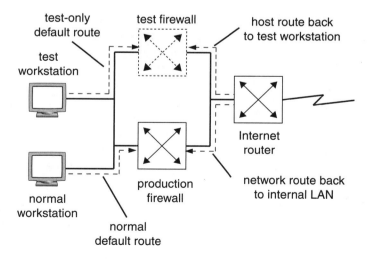

Figure 7.7 Test Firewall Network Topology

```
root@drone3:~# iptables --table filter --check INPUT            \
            --source 192.168.18.1 --destination 192.168.18.13  \
            --proto tcp -in-interface eth0
iptables: Will be implemented real soon.  I promise ;)
```

But since it *should* be available RSN, let's at least talk about it for a minute. As you can see, creating a test packet looks very much like any other command used to enter, edit, or remove a rule. But because the Linux kernel doesn't invent information, you need to specify a source, a destination, a protocol, probably a source and destination port, and the interface which either receives or sends the virtual packet, depending upon the chain you are checking. Since I cannot show you output I don't have, I'll have to refer you to the reference material on the 2.2 kernel in Section 10.3.3 if you're interested in how it used to work. My assumption is that it won't be radically different but, like *netfilter/iptables*, most certainly will be better.

To speak generally about this type of testing, checking rules in this manner is a good way to review new configurations and configurations where you have reordered the rules for some reason—perhaps to improve performance as described later in this chapter. My recommendation is to develop a script which contains a comprehensive list of rules and compare the output of this script against the output of a control run which you know generates the correct results. You won't want to use --check as your only form of testing, because there are several drawbacks to testing firewall rules in this manner. For one, there is no virtual reply to the packet, which has to make it back through the firewall for the first rule to be useful (unless you're testing rules to block communications).

The second reason is based on my experiences in having to work alongside myself. Assume that you do code your set of check rules to include replies. Furthermore, assume that you have a test case (a --check command) for each rule of your packet filter. Because you wrote the packet-filtering rules, chances are that *your* rules will pass *your* checks. Most of the errors I have encountered when specifying rules for blocking or allowing a given protocol came from a lack of understanding (or adequate documentation) of the protocol. For this reason, I recommend that you test using a real environment whenever possible. When you run into problems, you can use a combination of a packet sniffer, the LOG target, and a review of the packet and byte counters for each of your rules to determine why something is passing or not passing. Thorough testing can be time consuming, so budget time for it. Sure, you can add a rule in 5 minutes, but if you do it on the fly and that rule produces a gaping hole in your firewall, how long is it going to take to clean up the mess? Refer to Appendix C for a general discussion of testing.

Firewall Performance Tune-Up

After running your packet filter for a while, you might want to look closely at the output of iptables-save --counters. It might be handy to print this out so that you can take a good look at it.

The byte counts will show you which rules are being used most often. Some (not all!) rules will be interchangeable with respect to position in the list without affecting the security of the firewall. You can highlight all rules of an equivalent ordering priority, and then shuffle these rules around in your firewall startup script so that the most frequently utilized rules appear further up in the list. The result is that the packet is either blocked or allowed to pass earlier, before unnecessary checking is done. Another way to tune is to check for rules which encompass other rules, or a set of rules which can be expressed by a single rule. An example is separate rules which are identical except for the source or destination specifications, where these specifications are consecutive subnets which can be aggregated into a CIDR subnet.

Hint: Printouts of Wide-Column Text

If you work in an environment where the usefulness of a wide-carriage dotmatrix printer is undervalued, you can get a reasonably good 132-column printout of an ASCII textfile using *a2ps*. a2ps -1 --font-size=9.5 --landscape --output=*outfile.ps infile*. If you need more columns, just adjust the font-size to be smaller.

Typically these methods will result in only small performance gains, but they can help, and in grossly misconfigured systems they can make a significant difference. Whatever you do, don't trade speed for security—that's not going to help for long!

7.4   Notification Systems

Pop quiz: Which is more inconvenient, being paged at 3:00 in the morning because your organization's Internet link is down, or coming into the office at 8:30 to deal with hordes of angry users, a thousand bounced emails, and another 500 or so in the outbound queue? The answer, of course, depends upon your particular situation, but, as uncomfortable as it is, I prefer the former. The more quickly a problem is addressed, the fewer negative repercussions there are to deal with later. This section is for those of you who need to know when your network is not well. As such, it is not only applicable to Internet routers. Your instincts may be able to whip up something clever to signal you when there is a problem, but before you get started designing your notification system, spend a moment and reflect on the following questions:

1. *What sort of failures should result in notification?* We will call this **detection**.

2. *How would you like to be notified? Are different methods of notification required for different types of failures?*

3. *How much money and time are you willing to spend to incorporate redundancy into your notification system?*

4. *What software and hardware are needed to implement the system you require? Are they available? Is there a current system in place with which you need to integrate?*

   Since all of these questions are interrelated, you may find that your answers to one change the answers to another. There are several ways to go about notification, ranging from simplistic to quite elaborate. Your choice will be dictated by your needs and individual tastes. A word of caution, however, to those who would implement a grand sophisticated notification system: How will you know if your system fails? For that reason, the simpler and more robust a notification system is, the better. Each of the questions above is discussed briefly in this section. The last discussion reviews some monitoring and notification software for Linux.

7.4.1   Failure Detection

Before we even worry about how we're going to send the message, we need to know what the message is. Here's a list of Bad Things for our Internet environment and certain requirements in order to be able to detect them:

power failure—To be able to detect power failures, you will need a UPS which can be connected to your notification system. That system, including its modem, must also be on protected power. As mentioned in Chapter 1, several UPS manufacturers have Linux support.

catastrophic router failure—If your router suffers a hardware failure, or if the kernel panics, it will no longer be able to alert you to its condition. For this reason, you should consider having a notification system in your environment separate from the resources being monitored. (See Section 7.4.2.)

Internet link down—If the link itself fails, but not the router, then your router will be able to detect this. It is probably sufficient to use *ping* in this instance (not so with other hosts, as we will see shortly), and your ISP should be OK with this, since you are paying for the service. However, it is bad etiquette to ping some other well-known Internet site at any regular interval. Pings generate *syslog* entries and use up bandwidth that is not yours. It's not a good idea anyway, since the well-known site could be down. If you're using *WANPIPE*, you can watch *syslog* for disconnect messages.

system under attack—This is a more difficult situation to accurately detect. There are, however, a few things which might signal a possible break-in: someone logging into the system or attempting to log in during nonbusiness hours or excessive pings or other connection attempts from an external or internal source—many attacks are launched from the inside source. A reboot is a sure sign of a problem. For this reason, you might want to have the startup scripts on the router send notification whenever the system restarts.

In any event, you are going to have to put on your coding cap to be able to detect that your system is under attack. To my knowledge, there are few packages readily available which will notify you of attacks in real time while they occur. (One exception is *iplogger*, discussed later, which can detect the FTP-bounce attack.)

excessive system load—This seems easy to detect because the system is up and able to communicate its status, but it's not always easy to tell when load becomes too high. What you monitor will depend upon the application(s) running on your router, but here are some ideas:

- **free disk space**—If you don't already know, do not let the root filesystem of a Unix system fill up—ever. You should also be concerned about the integrity of your logs; for this reason, make */var* its own filesystem.

- **memory/swapspace usage**—Don't let your system run out of virtual memory, either. For systems functioning strictly as routers, this should not be a problem because the system should be sized so that it does not normally swap. The system may occasionally swap, but it should be only during system maintenance functions, like loading packages, compiling a kernel, etc. You can get the information you need from */proc/meminfo* and */proc/swaps*, or with the command *free*.

- **number of users**—If your system allows users, there might be a limit to the number of simultaneous users allowed, e.g., some FTP daemons place a limit on the number of certain types of connections allowed.

- **number of free file descriptors**—Running out of file descriptors can ruin your whole day (even though the Linux kernel is surprisingly resilient and the problem can be fixed on the fly). Even if the kernel does not suffer, applications and daemons may not handle it as gracefully.

> ## Hint: Increasing File Descriptors on a Running System
>
> You can easily increase the number of file descriptors available to the system without having to recompile the kernel. Just write the number of file descriptors you would like to have to */proc/sys/fs/file-max*, with a command like `echo "8192" >/proc/sys/fs/file-max`. You can check the current usage with `cat /proc/sys/fs/file-nr`. The fields are: the current number of file descriptors in use, the number of unused file descriptors already allocated by the kernel, and the maximum number of file descriptors available. (The second value is not overly important; it merely indicates how many requests for file descriptors the kernel can service without having to stop and allocate more—up to the limit of *file-max*.)
>
> Another interesting place to check is the `filp` field of */proc/slabinfo* (for Linux kernel versions 2.2 and higher). The first column indicates the current number of file descriptors in use, while the second is the high water mark (the maximum number of file descriptors used at any time since the system was started).
>
> If you do run out of file descriptors, you can expect the following code to spit a message into *syslog*.
>
> ```
> printk("VFS: file-max limit %d reached\ n", max_files);
> ```
>
> Note that there is also a parameter set in */usr/src/linux/include/limits.h*, `OPEN_MAX`, which controls how many processes a single process can open. (If you change this, you'll probably need to recompile your applications.)

- **number of free ports**—Running out of ports is less likely, but possible. See the information on page 369 about checking the number of ports available for masquerading.

- **number of processes**—When the kernel is unable to fork additional processes, processing as we know it will end. Fortunately, the 2.4 kernel doesn't have a hard limit on the maximum number of processes; the ceiling is dictated by the amount of memory available. If you're running the 2.2 kernel, the pertinent variable is `NR_TASKS`, found in */usr/src/linux/include/linux/tasks.h*. Modifying it will require a kernel rebuild. The default value with the 2.2.x version of the kernel is 512, and for x86 the maximum number of processes when running a 2.2 kernel is 4096.

- **system load**—This should be evident. You don't need to use either *top* or *uptime* to get this value, just `cat /proc/loadavg`.

Most of these parameters can be easily read at regular intervals, perhaps as part of an SNMP monitoring system. If your mechanism supports it, you can record the values for trend analysis and system sizing. Of more immediate concern, set thresholds, and have your monitoring system either take corrective action or notify you (or both).

7.4.2 Methods of Detection

Most of the scripts you write to monitor the things listed above will run on the system being monitored, but you will probably need more for a complete solution. We have already mentioned that you need a monitoring system separate from the systems being monitored. This is not entirely true; the monitoring system can be configured to perform other tasks, too, but you should try to relegate some lesser duties to it. The principle here is that a production outage may ripple through your network—a router failing on one end of a link may result in two or more failures—so the monitoring system's function should be orthogonal to that which is being monitored.

You may be quick to point out that the notification system might also fail. Although possible, what is the likelihood of both systems failing simultaneously? (And if the notification system goes down, but the router stays up, then you do not have an outage.) Nevertheless, if you have the resources, monitor this one system with another system.

There are different ways of monitoring your router just to make sure that it is alive. One way which is **not** safe is to use *ping*. The reason is that, once an NIC has been configured with its IP address, the card often has the ability to respond to ICMP pings without the help of the host operating system as long as the card is physically powered on. (This is true for Unix flavors besides Linux, too.) For this reason, a better, and yet still very simple, test is to *telnet* one of the kernel services, e.g., time. `telnet` *inetrouter-ip* 13 should respond with the current date and time, as long as you haven't disabled this service in */etc/inetd.conf*. You can script this as follows, although your production version should have more error checking in case the call to *qpage* does not work, among other things:

```ksh
#!/usr/bin/ksh
#
# check_router.sh [<targetip>]
#    - very basic system health monitor
#
# modification history:
# 19990714/tm              initial release
############################################################
INTERVAL=60
LONGINTERVAL=3600
TARGET=${1:=192.168.22.13} # take $1 or default IP shown

while (( 1 == 1 ))
do
    telnet $TARGET 13 2>/dev/null
    retval=$?
    if (( $retval != 0 ))
    then
        # problems! - notify via qpage
        DATE=$(date '+%Y/%m/%d-%H:%M')
        qpage -f $0 -p dutypager "something is WRONG at $DATE"
        sleep $LONGINTERVAL
```

```
      fi
      sleep $INTERVAL
done
# not reached
```

There are issues with this script right away. First, you may not be comfortable opening TCP port 13, so you'll need to add a rule to limit access to this port from your monitoring system(s). In fact, you might not be running *inetd* at all, in which case you'll need to find something else to monitor (<cough> SNMP!). There are also several software packages that can give you monitoring without a lot of custom coding on your part. We'll talk about these after we talk about how to get the message out.

7.4.3 Methods of Notification

How you are notified of a (potential) problem will depend upon how you like to work, your budget, and how quickly you need to know about the problems. Different problems may have different priorities and may generate different forms of notification. Here are some ideas to get you started:

- **pager**—Alphanumeric pagers are a popular choice, and many providers have email gateways, making notification as simple as sending an email. Of course, if your Internet link is down, you need to do something else. The easiest thing might be to dial an alternate ISP and send your mail that way. If you are going to be doing a lot of paging, though, you should look into dedicated paging software that interfaces directly with the paging service's TAP/IXO gateway. **TAP** is the Telocator Alphanumeric input Protocol, the successor to IXO. On your side, the client side, you'll probably use SNPP for the protocol between your paging client and your TAP dial-out server. See RFC 1861 for more information on the protocol. An example of software that does just this is *QuickPage*, introduced later in this chapter. With the advent of two-way pagers, you may even be able to take corrective action from your pager. The plot thickens . . . .

- **email**—For many types of problems an email notification is sufficient, and it has the added bonus of being able to include information about the problem. Since we've all been conditioned to read our email before we sleep, bathe, or eat, the notification should not go unread for long.

- **logfile**—Since you will probably want to record the incident and some information about it, you can use *syslog* as a basis for your notification system. If you condense the amount of data written to the logfile sufficiently, you can review the data manually. Otherwise, use a logfile scanner to look for problems, and have it use another form of notification (e.g., emailing you an URL to access the logfile or paging you).

- **remote logfile**—As mentioned in the section on general host security, remote logging enhances security by forcing a hacker to compromise two systems to hide the evidence of an intrusion. It also means that you can perform archiving without adding a lot of disk space to your routers.

- **printout**—For certain systems, e.g., your firewall and other systems located outside the firewall, hardcopy printouts are priceless. If someone hacks into your system and deletes your logfiles, you will be an Unhappy Camper. Using the *syslog* facility to log certain things to a locally attached printer may provide the only clue after a successful break-in. An old-fashioned wide-carriage dot matrix printer with a nice box of fan-fold green-bar paper is perfect.

- **window popup program**—If you are typically glued to the screen, you can throw an X client to your workstation. If for some reason you do not have an X-server running on your desktop, you can use *linpopup*, a utility which will generate popup messages on Windows machines.

- **system management console**—An extension of the previous method, a system management console assumes that you have staff members on duty watching a status screen, ready to take action should one of the green lights turn red. This can be any sort of UI, but the trend is toward web-based interfaces. *Big Brother*, *NetSaint*, and *mon* all provide this sort of interface. Most network management systems provide some sort of management console, so you might be able to use the next method instead of deploying your own.

- **integration with another system**—Why recreate the wheel? And why unnecessarily separate yourself from other OS support groups in your organization? Part of making Linux work for you might include making it work in the data center, alongside the other production systems, and using the same tools. Of primary importance is the availability of SNMP for Linux. This software package is fully configurable and supports status queries through *snmpd*, generating exception conditions with *snmptrap* and acting as the data acquisition workstation with *snmpget* and *snmpwalk*. You can also set values using *snmpset*.

You will probably be happier with a system which is configurable to use more than one of these methods. How far you go with this is up to you, but don't forget that the more complicated the system, the more opportunities there are for bugs and failure within the system itself.

7.4.4   Notification Software

Monitoring and notification tools are often thrown together, since they share such a close relationship. For Linux, the strong monitoring players seem to be the three I've mentioned: *mon*, *Big Brother*, and *NetSaint*. All of these support HTML interfaces and are detailed in their own sections below. In addition, there are several *Big Brother* spin-offs, which you might like to use as they are or as a starting point for your own modifications.

- **angel**—The Angel Network Monitor (*http://www.paganini.net/angel/*) is similar to *Big Brother* and produces a very nice-looking status screen. The plugins are written in Perl, so you are invited to extend the system. There are plugins for TCP port services, low disk space, high system load, and ping roundtrip times. Unfortunately, it seems not to have been updated in quite a while.

- *Spong* is another *Big Brother*-esque monitoring package written in Perl which supports histories for machines. Check it out at *http://strobe.weeg.uiowa.edu/~edhill/public/spong/*.

- *snmptrapfmt* is a configurable SNMP trap daemon. As such, it is not a monitoring system by itself, but it could be a useful component if you decide to develop your own SNMP-based system or simply want to use the *snmptrap* client on different Unix systems to notify one central system that something is wrong. (Compare this to the old *snmptrapd* that performs the same task but does not support configurable output.)

Paging Software

The software packages in the previous section will detect system problems and maybe display the results via HTML, but they won't necessarily track you down and find you. For that, you will need to something to send a page. We've already mentioned the TAP interface for alphanumeric pagers (and many cellphones), but you may need support for SMS (Short Message Service) for GSM devices, depending on your equipment. There's a lot of different software out there, so browse around until you find a good starting point and customize from there. Many of the clients (and servers) are now available in interpreted languages, such as Perl or Python, which is a godsend if you have a diverse environment to support. As always, open standards are a must. (In my experience, once you get your paging set up right, folks will come out of the woodwork wanting to use it.) Here are a few tools that seem to stand out in the crowd:

- SMS/GSM Gateways

  - *Alamin (http://www.alamin.org/)*—written in Perl, this project provides both client and server software. The server is written to act like an MTA, but for SMS messages.

  - *smssend (http://zekiller.skytech.org/main.html)*—this is more of a client that sends the message directly, but supports configurable scripts so that it can interact with any service. There is also a Windows binary if you'd like.

  - *smstools (http://www.isis.de/members/~s.frings/*—this is the server half, but it provides some nice features, such as event handling and statistics reporting. Commercial support is also available.

- TAP/IXO Gateways

  - *qpage http://www.qpage.org/*—formally known as *QuickPage*, this software has been/is the backbone for many production notification systems. It's written in C and produces a single binary that can act as both the server and the client. For server-client communications it uses SNPP, so you can easily write your own client using the *Net::SNPP* module in *libnet-perl*.

  - *sendpage http://sendpage.cpoint.net/*—another SNPP server, like *qpage*, but written entirely in Perl and, notably, threaded to support driving multiple modems simultaneously. (Bad for your phone bill, but essential in large environments.)

Now that you have a way of sending messages, you need to generate them. But before you start coding, take a look at the three packages described below. They represent a lot of work and contain a lot of functionality, including some advanced features such as web-based output, grouping of machines, configurable error levels, pager and email notification. They come equipped with a nice collection of monitors and have support for system histories, reducing the amount of work required to maintain event logs on each system. They are also different enough from each other, not only in design, but in look and feel, to warrant a little investigation if you're in the market for a monitoring system.

Big Brother **as a System Monitoring Tool**

Big Brother provides a web-based *matrix* of servers and services, updated continuously, and accessible from almost any graphical web browser. It does not use SNMP but instead has its own client/server (monitoree/monitor) protocol and a collection of scripts. It has support for notification via email and paging; it uses *kermit* to send SMS messages to pagers and cellphones and to page numeric pagers. One interesting thing about *Big Brother* is that binaries are available for Novell and Windows NT, so it should cover most of what's in your data center. It can monitor the following without modification:

- DNS, NNTP, FTP, SMTP, HTTP, and POP-3

- network connectivity (ping)

- disk space usage, CPU usage, and uptime

- the status of processes and daemons you define

- messages logged via *syslog* containing a given string

Configuration is different from that of some other packages and may be taxing. Some people jibe well with *Big Brother* from the start, while others wrestle with it continually. Note that the most recent version of *Big Brother* is no longer free for commercial use. See *http://bb4.com/* for details. (I mention this because free software is about respecting licenses, not breaking them.)

mon **as a System Monitoring Tool**

mon uses a combination of its own service monitors and SNMP (where it's applicable) to perform the task of system monitoring. It is very capable and therefore very popular (or perhaps it's the other way around). It comes with a variety of interfaces, so it should please both web-browser jockeys and command-line diehards, and even those who aren't in the office. The descriptions are taken from the *README* which accompanies the distribution.

- *moncmd* is a command-line client which supports the full functionality of the client/server interface.

- *monshow* displays nicely formatted column output of the current operational status, groups, and the failure log.

- *skymon* is a SkyTel 2-way paging interface, allowing you to query the server's state and to manipulate it in the same manner as *moncmd*, right from your pager. Access is controlled via a simple password and an access control file.

- *opstatus.cgi* is a simple operational status webpage which highlights failures and shows things which are disabled. It is meant to be quick to use and to display the most critical information at the top.

- *mon.cgi* is the interactive web interface, allowing you not only to view status information, but to change parameters in the server while it is running.

mon includes alert scripts for sending alerts via email, alphanumeric paging via email, and *QuickPage*, although extending the system to support other forms of alerts is easy. It has a thorough collection of monitors, known as **service monitors**, ready for use. You should be able to cover most of your needs with these, but because *mon* is written 100% in Perl, extending it is relatively easy, and porting issues are all but nonexistent. Should *mon* not be available for your Linux distribution, you can find it at *http://www.kernel.org/software/mon/*. The current version includes the following service monitors:

- ICMP echo (ping), SMTP, telnet, FTP, NNTP, HTTP, POP-3, IMAP, LDAP, and DNS

- HPNP (for monitoring HP network printers)

- system disk space, uptime, and processes

- any (other) simple TCP-based service

- network appliance free space and quota trees

- dial-in terminal servers

mon even comes with a script that will convert a *Big Brother* configuration file for use by *mon*. See the file *README.Big-Brother* in the program documentation directory.

NetSaint for System Monitoring and Event Handling

I've used all three of these notification systems and find that *NetSaint* suits my needs very well indeed. At the moment, you can still find *NetSaint* at *http://www.netsaint.org/* (see the sidebar about sharks). It is a combination of a very sophisticated state machine that performs the monitoring using **plug-ins** (really, just scripts, not unlike the one we threw together on page 244 in Section 7.4.2). Then, depending upon the results of the service check, it can perform notifications (pages, emails, anything you can do on the command line) and/or **event handling** (firing another script as an automated response to the condition detected). All the while, it can log service-check data for performance and trend analysis, spacing out the service checks on the endpoints so as not to tax the monitoring server too heavily. Service checks may have dependencies—i.e., don't check X unless Y is up—including specific capabilities for not marking a host down if its upstream router is down (you'll be getting enough pages without the extra noise). It is extensible via a family of **add-ons** that are under active development. Some add-ons extend the monitoring capabilities with additional plug-ins and remote monitoring agents; others simplify the administration of the system. The most recent version even ports an embedded Perl interpreter for faster plug-in execution.

Of themselves these features would be sufficient, but some folks aren't impressed with a black box that does everything you need it to do. They want bells, whistles, and blinky lights. Perhaps *NetSaint*'s strongest point (at least in terms of corporate acceptance) is that it provides a very nice interface without the administrator having to spend inordinate amounts of time making it pretty. It is web based (although there is an add-on for command-line monitoring) and provides not only access to status, but also the ability to disable notifications for a host, a group of hosts, all of the hosts, and all the stops in between. It has hooks in the configuration file so that when an administrator pulls up a given host, you can already have links to your local documentation. Administrators can acknowledge service problems and leave notes about a given issue for others using the interface. The interface also provides service-history details, including graphs of service availability (a service being any datapoint you monitor with *NetSaint*). Varying levels of access to the user interface functions can be assigned to different users (without that access being a hassle to administer). All in all, it's just good stuff, and I right recommend it. If you want to get started with it, you'll want a system with enough CPU and memory to spawn a fair number of Perl scripts rapidly, run Apache (with SSL for security), and maybe support a database back end (*MySQL* or *PostgreSQL*). In my experience, a Pentium III/550 with 256MB of RAM does a pretty good job of keeping tabs on over 2000 services spread across about 100 hosts. By the time you read this, that will be considered a mediocre desktop configuration (at best), so it shouldn't be too difficult to dig on up.

> ### Shark Attack!
>
> Unfortunately, the future of *NetSaint* is not certain. The author, Ethan Galstad, was contacted by a commercial company with a software product with a *similar* name—no, not even the same name—and informed of a potential trademark violation. There was an attempt to assert the difference between the two names and the two distinct pieces of software, but the end effect is that the next release of *NetSaint* will be under another name (but still be the same fabulous product!). I believe that lawyers and software companies with nothing better to do than to smear their own image by harassing[8] the free software community couldn't do a better job of tattooing `ln -s /dev/null clue` onto their foreheads than they did in this case.

How you configure your notification system depends largely on your organization's needs and individual preferences. The larger the organization, typically the more advanced the notification systems need to be, including elements such as exception reporting (i.e., formally noting any system outage) and escalation procedures. Because different admins have different ideas about the right way to do notification, you may find that much of the available GPL code is almost what you want. The same is true for the expensive commercial systems. So be prepared to strike out on your own to get the system that you want.

7.5 Summary

This chapter started out simply enough—using a Linux router to connect to an ISP via synchronous PPP over a dedicated access circuit. Linux makes a very inexpensive and capable access router. Unfortunately, connecting to the Internet is not so simple. Security is a primary concern that has to be considered even in deciding where to place our Internet access router. In other words, we need to choose a network topology for the area outside our firewall. Once we have an idea where the system will be, we need to secure it. Because Linux is capable of acting as a server, we must take some precautions to ensure that we do not leave services running which can be used to launch attacks against our system—some tips were presented in Section 7.2. Even after we've locked down our router, we'd like to know when others are trying to access it and whether they can. Tools to detect this—IP event loggers—were the topic of Section 7.2.3, while tools to detect weaknesses—port scanners—were discussed in Section 7.2.4.

The next section covered IP firewalling, along with two different ways to think about it. The first is to control what can be forwarded by the firewall, which we called **conditional forwarding**. This is often appropriate for systems with more than two interfaces, such as

---

[8]My choice of words, not Ethan's.

a combination firewall/access router that supports a perimeter net via a second Ethernet interface and is applicable only to routers. The next method of firewalling is **IP packet filtering**, where we limit what can enter or exit the local system. This form of firewalling is appropriate for any Linux system. In practice, both types of firewalling are used together to achieve the desired goal. We then looked at some of *netfilter*'s match extensions you have at your disposal to make things simpler and more secure. When it comes to developing a ruleset for your firewall, the more input, theory, and advice you can digest, the better able you are to critically analyze what's out there and decide what works best for your environment. When in doubt, drop it and log it.

The final section introduced some concepts about notification systems and what is available for Linux. Depending upon the organization, an Internet link ranges in importance from a convenience to the lifeblood of the company, although I dare say that few organizations nowadays are going to shrug their shoulders at an Internet outage of more than a few minutes. Having a stable system is crucial—being able to detect a problem and notify the necessary personnel is important, too. This final section gave some ideas about how to detect an outage and send notification and suggested some tools that can aid you in that task.

Before we move on to the next chapter, which discusses a flexible WAN router, I would like to reiterate the importance of physical security as it relates to your routers and any system(s) you use to manage them. If you lock down your routers tight and never allow a password to traverse the network in cleartext, you've made a good start. But if the management station (the computer where you're typing that encrypted password) is not physically secure, you might not be helping yourself much. All it takes is a floppy and a few minutes to break into a desktop, and the attacker can use a tool such as *ttysnoop* to quickly ferret out every password you use as you type it into the keyboard. Therefore, you should subject your management workstation to the same level of scrutiny when it comes to security matters, especially if it is not physically secure.

Chapter 8

CALIFORNIUM—SATELLITE OFFICE ROUTER

```
californium:/root> uptime
2:36pm  up 244 days,  1:14h,  1 user,  load average: 0.05, 0.00, 0.00
```

Californium is the first Linux router I deployed which was remote to the headquarters office. The small project office had no IT staff onsite and the router was its lifeline to the corporate source-code revision system, the intranet, and through the firewall out to the Internet. I have to admit that I had some angst about the router's being so distant. Should anything happen to it, it would have been costly and time consuming to make a service call. There was a bit of pride at stake here, too—a professional rivalry with a colleague who was deploying traditional routers remotely. The argument goes that because the traditional router has no hard drive and runs more stable code, it is less likely to fail and is easier and therefore less expensive to support. My counterarguments are that the risk of hard drive failure can be managed and that the Linux code is plenty stable. Furthermore, the flexibility of the Linux platform warrants any additional administrative overhead.

Californium was also the first WAN router I configured to do more than just route. Because the remote office was lightly populated (and scarcely funded), the strategy was to try to do more with less—much less. To keep costs low, californium took over some duties normally relegated to non-Linux systems at my organizations, and some duties that a traditional router typically cannot handle. Additionally (no matter what the users believe), a WAN administrator always takes pity on the less bandwidth-fortunate. To this end, californium is configured to help make their plight more bearable by adding services which helped conserve bandwidth on the WAN connection back to the main office.

This chapter devotes a section to each of the capabilities and concerns surrounding californium. First, it reviews the configuration of a WAN link running CHDLC using Sangoma's *WANPIPE* software. CHDLC (Cisco High-level Data Link Control) is another protocol used for WAN links, similar to synchronous PPP. The next four topics cover the ways Linux routers can save hardware and bandwidth:

- Californium acts as the DHCP server for the site, issuing IP addresses and other network info to local clients.

- It runs a copy of the DNS daemon *named* (part of *Bind*) as a slave. In this configuration, it fetches copies of internal zones and caches any external name lookups made by its clients.

- Californium is configured with *Samba* to act as a local print spooler for a network attached printer.

- Californium provides a caching HTTP proxy so that frequently accessed pages are kept locally.

Then we take an excursion, exploring the possibilities with the traffic-shaping code in the 2.4 kernel. This will allow us to place rigid limits on the bandwidth that certain types of traffic are allowed to consume. We return to californium for discussions about monitoring system load and supporting Linux systems remotely. The section on remote support goes into methods of accessing the router when the primary connection is down as well as a few tricks for sites with redundant links, such as load balancing across two links. The chapter concludes with a few backup strategies for remote systems.

8.1 CHDLC Router Topology

After getting bogged down in CIRs, PVCs, ports, and DLCIs with Frame Relay, we find CHDLC a welcome surprise. It is simple to configure, and as such, it supports basic configurations. Hardwarewise, the router is configured much like Frame Relay or synchronous PPP. The main difference is how you use the access. CHDLC is a protocol useful when you have a digital access circuit connecting two sites directly. From this access, you allocate a subset of channels to be used for data, and you run CHDLC routers on both ends of the link. A typical scenario is a small office, which needs to have telephone service and data and perhaps access to the company voicemail system. If the point-to-point access circuit costs are reasonable, there is no need to pay for each of these services individually at the remote location. You can order a single digital circuit which connects the remote site to the main office. With a couple of fancy CSU/DSUs, multiplex the T1 by allocating some of the channels to the PBX (for voice) and others to your data circuit. The hardware costs may be higher up front, but you'll save money in the long run because:

- There are no port or PVC charges and no CIRs. The full bandwidth of the trunks allocated to data is available to the connection.

- You can reconfigure the allocation on the access circuit as you see fit. If data bandwidth becomes less important over time and you need more voice capacity, you can change the channel allocation yourself with no reconfiguration costs.

- Apart from your telco provider, there is no other vendor or service provider. This saves time during contract negotiations and reduces finger-pointing during an outage.

- You will not have to pay for toll charges for calls between the offices (if your telephone equipment supports it).

- Rerouting voice calls to/from the smaller location leverages the capacity at the main office, which is purchased in larger quantities and therefore costs less per channel or minute—for example, a toll-free support line which may reroute calls to a specialist at the remote office.

- Even if you have no need for voice circuits, a point-to-point access circuit may be less expensive than paying for two shorter access runs, ports, and CIRs, especially if you need a high CIR.

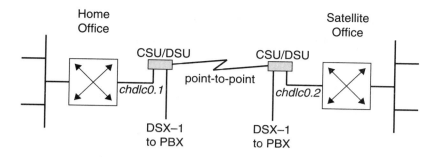

Figure 8.1 Satellite Office with CHDLC Router Topology

A typical topology is depicted in Figure 8.1. Because it is designed for point-to-point operation, configuring CHDLC is very similar to the synchronous PPP link described in Chapter 7. The only real difference is that you own both ends of the link and have to configure both routers. The hardware setup is the same as that presented previously for the Frame Relay and Internet routers running *WANPIPE*.

If you are intending to multiplex a T1 in the manner described, you shouldn't order WAN interface cards with the integrated CSU/DSUs. The integrated units are not designed for multiplexing. The type of CSU/DSU which supports this operation is referred to as **drop-and-add** and will have ports for both your router and the PBX. If you already have a Sangoma card (S508) in operation, you might be able to avoid purchasing another card for the home office. These cards have a second port, a DB9 connector underneath the DB25, which can be used to run CHDLC at up to 256kbps. Note that you MUST have a CSU/DSU with an RS-232 interface to use this port, or use a V.35-to-RS-232 converter. (Many CSU/DSUs come with a V.35 data port.) This port may be used only to run CHDLC, and you will need to order a cable from Sangoma to use it. Once you have a card in each router, and have the routers connected to their respective CSU/DSUs, it's time to configure the *wanpipe1.conf* file and the *interfaces* file.

8.1.1   Configuring *wanpipe1.conf* for CHDLC

Save yourself some time by copying a sample configuration (*wanpipe1.cpri*) from the appropriate directory over the default *wanpipe1.conf* (as long as you do not already have a working configuration!). The configuration presented here assumes that you are using the card solely for CHDLC, although it is not difficult to configure a card to run CHDLC on the secondary port (or a second card). If you would like to do this, refer to Sangoma's documentation.

Open up *wanpipe1.conf* in your favorite editor and get to work. I've prepared a configuration file with the nonessentials removed. The file is an example of a configuration where the IP address will be assigned to this node explicitly through the use of an interface file, which is dictated by SLARP_TIMER=0. The parameters in the example file are discussed in Section 8.1.2.

```
# /etc/wanpipe/wanpipe1.conf
# Protocol: Cisco HDLC  (CHDLC)
# -----------------------------------------------------------
```

```
#*****************************************
# Device Definition Section              *
#*****************************************
[devices]
wanpipe1 = WAN_CHDLC, Cisco HDLC


#*****************************************
# Network Interfaces Definitions         *
#*****************************************
#
# The [interfaces] section defines logical channels and corresponding
# network interfaces created by the router.  Each statement in this
# section has the following format:
#
#        {interface name} = {device}, {media_addr}, {function}, Comment
#

[interfaces]
chdlc0 = wanpipe1, WANPIPE, cisco hdlc connection on Port 0 (PRI)
#chdlc1 = wanpipe1, WANPIPE, cisco hdlc connection on Port 1 (SEC)



#*********************************************
# Link configuration section                 *
#*********************************************
[wanpipe1]
IOPort    = 0x360            # I/O port base
IRQ       = 11               # IRQ
Firmware  = /usr/lib/wanpipe/cdual514.sfm  # adapter firmware
CommPort  = PRI              # primary port (DB25 on the S508)
                            # use "SEC" for the DB9 port on the S508


#***************************************************************
# Logical channel (interface) configuration sections.         *
#***************************************************************
# To turn OFF Dynamic IP addressing set SLARP_TIMER to 0.


[chdlc0]
Interface            = RS232     # physical interface type, RS232/V35
Clocking             = External  # external clocking
BaudRate             = 256000    # 256k link
MTU                  = 1500      # for CHDLC, this can be 300 - 15354
HDLC_STREAMING       = NO        # use CHDLC
                                 # (YES == raw frames and no polling)
KEEPALIVE_TX_TIMER   = 10000     # interval to send keepalives
KEEPALIVE_RX_TIMER   = 11000     # interval to expect keepalives
KEEPALIVE_ERR_MARGIN = 5         # keepalive timeouts allowed
```

```
SLARP_TIMER               = 0          # (disable SLARP/dynamic addressing)
                                       # and use IPADDR and POINTOPOINT values
                                       # from /etc/wanpipe/interfaces/chdlc0
```

8.1.2   CHDLC Configuration Parameters for *WANPIPE* Explained

Now let's go over each of the parameters in more detail. The file is broken up into four logical sections: devices, network interfaces, link configuration (detailed device configuration), and logical channels (detailed interface configuration). Each of these is addressed separately.

CHDLC *wanpipe1.conf*—Device Definition Section

This section is the first in the file and begins with [devices] appearing on a line by itself. In previous releases of *WANPIPE* this section may have consisted of multiple lines, but now that each device (really, each port for the dual-port cards) has its own *wanpipe.conf* file, there is only one "device" line. Aside from the comment text, there are no options.

wanpipe1 = WAN_CHDLC, comment

CHDLC *wanpipe1.conf*—Network Interface Definition

This section begins with [interfaces] appearing on a line by itself. The section defines the interface name which is used by the kernel to access the link and associates it with a device. Although almost any interface name will do, you should stick to a name no longer than six characters—most networking commands do not expect a longer interface name than that. I recommend *chdlc0*. The line has the following format:

intf = device, port, function, comment

intf—whatever you want to name your interface (within reason)

device—the physical device name used above—normally wanpipe1

port—(no longer used). Don't forget to leave a blank here. Otherwise, your configuration file will have a syntax error.

function—use WANPIPE unless you're using the raw socket interface to the board, in which case you will use API.

comment—for your own use. Because this will show up in logfiles, you should make it descriptive.

CHDLC *wanpipe1.conf*—Link Configuration Section

The section begins with the device defined at the beginning of the file; for a single adapter, this is [wanpipe1]. Each of the allowable parameters is listed along with the possible values. If there is a default value, it is in bold.

IOPort = *0xNNN*—the I/O port address for the ISA board (S508 and S508/FT-1). The default is **0x360** unless you have modified the I/O port base jumper on the board. This parameter is required for the S508 and is not allowed for the S514.

IRQ = *irq* [3,4,5,7,9,10,11,12]—a free IRQ on your system. Required for the S508; not applicable for the S514.

Firmware = *pathname*—the pathname to the adapter firmware binary. This value should be set correctly in the sample configuration file. This parameter is required.

Memaddr = *0xNNNN*—the dual-port memory address used to read and write to the card. This value is detected by the OS automatically and is not needed unless you suspect some sort of memory conflict. See Sangoma's documentation for possible values.

UDPPORT = *port* [1–65534, default **9000**]—the UDP port used by the *WANPIPE* utilities for status information. There is no need to modify the default.

Interface = **RS-232** or **V35**, depending upon the physical interface type on your CSU/DSU. For an integrated CSU/DSU, use **RS-232**. (Required)

Clocking = **Internal** or **External**—always **External** unless you know better. For the Port 1 (secondary) interface on S508 cards, you set this via a hardware jumper as well as for any S514 device running RS-232—see the *WANPIPE_USER_MANUAL* for details. (Required)

BaudRate = [2048--2048000] for Port 0 interfaces, [2048--256000] for Port 1 interfaces. This should jibe with the CSU/DSU setting for the link. This parameter has no default value and is required.

MTU = [300--15354] for Port 0 interfaces, [**300–2048**] for Port 1 interfaces. Initially, you should leave it at the default of **1500** if you are using Ethernet on the other router interface. This prevents fragmentation of packets traversing the router.

TTL = [0x00--0xFF]. This is used only for the monitoring system and can be left at its default of **0x7F** (127) or omitted.

CHDLC *wanpipe1.conf*—**Logical Channel Section(s)**

This section consists of an interface-specific section for each interface specified earlier in the file. Starting with *WANPIPE* 2.1, this is typically a single interface, such as [chdlc0].

MULTICAST = **YES** or **NO**; used to enable multicasting via this interface.

IGNORE_DCD = **YES** or **NO**; the default is **NO**. This parameter decides whether DCD will be ignored or not when determining active link status for CHDLC.

IGNORE_CTS = **YES** or **NO**; the default is **NO**. This parameter decides whether CTS will be ignored or not when determining active link status for CHDLC.

IGNORE_KEEPALIVE = **YES** or **NO**; the default is **NO**. (Are you beginning to notice a pattern?) This parameter decides whether keepalive packets will be ignored or not when determining active link status for CHDLC.

KEEPALIVE_TX_TIMER = [0--60000]; the default is **10000** (milliseconds). This sets the interval between keepalive packet transmissions. If you are set to ignore keepalives, then this value is meaningless.

KEEPALIVE_RX_TIMER = [10--60000]; the default is **10000** (milliseconds). This tells the router how often to expect keepalive packets from the other router. If **IGNORE_KEEPALIVE=YES**, then this is of little use.

KEEPALIVE_ERR_MARGIN = [1--20]; the default is **3**. If you are not ignoring keepalives, and there are KEEPALIVE_ERR_MARGIN consecutive timeouts, the driver will bring down the link, assuming that something is wrong.

HDLC_STREAMING = **YES** or **NO**; the default is **NO**. If set to **YES**, this turns off CHDLC and uses raw HDLC frames.

SLARP_TIMER = [0--60000]. The interval between sending SLARP packages in milliseconds. SLARP packets are the mechanism by which the IP address of one side of the link can be dynamically assigned. The default value is **5000**; a value of 0 disables dynamic IP assignment. See Section 8.1.3 for related configuration information.

8.1.3 Configuring the Interfaces File for CHDLC

Just as with PPP and Frame Relay links running *WANPIPE*, both ends of the link need to be assigned an IP address in order to talk to one another. Unlike those protocols, CHDLC offers a mechanism to assign one end of the link automatically. To use this feature, decide which side will be the **master** and configure its IP address (IPADDR) in the *interfaces/chdlc0* file. Set POINTOPOINT to be the value of IPADDR incremented by one. You should also configure SLARP_TIMER=0 in the *wanpipe1.conf* on this system.

On the remote router, the **slave**, you should set IPADDR=0.0.0.0 (otherwise, you will have problems when *WANPIPE* starts) and leave POINTOPOINT blank. Make sure that you set SLARP_TIMER in the [interfaces] section of the configuration file on the slave. (If you do this, it will never ask the local router for its IP address.) Assuming that the timer value is nonzero, after the SLARP_TIMER expires, the slave sends an **inquiry** which says, *Please tell me your IP address*. When the master router replies, the slave takes the given IP address, increments its last octet by one, and assigns this to its CHDLC interface.

Note: SLARP-Assigned IP Addresses

When using automatic assignment of the IP address for a pair of CHDLC routers, the IP address that you assign to the master must have a host address of .1—for example, 192.168.64.1. The slave will be assigned the .2 address in the same network. Since this is so rigid, I prefer to set the IP addresses explicitly. Note that with explicit assignment, you may also use a subnet mask of 255.255.255.255 and a "0 node network" like the one described in Section 5.3.4.

If you want to assign an IP to both ends of the link explicitly, then set the SLARP_TIMER on both sides to be zero, and set the IPADDR and POINTOPOINT fields accordingly. In case you are wondering, besides being so phonetically pleasing, SLARP stands for Serial Line Reverse Address Resolution Protocol. It is often used in conjunction with ISDN links.

As you have seen, by virtue of the limited number of parameters, CHDLC is uncomplicated to configure and well suited for point-to-point links. Where you have access running directly between two of your locations, you can use any protocol you'd like. CHDLC should be considered along with PPP in this scenario. Frame Relay would work, too, but its DLCI overhead does not buy you anything when you have a two-node network. The CHDLC support in *WANPIPE* is also handy when you actually need to interface a Cisco (or some other CHDLC router). When you do interface a Cisco, be sure to configure it to "generate IETF packets only." This disables proprietary extensions such as CDP (Cisco Discovery Protocol). If you do not, the Cisco will generate non-IP packets that are logged in *syslog* as unintelligible by *WANPIPE*.

Another option you need to disable when interfacing a non-Linux router is any sort of packet compression. Not all of the vendors' compression protocols are open and therefore not implemented. To save bandwidth with Linux (until there are open standards for compression), you have to do more than set a parameter in a configuration file. You need to use your head. The next section talks about a couple of ideas to save bandwidth over your low-bandwidth links.

8.2   Conserving Bandwidth—Caches and Slaves

There is a group which calls itself the *Bandwidth Conservation Society*. As I understand it, its charter boils down to educating people to designing webpages without ridiculously large graphics so that browsing is comfortable for users without lots of bandwidth. They provide documentation on how to produce graphics which look good without being monstrous. Even if the techniques described there result in a modest 15% reduction in graphics size (and I suspect that you could do far better than that), you've saved 15%. Sometimes I get the feeling that people expect improvements in the computer field to be exponential in nature or else they are not worth the effort. Processor technology may follow Moore's Law,[1] but the bandwidth available to the average user has not. A 33.6kbps modem is only 100 times faster than the 300-baud modem I had in 1984, and a DSL circuit averages 10x again. (By Moore's Law, the increase in speed should have been a factor of 2^{16}!) You can visit the BCS at *http://www.infohiway.com/faster/index.html*.

Deep down, every WAN administrator is a latent member of a private mini-Bandwidth Conservation Society—sometimes, depending upon how loud the users' cries for more bandwidth are, a very active contributor. This section covers two things I did for the users on the far side of californium. The first is a DNS slave server for their site and the second is an HTTP caching proxy. Both of these can be used to save bandwidth without modifying your users' habits. (The best way to save bandwidth is to train your users to use it wisely. It's probably also the toughest. Good luck ....)

8.2.1   Slave DNS Server

Name resolution is part of almost every network transaction conceivable, anywhere, yet IMHO remains widely misunderstood by users (and sometimes administrators, too). For the administrator, the only excuse is ignorance. If you fall into this category, stop guessing and *thoroughly* read the manpage for `gethostbyname()` and whatever pages it may refer you to. On any flavor of Unix, this should get you on the right track to enlightenment.

For the user, a DNS outage means *the network's down* and DNS performance problems equate to *the network's slow today*. If you are lucky, the problem is a local configuration problem, such as a nonsensical domain search order, or a bogus DNS server entry. Oftentimes, however, poor performance is related to the time required for the DNS service to locate the

---

[1] See the Glossary.

requested information. The performance problems can be particularly acute for external (Internet) domains, where you have limited control over the latency and choice of server. The easiest way to alleviate the problem is to provide a caching DNS server close to the clients. (Any good ISP will do this; the lesser ones do not.) A properly configured DNS server can handle the client load and cache any successful lookups it performs. In that way, only the first resolution of a name is expensive (until the TTL associated with the lookup expires). One reason that emphasis is placed on the server is that most DNS clients typically do not cache any information. If you open three windows and type `telnet foo` in each, your machine will issue three DNS queries for the name *foo*, provided that it is not available in */etc/hosts* or via some other mechanism. This is one reason that some popular web browsers start *dns-helper* processes, which basically act as caching resolvers. Note that there is an *nscd*, or Name Services Caching Daemon, available for Linux, but it is intended to alleviate performance problems with NIS, NIS+, and LDAP. It is not a substitute for a DNS server.

The System Impact of a DNS Server

Providing a DNS server on the local LAN, instead of expecting our clients to access a DNS server across the WAN, is a big performance win that can be realized with little effort on your part. A DNS server is a relatively low-impact process to add to your router. It requires almost no disk space (unless you are acting as a secondary server for some massive zones) and not much processing power. The only thing you will need is some memory, and typically not much of that. I checked the memory footprint of the primary DNS server and mail exchanger for a site with over 1000 users—the daemon had been running for 110 days—and it was about 19MB. A satellite office will use considerably less than this, probably on the order of 2–4MB. If you are concerned about impacting the performance of your router, check the size of the process from time to time to make sure that it's not consuming too much of the system's resources. An easy way to check the memory footprint, especially from within a script, is look at the status file corresponding to the *pid* of the daemon in */proc*. An example on a system running *Bind* (*named*) looks like:

```
californium:/root> cat /proc/`cat /var/run/named.pid`/status
Name:    named
State:   S (sleeping)
Pid:     171
PPid:    1
TracerPid:        0
Uid:     0        0        0        0
Gid:     0        0        0        0
FDSize: 32
Groups:
VmSize:       2752 kB
VmLck:           0 kB
VmRSS:        1368 kB
VmData:       1032 kB
VmStk:          24 kB
VmExe:         460 kB
VmLib:        1200 kB
SigPnd: 0000000000000000
SigBlk: 0000000000000000
```

```
SigIgn: 8000000000000000
SigCgt: 0000000009015a0b
CapInh: 0000000000000000
CapPrm: 00000000fffffeff
CapEff: 00000000fffffeff
```

The field of interest is `VmSize`. Should it get out of hand, you can simply stop and restart the daemon. (Note, don't just *reload* it, because this will reread the configuration file but not release any memory.)

Bind, Linux's DNS Daemon

For DNS daemons for Linux, I am aware of only two choices, *Dents* and *Bind*. *Dents* (*http://www.dents.org/*) is a project to roll an RFC 1035-compliant DNS server with support for modular back-end modules so that zone files can be kept and managed in databases (or something other than flat files). Although the project got off to a great start, it seems to have lost steam in recent times. That leaves you with the good old standby, *Bind*, which is heavily documented and has been used on almost all Unix platforms since the early days, when we'd use a flat stone to pound out */etc/hosts* files all day long.

  A sample configuration file for *Bind*, or *named*, the actual process name (*Bind* is the name of the software package as a whole), for the slave server I use on californium follows. It is for versions of *Bind* $\geq$ 8.1. All it does is configure *Bind* to act as the master for the localhost (which is a convention) and to not try to perform resolution on its own, but to forward requests to the `forwarders` listed. Once it performs a lookup, it caches the value for future reference.

```
//  /etc/named.conf

// "forward only" indicates that we are a slave
// "forwarders" are DNS servers "in the know"
options {
    directory "/var/named";
    forward only;
    forwarders {
        192.168.16.1;
        192.168.18.2;
    };
};

// local zone information
zone "localhost" {
    type master;
    file "named.local";
};

zone "127.in-addr.arpa" {
    type master;
    file "named.rev-local";
};
```

After you reload *named* (with `/etc/init.d/bind reload`), you should update your DHCP configuration to reflect the new DNS server. For added protection against failures, configure your clients to use one of the forwarders as their secondary DNS server. (Make sure to list the caching DNS server first, because it is your clients' first preference.) Assuming a 30–100ms response time for DNS queries over the WAN, your users should see a noticeable improvement.

8.2.2 Caching HTTP Server

HTML and its underlying transport mechanism, HTTP, have changed almost every desktop everywhere. This has changed your job as a network administrator almost as much as it has changed the thin-client client/server world. Now, it is your job—no, your duty—to bring the World Wide Web to those desktops, and to make it quick, although you may find the statistics concerning how much of your precious bandwidth is clogged with Internet HTTP downright appalling. We would like to help our bandwidth-impoverished users on the end of a skinny network pipe in any way possible (so that they can accomplish real work while their colleagues are browsing the Internet).

A common approach is to deploy HTTP proxy servers which cache successfully retrieved pages. A proxy can be very effective for increasing browsing performance for your users, especially when they frequently access a particular page, or many users use common pages, such as search engines. Because you locate the proxy "netographically" near to the clients, cache hits are serviced at LAN speeds (almost as quickly as a webpage designer sees!). Misses cost the client only slightly more than the original lookup. Aha! The catch, you say. How *much* more is *slightly more*? The lookup and caching operations, when viewed from the vantagepoint of the user, are free. They take place at least an order of magnitude faster than any actual HTTP GET could be completed, regardless of how small, but certainly several orders of magnitude faster for a GET of any considerable size. Many browsers support user-level caches, achieving similar savings. The added benefits of a caching proxy are:

- The first miss for one user results in subsequent hits for all other users. This improves throughput substantially for commonly accessed pages like intranet pages. If you make a file accessible via an HTTP URL, the proxy will cache it, too, which is invaluable when you need to update dozens of client machines with a virus definition file or new piece of software.

- Caching provides a useful excuse for simultaneously logging user activities. While you shouldn't use these data improperly, logging can be useful for studying bandwidth usage and following an audit trail in case a user does something improper on the web.

- Caching can be run in conjunction with *Apache*, making the additional overhead for web server minimal. Although you might not want to deploy a large website on your router, you can provide a general information page for the office, a telephone directory, or something similar quite easily.

Several caching proxies are available for Linux; I have used *Squid* and *Apache*. Either of them will serve your need, and your choice is a matter of preference. I tend to use *Apache* because I am more familiar with its configuration, but *Squid* has more options, including support for hierarchical caching configurations. Below are some general notes on using them.

Apache

Apache is best known as a web server, but it is also quite capable as a proxy. If you already have it installed, you need to do the following to modify it to act as a proxy:

- Modify */etc/apache/httpd.conf* to load the proxy module and enable proxying, with statements like:

```
LoadModule      proxy_module /usr/lib/apache/1.3/libproxy.so
ProxyRequests   On
CacheRoot       /var/spool/apache_cache
CacheSize       2000000              # cache size in kb (2GB)
CacheGcInterval 4
```

After these changes, you need to stop and restart *Apache* with */etc/init.d/apache restart*. The parameters you added do the following:

- `LoadModule` tells *Apache* to include certain code/functionality—in this case, the proxy module. The first argument is the name of the module, `proxy_module`, and the second argument is the path to the object file containing the code for the modules. (The path may vary on your system, depending upon your Linux distro and version of *Apache.*)
- `ProxyRequests On` enables proxying of requests. (Having the module loaded gives you the potential to proxy requests.) This statement cannot appear in the configuration file before `LoadModule proxy_proxy` or else it will not be understood.
- `CacheRoot` *pathname* tells the module where to cache successful proxy requests.
- `CacheSize` *sizekB* sets the maximum size of proxy's cache. You will feel sheepish if your router runs out of disk space because the proxy cache filled an important system partition. If possible, you should have a separate partition for the cache. If you're worried about performance, then a separate spindle (drive), preferably on a different controller from the OS, would help, too.
- `CacheGcInterval` *hours* tells the daemon how often to run its garbage collection routines on the contents of the cache. If you're clever about when you start the daemon, you can ensure that this takes place only once a day in the evening, or something like that. (Hopefully, future versions will let you indicate *when* to perform garbage collection.) There is no default, so if you do not have this enabled, garbage collection will never occur. This is Not Good, because it means that there is no way to enforce the limit set by `CacheSize`. On a high-load system with limited cache space, you need to tune this parameter to make sure that it runs often enough, but not continuously.

- Optionally, you can add the `NoProxy` and `ProxyBlock` statements to *httpd.conf*. The first of these tells the proxy not to proxy requests to the listed IP addresses or hostnames; instead, the client should contact the server directly. The second says not to allow connections to certain sites.

```
# no proxying for internal webservers
NoProxy       192.168.0.0/16 172.16.0.0/12 10.0.0.0/8
ProxyBlock    .dontgothere.com
```

- You can also adjust `MaxClients` *value* to the maximum number of clients. *Apache* considers proxy users to be web server users, and thus may limit the number of simultaneous connections. You can use this either to allow more concurrent sessions or to purposefully limit the number of sessions to a reasonable number.

- If you would like to run your proxy server on a port other than port 80, you can use the `Listen` parameter in *httpd.conf* to do so. 8080 is a popular choice.

- Access control works just as it does for *Apache* configured as a web server. You should refer to the Apache documentation at *http://www.apache.org* for the different options available to you.

Troubleshooting is easy, because logging is performed for proxy requests just as it is for web server requests. This has the added benefit that any existing scripts and procedures you already have in place to analyze your *Apache* logfiles will work on the proxy. Take a look at *analog*; its main site is *http://www.analog.cx/*. It is a very configurable logfile analyzer and report generator. It might take a few minutes to wade through the myriad of options, but once you have it set up, it produces nice-looking detailed reports. Another good *Apache* logfile analyzer is *AWStats*, available at *http://awstats.sourceforge.net/*. It is a CGI script that out of the box produces nice-looking usage reports.

Squid

With a name like *Squid*, it's gotta be good. At least if you're talking about the high-performance caching HTTP proxy, it is![2] Unlike *Apache*, which offers proxying as an add-on, *Squid's* prime directive is to proxy and cache lookups. As such, it provides some advanced features not available elsewhere.

- It supports deploying a hierarchy of caching servers. Server A may not have the document cached, but it can ask Servers B, C, and D if they have a copy. In californium's case, it may refer to the other servers before going to the Internet to retrieve the requested document. This is not limited to a hierarchy within your site. You may apply to connect to an upstream NLANR (National Laboratory for Applied Network Research) cache using the ICP (Internet Cache Protocol).

- It supports a variety of authentication mechanisms, enabling you to limit access to the proxy. You can define ACLs (Access Control Lists) and then use them to dis/allow access to certain functions. You can also use one of the security modules (an **auth_module**) to identify proxy users. This is fantastic if you need security and do not have fixed IP addresses (or do not want to have to keep up with who has what IP address). These include:

  1. Authenticating against an SMB source (a Windows NT domain server) with the *smb_auth* module.

  2. Authenticating using the OS's `getpwnam()` routines. In short, this means that whatever authentication mechanism you are using for */bin/login* can be used. On Linux, this may include NIS(+), LDAP, PAM, or the contents of */etc/passwd* (or */etc/shadow*). This uses the *auth_getpwname* module.

---

[2]Apologies to those of you who enjoy eating squid.

3. Authenticating against an NCSA httpd-style password file, perhaps prompting reuse of an already developed system.

- Runtime parameters, such as how much memory *Squid* is allowed to allocate, are tunable.

- *Squid* can act as an **httpd-accelerator**, a mode in which it caches outgoing data from your HTTP servers. These data would normally be sent directly from your servers, but *Squid* acts on their behalf, potentially improving response time and adding resilience to your configuration (because you can have multiple *Squid* caches communicating with each other via ICP).

- *Squid* provides CGI scripts for management of the cache through a web interface, getting you off the command line. For this to work, you will have to have an HTTP server with CGI support, e.g., *Apache*.

- URL **redirectors** are supported. A redirector rewrites a URL according to some rules defined by you. Many of these redirectors (they are implemented externally to *Squid*) support using regular expressions. For example, you can tell the redirector to rewrite any URL containing the string "donotgothere" to be *http://company-policy.yourcompany.com*. One of these is *Squirm*, available at *http://www.senet.com.au/squirm/*. Debian offers one of these already packaged and ready to go in the **urlredir** package.

- Commercial support is available! (*Apache* has this, too.) See the package documentation for details.

If a *Squid* package is not included in your distribution, you can find it at *http://squid.nlanr. net/*. It is offered under the GPL. *Squid* also has its own logfile analyzer, named, aptly enough, *Calamaris*. The upstream source can be obtained from *http://calamaris.cord.de/*.

8.3 Replacing Servers—Multifunction Routers

You cannot always limit bandwidth used by a remote site. There is a certain amount of bandwidth that it will always use; typically, this value seems to be "all of it." If your router cannot cut down on the amount of traffic, perhaps it can save you money and effort in other ways. Maybe it can reduce the number of network infrastructure systems you need to support at the remote site. The next two subsections are about little ways in which you can squeeze more value out of your technology investment dollar. System administration costs your company money—money as real as commercial software licenses or floppy disks. When Linux flaunts its flexibility and saves more than others, it ingratiates itself (and you, by association!) even more to management and the bean counters.

8.3.1 DHCP Server

Acting as a DHCP server is nothing new for either Linux or traditional routers. But at my organization, the task was traditionally assigned to the Windows NT domain controllers. Californium was a good chance to show that Linux can easily do the job. If it couldn't, there would have to be another system deployed at the site. Configuring a DHCP server for Linux is even easier than configuring Linux to act as a DHCP client. If you have Windows workstations in your network, don't worry; the Linux DHCP daemon supports a slew of options so that your clients will not know the difference.

A router is the right place to have the DHCP server, anyway. With non-routers, issues crop up when you have more than a single subnet—you need to start configuring BOOTP relay agents (daemons which listen for DHCP requests on a given subnet and forward them to a different subnet where the DHCP server is located). Because this requires a reconfiguration on the router, why not configure it as the DHCP server? Such a relay agent is available for Linux. It is packaged in Debian as **dhcp-relay**. The original source is available from the *Internet Software Consortium* at *ftp://ftp.isc.org/isc/dhcp/*.

To get started, load the Debian package **dhcp** or get the source from the same site listed for **dhcp-relay**. Before using the package, you have to configure a few options into your 2.2.x or 2.4.x version of the kernel.[3] You need:

```
Networking options --->
  <*> Packet socket
  [*] Socket Filtering
```

Configuring the DHCP Daemon

The default configuration is completely worthless to you, so the Debian package comes configured to not start *dhcpd* until you edit */etc/init.d/dhcp* and set run_dhcpd to 1. After you edit the configuration file (*/etc/dhcpd.conf*), you can start the DHCP server with /etc/init.d/dhcp start. Editing the configuration file is simpler than it looks, even though the sample file reads like it came from a Douglas Hofstaedter book. If you get stuck, there is a manpage for *dhcpd.conf*. (It reads like a Douglas Hofstaedter book, too.[4])

> The *dhcpd.conf* file is a free-form ASCII text file. It is parsed by the recursive-descent parser built into *dhcpd*. The file may contain extra tabs and newlines for formatting purposes. Keywords in the file are case insensitive. Comments may be placed anywhere within the file (except within quotes). Comments begin with the # character and end at the end of the line.

Instead of drilling into the configuration in all of its complexity (and capability), I summarize what you need to configure to get started. For a small office like the one californium is in, we have only a single interface on the router (not including the WAN interface). Still, *dhcpd* wants to know about *all* of the interfaces. One way to skirt around the issue is to use a zero-node subnet like that described on page 154 in Chapter 5. By doing this, you trick the DHCP daemon into thinking that it's taking care of all of the interfaces when it takes care of the LAN subnet. If you have multiple subnets for your interfaces, you must declare each of them.[5] A sample configuration file looks like this:

```
# a name by which we may identify this DHCP server
# you should set this to the DNS canonical name of the box
server-identifier californium.mancill.com;

# options for all subnets connected to this server
option domain-name "mancill.com";
```

---

[3] This does not apply to the 2.0.x versions.

[4] If you're not familiar with Hofstaedter's work, you need to start with *Gödel, Escher, Bach: An Eternal Golden Braid*.

[5] The 1.x version of the DHCP software does not get along with Linux on systems with multiple interfaces (except in the case I describe here). Make sure you use a version $\geq$ 2.0.

```
option domain-name-servers 192.168.34.1, 192.168.16.1;
option time-servers 192.168.16.1;

# windoze stuff - see "man dhcp-options" for the full list
option netbios-name-servers 192.168.16.4;

# subnet definition
subnet 192.168.34.0 netmask 255.255.255.0 {
    range 192.168.34.128 192.168.34.254; # the actual scope
    option routers 192.168.34.1;
    option subnet-mask 255.255.255.0;
    option broadcast-address 192.168.34.255;
    default-lease-time 36000;          # 10 hours
    max-lease-time 72000;              # 20 hours
}
```

The preceding example will dole out IP addresses and assign the WINS server, but it scratches only the surface of what you can do with the DHCP daemon. Other possibilities are:

- Assigning fixed IP addresses, using the BOOTP or DHCP. This can be handy for things like network printers and Xterminals.

- Assigning other NetBIOS-specific settings, such as **netbios-node-type**, **netbios-scope**, and the **netbios-dd-server**.

- Assigning values for the following server types: NTP, NNTP, SMTP, IRC, POP3, WWW, finger, NIS, lpr, syslog, and others.

- You can assign DHCP addresses for clients of multinets such as those described in Section 3.2. This is known as a **shared network** in DHCP parlance.

The DHCP daemon will log information about requests via *syslog* using the LOG_DAEMON facility. You can have it log directly to *stderr* by using the -d switch when starting the daemon. If the daemon detects configuration file errors, it will show them immediately. (This is unlike many other daemons which expect you to look in *syslog*, e.g., *bind*.) Let's see ... software source, kernel configuration, software configuration, and logging—that about wraps it up for DHCP. Keep in mind the DHCP-relay for situations where you want to use the existing DHCP server for remote subnets.

8.3.2 *Samba* Print Spooler

The next thing we are going to do with our router is definitely *not* something that you can do with a traditional router. Before we dive right into setting up a print spooler on our router, the matter bears a little consideration. First of all, you are adding processing overhead to your router. If you believe that it is already heavily loaded, then you should pass on the idea. Above all, you will need more memory and more disk space. (*Samba* recommends about 1MB of real memory per active session.) You also need disk space for print spooling. The partitioning scheme recommended throughout the book fits well with this, because your print jobs will be spooled on the */var* partition. If you intend to run a heavyweight protocol conversion filter such as *Ghostscript* (the **gs** package) and the spooler will be busy, plan to have some additional processing power, too.

One last thing to consider: *Samba* has several different security models, some of which require that user IDs and passwords are stored on the local system (i.e., these users must exist). If you require this security, you should really start asking yourself whether your router should be your print server as well. In most organizations, printing is a basic user right, so there is little need to protect it with authorization mechanisms. If a user monopolizes the printer or otherwise takes advantage of it, he runs the risk of being pummeled by his co-workers. So for a small office, I would recommend that you forego the complexity of named user accounts for printing and allow all printing to be performed by single UID on the router. Why use *Samba* at all? In a small office with a network printer, you can configure each system to print to the printer directly. In my case, it was an issue of configuration uniformity. Other offices used SMB print queues to service user requests, so why not this one, too?

Now we need to choose a spooler. Actually, depending upon your printer, a spooler may not be necessary. You can use the *netcat* toolkit to print directly to port 9000 of HP printers with JetDirect interfaces. But we are going to use old-fashioned LPR queues, since JetDirect supports this also. (LPR refers to either the **lpr** or the **lprng** software packages available for Linux.) Remember that you want to keep things simple, as in the example files shown below.

```
;
; /etc/samba/smb.conf
;
; simple configuration to allow anonymous

[global]
    ; printing
    printing = bsd
    printcap name = /etc/printcap

    ; logging
    log file = /var/log/samba/log.%m
    debug level = 2

    ; security (or the lack thereof)
    guest account = nobody

; a printer definition
[itprinter]
    printer name = itprinter
    comment = printer in IT area on 3rd floor
    printer driver = HP LaserJet 5N
    path = /var/tmp
    printable = yes
    browsable = yes
    public = yes
    valid users =

### LPR configuration
#
# excerpt from /etc/printcap for an LPR system
# the "rm" parameter is the IP address of the JetDirect card
```

Hint: Troubleshooting *Samba*/**LPR Spools**

If this were a book on *Samba*, LPR, or network printing, I might go into some detail about troubleshooting. Here's a quick hint anyway. If you can print from the router to the printer, then the problem is with *Samba*. If the problem is with *Samba*, then you should look in the `log file` (defined in the *smb.conf* file) to see what is happening—nine times out of ten it will have to do with either security (insufficient permissions) or the interface to the spooler (**cooking** the job—not passing the spool job in raw binary is often the culprit here). For more information, turn up the `debug level` parameter in *smb.conf* and restart *Samba*.

```
mailroom27|mailroom27:\
        :lp=:\
        :rm=192.168.16.82:\
        :rp=raw:\
        :sd=/var/spool/lpd/mailroom27:\
        :mx#0:\
        :sh:
```

Once you restart *Samba* and LPR, you should be able to print through the SMB print queue on your router to the network printer. Small installations notwithstanding, print spooler configuration can be very involved, and it is a function generally better left to systems other than your routers. That is not meant to scare you away from such a configuration—only to remind you to keep system load in mind.

8.3.3   How Much Additional Load Is Too Much?

You need not be overly paranoid about breaking your router by extending its capabilities beyond those traditionally attributed to a router. In the print spooler case, the performance issue is more likely to come from memory use by *Samba* than anything with LPR. Routers tend to not use their drives much when then are just routing. Most of the disk access will come from the host operating system maintaining itself. (For example, the Debian distribution needs to update the database used by the *locate* command daily. The cron job which does this [*/etc/cron.daily/find*] invokes *updatedb* and generates a substantial amount of disk access.) Many of these system management features can be trimmed or cut out entirely, if you see the need.[6] The point is that disk I/O contention is rarely an issue for routers that only route, so you should be able to add some I/O without worry of bringing the system to its knees. I/O bus contention is another matter for heavily loaded LAN routers, but unlikely for a typical WAN router. When you are debating whether or not to add some functionality to a router, you should take into account these potential system bottlenecks:

- **Memory**—Insufficient memory leads to swapping, which leads to disk I/O, which takes time. Time leads to packet latency. The kernel is **locked** into memory, as are its buffers and the routing table. (Locked memory pages cannot be swapped out to disk.) When

---

[6]I never have.

the kernel receives packets, it needs some (real) memory for them so that it can take a look at them and then forward them. If you have other processes consuming all of the available memory, then the kernel will choose to swap out a few pages from one of those processes. This is neither Good nor Bad, it just takes time. If there is already contention for the disk due to other activity on the system, then it will take some time to swap the page.

- **Disk I/O**—Swap is just one of the system's uses for the disk. You may be performing heavy logging, or print spooling, or logfile analysis. (Of the three of these, you can move all but the first to a different system.) Tools which measure disk I/O interactively have been somewhat scarce for Linux when compared to proprietary Unix releases. Only relatively recently has the Linux community turned an eye toward benchmarks and tuning. At the time of writing, several hard-drive benchmarking programs are available, as well as a few programs designed to flag performance problems during normal system operation. Some of these are listed below with other performance tuning tools.

- **CPU**—If you are **CPU-bound** on your router, then you need to spend time investigating what is using so much CPU. *CPU-bound* is a term used for systems which have processes being repeatedly put to sleep by the kernel because their timeslice has expired. Normally, a process will relinquish the CPU by some other natural cause, such as blocking on an I/O request or waiting for input.

    A simple check for this is to use either *uptime* or *top* (or go to the source, */proc/loadavg*). If the load average is consistently ≥ 1.0, then there is more happening on the system than can be successfully scheduled and completed. The system will continue to route, but other things will have to wait. Normally, you can locate the problem quickly using *top* or by repeatedly looking at process listing with *ps* to determine which processes are quickly accumulating CPU time, as seen in the `TIME` field of `ps fax`.

- **Interrupts and DMA**—Interrupts are a bit different, because they span different types of devices and are more related to the design of the device; i.e., how much buffer space it has, and how sensitive it is to variations in the time it takes to service the device after it raises the IRQ line. If you load the Debian **hwtools** package and read the documentation for *irqtune*, you will see that sometimes relatively low-speed devices are very sensitive to IRQ latency. (You can get *irqtune* at *http://www.best.com/~cae/irqtune/*.)

    DMA is the anti-IRQ. It is a Good Thing, and should be used whenever you have a choice to use it, because it allows data to move between devices and memory without having to shuffle through the processor using `inb()` and `outb()` calls.

- **PCI, and Other Bus-related Issues**—There are a few ways to tune PCI, typically via settings in the driver. Because there are so many different PCI devices, the tuning may improve performance for any type of device. Recently announced is *Powertweak*, which has been available for Microsoft Windows for a while, but is now ported to Linux and free software (for Linux only). See *http://linux.powertweak.com/* for more information.

    When performance tuning, you should consider the system bus(es) to be a resource just like any other device. Most of the proprietary Unix architectures go to great lengths to ensure that the bus architectures on their systems are capable of moving large amounts of information quickly. When a bus becomes overloaded, it is often possible to add another bus interface to the backbone bus (the **backplane**) and to partition I/O channels by redistributing the load across multiple buses. The PC platform does this to a certain extent with things like the AGP bus, a separate memory bus, and having both PCI and ISA buses. Unfortunately, there is no magic way to know everything that is happening on your bus without purchasing a logic analyzer and spending months learning how to use it and what to look for. For the PC, the bus implementation depends upon the motherboard chipset used. If you intend to use disk-intensive or graphics-intensive operations, you should do some research on the different chipsets themselves. Not all chipsets (or their features) are supported equally under Linux; you'll have to do even more homework to find out what works best.

- **Network**—Network performance is a separate animal from the other topics listed here because it depends largely on what is happening outside the system. If you want to tune the machine itself, then you should focus on things like drivers and buses. The IP stack is also tunable via the */proc* filesystem. See */usr/src/linux/Documentation/networking/ Configurable* (in the kernel source tree) for pointers to the lists of tunable parameters. Sometimes network performance of an individual link is important, in which case you may tune the MTU of the interfaces on each end to correspond to the most frequently used packet size. Chatty protocols normally prefer smaller packets, while large data transfers like larger packets.

Once you are outside your system or a single link, you will have to look at the networking environment itself. If you are retrieving software from a mirror site, use tools like *netselect*, *traceroute*, *bing*, and *pathchar*[7] to find the best path—a function of both the number of hops and the bandwidth between the hops.

Hint: Locating *pathchar* for Linux

pathchar is a great tool for very easily determining the characteristics of the various network hops between two points. It was developed by Van Jacobson, who is also responsible for *traceroute*, one form of PPP compression, and others. Unfortunately, the command is not available in source form, nor is its license clear. A statically linked binary for Linux (in ELF format) can be found at *ftp://ftp.ee.lbl.gov/pathchar*. The tarball comes with a short *README*, but the tool is so widely used that others have taken the time to document it. One such site is: *http://www.caida.org/tools/utilities/others/pathchar/*. When you first use the tool, be sure to use the -m *MTU* switch to disable MTU detection. Otherwise, the command will produce no output while it determines the MTU, making you think that it's not doing anything.

General Performance Tuning Tools

I will offer a few pointers to commonly available tools not mentioned above. As the experienced can attest, performance tuning is as much of an art as a science. (Really, it's an art based on a science.) I caution you to not blindly follow every recommendation made by these utilities, but to take them in the context for which they were intended, which may be very different from your configuration. Nor would I start tuning systems with acceptable performance unless

---

[7]See the hint on *pathchar* later in this chapter.

you foresee considerable system growth or change in functionality. There is surely a wealth of information available just from the *proc* filesystem alone, but I am not aware of a comprehensive resource for how to interpret it. In the meantime, you can use the information at *http://tunelinux.com*, a site dedicated to sharing Linux performance tuning information, as well as *http://linux.com/enhance/tuneup/*.

- To get a basic idea of what your system is spending time doing, invoke the *vmstat* command, which is available on all flavors of Unix. The different fields are covered in the manpage. They will show you the number of processes which are waiting to run, and virtual memory statistics (including the `si` and `so` fields, which indicate whether your system is swapping). Also of interest is the amount of I/O performed by the kernel and the number of interrupts and context switches per second.

- *systune* and its companion program *systunedump* are used to examine the current state of kernel parameters tunable via the *proc* filesystem, as well as provide a convenient way of setting these parameters to desired values at boot time (without having to go and edit the kernel Makefiles or includes to modify the defaults). It is a "native" Debian package—**systune**—but as always the source is freely available and it should work under any distribution. You might want to note the sample configuration files in */usr/share/doc/systune/examples/*, particularly *systune.router.conf*, for some ideas.

- *hdparm* performs some benchmarking on drive performance and allows you to modify settings in the driver to greatly increase performance of the disk system. It will also let you slightly decrease filesystem performance while improving interactive performance by changing how interrupts are processed. It is of little use for SCSI users but very valuable for IDE systems.

- *tune2fs* can be used to modify the tunable parameters of ext2 filesystems. Although the parameters are necessarily related to raw performance, they can be quite useful for tweaking your production environment. They are part of the **e2fsprogs** package.

- *VTad* is a rule-based performance monitoring package which can be used to collect statistics during normal system operation. It is written in Perl, and, according to its author, is similar to the *SE Performance Toolkit* distributed by Sun Microsystems for use under Solaris. It gets its information from *proc* and comes with a sample ruleset which should get you started. It would be a flexible framework for use in many different types of tuning situations. It even offers suggestions based on tuning principles. See *http://www.blakeley.com/resources/vtad/*.

One of the biggest problems for the performance tuner can be correlating what is happening in the system to what is happening in user-space for multitasking operating systems. Good luck!

8.4   Linux Traffic-Shaping Walkthrough

Traffic shaping gives the network administrator the ability to control bandwidth utilization of a single shared physical link based on some criterion of the traffic in the same manner that filtering does. This is necessary because TCP/IP was not originally designed to support bandwidth management and requests within the protocol itself, like, say, SNA. Unregulated, TCP/IP clients will use bandwidth until they are sated, or there is no more available. Thus

TCP/IP-based networks provide *best-effort* service. **QoS**, or Quality of Service, is a close relative to traffic shaping; it provides network clients a mechanism by which they request an allocation of bandwidth for their session. This request is made of the upstream router, which will then try to guarantee that the bandwidth is available throughout the network, or at least to the extent that the router has influence. There are two protocols for providing QoS: Differentiated Services, commonly known as **DiffServ**, and **RSVP**, the Reservation Protocol. The Linux kernel provides support for both of these protocols and for traffic shaping. In this section we'll concern ourselves with the latter; it doesn't require any change to our client system configurations, and on californium we're more concerned about limiting certain types of traffic, so that no single protocol gets starved, than about guaranteeing that the boss in the satellite office will be able to watch streaming video without flicker.

QoS/traffic-shaping support for Linux is another feather in the Linux networking cap. It differentiates Linux not only from other server operating systems, many of which can perform routing, IP aliasing, and sometimes even NAT, but also from many networking-centric operating systems and a good many traditional routers on the market. That it is all done in kernel space is another feat, and in terms of Linux's commercial significance in the networking world, I'd have to rank QoS capabilities second only to the full NAT functionality in the 2.4 kernel. (This takes for granted that packet filtering has long been available and was already checked off the list.) What's interesting is that the QoS features have been available since the 2.2.x kernel series (although in 2.4 you get all of the functionality without searching around for patches) but still aren't widely used. The reason most likely is that they are only minimally documented, and even then you have to piece together information from several sources to get everything you need. I wish I could say that this section would change all that and provide you with soup-to-nuts coverage of the topic. But first my wish that I could buy a week of Alexey Kuznetsov's time would have to come true. (And while I'm wishing, a week of Rusty Russell's time too!) But the fact that upstream documentation is limited doesn't mean that we can't start using QoS and, more importantly, achieve immediate results.

8.4.1   Traffic-Shaping Warmup: The *shaper* Module

Before we jump into the QoS swamp, let's stroll down memory lane and get some basic relief for our users of californium. The *shaper* module has been part of the kernel since the 2.0 days. It provides us some basic shaping functionality through the creation of a virtual interface that is attached to a physical interface, but imposes an upward limit on the rate at which it will transmit. There is a very important point here that applies to all traffic shaping. **You can shape traffic only when you transmit.** This is true for simple shapers as well as complex, because you're not really in control of what you receive at the router. Remember, the router is just passing traffic; it doesn't participate in the adjustment of TCP window sizing and the like. So if you're receiving too much at the router, about the only thing you can do is either queue it or discard it. Therefore, to have effective traffic shaping and guarantee no congestion on the line, you should perform it on both sides of the router.

However, many protocols have asymmetrical traffic usage patterns. For example, browser traffic pulls much more than it pushes. In the workplace, people normally receive more email than they send. We're going to take advantage of that, plus the fact that, despite our efforts to conserve bandwidth, californium still pulls more traffic toward the satellite office than it pushes back to the main office. Since we have developers out there using *ssh*, telnet, and other interactive protocols, we want to make sure that the HTTP traffic doesn't consume 100% of the available bandwidth. Because we're worried about downstream traffic (traffic headed toward californium), we need to do our work on the other end of the WAN link. Let's call that system *iron* and use the polar bear swim club method to introduce this configuration.

```
# use netfilter to mark packets from HTTP ports bound
# for the satellite office with the mark "5"

iron:~# modprobe iptable_mangle
iron:~# modprobe ipt_MARK
iron:~# modprobe ipt_multiport
iron:~# iptables --table mangle -I PREROUTING -j MARK       \
                 --destination 192.168.64.0/24 --proto tcp  \
                 --match multiport --sport 80,443,8080      \
                 --set-mark 5

# configure policy routing by adding a rule to match
# packets with the mark of "5"
# (the priority and choice of routing table name are arbitrary)
iron:~# echo "505 httpcali" >>/etc/iproute2/rt_tables
iron:~# ip rule add fwmark 5 table httpcali priority 200

# check to see that things look ok
iron:~# ip rule list
0:       from all lookup local
200:     from all fwmark      5 lookup httpcali
32766:   from all lookup main
32767:   from all lookup default

# configure our shaper device to transmit at 128kbits max
# and add a route to the httpcali to use dev shaper0
iron:~# modprobe shaper shapers=2
iron:~# shapecfg attach shaper0 chdlc0.1
iron:~# shapecfg speed shaper0 128000
iron:~# ip addr add dev shaper0 192.168.64.3/24
iron:~# ip link set dev shaper0 up
iron:~# ip route add table httpcali dev shaper0
```

Kick off a nice large HTTP pull and watch the throughput on an otherwise quiescent link bounce around between 14.5kB/s and just over 16kB/s. Telnet and *ssh* in peace. If you're wondering what just happened, this configuration is the synthesis of three separate kernel mechanisms, none of which we've talked about in any detail.

1. We utilize *netfilter's* `mangle` table to **mark** the traffic we'd like to bandwidth-limit. The mark is a tag that stays with the packet during its path through the kernel of the local system and no longer. In other words, we're not modifying the packet headers in any way; we just want to classify this packet so that later on we can treat it differently. In this case, we care about packets headed for the IP address range in the satellite office from a source port that is most likely a web server. The rest of the rule is no different from the packet-filtering rules we used in Chapter 7. We are using a new target, *MARK*, and its corresponding module *ipt_MARK*, and we need the module for the `mangle` table itself.

2. Ah, more *iproute2*—showing off once again by doing something we truly cannot do with the traditional routing tools. First we create an entry in */etc/iproute2/rt_table* for the

name of our new routing table. We need this piece so that we can assign to our marked traffic a route different from the one we use for unmarked traffic. The name *httpcali* and the value 505 are completely arbitrary. (OK, the 505 is meant to remind the humans which firewall mark we're intending to route.) Take a look at the file and you'll see that there are a few reserved numbers for the kernel; everything else is available. Why exactly this mapping is required, I'm not sure, but my guess is that it's for performance reasons (just as we use */etc/services* to map TCP/IP protocol names to numbers). We then add a routing rule that matches the firewall mark 5 and tells the kernel to look into the routing table *httpcali* for routes for these packets. The priority is also arbitrary, at least in that it doesn't affect the flow of the packet, and we are well warned by the *iproute2* documentation to assign a unique priority to each rule. The last command simply lists the routing ruleset to make sure that we have the rule and that it points us to the *httpcali* table.

3. Now that the stage is set, we need something to actually limit the traffic. We load the *shaper* module and pass it a parameter to say that we'd like two virtual shaper devices created. We're only using one here, but I've noticed some nastiness in the kernel when trying to unload the shaper module, so we want to avoid that if at all possible. Then we use the *shapecfg* utility to attach our first shaper device to the appropriate physical device (the WAN link that's connected to californium). Note that the shaper devices are named *shaper0–shaperN*, up to the number of shapers you indicated when you loaded the module. Then we assign a speed, which must be in the range of 9600–256000,[8] meaning kbps. (As you can see, here's a pretty serious limitation of *shaper* already. I suppose you could use TEQL to talk over multiple shapers simultaneously, but <shudder> that's ugly.) Now we configure our shaper device with an IP address and add a route to the *httpcali* routing table over that device. Note that, without specifying any sort of address, this command adds a default route. (See for yourself with `ip route list table httpcali`.)

The technique used here can be extended to clump other traffic into that same 128kbps bucket by marking it with the same firewall mark. Or, you can use another mark to route other traffic into another routing table, and then out another shaper interface. The policy-based routing with *iproute2* can be used with any type of device to accomplish almost any packet flow you desire. Let your imagination run wild. If you'd like to run a configuration like this, the kernel module for *shaper* is found under `Network device support ---> <M> Traffic Shaper (EXPERIMENTAL)`.

8.4.2   Linux Network Queuing Terminology

Perhaps one reason why traffic shaping hasn't seen more use on Linux is that, unlike some earlier mechanisms, it is designed from the start to be suitable for all kinds of applications going forward. In this regard, it is much like *netfilter*; the various queuing disciplines are implemented as modules, and the entire queuing subsystem is extensible. Note that from here on out, we're no longer referring to the *shaper* kernel module (or anything close to it) but instead to the `QoS/fair-queuing` support in the later 2.2.x kernels and the 2.4 series.

---

[8] The upper bound is from the documentation, which I think might be a little old. I decided to test it and got good results pushing the speed on up into the megabit range.

There are three main objects that you need to be able to differentiate among to be able to set up class-based queuing on Linux. First, we have a **queuing discipline**, sometimes called a **scheduler**. This is like a queuing algorithm; it tells the kernel how to choose the next packet for transmission based on parameters you use to configure the queue. A **queue** is what you get when you attach a queuing discipline to a device. The next entity is a **class**, which is an administrative tag applied to grouping of packets within the queuing discipline. By that, I mean that a class is nothing more than a label that we can use to manage packets flowing through our queue. We need some sort of label so that we can instruct the kernel on how to pick the next packet for transmission. Finally, there is a **filter**, which is a means of shuffling packets into a class. Filters are also known as **classifiers** (unfortunately so, in my opinion, for those of us who would immediately associate classifiers with classes). Now, all that would be straightforward enough if there were a rigid hierarchy for these objects to follow, such as: *A queuing discipline contains one or more classes, each characterized by a filter.* But that won't do. Each class may have its own queuing discipline (so you have a queuing discipline containing several classes, each of which may be another queuing discipline). And the filters are not merely a set of arguments for packet-matching criteria, as they are with *netfilter*, but instead imply a method of matching or classifying (there's that word again), which may in fact be *fwmark* from *netfilter*.

Now, we need a way to refer to all of these various objects when we use commands to set them up. For this, we use **handles** and **classids**, which consist of two integers expressed as a *major:minor*. The difference between them is that a handle is used to refer to the **root** of a class, the point where a queuing discipline is associated with a physical device. The root handle always has a minor number of 0 (which you may see omitted in some of the literature available on CBQ). A classid refers to any of the classes below the root, which must have either the root queuing discipline or another class as its **parent**. You'll find that, in all of the examples, there is always a single **root class** that is the child of a root handle and serves as the parent for all the classes where we're actually going to start assigning filters and limiting bandwidth. Within a class hierarchy (or *family*, although this is not a CBQ word), descendant classes share the same major number, but relations below the root are not discernible by looking at the classid alone. You can list the classes using the `tc class list dev device`, which we'll use later. One more note about classes and root handles: the namespace (or numberspace) for classes is not systemwide, but must be unique only devicewide. This means that you can have a 5:15 descended from *eth0* (which would necessarily have a queuing discipline with root handle 5:0), and the exact same class hierarchy attached to *eth1*.

Before we dig into the various queuing disciplines available, we'll need a few more terms. A queuing discipline class is known as a **leaf** if it contains no further classes (you'll also note that the kernel will assign an arbitrary root handle to these objects). A class is **bounded** if it is not allowed to borrow bandwidth from a parent class. An example would be a client who has paid for certain amount of bandwidth, and although you have excess capacity at the time, you don't want that client getting used to the extra bandwidth, because down the road you intend to run the link at capacity. So a bounded class must not exceed its assigned rate, even if the parent class has additional bandwidth available. An **isolated** class will not lend unused bandwidth to other classes, which I like to think of as *dog-in-the-manger mode*. That's a goodly portion of terms and definitions. I include them here not to drive you nuts, but to try to increase your comprehension when reading the available documentation and also to introduce you to some of the keywords used in the commands.

8.4.3   Queuing Disciplines

We've already talked quite a bit about class-based queuing, and we haven't said anything about the queuing disciplines available. Maybe it's not worth the trouble to put this stuff on your router after all! I don't think you'll conclude that after this section. There are some very interesting options available to CBQ users—far beyond what the *shaper* could do.

- TBF (Token Bucket Filter)—this is a queue to limit bandwidth to some upper bound. You can specify the constant rate at which data can pass through the filter (`rate bps`), along with parameters such as the maximum number of bytes to queue (`limit bytes`), which controls the depth of the queue, and the maximum burst allowed through the queue (`burst bytes`). You may also specify a peak rate (`peakrate bps`) to allow packets through the filter. Why this in addition to a regular rate? Well, 256kB/s is the same thing as 1MB in 0.25 seconds. You may not want to ever allow more than 256kB/s, down to the smallest quantum the kernel will allow. This queue works very much like the limit match we discussed for *netfilter* back in Section 7.3.6; it feeds tokens in at a given rate, and each packet entering the queue needs a token to exit the queue. If there are no tokens available, the packet at the head of the line must wait until a token arrives, while subsequent packets queue up in the meantime (up to the limit). Because this algorithm is very accurate, it can chew up CPU cycles in a hurry.

- SFQ (Stochastic Fairness Queuing)—this algorithm looks at IP protocol flows (source and destination addresses plus ports) and attempts to fairly service each flow in a round-robin fashion. Although it's not 100% accurate—it stuffs the connections into a hash table— it provides a fair approximation and is meant to prevent one stream from completely starving out other streams. As such, it doesn't require any parameters, although it likes to know the average chunk it will be dealing with (`quantum bytes`) and how frequently it should stir up the hash table (`perturb seconds`) to try to break up sessions that are camped.

- FIFO (First In, First Out)—this is a simple queue that works just like its name, but consists of multiple bands, numbered 0–15 (`TC_PRIO_MAX` in the kernel). As long as there are packets in band 0, nothing will transmit from band 1, and so forth. You can use this to give interactive traffic the utmost priority and batch transfers the lowest. The only parameter here is the size of the fifo. For a pfifo, allow `limit packets`; for a bfifo, allow `limit bytes`.

- RED (Random Early Detect)—this a queuing algorithm for backbone routers where you want to pass traffic as quickly as possible, but you never want to find yourself so low on memory that you have to just start dropping incoming packets. This is known as **tail-drop**, and the reason you want to avoid it is that you're dropping a disproportionate amount of the traffic that just happened to get to the router at the wrong moment. The traffic that caused the congestion in the first place is queued on the router, happily waiting to be sent. The RED algorithm addresses this by randomly dropping packets before the situation gets critical. It does this with a parameter for the minimum queue length (**min**), below which no packets are dropped, and above which packets may be randomly dropped; a parameter for the maximum queue length, or the absolute upper bound for the queue (**limit**); and the target length for the queue or the queue length the algorithm will strive not to exceed (**max**).

- ingress—do you recall when I said you could only control what you send, not what you receive? Well, this queuing discipline sets out to do just that by dropping packets once the desired rate has been exceeded. This can be used to rate-limit a given connection or host if we cannot control the host and there isn't a Linux router in between. You would use it much like we used *shaper*. Mark the packets you want to limit as they traverse the PREROUTING chain by using -j MARK in the `mangle` table. Attach the ingress queuing discipline to the input interface, and then add a filter to match the firewall mark you set. (No classes are needed here—see the example in the *Cookbook* section of the *Linux 2.4 Advanced Routing HOWTO*.)

- CBQ (Class-Based Queue)—last but not least, we have the class-based queue. This queuing discipline implements a weighted-round-robin (WRR) algorithm based on the relative priorities (`prio` *priority*) of the component classes. For this reason, it is used as a connector to shuttle packets to children classes that may have queuing disciplines (or simple fifos) inside. It needs to know how much bandwidth is available to it (`bandwidth bps`), what the average packet size is (`avpkt bytes`), and the rate at which it should pass data (`rate bps`). It also requires a `weight bps`, which is a tunable parameter that should be set to about one-tenth of `rate`. If you dig into the code, it needs these figures to be able to wake itself up at appropriate intervals in order to service the classes and queues. Take a look at the files in *./net/sched/* under the kernel source tree.

This list isn't comprehensive, but it should give you a good idea of what's possible. Remember that you can build arbitrary structures out of these. For example, you may want to have a device host several RED queues and one token bucket filter. Or you may decide to place TBF queues inside your fifos. The best way to get an idea of what you'd like to do is to start experimenting.

Kernel Support for QoS and Fair-Queuing

As always, we have to let the kernel know that we intend to ask it to do these special things. Because fair-queuing is specialized, your distribution kernel may or may not have that support compiled into its stock kernel. No need to take chances. In order to use fair-queuing, you're going to need to be able to *ip* (hence `netlink socket`), and you may want to use *iptables* with the `mangle` table. Actually, by this time, you're probably going for half of the networking options or better, so tack on QoS and be done with it. Let's look at the the QoS kernel options available in the 2.4.16 kernel:

```
Networking options --->
  <*> Packet socket
  [*] Kernel/User netlink socket
  [*] Network packet filtering (replaces ipchains)
  IP: Netfilter Configuration  --->
     <M> IP tables support (required for filtering/masq/NAT)
     <M>    netfilter MARK match support (NEW)
  QoS and/or fair queueing  --->
     [*] QoS and/or fair queueing
     <M>    CBQ packet scheduler
     <M>    CSZ packet scheduler
     <M>    The simplest PRIO pseudoscheduler
```

```
<M>    RED queue
<M>    SFQ queue
<M>    TEQL queue
<M>    TBF queue
<M>    GRED queue
<M>    Diffserv field marker
<M>    Ingress Qdisc
[*]    QoS support
[*]       Rate estimator
[*]    Packet classifier API
<M>       TC index classifier
<M>       Routing table based classifier
<M>       Firewall based classifier
<M>       U32 classifier
<M>       Special RSVP classifier
<M>       Special RSVP classifier for IPv6
[*]       Traffic policing (needed for in/egress)
```

8.4.4   Configuring CBQ with *tc*

Let's get familiar with *tc*, or *traffic control*, which comes as part of *iproute2* package. This is the single command you use to configure your queues, classes, and filters. As when we were learning to use *ip*, you can ask *tc* for context-sensitive help. For example, `tc qdisc add help` will tell us about adding queuing disciplines, and `tc qdisc add cbq help` tells us something about the CBQ discipline itself. Just as there are three main objects, there are three basic commands: `tc qdisc`, `tc class`, and `tc filter`. The standard procedure to set up one of these jobbies is:

1. Attach a CBQ queuing discipline to the device. Do not specify a rate at this point.

2. Create a root class, specifying the handle of the queuing discipline you just created as the parent. This root class has the same rate and bandwidth information as the queuing discipline and is also a *cbq* queue.

3. Create a class for each logical division or queue you'd like to create. Once again, *cbq* queues.

4. Create your leaf queuing disciplines, one for each class in the step above.

5. Create your filters, which make sure that the traffic gets into the queues.

   For a quick example, we're going to set up our router to limit incoming HTTP to 128kB/s with a token bucket filter, using firewall marks to mark our packets. Recall that we want to limit traffic on the sending interface, so we'll once again be working on iron. (If we did this work on the LAN interface on californium, we'd still be saturating the link and asking CBQ to queue on californium.)

```
# create our root handle queueing discipline
iron:~# tc qdisc add dev chdlc0.1 root handle 1:0          \
       cbq bandwidth 256Kbit avpkt 1000
```

```
# create our root class
iron:~# tc class add dev chdlc0.1 parent 1:0 classid 1:1  \
        cbq bandwidth 256Kbit avpkt 1000 allot 1514        \
        weight 26Kbit

# create a class for our rate limited traffic
iron:~# tc class add dev chdlc0.1 parent 1:1 classid 1:80 \
        cbq bandwidth 256Kbit avpkt 1000 allot 1514        \
        rate 128Kbit weight 13Kbit prio 8

# create a TBF queue within this class
iron:~# tc qdisc add dev chdlc0.1 parent 1:80              \
        tbf rate 128Kbit buffer mtu 1514 limit 4M

# create a filter that looks for firewall mark "80"
iron:~# tc filter add dev chdlc0.1 parent 1:0              \
        prototcol ip handle 80 fw classid 1:80

# set up the mangle table to mark those packets
iron:~# iptables -t mangle -I PREROUTING -p tcp --sport 80 \
                -j MARK --set-mark 80
```

You can take a look at the classes, filters, and queuing disciplines by using `tc class list dev chdlc0.1`. Add `-s` to get statistics such as how many packets are in the queue, how many have been dropped, how many times the rate was exceeded, etc. If you'd like to drop a queuing discipline from a device, use `tc qdisc del dev device root discipline`. Don't forget to include the physical device on the command line, since these commands won't work without it. Note that there is another way to achieve what we did above without having to use firewall marks. Several packet classifiers are available for use with filters. We used **fw**, which is for the firewall marks (and hence *netfilter* integration). Others include:

- **u32**—this is another method of matching IP header fields but implemented for low system overhead on very high-speed/high-performance routers. You can read up about it, as well as the other classifiers, in the documentation links at the end of this section.

- **route**—this integrates with routing realms, also part of *iproute2*. The idea is that you can *mark* packets when they pass through the routing table by adding realms to routing-table entries. This is as simple as specifying a realm (just an integer number) when adding the route—for example, `ip route add default via 192.168.16.1 dev sppp0 realm 52`. Now you can use `route to 52` when specifying your filter to classify anything heading out over the default route.

- **rsvp**—this classifier is for QoS-style RSVP on Linux.

8.4.5   Using the *cbq.init* Script

There is a lot to CBQ and, like some things with Linux, it takes a lot of browsing, a flagon of coffee, and sometimes even much puzzling over the source code to be fully comfortable with the functionality. On the other hand, if something works without your having to peel the onion, why not use it? The *cbq.init* script is not a panacea—it cannot address every queuing need you're likely to have—but it takes care of a general class of QoS problems. It's written and tuned to rate-limit traffic flows using TBF on a router with a pair of 10Mbit Ethernet adapters. It can also use SFQ as a leaf-queuing discipline (if you'd like to try to avoid starving any of your clients). Best of all, it handles building u32 packet classifier rules for you, and it does all this in one neat, well-documented shell script.

You can find the script at *ftp://ftp.equinox.gu.net/pub/linux/cbq/* (or in the Debian package **shaper**—it's likely to be packaged for other distributions as well). You'll need to install it where you can call it from your system initialization scripts, say */etc/init.d/*. Then create */etc/sysconfig/cbq/* to store your configuration files (*/etc/shaper/* for Debian users). Now, much of that verbiage so far on CBQ is compressed into some simple configuration files you place in this directory. A sample file looks like this:

```
root@drone3:/etc/shaper# cat cbq-400.drone2
DEVICE=eth0,10Mbit,1Mbit
RATE=1Mbit
WEIGHT=100Kbit
PRIO=8
BOUNDED=YES
RULE=,192.168.16.12
```

First of all, note the filename. It must be in the format *cbq-minor.comment*. The minor number there is used to create the classids, so in the case of multiple files, they must be unique for any given device. That is, you may have two *cbq-400.drone2* files, but they may not reference the same **DEVICE**. Moving on to that line, we have the device, its bandwidth, and then the weight parameter for the root class. Once again, use one-tenth the bandwidth until you know better. The **RATE** and **WEIGHT** parameters tell the script that we want to rate-limit this class to 1Mb/s and tune accordingly. The priority is a relative priority for the CBQ classes. Then we get to the *RULE*, used to generate the u32 packet specifier. The format is **RULE=*srcaddr/mask:port,destaddr/mask:port***, and all of those values are optional. If the comma is omitted, the value is assumed to be a source. In the case of the file above, the rule above simply matches any source with a destination of 192.168.16.12. So, overall, the file limits traffic to 192.168.16.12 to 1Mb/s, bounded. By the way, if we hadn't specified bounded, it would be assumed. Let's define another rule:

```
root@drone3:/etc/shaper# cat cbq-200.httpclients
DEVICE=eth0,10Mbit,1Mbit
RATE=6Mbit
WEIGHT=600Kbit
PRIO=7
BOUNDED=no
RULE=:80,192.168.0.0/16
LEAF=sfq
```

In this file we allocate up to 6Mbit for our HTTP clients (we're no longer talking about californium!), assign a relatively higher priority than what we gave traffic bound for drone2, and indicate that the class shouldn't be bounded (use it if you have it) and that it should attach an SFQ filter to the leaf node. The idea here is not to limit our HTTP users but to try to make the access more consistently fair. We could continue on like this, perhaps creating another class with a higher priority (lower number) for our interactive traffic, but I think you get the idea. It's a great script that will get better with time. At the time of writing, *cbq.init*-0.6.2 is the latest (and thus what's documented here).

And with that, we bring to an end our tour of traffic control under Linux. As I said at the beginning of the section, I regret that the material here isn't more comprehensive. But it's a big topic, and I'd hope to see a book or the majority thereof dedicated exclusively to it. If you'd like to start working with QoS on Linux, please take a look at the documents below, as well their references.

- *http://www.linuxdoc.org/HOWTO/Adv-Routing-HOWTO.html*—the *Linux 2.4 Advanced Routing HOWTO* is where I would go first to start working with queuing on Linux. It's a great document, loaded with difficult-to-find information and pointers from folks who do this stuff everyday.

- *http://qos.ittc.ukans.edu/howto/*—an academic paper with some emphasis on how the code works under the covers. You'll want this for sure if you're going to dig into the code, and it's good reading for general understanding, too.

- *ftp://ftp.equinox.gu.net/pub/linux/cbq/doc/*—the same source as the *cbq.init* script, where there is a paper entitled *Linux Traffic Control—Implementation Overview* by Werner Almesberger that is definitely worth the read, despite its age (1998).

8.5   Remote System Support

Technically speaking, unless you have very special security considerations, almost all of your support will be remote support, meaning that it is not performed on the system console. This section is not about remote system support when everything is working, but about planning for problems at remote locations. It is roughly divided into two topics: strategies to quickly restore functionality when links fail, and methods to minimize restore times after hard-drive failure.

8.5.1   Redundant WAN Links

What to do when your WAN link fails is a problem for anyone, regardless of the router platform. Your service provider may have internal network outages which cannot be rerouted, your access provider(s) may have problems, or it may just be a case of bad weather. In any event, despite any SLA (Service Level Agreement) you may have with your provider, you need to be prepared for a link outage. Redundant links are one of the most common solutions; if you have the economic means, they protect against provider outages and hardware failures at the same time.

In a typical scenario, there are two routers, each connected to different circuits, ideally from different service providers. With some creative routing, you can even use both of the circuits normally, and then operate in a degraded mode when a link is unavailable. While this looks good on paper, there are some potential pitfalls. For one, there might not be multiple (economically feasible) service providers at a given location. Ordering redundant links from a single provider does nothing in the case of a provider outage (and there have been a few *significant* provider Frame Relay outages in the past few years). The second concern is that, although there might be different service providers, they may use the same access provider to deliver service to your site. In this case, a construction crew up the road cutting a piece of fiber-optic might render both of your circuits useless. (If you have a large enough installation, you should be able to impress upon your service provider the need to ensure that the access circuits are sufficiently redundant. But if you are dealing with smaller sites, good luck.) Before you leap for the panacea of redundant links, you may want to do some homework about available options at your different sites.

It may be that different locations call for different strategies. One way to mix things up is to have redundant links which use different types of access, in hopes that partial access providers' outages will not affect both types of circuits. If you have digital access for normal conditions, and ISDN or analog access as a backup mechanism, then you might be spared when a backhoe misses its intended target. Most sites with redundant access have dial-in access as an additional line of defense.

Equal Cost Multipath over Redundant Links

It may be that using an analog or ISDN circuit as the only form of redundant access is simply too uncomfortable for your users or detrimental to your organization's business model. If you have a second link, you should use a second router (it might be a system which normally serves another function) to protect against hardware failures, too. If you are paying for a second link (with the associated access and port costs), you certainly want to use it 100% of the time, and then have your site operate in a degraded mode when one of the links/routers fails. (Don't forget the prior discussion of adequate redundancy for access circuits, and don't forget about redundancy on the other end.)

If you are running a dynamic interior routing protocol more capable than RIP, such as OSPF, then you can design the redundant paths into your routing topology. This would be the traditional way of doing things, but with Linux there are other methods of accomplishing the same goal. There is functionality in the 2.2 and 2.4 kernels called IP: equal cost multipath which will forward packets over multiple pathways in a *nondeterministic* manner. To enable it, you need to compile your kernel with:

```
Networking options --->
    [*] IP: advanced router
    [*] IP: equal cost multipath
```

Once you have the kernel support, you'll need our friend *ip* from the *iproute2* package to configure it. You can add a multipath route by listing both of the next hops for the route in a single command, like:

```
ip route add net nexthop dev dev1 via ip_gw1 nexthop dev dev2 via ip_gw2
```

By default this won't randomize the traffic too much, as it tries to alternate based on flows (pairs of source and destination addresses). You can add the equalize keyword before you start listing your nexthops to ask the kernel to stir things up more. We're telling the kernel what two paths it can take to satisfy a request for a given route. If you don't do something similar on the other end, don't be surprised when everything comes back over one interface and link. For both sides, every time this router receives a packet that matches *net*, it rolls the dice. Depending upon the outcome, it forwards the packet directly over its interface, or forwards it to the secondary router as the gateway. The secondary router does not need to know that this is happening. It just forwards any packets it receives, which will statistically

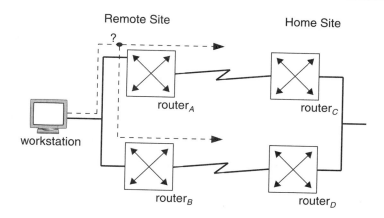

Figure 8.2 Redundant Routing with Multipath

(hopefully) be about 50% of the load. You perform the same routine on the other end of the link. I've included Figure 8.2. If you don't have two separate routers, but instead just two interfaces on the same router, things work just as well.

There are two things to note here. First, you'll need to use `ip route list` to view your routes. If you use the regular *route* command, you're not going to see everything, and this could lead to confusion. If you work in an environment with other administrators, you might want to alias *route* to a friendly reminder message about the correct command. Second, when I tested this functionality recently on a 2.4 system, I ran into a bit of trouble, with the first choice always being marked as **dead** by the kernel as soon as it was added. My guess is that there is some **bit rot** afoot here, perhaps with my version of *ip*. In any event, trust the output when it says a route is dead; it will not be used.

```
drone2:~# ip route list
192.168.18.0/24 dev eth1  proto kernel  scope link  src 192.168.18.12
192.168.64.0/24 dev eth2  proto kernel  scope link  src 192.168.64.12
192.168.16.0/24 dev eth0  proto kernel  scope link  src 192.168.16.12
default equalize
        nexthop via 192.168.18.1  dev eth1 weight 1 dead
        nexthop via 192.168.64.1  dev eth2 weight 1
        nexthop via 192.168.18.1  dev eth1 weight 1
```

You'll need to do one more thing before you try this out yourself. Realize that we're creating a situation where **asymmetrical routing** can occur. You may send a packet out over one link and have it return over the other. Depending upon which IP address you're accessing from where, you may activate the kernel's anti-IP spoofing mechanism by accident (a.k.a. **return path filtering**). You can tell the kernel to not be so picky about what IPs are being received on what interface by disabling this with:

```
drone2:~# echo 0 >/proc/sys/net/ipv4/conf/eth0/rp_filter
drone2:~# echo 0 >/proc/sys/net/ipv4/conf/eth1/rp_filter
```

It should be done for both sides of the link for each interface involved in the load balancing.

Note that *rp_filter* is going to default to being set to 1 when the system boots—this is a Good Thing for safety—so you'll need to explicitly set these values to 0 during system startup.

TEQL over Redundant Links

There is another way to load-balance. It was introduced along with the QoS code in the 2.4 kernel. Unlike the previous example, where we do something special to the routing table, the **TEQL** (Trivial link Equalizer) pools physical devices into a virtual device over which we can route our packets. To configure it, you'll need to `modprobe sch_teql`, which requires these options to have the module.

```
Networking options --->
   QoS and/or fair queueing  --->
      [*] QoS and/or fair queueing
      <M>   TEQL queue
```

You set it up by adding the appropriate queuing discipline to the devices you'd like to pool, then configuring your new *teql0* interface with an IP address and adding a route to it. As an example, I'll set up a couple of Ethernet adapters together tied together. This is not the same as physical-device trunking, but it nearly accomplishes the same purpose.

```
# pooling physical devices to use the teql device
drone3:~# tc qdisc add dev eth1 root teql0
drone3:~# tc qdisc add dev eth2 root teql0

# add an ip address to our newly created virtual device
drone3:~# ip addr add 172.16.1.2/24 dev teql0

# set the link state to up (don't forget this step!)
drone3:~# ip link set dev teql0 up

# clear reverse path filtering for these interfaces
drone3:~# echo "0" >/proc/sys/net/ipv4/conf/eth1/rp_filter
drone3:~# echo "0" >/proc/sys/net/ipv4/conf/eth2/rp_filter

# change our default route
drone3:~# ip route change default dev teql0 via 172.16.1.1
```

You can then perform the same steps on the other side of the link. BTW, did you note the ability to change a routing entry? This beats deleting the old route and then adding a new one, particularly when you're working from remote over the route you're using to access the box.

There is no real magic going on here. The *teql0* device depends on the fact that, when it hands the packet off to one of the physical devices, it will be able to get the packet to where it needs to go. It does this by issuing ARP requests on both of the physical links for the address of the gateway given in the **via** *ipaddr* portion of the route over the *teql0* device. The physical devices that are part of the TEQL pool on the other end know to listen out for these requests and to respond with their real link-layer addresses accordingly. So, if you're running TEQL on both sides, this is not such an issue. If the packet originated from the

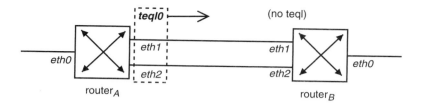

Figure 8.3 An Asymmetrical TEQL Topology

TEQL router itself, realize that it will bear the IP address you assigned to the *teql0* device, so take this into consideration when doling out IP addresses. Furthermore, resist the temptation to remove the IP addresses from the real interfaces themselves. When you do that, all of the information in */proc/sys/net/ipv4/conf/device/* disappears.

Note that you don't have to have the other side set up the same way. For point-to-point link, you can use TEQL to bond two or more interfaces together into a virtual interface, and then point routes at the interface. However, if the real physical devices don't have routes on them for the packet destination, then the kernel doesn't know what to do, since there's no gateway. You can get around this by using the `onlink` option together with a gateway in your route statement. This option tells the kernel to ignore the fact that the IP address is not part of the subnet range of the sending interface (in this case, none of the three *eth1, eth2,* or *teql0*) and ARP for it anyway. It may help to look at the topology in Figure 8.3 to follow what's happening here.

Router$_A$ has TEQL set up and will use *teql0* to send packets toward subnet$_B$ and beyond, assuming that we've configured routes that use the *teql0* device. But we need to specify a gateway to reach addresses that aren't on the physical link, and in this setup, router$_B$ isn't running TEQL. The trick is to specify the IP address of *eth0* on router$_B$ (say, 192.168.18.1) and tell the kernel to send the packet anyway. The command is:

```
routerA:~# ip route change default dev teql0 via 192.168.18.1 onlink
```

Now, this will let you send over both physical devices from router$_A$. The return path of the packet is determined by its source address and the routes available on router$_B$. If there's nothing fancy on router$_B$, the return traffic will be restricted to only one link. This may or may not be OK, depending on the traffic patterns. For grins, I set up a test link like this with TEQL on one side and using equal cost multipath on the other. Why you'd want to do this is beyond me—I'd use TEQL on both ends of the link if possible—and just because you *can* doesn't mean you should. But when you're learning, try whatever you dream up. The process of implementing an idea and then troubleshooting it until you get it working is more valuable than almost anything you're going to read. Now let's resurface from our dive into the technical details and talk about remote sites and routers in general.

Configuring Your Environment for Multipath

To have complete redundancy, you need to have two routers (on both sides) with a mechanism so that each watches its peer using a script somewhat like the one introduced in Section 7.4.1. Let's assume that you are set up as in Figure 8.2 and that the clients think router$_A$ is their default gateway. If router$_A$ fails, router$_B$ will need to configure an IP aliased interface with router$_A$'s IP address so that the clients do not need to be reconfigured. (The converse is not true.)

The configuration at the home office (router$_C$ and router$_D$) is similar. The multipath configuration will randomize which link is used. Alternatively, you can configure the remote office routers to perform masquerading. Because the homebound packets will be marked with the IP address of the WAN interface on the sending router, they will be returned over the same link to that router. (You need to configure host routes for each of the WAN interfaces in order for this to work correctly.) Another alternative is to masquerade/NAT inbound traffic at router$_C$ and router$_D$. In any case, you'll want to have scripts at the home office which monitor their link peers so that they can take the appropriate action—essentially the same action you took at the remote site—should a link fail.

Another method, possibly easier to conceptualize and debug, is to have a single monitoring system with the ability to *rexec* (or preferably, *ssh*) routing changes on the systems it monitors. It would be located at the home office and would have host routes to each of the IPs of the WAN interfaces so that it would not get caught up in any multipath configuration you may have. (The kernel always services the other end of a point-to-point link, using the host route registered when the interface is configured up. This host route has a more restrictive subnet mask than the general network route for the remote site, so it will match the destination first.) When the monitoring system notices a link down, it takes appropriate action on the required routers for a reroute. If it sounds like a mess, just consider what you would do manually to reroute traffic and script it on these machines.

Configuring for Redundant Links without Multipath or TEQL

You can use the above strategy without the multipath routing by dividing your clients into two groups and assigning one group on the remote site to use router$_A$ as a gateway and the other group to use router$_B$. It may be easiest to do the assignments with DHCP. You will not really divide the traffic in half or perform any sort of load balancing, but the approximation should be sufficient. Using the same sort of monitoring scripts, you can take sensible actions depending upon the situation, similar to what you would do with multipath. Examples include:

- If the WAN link fails, but the router is still up, have it add the route using the other router as a gateway. Then have it mail you a message that the remote site is running in a degraded state. This covers situations where the link itself dies (for whatever reason) and those where the router on the other side is unexpectedly offline. Because this router is still running, as soon as it detects that the WAN link is once again useful, it can reconfigure its routes back to the normal state.

- If one router fails entirely, the other router should notice and assume its IP address.

- If both links fail, the scripts will configure both routers to use the other as a gateway. For this reason it may be preferable to do something to the packets as they are forwarded to the other router for gatewaying so that you can detect this situation. Modifying the TOS of a packet is perfect for this. The scenario works as follows:

  1. A client sends a packet to router$_A$, its gateway, for forwarding.

  2. Router$_A$ knows that its link to the home office is down, so it forwards the packet using router$_B$ as a gateway. But before it does this, it modifies the TOS field to some magic number.

3. Router$_B$ receives the packet, but its link is also down, so it forwards the packet using router$_A$ as a gateway (*deja vu!*).

4. Router$_A$ receives the packet, but notices the magic number in the TOS field. Using the *ip* command, you can configure a route which will respond to the sender with an ICMP host unreachable message. (This is done by adding an *unreachable* route type entry to the table.) In this way, you tell your clients that things are bad without generating a storm of packets being bounced between router$_A$ and router$_B$.

If one of the routers has an alternate form of access to connect back to the home office, you can add the route over this alternate form of access, using the TOS strategy described above.

Making the Most of a Little Bandwidth

Should your WAN link(s) fail, you need to establish some sort of connectivity during the interim. If this is an analog modem-based connection, you may want to take some measures to prioritize the traffic to and from the remote site. One idea is to configure a few IP firewalling rules to prevent surfing and FTP and other noncritical functions (what these are will depend upon your office).

How you use the analog bandwidth depends upon your needs. If the remote site is primarily interested in browsing, then you can have the modem dial a local ISP (and avoid toll charges back to the main office). Users can access the Internet over that link (be sure to configure masquerading on the router). Users can use PPTP or some other VPN software to connect back to the main office as if they were on the road. Since VPN is easy to set up for Linux, the router itself could establish this link, too. This has the added bonus that VPN software typically compresses its payload, which will squeeze a little more out of the limited bandwidth.

The multipathing code can be used with PPP route running on analog modems. If you have multiple modems, have them both dial into ISPs, configure the kernel to masquerade over both links and then to multipath over both links. Now you're really talking. So that mail (and other things) will function properly, don't forget about changes to the DNS server configuration when you're running in a degraded mode. In any event, have the remote router send you an email after it's connected to the ISP so that you know where to find it in the Internet.

All this is well and good, but failover scripting can be complicated, so there is always the chance that something with it will also fail. For this case, and the general case of gaining access to your remote systems without opening them up to the Internet, configure a way *into* your remote site, which is the next topic.

Gettys—Another Way In

Assuming that your normal link is down but the router is still running, you can connect back into your system if you have a modem and a **getty** running. A **getty** is a process which allows login to the system via a tty (serial port) or via the console. Before networking was a big thing, this was the only way to access the system. Since then, however, the arcane arts have been maintained and advanced by the diligent few. Gettys are available now which can handle dial-up (with ringback), virtual consoles, fax, and voicemail. If you intend to be dialing into your system, you will probably want to exchange the system's default getty for one sporting more features.

Hint: Gettys Are Spawned from *init*

If you are not used to working with gettys, you need to know that they are not started where most of your system services are started—that is, they do not start as standalone daemons out of the */etc/init.d/* startup scripts or via *inetd*.

Instead, they are started by *init*, which reads its configuration out of */etc/inittab*. If you look at *inittab*, you will see that it has four colon-delimited fields: `<id>`: `<runlevels>`:`<action>`:`<process>`. When you add lines for the dial-in getty process, select a unique `<id>`, choose the runlevels in which it should run (probably two and three), and configure it with an action of `respawn` (so that the process is restarted once it dies and exits). The `<process>` field contains the program to execute along with any options. Therefore, it depends upon the getty and should be described in the getty's documentation.

To signal *init* to reread the contents of *inittab*, issue the command: `telinit q`

Linux Getty Replacements

- **getty_ps**—The *getty_ps* package contains two versions of a serial-capable getty. The first is *getty_ps*, the second *uugetty_ps*. You should use the latter, as it supports UUCP-style lockfiles for serial devices. This is important if you want to be able to use the same modem for dial-out. In this configuration, you are able to use a single modem for dial-in (in a support scenario) and automatic dial-out (in a link-failure scenario). *getty_ps* is available from Sunsite or your distribution. Ample documentation is included with the package to get things running.

- **mgetty** is another full-featured getty replacement that even comes preconfigured to allow dial-up from PAP clients. The source is available at the site *ftp://alpha.greenie.net/pub/mgetty/source/* or you can load the Debian package **mgetty**. There are also add-on Debian packages available, **mgetty-voice** (voicemail support) and **mgetty-fax**.

- **mingetty** is *not* for use with modems or serial lines. It is only for running your console from virtual consoles, which is sufficient for most applications where the console is not on a serial port. It is a lightweight alternative to the default getty shipped with most distributions.

- **fbgetty** is also not useful for modems, but it can be used with frame-buffer consoles. The upstream source is at *http://fbgetty.meuh.eu.org*.

After you have configured your replacement getty, test the configuration. Then test it again. Getty configuration can be unkind to the uninitiated and to fat fingers (typos). The following is taken from the README that accompanies *getty_ps*.

After the sources are compiled, MAKE A BACKUP COPY OF YOUR EXISTING WORKING GETTY PROGRAM! I cannot stress this enough. There is a good chance that you will not have things configured correctly the first time around and will not be able to log into your machine. This is also probably a good time to get one of those bootable rootdisks. In any case, be sure you can boot your system in single-user mode before you install anything.

Hint: Running the System Console on a Serial Port

There is a kernel setting in the 2.2.x and later kernels to enable your console on a serial port. Select the following during kernel configuration and regen the kernel:

```
Character devices --->
<*> Standard/generic (dumb) serial support
[*]     Support for console on serial port
```

You also need to add a line such as `"console=ttyS1"` to your bootloader configuration (probably the `append=` line in */etc/lilo.conf*). When you boot with the new kernel with this setting, you'll be able to use a dumb terminal or terminal communication program to access the system console. No more expensive KVM switches or monitors!

Automatic Dial-Out by the Remote Router

Dial-out via either an analog or an ISDN link is not covered in depth here because there is so much general experience with PPP and information about it on the Internet. On the remote system, which should dial back into the home office, you can use any of the PPP configuration tools mentioned in Chapter 4, Section 4.1.3. On the home office side, you'll be using whatever normal dial-in solution you have implemented, which brings up a few issues:

- The access password must be scripted into the remote router, so pick a secure password (it doesn't need to be easy to remember if it's stored in a script) and change it periodically.

- Most dial-in solutions issue IPs from a pool of addresses (unless you are connecting to a separate dial-in solution from that normally used for remote access). Because you need to know the IP address assigned to the remote router's PPP interface to log into it, you should have the router send an email to your account as soon as the link is up with the IP address of the PPP interface.

- The home office doesn't expect that the remote office will be connected via the dial-in solution, so configure the remote router to masquerade the traffic that it sends back to the home office. Although this is not a 100% solution, it takes care of most protocols.

As you can see from the examples given, things can get esoteric quickly when you are trying to strike a balance between efficient use of resources and flexibility. The *iproute2* has some very advanced features which will aid you. My point in this section is not to feign to provide you with a comprehensive solution, but to stress the idea that creativity and planning will serve you better during a system outage than mountains of hardware and circuit redundancy. The previous discussion dealt with what to do when network paths fail. What about when hard drives and entire machines fail? You will need a backup and recovery plan for your production environment. Otherwise, it's just a matter of time. The next section has some pointers.

8.5.2   Backups and Restores

Backups are a part of life, not unlike taxes or the inevitable demise of hard drives. One day (hopefully soon) there will be a breakthrough in nonvolatile memory density and price which will make disk drives a thing of the past. Most traditional routers already operate with flashable ROMs and NVRAM or flash cards. LRP (Section 3.5) nicely circumvents this issue but leaves most admins wanting more disk space. Instead of discussing the relative merits of backup software and media formats, I will propose some alternative ways to approach the issue. First, let's list some reasons why we wouldn't want to use full backups to tape:

- Restoral times are typically long, especially when users/systems are down.

- Backup media and equipment are expensive, as is correct handling of them. Even the bare minimums, such as keeping tapes offsite and manually changing a tape every day (or week) are expensive in terms of time.

- Backups are worthless unless they and their procedures are regularly tested. This is also time consuming and prone to operator error (or sloth).

- For a router, there are very few *data* which are not easily reproducible.

- There is something about Murphy's Law and backups ... they have this affinity for each other that defies the laws of probability. (Call me paranoid, but the potential for weirdness seems to increase drastically when you actually insert a backup tape in the drive for restoral.)

For the reasons above, and because downtime is expensive, I propose some entirely different methods for backup and restoral. Routers are admittedly easier to back up than other types of machines because they do not have user accounts or user data on them. They should consist of the OS software plus configuration files, and nothing more.

Brute-Force Backups

For the price of DAT drive and a handful of DAT tapes, you can buy half a dozen 1GB disks. For remote sites like californium, you can add a second hard drive on the secondary controller. You should use the same partition layout you did on the primary disk (although the sizes do not need to match exactly). Every so often (only after configuration changes), you can run a script such as:

```
############################################################
# brute-force backup
############################################################
# this part really only needs to happen the first time
# separate this out into another script if you'd like
mkfs.ext2 -c /dev/hdc1
mkswap -c /dev/hdc2
mkfs.ext2 -c /dev/hdc3

# mount the hot spare
mkdir /tmp/root 2>/dev/null
mount /dev/hdc1 /tmp/root || {echo "abend!" && exit 1}
mkdir /tmp/root/var
mount /dev/hdc3 /tmp/root/var || {echo "abend!" && exit 1}
```

```
# copy the entire contents
cd /var
find . | cpio -pdmv /tmp/root/var
cd /
find . -mount | cpio -pdmv /tmp/root

# fix fstab
cat /etc/fstab | sed 's/\/dev\/hda/\/dev\/hdc/' >/tmp/root/etc/fstab

# leave a trace of our actions
touch /tmp/root/root/$(hostname)_clone_on_$(date '+%y%m%d')

# unmount
umount /tmp/root/var
umount /tmp/root
```

Sure, it's overkill, but it is almost foolproof. *cpio* will not bother to overwrite files with identical timestamps, so subsequent backups will run very quickly (assuming that you do break out the *mkfs* of the script and only run it the first time). To make our new disk usable, leave the floppy in the drive which will boot off the backup drive. When things go south with the primary drive, ask one of the employees onsite to pop the floppy disk into the drive and reset the hardware. Because the backup partitions are not mounted, the abrupt reset will not damage their filesystems. The floppy is required to keep LILO from trying to boot from */dev/hda*. There are several different ways to generate such a floppy:

1. You can write a kernel image to it with **make zdisk** and then use *rdev* to set the root and swap devices with **rdev /dev/fd0 /dev/hdc1** and **swapdev /dev/fd0 /dev/hdc2**.

2. You can use *loadlin* to build your boot disk on a DOS foundation. This is a simple way to leave the disk in the drive (so that you can mount it as a FAT partition and write new versions of the kernel to it), and then have a short batch script which will *loadlin* and point the root to */dev/hda1* after some timeout, but if someone interrupts the boot sequence, then boot from */dev/hdc1*. Or, reverse the defaults to suit your tastes.

3. Use one of the other half-dozen ways there are to boot Linux from a floppy. *syslinux* is an example.

Backups Based upon Filesystem Orthogonality

If you do not want the heat or cost of a second drive inside your router, then we can take a more civilized approach to the matter. There are only a handful of files which separate one Unix machine from another. If you load two machines from the same sources using the same package selections, they have the same software on them. The only differences are the things which you configured. Because the software load is readily reproducible to a very high degree of accuracy, you need to back up only those configuration files. This is not always as easy as it sounds.

The first idea is to touch a file just after the OS is loaded, and then back up any files modified after that timestamp (using **find -type f -newer** *touchfile*). The problem is that most of the current distributions ask you questions while they install files, so it may not be so easy to differentiate between what is part of the OS and what is part of your configuration.

Still, it is better to err on the side of too much than too little. You can note the system time when you start your load and use this to create your *touchfile*. What you back up will probably be too much, including some directories created during the install and other various things, like logfiles, but it is much better than everything. It will NOT include all of the binaries. You can create a compressed tarball of these newer files and store it on another system.

You can take a more conventional approach than the one used above and back up everything under */etc/* and */usr/local/*. If you are diligent about where you place your site-specific customizations (preferably under */usr/local/etc/*), this should not cause any harm. If you have the habit of dropping things in your home directory, you'll need to get */home/* and */root/*. But ... if you built your own kernel, you might have special modules under */lib/modules/*. (I wouldn't back up the kernel source, just the file */usr/src/linux/.config.*)

Restoral consists of taking a spare drive which already has the base image of your OS install on it and uncompressing the backup tarball on top of it. Creating this image can be as simple as using the brute-force script mentioned previously. You might also place the image on a CD and then distribute the CD with a bootable floppy which loads it onto the hard drive. For this to be useful at a remote site, you'll need to have the spare drive and image already there! This is also a way to save time when loading systems; you don't need to always install from the source media. If you have time, learn where *all* of the configuration files are for your distribution.

No backup strategy will work if you are not diligent about backing up the system after changes take place. You should also be prepared in case you lose your image. You can build another image, but only you know what was on it. You can do this by using your distribution's package maintenance program to print out a list of everything that you loaded on the system. For Debian, `dpkg -l` will produce this list. Be sure to note any other items which you may have compiled and installed by hand.

Until Unix installations can be completely orthogonal with respect to configuration files and OS files, this will result in some extra files being backed up, but that's not (too) bad. I created such backups for several of my systems, and they averaged between 300 and 400kB when stored as a gzipped tarball, an easily manageable size. Just keep in mind the concept of orthogonality when adding things to the system. It goes without saying that you should have spare IDE disks and cables on hand, suitable mailers in case both drives in a router fail, and possibly some of those itty bitty jumpers used to configure the drive for the controller. You should also back up the tarballs and images using a "real" backup system.

Other Backup Tools

Should you desire to generate a "real" backup, there are literally dozens of choices of tools and equipment, with constantly more options becoming available.[9] I recommend that whatever you choose, you become familiar with it to the point that you have a high degree of confidence in it, and then stick with it. This means that you need to do more than just back things up—you must also rigorously test restores in as many distinct scenarios as possible, as well as at scheduled intervals (to account for system configuration changes and to test media integrity).

If you're not sure where to start, you should shy away from solutions that are tied to a particular type of backup medium. Backup technologies change often and come in several different scales. By this I mean that what is inexpensive per MB for 2GB backup solutions may be prohibitively expensive for backing up 100GB, but at the same time you cannot justify the cost of a 100GB solution if you never back up more than 1GB. Your needs will change

---

[9]For example, when I started writing this book, there were no writable-DVD drives on the market.

over time (either growing due to environment growth or shrinking due to things such as better filesystem orthogonality), and you don't want to be using backup software tied to a certain type of device. (For example, sometimes you'll want to back up directly to another disk.) In any event, take a look at the traditional standbys as a starting point and assess your needs from there.

- *tar* and *cpio* are your basic system primitives for backup and restore. Because they are so general-purpose, they may fall short of your needs, but they are typically utilized far short of their capabilities. As an example, they can be used together with *rmt* to manipulate a remote tape device for either reading or writing.

- The BSD *dump* and *restore* utilities are more in line with what people think of when they imagine a backup tool. They support incremental backups via levels and use of a remote tape device through *rmt* like *tar* and *cpio*.

- *taper* gets you off the command line and into using an *ncurses*-based user interface, while supporting the same generic functionality as *dump*.

- If none of these suits your tastes, there are several good commercial products available for Linux. These typically provide the added features of verifying backups after they occur, counting the number of times a piece of media has been used, a GUI interface, and so on. You may also find some of the big-name companies offering Linux clients that interoperate with their backup server code.

8.6   Summary

How often does your naming scheme work out to describe the physical location of a system? Californium happened to be located in northern California. It performed its tasks so well and so quietly—as if it belonged there—that it was the sort of router that made you feel good about Linux. This is exactly the ease of maintainability that the traditional routers brag about, and with extra functionality, too. I consider the entire project to be a complete success, and this chapter documents what californium brought to its office, and what I did to allay my fears of a support nightmare. This chapter covered a new WAN protocol, CHDLC, useful for point-to-point access links; configuring a slave DNS server, a caching HTTP proxy, DHCP, and a *Samba* print spooler; how to get back into your systems when links fail (with a modem and a *getty*); some basic strategies for routing over redundant links; and a different way to think about backups. Hopefully, you will have a californium somewhere in your fleet of systems—a system where things work better than planned, and are configured once and then forgotten.

Now that's the warm and fuzzy summary. What about that section on the black arts of traffic control and queuing disciplines? To be honest, the first time I tried to set up a bandwidth limiter using *tc*, I felt about as confident as I did the first time I had to edit *sendmail.cf* by hand. If you don't feel as if you're ready to go out there and tune your network to within a few bits per second of where you want it, take heart. (a) It's not a simple topic, and (b) the best way to achieve facility with it (and with everything in this book) is to use it. This is an easy facility to test because you can throttle traffic at egress from your workstation. Perform a couple of benchmarks without any queuing—say, a large ftp and scp at the same time (the Linux kernel works great for this). Then limit the one and/or both. Work your way up from there.

If you have more complex scenarios in mind, you're going to need to spend some time searching on *google.com* and wading through the source. Post questions to forums and mailing lists, join IRC chat rooms, share your own findings with others, get involved. If that sounds like a sales pitch, maybe it is to a certain extent. If my management asked me right now how we'd get support on Linux CBQ if we needed it, I couldn't write up a business-case-style answer that would go very far. Does that mean it shouldn't be used in business? Not at all. Truth be told, most support in the computer industry is community based. If you don't believe me, look at Oracle's *TechNet*. Linux is no different, but it takes a community to support a community. So if you need help, ask for it. If you can offer assistance, do so. And pretty soon, class-based queuing will no longer be a black art, just as *sendmail* no longer is . . . .

Chapter 9

HAFNIUM—INTERNET SERVICES ROUTER

With its impressive uptimes, ease of administration, and meager hardware appetite, Linux may lead one to boastfulness—the origin of hafnium's name. In this case, a co-worker was loading a web server using a popular commercial web server application and operating system and was adding copious amounts of memory to the system so that it would be "usable." I snidely remarked that Linux could provide the same functionality using "half the hardware." Thus, hafnium was born. In Chapter 7 we focused on connecting to the Internet, security, and keeping our routers running. Now we're going to do more with our routers. Because one strategy to reduce the TCO (Total Cost of Ownership) of an environment is to reduce the overall number of systems, there is economic merit to such efforts. For this chapter, you could almost say that we're building network servers and adding routing as an afterthought.

There are a few issues to keep in mind when you start mixing routing with network services; this chapter addresses some of the more common problems. For small environments (say, a website run from a cable modem in your house), these techniques will help you get by with less equipment. For larger installations, they increase potential for high availability by allowing network servers to act as backup routers and routers to act as backup network servers. Beyond combining services, the chapter shows methods for sites with limited amounts of Internet-routable address space, either for your clients or for servers which provide Internet services. It goes on to introduce dynamic routing daemons for Linux, and finally, it explains what to do when your system is down. The chapter is divided into the following sections:

- proxies—making external resources available to users on the inside

- redirecting Internet services from one host to another, including using **DNAT**, or Destination NAT

- general Internet services which may coexist with routers

- dynamic routing daemons

- emergency down procedures

9.1 Allowing Access to the Outside—Proxying

We've already discussed the caching HTTP proxy in Chapter 8. This type of proxy can increase HTTP performance for your users by saving bandwidth. Although this is one reason to deploy proxies, it is neither the only nor the original reason for proxies. The impetus for the development of proxies was the need for security and control. Let's call these **firewall proxies**, or, as they are frequently referred to, **application proxies**. Like a caching proxy, these proxies accept HTTP requests and perform them on behalf of the user. Additionally, they perform authentication and access control, limit who may access what sites, and log all transactions in (configurable) detail. Firewall proxies are also useful for environments where IP masquerading is not possible.

As you might guess, there are proxies for protocols other than HTTP; almost any TCP protocol can be proxied. To eliminate having to write a proxy for every protocol, generic proxy servers are available. (We will talk about the difference between generic proxies and protocol-specific proxies later in this section.) UDP can also be proxied but presents its own challenges. Because it is connectionless, you might have to perform authentication for every packet to make sure that the same person who initiated packet exchange is the same one sending the nth packet. A reasonable compromise is to specify a timeout for the valid session, as is done with ticket-granting security models, such as Kerberos. For UDP application protocols—common ones include IRC, ICQ, DNS, and some RealAudio applications—there is another form of server which is like a generic proxy, called a SOCKS server. SOCKS, covered in Section 9.1.3, requires a **SOCKsified** client (these are common) and offers the possibility of encrypting the internal session (between the client and the proxy).[1]

Any of these proxies may coexist on your Linux router, although those which require local user accounts, significant disk space, or considerable CPU cycles are candidates for their own server. Be forewarned that some network security purists will abhor the idea of mixing proxies and packet filtering. In a perfect security-minded world, you would have either a firewall that is purely a packet filter, or a dual-homed nonrouting machine with only proxies. In either case, the idea is to keep you focused on the concept of forwarding packets *or* proxying services, without worrying about the other. Of course, the proxies described here are not limited to use on routers, but you will often find the functions combined. Furthermore, I believe that benefits outweigh the security risks, as long as you keep your mind on what you're doing. With that word of caution, let's look at some different protocol proxies.

9.1.1   The *TIS Firewall Toolkit—FWTK*

The *TIS FWTK* (Trusted Information Systems FireWall ToolKit) seems to have started it all. (If there were others before it, they were not as widely used and distributed.) It is a collection of proxy programs which work together and focus on firewall security. Note that the software is not free, in the sense that GPL or BSD software is free, but you may retrieve the sources if you agree to comply with the license. See *http://www.tis.com/* for more details. Even if you do not want to take a look at the source, there is a very good document about the design and use of the "toolkit" available at that same website entitled *TIS Internet Firewall Toolkit Overview*. If the concept of firewalling and proxying is new to you, then this will be good reading.

TIS Toolkit **Concepts**

The toolkit consists of a set of servers and clients which all use a common permissions file or authentication mechanism. These clients and servers are proxies for different network services you may provide to your internal users. Think of a proxy as a ferry, which transports users' requests from the internal interface (where the proxy is bound and listening) to the services

---

[1]SOCKS V5 only.

they are requesting on the remote servers. Introducing this step allows you to control and log all access attempts to the ferry. Furthermore, because you have control of the packets, you may inspect their contents, as well as the contents of replies. This is where firewall proxies can set themselves apart from generic proxies (whose main focus is acting as an alternative to masquerading). You wouldn't want someone transporting contraband using your ferry, nor should you allow someone to sneak a bomb in via one of the reply packets. (In this case, a bomb is anything which the sender's client is not expecting and therefore may not handle gracefully.) For protocol-specific proxies, this is done by making sure that the response follows the state machine of the application protocol. Any commands which are not known by the proxy can be discarded (or at least logged), since there is no way to know whether or not it is safe to "transport" them to the inside. There are also ways to make the ferry itself safer, should someone attack it directly. It can be run in a chroot()'ed environment so that a vulnerability in the proxy or the application protocol provided by the proxy does not endanger the proxy host.

At what cost, security? Operating a ferry obviously requires more overhead than just routing or filtering the packets. The packets must be copied into user-space and dissected by the proxy, the proxies themselves are statically linked (not necessarily detrimental to execution speed, but expensive in terms of memory), and you will need a separate proxy process for each connection. The proxies also like to perform logging—perhaps a great deal of it—which further increases the overhead. As a firewall administrator, you have to make this sort of trade-off, depending upon the needs of your environment. Slow response times might be preferable to less security in some situations, in others not. Where you draw the line is a difficult decision, and this is what differentiates you from other firewall administrators. No defense is 100% complete; remember that you're connecting your network to a network filled with potential attackers who, relative to you, are infinite in number, have infinite time, and typically have superior knowledge and tools. (Try telling your management that!) Instead of waxing philosophical about security any longer—that topic is better left to a security book—let's review the tools available to you in the *FWTK*.

TIS FWTK **Modules**

auth—the authentication server and libraries. These allow you to develop a database of proxy users and provide support for authentication mechanisms based on several popular schemes in addition to plain old (insecure) passwords. This database is also useful if you have external users whom you would like to allow into your network. Authentication against the server is available to the user-based proxies in the toolkit.

ftp-gw—the FTP proxy server.

http-gw—the HTTP and gopher proxy. (No caching here!)

netacl—the TCP/IP access control wrapper, similar in function to the *tcpd* package, but with a different file format. You can use this to integrate additional application proxies into your existing configuration without a lot of rework.

plug-gw—the "plug-board" proxy server. It is a generic TCP protocol proxy, allowing you to ferry traffic across your firewall for application protocols which do not have their own proxy. It doesn't provide the level of protection that the application-specific proxies do because it doesn't know how to detect that there is a "bomb" in the boat. It does integrate with the rest of the access control and authentication information available in the toolkit. Viewed this way, at its worst, it is still as secure or more so than any other generic TCP proxy.

rlogin-gw—the rlogin proxy server.

smap—the SMTP proxy, used in conjunction with **smapd** (the *sendmail* wrapper daemon) to provide a way to shield SMTP daemons on the inside from SMTP daemons on the outside.

tn-gw—a telnet proxy server.

x-gw—a proxy for X11 traffic.

Additional tools and patches are not officially part of the *FWTK* but have been contributed by users and are available along with the source distributed by TIS. TIS is also kind enough to provide a mailing list for *FWTK* users. You can see their website for details. If you are considering using the *FWTK*, you should also visit *http://www.fwtk.org/*, which is a good source of information about the toolkit, FAQs, patches, and more.

9.1.2   Other Proxies for FTP, Telnet, and HTTP

Although you can configure packet filtering and/or masquerading to allow user access to the outside, you lose the logging and the ease of troubleshooting user problems offered by a proxy server. If your mode of operation is incompatible with the *TIS FWTK* license and you need proxying, then you will need to look elsewhere. However, when you go searching for a generic proxy server for Linux (SOCKS withstanding, which is covered in the next section), you might come to the same conclusion that I did: Most corporate cultures which require detailed logging of client accesses to the Internet either do not use free software or do not share their developments with the free world. When searching for a telnet proxy on *freshmeat.net*, I was able to find only one with a free license. Of course, the one I found is capable of doing everything I was looking for and more. It built *right out of the box* and starting proxying telnet sessions for me five minutes later. It is called *DeleGate*; its homepage is *http://www.delegate.org/*.

> DeleGate is a multipurpose application-level gateway, or a proxy server which runs on multiple platforms (Unix, Windows, and OS/2). DeleGate mediates communication of various protocols (HTTP, FTP, NNTP, POP, Telnet, etc.), applying cache and conversion for mediated data, controlling access from clients and routing toward servers. It translates protocols between clients and servers, merging several servers into a single server view with aliasing and filtering.

If you don't need the *emacs* of proxy servers and telnet is not your worry, several different special-purpose proxies are available. Keep in mind that another term for **proxy** in this context is **application-level gateway**. Many application-level gateways concentrate on proxying a single application, just as the individual proxies in the *TIS FWTK* do. Because masquerading and packet filters are so widely used, you are most likely to find application-level gateways for protocols which cannot be provided easily using those methods. Here is a partial listing by protocol:

IRC—This is UDP-based which requires inbound as well as outbound connections. One such proxy is *tircproxy*, a fill-featured IRC proxy whose homepage is *http://bre.klaki.net/ programs/tircproxy/*:

It can proxy DCC CHAT, DCC SEND, and other DCC requests transparently to the user, block common trojans (such as script.ini), hide the user's identity, and more. It can be used with the Linux kernel or IPF transparent proxy features to transparently proxy IRC sessions.

ICQ—I am not aware of an ICQ proxy, but many clients support use of a SOCKS server, covered in the next section.

NNTP—Because most newsfeeds are not open, news is not something you really proxy all of the time. Still, there may be a need to allow access to a vendor's news server. You can use a package like *DeleGate* or *plug-gw* (in the *TIS FWTK*). Otherwise, look into a lightweight NNTP server such as *NewsCache* (*http://www.infosys.tuwien.ac.at/ NewsCache/*).

FTP—This can be a problem. Apart from the *FWTK* (or *DeleGate* again), I am not aware of a standalone FTP proxy server. Fortunately, many HTTP proxy daemons support use of *ftp://* URLs implicitly.

HTTP—These proxies are wildly abundant. In addition to the *TIS FWTK* and the caching proxies described in Section 8.2.2, there are literally dozens of others. Some are very lightweight and simple, while others provide features not available in many clients. For example,

> Junkbuster is an instrumentable proxy that filters the HTTP stream between web servers and browsers. It can prevent ads and other unwanted junk from appearing in your web browser.

Junkbuster's homepage is *http://internet.junkbuster.com/*. It is available as a Debian package of the same name.

POP—*pop3gwd*[2] is available, along with the support built into *DeleGate*.

RealAudio—This has an application gateway which is made available by RealNetworks. It is disguised on their website under a section for firewall developers. See *http://service.real. com/firewall/fdev.html*.

There are many other application gateways for these and other protocols. The list above is only a starting point for your search. If you cannot locate a suitable proxy, then you may be able to use a SOCKS server. If SOCKS, masquerading, and proxying are out of the question, then you might be breaking new ground on the protocol field. In a vast majority of cases, however, someone has run across the problem before you and has been generous enough to make his or her tools available. If the application is one under development, so that a specific user needs access to a specific site or short list of sites, see Section 9.2 for information about redirecting that traffic.

9.1.3   A SOCKS Server

Another way to approach proxies is to use a SOCKS server. Unlike other proxy mechanisms, SOCKS does not try to make the presence of the proxy server transparent to the user. To use the proxy, you need SOCKS-capable (or **SOCKsified**) clients. In other words, you cannot use

---

[2] *http://caristudenti.cs.unibo.it/~borgia/homepage/Software/Software.html.*

a standard telnet client to connect to the SOCKS proxy server and then continue out to your Internet destination. This is not as bad as it sounds, since many popular clients have SOCKS support built into them, including browsers and most modern Internet clients (e.g., ICQ, IRC, FTP GUIs, etc.) On the command line, use one of the *rclients*, such as *rtelnet*, *rftp*, *rfinger*, and *rwhois*. There is library support for building your own clients on a variety of platforms.

The need for special clients can be viewed in a positive light, as it requires your users to understand the difference between connecting to an internal machine directly and using resources on the Internet. In the case of command-line clients, you can hide this from the user completely by aliasing the SOCKsified clients to the names of the standard clients and configuring the location about the SOCKS server(s) in */etc/socks.conf.* The SOCKS clients will revert to direct (normal) connections for their application protocol if no SOCKS server is available for the service you are using. You can also use the *runsocks* scripts (available for both SOCKS V4 and V5—part of the **socks4-clients** Debian package). The description below is taken from the manpage for the Linux version of *runsocks*:

> *runsocks* is a shell script that initializes environment variables to ensure that the linker uses the SOCKS shared library when you link at runtime. Use *runsocks* to SOCKSify an application without recompiling. *runsocks* only works if you dynamically link and the operating system supports all the runsocks features.

SOCKS V4 vs. SOCKS V5

There are two versions of the protocol in circulation: SOCKS V4 and SOCKS V5. Both have the following advantages:

- SOCKS alleviates the need for any sort of masquerading or NAT for outgoing connections and provides the logging available with other proxies.

- Even if you don't need any sort of address translation, using a SOCKS daemon protects the (IP) identity of your clients (as any other proxy would).

- SOCKS is not application protocol dependent, and it includes extensions for more complicated TCP protocols, such as FTP.

Whether or not you decide to deploy SOCKS V4 or V5 depends upon your needs (and license issues). Table 9.1 lists the primary differences between the versions.

SOCKS is well supported for Linux. You can retrieve the sources listed above and be up and running in less than a half hour. If you run into problems, NEC hosts FAQs and mailing lists and in general has a well-designed site with lots of information about using SOCKS. If you choose it for your primary method of providing user access to the outside, you will not be alone.

Dante—A Free SOCKS Implementation

If you are not partial to NEC's implementation or license, then there are alternatives. Check out *Dante*, which has a BSD-style license. You can visit its homepage at *http://www.inet.no/ dante/.* The following description is taken from *freshmeat.net*:

> Dante is a free implementation of the proxy protocols socks version 4, socks version 5 (rfc1928) and msproxy. It can be used as a firewall between networks. It is being developed by Inferno Nettverk A/S, a Norwegian consulting company. Commercial support is available.

Table 9.1 Primary differences between SOCKS versions

SOCKS V4	SOCKS V5
• Supports client authentication only through *ident* or via username information provided by the client. You can also check the client's IP address against an access control list similar to most proxy servers.	• Provides for strong client authentication through the GSS-API (Generic Security Service Application Programming Interface) in addition to *ident* and IP-based access. The GSS-API specification as it relates to SOCKS V5 (RFC 1961) also allows for encryption between the client and the proxy server.
• Supports TCP connections only.	• Supports both TCP and UDP connections.
• Has a free license, as in the definition of free software. You can retrieve the sources from *ftp://ftp.nec.com/pub/socks/socks4/*, or use the Debian package **socks4-server**.	• Source code is available free of charge, but the license restricts certain types of use. (Because of this, you will not find a Debian package for it.) If your use is compatible with the license, it is easily retrieved and built. See *http://www.socks.nec.com/* to retrieve the sources.
• Is compatible only with SOCKS V4 clients.	• Depending upon the implementation, can be backward compatible with SOCKS V4. The NEC implementation is.
	• Has extensions which support ICMP applications like ping and traceroute.

In summary, SOCKS is a good way of providing proxies if you do not mind dealing with modified clients. If you use a dual-homed SOCKS server with routing disabled and properly configured access control lists, it is an effective firewall and can alleviate the need for masquerading (as long as the external interface on the SOCKS server has a Internet-valid IP address).

9.2   Redirection of IP Traffic—Smoke and Mirrors

This section is about methods to take traffic that is headed to one destination and point it toward a different destination without the sender (and sometimes the receiver) ever being aware that any such activity is taking place. The action does not necessarily have to be covert; it may be the only way to allow access from the outside to systems inside a masquerading firewall. Redirection is like the Perl slogan in the Camel book,[3] TMTOWTDI (*There's More*

---

[3]See *Programming Perl* in the Bibliography.

Than One Way To Do It). The options run the gamut from simple user-space processes to kernel firewalling rules, a combination of these two, and then finally some more complex kernel rules which perform reverse masquerading. We cover each of these with an example.

9.2.1   User-Space Redirection—The Illusion of the Facade

The first, and likely the most common, method of redirection is to use a user-space process to listen to networking requests on the desired interface and port, and then to forward these unaltered to the destination system and port. To a large extent, these processes are like the proxies discussed in Section 9.1. In fact, these processes are often referred to as **proxies**, although I think that **redirector** is more precise. If all goes well with the redirection, the user cannot tell the difference between connecting to the redirecting and to the true destination. (Note, however, that the destination sees the connection attempt come from the redirecting server.) One positive upswing of all this is that servers with private IP addresses can still be used to provide services to Internet clients. The topology is depicted in Figure 9.1.

Because this type of topology is frequently used (or at least frequently desired), and in many cases admins do not choose to run HTTP daemons on their firewall or external routers, people have invested some time in developing redirection solutions. Several popular redirection packages are available, some of which are listed here.

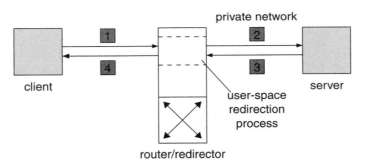

Figure 9.1 User-Space Redirection of Traffic

transproxy

transproxy provides a daemon, *tproxy*, which is easy to set up and use. It has no configuration file—all options are passed as command-line arguments. It is very simple to configure after you take a look at the manpage, so I won't go into detail. But since I've used it a lot, here are some notes on things that may not be immediately obvious.

- It can be run either from *inetd* or as a standalone server (the absence of -s *port* indicates that it should run from *inetd*).

- You need to specify -t when you are not proxying HTTP—the default mode is for *HTTP translate*, which is for use when connecting to HTTP proxy servers *Squid* or *Apache*.

- Use -r *username* to have the proxy run as a nonroot user. This is valid even if the listening port is ≤ 1023.

- You can use *-b ipadress* to force the daemon to bind to a particular interface or IP address.

transproxy is available from the upstream source *http://www.transproxy.nlc.net.au/*. Some instructions floating around out there note incorrectly that you need to have transparent proxying enabled in the kernel to be able to use the daemon; you can safely ignore this. Note that *transproxy* is for "simple" TCP connections, so it will not work for every application protocol. You will have to use something like the next tool for FTP.

redir

redir, like *transproxy*, is only for TCP connections. It does everything *transproxy* does and adds some nice capabilities. You used to be able to download the source from the author's homepage: *http://users.qual.net/~sammy/hacks*, but recently I've been unable to find it either there or on the old Sunsite archive. As I mentioned in the sidebar back on page 105, if a piece of software is included in Debian, you can always retrieve the original upstream source from the Debian archive. The Debian package is *redir*—kept there for the very reason that people and homepages move. The functionality above and beyond *transproxy* is listed here by the command-line switches used to invoke it:

- —`ftp` will handle passive-mode FTP connections.

- —`timeout=`*n* will close the connection after *n* seconds of inactivity.

- —`syslog` enables logging via *syslog*. It's not in the manpage, but it will log to the facility *daemon* at the level *notice*.

- —`name=`*string* or —`ident=`*string*[4] will use *string* instead of *redir* in the *syslog* entries.

- —`debug` will write debugging information to *stderr*, or to *syslog* if you are using the `--syslog` switch.

- —`transproxy`, in conjunction with a kernel running transparent proxying,[5] will report the original sender's address and port to the proxied destination.

Here is an example. When machine$_A$ connects to the redirector running on router$_B$ which forwards the traffic to machine$_C$, machine$_C$ will see the packet as having originated from machine$_A$. When machine$_C$ goes to reply to machine$_A$, the packet will be intercepted by router$_B$, which bound itself to the sender's interface IP and port. This is possible only if *redir* is running as root and IP: `transparent proxy support` is compiled into the kernel. Furthermore, it will work correctly only for connections which are symmetrically routed (i.e., in both directions) by the system running *redir*. Lastly, there is always the chance that the sender's port is already in use on the firewall and will not be available for use. Nonetheless, it's a neat and useful trick. One benefit is that things like web-server logs will contain the correct source address for generating access statistics. See the *transproxy.txt* file accompanying the distribution for more information.

rinetd

rinetd is a multiheaded (and multithreaded) server which acts like *redir* and *transproxy*. Like these, it redirects only TCP connections (but not FTP, so keep a copy of *redir* around!). *rinetd* sets itself apart with its configuration file. Unlike the previous two, it can listen to an arbitrary

---

[4]Not noted in the manpage for the version I have, but it works fine.

[5]Transparent proxying is a 2.2.x kernel feature covered in Section 9.2.2.

number of ports simultaneously, each of which may be bound to a (possibly different) interface address on the router. These port/address tuples are specified in the configuration file with lines in the format of *bindaddress bindport connectaddress connectport*. The addresses may be hostnames, and the ports may be service names. *rinetd's* configuration file may also include global and service-specific "allow" and "deny" lines, reminiscent of the configuration file used by the *TIS FWTK*. Any connection from a source which is explicitly denied or is not found in a global allow will be immediately rejected. The next feature is a choice of logfile formats. You may choose to have no logfile whatsoever, use *rinetd's* format, or use a common web-server format. Like *inetd*, *rinetd* can be caused to reload its configuration by sending it a SIGHUP.

If you would like to try *rinetd*, it can be found at *http://www.boutell.com/rinetd/*. There is also a Debian package of the same name. The following is an excerpt from the manpage which provides a good synopsis.

> *rinetd* redirects TCP connections from one IP address and port to another. *rinetd* is a single-process server which handles any number of connections to the address/port pairs specified in the file */etc/rinetd.conf*. Since *rinetd* runs as a single process using nonblocking I/O, it is able to redirect a large number of connections without a severe impact on the machine. This makes it practical to run services on machines inside an IP masquerading firewall.

The software listed in this section represents just a few of the user-space redirectors out there, but these have been around for a long while and are amazingly useful. If none of them fits your needs, you can always roll your own, as many have chosen to do. (About five minutes on freshmeat will find you half a dozen more.) If the nitty-gritty network programming scares you, use one of the general-purpose socket utilities such as *socket* or *netcat*. They should be available anywhere, but if you have problems finding them, refer to the **socket** and **nc** Debian packages. Otherwise, grab the Camel book and try your hand at some Perl; rewrite later in C if needed for performance. The next section is about using the kernel to do some of the work of redirection, normally in conjunction with a user-space redirector.

9.2.2   Transparent Proxy Support—Sleight of Hand

This form of redirection augments the kernel with the ability to redirect traffic encountered by the router to a local port. The redirection code is integrated with the firewalling code for input filters. As with any other firewall rules, you have to specify some packet-matching criteria, in addition to the local port to receive these packets. On any router located along the flow of traffic, you can take traffic headed for a particular host or subnet, from a particular subnet— anything which can be specified as an input firewall rule—and redirect it to a local port. A process server capable of dealing with the packet should be running on that port (otherwise the client will get a `Connection refused` message). This is depicted in Figure 9.2.

Instead of a service process, you might have a user-space redirector running on the local port, which then forwards the traffic to some remote *system:port*, such as *transproxy* (introduced in Section 9.2.1). If you would like to enforce the policy of using proxy servers, you can use transparent proxying to forward all outbound requests for direct connections to the internal proxy server. Figure 9.3 is an illustration of this.

Strictly speaking, the system does not need to be a router, because the firewalling rule must be specified as part of an input rule. In that case, you would redirect traffic from certain sources (the destination will be you, since you're not anybody's gateway) to a particular port, and traffic from other sources to a different port. This is the poor admin's (easy) way to enforce IP-based security (useful for things like inside vs. outside) on an ident or finger server by running two separate daemons on different ports, but on the same server.

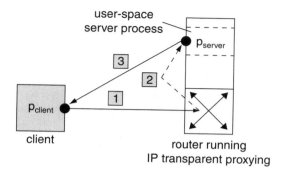

Figure 9.2 Kernel Redirection Using IP Transparent Proxy

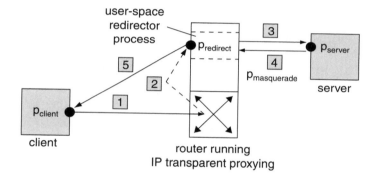

Figure 9.3 Kernel + User-Space Redirection of Traffic

IP Transparent Proxy Support with the 2.4.x Kernel

It will come as no surprise that *netfilter* provides a mechanism for this redirecting of packets to a port of your choosing. In this case, it comes in the form of another target, REDIRECT. A great feature of *netfilter* is that the authors carefully considered *when* (or more precisely, *where* along the packet's path of travel through the kernel) a particular feature would be most useful. Now, where do you think it makes the most sense to have a feature that takes traffic and redirects it to a process running on a local port? It might be helpful to take a look at Figure 4.5 to see the possibilities, the places where hooks exist. If you guessed PREROUTING, you're thinking like a Linux kernel guru. (If you didn't, don't let it bother you.) REDIRECT hooks into the PREROUTING so that you can catch all traffic passing through the system, regardless of its destination, i.e., local or not. The target is appropriately part of the nat table, since it modifies the destination address of the packet, and frequently the destination port too. The kernel modules you'll need to redirect are shown below:

```
Networking options --->
   [*] Network packet filtering (replaces ipchains)
   [*] TCP/IP networking
     IP: Netfilter Configuration  --->
```

```
<M> Connection tracking (required for masq/NAT)
<M> IP tables support (required for filtering/masq/NAT)
<M>    Full NAT
<M>       REDIRECT target support
```

Once you `modprobe ipt_REDIRECT`, you're ready to get busy with *iptables* (or simply configure a rule with redirection if you have kernel support for auto-loading modules...). The `REDIRECT` target adds one command-line option to your *iptables*, `--to-ports port[-port]`, which can be used as in the following examples:

```
# we want all HTTP traffic to use the squid proxy on hafnium
hafnium:~# iptables --table nat -j REDIRECT -A PREROUTING      \
                    --match multiport --destination 0.0.0.0/0  \
                    --proto tcp --dport 80,443,8080            \
                    --to-ports 3128


# redirect ssh, telnet, and smtp to the local box
hafnium:~# iptables --table nat -j REDIRECT -A PREROUTING       \
                    --source 192.168.0.0/16 --in-interface eth0 \
                    --proto tcp --dport 22:25 --to-ports 22-25
```

The first command is a fairly common way to redirect traffic to a local *Squid* proxy daemon running on port 3128 of this system. It matches traditional HTTP service ports for any destination. We could have just as well left off the `--destination 0.0.0.0/0`, but I specify here explicitly so you can see it. The second command matches telnet, *ssh*, and smtp connection attempts and redirects them to local ports on the same system, where *TIS Toolkit* equivalents are ready and waiting. We match source addresses from our internal address space and coming from an interface on the inside. We don't want to redirect someone coming from the outside spoofing our internal address space. On firewall boxes, keep this in mind, because `PREROUTING` rules match before `INPUT` or `FORWARD`. Note the slight syntactic discrepancy between the specifications for a range of destination ports and the range of ports to redirect to. The rule works the way you'd expect, mapping the ports sequentially from the destination to the redirect. That is, destination port 22 becomes local port 22, destination port 25 becomes local port 25, and no, port 24 doesn't get you anything except a *connection refused message*. The use of ranges here is to illustrate how the lazy network admin can escape specifying three separate rules or using multiport matching. Now we'll take a look at another example using the 2.2 kernel facilities for redirection.

IP Transparent Proxy Support with the 2.2.x Kernel

The drill for the 2.2 kernel is similar to configuring any of the 2.2 firewalling rules with *ipchains*. Akin to the `MASQ` target used for masquerading, *ipchains* allows you to specify `REDIR` as a target of a rule. You may optionally specify a port, and specifying no port means to use whatever port was in the original packet's destination field. Before configuring rules, you will need support in the kernel:

```
Networking options --->
    <*> Packet socket
    [*] Network firewalls
```

```
[*] TCP/IP networking
[*] IP: advanced router
[*] IP: firewalling
[*] IP: transparent proxy support (EXPERIMENTAL)
```

For our example, we want to let everyone know that a server is down, should anyone try to access it. Note that you can use the flexibility of *ipchains* to redirect traffic from different sources to different destinations.

```
### redirect all traffic headed for port 80 on moose.mancill.com
### to local port 12970, where a user-space proxy will send the traffic
### to another web server while moose gets a brain transplant

ipchains -A input -p tcp -j REDIR 12970   \
        -s 0.0.0.0/0 -d moose.mancill.com/32 80


### configure transproxy to listen on port 12970 as user "nobody"
### anything received by the proxy is sent to port 80
### on cow.mancill.com, which has get-well message about moose
### when people access it with an http://moose... URL

tproxy -s 12970 -r nobody cow.mancill.com 80


### management says that the message is too casual for the external
### customers who use moose, and that it would be better if the
### server were just down with no error message
### (?!? - I'll never understand mgt)

# assuming that our internal addresses are 192.168.0.0/16
ipchains -I 1 input -p tcp -j REJECT              \
        ! -s 192.168.0.0/16 -d moose.mancill.com/32 80
```

The above example works well for "onesy-twosy" situations, when there are only a few ports to redirect. However, when the server process is not local to the router, you incur the overhead of user-space redirection. For high-bandwidth applications, it seems like a lot of work to ask the router to review all of the packets with firewalling rules and then to copy them into user-space to be redirected. Is there a better way? The next section covers pure user-space redirection, and the following presents a kernel-only solution.

9.2.3   Remote Redirection with DNAT

In review of the previous two sections, **IP transparent proxying** could have been named **firewall port redirection**. Its purpose is to redirect traffic to a local port, regardless of its destination. In contrast, the user-space redirectors take traffic bound for a local port and forward it to a predetermined destination. Neither of them directly addresses the case where we want to take traffic bound for destination$_A$ and ship it off to destination$_B$. We noted that you can achieve this affect with a combination of `REDIRECT` and a user-space redirector, but this is going to feel like a kludge for high-bandwidth applications. Starting with the 2.4 kernel, you can use the `DNAT` target to accomplish the same thing all in kernel-space. Short for Destination

Network Address Translation, DNAT fulfills the promise of the *netfilter* code by giving Linux the last significant tool required in order to play in the traditional firewall arena.

Also noteworthy is the fact that DNAT is not connected to masquerading and SNAT. If you dealt with some of the 2.2 kernel hacks that delivered a subset of DNAT, you can appreciate the orthogonality in their treatment on 2.4. If you need to implement this feature on a 2.2 kernel or are just interested, refer to Section 10.7. Like `REDIRECT`, the `DNAT` target is available for matches in the `PREROUTING` chain, before the packet touches any of the other chains. Therefore, the same security precautions apply, too. The kernel module requirements are about the same as for `REDIRECT` in Section 9.2.2, except that you won't need the *ipt_REDIRECT* module itself, and you may find it useful to have `Connection state match support` (*ipt_state*) at your disposal. So, without further ado, let's look at the topology in Figure 9.4 and start writing some rules for it. It is similar to the setup we had in Section 7.3.2 when we discussed conditional forwarding. The difference now is that the IP addresses of our servers on the DMZ segment are private. Thus, they don't have to correspond to the DNS A records we publish to the Internet, because we can translate those addresses with DNAT.

The first thing we're going to do is get that *Squid* proxy server from our `REDIRECT` example off our firewall. (We didn't really like it there in the first place.) We'll use DNAT to transparently move all of our proxy services over to a dedicated proxy server. Is one proxy enough? What if we want to load-balance across several proxy servers? All we have to do is simply add the additional proxy servers to our list of addresses to map to, as indicated in the help for DNAT. Finally, we take care of FTP, telnet, and SMTP, redirecting it to the one proxy server set up for that, and indicating that the rule matches the *RELATED* state, which catches FTP data connections related to FTP control sessions based on the code *ip_conntrack_ftp*:

```
hafnium:~# iptables -t nat -j DNAT -help
DNAT v1.2.3 options:
  --to-destination <ipaddr>[-<ipaddr>][:port-port]
                  Address to map destination to.
                  (You can use this more than once)
```

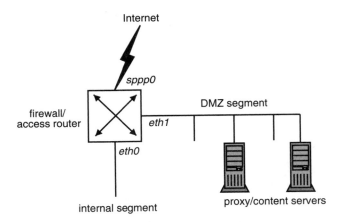

Figure 9.4 Basic DNAT Firewall Topology

```
# all outbound HTTP goes to our one proxy server
hafnium:~# iptables --table nat -j DNAT -A PREROUTING              \
                    --match multiport --in-interface eth0         \
                    --proto tcp --dport 80,443,8080               \
                    --to-destination 192.168.99.5:3128


# whoops, we want load balancing.  which rule should we replace?
hafnium:~# iptables --line-numbers -t nat -L PREROUTING | grep DNAT
6    DNAT        tcp --  anywhere           anywhere          \
          multiport dports www,https,webcache to:192.168.99.5:3128


# replace rule 6 on the PREROUTING chain with our new rule
hafnium:~# iptables --table nat -j DNAT -R PREROUTING 6           \
                    --match multiport --in-interface eth0        \
                    --proto tcp --dport 80,443,8080              \
                    --to-destination 192.168.99.5:3128           \
                    --to-destination 192.168.99.15:3128


# redirect outbound ftp, telnet, and smtp to the proxy server
hafnium:~# iptables --table nat -j REDIRECT -A PREROUTING         \
                    --source 192.168.0.0/16 --in-interface eth0 \
                    --proto tcp --match multiport --match state \
                    --state NEW,ESTABLISED,RELATED              \
                    --dport 20,23,25 --to-destination 192.168.99.15
```

Now that we're taking care of some outbound connections, what about inbound? It's just as common to want to redirect inbound connections as outbound, since this allows you to deploy Internet servers on private address space, conserving your Internet-valid IPs. By matching source ports, you can also spread out services across servers while publishing only one IP address to your external clients (and in some cases perform round-robin load balancing for those services, depending on how complicated the service is from a client-server standpoint). Let's say we're running an instance of *Apache* on one of the servers in the DMZ with the IP address 192.168.99.20, and we'd like external users to be able to access that server using one of our Internet-valid addresses, 172.18.1.10. In fact, we may add other services later, so we'd like to map that IP for all ports and protocols:

```
# info.mancill.com -> 192.168.99.20
hafnium:~# iptables --table nat -j DNAT -A PREROUTING            \
                    --destination 172.18.1.10                   \
                    --to-destination 192.168.99.20
```

This works like a charm for connections made *to* this server. The rule matches during pre-routing and modifies the destination, and the connection tracking code takes care of modifying the source address of reply packets. In other words, you don't have to worry about setting up rules to SNAT the reply packets from 192.168.99.20; from the client's perspective, they are having a conversation with 172.18.1.10 (given that the client is not on that same DMZ segment, of course). If 192.168.99.20 were to initiate a connection, say send some outgoing SMTP, this rule would not get involved. If you need this connection masqueraded or source-nat'ed, you'll need to take care of that with another rule. This is fortunate, because it separates the rule-space used when the system in question acts as a client and when it acts as a server. Very flexible . . . .

Now, let's consider the when your topology isn't as simple as that depicted in Figure 9.4. Many times, there will already be an access router in place, perhaps not a Linux device, as it is in Figure 9.5. Many times folks insert a firewall between the access router and their DMZ as an additional layer of protection or to overcome some of the shortcomings of their access router. In this case, traffic for 172.18.1.10 will arrive at the access router. What happens next depends upon the nature of that segment between the access router and the firewall. If the access router has a route for 172.18.1.0/29, say, that uses the IP address of *eth2* on the firewall as the gateway, we're fine using the configuration above. The packet will be forwarded to our firewall; the prerouting hook will catch the destination address and perform the destination NAT to send the packet into the DMZ.

But quite frequently in smaller shops that have experienced growth, this is not the scenario. Many times, the access router was originally the only firewall and is configured such that the segment directly connected to its *eth0*, the *no-man's land segment*, is the 172.18.1.0/29 segment. If the router is vendor managed or run by the jerks up at HQ, you might not have much say in reconfiguring it. Another common case is when the organization originally started with a very small allocation of addresses. 172.18.1.0/29 has six usable addresses after you account for the network and broadcast address, and the access router needs one of them. Back when Maw and Paw were taking 5–10 orders a week via that high-tech Internet thingie, the outfit had more than enough address space. This is the *What would we ever do with more than one server?*[6] syndrome. Asking yourself how you got into this situation may be be useful for planning a complete topology overhaul, but dwelling too long on questions like this will turn you into a bureaucrat and doesn't get the job done. We're taking another one of the IP addresses for the *eth2* interface on the firewall/NAT router, which leaves us with four. We shouldn't fret

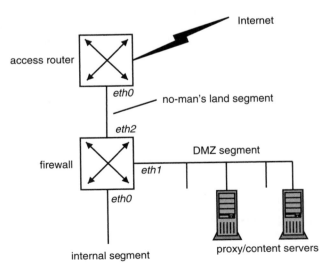

Figure 9.5 DNAT Firewall with a Separate Access Router Topology

---

[6]Or more than 640K?!?

the one for *eth2* because it's the address we're using to masquerade our outgoing traffic, and therefore well worth it.

To deploy our web server to be accessible from the outside with an address of 172.18.1.4 means that the server needs to exist on that no-man's-land segment, right? Let's think about what's going to happen. The access router is going to receive a packet with a destination of 172.18.1.4. Because this is part of the network directly attached to its *eth0*, it will assume that it can ARP for this address on that segment. But the web server is physically on the DMZ segment, so it will never see the ARP request, and it has another IP address anyway. Are we stuck? Never! All we need to do is to add the 172.18.1.4 address to the firewall's *eth2* interface with `ip addr add 172.18.1.4/32 dev eth2`. Now the firewall will respond to ARP requests for this IP address and will receive the packet. Because the `PREROUTING` chain is traversed before `INPUT`, we don't have to worry about our input rules, which should drop almost everything, adversely affecting the web server. We can do this with multiple IP addresses and, because we can match destination ports with our `DNAT` rules, spread out those four available server addresses into 5 × *number of services* servers, assuming that we can use the IP address of the firewall's *eth2* for any services we're not providing via the firewall. This is probably worth about twenty IP addresses for a typical shop.

9.2.4   Alternatives to DNAT

Configuring your firewall's physical interface with multiple IP addresses is not the only way to address this issue. Another popular method is through the use of **proxy ARP**. This is close to what we just did with destination NAT, but a twist. Instead of using private address space for our DMZ, we're going to use the same Internet-valid address space on both the DMZ and the no-man's-land segments and trick the access router into forwarding its packets to the firewall. Er, sorta. Proxy ARP is nothing new; it's the way in which a client dialed into a modem server can access a gateway that's not directly part of the modem server. In that situation, the modem server proxy ARPs the gateway address on behalf of the dial-in client. To achieve this configuration is a bit subtle, consisting of the following steps for our topology in Figure 9.5:

1. The access router isn't touched. Let's say its *eth0* has the IP address 172.18.1.1.

2. We configure both the *eth1* and *eth2* interfaces on the firewall with the same IP address, 172.18.1.2. You'll want to be on the console when you do this, or be using another private IP address to access the firewall.

3. OK, we're in a bit of pickle, because nothing works very well now. Let's remove the routes for the 172.18.1.0/29 network from both *eth1* and *eth2* with `ip route del 172.18.1.0/29 dev eth1 ; ip route del 172.18.1.0/29 dev eth2`.

4. With this configuration, we can't talk to the access router at all, so let's add a **host route** for the access router with `ip route add 172.18.1.1/32 dev eth2`.

5. Now here comes the sly part. Add the route for the Internet-valid address space back to the DMZ segment (*eth1*) in the normal way. `ip route add 172.18.1.0/29 dev eth1`.

6. At this point, the firewall can speak to the systems on the DMZ network, but the access router still can't. Here's where we finally get to the proxy ARP part. You can enable proxy ARP for an interface by writing "1" to the */proc/sys/net/ipv4/conf/**device**/proxy_arp* file. In our case, substitute *eth1* and *eth2*, and we're done.

There's a nice example of this type of configuration available at *http://www.sjdjweis.com/ linux/proxyarp/* along with a script suitable for firewall use. In the last step, note that we enabled proxy ARP on both interfaces. This is necessary because the hosts on the DMZ segment are still going to use the IP address of the access router for their default gateway. So *eth1* needs to proxy those ARP requests for the access router, just as *eth2* will be proxying ARP requests for the machines on the DMZ segment. This technique can be used to insert a firewall without having to touch the existing access router or the servers on the DMZ segment. Pretty neat, eh?

> ### Hint: Firewalling with Proxy ARP
>
> At this point you should be asking yourself, *If we decide to deploy the proxy ARP topology, how do we build our firewall?* It's a valid question. The answer is that, despite the proxy ARP, the packets are still being forwarded by the kernel. (So make sure IP forwarding is enabled.) Thus we can address our filtering needs using the `FORWARD` chain in the `filter` table, just as we did when we spoke of conditional forwarding in Section 7.3.2.

For our proxy ARP stealth firewall, do we lose anything over the DNAT configuration? Not really. We can still use DNAT rules in the `PREROUTING` chain, and we can always IP alias *eth1* on the DMZ and multinet that segment with another subnet of private address space. There is yet another approach to this that utilizes the bridging support in the Linux kernel along with some extensions to *netfilter/iptables* to allow your Linux system to act like a filtering switch. At the time of writing, the project is still under development and is available as a patch against the 2.4 kernel source. I haven't used this facility, so I won't pretend and walk you through a sample configuration here, but it's an interesting approach. In my mind, any functionality that helps you conceptualize a solution is worth knowing about. You can read up on bridging+firewalling at *http://bridge.sourceforge.net/*.

And that concludes our discussion on the various forms of redirection, destination NAT, and proxy ARP. Hopefully it gives you a good idea of how to think about firewalls providing services and flexibility at the same time they protect from unwanted traffic. They can even solve some sticky topology migration problems for us, using techniques that can be used in other situations as well. One word of caution before you go out and proxy ARP your network to bits. While technically there's nothing wrong with doing lots of proxy ARP and DNAT around the inside of your network, keep in mind that an easy-to-follow, intuitive topology will make documentation and sharing your work with others less stressful for all involved. Fortunately, things are getting better with Linux and complex topologies. If you're interested, take a look at Section 10.7, which includes the materials from this section in the first edition of the book. You could do a fair amount with the 2.2 kernel, but things could become rapidly obfuscated if you tried to do too much. But for firewall topologies, ignore all that and do whatever gives you the best combination of security, performance, and flexibility. The next section takes us up a level to talk about Internet services. After all, what good is a fancy TCP/IP stack if you cannot do anything with it?

9.3 General Internet Services on Routers

This book has intentionally tried not to get overly involved with how to run a particular type of router. The topics were chosen, for the most part, because they are applicable to many router applications. If you need to run an Internet shop and have questions, you should refer to the *LDP* documentation or one of the books already published about using Linux as an Internet system. However, I would be remiss not to share some knowledge I have gained about running Internet services on Linux routers. The section is divided into different services which are likely to coexist with a router, and it includes points I learned during my encounters with these.

9.3.1   Internet DNS on a Router

We have to cover this one first, because it can be the main sticking point concerning the other services. DNS daemons run fine on routers; we covered this in Section 8.2.1. The potential issue has to do with how packets are formed by the IP stack. Remember that when Linux originates a packet, it populates the IP source address field of the packet to be the IP address of the sending interface. The point to remember when planning to use DNS is that you run your daemon on your Internet router; the default route points out over that router interface on the Internet link. This is worth mentioning, because this address space may not be part of the address space allocated to you by your ISP. Consider the following situations:

- The Internet link runs PPP. The point-to-point IP addresses may or may not belong to you—meaning that you may not have authority to register them with the InterNIC. If this is the case, and your ISP will not cooperate with you on registering the IP address to correspond to your domain name, you need to work around the problem. The easiest solutions are either to run DNS on a different system or configure the DNS daemon on the router to bind to a specific interface which *is* part of your address space. (Most DNS daemons support this; see the hint below.)

  If you do not own any IP address space of your own whatsoever, you have issues. (This is the case for many sites operated using cable modems or noncommercial DSL providers.) The issue is, when you go to register your IP address with the InterNIC as the primary nameserver for your domain, you'll have to give them the (Internet-valid) IP address of the system, i.e., the PPP or cable modem interface. When they perform a reverse lookup on this (i.e., resolve the IP address into a name), they will see that the name is already registered with the InterNIC, and it belongs to a zone which is not yours. You will not have authority to register that IP address as a nameserver for your domain without permission from the IP's owner (your ISP). Your ISP may be helpful and submit the nameserver request on your behalf. However, the ISP may refuse, or charge you a handsome sum.

- The Internet link runs Frame Relay. In this case, the address at both ends of the Frame Relay PVC may not be intended to be Internet-routable (and you must have some Internet address space). This has no effect on traffic which flows through the point-to-point, but it has serious consequences for traffic which may originate from your router. If you run DNS on this system, people will be able to send you queries, because they will be using the Internet-valid IP address of the router (most likely on the *eth0* interface). They will receive your replies, even if the Frame Relay interface does not have an Internet-valid IP address, because it has the right destination address and is headed in the right direction. When your machine makes queries, however, they will be from your unroutable address. They will go out into the Internet with bogus source addresses, never to be heard from again. The same fate would befall any masqueraded internal traffic bound for the Internet. If the address is Internet-routable but does not belong to you, then the situation is the same as described above for PPP.

It all seems like a rip-off, eh? Not only do you have to purchase your domain name, pay for a port at the ISP, pay for access, buy the router, pay a bunch of setup fees, but now you can't even do anything without buying some address space! (And registering it ... and waiting ....) If you truly have a single IP address, or an address (or addresses) which belongs to your ISP, you are going to have to find someone else to host your DNS, do without, or break down and get some IP addresses.

Hint: Binding Services to a Specific IP Address

TCP/IP allows you to use the `bind()` system call to bind the socket to a particular interface (really an IP address); you can force the outgoing packets to contain your source IP of choice, provided that it belongs to an interface directly attached to that machine. (BTW, do not confuse `bind()`, the system call, with *Bind*, the DNS daemon.) Properly coded Unix network applications should allow this to be configured, and default to binding to address *0.0.0.0* if no address is specified. (Binding to address is done by binding to `INADDR_ANY`.) Still, many do not.

The *Bind* daemon does, which is extremely useful in situations like those described previously in this section. Refer to the documentation; the keywords you need are `query-source listen-on`, which are part of the `options` statement. After editing the configuration file and restarting the daemon, take a look at *syslog* to make sure that the configuration does what you want it to.

If you would like more information on the topic, or are coding your own Internet-capable daemons, see the manpages for `bind()`, `accept()`, `listen()`, and `connect()` (all in Section 2 of the man database), or pick up a copy of the classic and authoritative work on the subject by W. Richard Stevens, *Unix Network Programming: Networking Apis: Sockets and Xti (Volume 1)*.

9.3.2 HTTP and NNTP on a Router

The issues you may have with running a web server on your Internet router are, in essence, the same as those for DNS, but they are, for the most part, not as severe. For one, many HTTP daemons also allow you to specify the IP address(es) they should bind to. Even if yours does not, people accessing an HTTP server rarely perform a reverse lookup on the IP address of the web server to make sure that it matches the forward name lookup.

This may not be the case for other services, though, such as NNTP (used for a Usenet news feed). Let's say that you have only the single fixed IP address that your ADSL provider issued you, and you have found someone else with an established nameserver to provide forward resolution for your domain. Therefore, when people connect to *www.yourdomain.com*, their system will query DNS for the IP associated with that name. Their DNS system will find your NS and then your A record, and return *w.x.y.z*, the IP address of your ADSL interface. So far, so good ... but if an upstream news server were to perform a reverse lookup on this IP address, it would return *someip.at.adsl.provider.com*, which does not match *www.yourdomain.com*. If you connect to an upstream server that uses DNS-based access control, be sure to give them the **canonical** name of your system, i.e., the *someip.at.adsl.provider.com* address.

HTTP daemons also allow you to indicate which server name you would like to use for the server. Although the name should correspond to a valid DNS name (either an A record or a CNAME) for that web server, it does not need to be the canonical hostname, nor necessarily a name which corresponds to the IP which will be used to service the requests.

9.3.3   FTP on a Router

Serving FTP should be no problem. There is one "gotcha," again with DNS, but this time affecting clients. The FTP daemon may want to perform a successful reverse DNS lookup (IP to FQDN) for all client connections.

> ### True Story: Lousy FTP Server Performance
>
> I once had a call about a performance problem with the FTP server. The client complained that when he tried to connect to the service, it would hang for several minutes and then time out. I checked the server and there was no load, and no mention of connections from the client's domain in the logfile. As it turns out, the problem was that the client's firm had just switched over to a new Internet link and did not have a IP-to-name mapping for the external IP address their firewall was using to access the FTP server. Before the FTP daemon would do anything with the incoming connection, it would attempt a reverse lookup for the connecting IP to place this in the log. In this case, it took several minutes for the lookup to time out, and the client would drop the connection before the lookup timed out, so the FTP daemon was not even logging the connection attempt. A couple of entries in */etc/hosts* fixed things up until the client's DNS zones were configured correctly. In this situation, being able to take a look at the *ftpd* sources was very useful.

BTW, the requirement that a connecting system have a DNS resolvable IP address is something that can be enforced by *tcpd* and its configuration files, */etc/hosts.allow* and */etc/hosts.deny*. If you are having trouble connecting to a server which you know is running the service you are requesting, it could be a routing problem, it could be a masquerading problem, but many times it's either DNS or the *tcpd* configuration on the target.

9.3.4   *Sendmail* on a Router

Sendmail (and other MTAs) may be a mixed bag. Let's think about about the functions that they need to perform. First, they have to send mail (prophetic, eh?). Next, they have to be able to receive mail and to forward it as necessary, also known as **relaying**. (I am not addressing the case when mail is to be delivered locally and stored on server; IMO, except for small installations, it is not very appropriate for a router.)

Receiving mail should not be a problem. Your DNS configuration needs only an MX record which lists your router as an appropriate Mail eXchanger for your domain. Some senders may be disturbed by the fact that your forward and reverse DNS lookups do not match; they may generate a warning message, but they probably won't refuse to deliver mail to you on these grounds.

Sending mail, however, has issues similar to serving DNS. Furthermore, because of the recent campaigns against spam, some other problem situations may occur. First, you are likely to find mail systems refusing to accept mail from servers which are not properly resolvable in DNS. Second, some mail servers may reject your mail based on the sender address (or **domain**), if that domain does not correspond (once again, in DNS) to the domain of the sending system. Finally, you may have problems if your point-to-point link to the Internet is not routable, since not all MTAs allow configuring a bind-to address as we discussed for our DNS daemon.

The DNS and routing issues listed here are applicable to most Internet services. To summarize, some services like to be able to validate that the IP address and hostname are a matching pair in DNS. More specifically, the canonical hostname should match the IP address being used to send traffic to the Internet. This is probably a holdover from earlier times when the predominant security mechanisms were IP-based. The idea still has merit, because it means that the machines on the other end were configured by someone who took the time to configure their DNS properly, and when required, registered their servers with the InterNIC. However, with the explosive growth of the Internet, things have changed. Many people running domains have never even read an RFC. In their defense, they (we) are asked to support an environment with more protocols, less knowledgeable users, and significantly more volume than before. Still, it never hurts to know what you're talking about.

A subtle variation on this theme, not related to DNS, may occur for internal WAN links which use "unroutable" IP addresses for the point-to-point interfaces. An administrator sitting on a router tries to *telnet* to a host on a remote network to test the link. The link seems to be up, but the host never replies. This is because the *telnet* client binds its socket to address INADDR_ANY when trying to connect to the remote host. Instead of using the hostname IP for the source field in the packet, the kernel places the IP address of the interface used to send the packet. The packets reach the intended destination, but that destination may not be able to find a route back to the IP address of the point-to-point interface on the router. The frustrated network admin is confused, because there does not appear to be anything wrong with the link or its routing configuration. For internal links, one solution was offered in Chapter 5 on page 154. Another solution is to ensure that all internal IP addresses, including those that are part of the point-to-point, are routable by getting the right information into the routing tables on all of your routers. Daemons which take care of this are the topic of the next section.

Hint: Zero-Node Networks Revisited

You may recall back in Section 5.3.4 that we said that we could "stretch" a subnet to include a WAN interface on the other end of a point-to-point link. We did this by assigning an address out of that subnet to both the near and far ends of the point-to-point and using a subnet mask of 255.255.255.255. The motive was to save address space by not assigning a distinct subnet to the link itself.

The Linux kernel will let you take this one step further. Because network interfaces are known to the kernel by their names, and not just by their IPs, two different interfaces on a single system may have the same IP address.[7] This makes the most sense for Internet routers and other WAN routers, where the distinction between the WAN interface and the Ethernet interface is necessary only for the routing table. In other words, users of the system don't care which of the interfaces they are using.

To use this feature, assign the IP address to the Ethernet interface along with its regular subnet mask. Assign the same IP address to the near end of the point-to-point and use a subnet mask of 255.255.255.255. (The far end can share the IP of its router's Ethernet interface, too.) Presto—no more worries about two IPs in DNS, or IP-based authentication confusion!

---

[7]Thanks to David Mandelstam for sharing this tidbit with me. I wish I had known it sooner!

9.4   Dynamic Routing Daemons

For some applications, it is not possible to manually configure your routing table with a series of *route add* statements. It may be that the entries will frequently change, or that there are simply so many entries that you cannot enter them all by hand. Or you might simply find typing routing statements into scripts and having to maintain those scripts on all of your systems tedious. Several alternatives are available to set up your Linux router for dynamic routing. They take the form of user-space daemons which read their configuration from local files, listen for routing updates on a network socket, and periodically broadcast their routing table out over their interfaces to their **neighbors**. Machines interested in routing information will receive these broadcasts and update their routing tables accordingly. In this manner, you do not have to type in much of anything, and as long as everything is configured correctly, your network should quickly converge upon a stable routing configuration.

Before you load one of these on your router, understand that they are not for everybody. Certain types of network topologies lend themselves more readily to certain routing protocols; others do not lend themselves to being managed by daemons at all. If you are new to routing protocols, you should do some homework with a book before you crank one up and bring down your network. Also keep in mind that for many topologies, a well-designed internal network can be managed with static routes with less overhead and greater ease than with these daemons. But that is admittedly a manner of opinion.

9.4.1   The *routed* Routing Daemon for Linux

routed is the original, if you will, of routing daemons. It supports **RIP**, the Routing Information Protocol, which was originally designed by Xerox and implemented by the program *GWINFO*. This was renamed *routed* and brought to the mainstream Unix world via BSD 4.2. It is originally described in RFC 1058 (which is known as **RIPv1**) and has the variants **RIPv2** (RFC 1388 → 1723 → 2453) and **RIPng** (for use with IPv6, documented in RFC 2080). The version distributed with Linux covers **RIPv1**.

If you want to load it on your system, check to see if it is already there. It is part of the original *NetKit* for Linux and is typically distributed as part of the base installation. Under Debian, it is part of the **netstd** package. By default, it is disabled, but you can enable it by editing */etc/init.d/netstd_init* and then starting the service with `/etc/init.d/netstd_init start`.

Configuring *routed*

There is no configuration file per se, but there are a few options you might want to modify. You can set these in *netstd_init* so that they will be set to your liking the next time that you stop and start the service.

-d enables debugging, which will log some extra information via *syslog* (by default into */var/log/syslog*).

-g instructs the daemon to advertise routing information about its default route gateway (if it has one). Use this with care, as your topology might not take well to having one default route replaced with another.

-s | **-q** control whether or not *routed* will generate information about its machine's interfaces and routes. The choice is either to say (-s) or remain quiet (-q). Note that the default is to say for machines with multiple network interfaces (i.e., routers) and to remain quiet on machines with a single interface. Either switch will override the default behavior.

In addition to these switches, you can affect *routed* by configuring the file */etc/gateways*, which is read when *routed* starts. Each line in */etc/gateways* indicates whether a certain gateway should be considered **passive**, **active**, or **external**.

- An **active** gateway is treated like any other active interface on the system, i.e., routing information about it is shared with others, and an entry for it is entered into the running kernel.

- A **passive** gateway will be added to the routing table, but it will not be broadcast as part of the RIP packets.

- An **external** gateway is neither advertised nor added to the kernel's routing table.

A line in */etc/gateways* very closely corresponds to a `route add` statement, as you can see in the following format (or by reviewing the manpage for *routed*):

<net|host> *destIP* **gateway** *gwIP* **metric** *value* **<passive|active|external>**

One final comment about the *routed* process itself. It does not fork and detach itself from the shell where you start it (i.e., it doesn't go daemon). If you start it in the foreground and then want to detach it from your terminal, you can hit **CTRL-Z** and then the command **bg**. Another thing you should know about *routed* is that it will make its own entries into the routing table as it sees fit for anything that isn't marked **external**, regardless of what is currently in your running routing table. If you have static routes already set up, this is an annoyance, so you will either want to adjust */etc/gateways* or quit walking the fence—use either static or dynamic routing, but not both. You may notice that *routed* creates routing entries for net routes for directly attached networks the traditional way, with an explicit gateway IP address. This will look either peculiar or familiar to you, depending upon where you earned your router wings.

ripquery

Say that you would like to know what a router running *routed* is advertising to the world (without running one of the packet sniffers covered in Section 3.3). You can use the *ripquery* command to get the contents of that system's routing table according to *routed*. If you are on the router itself, issue the command `ripquery localhost`. For a remote router, use the hostname or IP address of that router in the place of *localhost*. The command also supports a single switch.

-n is the ubiquitous **n**o **n**ame lookups. On my setup, this seemed to be of little use except to prevent `name ???` from being spit out after each line in the results of the query. No amount of prodding of */etc/networks* or */etc/hosts* or their associated configuration files seemed to help. (You should be able to recognize the subnets returned by the query anyway.)

Additional information about *routed* can be found by reviewing the applicable RFCs or the source code itself. When you go to look for it, remember that it is part of the *NetKit*.

9.4.2   The *zebra* Routing Daemons for Linux

zebra is the first full-featured routing daemon to gain popularity and be 100% free (GPL). At the time of writing, it is still beta software, but it is functional. It is being developed by some talented programmers and could surely use the support of the free software community to help test and contribute patches. The following is taken from the website at *http://www.zebra.org*:

GNU Zebra is a free software (distributed under GNU Generic Public License) which manages TCP/IP based routing protocols. It supports BGP-4 protocol as described in RFC 1771 (A Border Gateway Protocol 4) and RIPv1, RIPv2 and OSPFv2.

Zebra uses multi-thread technology under multi-thread supported Unix kernels. However, it can be run under non-multi-thread supported Unix kernels.

Zebra is intended to be used as a Route Server and a Route Reflector. Zebra is not a toolkit; it provides full routing power under a new architecture. Zebra is unique in design in that it has a process for each protocol.

It also contains support for IPv6, although it's not listed in the description. There is a Debian package (*Zebra*) available, but if you have to build it from the sources, don't despair. They are an excellent example of using the GNU tools to their fullest potential. I was able to build the executables and produce the documentation in ten minutes. The configuration of *Zebra* is covered in the documentation (distributed in TeX format; the `.texi` file). As a bonus for those of you with experience with Cisco, the configuration syntax is similar.

```
### note: you must have the tetex-bin package installed
$ cd zebra-0.92a/doc
$ tex zebra.texi


# to view the documentation
$ xdvi zebra.dvi


# to print it out, assuming that you have
# magicfilter installed properly for your default printer
$ dvips zebra.dvi -o /tmp/zebra.ps
$ lpr /tmp/zebra.ps
```

As mentioned on *Zebra*'s homepage, *Zebra* is different from other routing daemons in that it provides a separate daemon for each routing protocol. The *zebra* daemon itself handles communicating routing updates between the various routing protocol daemons and the kernel. This means that you can run multiple dynamic routing protocols simultaneously, if you are so inclined. Like many routing daemons and router systems, *Zebra* supports a telnet session running on a special port, known as the **VTY** interface. Each of the protocol daemons runs on its own TCP port. If you are using the Debian package, the documentation is in */usr/share/doc/zebra/*. A few other points about the Debian package:

- All of the configuration files are in */etc/zebra/*.

- You control which routing daemons start by listed them in */etc/zebra/daemons*.

We will work through a sample configuration using *Zebra* in Section 9.5, when we'll work through a basic OSPF configuration.

9.4.3 The *Multi-Threaded Routing Toolkit*

If *Zebra* doesn't strike your fancy, you can try *MRTd*, the **M***ulti-threaded* **R***outing* **T***oolkit* **d***aemon*, which is made possible by grants from the NSF and the Intel Corporation.[8] The

---

[8]Although it *sounds* commercial, this sort of sponsorship is really in the grand tradition of TCP/IP itself, which has its roots in DARPA.

presence of money means that everything is organized and there is pretty documentation
(which is also pretty good); they even have a release schedule. *MRTd* is not developed natively
in Linux, so it does not always compile on the first try. On the other hand, it is available for
other platforms.

The latest version at the time of writing includes support for **BGP4+**, **BGP**, **RIPng**,
and **RIP2** (which includes support for **RIP1**), with plans to support **OSPF** for IPv4 and
IPv6 soon. Like *Zebra* and *GateD*, you can interface the daemon via telnet to a well-known
port.

MRTd also comes with a suite of test programs:

- *sbgp*—a utility which can receive BGP4+ messages as well as generate them and inject
  them into the network.

- *sospf*—a simple OSPF speaker and listener, similar in function to *sbgp*.

- *route_btoa*—a utility to convert binary *MRT* messages to ASCII.

- *route_atob*—the other direction of *route_btoa*. This is useful because *MRT* messages can
  be piped into other *MRT* utilities.

- *bgpsim*—a BGP4+ traffic generator for performing simulations.

You check out the documentation and mailing lists and retrieve a copy of the source from
http://www.mrtd.net.

The *GateD* Routing Daemon for Linux

The first edition of this book included material on how to retrieve and compile the *Public
Release for Unicast* version of *GateD*. At that time *GateD* was hosted by *Merit GateD Consortium* at *http://www.gated.org/*. While the URL is still good, it seems that the code is now
the property of *NextHop Technologies*, and there's no openly available version for research or
noncommercial use. If for some reason you just have to look at the *GateD* source, you can
try you luck by emailing *research@nexthop.com*. According to *NextHop's* product literature,
the software has been ported to Linux but is not available precompiled or tested for Linux.
In my opinion, if you're in the market for a commercially supported dynamic routing daemon
for Linux, spend your dollars on support from an organization that supports one of the open
projects. Another excellent way to benefit your company and the community at the same time
is to purchase support directly from the open software developers, when possible. The support
will be directly from the author, and your patronage improves the software, making it more
stable and you more self-reliant.

9.5   OSPF Walkthrough Using *Zebra*

We've made it a long way into this book and accomplished much with our Linux routers
using static routes. But static routes won't always get the job done. Often, a service provider
or business partner will require that you run a dynamic routing protocol to interface with
their network. Particularly, if you are multihomed on the Internet—i.e., you have more than
one firewall/router connecting your internal network to the outside—you may find that the
outside needs you to present your internal routes in a protocol it understands (often BGP4). In
general, if you control only part of a changing, growing network, but need to to communicate

with all of it, you will find it difficult to keep up with the static routing changes. Nor are you likely to find others interested in adding static routes toward your network. Dynamic routing protocols can exchange routes as well as additional information, such as link bandwidth or the number of hops between two networks. The use of dynamic routing daemons can achieve certain functionalities, such as automatic failover, without going through the rigamarole in Section 8.5.1. Oh yeah, and they keep you from having to manually configure static routes on your routers, too. To illustrate some of the capabilities of these daemons, we're going to configure *Zebra* to run the **OSPF**, or Open Shortest Path First, protocol in a test environment.

9.5.1   OSPF 101

OSPF is link state protocol designed to perform interior routing on TCP/IP networks. **Link state** means that the protocol keeps tabs on all of the links within an **area**, and each router running the protocol computes the optimal route based its own internal representation of the network topology. The other main family of routing protocols are **distance vector** protocols, which operate by trading information with other routers about the "distance" (often the number of hops) to a given subnet from their current location. These protocols learn routes over time, as the relative distances to destination networks are gleaned from the information shared by their **neighbors** (routers with interfaces on the same segment). Examples of this type of protocol are RIP, IGRP, and EIGRP.

We also stated that OSPF is an interior protocol; this implies that it is designed for use within an **AS** (Autonomous System), which really means nothing more than within your own network, as opposed to between your network and some other network you don't control. Finally, the term **area** is actually a keyword used in the configuration of OSPF that refers to an administrative domain or portion of your network. Dividing the network up into areas is done for two reasons: First, link state protocols can chew up a lot of memory and CPU calculating routes based on the state of every link in your network. Second, transmitting link states, also known as **LSAs** (Link State Advertisements) to every router, even the ones way over there, can become bandwidth intensive. This is especially true if your areas are separated by WAN links, which implies that the only way to get over there is via that link, and those two routers already know about each other. So you can divide your network into areas which correspond to one or more larger subnet groupings, similar to the way we divvied up the RFC 1918 private address space in Section 2.1.5. Finally, we stated that OSPF is for TCP/IP networks. It pretty much has to be, because it uses raw IP protocol 89 (0x59).

OSPF has a number of other features, such as the ability to assign a designated router (DR) and backup designated router (BDR) on network segments that support broadcasts, such as your standard Ethernet segment. Once a DR is elected, it handles sharing updates with other routers on the segment. This saves bandwidth when there are more than two routers on that single segment; without it, every router would need to transmit its latest LSA information to all of its neighbors (i.e., every other router on that segment). The [B]DR router is elected through a process that suspiciously resembles the way that Windows NT servers hold Master Browser elections. Bandwidth is also conserved by the use of multicast addresses instead of broadcast. There is also a concept of internal routers versus backbone routers (BRs) versus area border routers (ABRs) versus autonomous system boundary routers (ASBRs). These classifications differentiate between routers within a given area, routers connected to area 0 (designated as the backbone), routers with interfaces in more than one area, and routers on the edge of the autonomous system, which may mean that they trading routing tables with a router running a different routing protocol. OSPF supports the idea of a link **cost**, or a relative metric to determine which route is preferable (or "shortest"). This value normally is based on the amount of the bandwidth but may also be tuned to account for per-byte charges or reliability issues. The protocol can even split traffic across two paths of equal cost. Furthermore, OSPF supports authentication for messages passed between routers to prevent curious users from playing along. While these are good things to know about OSPF, and there is a great deal more to study, let's wrap up the introduction and get ready to use it.

9.5.2 A Minimal Test Topology for OSPF

In order to start working with dynamic routing protocols, you'll need to construct a test environment. If there is a potential for your testing to disrupt your production environment, make sure the environments are sufficiently isolated from each other. Also, because most dynamic routing protocols use either broadcasts or multicasts to communicate among themselves, several hubs of switches and a fistful of patch cables will help you simulate hierarchical network topologies. Another option I use for simple topologies is to build my test environment using several VMware instances running on a decent workstation. (VMware is covered in Section C.4.)

For OSPF, you can get away with a just a pair of machines if you'd like to watch them trade their routing-table information. For our example, we're going to use the topology depicted in Figure 9.6, which is the simplest example I could concoct that would not only illustrate sharing of routing-table information but also demonstrate the use of a dynamic routing daemon to handle interface failure. In this case, osmium is our gateway to the world, as depicted by the link on the left. It normally communicates with sulfur and copper over its primary interface on the 192.168.168.0/24 segment, but should that interface fail, sulfur and copper would be able to reroute traffic bound for the outside world over the 192.168.18.0/24 link. Admittedly, it could just as well be the 192.168.16.0/24 segment that fails, but the idea here is to build a test lab without having to go shopping (or particularly, adding another interface to sulfur). In this topology, sulfur need not be a proper router with multiple interfaces and workstations using it as a gateway. Even as a single-homed workstation, sulfur will still see the benefit of receiving dynamic routing updates from *ospfd* running on the other two machines; it's just not likely to have anything to contribute.

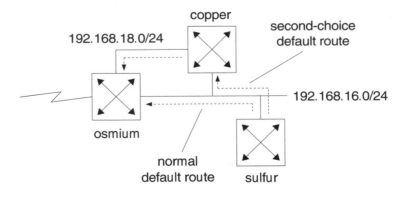

Figure 9.6 OSPF Test Topology

2.4 Kernel Configuration for *Zebra* and OSPF

Next, we may need to do a little work to prepare our workstations to run *Zebra* with OSPF. To be quite truthful, I pulled a little hair out over this. To support *Zebra*'s ability to communicate with the kernel's routing table and multicast, you would think that you'd need CONFIG_NETLINK, CONFIG_RTNETLINK, and CONFIG_IP_MULTICAST, just as the *Zebra* documentation suggests—that is, something along the lines of:

```
Networking options --->
   <*> Packet socket
   <*> Netlink device emulation
   [*]    Routing messages
(OR, depending upon your exact 2.4 kernel version)
   [*] Kernel/User netlink socket
   [*] TCP/IP networking
   [*]    IP: multicasting
(and perhaps even these)
   [*]    IP: multicast routing
   [*]       IP: PIM-SM version 1 support (NEW)
   [*]       IP: PIM-SM version 2 support (NEW)
```

However, all seemingly plausible permutations of these options resulted in the following error message when starting the *ospfd* process, but only on some of my systems:

```
ZEBRA: can't create router advertisement socket:
Address family not supported by protocol
```

In practice what I discovered is that if *Zebra* is built with support for IPv6,[9] even when running the IPv4 versions of the daemons, you can do away with all of the netlink and multicasting options and just enable IPv6 in the kernel. If you'd rather not run IPv6, build your *Zebra* accordingly and enable Kernel/User netlink socket and IP: multicasting.

9.5.3   Configuring and Using *Zebra*

This section is written based upon *Zebra* version 0.92a and using the binary pathnames dictated by the upstream tarball's make install. If you're using your distribution's packaging of *Zebra*, refer to the local README for the correct pathnames. One thing you may find interesting about *Zebra* is that it can be configured entirely after the daemons are running. You do this by connecting to the terminal interface of the daemon(s) running on your system and then giving yourself the needed privileges with the **enable** command. If you have ever worked with a Cisco router, you'll find the interface to be almost identical. However, to be able to use that interface, you'll need to set the enable password, which is controlled via the configuration file.

The makefile installation drops sample configuration files into *∕usr∕local∕etc∕*, and for our example we'll want to copy the *zebra.conf.sample* and *ospfd.conf.sample* over to *zebra.conf* and *ospfd.conf*, respectively. If you take a look at these files, you'll notice that the '!' character is used at the beginning of a line to indicate comments. For the *zebra.conf* file, it should be ready to test as is, with passwords set for both the basic interface and the enabled interface to "zebra" and the name of this router set to "Router." (*Note:* If you are running *Zebra* in

---

[9] As is the case with the Debian *Zebra* package.

a production environment, do not use these default passwords. In fact, because the telnet interface will pass your authentication in the cleartext, you should firewall off the ports the daemons listen on and use only the terminal interface by connecting from the localhost.) I'd recommend changing the **hostname** to match the hostname of your machine. It will make it easy to keep track of once you have a half-dozen telnet windows into your various router daemons. So *zebra.conf* should look like:

```
! -*- zebra -*-
!
hostname osmium
password zebra
enable password zebra
!
! log should be a path to a filename or "stdout"
log /var/log/zebra/zebra.log
```

This file can also contain information about the interfaces on this box such as descriptions and bandwidth, but they aren't required for our example. You can go ahead and start up the *zebra* daemon now, which the install should have placed into */usr/local/sbin/zebra*. By default, it will pick up the configuration file from */usr/local/etc/zebra.conf* (use **-f** *file* to override this) and begin listening for network connections on port 2601 (specify **-P** *port* to use a different port). You can even go ahead and connect to this process using *telnet*:

```
tony@bach:~$ telnet osmium 2601
Trying 192.168.16.1...
Connected to localhost.
Escape character is '^]'.

Hello, this is zebra (version 0.92a).
Copyright 1996-2001 Kunihiro Ishiguro.


User Access Verification

Password: *****
osmium> show ip route
Codes: K - kernel route, C - connected, S - static, R - RIP, O - OSPF,
       B - BGP, > - selected route, * - FIB route

K>* 0.0.0.0/0 via 192.168.1.1, eth0
C>* 127.0.0.0/8 is directly connected, lo
C>* 192.168.1.0/24 is directly connected, sppp0
C>* 192.168.16.0/24 is directly connected, eth0
C>* 192.168.18.0/24 is directly connected, eth1
osmium>
```

In the output above, we connected to the running instance of *zebra*, supplied the password from the configuration file, and then issued the **show ip route** command, which shows us the current routing table. The routes designated with C correspond to interfaces on this system, and the K route is the default route from the kernel. Among other facts about the configuration of osmium, we can ascertain from this output that 192.168.1.1 is on the other end of the link connected to *sppp0*. Now, there are many commands you can issue at the prompt—it is really like learning another shell—but here are the bare minimum you need to know if you are new to this type of interface:

- `list`—display all applicable commands. As you work with the interface, you'll notice that the list of commands available depends upon your current context. For example, are you running in privileged mode? Are you currently configuring the running daemon?

- `show ?`—display the list of valid arguments for `show` in the current context. You can actually use `?` after any command, or command with partially supplied arguments, to see what arguments are allowed. Try this with `show ip ?` and you'll discover that you can display either the routing table or the status of IP forwarding on the system. One gotcha is that after using `?`, your command and argument line will be repeated on the next prompt up to the point where you hit `?`. (This can be annoying until you get used to it.)

- **TAB**—autocompletion. If you are accustomed to using *bash*, then you'll feel at home with this feature, as with the up-arrow key, which will walk through the command history. If an unambiguous amount of the command or argument has been specified, hitting the TAB key will autocomplete it for you. If the completion is still ambiguous, you'll see the possible completions listed out. If only one argument is possible, hitting TAB will retrieve it for you. In general, you have to specify only enough of a command and argument such that it is unambiguous to the interface. For example, try `sh in<TAB>` and then specify an interface on your box. This will give you *Zebra*'s version of *ifconfig*.

- `enable`—enable privileged commands. This will get you to a prompt where you can turn on debugging and configure the daemon directly through this interface. It will prompt you for the password you set in the configuration file, and once you're in this mode, the prompt will change to `bach#`.

- `quit`—drops you out of the interface.

9.5.4   Configuring *ospfd* for *Zebra*

Recall from Section 9.4.2 that the *zebra* is merely an interface between the various dynamic routing protocol daemons and the kernel. So we aren't running a dynamic routing protocol until we configure one of these. Since we're working with OSPF, we need to start up */usr/local/sbin/ospfd*, but not before we spend a little time with the configuration file. Besides setting the passwords for the terminal interface, we need to tell OSPF which network interfaces it should use to advertise LSAs. This is done by first specifying `router ospf`, because without it, the daemon will start but it won't actually speak OSPF with anybody. Next, add a `network` *subnet/mask* `area` *area* line for each interface that is to be used by the daemon. Note that the network address and subnet mask should match that of the interface or else it won't be used. The configuration file for osmium is:

```
!
! Zebra configuration saved from vty
!   2002/01/24 22:30:20
```

```
!
hostname osmium-ospf
password zebra
enable password zebra
log file /var/log/zebra/ospfd.log
!
router ospf
 network 192.168.16.0/24 area 4
 network 192.168.18.0/24 area 4
 default-information originate
```

Notice that we specify an area of 4, but that this is completely arbitrary. We could have used 0, the backbone, or any other area. Just remember that OSPF routers will construct a topological database for all of the link states/interfaces in that area, so you can use this to partition larger networks based on your needs. (You can also specify the area as a dotted-quad, just like an IP address.) For now, let's assume that osmium is in a satellite office that we're designating to be area 4. I've also thrown in another configuration option, `default-information originate`, which tells the daemon that this router should share default routes if it has them. Go ahead and start *ospfd* and *tail* the logfile.

You'll want to configure sulfur and copper similarly. Just replace the hostname as appropriate and leave out the `default-information originate` as well as the network statement for 192.168.18.0/24 on sulfur (although the daemon will just ignore it, since there is no interface to which the network can be mapped). For maximum effect—i.e., to give yourself a better indication that the daemons really do something for you—remove the default routes from both sulfur and copper, and make sure there isn't a route for 192.168.18.0/24 on sulfur. Both of these boxes should be able to speak only on their directly connected networks. (Er, if you're not on that 192.168.16.0/24 segment, set yourself up so that you are, or you're going to lose your connection.) Now, crank up *ospfd* on both copper and sulfur. *Voila!* You will have default routes on both copper and sulfur. Notice how using *ip* to list your routes on the regular command line will indicate routing entries from *Zebra* with **proto zebra**; **proto kernel** is the route we had previously for segments connected directly to the interface.

```
tmancill@sulfur> ip route list
192.168.18.0/24 via 192.168.16.1 dev eth0  proto zebra  metric 20
192.168.16.0/24 dev eth0  proto kernel  scope link  src 192.168.16.55
default via 192.168.16.1 dev eth0  proto zebra  metric 10
```

9.5.5 OSPF in Action

If you didn't get that *voila* feeling from simply distributing the default route (and a route for 192.168.18.0/24 to sulfur), maybe some of the features in this section will be more impressive. If you didn't get a default route at all, check to make sure that *ospfd* is still running on each system and check the logfiles. Use the telnet interface to connect to port 2601 to compare the routing table *zebra* has with the table shown, using either *ip* or *route* on the command line. You can also start to get comfy with the terminal interface to *ospfd* by using *telnet* to connect to port 2604, the default port for *Zebra*'s *ospfd*. Use the commands **show ip ospf neighbor**, **show ip ospf database**, and **show ip ospf route** to glean a better picture of what is occurring. You might also want to fire up *tcpdump*, which should show plenty of OSPFv2 packets of various flavors and intent flying back and forth. (After your configuration has stabilized, you'll catch only the occasional **OSPFv2-hello**. Just restart the daemons to get another glimpse.)

```
sulfur-ospf> show ip ospf route
============ OSPF network routing table ============
N     192.168.16.0/24      [10] area: (0.0.0.4)
                           directly attached to eth0
N     192.168.18.0/24      [20] area: (0.0.0.4)
                           via 192.168.16.1, eth0
                           via 192.168.16.13, eth0


============ OSPF router routing table ============
R     192.168.18.1         [10] area: (0.0.0.4), ASBR
                           via 192.168.16.1, eth0


============ OSPF external routing table ============
N E2 0.0.0.0/0             [10/10] tag: 0
                           via 192.168.16.1, eth0
```

According to *ospfd* on sulfur, we can reach 192.168.16.0/24 with a metric of 10 via our directly attached interface. 192.168.18.0/24 is accessible via both 192.168.16.1 (osmium) and 192.168.16.13 (copper), in both cases with a metric of 20 (or the default metric of 10 for a hop times 2). Also note that the area is displayed in dotted-quad notation, so don't be confused when area 1000 shows up as (0.0.3.232) or $(3 * 256 + 232)$. If you're going to use a lot of areas, it'll certainly be easier to specify them in dotted-quad notation directly in the config file.

Now, get on sulfur and start a ping of something on the far side of osmium—something that requires that default route we've worked so hard to set up (when all we had to do was run a single *route add* on sulfur in the first place). On osmium, issue *ifconfig eth0 down* and watch your ping on sulfur hang. But OSPF daemons are busy (watch your sniffer traces, too, if you have them), and within a short period of time the routing tables on the affected systems will once again converge on a new path to reach to the default gateway if one exists. In this case, the packets can be forwarded via copper, and the convergence in my test environment took between 10 and 30 seconds.

At this point, we've really only started exploring the features of OSPF and *Zebra*. I'll leave it up to you to develop similar test environments using RIP (watch out, version 1 of the protocol doesn't support variable-length subnet masks [CIDR]) and BGP, add authentication support to all three, configure weighted metrics and costs such that certain links are preferred over others, and so on. *Zebra* will also allow you to work with IPv6-aware versions of the RIP and OSPF protocols (*ripngd* and *ospf6d*). Finally, you can set up the *zebra* to run multiple dynamic routing protocols on the same system and configure them to exchange information with each other, say in the case where you run BGP4 on your Internet gateways but OSPF internally.

A full coverage of the configuration possibilities of any of the dynamic routing daemons fully would range from several chapters to an entire book. If dynamic routing protocols are new to you, do some research and testing before configuring and deploying routers running these daemons. Many good books are available on the topic, either covering the protocols in general or going into explicit detail about configuring them, typically for the Cisco platform. In this, it is fortunate that *Zebra* uses a very similar interface and identical keywords where possible. In any event, don't think that you cannot coexist with *real* routers just because you're running Linux. You can run a real routing daemon on Linux just like anyone else running Solaris boxes or a Cisco r⌐

9.6   Emergency Down Procedures

Pray to God, but keep rowing to shore.
                    — Russian Proverb

So you're running a Linux shop, and everything is peachy. Linux stays up when it's up, and when it fails, there is a logical explanation, and it comes right back up. But what about the one time that it doesn't?—the time when your hard disk gets tired of holding heads away from the platters and decides to let them rest for just a few seconds ... or the time when you kick the power cord out of the machine while it's *very* busy? Some planning and advance preparation, coupled with quick thinking and creativity, will keep your environment running when the outside world conspires to make it do otherwise.

This section contains ideas about how to make your Linux production environment more highly available. You may find some of the strategies uninspiring, or you may disagree with all of them entirely. If you already know better ways, you should use them, and if possible, share them with others. The disclaimer is that they represent what has worked for me in the past. YMMV . . . .

9.6.1   Redundant Services and Servers

Deploying multiple machines, each capable of performing the same task, is the idea behind most of the commercial Unix high-availability suites. Two or more machines perform an orthogonal set of duties when everything is running properly, and they share a common data source (typically a dual-ported SCSI RAID array) for the times when machine$_A$ is down and machine$_B$ needs to take over for a while. During this time, machine$_B$ assumes as much of the identity of machine$_A$ as is feasible. Most clustering software operates upon this same principle, but varies in how it tricks the user into thinking that she is still using machine$_A$. Whether it changes the DNS record being used to access machine$_A$, or performs some sort of transparent proxying, as we configured earlier in this chapter, the idea is still the same. Most of this software is aimed at applications instead of routers, but, as discussed in Chapter 8, a few shell scripts and you can roll your own with routers. Now we extend upon this idea and talk about more ways in which you can bolster the illusion of 100% uptime—the illusion of uptime being far more important than the reality.

Redundant Routers

Because every Linux system can act as a router by using a few simple statements, you can easily have several of your other production machines as potential failovers in times of need. For routers, the key issue is one of connectivity. If you keep this in mind, you will be able to quickly configure one of your other machines to take over the duties of a local network router or a WAN router, should a production router go belly-up. Look at the network topology in Figure 9.7 for one way to do this. The idea is very basic—have machines with an extra NIC available to assume the same connectivity displaced by the down router. To be adequately prepared, you should have a script already written which will configure standby$_A$ to *become* router$_A$. During nonpeak hours you can test your configuration by configuring the interfaces on router$_A$ down and running the script. Once you trust your script and its ability to make standby$_A$ become router$_A$, you can go ahead and work on ways to automate the failover. Because NICs are inexpensive, and scripts are free, there is no reason not to use Linux servers as standby routers at every point in your network.

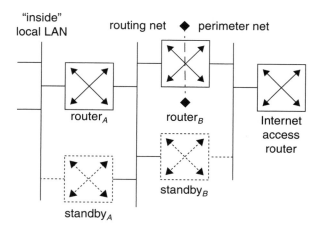

Figure 9.7 Redundant Router Connectivity

Redundant Firewalls

Firewall failover is another story altogether because of security concerns, and what you can do here is largely dependent upon your firewall topology. If you are using proxies, then a second (nonrouting) proxy machine should not pose much of a security risk. You're no more susceptible to attack through one than through the other, and having two (or more) machines might be necessary for your amount of client load. In this case, you might want to use an $N+1$ approach toward allocating backup machines. The configuration of safe packet-filtering rules while allowing ample access to the proxies can get complex. In particular, you will need to forward traffic which traverses the packet filters, but you do not necessarily want to forward traffic which should use only the proxies. If you really need to do this, focus on using forwarding rules to limit traffic instead of input or output filters.

In the case of a packet filter, you probably do not want to have an extra machine connected to your perimeter net at all times. Because a firewall failure is probably important enough to warrant a personal visit, you can have a standby$_B$ ready to take over, but leave it disconnected from the perimeter network. When you need the machine, you can physically connect it to the perimeter network. If you're less paranoid about internal attacks, you can keep the interface connected but configured down.

To summarize, firewall redundancy is well and good, but you should not compromise your overall security model for it. In my opinion, a good firewall might be one that goes down and stays down until an attack is over, and you've had a chance to verify that your system was not violated. An automated failover system which pops up in place of the downed firewall will have the same weaknesses and will suffer the same fate. The issue is that you will not be sure whether the firewall suffered a hardware failure or a software failure except in very special cases. Sometimes a trustworthy human is worth a lot more than clever scripting.

On the other hand, outages are often attributable to human error. Don't cause one because you introduce a shell script syntax error when you make changes to your firewall rules startup script. After any change, you should use `bash -n` *scriptname* or `ksh -n scriptname` to check for typos. Consider what happens if your firewall is restarted with an error in the configuration script. If the script does not configure masquerading, then you have a production outage. If your filters are not in place, then you are running without a firewall.

9.6.2   The Support Server—A "Safe Place"

When you plan for redundancy, do not neglect other important network services. As far as the users are concerned, a DNS or DHCP outage is as tragic and disruptive as a hard-drive crash in the router. As you design your network infrastructure, keep in mind the handiness of being able to copy all of the configuration files around in an automated fashion. If you make changes to the DHCP daemon configuration file, a copy of that file should be transferred to a safe place, as well as to the machine designated to be the standby DHCP server. (DNS takes care of itself with the designation of secondary servers.) Any service crucial to the day-to-day operation of your network should be handled like this. An additional precaution to consider is the habit of saving revisions of these files, if you need to fall back to a previous revision quickly. This might sound like a case for doing away with traditional backups. It almost is. The problem with anything on a tape is that it takes a while to get to it, and you cannot manipulate tapes from a remote location. So where is a good place?

For an environment of any size (more than a couple of machines), I recommend dusting off that old 486/16M machine in the corner, installing a fresh hard drive (and possibly a tape drive), and using this machine as your "Linux environment support server." You can use this server as a software repository; it may be the only machine in your fleet with a CD-ROM drive (so that you can keep a copy of your distribution online and NFS mountable). It will also have any software you use which is not part of your distribution, kernel source and packages, and the configuration files I mentioned previously. You may also want to copy system logs over to this machine for archiving. In fact, this may be the only machine on your network for which you perform full backups.

In most cases, you can use NFS as your configuration-file backup mechanism. If you do this, be sensible about what is backed up and how. For one, you're going to be exporting part of the support machine's filesystem as writable to all of your servers. Export a directory like */usr/local/etc/envbackups*, which may contain a subdirectory for each of the machines in your environment. Your production machines would then mount *carbon:/usr/local/etc/envbackups/ $(hostname)* and copy the files while preserving the modification date (*cp* with the -p option, *cpio* with -m, or *tar* just the way it is). What you copy is up to you, but you could start with the things listed in Section 8.5.2. When you mount the support server, make sure that you use the -o soft option to *mount*, so that your production boxes will not be unhappy should the mount point be temporarily unavailable. Because the files being copied may contain sensitive configuration information, do not neglect to protect the mount points from prying eyes—to keep your "safe place" truly safe. For a less home-grown approach, look into using a centralized CVS server as your central repository and loading the cvs client on all of your production systems.

9.6.3   Minidistributions for a "Warm" Standby

Keep in mind that any machine with a couple of network cards will suffice in a pinch for a LAN router or packet filter. You just need to have a minidistribution which will boot and configure the interfaces and have the firewalling commands available on it. In the case of a simple router, most distributions' rescue floppies are good enough. In particular, you need IP firewalling (and perhaps IP masquerading) support in the kernel plus the configuration binary which corresponds to particular version of the kernel you are running, i.e., *ipfwadm* or *ipchains*. The *Trinux* and *LRP* minidistributions come to mind—refer to the list on page 20 for more choices. In all cases, you will want to have the most recent copy of your firewall rules *easily* accessible. Consider incorporating something like the following step into your firewall change-control procedures:

Every time you change your firewalling rules, make a backup of the previous version of the file and document the changes. The *savelog* command (native to Debian) is a handy way of making backup versions of a file. You should also save a copy of the new rules in a safe place, which means not on the firewall itself. You will need the most current ruleset if you have to configure a new router in a hurry. If you're prone to forget to save a copy, set up a cron job to check the file daily for changes and to mail you the file when it does change. (This is a good idea for the sake of security, too.)

Those of you familiar with change control will recognize this as its simplest and most basic form. There is more text on this in Appendix C, Section C.3.

9.6.4   Rescue Disks

Sometimes you will find yourself (stuck) in the position of having to decide between trying to repair your primary system or falling back to a standby—especially if you know you don't have backups as recent as you might like ... or you know what the problem is and just need a way into the system to patch things up. If you decide to operate to try to save the patient, you will have to start with a rescue floppy (or CD-ROM).

Use of rescue disks refers to placing a copy of the Linux kernel along with some common tools as a compressed image on a floppy disk. When you boot from this floppy, it creates a RAM disk, extracts the compressed root image onto the RAM disk, and then boots using this as the root. Once you're booted (you should not have any hardware problems with just memory and your floppy drive—if you do, get your hands on some more hardware quickly), you can take whatever actions are necessary to repair your system. Typically, this involves mounting the root partition (and possibly others) of your hard drive(s) somewhere underneath the root of the RAM disk. You can then edit files, move/rename files, replace a file with another version, unmount the filesystem, and reboot. (Don't forget to unmount the filesystems before the reboot!)

There are a variety of rescue systems out there; which one you use will depend on your tastes and what you happen to have on hand when you need it. I encourage you to experiment with several so that you are familiar with their particular capabilities and shortcomings. For the most part, they are all impressive feats of space management, but you will find that some have more of what you need for repairing filesystems, while others have what you need to get back on the network just long enough to copy some files from your backup server. They are useful for more than just hardware outages, too. Here are a few common "whoops, I just shot myself in the foot" situations (not really emergency down) where you might find them useful.

- It is embarrassing, but it happens. Lost password(s) can put you in a precarious situation. The best way I have found to deal with them is to wait for an off-peak period, bounce the box (from the console with **CTRL-ALT-DEL**), and boot using a rescue floppy. Let the rescue floppy boot the system and then execute a shell. In this shell, create a directory */tmp/root* and mount the root partition of the hard drive here. Now just `cd /tmp/root/etc` and use the editor on the rescue disk to remove whatever is in the password field for `root` in *./passwd* and *./shadow*. Now `cd /`, `umount /tmp/root`, eject the floppy, and reboot the system. As soon as it it comes up, login as "root" (just hit **ENTER** for the password) and set the password to something you can remember. If you procrastinate fixing the problem, you may find yourself explaining to a user or manager why you cannot make the requested configuration change in the middle of the day without disrupting normal activity.

- Almost as embarrassing as a lost password is a bad kernel gen. If you generate a kernel which will not boot your machine and do not have a backup kernel image configured in your boot loader, you'll have to boot from something standard to get going again. In this case, boot the system from a different kernel, but mount the root filesystem as itself. For the Debian rescue floppy, you can type `rescue root=/dev/hda1` (substitute your root partition for *hda1*) at the `root:` prompt to boot from the same kernel you used to initially load the machine. Once booted, you can log in, clean up the kernel mess, and try again.

- You may encounter a similar situation to the one explained above if you image hard drives from one drive to another. This will confuse your boot manager and prevent it from finding the kernel when you attempt to boot from the newly imaged drive. Once again, boot from rescue media and indicate what the root partition should be. As soon as you're up, issue the command `lilo -v` (or whatever is appropriate for your machine) and then reboot.

Hard-Drive Problems

OK, stupid admin tricks aside, there are problems of another, entirely different class which require rescue disks—namely, any sort of filesystem corruption which renders the root filesystem unmountable. Filesystem corruption typically takes one of four forms.

1. Filesystem metadata are inconsistent due to disk buffers not being flushed before the system was halted. This sort of corruption will occur any time that the system reboots unexpectedly. The *fsck* program will usually set things straight again, as long as it is able to execute (i.e., the root filesystem can be mounted read-only).

2. The hard drive detects a bad block and the controller is unable to relocate it to a good block.[10] Any files or inodes with data in that block are now unreadable. In this case, the severity of the problem depends entirely on where the bad block is located. If it is underneath */lib/ld.so* or */etc/inittab* of */bin/mount*, things will get worse before they get better. On the other hand, it could be located in the middle of nowhere, and you may never notice it. It does not necessarily mean that the drive is failing or that more bad blocks are to be expected.

3. The hard drive is under duress due to any number of physical factors such as failing bearings, excessive heat, etc. This may result in intermittent problems, or it may be the beginning of the very short journey known as "head crash." In this case and in the one above, the best thing to do is to revert to a standby system, try to mount the drive read-only, and salvage what you can (if you need to).

4. Incompatibilities may exist between the kernel and the chipset on your disk controller. I used Linux for five years before I ever experienced anything like this. Boy, was I surprised! The problem was easily corrected, but it was costly in terms of lost time. While these types of incompatibilities are not commonplace, they do exist, as I learned when I appealed to others for reasons why my system had suddenly lost its mind.

   The best way to prevent these is to take heed of the configuration help which comes with the kernel, and to be careful when tuning with *hdparm*. If such a failure occurs,

---

[10] A function of IDE drives.

you will probably know it right away. What typically happens is that the kernel notices the problem and remounts the root filesystem as read-only (as per `errors=remount-ro` in */etc/fstab*). This will break things such as system logging, being able to edit files, and perhaps being able to view manpages but will prevent the bug from destroying the filesystem any further. If you notice something odd with your system all of a sudden, if `touch /tmp/moomoo` fails, then you ought to take a close look at */var/log/kern.log* and */var/log/syslog*.

These problems are of varying degrees of badness, depending upon what is affected. The Linux system tools will patch up problems with the metadata as long as the drive itself is capable of storing and retrieving information accurately. If the drive can boot from itself and clean itself, then you do not have anything to worry about. If the system can mount the root partition read-only but cannot successfully complete a *fsck* run without interaction, then you will be prompted for the root password and will have to run *fsck* manually. This typically amounts to answering "yes" to a slew of arcane questions. (You can save yourself time by specifying `-y` on the command line.) Once the run is complete, you can hit **CTRL-D** to continue.

Things get more interesting if the filesystem cannot be cleaned using the copy of *fsck* on the hard drive. Now you bring in the rescue media, boot from it, and try to clean the filesystem. If this is successful, you may be tempted to mount the partition and take a look, just to see if everything seems to be intact. This is reasonable enough. Furthermore, you can use any of the tools provided with the rescue media to move things around, view the contents of the *lost+found* directory, etc.

Rescue Disks and Dynamically Linked Binaries

Less experienced administrators may get into trouble when they try to use binaries on the mounted root partition. The problem is that those binaries are dynamically linked, and their libraries are not available. If you are not familiar with the difference between dynamically and statically linked binaries, refer to a good text on operating systems concepts. Here is my terse synopsis:

> There are statically linked executables and dynamically linked executables. The static ones are typically much larger but are wholly independent entities. Dynamic executables have advantages in terms of memory and binary size but require a functioning linker-loader and libraries in order to be useful. The end.

Rescue disks typically consist either solely of static binaries or of a pared-down set of dynamic libraries. If there are dynamic libraries on the rescue media, they are almost certainly not the versions against which the binaries on the hard disk are linked. This means that you cannot use the binaries on the disk, or any script requiring an interpreter (or shell) which is not on the rescue media. What's the moral? Don't be fooled into thinking that, once your root filesystem is mounted, you're free and clear to crank up an FTP or *ssh* client. (As a side note, it might not be a bad idea to have printed copies of the *fsck* and *mount* manpages handy. You probably will not be able to access manpages on your crippled system. You should also be aware that the versions of these commands on the rescue media will not always match the versions you are familiar with from everyday use, so be prepared for differences and/or limitations.)

There is another related point to be made about dynamic libraries. Those of you who have experience with other Unices may be surprised to discover that, for most Linux distributions, even the basic system tools are not statically linked.

```
hafnium:/root> ldd /sbin/fsck
        libc.so.6 => /lib/libc.so.6 (0x40010000)
        /lib/ld-linux.so.2 => /lib/ld-linux.so.2 (0x40000000)
```

This means that if cruel fate decides to flip a bit in a sector in a block which contains a file, which is called *libc.so.6*, you **will** be using rescue media to work on your system.

Other than these general guidelines, I cannot tell you how to use rescue media to revive your fallen routers. There are simply too many variables to make an "if A, then do B" flowchart feasible. Fortunately, aside from the three "stupid admin tricks," I have had very little use for rescue media. Most situations can be handled more quickly by performing services elsewhere than by trying to repair a badly damaged system.

9.7 Summary

This concludes our chapter about routers that do more than just route. Some descriptions of firewalls depict them as nonrouting dual-homed hosts running proxy services. Others consider them packet filters, and still others NATs. A Linux system can be all three of these simultaneously, if needed. Like the variety of emergency down situations you will encounter as a network admin, Linux deployments, too, cannot be pigeonholed into any single role. Hopefully, this chapter has conveyed the wide range of options you have when using Linux as a network component. Some of the topics covered are the following:

- Different types of proxy services you can provide to your users, either to heighten security or to provide access for private IP addresses other than by masquerading.

- Deploying Internet-accessible web servers using private address space, making use of port redirectors, such as *rinetd*, the kernel's **REDIRECT** target, or a combination of the two with a user-space redirector such as *redir*.

- Making efficient use of Internet address space if need be, while not sacrificing security, by using *DNAT* and/or proxy ARP on your firewall.

- Dynamic routing daemons available for Linux.

- Methods to keep your environment available, and what to do when you have system outages.

Chapter 10

YE OLDE KERNEL SHOPPE—LINUX 2.2.X

This chapter includes materials from the first edition of the book specific to the 2.2.x version of the kernel. Specifically, folks still using 2.2 kernels can find information on configuring *ipchains*, the predecessor of *netfilter*, and the tools used to configure it. The topics include masquerading, some early forms of NAT that were available in the kernel, firewalling, and IP accounting. Even if you've already made the jump to the 2.4 kernel, you may find yourself using tools that require the older *ipchains* interface, in which case you can load the *ipchains* module and use *ipchains* just as if you were running on a 2.2 system. The basic kernel configuration on a 2.4 system would be:

```
Networking options --->
    [*] Network packet filtering (replaces ipchains)
    IP: Netfilter Configuration  --->
       <M> ipchains (2.2-style) support
```

The order of topics in this chapter is: IP accounting, taken from the original Chapter 3; conditional IP forwarding, taken from the material in Chapter 7 (this section also contains an introduction to the basic *ipchains* command forms); the more general case of packet filtering using the *ipchains* tools, also from Chapter 7; and finally, tricks and tools needed to overcome some of the limitations of the masquerading code in the 2.2 kernel to perform things such as DNAT, taken from Chapter 9 in the first edition.

10.1   IP Accounting

IP accounting is a facility available in the Linux kernel which will accumulate the number and sizes of network packets that match a given set of criteria. By specifying particular combinations of pattern-matching criteria, also known as **rules**, you can collect all kinds of statistics about the packets flowing through your router. Examples include what percentage of the network traffic crossing the router consists of people using HTTP browsers, or what percentage is inbound FTP, or NFS traffic between servers. The only trick is learning how to configure the rules, which are called that because they are set up in the same manner as packet-filtering rules. In fact, IP accounting is just a piece of the **IP firewalling**, **IP forwarding**, and **IP masquerading** facilities in the kernel. The same kernel code is used to determine if a packet matches the specified criteria—in the case of accounting, a counter is incremented; for firewalling, forwarding, and masquerading, more sophisticated actions are taken.

The underlying kernel code which supports IP accounting changed between versions 2.0.x and 2.2.x of the kernel. The 2.0.x facility is known as **ipfw** and uses *ipfwadm* to configure the rules. The 2.2.x facility is **ipfw_chains** or simply **ipchains** and uses the command *ipchains* to configure the rules.[1] For a good understanding of the interaction between rules and packets, you should review the copies of the manpages for these facilities and commands.

Hint: Nice Printouts of Manpages

An easy way to generate nice-looking printouts of manpages is to use `man -t` *manpage* `>/tmp/`*manpage*`.ps`. This will produce a PostScript file which will be nicely formatted when printed. If you do not have a PostScript-capable printer, use the **magicfilter** package to configure your printer to automatically invoke *ghostscript* before spooling the file for printing.

10.1.1   Summary of IP Accounting Concepts

Before we get into configuring IP accounting, let's quickly summarize the concepts.

- IP accounting is built into the Linux kernel. Because of this, there is no process which must be running to collect the statistics.

- Counters may be incremented any time a packet traverses the networking stack. A counter is incremented depending upon whether or not the packet meets a certain set of criteria.

- These criteria are called **rules**. Rules are specified by using a command-line interface which enters the rules into the running kernel. (Other interfaces are available for entering rules, but they are all based upon the command-line interface.)

- Packets can be matched based on the contents of the TCP/IP protocol headers, such as source IP address and destination port.

- The kernel code which supports IP accounting changed between versions 2.0 and 2.2 of the kernel. The old code used *ipfwadm* as its configuration tool; the new code uses *ipchains*.

Compiling Support for IP Accounting into the 2.2.x Kernel

The only additional option required to use IP accounting with the 2.2.x version of the kernel is to enable IP firewalling.

```
Networking options --->
    [*] IP: IP firewalling
```

---

[1] There is an implementation of *ipchains* for the 2.0.x kernel. It is distributed as a set of patches. Visit the IPCHAINS homepage if you need this functionality.

10.1.2   Configuring IP Accounting Rules with *ipchains*

If you are comfortable with *ipfwadm*, then the flexibility of *ipchains* can take a bit of getting used to. It might help to think of *ipfwadm* as a subset of *ipchains* where there are only four chains (accounting, input, output, and forwarding) and these chains are always configured. Unlike the situation with the 2.0 kernel, *ipchains* does not come preconfigured with a chain for accounting; it is up to you to create one (or more). The chains it does have are **forward**, **input**, and **output**, plus any that you create.

Another difference between 2.0 and 2.2 with respect to IP accounting is that the *ipfwadm* accounting "chain" allowed you to differentiate specifically between **in**, **out**, and **both** directions for packets. In this regard, it was sort of special. With *ipchains*, you need to create the chains yourself, and you will need to create one each for inbound, outbound, and bidirectional traffic. We will feed our chains by adding rules to the built-in chains **input** and **output** that target our chains. This means that any packet which traverses the input and output chains (by definition, *all* packets must traverse these) will also be forwarded down (or visible to) our user-defined chains.

Here is a list of ways in which you can manipulate chains:

- `ipchains -N` *mychain* creates a chain named *mychain*.

- `ipchains -X` *mychain* deletes a chain named *mychain*. *mychain* must not be referenced by (be the target of) another rule.

- `ipchains -F` *mychain* deletes all rules on the chain named *mychain*.

- `ipchains -L` *mychain* lists all rules on the chain named *mychain*. There are several display options related to `-L`.

    - `-v` generates verbose output.

    - `-n` generates numeric output. In other words, it supresses any name or services lookups.

    - `-x` expands numbers in the packet and byte counter fields. No more pesky K, M, and Gs to try to hack around in your Perl script!

- `ipchains -A` *mychain* *myrule* **A**ppends *myrule* to *mychain*. Rule specification is similar to rule specification with *ipfwadm* but has been expanded with some nice features.

    `-p` [!] *protocol* specifies a protocol, which must be **tcp**, **udp**, **icmp**, or **all**. '!' does what you think it would; it is the logical opposite of the condition. For someone used to *ipfwadm*, this jumps out immediately as a useful improvement.

    `-s` [!] *address[/mask]* [!] *[port. . .]* specifies a source address as with *ipfwadm*. The port can be an ICMP type (`ipfwadm -h icmp` will list them for you). Nice enhancements are that the ICMP type can be listed by name, and inclusive port ranges—specified with ":"—default to either 0 or 65535 if the lower or upper bound is omitted.

    `-d` [!] *address[/mask]* [!] *[port. . .]* specifies the destination address in the same way as `-s`.

-i [!] *interfacename* indicates that the packet must (not) traverse *interfacename*. A wildcard can be specified by ending an interface name substring with "+". For example, *eth0+* will match eth0 and any IP alias of *eth0*.

-b makes the rule apply bidirectionally. What really happens is that two rules are entered—one the way you specified it on the command line and the other with -s and -d reversed.

[!] -y matches packets where SYN=1 & ACK=0 & FIN=0, in other words, packets initiating a TCP connection (or ! not).

[!] -f matches packet fragments 2–N of a fragmented packet. This is necessary because fragments do not contain ports (neither source nor destination) or ICMP types, so it is not possible to match them with other rules.

[-j] *target* sends the packet to a chain called *target* if it matches it. This is how we send packets through our user-defined accounting chains. Besides a user-defined chain, *target* can be one of the built-in targets. These are **ACCEPT**, **DENY**, **REJECT**, **MASQ**, **REDIR**, and **RETURN**. Of these, **RETURN** is of interest for IP accounting. This is a way to not count packets which match the criteria specified in the rule, because it returns the packet to the calling rule on the calling chain.

- ipchains -D *mychain* {*myrule* | *rulenum*} **D**eletes *myrule* from *mychain* or *rulenum* from *mychain*. Rules are numbered consecutively starting with 1.

- ipchains -R *mychain rulenum myrule* **R**eplaces *rulenum* with *myrule* in *mychain*.

- ipchains -I [*rulenum*] *mychain* **I**nserts *myrule rulenum* into *mychain*. If *rulenum* is omitted, then the beginning of the list is assumed.

Phew! *ipchains* packs a lot of functionality, and we have only scratched the surface. We need to do something with it before we lose track of all those options.

10.1.3   Choosing Packet Criteria for IP Accounting

Let's continue to introduce the concept of IP accounting by deciding on some packet criteria and then configure the system to count all matches. Fundamental to making sense of IP accounting is understanding TCP/IP's use of different source and destination ports to differentiate between protocols. In other words, IP accounting is not going to configure itself; you have to know what you are looking for, and what that means at a protocol level. For example:

- establishing a TCP socket connection to port 23 is the first step in starting a *telnet* session.

- sending a UDP packet to port 53 gets things going with DNS.

- connecting to TCP port 110 implies that you want to talk to a POP3 daemon.

- talking to TCP port 80 will more than likely get you a connection to an HTTP daemon.

Several books cover this topic in considerable detail and clarity; *Building Internet Firewalls* by Chapman and Zwicky does an excellent job of putting the pieces together.It is important to have a good understanding of the protocol to configure accounting rules which detect the *network events* you are interested in capturing.

For our example, we are going to configure our router to keep track of the number of packets (and bytes) traveling between subnet$_A$ and subnet$_B$. Furthermore, because all of our intranet web server is located on subnet$_A$, we would like to know the volume of traffic generated by users in subnet$_B$ accessing web services in subnet$_A$.

10.1.4   IP Accounting in Action—An Example

To implement the example, follow the script below. The first few steps are just to set up the user-defined chains. Next are the accounting rules which keep track of the traffic between our two subnets. The configuration is depicted in Figure 10.1.

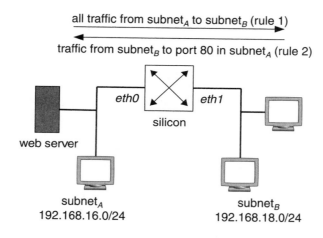

Figure 10.1 IP Accounting Example

```
# create accounting chains "in", "out", and "both"
# and hook them into the built-in chains (input and output)
# by making them targets of these (the built-in) chains
#############################################################

# create a (N)ew chain "in"
ipchains -N in

# (I)nsert a rule for the input chain
# which (j)umps to target chain "in"
ipchains -I input -j in

# create a (N)ew chain "out"
ipchains -N out
ipchains -I output -j out

# create a (N)ew chain "both"
ipchains -N both
```

```
# (I)nsert a rules into the input and output chains
# that (j)ump to target chain "both"
ipchains -I input -j both
ipchains -I output -j both


# acct rule 1
#############
#
# monitor traffic from subnetA destined for subnetB
#
# (A)ppend a rule to the "in" chain which counts all inbound packets
# from (s)ource 192.168.16.0/24 to (d)estination 192.168.18.0/24
#
# note that this could have been an "out" rule, too

ipchains -A in -s 192.168.16.0/24 -d 192.168.18.0/24


# acct rule 2
############
#
# monitor HTTP traffic between clients in subnetB and
# servers in subnetA
#
# (A)ppend a rule to the "out" chain count all packets
# from (s)ource 192.168.18.0/24 (generic client port)
# to (d)estination 192.168.16.0/24 (HTTP server port)
# of (p)rotocol tcp, and (-b) vice versa (server to client)
# and entering/exiting the router via (i)nterface eth0
#
# note that the (s)ource port range upperbound defaults to 65535

ipchains -A out -s 192.168.18.0/24 1024:          \
                -d 192.168.16.0/24 80             \
                -p tcp -b -i eth0


# acct rule 3
############
# count the number of telnet sessions initiated in subnetA
# to hosts located in subnetB
#
#
# (A)ppend a rule to "in" to count all packets
# from (s)ource 192.168.16.0/24 (generic client port)
# to (d)estination 192.168.18.0/24 (telnet daemon port)
# and entering/exiting the router via (-W) interface eth0
#
```

```
# as in rule 2, an interface (or direction) is
# specified to avoid counting the traffic twice

ipchains -A in -s 192.168.16.0/24 1024:          \
                -d 192.168.18.0/24 23            \
                -p tcp -i eth0
```

10.1.5   Viewing IP Accounting Rules with *ipchains*

IP accounting rules created with *ipchains* are viewed using the −L switch and its various options
as listed above. For our example rules, sample output looks as follows:

```
### first list the rules for each user-defined chain

silicon:/root> ipchains -L in
Chain in (refcnt = 1):
target prot opt     source            destination       ports
-      all  ------  192.168.16.0/24   192.168.18.0/24   n/a
-      tcp  ------  192.168.16.0/24   192.168.18.0/24   1024:65535 -> telnet

silicon:/root> ipchains -L out
Chain out (refcnt = 1):
{\lpage{1}}
target prot opt     source            destination       ports
-      tcp  ------  192.168.18.0/24   192.168.16.0/24   1024:65535 -> www
-      tcp  ------  192.168.16.0/24   192.168.18.0/24   www -> 1024:65535

### we did not add any rules to the "both" chain
silicon:/root> ipchains -L both
Chain both (refcnt = 2):

### (L)ist the rules in chain "in" (v)erbosely with (n)o name lookups
silicon:/root> ipchains -L in -vn
Chain in (refcnt = 2):
 pkts bytes target prot opt   tosa tosx ifname mark  outsize \
 624 24960 -        all  ------ 0xFF 0x00 *                   \
 606 24240 -        tcp  ------ 0xFF 0x00 eth0                \

        source            destination          ports
        192.168.16.0/24   192.168.18.0/24      n/a
        192.168.16.0/24   192.168.18.0/24      1024:65535 -> 23

### hmm... telnet traffic accounts for most of the packets

### list the "out" chain with statistics
silicon:/root> ipchains -L out -v
Chain out (refcnt = 2):
```

```
pkts bytes target  prot opt    tosa tosx  ifname  mark   outsize  \
   6   264 -       tcp  ------ 0xFF 0x00  eth0                     \
   0     0 -       tcp  ------ 0xFF 0x00  eth0                     \

        source              destination          ports
        192.168.18.0/24     192.168.16.0/24      1024:65535 -> www
        192.168.16.0/24     192.168.18.0/24      www -> 1024:65535
```

```
### wow, our webserver must be down.  There were 6 packets sent to the
### www port, but no replies.
```

The counters can be reviewed in two ways. You can use the commands as illustrated in the examples. Alternatively, you can access the counters directly by reading the contents of the appropriate file in the */proc* filesystem. For kernel version 2.2.x, that file is:

/proc/net/ip_fwchains

Of course, keeping detailed statistics either with *ipchains* or by periodically reading from the */proc* filesystem will require some additional development on your part. Before you start on that project, you might want to conduct some research and perhaps try some of the packages listed below.

Debian Packages/Commands Related to IP Accounting

ipac is a set of commands which script the things that you would most likely end up scripting on your own, if you wanted to use IP accounting to generate reports on a regular basis. To use it, load the **ipac** package and read the manpages for *ipacset, ipacfetch,* and *ipacsum.*

netbase contains a command called *ipfwadm-wrapper.* This package will be installed on your system as part of the base OS, but it is nice to be aware of the ipfwadm-wrapper when converting to *ipchains.*

net-acct provides a user-level daemon, *nacctd,* that logs all traffic passing the machine it runs on. It does not require IP accounting support in the kernel; instead, it functions more like a sniffer (by placing the interface in promiscuous mode).

wmnet is a network monitor for WindowMaker using kernel IP accounting. It polls */proc/net/ip_acct* and displays the results as an X client. One nice feature is that it works with both *ipfwadm* and *ipchains,* so it works for both 2.0 and 2.2 systems.

dotfile-ipfwadm (requires **dotfile**). This package uses a Tcl/Tk interface to allow you to graphically "build" your own accounting, forwarding, input, output, and masquerading rules. It can be very helpful for quickly developing a set of rules, which it outputs to a file. You can then tweak the rules if needed. *Note:* It allows you to select only options which are applicable to your running kernel. Because of this, you need to have options which you will be using already enabled. This is currently useful only for 2.0 kernel users, or for 2.4 kernel users employing the *ipfwadm* module under *netfilter.*

That concludes the introduction to *ipchains* for use with IP accounting. For an alternative discussion of *ipchains,* and information about migrating from *ipfw* to *ipchains,* please see the *IPCHAINS-HOWTO* either at the *LDP* site or at *http://netfilter.samba.org/ipchains/HOWTO.html.*

10.2   Conditional IP Forwarding for Linux 2.2.x

Conditional IP forwarding is a term used where a router is configured to reject the forwarding of certain packets or, vice versa, to allow only certain packets to be forwarded. It evaluates packets which are to be forwarded to see if they meet the criteria specified in the rule(s). When a match occurs, the target of the rule is invoked; if no rule matches, the policy for the appropriate chain is invoked. We still cannot predict the final fate of the packet at this point, because we do not know if the default action—the action taken when no rules match—is to forward the packet or to reject it. In any case, your system must be configured with IP: `forwarding/gatewaying` set to **yes** in the kernel for 2.0 kernels; */proc/sys/net/ipv4/ip_forward* = 1 for 2.2 kernels and later. Otherwise, the packet will never be examined by the forwarding chain at all.

In the case that forwarding is enabled, a default policy will be associated with it. The default policy, when no firewalling rules have been specified whatsoever, is **ACCEPT**. If the router can forward the packet, it will. The default policy can be set using *ipchains* to one of these three values: **ACCEPT**, **REJECT**, or **DENY**. The second two are equivalent, in that the packet is discarded. **REJECT** notifies the sender that the packet could not be forwarded via an `ICMP host unreachable` message. For denied packets, no such message is sent. Typically, you use **DENY** for packets originating outside your network (so the sender is not sure what happened to the packet) and **REJECT** for internally rejected packets as a polite way of saying "no." As you can easily surmise, there are two basic ways to go about configuring your rules.

1. You can expressly list the types of traffic which should not be allowed to traverse the system by using the default policy of **ACCEPT** and then specifying the traffic to be blocked with either **REJECT** or **DENY** rules.

2. The other way is to alter the default policy to be either **REJECT** or **DENY** and then explicitly list the types of traffic which are allowed to pass with **ACCEPT** rules.

Which of these you choose will depend upon the desired effect and your skill level. The more secure of the two is undoubtedly refusing all traffic by default, and then listing traffic which may pass in **ACCEPT** rules. However, this can be difficult (read: *maddening*) until you are familiar with the types of traffic you expect and understand all of the protocols which will be in use in your network. It is a time-consuming process to get the rules right the first time, and if you are in a time-critical situation, you might have to defer this type of configuration until later. Still, I recommend it, as it provides more protection and is an excellent way to earn your IP protocol "wings." If the default policy is to accept traffic, then you must explicitly block everything which should not be allowed to pass, which may be quite a lot. It also means that you have to test to make sure that services are blocked.

An example for 2.2.x systems using *ipchains* is presented below—configuring the default policy to reject all traffic and to allow two services, HTTP and telnet. You use the same syntax to specify packet-matching criteria to build rules as you did while configuring IP masquerading. You should recall the definition of **forwarding interface** from the discussion of IP masquerading (Section 10.6). When specifying an interface with any type of forwarding rule, the **forwarding interface** is the interface via which the packet leaves the router, not the one that received it.

The example refers to Figure 10.2. As you see from the diagram, it represents one basic configuration of the oxygen router. For our forwarding example, we will use a system with three

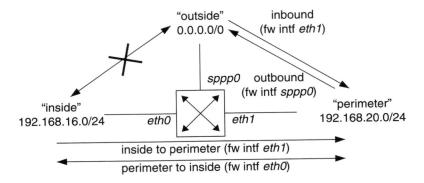

Figure 10.2 Conditional Packet Forwarding Example

interfaces. (Forwarding rules with only two interfaces are not very different from input/output rules.) Our system is a combination firewall and Internet router with a perimeter net to boot. The *sppp0* interface is our point-to-point connection to our ISP and is configured as the default route in the kernel. The perimeter net (*eth1*) hosts our site's proxy servers. The inside (*eth0*) should have access only to the perimeter net, and for now, we will allow the perimeter net to speak freely to the Internet.

10.2.1   Conditional IP Forwarding with *ipchains*

If you are accustomed to working with *ipfwadm* and the 2.0.x kernel, *ipchains* provides a more powerful interface than *ipfwadm* for rule specification. Just keep in mind when working with forwarding rules that they must be either part of the built-in **forward** chain or on a user-defined chain which is the target of that chain. For our example, we add rules to the built-in chain. But first, let's review the syntax of *ipchains* (Tables 10.1–10.5).

Table 10.1 *ipchains* General Forms

	general usage
ipchains	-[**ADC**] *chain rule [options]*
ipchains	-[**RI**] *chain rule [options]*
ipchains	-**D** *chain rulenum [options]*
ipchains	-[**LFZNX**] *[chain] [options]*
ipchains	-**P** *chain target [options]*
ipchains	-**M** [**-L**|**-S**] *[options]*
ipchains	-**h** *[icmp]*

Table 10.2 *ipchains* Commands

command	description
-A *chain*	append to *chain*
-D *chain rule*	delete rule-matching *rule* from *chain*
-D *chain rulenum*	delete rule *rulenum* from *chain* (rules are numbered starting at 1)
-I *chain [rulenum]*	insert rule into *chain*, optionally at position *rulenum* from the start (rules are numbered starting at 1)
-R *chain [rulenum]*	replace rule *rulenum* in *chain* (rules are numbered starting at 1)
-L *[chain]*	list all rules, or, if a chain is specified, list all rules in chain *chain*
-F *[chain]*	flush all rules, or, if a chain is specified, flush all rules in chain *chain*
-Z *[chain]*	zero counters for all rules, or, if a chain is specified, zero counters for all rules in chain *chain*
-C *chain rule*	test the packet defined by *rule* in chain *chain*
-N *chain*	create a new user-defined chain *chain*
-X *chain*	delete a user-defined chain *chain*
-P *chain target*	change the policy (default target) for chain *chain* to *target*, which must be one of the built-in targets: • ACCEPT—allow the packet to pass • DENY—swallow the packet • REJECT—swallow the packet but notify the sender with an ICMP host unreachable message • MASQ—masquerade the packet • REDIR—redirect the packet to a local port • RETURN—return to the calling chain (not valid for built-in chains)
-M -L	list current masquerading connections
-M -S *tcp tcpfin udp*	set masquerading timeout values (in seconds—all three must be specified; use a value of 0 to indicate no change)

Table 10.3 *ipchains* Options That Affect Packet-Matching Specifications

option	description
`-p [!]` *proto*	match protocol *proto*, which is one of **tcp**, **udp**, **icmp**, **all**, or an IP protocol number
`-s [!]` *addr*`[/`*mask*`]` `[!]` `[`*port(s)*`]`	the IP source specification. The address can be a dotted-IP address or a hostname, the mask can be in dotted format or / format, and the ports can be a range *low:high*, or a space-delimited list. The '!' reverses the sense of the comparison.
`-d [!]` *addr*`[/`*mask*`]` `[!]` `[`*port(s)*`]`	the IP destination specification
`-i [!]` *intf*`[+]`	the name of the network interface, which may end in '+', which acts as a wildcard. The sense may be reversed with '!'.
`[!] -f`	match second or further fragments only (or not)
`[!] -y`	match TCP packets only when SYN set (or not)

Table 10.4 *ipchains* Options That Affect Chains and Rules

option	description
`-b`	insert two rules: one with -s & -d reversed
`-j` *target [port]*	specify a target rule of *target* for this rule, should it match. Valid targets are other user-defined rules, **ACCEPT**, **DENY**, **REJECT**, **MASQ**, **REDIR**, or **RETURN**. When using **REDIR**, you must specify a *port*, which can be 0 (which indicates that the destination port in the packet header will be used to determine the local port), or any other port.

Table 10.5 *ipchains* Options That Affect Output and Misc.

option	description
-n	numeric output of addresses and ports
-v	verbose mode
-x	expand numbers (display exact values)

other options

option	description
-l	enable kernel logging (via *syslog*) for matching packets
-o *[maxsize]*	Copy matching packets to the user-space device. This is currently mainly for developers who want to play with firewalling effects in user-space. The optional *maxsize* argument can be used to limit the maximum number of bytes from the packet which are to be copied. This option is valid only if the kernel has been compiled with CONFIG_IP_FIREWALL_NETLINK set.
-m [+-] *markvalue*	Mark matching packets. Packets can be marked with a 32-bit unsigned value which may (one day) change how they are handled internally. If you are not a kernel hacker, you are unlikely to care about this. If the string *markvalue* begins with a + or -, then this value will be added to or subtracted from the current marked value of the packet (which starts at zero).
-t *andmask xormask*	Masks used for modifying the TOS field in the IP header. When a packet matches a rule, its TOS field is first bitwise AND'ed with first mask, and the result is bitwise XOR'ed with the second mask. The masks should be specified as hexadecimal 8-bit values. As the LSB of the TOS field must be unaltered (RFC 1349), TOS values which would cause it to be altered are rejected, as are any rules which always set more than one TOS bit. Rules which might set multiple TOS bits for certain packets result in warnings (sent to *stdout*), which can be ignored if you know that packets with those TOS values will never reach that rule. Obviously, manipulating the TOS is a meaningless gesture if the rule's target is DENY or REJECT.

10.2.2   2.2.x Kernel Support for IP Firewalling

Before you start building rule chains, you will need to make sure that your kernel has support for IP firewalling built into it. The support is enabled by using the following options and recompiling the kernel:

```
Networking options --->
    <*> Packet socket
@   [*] Kernel/User netlink socket
@   <*> Netlink device emulation
    [*] Network firewalls
    <*> Unix domain sockets
    [*] TCP/IP networking
```

```
[*]  IP: advanced router
[*]  IP: firewalling
@    [*]  IP: firewall packet netlink device
[*]  IP: always defragment (required for masquerading)
```

The options denoted by the @ character are not required but are highlighted for our discussion of features in progress in the Linux kernel. The `Kernel/User netlink socket` is a mechanism by which user-space programs can interact with the kernel via a device file. Among other things, it provides an alternative to logging kernel packet headers via *klogd*, which is one of the options available when a firewalling rule makes a match. In the case of IP firewalling, the netlink copies the entire packet to a character special file under */dev* with major number 36 and minor number 3. The upshot is that this can be used to detect attacks in real time, and possibly even take some form of action against the attack (or the attacker!). By creating device files with different minor numbers, other types of packets, e.g., raw Ethernet (as an alternative to using *libpcap*) and routing messages can be monitored. At the time of writing, only minimal application support is available for this, so we're going to stick to the mainstream features, such as selectively forwarding packets with *ipchains*.

10.2.3 An Example of Conditional Forwarding with *ipchains*

We will now configure our three-way router, depicted in Figure 7.6. We want to prevent traffic from flowing between the *inside* and the *outside* in either direction, but to allow traffic to flow between the *perimeter* and the *inside* and between the *perimeter* and the *outside*.

1. This rule initializes us in a known state. All rules in the built-in **forward** chain are flushed.

   ```
   ### (1)
   ### flush any existing rules on the "forward" chain
   oxygen:root> ipchains -X forward
   ```

2. Configure the default policy for forwarded packets to be **REJECT**.

   ```
   ### (2)
   ### our default forwarding policy is "deny"
   ### after this, nothing works
   oxygen:root> ipchains -P forward DENY
   ```

3. Prohibit any direct communication between the inside and the outside. The forwarding rules will be executed in order until a match occurs, so, even though the default policy already excludes this communication, a misplaced rule could "open up" the firewall again.

   ```
   ### (3)
   ### expressly prohibit those on the inside from reaching
   ### the outside, but be polite about it ("reject")
   oxygen:root> ipchains -A forward -j REJECT -i sppp0        \
                        -s 192.168.16.0/24
   ```

4. Allow both the outside and the inside to send TCP packets (from any port to any port) to the perimeter net. This gives the inside access to the proxies and allows the outside to deliver mail, etc.

```
### (4)
### allow anyone to send TCP to the perimeter net
oxygen:root> ipchains -A forward -j ACCEPT -p tcp -i eth1 \
                        -d 192.168.20.0/24
```

5. Allow the perimeter net to respond to TCP connections when talking to the inside.

```
### (5)
### allow the perimeter net to send to the inside
### when responding to TCP connections
oxygen:root> ipchains -A forward -j ACCEPT ! -y -p tcp -i eth0 \
                        -s 192.168.20.0/24                      \
                        -d 192.168.16.0/24
```

6. Allow the perimeter net to send freely to the outside. Note that this doesn't mean that everything can be answered. In other words, you're not done yet. Although you can send out all protocols, only TCP replies will be forwarded back to the perimeter net (as per rule #4).

```
### (6)
### allow the perimeter net to forward to the outside
oxygen:root> ipchains -A forward -j ACCEPT -i sppp0 \
                        -s 192.168.20.0/24
```

So that's all there is to forwarding. Forwarding rules are more useful when you have three or more interfaces. In many cases, you will find that input (for systems which only route) and output rules (if there are services running on the system too) are sufficient to configure your packet-filtering needs. Still, conditional forwarding can quickly realize configurations which would be more complicated using only input rules. One example which comes to mind is to prevent forwarding of ICMP but to still allow the internal interface(s) to respond to pings. You can disable ICMP forwarding with a single rule, and all interfaces will still be able to respond to pings. If you want to prevent external interfaces from responding to pings and traceroutes, you could use an input rule on that interface to block ICMP. Even better, use an output rule on that interface, so that the sender never sees a reply, but any IP event logging occurring on the system will still take place.

Anyway, keep conditional forwarding in your little bag of magic tricks. When you need it, sometimes nothing else will do. If I'm allowed one complaint, it's that the default listing format does not show the interface (nor did it for *ipfwadm*). For this reason, you should get into the habit of opening wide windows into any system which will be using any of the kernel firewalling features and using the -v switch for *ipchains* (and -e for those who use *ipfwadm*).

10.3 IP Packet Filtering for Linux 2.2.x

Packet filtering is a term that often goes hand-in-hand with firewalls, although that is only one application of its usefulness. But before it can be used, we should answer the question, "What is packet filtering?" Everything that enters and exits our routers via the network is in the form of a packet. Normally, there are no restrictions on which hosts may use a system as a gateway. If the system can forward the packet, it will. Aside from systems with *tcpd*, there are few restrictions as to which hosts may attempt to contact a system on any given port via any particular protocol. If the system can answer, i.e., it has a daemon or service ready to answer on that port, it will. **Packet filtering** allows us to restrict the flow of packets entering and exiting our system, based on the properties of the packets themselves. It differs from IP masquerading and conditional forwarding in that it operates only on input and output from the system, not on packets selected for forwarding by the kernel's routing table. This is not to say that rules cannot match packets which are being forwarded; they can. The difference is that the matching occurs when the packet enters (or exits) the system. As you've come to expect, the rules are specified using *ipchains* with its usual syntax.

For simple routers, we talk primarily about **input** rules; **output** rules are equally valid, but I find it conceptually easier to think about blocking things on the way into the machine rather than on the way out of it. This also seems as if it would mean less work for the machine. If you reject packets on the way in, you can potentially short-circuit a lot of the filtering rules. That is, you do not have to compare the packet to the remainder of the input chain, the forward chain, and then the output chain before finally rejecting the packet with the output rule.

The situation changes on a system with services, e.g., proxies, and/or users. In this case, output rules may be the only way to prevent certain traffic from originating from your system. (Packets originating from a system are never considered to be forwarded.) Keep this in mind when configuring proxies. In either case, input or output, you can alter the default policy of the **input/output** rules chain, just as with forwarding. Once again, specifying a default policy of **REJECT** or **DENY** is recommended.

I find it very helpful to draw pictures of what's going on when working with packet filtering. One reason is that the definitions of **input** and **output** are relative to your position. Input with respect to an external interface means a packet from the outside of your network, while input rules on an internal interface apply to outbound packets. Figure 10.3 illustrates the difference. I often refer to your perspective on packet flow as "where you stand." For example, if you are "standing" outside of the firewall, all input rules apply to *eth1*.

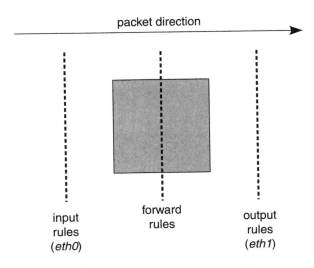

Figure 10.3 Packet Filtering for Two Interfaces

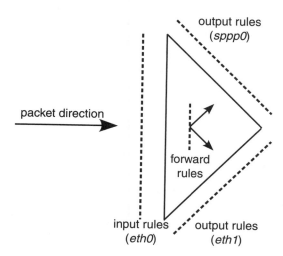

Figure 10.4 Packet Filtering for Three Interfaces

Realize that the picture becomes more complicated when you have more than two interfaces, so keep this in mind when designing your network topology around your firewall and Internet router. To give you an idea, take a look at Figure 10.4.

Packet filtering is just another example of how there are many ways to accomplish a given task with Linux. I believe this to be part of its Unix heritage—part of the toolbox philosophy. Your solution to a problem depends upon how you look at it. In the case of packet filtering and firewalling, there are many "correct" answers; use the one that you understand.

10.3.1   Packet Filtering with *ipchains*

ipchains provides a very powerful mechanism for limiting traffic into or out of a system or between networks. (Later, it is also the tool used to take advantage of some of the kernel functionality like port forwarding.) This section provides a short introduction to using *ipchains* to configure input and output firewall rules. You can refer back to Tables 10.1–10.5 for help with the syntax or run `ipchains -h` to see all of the options available. Let's work through a couple of examples.

Packet-Filtering Example 1

First, we need to prevent the training workstations in the training department from browsing the Internet. The instructors have complained that the users are browsing instead of paying attention to the course material. Fortunately, you planned for this when designing the company network, and the training workstations are all located on a separate (possibly virtual) subnet. That subnet is 192.168.36.0/24.

```
# ipchains input/output firewalling example #1
###############################################################
# set up a few variables
```

```
INSIDE="192.168.0.0/16"        # all of our internal address space
TRAINING="192.168.36.0/24"     # training workstations

                               # eth0 is the "inside"
                               # eth1 is the "outside"


# set up default policies for the chains
#    by default, no input is allowed
#------------------------------------------------------------
     ipchains -P input REJECT

# allow _our_ address space to access the outside
#------------------------------------------------------------
     ipchains -A input -i eth0 -j ALLOW -s $INSIDE

# prevent the training workstations access to the outside
# (have to "Insert" this before the previous rule)
#------------------------------------------------------------
     ipchains -I input -j REJECT -s $TRAINING
```

This will prevent workstations in that subnet from accessing the outside. But because this has been such a problem for the instructors, they would also like to know which workstations are trying to access the outside during class. We can easily fulfill this request by enabling packet logging for matching packets. We do this by adding the -l (for "logging") switch to our REJECT rule above. When someone on a training workstation tries to access an external website, we'll see an entry like this in */var/adm/messages*:

```
Jun 30 12:00:19 oxygen kernel: Packet log: input REJECT eth0 PROTO=6
          192.168.36.21:4306 207.200.75.204:80
          L=60 S=0x00 I=28632 F=0x4000 T=64 SYN (#1)
```

That first line tells us when and what happened. At the time given, a packet trying to enter *eth0* of protocol "6" (which is TCP) was rejected. The second line lists the source IP:port and destination IP:port of the packet. The third line contains more information about the packet. It is produced by the code in */usr/src/linux/net/ipv4/ip_fw.c*. The fields have the following meanings:

- L=n is the length of the packet (in bytes).

- S=0xnn is the value of the TOS (Type Of Service) field in the packet.

- I=n is the identification field of the packet.

- F=0x$nnnn$ is the fragment offset.

- T=nn is the value in the TTL (Time To Live) field of the packet—the number of hops the packet can take before being discarded.

- The presence of SYN indicates that this bit is set; the (#1) is the absolute sequence number for the TCP sequence.

With this information logged via *syslog*, we can quickly scan for any attempts, all attempts made by each individual IP, and the times of those attempts.

Packet-Filtering Example 2

Our second example is to use packet filtering to prevent direct access to FTP sites. Instead, we want to force users to use an FTP proxy client. The motivation is that management wants us to keep a log of all transfers in case a disgruntled employee decides to FTP a copy of our trade secrets to a competitor.

We are going to load a FTP proxy directly on the firewall and instruct the users to connect to the proxy when they need to access external sites. We will not cover configuring the FTP proxy itself, which is simple enough, but will focus on the rules needed to allow the proxy to get outside the firewall, but not any internal systems. Drawing a picture helps—see Figure 10.5. From this, we can write out the high-level rules required.

- Allow FTP access from the inside to the FTP proxy service running on oxygen.

- Prevent direct FTP access to the outside for any clients on the inside.

- Prevent external clients from connecting to the FTP proxy.

- Allow FTP access to the outside from the FTP proxy service.

- Prevent any other traffic from traversing the firewall.

But before we can write the packet-filtering rules to block direct FTP (or any protocol), we need to understand how the protocol works:

- FTP in "normal" mode

  1. The client uses a client port (a port in the range between 1024 and 65534) to contact the FTP server on port 21. This is called a **control connection**.

  2. Authentication occurs over the control connection, as do any client-issued commands and server acknowledgements of those commands.

  3. However, if one of those commands results in a data transfer (including getting a directory listing), then the client prepares for it by opening a second client port and sending this port number to the FTP server over the control connection.

  4. The FTP server opens a connection from port 20 on the server to the second client port on the client system. This port is used to transmit the data.

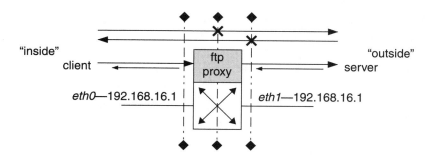

Figure 10.5 Providing a Secure Environment for an FTP Proxy

Because you do not know the port to allow for the data transfer beforehand, you have to allow all external sites to use port 20 to connect to your internal clients. Thus anybody on the outside can probe your network by sending packets from port 20 on their system.

- FTP in passive mode

  Because of the dangers of normal FTP, some bright people came up with the idea of passive-mode FTP, which works as follows:

  1. The control connection works as before. However, when a data transfer is initiated, the client asks the server to open an additional port on the server for use by the data transfer.

  2. The server finds a free port and sends this value back to the client over the control connection.

  3. The client then makes an outbound connection to the port the server just gave it, and the data transfer takes place over this connection.

The server thinks that this is cool because it has already authenticated the client (as much as it wanted to), so it does not mind the inbound connection—it has to allow these anyway to offer the FTP service. The firewall likes the idea because it doesn't have to accept inbound connections from the outside. The client likes the idea because it gets its file.

Back to the problem at hand: Aside from the obvious requirement that we need to protect our network, we have the management mandate to log all transfers. An FTP proxy can help us do this and more. (Several proxies for Linux are covered in Section 9.1.) The idea of a proxy is to have a process running which handles connection requests and data transfers to the outside on behalf of the client. This offers the following advantages:

1. FTP proxies run on a single system, which means that if you do have to allow normal-mode FTP, it is only to a single system.

2. They log all transfers, connection attempts, etc.

3. Most of them have access-control mechanisms to prevent just anybody from using the proxy.

4. They provide "application"-level protection. Because they are proxying the FTP commands (i.e., they converse with the client, then turn around and converse with the FTP server, in such a manner that the client believes that the FTP proxy is the FTP server, and the FTP server believes that the FTP proxy is the client), FTP proxies can examine the commands for illegal commands, buffer overflow attempts, and other assorted unscrupulous actions an FTP server (or client) might attempt.

For our rules, we will NOT assume that the FTP proxy always operates in passive mode on the client side (client proxy), because a user may neglect to configure his FTP client to automatically request passive-mode transfers. The proxy will use passive-mode data transfers between it and the server. A sample set of rules is listed below. The section before each rule documents its role in preventing (or allowing) access through the firewall system.

```
#
# ipchains input/output firewalling example
##############################################################
# set up a few variables
INSIDE="192.168.0.0/16"            # all of our internal address space

ETH0=192.168.16.1/32       # fw intf on the inside
ETH1=192.168.20.1/32       # fw intf on the outside
ANY=0.0.0.0/0


# create new user-defined chains, "eth0in" and "eth1in"
# these get first dibs on anything that enters the system
ipchains -N eth0in
ipchains -N eth1in
ipchains -I input -i eth0 -j eth0in
ipchains -I input -i eth1 -j eth1in


# also create output chains, eth0out and eth1out
ipchains -N eth0out
ipchains -N eth1out
ipchains -I output -i eth0 -j eth0out
ipchains -I output -i eth1 -j eth1out


# set up default policies for the chains
#    by default, no input is allowed
#    by default, no output from eth1 is allowed
#        (note, this rule should remain the LAST rule on
#         the eth1out chain, so insert all other eth1out rules)
#------------------------------------------------------------
   ipchains -P input REJECT
   ipchains -A eth1out -j REJECT


# turn off any forwarding of FTP
#    nothing on the inside may forward to port 21 on the outside
#    not allow anyone to forward traffic to ports 20 or 21
#------------------------------------------------------------
   ipchains -I forward -j DENY -p tcp -s $INSIDE -d $ANY 21
   ipchains -I forward -j DENY -p tcp -s $ANY 20 21


# now that we know that FTP traffic cannot bridge the gulf
# of the forwarding code in the kernel, we can
# be a little bit more relaxed with our rules


# CLIENT <-> PROXY, control connection
#    client * -> proxy 21
#    proxy 21 -> client * (ACK set)
#------------------------------------------------------------
# allow the internal machines to connect from a client
# port to port 21 of the proxy service
```

```
    # client -> proxy
    ipchains -A eth0in -p tcp -s $INSIDE 1024: -d $ETH0 21


    # proxy -> client
    # none needed - the proxy can answer because there is no
    # output rule restricting flow on the output of eth0

# CLIENT <-> PROXY, data connection (normal mode)
#    proxy 20 -> client *
#    client * -> proxy 20 (ACK set)
#------------------------------------------------------------

    # proxy -> client, none needed,
    # the proxy is free to speak with the client

    # client -> proxy
    ipchains -A eth0in -p tcp ! -y -s $INSIDE 1024: -d $ETH0 20


# CLIENT <-> PROXY, data connection (passive mode)
#    client * -> proxy *
#    proxy * -> client * (ACK set)
#------------------------------------------------------------
    ipchains -A eth0in -p tcp -s $INSIDE 1024: -d $ETH0 1024:
    # the proxy is open to talk to the client
    # (if it were not, we would use a bidirectional (-b) rule)

# PROXY <-> SERVER, control connection
#    proxy * -> server 21
#    server 21 -> proxy * (ACK set)
#------------------------------------------------------------
    # proxy -> server
    ipchains -I eth1out -p tcp -d $ANY 21

    # server -> proxy
    ipchains -I eth1in -p tcp ! -y -s $ANY 21
    # there's no need to specify a destination, since the
    # forwarding code will discard anything not for the proxy
    # "! -y" means the packet must be an ACK

# PROXY <-> SERVER, data connection (always passive mode)
#    proxy * -> server *
#    server * -> proxy * (ACK set)
#------------------------------------------------------------
    # proxy -> server
    ipchains -I eth1out -p tcp -d $ANY 1024:

    # server -> proxy
    ipchains -I eth1in -p tcp -k -s $ANY 1024:
```

Whew! FTP is relatively difficult to provide with a packet filter and a proxy together. If you look at the connections we allow between the proxy and the server, you should understand why we want to use a proxy. Fortunately, most protocols are much easier to block and proxy. For example, a protocol such as telnet uses only a single server port, similar to FTP's control connection. (A notable exception is DNS when you have to deal with servers and clients, which points out a caveat about the example above. It won't work in most situations as written. The FTP part will work, but you will need DNS name resolution available to the proxy before it will be useful.)

Before you throw up your hands, there is a lot of help available out there. To start, most protocols are well documented, so you can get the details of the protocol and use that to write your own rules. There are several packages out there where someone has already come along and written most of the rules for you. Some of these are introduced in the section on masquerading (Section 10.5.3). A few more available are **mason**, **gfcc**, **fwctl**, and **ipmasq**. If you use one of these tools, you leverage all of their experience with a few keystrokes (or mouse clicks).

The point in the painful example is to show you what went into rules and what the automated tools need to go through. No amount of slick GUI should replace understanding what is happening at the system level. You should "take the rules apart," look at what each does individually, and then start piecing them together to see how the entire chain works. This knowledge will help you during configuration of firewall tools, and it is the basis of any troubleshooting you may have to do when these tools don't work as expected. For more information, refer to the *LDP* for several appropriate HOWTOs.

But we're not out of the firewalling forest yet. The next section covers a little necessary housekeeping when configuring your own rules.

10.3.2   Scripting Firewalling Rules

As you play with IP firewalling, you may be tempted to enter rules one by one on the command line to build up your configuration and test ideas. You may quickly find this to be a frustrating method of working. For one, there is no easy way to list out your rules in a format that is easy to enter into a script to reproduce the same environment. Say you spend a few hours testing various rules and have them just the way you like them. Now you want to save them into the script that will be run at boot time to configure your packet filter. There is no easy way to list the rules with *ipchains* so that you can reproduce the switches used in the commands to configure the rules. (A shell with a history file might help here, but because the process involves adding rules and then deleting them again to enter a slightly different variant of the same rule, you will have to spend a while poring over the history to find out which commands negated each other.)

Finally, and most significantly, packet-filtering rules function as a set and are adequately tested only when they are tested as a single unit. Therefore you should get used to the idea of working with them as a set. For these reasons, I recommend that you enter all rules into a shell script and then edit → run → test → edit ... this shell script until you have what you want. In this way, you can document your rules and design trade-offs as you go along and have a script ready to add to your system startup. If you use a script like the skeleton below, you can edit the script, `stop` it, and then `start` it again so that you are always testing the rules as a group.

```ksh
#########################################################
#!/usr/bin/ksh
#
# firewall_rules.sh
#
# modification history:
# 19990524/tm              initial release
# 19990624/tm              added rule 1 to combat HackerX, who
#  attacks from RFC1918 private IP addresses
# kernel version check
if [[ $(uname -r) == 2.0* ]] ; then
   USE_IPFWADM=1
else
   USE_IPFWADM=0
fi

# specify interfaces in rules as either $I or $E
I=eth0                    # Internal interface (inside the firewall)
E=eth1                    # External interface (outside the firewall)


###########################################################

# Install_input_rules configures input packet-filters
######################################################
Install_input_rules()
{
   # rule 1
   # disallow IP spoofing of private subnets
   # (i.e., they must not originate from the outside)
   ################################################
   for subnet in  192.168.0.0/16 \
                  172.16.0.0/12  \
                  10.0.0.0/8

   do
      # ksh shorthand for mask=$(echo $subnet | cut -f2 -d'/')
      mask=${subnet#*/}
      network=${subnet%/*}
      if (( $USE_IPFWADM == 1 ))
      then
         ipfwadm -I -a deny -S ${subnet}/${mask} -W $E
      else
         ipchains -A input -j DENY -s ${subnet}/${mask} -i $E
      fi
   done

   ########
   # rule 0
   # default rule is to prevent any packet from flowing
   # any packet into the firewall
   # not specifying a src or dest is the same as using
   # -S 0.0.0.0/0 and -D 0.0.0.0/0
   ###################################################
```

```
    if (( $USE_IPFWADM == 1 ))
    then
        # default reject (internal client receives ICMP failure)
        ipfwadm -I -a reject -W $I

        # default deny (no ICMP error sent)
        ipfwadm -I -a deny -W $E
    else
        ipchains -A input -j REJECT -i $I
        ipchains -A input -j DENY -i $E
    fi

} ### end Install_Rules()

###########################
# main script starts here
###########################
case "$1" in
    start)
        # load any modules required for IP masquerading rules
        modprobe ip_masq_ftp
        modprobe ip_masq_irc
        Install_input_rules
        #Install_forward_rules
        #Install_output_rules
        ;;
    stop)
        # unload IP-masquerading modules
        modprobe -r ip_masq_ftp
        modprobe -r ip_masq_irc

        # flush all input rules
        ipfwadm -I -f && echo "INPUT RULES FLUSHED - FIREWALL INACTIVE"
        #ipfwadm -F -f
        #ipfwadm -O -f
        ;;
    reload|restart)
        echo "$1 of $0"
        $0 stop
        $0 start
        ;;
    *)
        echo "Usage: $0 {start|stop|reload|restart}"
        exit 1
        ;;
esac

exit 0
```

10.3.3 Testing Packet-Filtering Rules with *ipchains*

What do you do if you want to test your packet filter before placing it in production? There are several alternatives. Perhaps the most thorough is to set up an identical environment and test. The problem with this, as when testing any sort of Internet service, is that it is difficult to simulate the Internet without really having the Internet. If you have perimeter net topology, this is still an option. You can configure a test firewall and add a route to your Internet router for your test workstation via the test firewall. The test workstation will use the test firewall for its default gateway. See Figure 10.6 for the topology. This will work, but you should be careful not to weaken your security by allowing another way into your network via the test firewall. It is also a lot of work. The pros are that it is an accurate test of many client-server type connections and that your method of testing/problem detection is identical to your day-to-day firewall activities.

If this is too time consuming, or if you would like to quickly test a rule, there is an easier option. *ipchains* has the ability to generate test packets which will be checked against the rules configured in the kernel. The command to create a test packet looks very much like any other command used to enter, edit, or remove a rule. Because the Linux kernel is not known for its ability to invent information, you need to specify a source, a destination, each with a port, a protocol, and the interface which *receives* the virtual packet (for **input** and **forward** rules) or the interface which should send the virtual packet (for an **output** rule).

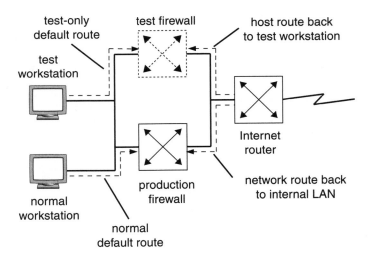

Figure 10.6 Test Firewall Network Topology

For *ipchains* use the -C *chain* (or --check *chain*) switch in addition to:

argument	comments
-s *address port*	a regular dotted IP + port
-d *address port*	a regular dotted IP + port
-p *protocol*	**tcp**, **udp**, or **icmp**
-i *interface*	interface to receive/send the packet

Results from **check**ing include:	
accepted	The packet matched a rule with a policy of **accept** and would have been forwarded, allowed to enter (input rule) or exit (output rule) the firewall.
denied	The packet matched a rule with a policy of **deny**, and an ICMP denied would have been sent to the sender.
rejected	The packet matched a rule with a policy of **reject** and would have been thrown into the bit bucket.
masqueraded	The packet matched a forward rule with a policy of **accept** and with the -m switch and would have been forwarded and masqueraded.
redirected	The packet matched an input rule which indicated that it should be redirected to a local port.
caught in loop	The packet matched a rule with a *target* which consequently resulted in the packet returning to that same rule. This will result in nothing but wasted CPU cycles in production and is a good example of how checking rules can be helpful.
passed thru chain	The packet passed through the chain without jumping to another chain.

Checking rules in this manner is a good way to review new configurations and configurations where you have reordered the rules for some reason—perhaps for performance reasons as described later in this chapter. My recommendation is to develop a script which contains a comprehensive list of rules and compare the output of this script against the output of a control run which you know generates the correct results. The reason that I suggest using only the check functionality for testing changes in sets of rules is that I think there are several drawbacks to testing firewall rules using *ipchains*. For one, there is no *virtual reply* to the packet, which is important for any realistic network communication.

The second reason is related to the first. Assume that you do code your set of check rules to include replies. Furthermore, assume that you have a test case (a **check** command) for each rule of your packet-filter. Because you wrote the packet filtering rules, chances are that *your* rules will pass *your* checks. Most of the errors I have encountered when specifying rules for blocking or allowing a given protocol came from a lack of understanding of the protocol (or from a lack of adequate documentation of the protocol). For this reason, I recommend that you test using a real environment whenever possible. When you run into problems, you can use a combination of *tcpdump* and reviewing the packet and byte counters for each of your rules to determine why something is passing or not passing. Thorough testing can be quite difficult and time consuming. Refer to Appendix C for a general discussion of the topic.

10.4 IP Masquerading with the 2.2 Kernel

IP masquerading is the predecessor to full network address translation (NAT) in the Linux kernel. There is a great body of knowledge accumulated around this topic—coaxing the router to masquerade what you need it to without sacrificing security or other needed functionality became somewhat of an art. Because there are limitations that inevitably led to trade-offs, I can assure you that the *netfilter* NAT code is a welcome enhancement to 2.4. Nevertheless, sophisticated configuration can be accomplished with the masquerading code in the 2.2.x kernel, and its study can be beneficial to understanding what goes into TCP/IP network address translation. Although it is somewhat of an oversimplification, the 2.2.x. masquerading code is able to cope with simple client → server TCP/IP protocols and masquerades the packet source as the forwarding interface on the router.

10.4.1 Protocol Masquerading Support with Linux 2.2

The 2.2 version of the Linux kernel handles the differences between various TCP/IP application protocols with the kernel option `Protocol-specific masquerading support`. Code, in the form of modules, can be loaded into the running kernel to provide masquerading for the less well-behaved protocols. These modules are automatically built when you select `IP: masquerading` during kernel configuration—all you have to do is load them, if you want them, and prevent their being loaded if you don't want that support. Pretty spiffy, eh? The list of modules and protocols supported includes, but is not limited to:

- **CUSeeMe** with the module `ip_masq_cuseeme.o`

- **FTP** with the module `ip_masq_ftp.o`

- **IRC** with the module `ip_masq_irc.o`

- **Quake** with the module `ip_masq_quake.o`

- **RealAudio** and **RealVideo** with the module `ip_masq_raudio.o`

- **VDO Live** with the module `ip_masq_vdolive.o`

To use one of the protocol modules, simply load it with `insmod` *modulename*. Because they need to be loaded to be useful, I add them to my */etc/init.d/local_network* file so that they are loaded during the startup sequence. Although you may rarely need to use it, several of the modules support the ability to listen to more than just the well-known port for their respective protocol. This is useful if you would like to provide FTP services on more ports than just port 21 by adding the argument to `ports=x1,x2,x3...` to the command line when using *insmod* to load the module. If you want to specify more than `MAX_MASQ_APP_PORTS` different ports, you will have to modify the value in */usr/src/linux/include/net/ip_masq.h* and recompile the kernel and the modules. Several other masquerading modules related to **IP port forwarding** are covered in Section 10.7 and **transparent proxying** in Section 9.2.2.

10.5 Configuring IP Masquerading for Linux 2.2.x

Now that you know what masquerading can do, and have an idea about how it does it, you need to know how to go about enabling support for it and configuring masquerading rules. As with other kernel facilities, you must select it during the kernel configuration process, compile a new kernel, and then reboot to be able to use IP masquerading.[2]

The generic IP masquerading code is in */usr/src/linux/net/ipv4/ip_masq.c* and handles the straightforward TCP, UDP, and ICMP protocols. When you compile a kernel only with `IP: Masquerading`, you will have support for TCP and UDP. You should set `IP: ICMP masquerading` if you also want ICMP packets to be masqueraded. (This enables some conditional parts of the code in *ip_masq.c*.)

In either case, be sure to set `IP: always defragment` whenever using masquerading. This has the effect of coalescing any packet fragments into the original (larger, unfragmented) packet before handing them to the kernel's forwarding code. This is necessary because the masquerading code in the kernel will not be able to recognize fragments from masqueraded connections without knowing the source and destination IP and ports. Additional protocol support is automatically built as modules when you build a kernel with masquerading support. (Just don't forget to load the modules into the running kernel before using them.) The full set of options follows:

Compiling Support for IP Masquerading into the 2.2.x Kernel

```
Networking options --->
    <*> Packet socket
    [*] Network firewalls
    <*> Unix domain sockets
    [*] TCP/IP networking
    [*] IP: advanced router
    [*] IP: firewalling
    [*] IP: always defragment (required for masquerading)
    [*] IP: masquerading
    --- Protocol-specific masquerading support will be built as modules.
    [*] IP: ICMP masquerading

Filesystems --->
    [*] /proc filesystem support
```

10.5.1   Configuring IP Masquerading with *ipchains*

As with IP accounting and firewalling, once you have a kernel with masquerading support, you use *ipchains* (for 2.2.x kernels) to configure **rules**. In this case, the rules are part of the packet-forwarding mechanism (as compared to the input, output, or accounting mechanisms). The syntax for *ipchains* is identical to that covered in Section 10.1.2, but we use some different arguments for masquerading.

Managing rules consists of entering, viewing, editing, and removing them. Entering them involves specifying pattern-matching criteria along with the option(s) to tell the kernel to perform masquerading when a match occurs. Recall that *ipchains* uses the concept of **targets**, so masquerading occurs when a packet matches a rule with a target of `MASQ`. Furthermore, only packets that are being forwarded can be masqueraded.

---

[2]The stock Debian kernel comes with masquerading enabled, as may others.

Adding IP Masquerading Rules with *ipchains*

All packets being forwarded automatically traverse the built-in `forward` chain. To masquerade them, add a rule to the `forward` chain with a target of `MASQ`. Alternatively, you can add a rule to the `forward` chain which has a user-defined chain as its target, there being somewhere along this chain a rule with the built-in target `MASQ`. Perhaps a few examples will clear this up:

```
# masquerade EVERYTHING
### insert a rule that masquerades everything that the
### kernel forwards, using the built-in "forward" chain
###
### (note that not specifying any matching criteria means
### that all packets will be matched)
erbium:/root> ipchains -I forward 1 -j MASQ


# masquerade packets forward out over ppp0
### create a user-defined chain named "ipmasq" and append it to
### the built-in "forward" chain, and then add a rule to masquerade
###  packets which will be forwarded over the ppp0 interface
erbium:/root> ipchains -N ipmasq
erbium:/root> ipchains -A forward -j ipmasq
erbium:/root> ipchains -A ipmasq -i ppp0 -j MASQ
```

You may want to masquerade traffic only from certain subnets or traffic destined for a particular subnet. To do this, use the `-s` and *-d* switches (among others) to specify some packet-matching criteria. For example, for erbium, we might find it conceptually simplest to masquerade only traffic bound for the client's network instead of trying to figure out what interface is forwarding the traffic. So we would use rules such as:

```
# masquerade packets destined for host 10.10.34.216
### use the /maskbits notation for the subnet mask
erbium:/root> ipchains -A forward -d 10.10.34.216/32 -j MASQ


### is equivalent to:
erbium:/root> ipchains -A forward -d 10.10.34.216/255.255.255.255 -j MASQ


### is equivalent to:
erbium:/root> ipchains -A forward -d 10.10.34.216 -j MASQ
```

Sometimes it is easier to specify what you do not want to masquerade. For example, you may have a topology where the firewall is performing masquerading, but several machines located outside the firewall that routes for your internal networks. You do not want connections to these machines from internal machines to be masqueraded, because any meaningful information about the source IP address is lost. If the internal network you need to masquerade is 192.168.0.0/255.255.0.0, and the external network is 210.56.12.64/255.255.255.192, you can set the rules as follows:

```
# masquerade everything from the internal network
# to everywhere except the perimeter net
```

```
### masquerade for almost all destinations
erbium:/root> ipchains -I forward -s 192.168.0.0/16      \
              -d ! 210.56.12.64/25 -j MASQ

# OR, an alternative solution

### masquerade for all destinations
erbium:/root> ipchains -A forward -s 192.168.0.0/16 -j MASQ
### forward _without_ masquerading to the perimeter net
erbium:/root> ipchains -I forward -d 210.56.12.64/25
```

By using user-defined chains and the special targets **MASQ** and **RETURN**, you can create very intricate rulesets which masquerade only certain types of connections and provide accounting for different aspects of the process. Refer to the manpage for more information about managing rules using *ipchains*.

Modifying IP Masquerading Rules with *ipchains*

Spend a little time with the *ipchains* manpage and you will grow familiar with methods of manipulating existing rules. Being able to make modifications to chains, such as inserting rules into chains at arbitrary locations, is quite handy, since, unlike IP accounting, masquerading rules are sensitive to order. Here's a synopsis of useful command forms:

ipchains -R *chain n rule*   replaces the *n*th rule for chain *chain* with the new rule specified by *rule*. (Rules are numbered starting at 1.)

ipchains -D *chain n*   deletes the *n*th rule from chain *chain*. If you'd rather specify the rule explicitly, just use it in place of the number.

ipchains -I *chain n rule*   inserts the rule given into the *n*th position for chain *chain*, moving each of the existing rules down. (Rules are numbered starting at 1.) Omitting the position argument defaults to the first position in the list.

Viewing IP Masquerading Rules with *ipchains*

You can view the counters associated with rules by listing (-L) the rules on a chain along with some switches to increase the amount of detail (normally -v, -n, and -x).

```
### list masquerading rules
### (headers/output split into two lines)
erbium:/root> ipchains -L forward -n -v
Chain forward (policy ACCEPT: 33 packets, 1686 bytes):

 pkts bytes target  prot  opt     tosa tosx  ifname      mark    outsize
   33  1686 MASQ    all   ------  0xFF 0x00  eth1

            source       destination  ports
            0.0.0.0/0    0.0.0.0/0    n/a
```

Some additional notes about viewing the rules:

- `-n` prevents name resolution from occurring.

- `-v` makes the output more verbose, adding the packet (`pkts`) and byte (`bytes`) counter fields, the interface field (`ifname`), the TOS masks (`tosa` and `tosx`), and the `mark` and `outsize` fields.

- `-x` is useful only in combination with `-n`. It prevents conversion of the byte and packet counters into larger units of K, M, or G.

- If you do not specify a *chainname*, all chains will be listed. If you want only to see rules which result in masquerading, *grep* the output for `MASQ`.

- If you do not specify the verbose switch, you will not see the interface field (an oversight, in my opinion), which is important unless you do all of your masquerading based solely on source or destination address.

Viewing Active Masqueraded Connections

You may view the current list of masqueraded connections with *ipchains*. The syntax is:
ipchains -M -L [-n] [-v]:

- The `-n` (once again) switch prevents hostname and portname lookups. Its use is optional.

- use `-v` (verbose) if you would like to see the `initseq delta prevd` fields in the output.

  — `initseq`—the initial sequence number
  — `delta`—the difference between the client's opinion of the current sequence number (read from its most recent packet) and the server's opinion of the current sequence number.
  — `prevd`—the previous delta value

```
#  ipchains -M -L
IP masquerading entries
prot expire   source              destination         ports
TCP  03:57.94 192.168.107.223     195.20.227.241      3160 (62041) -> 80
TCP  01:22.40 192.168.104.221     193.71.196.106      1185 (62057) -> 80
TCP  01:22.46 192.168.104.221     193.71.196.106      1182 (62054) -> 80
TCP  14:27.44 192.168.104.221     193.71.196.101      1184 (62056) -> 80
TCP  11:58.10 192.168.108.220     204.71.200.55       1099 (63099) -> 5050
UDP  01:57.29 192.168.101.14      24.112.240.60       1076 (62219) -> 53
```

Each line of the output represents a masqueraded connection. As you can see, there are five actively masqueraded connections at this time. Looking at the 192.168.104.221 client, you will notice that a **masqueraded connection** refers to every unique port pair between a client and server; there are two active connections from this client to the same server.

Two fields should be noted. The `expire` field is the wall-clock time remaining before the masquerading is taken down for this connection. It is in *minutes:seconds.hundredths*. The `ports` field is in the format *client (router) → server*. The router port is the port to which the server will reply to a client request. After unmasquerading the packet, the router sends it back to the client at the client port.

What Is the Expire Field and Why Is It Necessary?

If someone initiates a TCP connection, but then some evil befalls him/her and he/she is not able to take down the connection gracefully, the masquerading router will sit there forever waiting for more packets, because it never saw the stream taken down properly. Since UDP is stateless, the situation is even more dire; the router is never able to intercept any information about the final packet in a UDP sequence. However, during their normal operation both types of masquerading use up ports on the router. If the masquerading never timed out, some of these ports would linger forever ... or until the next reboot, which would probably have to occur when all 65535 ports on the system were exhausted. The expire timers are reset each time the connection is used. They then start counting down. If they reach zero before another packet is sent or received via the connection, the masquerading for that session is torn down.

Modifying Masquerade Expiration Timeouts with *ipchains*

You can modify the expire timeout values to something other than the defaults set in *ip_masq.h*. Those defaults are 15, 2, and 5 minutes for TCP sessions, TCP in the FIN WAIT state (after receiving a FIN packet), and UDP packets, respectively. There is also a default for ICMP (about two minutes), which may be set only by modifying the header file and recompiling the kernel. The syntax to modify the TCP and UDP values is:

ipchains -M -S *tcp tcpfin udp*

Note that you must specify all three of the timeout parameters, which have the unit of seconds. If you want to leave a value set to its current value, you can specify a timeout of 0. You may find tuning this useful if you have the habit of logging into a remote site over a masqueraded connection and do not want to be logged out after 15 minutes of inactivity.

10.5.2   IP Masquerading Information in */proc*

Another way to view rules, counters, and expire timeouts is to poke around in the */proc* filesystem. The amount of information you can find here has been increased with the 2.2.x kernel. Some highlights are listed in Table 10.6.

Probably the most interesting of these for day-to-day use is */proc/net/ip_masquerade*. Besides displaying the actively masqueraded connections in raw format, it shows the number of ports available for masquerading each type of connection.

```
erbium:/root> cat /proc/net/ip_masquerade
Prc FromIP    FPrt ToIP      TPrt Masq Init-seq  Delta PDelta Expires
(free=40959,40956,40960)

TCP C0A80102:0464 D08C7063:006E F658 00000000       0      0     479
TCP C0A80102:0466 1801F046:006E F65A 00000000       0      0    1145
UDP C0A80102:0434 1801F021:0035 F30B 00000000       0      0   18839
TCP C0A80102:0448 D0EDB215:0050 F65B 00000000       0      0   88925
TCP C0A80102:0465 D11E0216:006E F659 00000000       0      0     847
```

From this output, we see that 40959 ports are available for masquerading UDP connections, 40956 for TCP connections, and 40960 for ICMP connections. We also see the five connections currently masqueraded and the number of clicks remaining for their expire timers (expressed in hundredths of a second).

Table 10.6 Some Information You Can Find in the */proc* Filesystem

file[a]	description
ip_fwnames	lists all chains, including the chain name, default policy, reference count, packet count watermarks (high and low), and byte count watermark (high and low).
ip_fwchains	contains all rules from all chains (the chainname is the first field). This is merely a quick way to list all active rules.
ip_masquerade	lists the current masqueraded connections in raw format, along with the number of free ports available for UDP, TCP, and ICMP masquerading. (See the sample output in Section 10.5.2 for more information.)
ip_masq/app	contains the active reference counts for the kernel built-in masquerading protocol modules. It has four fields:

- **prot**—one of `TCP`, `UDP`, or `ICMP`

- **port**—the port which needs to be monitored to properly masquerade the protocol

- **n_attach**—the number of active masquerading connections using the module and port

- **name**—the protocol name, i.e., the protocol modules name *sans ip_masq_*

ip_masq/icmp	available when `CONFIG_IP_MASQUERADE_MOD` is enabled in the kernel—provides support for special modules that can modify the rewriting rules used when masquerading. It gives the userspace program *ipmasqadm* access to the kernel data structures.
ip_masq/tcp	see *ip_masq/icmp*
ip_masq/udp	see *ip_masq/icmp*

[a]All pathnames are relative to */proc/net*.

If you suspect that you are low on ports for masquerading, you: (a) might want to remember to check here to see what the kernel thinks, (b) might have a busy site, and (c) may want to compile a new kernel to adjust the number of ports available. The values you need to change are `PORT_MASQ_BEGIN` and `PORT_MASQ_END` in */usr/src/linux/include/net/ip_masq.h*. After modifying the source, you will have to recompile the kernel and reboot for the change to take effect. (For those of you who worked with the 2.0 kernel, you'll notice that the number of free ports assigned to masquerading by default is increased by a factor of 10 for the 2.2.x kernel versions.)

One last note about using *ipchains* to configure your rules. You will need to store the rules in a script once you get them the way you want them or else they will be lost during the next reboot. You may even want to save a hard copy of the forwarding/masquerading rules.

If you don't like the idea of configuring these rules by hand, check the following section for information about configuration tools.

10.5.3   IP Masquerading Configuration Tools

IP masquerading is a very commonly performed task. As such, a lot of work has been put into making it easier to configure. Now that you know what lies underneath, here are some packages which might aid you in configuring it for your system.

ipmasq is a native Debian package based on the scripts in the LDP's *IP Masquerade mini-HOWTO*. If you would like to use the package without running Debian, you can retrieve the source from any Debian mirror site. The following is taken from the description which accompanies the package:

> By default, this package configures the system as a basic forwarding firewall, with IP spoofing and stuffed routing protection. The firewall will allow hosts behind the firewall to get to the Internet, but not allow connections from the Internet to reach the hosts behind the firewall. However, **ipmasq** now features a very flexible framework where you can override any of the predefined rules if you so choose. It also allows you to control if the rules are reinterpreted when *pppd* brings a link up or down. This package should be installed on the firewall host and not on the hosts behind the firewall.

dotfile-ipfwadm is a module for **dotfile**. This package uses a Tcl/Tk interface to allow you to graphically build your own accounting, forwarding, input, output, and masquerading rules. It can be very helpful for quickly developing a set of rules, which it outputs to a file. You can then tweak the rules as needed. It allows you to select only options which are applicable to your running kernel. For non-Debian systems, check to see if *dotfile* is available, otherwise visit *http://www.imada.ou.dk/~blackie/dotfile/*. (Note, this currently supports only *ipfwadm* commands for the 2.0 kernel.)

netbase contains a command called *ipfwadm-wrapper*. This package will be installed on your system in any event, but it is nice to be aware of *ipfwadm-wrapper* when converting to *ipchains*.

MasqDialer (Debian package **masqdialer**) is suited to replace the scripting work I had to do by hand for erbium. The description from the Debian package is shown below. I wish it had been available back when I started on that. <sigh>.

> The masqdialer system is designed to provide easily accessible control of multiple dial-out modem connections to the members of a LAN using IP Masquerade for their Internet connectivity. The system is a client/server design, so as long as a client can be written for a particular platform, that platform can take advantage of masqdialer's offerings. The masqdialer daemon runs on the Linux machine, and upon an authorized client request, carries out the user's request.

MasqDialer's home website is *http://cpwright.villagenet.com/mserver/*. There is a GUI front end for managing the server available in the Debian package **tkmasqdialer**. You will also need the **mclient** package, which is a command-line client used to communicate with the server.

10.6   Using IP Masquerading Every Day

Masquerading is great when it works and can be miserable to troubleshoot when it doesn't. Things can go wrong if you've specified rules that masquerade too much, not enough, or in the wrong direction. It may also be that the protocol doesn't lend itself to masquerading and is not supported via a protocol module. But in my experience, bad rules are often to blame.

First, think about what you want to accomplish. For a dial-up connection into another corporation, you will probably want to masquerade everything headed from your network into theirs so that it can be returned back to you. The easiest way to do that is to masquerade everything leaving that interface. Something like `ipchains output -I -j MASQ -i ppp0` seems like it would do the trick. The rule means that everything that leaves the system over interface *ppp0* is masqueraded, regardless of its source or destination. Unfortunately, that will not work because the `-j MASQ` target is valid only for rules on the **forward** chain. If you use the same format with a forwarding rule (without specifying a source or a destination), you will be masquerading in both directions, or will you? And should you be masquerading in both directions anyway? (This *might* be OK, but before you jump on it, you need to determine if you want traffic coming back into your network from the PPP link to appear to originate from your extranet router.)

Instead of waxing philosophic about how to provide rules, I believe that they are easiest to understand by looking at pictures of what works and what doesn't. Masquerading is a topic with a lot of subtleties, and for me it was sometimes easier to grow accustomed to how to use it than to understand all the details of how it worked. Throughout this section, the router is shown to have two Ethernet devices, *eth0* and *eth1*. That both of these are Ethernet devices is purely arbitrary. The concepts would be valid if either of the interfaces were replaced by an interface of another type. The convention in the drawings is that *eth0* is on the *inside* and *eth1* is on the *outside*, when such a distinction is applicable.

Secret #1

The Linux kernel is smart about what to masquerade. When you have a rule that instructs the kernel to masquerade packets matching a particular source network/mask, it chooses the IP address to place in the headers, depending upon which interface is used to forward the packet. As an example, see Figure 10.7.

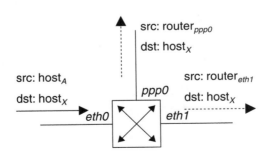

Figure 10.7 Masquerading Interface Is Chosen Based upon Packet Destination

Instead of replacing the packet's source IP with any IP on the system, it always uses the IP of the interface over which the packet will be sent.[3] This is the same interface that appears in the routing table for either the gateway route or network route which must be used to reach the destination IP. If you think about it, this is exactly what you want to happen. Any other action would be nonsensical, because the packet would not be routed back to you over the same interface, if at all.

Secret #2

Masquerading is directional with respect to client-server transactions. A client-sever transaction refers to the paradigm where the client initiates the connection to the server, sends to the server, and the server responds. As shown in Figure 10.8, we can represent such a connection as a pair of arrows, first from client to server and then from server to client. The router in this picture is configured to masquerade any packets with a source address in subnet$_A$. The masquerading bends the arrows a bit (because of the port changes), but the connection proceeds correctly.

It should not be surprising that, if the packet source address does not match, then the packet is not masqueraded. What about the reply? It has a source address from subnet$_B$, not from subnet$_A$. However, the reply is unmasqueraded correctly because the kernel is expecting and because it arrives on a special port.

What's interesting is when a client on subnet$_B$ tries to *open* a connection to a server on subnet$_A$, as depicted in Figure 10.9. (For this example, let's assume that the host on subnet$_B$ has a valid route to subnet$_A$, which will not always be the case.)

The packet passes from client to server untouched by the router because the source address did not match any of the packet criteria for masquerading. The server on subnet$_A$ formulates a response to the client and sends it. But now the packet matches the masquerading code. The kernel knows that something is amiss, since this is not the *direction* implied by the arguments given when establishing the rule, and it throws the packet into the bit bucket. The same situation depicted differently is shown in Figure 10.10.

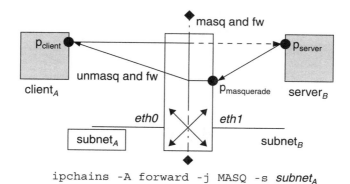

```
ipchains -A forward -j MASQ -s subnet_A
```

Figure 10.8 Masquerading Is Directional—Inside Out

---

[3]If you want to explicitly specify the interface to be used, then you can do so when you configure the IP masquerading rules with *ipchains*. However, you will see that it is unnecessary, unless you want every connection going out over that interface to be masqueraded.

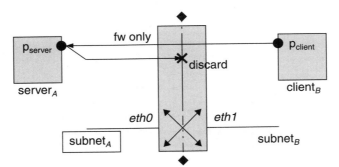

ipchains -I forward -j MASQ -s *subnet_A*

Figure 10.9 Masquerading Is Directional—Outside In

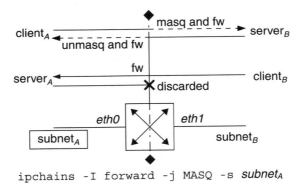

ipchains -I forward -j MASQ -s *subnet_A*

Figure 10.10 Masquerading Is Directional

You can verify this independently using packet sniffers—the server on subnet$_A$ will respond, but the response never gets forwarded by the router. One reason to mention this case is that not all masquerading routers are positioned between only two networks. If you used source-based rules without explicitly defining forwarding rules for the nets which should be able to communicate unmasqueraded, you might experience problems. This can be further compounded by the fact that ICMP (e.g., *ping*) and UDP (e.g., *traceroute*), which use both, will traverse this configuration in both directions without a problem. This can be alleviated by using interface-based masquerading rules, but be aware that they also have an implied direction and nuances.

Secret #3

Masquerading for an interface occurs only when the interface specified is the **forwarding interface**. Figure 10.11 depicts a configuration where masquerading is set up to be performed on the *eth1* interface, which we will call the *outside*. The interface on the inside is *eth0*.

As you can see from the arrows in Figure 10.11, connections from the inside out are masqueraded, but those from the outside in are not. To complete our terminology, the **forwarding interface** is the interface on the router that *sends* (forwards) the *outbound* (inside → out) connection. The packets which emerge from this interface will be masqueraded, provided that they met any other criteria in the masquerading rule (such as protocol, source, or destination addresses). For an *inbound* connection, *eth1* is the receiving interface, not the forwarding interface. Note, in addition to the definition of the forwarding interface, that the situation is identical to the source-based masquerading example with respect to direction. Client-to-server connections which are forwarded by the masquerading interface will succeed. Client-to-server connections which use the masquerading interface as a receiving interface for packets in the client → server direction will be swallowed by the kernel.

So what do the secrets mean? That depends upon your masquerading application. Perhaps they might save you some time when configuring masquerading on your system. Packet sniffing, presented in Section 3.3, is an excellent way to troubleshoot masquerading problems, but you'll need to be monitoring on both sides of the masquerading router to get the complete picture of what is happening. Other things to keep in mind when troubleshooting masqueraded connections so that you don't spend all day chasing ghosts are:

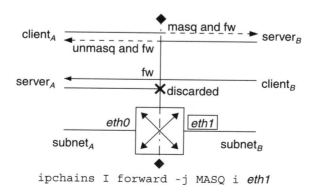

ipchains I forward -j MASQ i *eth1*

Figure 10.11 Interface Masquerading Must Occur on the Forwarding Interface

- The problem may not be with your rules configuration, but may be that you have failed to load the correct module to masquerade the protocol being used.

- The protocol you are using might not have masquerading support in the kernel at all. Watch out for protocols where the server tries to open a connection with the client.

- When dealing with extranet connections, sometimes the problem is either the NAT or some firewalling on the remote side (although masquerading a masqueraded connection does work when correctly configured).

- Firewalling rules and masquerading rules are executed sequentially, in the order defined by your configuration. Take care that you are not filtering out part of the masqueraded connection (perhaps by blocking part of the masquerading port range).

- Proxies are an excellent way of avoiding the issue for Internet masquerading. One drawback is that you may have to give up some of the standard services you run on that system (e.g., telnet) or train your users to telnet to a different port when connecting to a client. However, not everything can be proxied. See Section 9.1 for more information.

- Tools are available to aid you in configuring masquerading—sweet, nourishing tools! (See Section 10.5.3.)

10.7   Kernel Port Forwarding—High Wizardry

Now we are about to come full circle on TCP/IP stack tricks. Some clever kernel folks decided that the functionality being performed by the user-level processes we've discussed could also be implemented completely in the kernel. In review of the previous two sections, **IP transparent proxying** could have been named **firewall port redirection**. Its purpose is to redirect traffic to a local port, regardless of its destination. In contrast, the user-space redirectors take traffic bound for a local port and forward it to a predetermined destination. This section covers extensions to the IP masquerading code in the kernel which can perform a mixture of these functions. But before we dive in, there are a few things you should know about kernel port forwarding.

- This functionality is available only in the 2.2 kernel or later. (This is not entirely true. There are patches for the 2.0 kernel available which support IPPORTFW, one of the functionalities discussed here. If you want to use this on the 2.0 kernel, retrieve the Debian packages **ipportfw** and **kernel-patch-ipportfw** to get started. You may also want to refer to the documentation at *http://www.monmouth.demon.co.uk/ipsubs/ portforwarding.html*. This section will not cover the 2.0 kernel.)

- You will need the *ipmasqadm* package if your distribution does not include this binary. The source is *http://juanjox.linuxhq.com/*. Debian users already have it; it is included in the **netbase** package.

- This code is still considered experimental. This means that YMMV, and in some places the documentation is still a little spotty. The 2.3 kernel coders are working on an entirely new functionality called *netfilter*,[4] which will replace this code and *ipchains*. I mention this because you may not see a lot of additional development for these modules.

---

[4]Those of you who like to be on the bleeding edge (and who can tolerate a kernel panic or two) can check out the new development at *http://netfilter.kernelnotes.org/netfilter-hacking-HOWTO.html*.

To use kernel port forwarding, you must compile support for it into your kernel. Each of the IP masquerading special modules may be compiled as a module or directly into the kernel. The options required are given below.

10.7.1   Compiling Support for Kernel Port Forwarding into the 2.2.x Kernel

```
Code maturity level options --->
    [*] Prompt for development and/or incomplete code/drivers

Networking options --->
    <*> Packet socket
    [*] Network firewalls
    [*] TCP/IP networking
    [*] IP: advanced router
    [*] IP: firewalling
    [*] IP: always defragment (required for masquerading)
    [*] IP: masquerading
    [*] IP: masquerading special modules support
    <*> IP: ipautofw masq support (EXPERIMENTAL)
    <*> IP: ipportfw masq support (EXPERIMENTAL)
    <*> IP: ip fwmark masq-forwarding support (EXPERIMENTAL)

Filesystems --->
    [*] /proc filesystem support
```

The last three options are the ones of interest—they are actual "special modules." To differentiate among them through the end of this section, I will refer to them as **AUTOFW**, **PORTFW**, and **FWMARK**, respectively.

10.7.2   Kernel Port Forwarding—AUTOFW

The first of these, AUTOFW, allows for the masquerading of protocols which do not have their own protocol helpers. The list of masquerading protocol helpers (i.e., protocols which already have support in the kernel) can be found in Section 10.4.1. The idea is that sometimes an internal (masqueraded) client will connect to an external resource via a control connection (typically TCP), but the external resource returns data on a range of ports, possibly UDP ports. This is often the case for streaming media protocols, such as RealAudio and Netmeeting. When the router masquerades the outgoing connection, it expects traffic to return only from the server port to which the client sent. The situation is depicted in Figure 10.12.

AUTOFW attempts to mend this situation by allowing a range of ports to be forwarded to the internal system, also known as the **hidden system**. There are two ways to specify which internal system should receive the packets. The first is to explicitly define the IP address of this system (using the **-h** *hiddenhost* option). The second is to use an autodetection technique which watches for traffic to traverse a specified control port. The (internal) sender of that traffic is then noted as the correct recipient of the inbound data destined for the range of ports. If you take a moment to consider either of these two options, you'll notice (at least) one serious problem. Namely, the functionality is not designed for use by multiple internal clients connecting to a single external server simultaneously. Any single client can use the service, and as soon as it is finished, a different client (assuming that you're using the autodetection

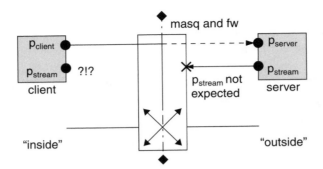

Figure 10.12 An Application for AUTOFW

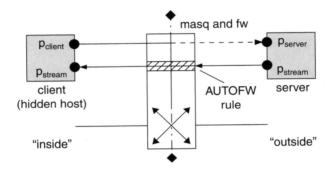

Figure 10.13 AUTOFW at Work

mechanism) will be able to use the service. By specifying the hidden host explicitly, only one client can ever use the service (until you reconfigure the AUTOFW rule). When it does its thing, port forwarding looks like Figure 10.13.

Its limitations aside, the AUTOFW functionality may have usefulness, and it is a handy thing to have in your bag-o-tricks. In order to use it, make sure that you have support for it in your kernel, and that you've loaded the `ip_masq_autofw` module if you compiled it as a module. Next, you need to masquerade the outgoing (control) connection as you normally would with *ipchains*. Now you need to add your autoforwarding rule with `ipmasqadm autofw` `-A`. Documentation on this is a little sparse. If you invoke `ipmasqadm autofw` (with no arguments), then you will evoke a usage statement. (Note that the option syntax is the same as for the *ipautofw* which was used for the AUTOFW patches running on the 2.0 kernel.)

```
hafnium:/root> ipmasqadm autofw

Usage:
    ipautofw <command> <options>

Valid commands:
```

`-A`	`add new autoforward entry`
`-D`	`delete an autoforward entry`
`-F`	`flush the autoforward table`

`(and so on)`

It supports three basic commands, similar to *ipchains*, plus options that specify how you want the autoforwarding to work. Remember that there are two ways to use autoforwarding. The first specifies the hidden host explicitly; the second infers it from activity on the control connection.

<code>ipmasqadm autofw -A -r proto lport hport -h ipaddr -u</code>

The first syntax always names the hidden host with `-h`. `-A` indicates that a rule should be added. The `-r` specifies the protocol (either `udp` or `tcp`) and the range of ports to be autoforwarded to the hidden host. The `-u` tells the kernel to allow timeouts longer than the default of 15 seconds.

<code>ipmasqadm autofw -A -r proto lport hport -c proto port -u</code>

The second command is the same as the first, except that instead of specifying a hidden host, `-c` indicates the control connection of protocol *proto* and port *port*. Once you establish rules, look at */proc/net/ip_masq/autofw* to get an idea of what is happening.

10.7.3   Kernel Port Forwarding—PORTFW

The PORTFW feature has a different focus (and is less complicated!) than AUTOFW. Its aim is to replace user-space redirectors by performing the same task in kernel-space. If done correctly, it should have lower resource requirements than the user-space equivalents. The drawback is that some features, such as configurable logging formats and access control lists,[5] are not implemented to prevent bloating the kernel code. (The developers did manage to include support for preferences and load balancing.) There is much less to discuss about using this option, because you should already be familiar with the concepts from the discussion on user-space redirectors. PORTFW has the added feature of preserving the original sender's IP address when forwarding the connection (like *redir* using the `--transproxy` option).

There are a couple of details you should keep in mind when using PORTFW. First, because this code is an extension to the masquerading code in the kernel, it may occur only during the forwarding of a packet. This means that you cannot use PORTFW on a firewall to redirect an internal to a local port on that firewall. Because the packet remains on the "inside" of the firewall, no forwarding occurs. In practice, this is not the sort of thing you would want to do with PORTFW anyway, but it might cause some confusion when you test your port forwarding from an internal address. (You can achieve the desired effect with transparent proxying anyway.) The second point is that the PORTFW rules, by themselves, do not masquerade the outgoing (internal) server → (external) client replies. This means that if you port forward inbound requests (from an external client to an internal server), you may want to masquerade the outbound reply. Otherwise, the client will see the reply from a different server (the internal address) than the one it sent the request to (the external firewall address). This may or may not pose a problem. If it does, add a masquerading rule for these packets, similar to one you would use for connections in the other direction.

---

[5] Which is not a distinct limitation, since only the connections specified by the masquerading rule will be matched.

To make use of PORTFW in production, you advertise the IP address of your web server to the world via DNS as the IP address of the external interface on the firewall. If internal users are to use the same resource, you can overload this name on the internal DNS server with the internal IP address. Then configure the PORTFW rule to redirect inbound connections to the IP address(es) of the web server. You set up your forwarding rules using the following syntax:

```
hafnium:/root> ipmasqadm portfw -h
Usage: portfw -a -P PROTO -L LADDR LPORT -R RADDR RPORT [-p PREF] add entry
       portfw -d -P PROTO -L LADDR LPORT [-R RADDR RPORT]         delete entry
       portfw -f                                                  clear table
       portfw -l                                                  list table
       portfw <args> -n                                           no names

PROTO is the protocol, can be "tcp" or "udp"
LADDR is the local interface receiving packets to be forwarded.
LPORT is the port being redirected.
RADDR is the remote address.
RPORT is the port being redirected to.
PREF  is the preference level (load balancing, default=10)
```

Notice that the −a (add), −d (delete), and −f (flush) options are in lowercase, unlike for AUTOFW (<frown>), and that you always precede these options ipmasqadm portfw. The usage is straightforward, but there are a few additional tips in Table 10.7.

Table 10.7 *ipmasqadm* PORTFW Options

option	description
-l	lists not only the rules but also the pcnt and pref fields, which are explained along with the -p option.
-n	suppresses name resolution, as it normally does. It makes sense to specify this in conjunction with -l.
-p *preference*	load balancing is implemented via a simple counter. The rules are stored in the kernel as a linked list, and by default, each rule is initialized with a preference count (pcnt) of 10. Each time the rule is used, the preference count is decremented. When the counter reaches 0, the rule is moved to the end of the list. In the degenerate case of a single rule, this doesn't change anything. But if there are multiple rules for a given LADDR:LPORT pair, then shuffling the list will result in the next entry (with a different RADDR:RPORT value) being used on the next request. Use -p 1 to implement a simple round-robin scheme. If one server is more capable than another, you can weight your preference values according.

The following sequence of commands is a simple example of usage:

```
# kernel PORTFW for inbound requests

### set up the port forwarding
# the .27 system gets the bulk of the requests because it
# has the new UltraPANTHEON 4692 HTTP coprocessor chip
ipmasqadm portfw -a -P tcp -L extip 80 -R 192.168.16.27 80 -p 15
ipmasqadm portfw -a -P tcp -L extip 80 -R 192.168.16.28 80 -p 5

### need masquerading rules too!
ipchains -A -p tcp -s 192.168.16.27/32 80 -j MASQ
ipchains -A -p tcp -s 192.168.16.28/32 80 -j MASQ
```

Remember that you can perform a sort of load balancing by specifying preferences for your rules. Test your setup by telnetting to an external machine and then trying to telnet to the firewall at port 80. You should connect to the internal system. Issue the command quit to disconnect. As with most things in the kernel, you do not have to use the commands provided to get an idea of what is going on. In this case, you can view the contents of */proc/net/ip_masq/portfw*.

10.7.4   Kernel Port Forwarding—FWMARK

FWMARK basically accomplishes the same goal as PORTFW—to redirect traffic to an internal host using private address space—but adds a more powerful way to specify which inbound connections are to be forwarded. It does this by operating in conjunction with *ipchains*, which is used to **mark** packets with a label (actually, an integer). A FWMARK rule can then act upon a packet bearing a certain mark, with different rules operating on each type of mark.

Consider the case where you would like a certain set of users to be redirected to one web server (perhaps with privileged information) while the rest always use another server. With PORTFW, there is no way to specify any sort of source criteria; this also goes for transparent proxying. So you would have to publish a second IP address (and therefore DNS record, etc.), use PORTFW or a redirector bound to the second interface, and then perform some sort of filtering to make sure that unprivileged machines could not connect to the restricted redirector. As long as you can differentiate between clients based on IP address, FWMARK allows you to do this sort of selection without leaving clues as to the different forms of access.

The command syntax is similar to that for PORTFW (except that most of the options have changed from lowercase to uppercase and vice versa). There is no need to specify the local address or port, because *ipchains* syntax takes care of that with the criteria it uses to mark the packet.

```
hafnium:/root> ipmasqadm mfw
Usage: mfw -A -m FWMARK -r RADDR RPORT [-p PREF]  add entry
       mfw -D -m FWMARK [-r RADDR RPORT]          delete entry
       mfw -E -m FWMARK [-r RADDR RPORT]          edit entry
       mfw -S -m FWMARK                           force scheduling
       mfw -F                                     clear table
       mfw -L                                     list table
       mfw <args> -n                              no names
```

The syntax is straightforward, but the option -S does bear explanation. The round-robin scheduling mechanism used in PORTFW is also available for FWMARK, but with an extension. If a rule's preference is set to 0, no scheduling is performed, and that rule retains its position in the linked list of rules. If there are other rules with nonzero preferences, the zero-preference rule will eventually become the first rule in the list for that mark and will stay there. This will remain so until you force scheduling to occur by invoking `ipmasqadm mfw -S`. At this time, whatever rule is at the head of the linked list will be moved to the back, promoting the next rule. An application of this is to perform failover from one RADDR to another—set all preferences to 0 and, if the primary server is detected to be down, force scheduling of the rules to select the next in line.

Marking packets with *ipchains* is not difficult either. You mark them with an integer value using -m *markvalue*. Below is a sequence of commands which will enforce a policy like the one we described at the beginning of this subsection.

```
# kernel firewall mark forwarding for web access
#
# use these symbolic names to keep everything straight
MARK_FRIEND=1
MARK_NEUTRAL=3
FRIEND=209.81.8.0/24
FRIEND_SVR=192.168.17.3/32
NEUTRAL_SVR=192.168.15.46/32

# mark packets as they enter the system
ipchains -I input -s ${FRIEND} -m ${MARK_FRIEND}
ipchains -I input -s ! ${FRIEND} -m ${MARK_NEUTRAL}

# establish forward/redir rules based on marks
ipmasqadm mfw -I -m ${MARK_NEUTRAL} -r ${NEUTRAL_SVR}
ipmasqadm mfw -I -m ${MARK_FRIEND} -r ${FRIEND_SVR}

# make sure that the replies are masqueraded, too
ipchains -I forward -d ${FRIEND} -s ${FRIEND_SVR} -j MASQ
ipchains -I forward -s ${NEUTRAL_SVR} -j MASQ
```

The script is a pretty simple case, but not so trivial that it cannot have interesting uses. Note the lack of -p *protocol* and port specifications in the *ipchains* commands and the lack of a `rport` in the *ipmasqadm* statements. Because they are not specified, the commands will forward traffic for all ports (TCP, UDP, and ICMP) to the corresponding internal server. The same is true for the masquerading rules on the return trip. You could have just as easily added specific ports—it is up to you.

10.8 Summary

That concludes our tour of some of the redirection facilities available for Linux and, with it, the specific material for accounting, firewalling, and masquerading using the 2.2.x kernel. The differences in capabilities between Linux 2.0, 2.2, and 2.4 are significant, as is the learning curve to move from one to the other. Give yourself a correspondingly appropriate amount of time to become familiar with the facilities you'll be using, and remember that you're not alone, especially if you're using the 2.2 kernel. A *lot* of good information about *ipchains* is freely available in the HOWTOs and on people's private pages. If you have questions left unanswered, hit *google.com* and start searching.

Chapter 11

CONCLUSION

Wow! You've made it this far, and I sincerely hope that *Linux Routers* has advanced your knowledge and given you some ideas about how to run Linux in your environment. For the most part, the scenarios presented in this book are "real-life"—that is, I've used Linux to deploy them in production. As such, I feel confident that they are realistic applications of Linux routers, but I'm certain that they are merely a small subset of practical Linux production uses. Therefore, the omission of an application scenario that meets your needs should not deter you from such a deployment. In fact, I am constantly fine-tuning my production Linux systems to find the right match of security, functionality, and ease of administration.

When developing new types of Linux routers, my suggestion is to keep an eye toward fundamentally sound system administration practices. If you recall the first chapter in this book, when we discussed hardware selection and choice of Linux distribution, the emphasis was not on cutting-edge technology, nor on the distribution with the most bells and whistles. In my opinion, technology for the sake of technology has its place, but not in router closets or data centers. And stability goes beyond hardware and software—they are merely a foundation. Best practices for system administration include good documentation and change management, plus a level head concerning when to deploy what, and how to expeditiously address outages.

I'm not going to review each of the chapters, since hopefully they speak for themselves and you can refer back to them as you like. A few comments surfaced during the technical reviews of this book that I would like to include now. First, the portions of the text that deal with hardware selection illustrate that I am guilty of an i386 bias with respect to Linux. Actually *bias* isn't really the correct term—it just so happens that the bulk of the Linux routers represented in the book are indeed 32-bit Intel boxes. I have, much to my delight, worked with Linux on the Alpha, SPARC, and StrongARM platforms. Whether or not one hardware architecture is superior to another is immaterial. The fact that you can use a common toolset across all of them is simply amazing. It has spoiled me and redoubled my complaints about having to work around the arbitrary differences that separate the commercial Unices. A penguin in every processor, or something like that . . . .

Another point brought to my attention is this book's lack of emphasis on security. My first instinct is to point the finger back at "traditional" routers that can be booted via *tftp*, have documented back doors, and have administrative interfaces running on unencrypted protocols. This, however, is merely a defensive parry. In truth I believe that any more discussion about security would have clouded the main topic of Linux router configuration. What good is a secure network that doesn't function? That should by no means lessen the importance of security in your mind. If you do not already have a handle on Unix, network security, and firewalling (the topics of several books longer than this), then you should do further research on these topics. There are references in the Bibliography and Appendix A.

Finally, a few people wanted to know why I presented such kooky router scenarios and examples. Once again, all I can say is that the book is very true to life. Unfortunately, this means that the router applications were not concocted to most clearly illustrate their functionality and the Linux features they employ. (Chapter 4, "Erbium," is certainly a good example of this.) There are some good straightforward NATs and firewalls in the *LDP*. I hope that the information there plus what is in this book will help you build newer, more advanced configurations than you find in either.

Except for Appendix A, which contains URLs and some support information, the appendices cover topics that either are too general or otherwise do not fit the flow of the main text. I encourage you to thumb through them to see if anything strikes your fancy. Happy routing!

tony mancill   *January 2002*

Appendix A

HELPFUL LINKS

Perhaps the greatest challenge facing a network administrator is being able to find the right information in a timely manner. I have listed links which you may find useful.

A.1 General

- *http://www.linuxdoc.org/* is home to the *Linux Documentation Project*, or *LDP*. This is an excellent resource for up-to-date HOWTOs.

- *http://www.faqs.org/rfcs/* is a good site for retrieving RFCs. RFCs are scattered all over the Internet, so any search should return a long list of hits, but not all of them are as well organized or formatted as this site. For Debian users, you can load the RFCs locally by installing the **doc-rfc** package.

- *http://www.linux.org/* and *http://www.linuxlinks.com/* are both good places to start out if you're not sure where you need to go for certain information.

- *http://www.freshmeat.net/* is a wonderfully current directory of software and software development projects for Linux (and other free operating systems). When someone says, "Have you used *X*?" and there isn't a Debian package for *X*, this is the first place I go.

- *http://www.fsf.org/* is the home of the *Free Software Foundation*. Here you can find authoritative documentation for the GNU tools in both electronic and hardcopy form. If you appreciate free software, drop in and make a tax-deductible contribution.

A.2 The Linux Kernel

- *http://www.kernel.org/*—the main kernel source repository.

- *http://edge.linuxhq.com/* is another site that posts information about changes in the kernel, patches, etc.

- *http://lwn.net/*—more kernel news, perhaps not as terse or cryptic as the sites listed above. The *Kernel NewsFlash* can be helpful.

A.3 Security

- *http://www.cert.org/*—CERT (Computer Emergency Response Team) provides security bulletins affecting all common operating systems and applications. You can subscribe to CERT's mailing list to keep current on various threats and available patches.

- *http://www.cerias.purdue.edu/*—CERIAS (Center for Education and Research in Information Assurance and Security) is an excellent security site, including news, documentation, and tools. (Some of you may know it from its previous incarnation, COAST [Computer Operations, Audit, and Security Technology], which is famous for its security archive.)

- *http://www.linuxsecurity.org/* is more specific than the previous two sites and focuses on Linux vulnerabilities and security news.

- *http://www.wwdsi.com/saint/*—the *SAINT* (follow-on to *SATAN* website) hosts not only the *SAINT* network security tools, but also several vulnerability assessment and awareness tutorials.

- *http://www.securityfocus.com/*—this is an excellent overall security website for Linux, Unix, and Microsoft operating systems. Take some time and browse through the library section and the archive of the Bugtraq list.

- *http://munitions.vipul.net/*—this site contains much good information about cryptography software for Linux.

A.4   Networking

- *http://www.linuxrouter.org/* is the Linux Router Project's homepage. This site is a must for those who want to use a Linux router on systems without a hard drive.

- *http://netfilter.samba.org/*—the same folks who bring you *Samba* are hosts to the *netfilter* project. Along with the latest software versions, there are security announcements and lots of documentation.

- *http://www.linuxtelephony.org/* is not strictly a site about Linux routers, but wherever there is a network of any size, telephony integration is not far behind.

- *http://www.sangoma.com/* has some protocol and TCP/IP subnetting tutorials that are useful. Also see the troubleshooting page (*http://www.sangoma.com/linedebug.htm*).

A.5   Debian GNU/Linux

- *http://www.debian.org/* can tell you just about anything you want to know about Debian. If it doesn't, try `#debian` on *irc.openprojects.net* for real-time interaction. Alternatively, try one of the mailing lists.

- Books on Debian:

  — *Debian GNU/Linux: Guide to Installation and Usage* by John Goerzen and Ossama Othman. ISBN: 0-7357-0914-9 *http://www.newriders.com/*

  — *Debian User's Guide*, 2nd ed., by Dale Scheetz. ISBN: 0-9659575-1-9 *http://www.linuxpress.com/*

Last, and probably least too, *http://mancill.com/linuxrouters/* contains errata discovered in this text and as many helpful links I can keep current. If you visit here, you'll discover that webpages are not my forte.

Appendix B

BUILDING THE LINUX KERNEL

Those of you who are already intimate with Linux and dealing with the kernel will find nothing new or interesting in this section. But those of you who may have had less exposure to Linux— read on! This section covers the basics of retrieving, patching, and building the Linux kernel. It embodies the x86-bias that permeates the book, only because 99 of 100 kernels I've built have been on x86 systems (and most new users seem to be running on this platform).

Although it is one of the best-scripted and most finely done parts of Linux, compiling the kernel seems to be a daunting task for a newcomer. Fortunately, it only *seems* that way. Many Linux distributions come with their own mechanisms to compile the kernel, and even with kernel source as a package. I prefer the *old-fashioned* way of building the kernel from the upstream sources, which is the method I will present here. It is a matter of a few easy steps.

1. Prepare your system for the kernel build process.

2. Obtain a copy of the kernel source.

3. Update or patch the kernel source as required.

4. Configure the kernel.

5. Compile and install the kernel.

B.1 Preparing Your System to Build the Kernel

To build a kernel, your system needs two things—the tools required to build the kernel and enough disk space underneath */usr/src* to hold the kernel source tree. The disk space required on an x86 platform, including the sources and the object files created during the build, is as follows:

version	size
2.0.36	36MB
2.2.9	60MB
2.2.14	93MB
2.3.51	114MB
2.4.12	163MB

As you can see, the kernel keeps growing in size as more architectures are supported and more device drivers added. This is awesome and exciting, although at some point the thing is going to be so truly monstrous that the code will have to fork into several trees. (On the flip side, bandwidth, processor power, and disk space seem to be growing at a rate far greater than the size of the kernel source tree.)

The tools required are a subset of those used in a standard C development environment. Because you may not be familiar with these, or did not load a development model when you first loaded the system, here is a list of the bare essentials which may not be part of the base install of your Linux distribution:

bin86—the 16-bit assembler and loader. (*Note:* This is x86-specific. There are other packages for the other architectures.)

binutils—the GNU assembler, linker, and binary utilities.

gcc—the GNU C compiler.

make—the GNU version of the *make* utility.

Every now and then it seems that I can't build a kernel without a copy of *bison* and *flex* on my system. I'd have them just in case. One nice thing about the kernel build is that you do not have to fully understand how to use these tools—the commands to invoke them have been scripted for you. In addition to those listed above, you may want to have the following packages on your system:

gnupg is the GNU Privacy Guard package and contains the *gpg* binary used to verify the kernel source after download.

bzip2 is a file-compression utility that gives better results than *gzip* (and therefore can save you some time and/or bandwidth when downloading the kernel source).

libncurses-dev is used to produce a menu-driven text interface to the kernel configuration scripts.

tk and **tcl**, both runtime and development packages, are needed to use the full-blown X-based GUI for kernel configuration.

superfloppy is used for formatting floppy disks.

B.2   Retrieving the Kernel Sources

The first time around you will need to retrieve a full set of kernel sources. If this is available as a package for your Linux distribution, feel free to use it instead (but read the instructions that come with it for details). I normally go to the nearest mirror of *ftp://ftp.kernel.org/*, `cd /pub/linux/kernel/v2.x`, and retrieve the latest stable *linux-w.x.y.tar.gz* or *.tar.bz2*. While you're there, also retrieve the *.sign* of the same name; we'll use this to verify that the kernel source we downloaded matches the one uploaded by the kernel maintainer.

Keep in mind that the stable versions of the Linux kernel have minor release numbers that are even (e.g., 2.0.x and 2.2.x) and the unstable/development versions have odd minor release numbers (e.g., 2.1.x and 2.3.x). Stick to stable versions of the kernel for your routers when possible. In fact, you may not even use the most recent major version. At the time of writing, version 2.4.x is out and stable, but small issues keep popping up with various functionalities or interactions between subsystems. If you have the resources, you can track the latest kernel on hardware similar to what you're running in production. Once you have some confidence, you can upgrade.

Kernel Versions

The *official* versioning scheme used in the kernel *Makefile* is *Version.Patchlevel. Sublevel*, but I've never heard anyone use this nomenclature. I think that you are more likely to be understood by others if you use *Major.Minor.Patchlevel* or *Major.Minor.Pointrelease*.

Before we extract the kernel source, we should verify that it matches what the kernel developer uploaded into the archive. Some sites do this with md5sums, but using GPG adds another layer of protection. Assuming that someone did hack into the archive and replace the kernel source with a trojaned version, they would then have to produce signatures that matched the key you're about to install into your keyring. Once you have the **gnupg** package loaded, you'll need to retrieve the *Linux Kernel Archives Verification Key <ftpadmin@kernel.org>* public key from a key server as follows:

```
bach:~$ gpg --keyserver wwwkeys.pgp.net --recv-keys 0x517D0F0E
gpg: requesting key 517D0F0E from wwwkeys.pgp.net ...
gpg: key 517D0F0E: public key imported
gpg: Total number processed: 1
gpg:               imported: 1
```

Or, if you don't have access directly to the outside, you can visit *http://www.kernel.org/ signature.html* and obtain the public key there. If you run into problems, there are more instructions on the verification process there too. Assuming that you have the key, you can now verify signatures from the kernel archive using **gpg --verify** *signfile binaryfile*. A bad signature will result in an error like one of the following:

```
bach:~$ gpg --verify linux-2.4.12.tar.bz2.sign linux-2.4.12.tar.bz2
gpg: CRC error; 45b265 - d9af5e
gpg: packet(2) with unknown version 67
```

OR

```
bach:~$ gpg --verify linux-2.4.12.tar.bz2.sign linux-2.4.12.tar.bz2
gpg: Signature made Thu Oct 11 01:05:25 2001 MST using DSA key ID 517D0F0E
gpg: BAD signature from "Linux Kernel Archives Verification Key <ftpadmin@kernel.org>"
```

In the first case, the signfile itself is suspect, since it failed a checksum test. In the second case, the signfile is a valid one from ftadminkernel.org, but it isn't a signature for the binary file specified (in this case, because I modified the binary file and repacked it). A good signature will look like the following.

```
bach:~$ gpg --verify linux-2.4.12.tar.bz2.sign linux-2.4.12.tar.bz2
gpg: Signature made Thu Oct 11 01:05:25 2001 MST using DSA key ID 517D0F0E
gpg: Good signature from "Linux Kernel Archives Verification Key <ftpadmin@kernel.org>"

Could not find a valid trust path to the key.  Let's see whether we
can assign some missing owner trust values.

No path leading to one of our keys found.
```

```
gpg: WARNING: This key is not certified with a trusted signature!
gpg:          There is no indication that the signature belongs to the owner.
gpg: Fingerprint: C75D C40A 11D7 AF88 9981  ED5B C86B A06A 517D 0F0E
```

The bit about the *valid trust path* is part of the game when using public-key signature software. After all, you don't *know* for a fact that the key belongs to ftpadminkernel.org, and *gpg* makes this point clear. You can establish a trust path (or **web of trust**) by getting out and meeting people at Linux conventions and the like, and attending or hosting key-signing parties. The idea is to have met the guy who is friends with one of the grad students of Professor Tux who's met a big OpenSource advocate who had just been at convention and met the FTP administrator for *kernel.org.* Oh yeah, and they all signed each other's keys.

On the other hand, you may find it improbable that both *wwwkeys.pgp.net* and *kernel.org* have been hacked simultaneously, and once you have the public key, someone would have to hack *kernel.org* and somehow produce signatures that matched that public key. In short, something is better than nothing, and this is a good start. But that should in no way dissuade you from building your web of trust. The more people there are participating in security, the more secure the community becomes, and the more difficult it becomes for mischief makers to try to damage that community. (Sort of like it is in real life, eh?) You can read more about this from the GnuGP website, specifically at *http://www.gnupg.org/gph/en/manual.html#AEN554.*

So, once you decide upon a kernel version, retrieve the sources, and are satisfied that they are what they claim to be, you need to extract the source tarball. The standard location is */usr/src/linux/.* The kernel source will create the *linux/* directory, so you should extract while */usr/src/* is your current working directory.

```
$ cd /usr/src
$ tar xzvf /path/to/linux-w.x.y.tar.gz
     OR, if you have the .bz2 file, use
$ tar xjvf /path/to/linux-w.x.y.tar.bz2
```

If you have an older version of *tar* you may have to specify -I to extract using *bzip2* (the story here is that -I conflicts with an option for Solaris' version of *tar*, and there are a lot of folks have to use both versions in their day-to-day).

To avoid confusion surrounding the version stored in your current source tree, you can annotate the directory name of the source to contain the current version, and then create a symbolic link so that */usr/src/linux* points to this directory. (If you're not sure what version of the source you have, you can check this quickly by viewing the first few lines of */usr/src/linux/Makefile.*)

```
$ cd /usr/src
$ mv linux linux-w.x.y
$ ln -s linux-w.x.y linux
```

B.3   Patching the Kernel

From time to time and for reasons mentioned previously, you will want to patch the kernel. Either you are upgrading from one point release (also called a **patchlevel**) to the next, or you have patches for a device driver that needs to be loaded.

With the kernel source as large as it is, you can save time once you have a full release by applying patches to upgrade between the point releases (e.g., from 2.2.1 to 2.2.2). This is done by retrieving the patch files from a kernel archive site and applying them to your source tree. (Don't worry ... your kernel configuration will not be overwritten.) These files are named *patch*-w.x.y.[gz|bz2] and are meant to be applied to a *w.x.(y-1)* kernel source tree. If you want to upgrade several by more than one patchlevel, apply the patches sequentially. As an example, let's say that we are running kernel 2.2.1. We need the following files to upgrade to the indicated kernel version:

2.2.2	**2.2.4**
patch-2.2.2.tar.bz2	patch-2.2.2.tar.bz2
	patch-2.2.3.tar.bz2
	patch-2.2.4.tar.bz2

Apply the patches with the following command:

```
$ cd /usr/src
$ bzcat ./patch-2.2.2.bz2 | patch -p0 -sEN
  OR
$ zcat ./patch-2.2.2.bz2 | patch -p0 -sEN
```

You don't have to use -sEN, but I like what they do most of the time. See the manpage for *patch* to learn more about them. If you keep your kernel source in a directory containing the version number, remember to update this directory name and point the symbolic link *linux* at it.

```
$ mv linux-{{\it w.x.y}} linux-{{\it w.x.y+1}}
$ ln -f -s linux-{{\it w.x.y+1}} linux
```

If you are installing patches which are not part of the official upstream kernel source, there should be accompanying instructions. For the most part, they will be similar to the procedure for the point-release patches, except that you might want to rename your kernel source tree something appropriate like *linux-w.x.y_mypatch*. Note that *patch* will create backups (prepatch versions) of files if you specify the -b option on the command line. It will also create *.rej* files for any touched hunk(s) of the patch that could not be applied.

B.3.1   To Patch or Not to Patch?

The decision to upgrade to the next patchlevel should be based on a need for either the functionality or protection that it provides. Most patches to the stable kernel tree are bug fixes, security patches, or driver support and are therefore a Good Idea. There are exceptions, such as one of the 2.2.x releases which had a memory leak in the memory management subsystem. Therefore, it is helpful to stay reasonably current with the state of the kernel. You can check out the changes between releases by visiting *http://edge.linuxhq.com* or the Linux Weekly News at *http://www.lwn.net*, which also offers a mailing list.

If these do not have sufficient information, then install the patch and check out */usr/src/ linux/Documentation/Changes*. This file contains pointers to other sources of documentation (and in several different languages). If you really want to see the differences, then download the patch file and *zcat* or *bzcat* it into a text file so that you can review the source itself.

B.4   Configuring the Kernel

Decisions, decisions .... Even if you're comfortable with hacking makefiles and applying patches, you still have to deal with the myriad of choices presented by the Linux kernel configuration tools. If at first you find it bewildering, do not fear. It amounts to nothing more than software configuration, so there's nothing you can break. If you mess up the configuration, **cd /usr/src/linux ; rm .config** and start your configuration over. If you gen a bad kernel, there's nothing you cannot fix by booting from a rescue floppy and generating a new kernel (or reverting to a previous one).

There are three different ways to specify your kernel configuration; they are equivalent in terms of result but vary in terms of user comfort. For all three, you should first **cd /usr/src/linux** so that you will be in the right place to start the configuration.

- **make config** is purely text based. It goes through the list of configuration questions sequentially, which is a drawback for beginners. If you make a mistake, you must start over from the beginning. On the other hand, you can run it on any type of terminal and easily over low-bandwidth connections. Help for most options is available by answering "?" to a question.

- **make menuconfig** is the menu-based configuration utility. It still runs in text mode but uses *ncurses* to create menus and dialog boxes. It works on the console and in nearly any type of recognized terminal emulator. It does require that you have the **ncurses** development libraries loaded on your system. The interface seems nonintuitive; note that you use <Exit> when you are finished with the menu selections currently on the screen.

- **make xconfig** is the graphical version of the configuration utility. It is based on the **Tcl/Tk** toolset (and therefore requires it to be loaded on your router) and requires that you have an X-server running on your workstation. It takes a few extra seconds to start up but is simple to use. Remember to export your DISPLAY to tell the router where to throw the X-client[1] and to tell the X-server to allow the client connection from the router.[2]

Regardless of the configuration method you choose, you will be presented with a list of questions to which you can answer (Y)es, (N)o, and sometimes (M)odule. "No" means, appropriately enough, that this functionality or driver is not accessible when running this kernel. "Yes" means that the code to support this functionality is compiled directly into the kernel. "Module," however, could be taken to mean "maybe." A module can be loaded into the running kernel at any time after boot-up, and it initializes itself at that time. Modules are a Good Thing—see Section B.6 on page 394 to find out more. My recommendation is to configure any device drivers which are not required to boot the system as modules.

The kernel options are divided into different sections and are hierarchical within each section. Selecting a certain option results in the ability to select suboptions which fall under it. For example, in the section `Networking device support`, you must select the option `3COM cards` to be able to select the suboption `3c509/3c579 support`. Some of the relationships are a bit more complex, but that is the basic gist. You will quickly get the hang of things and learn where drivers and options are found if you play with the *xconfig* version of the configuration utility, since the effects of your choices can be seen immediately (unavailable options are grayed out).

---

[1] **export DISPLAY**=*ip.address.of.workstation*:**0**
[2] `workstation>` **xhost** +*ip.address.of.router*

Once you select the desired configuration options, all three methods write the results to */usr/src/linux/.config.* If you have a kernel configuration you would like to move to another system, copy this file into */usr/src/linux/.* This is the only file in the kernel source tree which you must back up in order to be able to restore your configuration at a later date unless you're editing your kernel source by hand or have a complicated patching ritual that would be difficult to reproduce.

Which options should you choose? For the examples in this book, the required network-related options are spelled out. You also need driver support for the other devices on your system. You should not need esoteric filesystem drivers or support for soundcards or joysticks (on your routers, anyway).

B.5   Compiling the Kernel

To compile the kernel, you need a standard build environment loaded on your system. You're going to need this for lots of other stuff anyway, so I'm going to assume that you have it. There are five distinct steps:

1. Build the list of dependencies between the source files:

   ```
   $ make dep
   ```

2. Delete any of the object files from prior kernel builds:

   ```
   $ make clean
   ```

3. Build the kernel and automatically call *lilo* to update the master boot record with the new location of the kernel:

   ```
   $ make bzlilo
   ```

   or to place your kernel on a bootable floppy, use:

   ```
   $ make bzdisk
   ```

   or if you only want to build the new kernel, but not put it into place, you can use:

   ```
   $ make bzImage
   ```

   Actually, there are quite a few variations on this step, but these are the ones I find most useful. If you use LILO as your boot manager, `make bzlilo` will build the kernel, rename your current */vmlinuz* to */vmlinuz.old*, and then invoke *lilo* so that your system will find the new kernel upon boot-up. It's also quite simple to configure *lilo* to generate a label for your previous kernel; I keep three kernels around, one that matches the rescue/install media for the version of the distribution I'm running, my current kernel, and the version prior. Or you might want to build the kernel and write to a floppy disk, since this provides for simple fallback when testing a new configuration. Boot from the floppy to test the new kernel. If you do not like what you see, remove the floppy and boot the system from the previous kernel.

> **Hint:** `make bzlilo` and */boot*
>
> Boot loaders are not a very rewarding topic to document in my opinion, because there are so many variations on hardware, needs, and configurations out there, not to mention different boot loaders. I've stuck with *lilo* over the years, and as I started using larger and larger disks, I finally hit the point where *lilo* couldn't boot my kernel from my root partition. So, */dev/hda1* is now a small */boot* partition, and the easiest way I've found to stick to the five steps I outline here is to edit */usr/src/linux/Makefile* and uncomment the line with `export INSTALL_PATH=/boot`. If you forget to do this until after you do your `make bzImage` or *make bzlilo*, you'll essentially have to rebuild (since *make* will see that the Makefile has a newer date.)

4. Build the modules you selected during the configuration process.

   `$ make modules`

5. Install the modules into the */lib/modules/w.x.y/* directory, which is where the module utilities *insmod*, *modprobe*, and *depmod* will look for them. Note that *w.x.y* is the release of the kernel being compiled (not the one currently running). The module utilities look in the directory of the *running* kernel when loading modules.

   `$ make modules_install`

You can combine all of these into a single command line, such as **make dep clean bzlilo modules modules_install**, or type them into a script that you use every time you build your kernel. However you invoke the commands, you should watch to make sure they do not exit prematurely. For example, if you issue the commands `make bzlilo ; make modules` and `make bzlilo` fails, you may not notice error messages because the output of `make modules` did not result in errors.

If, after a reboot, you are not running your new kernel, make sure that you wrote the new kernel to your hard drive with the `make {b}zlilo` step. You can call *lilo* explicitly from the command line with **lilo -v** to see what is happening. You might also want to check whether perhaps you left either a rescue floppy or a boot floppy in your system during your reboot.

B.6   Why Use Modules?

Modular device drivers, commonly referred to as **modules**, are part of what sets Linux apart from other operating systems—maybe not so much in architecture, since most modern operating systems have a concept of modules, but because as a Linux system administrator, you interact with them. When we talk about modules, don't always expect them to automagically do what is required of them. Once a kernel is compiled with module support, you can load and unload device drivers at will using the *insmod* and *rmmod* commands, respectively, or *modprobe*. Aside from illustrating the programming prowess of the kernel developers, they are a fantastic boon for sysadmins. Here is a partial list of the useful properties of modules:

1. Both optional and required arguments are easier to specify when loading the module with *modprobe* or *insmod* than when having to specify them as a boot parameter in */etc/lilo.conf* and then rebooting the system to test the new parameter setting. This is particularly true when you're trying to configure a device for the first time . . . .

2. Modules can be unloaded and then reloaded. Sad but true, every now and then a piece of Linux code has a bug too. (Or maybe the bug is in the firmware on the controller card.) Without modules, reinitializing this device driver requires a reboot of the system. With the driver built into the kernel, it can be accomplished with a simple **rmmod** *module* ; **insmod** *module*.

3. Modules can be loaded in any order you see fit. This is nice for controlling the order in which the kernel creates the network devices (*eth0*, *eth1*, etc.). By dictating the order in which the modules are loaded or by specifying arguments while loading a module, you control the order in which the system detects the interfaces. On systems which have multiple NICs, this helps ensure that the physical card which you expect to be *eth0* really is.

4. Kernel builds can take a long time, and they can seem to take forever when your entire network is down. If an NIC fails, it's nice to have a driver for other types of NICs available. I always compile modular support for the most common cards used at a site. This way, you are back up and running in the time it takes to replace a card and reboot.

Modules' advantages go beyond these niceties for the sysadmin. Because the entire kernel must be **locked**[3] into physical memory, a kernel with lots of device driver support is large and consumes RAM which would be available for processes, routing tables, buffers, and so on. Compiling infrequently used device drivers as modules results in more efficient use of system memory.

Modules have furthered the cause of Linux with more than just their convenience. Linux supports a *lot* of network card drivers. If you are developing a Linux distribution, you do not know what type of NIC your potential user has, but you want to accommodate as many of them as possible. This means compiling a kernel with support for all of these (huge!) or the most popular of these (inconveniencing users who own a less popular NIC). If you're a developer, modules help device-driver development proceed more quickly, since consecutive tests of the driver can be made without rebooting the system (usually, unless you make a grievous mistake).

For all of these reasons, the use of modules has been assumed for all device drivers throughout this book, except where it makes overwhelming sense to have the driver directly in the kernel—e.g., IDE hard-drive support so that you can boot your machine. Do keep in mind that you cannot load modules until the kernel has booted and mounted the root filesystem. Actually, this isn't strictly true. Read up on **initrd** for options of booting your system from a ramdisk (that's created by your system when it first boots).

Hopefully you now feel comfortable obtaining kernel sources, upgrading them between point releases, specifying and saving your kernel configuration and compiling it. If you don't, find a test box and get busy experimenting!

---

[3]Locked memory cannot be swapped to disk.

B.7   Building Software from Sources

Building software for Linux will come naturally to those who have worked in Unix. For one thing, it is getting easier, thanks to almost everyone standardizing on the GNU *autoconf* toolset for configuration of makefiles.[4] Of course, no book can provide instructions for how to compile all of the software available. This section is merely an introduction for nonprogrammer types who are faced with compiling from sources for the first time.

Let's say that you've just downloaded *coolutil-x.y.tar.gz* and want to try it out. You will need to unpack, configure, compile, install, and then do your testing (**not** on your production router). Before you unpack it, take a peek at what is contained in the archive—commonly known as a **tarball**. Do this with **tar tzvf** *coolutil-x.y.tar.gz* | **more**. The t option tells *tar* to look at the contents of the archive, but not to unpack it. Omit the z option if the archive is not either gzipped (ends in *.tar.gz* or *.tgz*) or compressed (ends in *.Z*); use I if it is bzipped (ends in *.bz2*).

A well-behaved tarball will extract itself into a directory name, including the version of the software. Once you are satisfied that the sources will extract without overwriting something important on your system, extract them by using the -x switch in place of -t in the example above. You should now change the directory into the source.

Configuration prepares the makefile (often named *Makefile*) for compiling the software in your environment. How it is done depends upon the author of the software. Many authors include a script named *configure* which automates the configuration for you; start it with **./configure**.

If there is not a configure script, or if the configure script bombs out for any reason, you should break down and read the instructions that came with the software. There are typically files named *README* and *INSTALL*. If both exist, the former contains general notes for this current release while the latter has instructions for building and installing the software. If there is a *COPYRIGHT* or *LICENSE*, you should read that too. Not everything that is freely available is free for use in all situations, and as much as you may need the tool (and want both *free beer* and *freedom of speech*), violating the license is just that, not to mention being a crime in many countries.

Compiling the software is typically nothing more than typing **make**. Should this complete without errors, you can go on the next step of installing the software. Should it fail, you need to put on your programmer's cap and figure out what went wrong. Often, the software requires the development version of a library or headers which are not loaded on your system. Or it may be looking for the library or a C header file in the wrong location. (You can very quickly find files on your system using the *locate* command). If the build fails due to some problem with the source itself, check the *README* to see if there are any compiler or library version requirements you might have overlooked. If you still require assistance, try to get help locally or via a newsgroup or IRC, before contacting the author directly. Don't forget to check with your distribution to see if the package may already exist. More than once I've built software (and even packaged it as a *.deb*) only to discover that someone had already done it, and typically done a better job of packaging it than I had, too.

Installing the software seems to come in two forms. If the build results in a single executable, you can run it right from where you built it, or you might have to hand-lib it into place yourself. For more complicated software, consisting of multiple binaries or configuration files, you can probably use **make install** to install it. */usr/local/* is a good place to install software you build yourself, as it will not conflict with files in your Linux distribution (but remember to add */usr/local/bin* to your **PATH**).

---

[4] Thank GNU very much! ;)

After satisfactory testing, how do you get the software you built on your workstation installed on the router? I typically take a fresh copy of the tarball, copy it over to the router, and rebuild it from scratch. This ensures that the binaries built are linked against the versions of the libraries on your router, and it's easy. It also alleviates the need to have a compile environment on your workstation that perfectly matches the router, although for large environments, you should consider having a build system available for just this purpose.

Appendix C

TESTING STRATEGIES AND *VMWARE*

As a network administrator, you have to devise ways in which to adequately test new configurations, software, and equipment without adversely affecting your user community. The network is an integral part of most computer installations and requires uptimes an order of magnitude better than most applications—most applications use their maintenance windows to perform network-based backups!

Because nothing functions without the network, new routing configurations, new Ethernet drivers, and new versions of the proxy server all need to be right when they are first implemented. If anything breaks in production, it is not likely to go unnoticed. Testing network configurations gets complicated because:

- Lab environments which resemble production environments are costly. Resource contention can be very troublesome if you have a limited budget.

- It is difficult to simulate production load on the network.

- Test environments are designed by *you*, and chances are that you have already prepared your system(s) to cover the cases which you anticipate might occur. You may tend to do the same thing when conducting tests—in effect, testing only the cases for which you have already prepared.

- You will often be under pressure to deploy new configurations quickly or in response to problems or bugs. In this scenario, time is more of a resource constraint than money, and testing often takes a secondary role.

- Some parts of the environment are out of your control and cannot be duplicated. The ultimate example is the Internet itself. Adequately testing new SMTP mailer or DNS configurations is touchy stuff, since mistakes can have disastrous results. (Bouncing mail off your SMTP gateways for half an hour will require some explaining to your management.)

Dealing with these challenges requires creativity and a thorough understanding of your specific environment. Thus, it is difficult to present any sort of comprehensive test plan, and dangerous to assume that such a plan exists. Therefore, I present a few hints that have helped me in supporting a production environment.

C.1   Basic Testing Guidelines

Given the complex nature of performing comprehensive testing, here are some precepts to keep in mind:

- Don't do anything without having a way to undo it—properly stated, without having a fallback plan. This may be as simple as the backup of a configuration file (so that you can restore the prior configuration quickly). At the other extreme, you may want to load an entirely new system, copy over the pertinent data, and keep the previous system around for a week until you are sure that everything is OK.

- Switchovers which require a series of changes or changes on multiple systems should be "scripted," meaning that you should take the time to write out each required step and in what order. It is annoying to promise your users that you'll be back up in five minutes, forgetting that rebooting the DNS server first will cause daemons on other systems to hang on startup (trying to resolve names). By writing out a sequence, you are more likely to catch this sort of dependency. You can also retrace your steps if you run into problems, or you can have someone else help you implement the change.

- Testing new DNS functionality, such as load balancing, is best done with a test domain. (This can be a subdomain of your existing domain.) This is doubly true for *sendmail* and other MTAs.

C.2   Testing: The Buddy System

For the network administrator who works in an Internet environment, there is nothing more useful than having a shell account somewhere on the *outside*. Ideally, this system would be a Linux box external to your network and outside your buddy's firewall. If you can establish a rapport with another system administrator whom you can trust and who is willing to trust you, each of you can place a utility machine on the outside and allow the other access to it.

Having a shell account on the outside is almost indispensable for testing configurations as your external clients will see them (and for troubleshooting, too). Examples include testing FTP services, MX records and other associated DNS parameters. If you use *OpenSSH* or have some other means of tunnelling X clients, you can even see what your webpage looks like from the outside, using a graphical browser. Last but not least, you can probe your own systems for security holes—even launch full-blown attacks against your site to assess security risks. The advantages of this type of access are:

- Firewalling rules are generally not designed around preventing internal attacks (although perhaps they should be!), so it is more difficult to design an accurate test of how your systems will perform while under real attack.

- External routing problems are evident only when you're on the outside.

- When you access your own site, you are probably using your own DNS configuration, which works because you control it. Seeing how long it takes for updated DNS maps to propagate out to the rest of the world will give you an idea of how to coordinate changes and minimize client impact.

- You have an external account to which you can send mail *and* view that system's MTA's logs. The ability to view logfiles on both ends of a transaction can be very helpful.

Above and beyond these practical benefits is the fact that you have someone with whom you can discuss configuration problems and security alerts—basically, talk shop. If this is somehow impractical, a broadband connection or a shell account on a web-hosting service is your next best bet.

Using Kernel Compiles to Test Basic System Health

The kernel source is a very complicated piece of software, and compiling it requires a great deal of system resources. For this reason, it is good exercise for your system— *make* will spawn multiple copies of itself in addition to *gcc*; *gcc* will use all of the memory it can get its hands on and requires a lot of CPU, memory, and disk I/O.

For these reasons, I use kernel compiles to test memory chips and as a general benchmark of the CPU/disk/memory subsystem. Compiling the kernel is a good way to test for memory errors, because it will consume all of the memory on any reasonably sized system. If your kernel compile ends mysteriously with a SEGV error or signal 11, you should consider replacing the RAM in the system. If you are sure the memory is good and you still receive this error, it is sometimes caused by overclocking your CPU—you should consider setting it to operate within its designed specifications.

As for the benchmark, it provides a relative indication of system speed. For it to be useful, the system should be unloaded during the compile, and you should compare systems with equal amounts of real memory. Use the *time* command to time the entire build process, as in:

```
$ time make dep clean zlilo modules
```

C.3   Change Control

Change control is a large topic that consumes many books on its own. In fact, I've heard of all different types of change control—strong change control, fine change control, coordinated change control, etc. They are all essentially the same thing. When you implement changes, anyone (or anything) affected by those changes should be involved in the process of authorizing them, or at least be aware of them. The goals are to prevent unnecessary outages, ensure that procedures and documentation are updated correctly, and keep everyone in the loop. Your organization may already have some guidelines in place. If they do not, try to implement your own, even if they are nothing more than maintaining detailed documentation about all system changes and notifying your management before you make significant changes.

Whether you have a formal change-control process or not, anything you do is subject to Murphy's Law, and as a network administrator, you also confront the threat of network-based attacks. After all, you hold the keys to a valuable resource. Because of this, I recommend you deploy another type of change-control tool to detect the changes you *didn't* apply to the system. (As a side-effect, the same software will help keep you honest about normal change management.)

One such tool is *AIDE*, or Advanced Intrusion Detection Environment. It is a follow-on to the very popular intrusion detection tool called *Tripwire* and has the distinct advantage of having a GPL-free license. The following description is taken from the software's homepage:

> [AIDE] creates a database from the regular expression rules that it finds from the
> config file. Once this database is initialized, it can be used to verify the integrity

of the files. It has several message digest algorithms (md5, sha1, rmd160, tiger, haval, etc.) that are used to check the integrity of the file. More algorithms can be added with relative ease. All of the usual file attributes can also be checked for inconsistencies. It can read databases from older or newer versions.

As you can gather, the software detects any change to a file, and it can use several different checksum algorithms to detect changes that might elude a single checksum comparison (i.e., modifying a binary file so that its checksum is the same as the unmodified version). The software is straightforward to set up and use. It is, however, almost worthless if you don't really use it. The homepage is: *http://www.cs.tut.fi/~rammer/aide.html*.

C.4   Using *VMware* to Test Configurations

VMware, by VMware, Inc., allows you to create **virtual** machines which run within the environment of your host machine. The emulation of a full-blown PC is impressive, all the way down to the details of a working copy of BIOS which runs inside the virtual machine. A virtual machine runs a copy of the x86 operating system you load on it. Because the emulation is complete, the **virtual** copy of the OS is not aware of the differences, and many x86 operating systems can operate in this environment, including Linux, Solaris x86, FreeBSD, and several different versions of Microsoft Windows. The virtual machine believes itself to be running on a reasonably well-equipped machine, although it really exists as merely a couple of files and processes running on the host machine.

The upshot for system administrators is an entirely new way to think about testing. Instead of listing all of the product's capabilities, I will talk about a few different ways in which it is useful for testing router configurations and a few ways in which it is not. Note that I am not suggesting that you run *VMware* on your routers, but that you might find use for it on your workstation or testbed box to help test new software. First, let's cover what you cannot do with *VMware*:

Caveats

- Because the emulation provides for a single Ethernet adapter, you cannot test different Ethernet drivers. I cannot see why VMware, Inc., would want to change this, and I do not know how applicable such a test would be anyway, so I wouldn't expect this to change.

- Similar to the preceding issue, you cannot test any add-on board beyond determining whether or not the driver patch for the kernel (if one is needed) will compile. External modems, ISDN adapters, parallel port, and USB devices are a different story, as is addressed below under **Capabilities**.

- Because it is emulation and because you are sharing a single set of resources, things can get a little slow, especially if you do not have a lot of memory in your host system.

- You cannot test SMP functionality (yet, anyway).

Capabilities

- You can load a virtual machine with exactly the same configuration as your production router image and use this machine for compiles. This way, you no longer need to compile on your production machines, and you do not have to have a separate test/compile machine for every router image.

- You can make copies of the virtual machine before testing upgrades, so that there is no need to reload/restore the machine to fall back to a previous version of the image. Or you can use *VMware*'s nonpersistent disk mode.

- You can use items attached to the host machine as if they existed on the virtual machine. Currently, this list includes the floppy drive, an IDE CD-ROM drive, a PS-2 mouse port, parallel ports, an OSS compatible soundcard, and almost anything connected to a standard serial port, parallel port, or USB port.

- It is trivial to test new kernel versions and patches. It is nice to be able to build kernels and test them without having to reboot your real machine. This functionality is limited in its usefulness only by the fact that most network configurations depend heavily upon driver configurations for *real* Ethernet devices, so do not expect to test module parameter settings, etc.

- It is easy to test the minidistributions of Linux, which, owing to their nature, have a testing cycle that is Build $\rightarrow$ Boot $\rightarrow$ Test $\rightarrow$ Build $\rightarrow$ .... This can get annoying if you do not have a second (or third or fourth, depending upon how many hats you wear) workstation at your desk, which is annoying all the same because of the noise, second keyboard, monitor, etc.

- As with minidistributions, you can test full-sized Linux distributions, upgrades between versions, etc., without ever having to reboot your system. You can make copies of a harddrive image before you start an upgrade, or, if you are truly lazy, you can use *VMware*'s redo logs and not even worry about what you do to your virtual machine.

- You can test network and router configurations in several different ways. The section below details the different networking configurations available for virtual machines and how you can use them to test router settings.

- With up to seven virtual SCSI disks (and four virtual IDE disks), you can test kernel functionality like RAID and mirroring.

C.4.1   *VMware* **Virtual Network Configurations**

While configuring your VM (Virtual Machine), you are presented with several different options for your VM's network: **no network support**, **host-only networking**, **bridged networking**, **NAT**, and **custom**. These different types of connectivity are assigned by convention to different virtual Ethernet devices on separate virtual segments. The virtual Ethernet devices are known as *vmnetN* (for $0 \leq N \leq 255$) on the host computer, and each is attached to a distinct (switched) Ethernet segment.

Each of the virtual hosts, or VMs, can be attached to up to three of these distinct segments, which means that a VM sees an *eth0*, *eth1*, and *eth2* device. You control which virtual Ethernet segment they reside on by specifying the *vmnetN* to which that device is attached.

The conventions that VMware recommends are applied, as it were, via processes that run on the host system. The conventions you'll get out of the box (and from their tech support) are:

- *vmnet0* is bridged to the host machine's *eth0*. This is controlled via *vmnet-bridge*. Note that, starting with VMware 3.0, you can bridge to devices on your host computer other than just Ethernet devices. Although you're bridged, you're not sharing the host machine's IP address, just its net access. You'll need a free address on the same segment the host machine is attached to.

- *vmnet1* is *host-only*, which means that it acts like a normal Ethernet segment, and this segment is created by the *vmnet-netifup* process. In case you're wondering, the segments act like switches, but there is a *vmnet-sniffer* command you can use on the host machine to see everything. (Aside to the VMware folks reading this: is there any chance you could give that sniffer an option to write a standard tcpdump/libpcap compatible output file for use with tools like *ethereal?*)

- *vmnet8* is *NAT* (new with version 3.0), which I suppose was needed for operating systems that couldn't NAT packets from host-only segments. This type of device is created with *vmnet-natd*. (I've never used one, but I guess if you haven't configured *netfilter* on your host machines, this would fit the bill.)

- Everything else is *custom*, or *host-only* using a device other than *vmnet1*, and subject to your discretion.

To be honest, I was nonplused by the *VMware* network configuration *wizard* (although I readily admit that it's not intended for folks with a fair amount of network experience). If you want to customize things and not have to worry about losing your configuration every time a patchlevel for *VMware* is released, I recommend scripting at least the network portion of the *VMware* startup on the host machine for yourself. All of the network processes take the same style of arguments at invokation:

```
vmnet-netifup -d pidfile /dev/vmnetN localdev
```

where the local device may be a real network device in the case of a bridge, or the name of the virtual device (without the */dev*) for host-only segments or NAT'ed segments. Once the process is running, you can manipulate the *vmnetN* devices in almost any way that you can an Ethernet adapter, including adding firewall rules, setting options in */proc/sys/net/*, and what have you. You can even *ifconfig* them down (which I sometimes do). Note that a device must exist (i.e., its *vmnet-netifup* process must be running) when a virtual machine attached to that device starts, or virtual instances will gripe.

In previous versions of *VMware* where you could configure only a single network device within the virtual machines, you could configure your host machine to route between them if you wanted to separate them for a certain type of testing. Now that each can be connected to up to three different virtual subnets, and with 255 of these subnets, you can construct arbitrarily complex network topologies and test routing, queuing, and firewalling without a mess of wires or a half-dozen heaters cluttering up your test lab.

This isolation from your physical network can be used to test various types of attacks (and their patches), test monitoring techniques (things like *tcpdump* and *sniffit* work as well on vmnet interfaces as they do on real interfaces), and test things that you'd prefer not to have on your real network, such as beta versions of routing daemons, etc. Note, however, that the isolation exists only as long as you do not configure your host machine such that traffic may route out of it. If you have IP forwarding on and have configured IP masquerading, even if you are running in **host-only** mode, your VMs can very effectively communicate with the real world.

Pretty neat, eh? See Figure C.1 for a basic configuration where your host machine is a router. Figure C.2 is a simplified (really!) version of the *VMware* configuration on the system where I wrote this book and did some of the research. Strictly speaking, all of the virtual segments are attached to the VM host via the corresponding vmnet device. Note that *vmnet3* is not depicted as attached to my host system. This is because I configured this device down after it was started, so that virtual machines attached to it could not speak to the host system directly, but instead had to utilize the virtual router.

If the idea of having distinct operating-system instances on any number of virtual segments—all without having to find the first CAT5 cable—appeals to you, visit VMware's website at *http://www.vmware.com* for more information about *VMware*.

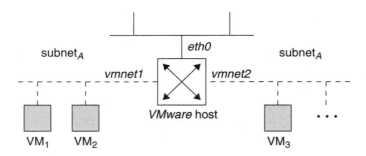

Figure C.1 A Simple *VMware* Network

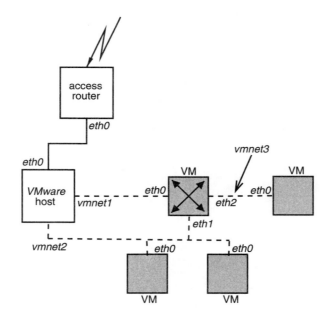

Figure C.2 *VMware* Network with Layered VMs

Appendix D

ETHICS AND OTHER CONSIDERATIONS

The sections in this appendix are essentially essays on topics related to being a network administrator with free software. They do not contain information about how to operate Linux routers, but I think that they are important topics for network administrators all the same.

D.1   Ethical Considerations of a Network Admin

Being a network administrator is not for everyone. It can be stressful at times. People who do not understand the network tend to blame it for application problems (which also they may not understand). You may have outages that are out of your control and cause you considerable work, while managers browbeat you and want to know why you did not have a contingency plan—the same managers who denied budget requests for backup links. Performance problems can be difficult to track down. Telcos can be maddening in their carefree attitude when it comes to installing your access circuits in a timely manner. All of this comes with the territory.

Another part of that territory is being in a convenient position to access the personal data of others. There is no need to go into detail about *how* you can do this; Linux comes loaded with enough tools to make anything from sniffing passwords to recording all email transmissions easily accomplished. My purpose is to dissuade you from doing anything like this, regardless of *why* you might decide to do so, and to avoid participating in any such activities asked of you. The ability to see into other people's activities, be they business or personal, may be tempting. We've all seen the sitcoms where people use telescopes to peek into the lives of others. I think the primary question boils down to one of right. Not in the sense of right or wrong, since it is not a question of good or evil—but right in the sense of privilege or permission. Does the ability to do something give you the *right* to do it? Some administrators I have worked with believed so. The typical rationalizations are, *They are (mis)using company resources* or *The company policy manual states that such monitoring may occur.* While these things may be true, and may even grant specific authority for the IT staff to engage in such activities, they rarely define sufficient and specific cause to perform such monitoring.

If your management requests such actions from you, I hope that you refuse upon moral grounds. I like to apply Kant's "categorical imperative," but the moral precept has several names, so you may call it what you like. The fundamental question you have to ask yourself is, "Would it be OK if everyone were to act as I intend to act?" I think that the answer is a resounding no. Some will maintain that they don't send sensitive personal information via email, so they wouldn't mind if someone monitored. But this evades the issue by limiting the principle of monitoring to a single type of monitoring. It would be a simple matter for telephone company technicians to monitor your telephone conversations, for PBX administrators to review your voicemails, and for the U.S. Postal Service to open your mail. Most of this could be done without your ever knowing—the first two without leaving the slightest trace. And it is trivial for your neighbors to point a telescope at your bedroom window, or use a camcorder to record your comings and goings. Society frowns upon these things both legally and socially, although the monitoring could be done with the same rationalization that you might use to watch a user's network activities. The telephone company might be listening to determine if customers are about to commit a crime. The PBX administrator might need to ensure that the system is not clogged with personal voicemails. The U.S. Postal Service could maintain they were simply trying to make sure that copyrights were not being violated, or to enforce laws concerning materials which may not be sent through the mail. Your neighbors may claim that they have a right to know if you are conducting dangerous activities in your house, since such acts could eventually result in grievous infringement of their rights. In these cases, I believe that most people would scoff at the rationalizations, debunking them as inane, paranoid, and/or intrusive. Is network monitoring (for content) any different?

Of course, not all ideals function flawlessly in the real world. What should you do if your management requests that you monitor the network activities of an individual? You have to be measured in your response, since you do not want to run the risk of being insubordinate. Nor will you always fully know management's reason for asking. Your response certainly should depend upon the severity of the situation, right? I do not believe so. When you are dealing with a corporate network that is owned by your employer and operated for business use, I think you have to draw the line and be willing to perform only certain types of monitoring. Specifically, you should agree to supply information about the source/destination of packets, but not the contents. In other words, if your employer would like to spy on employee 2112, then you might produce a report that includes the fact that employee 2112's workstation transferred packets to and from locations XYZ, YYZ, and XZZ. How is this different? For one, it takes you out of the position of having to peek at the packets themselves, so it is a purely objective assessment of employee 2112's use of the network. Also, it is a form of monitoring that is generally socially accepted. If management finds the destinations questionable, then may decide to confront employee 2112.

Let's use an analogy. The use of a company's postage machine for business mailings is an example of proper use of a company resource. On the other hand, using the postage machine to mail parcels to your friends in Germany is not. Does it matter what is in the parcels? Perhaps to employee 2112, but not to the company. The business-use-only policy for the postage machine was violated, and that is the act which should be punished. Employee 2112 does not need to suffer the further disgrace of having the contents (perhaps the motive) of the wrongdoing made public. The same should hold for potential network transgressions. Instead of snooping on employee 2112 until this person "digs his own grave," let management confront the employee so that he may (a) defend his actions, and (b) know that use of the system can be monitored.

I am not so naïve as to believe that every reader of this book has completely honorable intentions with regard to the information available by snooping. Some of you may have plans to generate J. Edgar Hoover files on colleagues or political enemies, since you never know when such evidence might come in handy. Others of you might be jealous of the promotion of a colleague and feel that you were overlooked. And some of you might just want to increase your popularity by being a source of interesting information and gossip. Regardless of your motive, these activities are a misuse of your skills. No one will be able to stop you; there is no one there to remind you of it. And this paragraph may not make much of a difference either, but doing these things is still wrong.

D.2   Management vs. Linux

Every time I deploy a Linux system or read about Linux being used at places like Cisco (as a print server) or the U.S. Post Office (as a high-speed mail sorter), the pronouncement "Linux in a production environment? It'll never happen!" echoes through my head. At a previous employer, this was the pat answer to all of my queries as to when we could try Linux out in our product evaluation lab. Admittedly, that was early on, but some of that mentality remains, and I am as happy to contest that statement now as I was then.

This book has focused on how to get Linux routers running and keep them running. But this is of little use if you never have a chance to test them and deploy them. If you work for an organization where you are the primary decision maker for technology, then you're fortunate. Many companies manage technical environments by committee, politics, tradition, and treachery. This section contains a few thoughts about why it makes good business sense to have Linux in your production environment.

D.2.1   How Much Does It Really Cost?

For a network infrastructure, everything boils down to the **TCO** (Total Cost of Ownership). A TCP/IP network is in most cases an entity independent of the applications and systems it supports. (The network does not change when you upgrade the operating-system revision of your development servers.) This means that the network can be composed of a squirrel-powered adding machine, and your management will not care so long as it is always up and delivers the required performance. Oh yeah, and it should be as inexpensive as possible. Although many technicians may find this philosophy unsavory (it certainly does not appeal to the idealist in me), the truth is that most finance departments are rarely interested in the technical elegance or excellence of their IT departments. In the eyes of those signing the checks, value is more important. Cost includes not just hardware and software, but all related personnel and maintenance costs.

In today's penny-conscious corporate environment, technicians need to be aware that many companies offer routing as a service, which may (at least on paper) look less expensive than your salary and equipment. Wouldn't it be nice if you could just say, "Linux routers are inexpensive, stable, and easy to maintain," and be done with it? This probably will not get you very far unless your management has a high level of confidence in you. The reason, IMHO, is that many middle managers today come from one of two backgrounds: (a) they were active technicians during the reign of Big Blue (IBM) *or* (b) they were managing during the late 1980s and early 1990s when the idea of a workstation on every desk started to take shape. In both cases, the heritage often contains conservatism. For the Big Blue fans, they know that big is good. For those who helped forge the personal computer revolution, I think many got burned by choosing anything other than Microsoft as their desktop operating system, so they also have a mistrust of the *small guy*. In a way, this sort of scrutiny of alternative technologies is good, or at least understandable. These managers are paid to develop infrastructures usable for several years, sometimes five years or longer. Mistakes can mess up stock options, retirement plans, and entire careers. To them, saving a thousand dollars on a piece of router hardware is hardly a bargain when they cannot hire someone to support it. And paradoxically, they are under constant pressure to keep costs low in the short term. So how do you alleviate their fears that Linux is only a flash in the pan, a strategic snafu waiting to happen? Mount a three-part offensive.

1. Make it well known how well known Linux is. Watch for press releases from reputable sources that mention another large company coming out of the Linux closet. These are effective for managers who use a "follow the leader" approach to technology decisions. Watch for articles from very well-known sources and about large-scale products. Examples that were helpful for me were Oracle's announcing the availability of their RDBMS on Linux and IBM's, announcing support of the Apache web server. Even better are items from IT consulting firms, such as the Gartner Group, about Linux in production. You might check *http://www.linux.org/business/index.html* for more of this type of news.

2. Make sure that the **total** cost of ownership of the current infrastructure is correctly documented. Don't forget things like:

   - Software licenses
   - Software maintenance
   - Software upgrades
   - Training
   - Downtime
   - Hardware requirements

   I have witnessed a shocking amount of piracy and licensing violation occurring in IT departments. Some people claim that the software vendors want it that way; otherwise, they would not make it so easy to do. I'm not sure what this has to do with the issue; it's the same sort of flawed rationalization some people make about network monitoring for content. And if software vendors really do want it that way, then they have their own ethical dilemma to face—they normally are in business to sell software.

   The point is that licensing represents a significant portion of many companies' IT budgets (or would, if it were done legally), and this cost (or liability) should be captured. If the industry trend of charging for server software while freely offering client software continues, the free server will have some distinct economical advantages. Not all of this directly applies to the router market, but Linux is not just a competitor of commercial routers. In general, software costs should be easy to capture, but you might find that people are not looking at the cost of the total cycle. For every upgrade, there are purchase negotiation costs, training costs (possibly for both the administrators and the users), and reduced user productivity costs due to server and/or workstation downtime.

3. If your IT shop is already in production with another operating system, you can start developing confidence in Linux by deploying it in non-mission-critical scenarios. After all, cautious managers don't leap without taking a nice long look first. You can ease their anxiety by letting them see Linux do things well over a period of time. Keep a detailed list of your time and cost investment. If it is your first time configuring such an application on Linux, note that reuse of both software and skills will lessen the costs in the future. You should not misrepresent your time investment. Remember that an expensive solution for your employer will eventually affect you, too. This trial period will also give you time to hone your Linux administration skills, if needed, and to consider how you would best

manage multiple Linux systems on a daily basis. If Linux does what needs to be done either better or more economically, then your management should eventually warm up to it.

D.2.2   Build vs. Buy

Working as a technician, I've seen IT staffs agonize over the "build vs. buy" question. The group has typically polarized into two camps: one believes that the software can be developed and maintained internally with a lower TCO than purchasing the software from an external vendor, and the other thinks that purchasing the software will result in lower costs for the company. Those who advocate *buy* cite the salaries of developers, quality problems, and conformance to industry standards as reasons to purchase a product instead of having it developed internally. They will also contend that an 80% fit, available immediately, is better than a 100% fit three to six months down the road. *Build* people take the stance that an 80% fit is generous, that off-the-shelf quality is often subpar and problem resolution takes longer, that planning the proper implementation of a system will take the same time or longer, and that the staff required to support the product internally along with the time spent negotiating contracts will easily outweigh the cost of developing the system in-house. If you cannot guess, I'm a *build* person, as many Linux and Unix people are.

Several stories come to mind where management clearly reached the wrong decision when they decided to *buy*. The one that is strongest in my mind involves software distribution tools in a large-scale Unix environment (3000+ servers). The company had already developed its own internal distribution system, which was very much like the package tools used with today's Linux distributions. It supported versioning, dependencies, verifying the integrity of an installation, and the use of scripts before and after the package installation to prepare the system and configure the software. It had some very advanced features, such as hierarchical distribution to reduce bandwidth requirements, the ability to push software to systems (via a nice Motif interface), and the option to revert to a previous version if something went awry. So what was missing? There were some GUI enhancements that everyone wanted, and the software needed to be ported to Microsoft Windows. This was just enough space to allow a vendor to come in and drive a wedge between the build and buy camps. If you detect a note of bitterness, it's not imaginary. The vendor courted upper management with promises of software that would do everything and more and would save hundreds of thousands of dollars. There were, of course, a few modifications required to make the software fit our needs, but these would be ironed out quickly.

"The Implementation Will Take Six Months."

There were a great many stern-faced meetings between the technicians and programmers, who were generally pro-build, and the managers, who were pro-buy. You might think that the technicians were just out to save their jobs, but the issue was much deeper than that. There were other jobs, other things to program. And the in-house system was not newly coded or deployed, but was fully in maintenance mode, so it wasn't an issue of wanting to work on the latest and greatest. When management made it clear that it was seriously considering replacing the in-house system, it was making more than a business decision, no matter it how classified it. Management was sending two clear messages to the software development staff: (a) what they had produced up to that point was not adequate, and (b) it had little faith in the team's ability to produce in the future. Meanwhile, there was plenty of input from non-programmers who believed that the off-the-shelf product would not be able to do the job.

Within the promised six months, more than $2.5M had been spent on the new software, but its implementation strategy was still being developed, and over half of the programming team resigned. This crippled the day-to-day operations of the current software and slowed deployment of the new software. Even so, the Windows port of the in-house software was completed and operational—on time, under budget. I was not part of the programming team, but I had interaction with them because I used the in-house tool to ship and install my systems software. The mess has severely damaged the team's morale, and not theirs only. Not just the programmers, but all of the technicians, voiced their disappointment in the decision to go outside for the software. And when managers do not listen to their employees about issues central to their jobs (after all, who was running the 3000 Unix servers here, the managers?), they send a clear message that either (a) they don't think we know what we are doing or (b) it doesn't matter to them whether or not we have the tools we need to perform our jobs.

Is there a happy ending this story? Only if you can take satisfaction in knowing that your instincts were correct. More than three years later, the in-house system was still being used, and despite the money and effort poured into the new system, it still was not able to replace the old one. What a waste . . . .

Love's Labor Found

People willingly work harder on solutions in which they take personal pride, and these are often the *build* solutions. Management, the stockholders, and the customers would all be better served if this psychology were better understood and utilized by those making the decisions. (Yes, I'm talking to **you**, all of you who take your minivan to any oil-change place but polish your 1972 MG with a diaper. Don't pretend that you don't understand what it means to take personal pride in your work.) In the case described above, ironically, the decision to go outside for the systems software was made while the department was publicizing its new mission statement, something to the effect "We will develop a world-class IT organization and set ourselves apart by the utmost quality of our information systems." What, by using the same off-the-shelf software that every company that *doesn't* have a world-class IT organization is forced to buy because it cannot build its own? Whatever happened to leveraging in-house software as a competitive advantage?

Busy Linux Bees

So where does Linux fit into all of this? Linux has been, and to a large extent still is, a solution for *builders*. I believe that this is what has brought it so far so quickly, and that it needs to be understood by those deploying it and managing it. If you have *buy*-type people (and there is no harm in this, I just believe that people tend to be one type or the other), then making them use Linux may have the desired results. Once Linux does reach the point where *buy*-types are advocating its use, I hope it will retain that "I can do it just as well myself" attitude. It is more important than some people realize. For one, Linux's support structure is heavily based upon people being enthusiastic about it. The same is true of its development. There will always be people interested in programming computers, and hopefully interested in programming computers running Linux. Finally, it takes builders to find creative ways to use Linux. Innovative buyers are builders at heart.

Appendix E

GNU GENERAL PUBLIC LICENSE

The GNU Public License is one of the basic tenets of the Free Software community. It is included here because most of the programs described in this book, from the kernel to my shell script examples, are covered (i.e., protected) by this license. I use the word "protected" because one of the best things about the GPL is that code licensed by it cannot be arbitrarily taken away from the users. This does not prevent the author from issuing new releases under a different license, but once a revision is released under the GPL, derivatives are allowed, so long as they are also released under the GPL (and distributed with source).

For a given piece of software, this means that a change in marketing strategy won't leave users stranded without source, and with no choice other than to succumb to the terms of the new license. The user always has the option to take the existing version and maintain and improve it for as long as it makes sense to do so. To a certain extent, this makes the GPL more important to companies than to individuals—corporations have a lot more to lose from draconian licensing practices than individuals do. In any event, this is why many people insist that all of the software they use be released under the GPL.

If you're relatively new to the Free Software world, this (in addition to the quality of the code itself) is what all the hubbub is about. The text of the license is included here; if you've never read it, here's your chance. If you have questions, there are plenty of netizens who would be happy to help you interpret it. To avoid confusion, I recommend going straight to the source: *http://www.fsf.org*.

Version 2, June 1991

Copyright (C) 1989, 1991 Free Software Foundation, Inc., 59 Temple Place, Suite 330, Boston, MA 02111-1307 USA. Everyone is permitted to copy and distribute verbatim copies of this license document, but changing it is not allowed.

Preamble

The licenses for most software are designed to take away your freedom to share and change it. By contrast, the GNU General Public License is intended to guarantee your freedom to share and change free software—to make sure the software is free for all its users. This General Public License applies to most of the Free Software Foundation's software and to any other program whose authors commit to using it. (Some other Free Software Foundation software is covered by the GNU Library General Public License instead.) You can apply it to your programs, too.

When we speak of free software, we are referring to freedom, not price. Our General Public Licenses are designed to make sure that you have the freedom to distribute copies of free software (and charge for this service if you wish), that you receive source code or can get it if you want it, that you can change the software or use pieces of it in new free programs; and that you know you can do these things.

To protect your rights, we need to make restrictions that forbid anyone to deny you these rights or to ask you to surrender the rights. These restrictions translate to certain responsibilities for you if you distribute copies of the software, or if you modify it.

For example, if you distribute copies of such a program, whether gratis or for a fee, you must give the recipients all the rights that you have. You must make sure that they, too, receive or can get the source code. And you must show them these terms so they know their rights.

We protect your rights with two steps: (1) copyright the software, and (2) offer you this license which gives you legal permission to copy, distribute and/or modify the software.

Also, for each author's protection and ours, we want to make certain that everyone understands that there is no warranty for this free software. If the software is modified by someone else and passed on, we want its recipients to know that what they have is not the original, so that any problems introduced by others will not reflect on the original authors' reputations.

Finally, any free program is threatened constantly by software patents. We wish to avoid the danger that redistributors of a free program will individually obtain patent licenses, in effect making the program proprietary. To prevent this, we have made it clear that any patent must be licensed for everyone's free use or not licensed at all.

The precise terms and conditions for copying, distribution and modification follow.

GNU GENERAL PUBLIC LICENSE
TERMS AND CONDITIONS FOR COPYING,
DISTRIBUTION AND MODIFICATION

0. This License applies to any program or other work which contains a notice placed by the copyright holder saying it may be distributed under the terms of this General Public License. The "Program," below, refers to any such program or work, and a "work based on the Program" means either the Program or any derivative work under copyright law: that is to say, a work containing the Program or a portion of it, either verbatim or with modifications and/or translated into another language. (Hereinafter, translation is included without limitation in the term "modification.") Each licensee is addressed as "you."

Activities other than copying, distribution and modification are not covered by this License; they are outside its scope. The act of running the Program is not restricted, and the output from the Program is covered only if its contents constitute a work based on the Program (independent of having been made by running the Program). Whether that is true depends on what the Program does.

1. You may copy and distribute verbatim copies of the Program's source code as you receive it, in any medium, provided that you conspicuously and appropriately publish on each copy an appropriate copyright notice and disclaimer of warranty; keep intact all the notices that refer to this License and to the absence of any warranty; and give any other recipients of the Program a copy of this License along with the Program.

You may charge a fee for the physical act of transferring a copy, and you may at your option offer warranty protection in exchange for a fee.

2. You may modify your copy or copies of the Program or any portion of it, thus forming a work based on the Program, and copy and distribute such modifications or work under the terms of Section 1 above, provided that you also meet all of these conditions:

a) You must cause the modified files to carry prominent notices stating that you changed the files and the date of any change.

b) You must cause any work that you distribute or publish, that in whole or in part contains or is derived from the Program or any part thereof, to be licensed as a whole at no charge to all third parties under the terms of this License.

c) If the modified program normally reads commands interactively when run, you must cause it, when started running for such interactive use in the most ordinary way, to print or display an announcement including an appropriate copyright notice and a notice that there is no warranty (or else, saying that you provide a warranty) and that users may redistribute the program under these conditions, and telling the user how to view a copy of this License. (Exception: if the Program itself is interactive but does not normally print such an announcement, your work based on the Program is not required to print an announcement.)

These requirements apply to the modified work as a whole. If identifiable sections of that work are not derived from the Program, and can be reasonably considered independent and separate works in themselves, then this License, and its terms, do not apply to those sections when you distribute them as separate works. But when you distribute the same sections as part of a whole which is a work based on the Program, the distribution of the whole must be on the terms of this License, whose permissions for other licensees extend to the entire whole, and thus to each and every part regardless of who wrote it.

Thus, it is not the intent of this section to claim rights or contest your rights to work written entirely by you; rather, the intent is to exercise the right to control the distribution of derivative or collective works based on the Program.

In addition, mere aggregation of another work not based on the Program with the Program (or with a work based on the Program) on a volume of a storage or distribution medium does not bring the other work under the scope of this License.

3. You may copy and distribute the Program (or a work based on it, under Section 2) in object code or executable form under the terms of Sections 1 and 2 above provided that you also do one of the following:

a) Accompany it with the complete corresponding machine-readable source code, which must be distributed under the terms of Sections 1 and 2 above on a medium customarily used for software interchange; or,

b) Accompany it with a written offer, valid for at least three years, to give any third party, for a charge no more than your cost of physically performing source distribution, a complete machine-readable copy of the corresponding source code, to be distributed under the terms of Sections 1 and 2 above on a medium customarily used for software interchange; or,

c) Accompany it with the information you received as to the offer to distribute corresponding source code. (This alternative is allowed only for noncommercial distribution and only if you received the program in object code or executable form with such an offer, in accord with Subsection b above.)

The source code for a work means the preferred form of the work for making modifications to it. For an executable work, complete source code means all the source code for all modules it contains, plus any associated interface definition files, plus the scripts used to control compilation and installation of the executable. However, as a special exception, the source code distributed need not include anything that is normally distributed (in either source or binary form) with the major components (compiler, kernel, and so on) of the operating system on which the executable runs, unless that component itself accompanies the executable.

If distribution of executable or object code is made by offering access to copy from a designated place, then offering equivalent access to copy the source code from the same place counts as distribution of the source code, even though third parties are not compelled to copy the source along with the object code.

4. You may not copy, modify, sublicense, or distribute the Program except as expressly provided under this License. Any attempt otherwise to copy, modify, sublicense or distribute the Program is void, and will automatically terminate your rights under this License. However, parties who have received copies, or rights, from you under this License will not have their licenses terminated so long as such parties remain in full compliance.

5. You are not required to accept this License, since you have not signed it. However, nothing else grants you permission to modify or distribute the Program or its derivative works. These actions are prohibited by law if you do not accept this License. Therefore, by modifying or distributing the Program (or any work based on the Program), you indicate your acceptance of this License to do so, and all its terms and conditions for copying, distributing or modifying the Program or works based on it.

6. Each time you redistribute the Program (or any work based on the Program), the recipient automatically receives a license from the original licensor to copy, distribute or modify the Program subject to these terms and conditions. You may not impose any further restrictions on the recipients' exercise of the rights granted herein. You are not responsible for enforcing compliance by third parties to this License.

7. If, as a consequence of a court judgment or allegation of patent infringement or for any other reason (not limited to patent issues), conditions are imposed on you (whether by court order, agreement or otherwise) that contradict the conditions of this License, they do not excuse you from the conditions of this License. If you cannot distribute so as to satisfy simultaneously your obligations under this License and any other pertinent obligations, then as a consequence you may not distribute the Program at all. For example, if a patent license would not permit royalty-free redistribution of the Program by all those who receive copies directly or indirectly through you, then the only way you could satisfy both it and this License would be to refrain entirely from distribution of the Program.

If any portion of this section is held invalid or unenforceable under any particular circumstance, the balance of the section is intended to apply and the section as a whole is intended to apply in other circumstances.

It is not the purpose of this section to induce you to infringe any patents or other property right claims or to contest validity of any such claims; this section has the sole purpose of protecting the integrity of the free software distribution system, which is implemented by public license practices. Many people have made generous contributions to the wide range of software distributed through that system in reliance on consistent application of that system; it is up to the author/donor to decide if he or she is willing to distribute software through any other system and a licensee cannot impose that choice.

This section is intended to make thoroughly clear what is believed to be a consequence of the rest of this License.

8. If the distribution and/or use of the Program is restricted in certain countries either by patents or by copyrighted interfaces, the original copyright holder who places the Program under this License may add an explicit geographical distribution limitation excluding those countries, so that distribution is permitted only in or among countries not thus excluded. In such case, this License incorporates the limitation as if written in the body of this License.

9. The Free Software Foundation may publish revised and/or new versions of the General Public License from time to time. Such new versions will be similar in spirit to the present version, but may differ in detail to address new problems or concerns.

Each version is given a distinguishing version number. If the Program specifies a version number of this License which applies to it and "any later version," you have the option of following the terms and conditions either of that version or of any later version published by the Free Software Foundation. If the Program does not specify a version number of this License, you may choose any version ever published by the Free Software Foundation.

10. If you wish to incorporate parts of the Program into other free programs whose distribution conditions are different, write to the author to ask for permission. For software which is copyrighted by the Free Software Foundation, write to the Free Software Foundation; we sometimes make exceptions for this. Our decision will be guided by the two goals of preserving the free status of all derivatives of our free software and of promoting the sharing and reuse of software generally.

NO WARRANTY

11. BECAUSE THE PROGRAM IS LICENSED FREE OF CHARGE, THERE IS NO WAR-RANTY FOR THE PROGRAM, TO THE EXTENT PERMITTED BY APPLICABLE LAW. EXCEPT WHEN OTHERWISE STATED IN WRITING THE COPYRIGHT HOLDERS AND/OR OTHER PARTIES PROVIDE THE PROGRAM "AS IS" WITHOUT WARRANTY OF ANY KIND, EITHER EXPRESSED OR IMPLIED, INCLUDING, BUT NOT LIMITED TO, THE IMPLIED WARRANTIES OF MERCHANTABILITY AND FITNESS FOR A PARTICULAR PURPOSE. THE ENTIRE RISK AS TO THE QUALITY AND PERFOR-MANCE OF THE PROGRAM IS WITH YOU. SHOULD THE PROGRAM PROVE DE-FECTIVE, YOU ASSUME THE COST OF ALL NECESSARY SERVICING, REPAIR OR CORRECTION.

12. IN NO EVENT UNLESS REQUIRED BY APPLICABLE LAW OR AGREED TO IN WRITING WILL ANY COPYRIGHT HOLDER, OR ANY OTHER PARTY WHO MAY MODIFY AND/OR REDISTRIBUTE THE PROGRAM AS PERMITTED ABOVE, BE LI-ABLE TO YOU FOR DAMAGES, INCLUDING ANY GENERAL, SPECIAL, INCIDEN-TAL OR CONSEQUENTIAL DAMAGES ARISING OUT OF THE USE OR INABILITY TO USE THE PROGRAM (INCLUDING BUT NOT LIMITED TO LOSS OF DATA OR DATA BEING RENDERED INACCURATE OR LOSSES SUSTAINED BY YOU OR THIRD PARTIES OR A FAILURE OF THE PROGRAM TO OPERATE WITH ANY OTHER PRO-GRAMS), EVEN IF SUCH HOLDER OR OTHER PARTY HAS BEEN ADVISED OF THE POSSIBILITY OF SUCH DAMAGES.

END OF TERMS AND CONDITIONS

How to Apply These Terms to Your New Programs

If you develop a new program, and you want it to be of the greatest possible use to the public, the best way to achieve this is to make it free software which everyone can redistribute and change under these terms.

To do so, attach the following notices to the program. It is safest to attach them to the start of each source file to most effectively convey the exclusion of warranty; and each file should have at least the "copyright" line and a pointer to where the full notice is found.

    <one line to give the program's name and a brief idea of what it does.> Copyright (C) <year> <name of author>

This program is free software; you can redistribute it and/or modify it under the terms of the GNU General Public License as published by the Free Software Foundation; either version 2 of the License, or (at your option) any later version.

This program is distributed in the hope that it will be useful, but WITHOUT ANY WARRANTY; without even the implied warranty of MERCHANTABILITY or FITNESS FOR A PARTICULAR PURPOSE. See the GNU General Public License for more details.

You should have received a copy of the GNU General Public License along with this program; if not, write to the Free Software Foundation, Inc., 59 Temple Place, Suite 330, Boston, MA 02111-1307 USA

Also add information on how to contact you by electronic and paper mail.

If the program is interactive, make it output a short notice like this when it starts in an interactive mode:

Gnomovision version 69, Copyright (C) year name of author Gnomovision comes with ABSOLUTELY NO WARRANTY; for details type 'show w'. This is free software, and you are welcome to redistribute it under certain conditions; type 'show c' for details.

The hypothetical commands 'show w' and 'show c' should show the appropriate parts of the General Public License. Of course, the commands you use may be called something other than 'show w' and 'show c'; they could even be mouse-clicks or menu items—whatever suits your program.

You should also get your employer (if you work as a programmer) or your school, if any, to sign a "copyright disclaimer" for the program, if necessary. Here is a sample; alter the names:

Yoyodyne, Inc., hereby disclaims all copyright interest in the program 'Gnomovision' (which makes passes at compilers) written by James Hacker.

<signature of Ty Coon>, 1 April 1989
Ty Coon, President of Vice

This General Public License does not permit incorporating your program into proprietary programs. If your program is a subroutine library, you may consider it more useful to permit linking proprietary applications with the library. If this is what you want to do, use the GNU Library General Public License instead of this License.

GLOSSARY

ACL Access Control Lists.

AFAIK As Far As I Know—the standard disclaimer.

AMI Alternate Mark Inversion (sometimes known as **bipolar**)—a protocol used on T1 circuits which alternates the polarity of ones being sent. This is done to save power on the transmission line by eliminating the residual DC component of the signal.

APM Advanced Power Management—a set of BIOS features which can be configured to implement power-saving features of the hardware, such as drive spin-down, after a defined period of inactivity.

ARP Address Resolution Protocol (for Ethernet, it's documented in RFC 826).

ATM Asynchronous Transfer Mode—a networking protocol characterized by very small packets.

B8ZS Binary 8 Zero Substitution—protocol used on T1 circuits to maintain the minimum density of ones (used so that clocking remains synchronized during long sequences of zeroes). It is an example of an intentional bipolar violation.

BGP Border Gateway Protocol, a dynamic routing protocol (RFC 1164).

BIOS Basic Input Output System, the code used to initially bootstrap the computer so that it can find the operating system. It can also perform functions such as assigning IRQs and base addresses to PCI devices. Some operating systems (e.g., MS-DOS) use functions provided by it for writing to system devices such as the screen or floppy drive.

bit-rot Allowing a piece of software to become antiquated and lose its usefulness by neglecting to maintain it properly.

bridge A network device that connects two segments of the same media type.

BTW By The Way.

CHAP Challenge Handshake Authentication Protocol—also commonly used for PPP authentication mechanisms. (*See also* **PAP**.)

CIDR Classless Inter-Domain Routing (RFC 1519).

CIR Committed Information Rate.

COTS Commercial Off The Shelf—term used to refer to widely available hardware (typically standard PC fare) that can be obtained quickly from a variety of distribution channels.

CPE Customer Premise Equipment—everything on your side of a digital telco circuit's demarc.

CSU Channel Service Unit—provides physical termination, performs signal amplification, and initiates loopbacks for a digital telco circuits. For T1 circuits, it also performs frame formatting and computes performance measurement statistics. Typically found in a **CSU/DSU**. (*See* **DSU**.)

D4 A framing technique used on T1 digital circuits. (*See* **ESF**.)

DDoS A Distributed Denial of Service attack—this is an even more heinous version of a **DoS** attack, since the attacker configures a large number of machines to attack the target simultaneously. (*See* **DoS**.)

DHCP Dynamic Host Configuration Protocol.

DLCI Data Link Connection Identifier—the link-layer address of a Frame Relay node within your network. Normally an integer between 16 and 1023.

DMA Direct Memory Access.

DMCA Digital Millennium Copyright Act—the end of the First Amendment as we knew it—*http://www.loc.gov/copyright/legislation/dmca.pdf.*

DNAT Destination Network Address Translation—used to mangle the destination address of packets (as opposed to the source address, as with **SNAT** and **masquerading**).

DoS Denial of Service (as in "DoS attack")—typically a network-based attack where the malicious party negatively impacts the system by consuming so many resources as to render the system useless to legitimate users/uses. (*See* **DDoS**.)

DSU Data Service Unit—is located between the CSU and terminal equipment (your router). It converts unipolar digital signals from terminal devices into a bipolar digital format for transmission over the digital network. The DSU also provides timing recovery, control signaling, and synchronous sampling. (*See also* **CSU**.)

EGP External Gateway Protocol, a dynamic routing protocol (RFC 904).

ESF Extended Super Frame—a framing technique used on T1 digital circuits which provides for collection of performance statistics of the circuit. (*Compare to* **D4**.)

FDDI Fiber Digital Device Interface—a physical network protocol which runs over optical fiber for LANs up distances greater than 100km.

FQDN Fully Qualified Domain Name—the combination of the hostname (sometimes called the "short name") with that host's domain name. For example, *pongo.mancill.com* is pongo's FQDN.

FSE Full Status Enquiry—a message format used between Frame Relay routers to let each other know that all is well.

FSF The Free Software Foundation. (*See* **GNU**.)

gen Jargon for "*generate a kernel*"—i.e., build a new kernel from the sources.

GNU "GNU's Not Unix." (The infamous lefthand recursive acronym.) A project started by the Free Software Foundation (**FSF**) "to develop a completely free Unix-like operating system." See *http://www.gnu.org/* for more information.

GRE Generic Routing Encapsulation—an IP over IP tunneling protocol developed by Cisco but published as an open standard and widely used.

GPL The GNU Public License. See *http://www.gnu.org/copyleft/gpl.html.*

GSS-API The Generic Security Service Application Programming Interface. A network programming API used with SOCKS V5. See RFC 1961 for details.

hand-lib Building and installing software by hand, as in "I had to hand-lib the latest copy of *foo* onto the box because there isn't a package available yet."

HDLC High-level Data Link Control—a layer 2 (link-layer) protocol which provides an error-free connection between two network nodes. All frames terminate with Cyclic Redundancy Check (CRC) bytes which are used to detect any data errors. Frames received correctly are acknowledged by the receiver while erroneous frames are ignored.

headless Used to describe a machine that does not have an attached monitor and keyboard. Typically, the console access is via a serial connection or a network-based remote management hardware.

hub A network concentrator that acts like a bus.

ICP Internet Cache Protocol, used by caching HTTP proxies such as *Squid.*

IDE Integrated Drive Electronics.

idiot image A precanned boot disk that is ready to go, hiding the more complex details of configuring the system.

IETF Internet Engineering Task Force.

IKE Internet Key Exchange—a public-key service used in conjunction with IPsec to exchange keys with other sites running IPsec.

IMHO In My Humble Opinion—certainly an oxymoron, since the speaker is not very likely to be humble after this lead-in.

IMO In My Opinion—brace yourself to receive someone else's idea(s).

IP Internet Protocol.

IPsec Internet Security Protocol—a security enhancement to IPv4 (and integral to IPv6) that allows for strong authentication and encryption.

IRQ Interrupt ReQuest.

ISA Industry Standard Architecture.

ISDN Integrated Services Digital Network.

ISO International for Organization Standardization—*http://www.iso.ch*.

ISP Internet Service Provider—someone who has more bandwidth to the Internet than you have and would like to sell you part of it.

ITAR International Traffic in Arms Regulations—the U.S. State Department's set of export regulations, wherein certain types of cryptography are deemed illegal for export under the pretext that they are *weapons*. For more information about this sort of thing, visit the *Electronic Frontier Foundation* at *http://www.eff.org/*.

kernel-space Refers to code that is executed by the kernel in its own environment, such as device drivers, routing, and packet filtering. Compare to **user-space**. Example of usage from *fortune*:

> Our OS who art in CPU,
> Unix be thy name.
> Thy programs run, thy syscalls done,
> In kernel as it is in user!

LAPB Link Access Procedure Balanced—a bit-oriented synchronous protocol that provides complete data transparency in a full-duplex point-to-point operation. It supports a peer-to-peer link in that neither end of the link plays the role of the permanent master station.

LBO Line Build Out—a CSU setting used to compensate for loss of signal strength over distance for T1 digital circuits interfacing CPE. For each 133 feet (40 meters) your CSU is distant from the terminating point of T1, you should increase this setting.

LDP Linux Documentation Project—a collection of freely distributable documentation including HOWTOs, mini-HOWTOs, and even some books. It is the brainchild of Greg Hankins and the result of hard work by many. Visit it at *http://www.linuxdoc.org/*.

LINUX Linux Is Not User Xenophobic—the obligatory lefthand recursive acronym (see **GNU**).

LMI Local Management Interface—the method by which Frame Relay routers keep each other notified regarding the status of the network.

lpr The command used to Line Print Remote—i.e., send jobs to a print spooler.

LRP Linux Router Project—a networking-centric Linux minidistribution. See *http://www.linuxrouter.org/*.

luser A not necessarily derogatory name for a nonadmin, nonprogrammer, nonguru. Reserve this term for a newbie for whom you felt a twinge of pity and compassion because of his or her computer ignorance. When you're having a bad day, everyone is a luser.

LVM Logical Volume Manager—a system utility that allows physical disk space to be allocated in terms of logical volumes, which may span multiple physical drives or represent only a fraction of the space available in a single physical partition. Filesystems are then created on the logical volumes, providing a layer of abstraction between the file systems and the physical disks below them.

MAC Media Access Control—as in *MAC address*, which refers to the 6-byte address assigned to each Ethernet adapter by its manufacturer.

MIB Management Information Base (RFC 1213)—a mapping of numbers to parameters used by **SNMP**. MIBs are databases of parameter descriptions with their associated MIB values.

MINIX A free Unix-like operating system created by and under the direction of Andy Tanenbaum. Much of the early history of Linux is intertwined with discussions on the *comp.os.minix* newsgroup. See *http://www.cs.vu.nl/~ast/minix.html* for more information.

Moore's Law The observation that the logic density of silicon integrated circuits has closely followed the curve *(bits per square inch)* $= 2^{t-1962}$ where t is time in years; that is, the amount of information storable on a given area of silicon has roughly doubled every year since the technology was invented.

MTA Mail Transfer Agent.

MTBF Mean Time Between Failure—the average operational life of a component before some part of it breaks.

MTU Maximum Transfer Unit—a network parameter defining the maximum packet size.

multihomed an adjective that refers to a system with more than one network interface.

NAT Network Address Translator—a network device that alters the source address in the IP packet headers along with the source port in either the TCP or UDP header so that the destination replies not directly to the source but to the IP:port of the NAT. This is typically done to obscure the true network address of the source, either because it is not routable from the destination's network or as a security technique.

netiquette Standards of politeness when interacting with other **netizens**. This is an undocumented code that used to be quite strong yet has somehow fallen by the wayside. You can often tell newbies by their (lack of) netiquette. A trivial example is having a *.signature* longer than four 80-character lines. A more serious example is flaming someone in a public forum (e.g., a Usenet newsgroup) without first discussing the matter with him or her via private email. Equally offensive is posting a private message to a newsgroup without the sender's permission.

netizens Others on the Internet.

NIC Network Interface Card.

OSI Open Systems Interconnection (sometimes known as the "OSI Reference Model" or the "OSI Stack")—an ISO standard for implementing networking protocols which logically separates the functions of the network and programs using the network into seven layers.

OSPF Open Shortest Path First—a dynamic routing protocol (RFC 1131).

OTOH On The Other Hand—whoops, I'm about to contradict myself.

OUI Organizationally Unique Identifier—a term employed by the IEEE to refer to the 24-bit field that is the first three octets of the MAC address of an Ethernet card. See *http://standards.ieee.org/regauth/oui/* for more information.

PAP Password Authentication Protocol—commonly used for PPP authentication mechanisms.

PCI Peripheral Component Interconnect.

PCM Pulse Code Modulation—a method used to convert an analog waveform to a series of digital pulses.

PIM Protocol Independent Multicast—this multicast routing protocol is used widely because Cisco supports it. You need special software to use it (pimd-v1); it comes in two flavors: PIMv1 and PIMv2.

POP Point Of Presence—this term describes locations where network service providers have installed equipment and are willing to let you connect to this equipment and their network via either a digital circuit or some form of dial-up. **POP** is also used for Post Office Protocol, as in POP3 for the third version of this protocol.

PPP Point-to-Point Protocol (RFC 1661).

PPTP Point-to-Point Tunneling Protocol—a method of encapsulating IP packets within IP packets for either security purposes (by encrypting the inner packet) or remote network access (by allowing the inner packets to have a source address on the destination network). Typically used simultaneously for both.

PTT Post, Telegraph, and Telephone—a generic term referring to providers of telephony services.

PVC Permanent Virtual Circuit.

RFC Request For Comments.

RFC 1983 This RFC contains the *Internet Users' Glossary*, which is a voluminous glossary of terms from an authoritative source.

RIP Routing Information Protocol—a dynamic routing protocol (RFC 1058).

RSN Real Soon Now—as, the time period within which a vendor promises to have a fix available. Typically meant sarcastically.

RTFM Read The Darn Manual. As a newbie, you may feel like a lightning rod for this statement. Give it time . . . .

SCSI Small Computer System Interface.

SLARP Serial Line Address Resolution Protocol.

SLIP Serial Line Internet Protocol—a predecessor to PPP for running IP over serial devices, typically modems.

SMS Short Message Service—a protocol for messaging GSM cellphones and handheld devices.

SMTP Simple Mail Transport Protocol.

SNMP Simple Network Management Protocol (RFC 1908) (plus RFC 1155, RFC 1156, RFC 1157, and others).

SNPP Simple Network Paging Protocol (RFC 1861).

SOHO Small Office/Home Office—a popular term describing organizations that need for a network with a small number of clients and connectivity to an external network (frequently the Internet).

TAP Telocator Alphanumeric input Protocol—an analog dial-up protocol used to send alphanumeric pages to pagers and cellphones.

TCO Total Cost of Ownership. For any sort of computing solution, this includes not only the initial hardware and software costs, but also the ongoing hardware maintenance and software license costs plus the time that must be spent keeping the system running (e.g., a system that runs on freeware, but requires 10–20 person-hours per month of system administration, will eventually cost a company more than a solution which costs $10,000 out of the box but needs one-tenth of the administration).

TCP Transfer Control Protocol (RFC 675).

TCP/IP A suite of protocols used over IP networks.

TDM Time Division Multiplexing—the practice of dividing bandwidth of a channel based on timeslots. Each timeslot is in a frame, which can then be allocated to different senders. The receiving side demultiplexes the signal back into its various components and passes each of these off to receiving applications/circuits.

TOS Type Of Service (RFC 1349)—a field in an IP packet header which indicates how network components should treat the packet if they are capable of providing different levels of service.

TTL Time To Live—in the case of an IP packet, this is the additional number of hops the packet can take before it is discarded as undeliverable. This is done to prevent misconfigured routers from bringing the network to its knees by routing a packet in circles infinitely.

UPS Uninterruptable Power Supply.

user-space Refers to processes running on a Unix system, whether they are daemons or normal user processes, and regardless of the UID of the process. If you can see it with `ps fax`, then it's a user-space process. (*See* **kernel-space**.)

WOL Wake-On-LAN—a network interface card feature that, upon the reception of a particular packet, can trigger the motherboard to "wake up" the system from a suspended or powered-down state.

WRD Weighted Route Damping (an extension to **BGP**).

YMMV Your Mileage May Vary—a disclaimer that states, "This worked for me, but its applicability to your environment is not known, and therefore it may or may not work for you."

BIBLIOGRAPHY

- CHAPMAN, D. BRENT and ZWICKY, ELIZABETH D., *Building Internet Firewalls.* O'Reilly & Associates, Sebastopol, CA, 1995. ISBN: 1-56592-124-0

- CROWCROFT, JOHN and PHILLIPS, IAIN, *TCP/IP and Linux Protocol Implementation: Systems Code for the Linux Internet.* John Wiley & Sons, New York, NY, 2001. ISBN: 0-47140-882-4

- GARFINKEL, SIMSON and SPAFFORD, GENE, *Practical UNIX and Internet Security, Second Edition,* O'Reilly & Associates, Sebastopol, CA, 1996. ISBN: 1-56592-148-8

- HATCH, BRENT, LEE, JAMES, and KURTZ, GEORGE, *Hacking Linux Exposed: Linux Security Secrets & Solutions,* Osborne/McGraw-Hill, Berkeley, CA, 2001. ISBN: 0-07-212773-2

- HELD, GILBERT, *Understanding Data Communications, Fourth Edition,* SAMS Publishing, 1994. ISBN: 0-672-30501-1

- PERLMAN, RADIA, *Interconnections: Bridges, Routers, Switches and Internetworking Protocols, Second Edition,* Addison Wesley Longman, Inc., 1999. ISBN: 0-201-63488-1

- RAYMOND, ERIC S., with STEELE, GUY L. JR., *The New Hacker's Dictionary,* The MIT Press, Cambridge, MA, 1991. ISBN: 0-262-68069-6

- STEVENS, RICHARD W., *Unix Network Programming: Networking APIs: Sockets and XTI (Volume 1), Second Edition,* Prentice Hall, 1999. ISBN: 0-13-490012-X

- TANENBAUM, ANDREW S., *Computer Networks,* Prentice Hall, 1996. ISBN: 0-13-349945-6

- WALL, LARRY, CHRISTIANSEN, TOM, and SCHWARTZ, RANDAL L., with STEPHEN POTTER, *Programming Perl, Second Edition,* O'Reilly & Associates, Sebastopol, CA, 1996. ISBN: 1-56592-149-6

INDEX

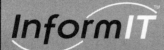